T0189323

# Lecture Notes in Computer Science 13189

More information about this series at https://link.springer.com/bookseries/558

Christian Wallraven · Qingshan Liu ·
Hajime Nagahara (Eds.)

# Pattern Recognition

6th Asian Conference, ACPR 2021
Jeju Island, South Korea, November 9–12, 2021
Revised Selected Papers, Part II

 Springer

*Editors*
Christian Wallraven 🆔
Korea University
Seoul, Korea (Republic of)

Qingshan Liu 🆔
Nanjing University
Nanjing, China

Hajime Nagahara 🆔
Osaka University
Osaka, Japan

ISSN 0302-9743          ISSN 1611-3349  (electronic)
Lecture Notes in Computer Science
ISBN 978-3-031-02443-6          ISBN 978-3-031-02444-3  (eBook)
https://doi.org/10.1007/978-3-031-02444-3

This Springer imprint is published by the registered company Springer Nature Switzerland AG
The registered company address is: Gewerbestrasse 11, 6330 Cham, Switzerland

# Preface

Pattern recognition stands at the core of artificial intelligence and has evolved significantly in recent years. This proceedings comprises the high-quality original research papers presented at the 6th Asian Conference on Pattern Recognition (ACPR 2021), which was successfully held in Jeju Island, South Korea, during November 9–12, 2021. The conference was planned to welcome all participants from around the world to meet physically in the beautiful surroundings of Jeju Island to exchange ideas, as we did in past conferences of the ACPR series. Due to the COVID-19 pandemic constraints, many of us could only join the conference virtually. Nevertheless, we tried our best to overcome various challenges to prepare and actually hold the conference both in person and online. With all your participation and contributions, we believe ACPR 2021 was a special and memorable conference!

ACPR 2021 was the sixth conference in the series since it was launched in 2011 in Beijing. ACPR 2011 was followed by ACPR 2013 in Okinawa, Japan; ACPR 2015 in Kuala Lumpur, Malaysia; ACPR 2017 in Nanjing, China; and ACPR 2019 in Auckland, New Zealand. As we know, ACPR was initiated to promote pattern recognition theory, technologies, and applications in the Asia-Pacific region. Over the years, it has welcomed authors from all over the world. This year, we had participants from 13 countries.

ACPR 2021 focused on four important areas of pattern recognition: pattern recognition and machine learning, computer vision and robot vision, signal processing, and media processing and interaction, covering various technical aspects.

ACPR 2021 received 154 submissions from authors in 13 countries. The program chairs invited 110 Program Committee members and a pool of additional reviewers to assist with the paper selection process. Each paper was single blindly reviewed by at least three reviewers. This rigorous procedure ensured unbiased review. The review committee made the hard decision to accept 26 papers for oral presentation and 59 papers for poster presentation. This resulted in an acceptance rate of 16.9% for oral presentation and 38.3% for poster presentation, giving a total acceptance rate of 55.2%.

The technical program of ACPR 2021 was scheduled over four days including four tutorials, a workshop, three keynote speeches, nine oral sessions, two poster sessions, and a spotlight.

The keynote speeches were given by internationally renowned professors. Lei Zhang, from Hong Kong Polytechnic University, talked about "Gradient centralization and feature gradient decent for deep neural network optimization", Andreas Dengel, from DFKI and the University of Kaiserslautern, talked about "Combining Bird Eye View and Grass Root View for Earth Observation", and Jure Leskovic, from Stanford University, talked about "Graph Neural Networks and Beyond".

Organizing a large event during the COVID-19 pandemic is a challenging task, requiring teamwork, intensive coordination, and collaboration across rather different geolocations and time zones. We would like to thank the organizing committee for their hard work and the steering committee for their guidance. The publication chairs, workshop chairs, tutorial chairs, exhibition/demo chairs, sponsorship chair, finance chair, local organizing chairs, and webmaster all led their respective committees and worked together closely to make ACPR 2021 successful. Our special thanks go to the many reviewers for their constructive comments on the papers. We thank all the authors who submitted their papers to ACPR 2021, which is the most important part for a scientific conference. Finally we would like to acknowledge all volunteers and students from our local organizing team.

Seong-Whan Lee<br>
Cheng-Lin Liu<br>
Yasushi Yagi<br>
Christian Wallraven<br>
Qingshan Liu<br>
Hajime Nagahara

# Organization

## Steering Committee

| | |
|---|---|
| Seong-Whan Lee | Korea University, South Korea |
| Cheng-Lin Liu | CASIA, China |
| Umapada Pal | ISI, India |
| Tieniu Tan | CAS, China |
| Yasushi Yagi | Osaka University, Japan |

## General Chairs

| | |
|---|---|
| Seong-Whan Lee | Korea University, South Korea |
| Cheng-Lin Liu | CASIA, China |
| Yasushi Yagi | Osaka University, Japan |

## Program Chairs

| | |
|---|---|
| Christian Wallraven | Korea University, South Korea |
| Qingshan Liu | Nanjing University of Information Science and Technology, China |
| Hajime Nagahara | Osaka University, Japan |

## Publication Chairs

| | |
|---|---|
| Unsang Park | Sogang University, South Korea |
| Wei Xiong | Institute for Infocomm Research, Singapore |

## Publicity Chairs

| | |
|---|---|
| Jean-Marc Ogier | University of La Rochelle, France |
| Umapada Pal | ISI, India |
| Richard Zannibi | RIT, USA |

## Workshop Chairs

| | |
|---|---|
| Soo-Hyung Kim | Chonnam National University, South Korea |
| Byoungchul Ko | Keimyung University, South Korea |

## Tutorial Chairs

Chang D. Yoo                    KAIST, South Korea
Jingdong Wang                  Microsoft Research Asia, China

## Exhibition/Demo Chairs

Sung Chan Jun                  Gwangju Institute of Science and Technology,
                               South Korea
Dong Gyu Lee                   Kyungpook National University, South Korea

## Sponsorship Chair

Soo-Hyung Kim                  Chonnam National University, South Korea

## Finance Chair

Wonzoo Chung                   Korea University, South Korea

## Local Organizing Chairs

Tea-Eui Kam                    Korea University, South Korea
Sungjoon Choi                  Korea University, South Korea

## Webmaster

Hyun-Seung Chung               Korea University, South Korea

## Program Committee

Alireza Alaei                  Southern Cross University, Australia
Sung-Ho Bae                    Kyung Hee University, South Korea
Saumik Bhattacharya            IIT Kharagpur, India
Michael Blumenstein            University of Technology Sydney, Australia
Sukalpa Chanda                 Østfold University College, Norway
Andrew Tzer-Yeu Chen           University of Auckland, New Zealand
Songcan Chen                   Nanjing University, China
Gong Cheng                     Nanjing University, China
Sungjoon Choi                  Korea University, South Korea
Jaesik Choi                    KAIST, South Korea
Michael Cree                   Waikato University, New Zealand
Jinshi Cui                     Peking University, China
Andreas Dengel                 University of Kaiserslautern, Germany

| | |
|---|---|
| Junyu Dong | Ocean University, China |
| Bo Du | University of Wollongong, Australia |
| Jianjiang Feng | Tsinghua University, China |
| Fei Gao | Zhejiang University, China |
| Guangwei Gao | Nanjing University, China |
| Hitoshi Habe | Kindai University, Japan |
| Renlong Hang | Nanjing University, China |
| Tsubasa Hirakawa | Chubu University, Japan |
| Maiya Hori | Kyushu University, Japan |
| Kazuhiro Hotta | Meijo University, Japan |
| Masaaki Iiyama | Kyoto University, Japan |
| Yoshihisa Ijiri | LINE Corporation, Japan |
| Kohei Inoue | Kyushu University, Japan |
| Koichi Ito | Chiba University, Japan |
| Yumi Iwashita | NASA, USA |
| Xiaoyi Jiang | University of Münster, Germany |
| Xin Jin | Peking University, China |
| Taeeui Kam | Korea University, South Korea |
| Kunio Kashino | NTT Communication Science Laboratories, Japan |
| Yasutomo Kawanishi | Nagoya University, Japan |
| Hiroaki Kawashima | Kyoto University, Japan |
| Sangpil Kim | Korea University, South Korea |
| Jinkyu Kim | Korea University, South Korea |
| Byoungchul Ko | Keimyung University, South Korea |
| Hui Kong | University of Macau, China |
| Shang-Hong Lai | National Tsing Hua University, Taiwan |
| Dong-Gyu Lee | Kyungpook National University, South Korea |
| Namhoon Lee | POSTECH, South Korea |
| Xuelong Li | Northwestern Polytechnical University, China |
| Zhu Li | University of Missouri, USA |
| Zechao Li | Nanjing University of Science and Technology, China |
| Junxia Li | Nanjing University of Information Science and Technology, China |
| Jia Li | Pennsylvania State University, USA |
| Weifeng Liu | China University of Petroleum-Beijing, China |
| Huimin Lu | National University of Defense Technology, China |
| Feng Lu | University of Virginia, USA |
| Jiayi Ma | Wuhan University, China |
| Yasushi Makihara | Osaka University, Japan |
| Brendan McCane | University of Otago, New Zealand |

# Contents – Part II

**Applications, Medical and Robotics**

**Computer Vision and Robot Vision**

# Contents – Part I

**Object Detection and Anomaly**

**Segmentation, Grouping and Shape**

**Face and Body and Biometrics**

**Adversarial Learning and Networks**

# Computational Photography

# Deep Rejoining Model for Oracle Bone Fragment Image

Zhan Zhang[1,2]([✉]), Yun-Tian Wang[1], Bang Li[1], An Guo[1], and Cheng-Lin Liu[2]

[1] Key Laboratory of Oracle Bone Inscription Information Processing, Ministry of Education,
Anyang 455000, Henan, China
zhangzhan161@mails.ucas.ac.cn
[2] National Laboratory of Pattern Recognition, Institute of Automation of Chinese Academy of
Sciences, Beijing 100190, China

**Abstract.** Image based object fragments rejoining can avoid touching and damaging objects, and be applied to recover fragments of oracle bones, artifacts, paper money, calligraphy and painting files. However, traditional methods are insufficient in terms of judging whether two images' texture are rejoinable. In this paper, we propose a deep rejoining model (DRM) for automatic rejoining of oracle bone fragment images. In our model, an edge equal distance rejoining method (EEDR) is used to locate the matching position of the edges of two fragment images and crop the target area image (TAI), then a convolution neural network (CNN) is used to evaluate the similarity of texture in TAI. To improve the performance of similarity evaluation, a maximum similarity pooling (MSP) layer is proposed in CNN, and the fully connected layer outputs the two-class probability of whether the rejoining is eligible or not. Our experiments show that DRM achieved state-of-the-arts performance in rejoining oracle bone fragment images and has stronger adaptability.

**Keywords:** Oracle bone fragment image rejoining · Deep rejoining model · Edge equal distance rejoining method · Maximum similarity pooling

## 1 Introduction

Object fragments can be rejoined by image analysis to avoid touching or damaging to them. This technology can be used to recover fragments of oracle bones, artifacts, paper money, calligraphy and painting files. There have been many oracle bone fragments found in the history, and the rejoining of them is important for archeology. Traditional methods, mostly based on heuristic rules and hand-crafted features, are human laborious and insufficient in performance, because oracle bone fragments are highly variable in bone size, texture, character size and position [1, 2]. Usually, a segment of edge of the source fragment image and that of the target fragment image are selected by exhaustive search to be matched for rejoining [3], and to judge the similarity of texture of the image pair is non-trivial. To search for the pair of edge segments, angle and chain code features in multi-scale image space have been extracted for matching [4]. The ratio of the gap between the boundaries of two fragment images has also been used [5]. The traditional methods [1–5] are insufficient in terms of accuracy, discrimination and adaptability, so they cannot satisfy the need of large-scale rejoining of oracle bone fragments. The keypoint extraction techniques in computer vision (such as [6–9]) are useful for matching images. But for oracle bone fragments rejoining, since two fragments are complementary in space with no overlap, such keypoints are not helpful for rejoining. Edge and corner based rejoining methods [3–5] would search more incorrect image pairs of oracle bone fragment, because it can not evaluate the texture similarity of image pairs, it is the challenges brought by rejoining oracle bone fragment (see Fig. 1).

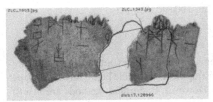

a. Oracle bone fragment images          b. Recovering of fragment images

**Fig. 1.** Oracle bone fragments

Deep learning models (deep neural networks, DNNs) have been widely used in computer vision tasks including object detection, classification and verification. To use DNNs for oracle bone fragments rejoining, there are two key issues: selection of the regions of two images to be compared, and calculation of similarity of two images in texture (whether two fragments are rejoinable or not). While the former step is accomplished using image processing techniques, the latter can be fulfilled using DNN. DNN models include encoding network (EN) [10, 11], regional convolution neural network (R-CNN) [12–15], inception network (GoogleNet) [16–18], VGG network (VGG-Net), YOLO [19] and graph network (GN) [20, 21], etc. To apply DNN to fragments rejoining, the fully connected layer needs to be re-designed since the two fragments are not overlapping in space.

This paper proposes a deep rejoining model (DRM) for oracle bone fragments rejoining. The model consists of two components: first, an edge coordinate matching method is used to locate the matching position of two oracle bone fragment images, and the target area image is cropped from the rejoined image to be evaluated by CNN. In the CNN, a max similarity pooling (MSP) layer is designed to calculate the similarity of texture feature in the target area image. The CNN functions as a two-class classifier, outputting the probability measuring whether two oracle bone fragments are compatible in texture or not. In our experiments, the DRM report accuracy of 99.56% and 99.81% on the training set and validation set, respectively. Applying the model to rejoining actual oracle bone fragments in the Lvshun Museum, the model has found 14 pairs of new rejoinable oracle bone fragment images, which were not found by human archeologists. The 14 pairs of images include images of cow bones, tortoise back carapace and tortoise belly carapace. This contributes tremendously to the area of archeology. This indicates that the DRM can be used for rejoining the fragments of tortoise shells, cow bones and other fragments, and is highly adaptable.

The rest of this paper is organized as follows. Section 2 reviews related works. Section 3 describes the proposed deep rejoining model. Section 4 presents experimental results, and Sect. 5 draws concluding remarks.

## 2   Related Work

The previous rejoining methods more or less rely on human knowledge or hand-crafted features. The edge-corner matching method evaluates the similarity of two fragment image edges according to the sum of the square of the edge length ratios [22]. This method covers three situations: one corner, multiple corners and three corners (see Fig. 2). Every triplet of adjacent points in the contour of the oracle bone fragment image can be used to calculate an angle [4], and in the case of multi-scale space, the feature vector is composed of the outline angle sequence to be matched with that of the target oracle bone fragment image. If the i-th angle of the source contour feature vector and the j-th angle of the target contour feature vector are equal at a certain scale, the two fragment images can be matched at the scale. This method is not suitable for matching those images whose edge has no corners, however.

On locating the target area of two fragment images to be rejoined, DNN can be considered to evaluate the similarity of the two fragment images. However, since two fragments are not overlapping in space, DNN cannot be used straightforwardly. We thus propose to revise the fully connected layer for fragment images rejoining.

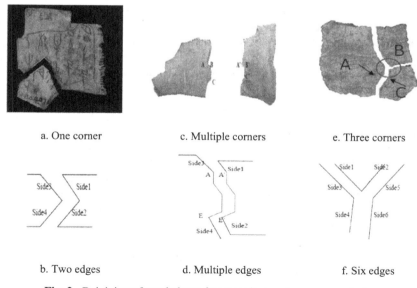

Fig. 2. Rejoining of oracle bone fragment images by corner and edge

## 3 Deep Rejoining Model

In order to solve the above problems, we propose the deep rejoining model to rejoin oracle bone fragment images. Our model consists of two parts: The first part is of a method for matching the edge point coordinates of oracle bone fragment images: an EEDR algorithm is proposed to locate the matching edge position of oracle bone fragment images and crop the target area in the rejoined image that have matching edge segment. The second part is a CNN based model for evaluating oracle bone fragment target area image texture similarity: the ResNet with proposed the maximum similarity pooling (MSP) layer is used to extract the texture features of the target area images, the MSP layer is used to replace the maximum pool layer to calculate the similarity of the texture feature in TAI and improve the accuracy of rejoining oracle bone fragment images. The fully connected layer is used as a two-category model, and to judge whether the oracle bone fragment images are complementary.

### 3.1 Image Edge Rejoining Method

When extracting the oracle bone fragment image's edge and the edge point coordinates (see Fig. 3a), the green curve is the edge of the source oracle bone fragment image, the pink curve is the edge of the target oracle bone fragment image. Aiming at matching the edge coordinates of oracle bone fragment images, this paper proposes a ways named edge equal distance rejoining method (EEDR), in order to make it easier to understand, firstly we give edge equal pixel rejoining method (EEPR). Generally, when the edge detection algorithm obtains the edge point coordinates, the point on the edge that is closest to the x-axis of the image is taken as the starting point, and the coordinates of the image edge points are achieved counterclockwise along the edge, the edge is stored into a list in form of point coordinate sequence. The downward arrow in Fig. 3a means to extract the coordinates of the image edge in counterclockwise direction. If two images could be rejoined together by their edges, the edge point coordinates in the list of the target image need to be reversed, its direction is shown in the upward arrow in Fig. 3a.

#### 3.1.1 Edge Equal Pixel Rejoining Method

As shown in Fig. 3a, the image EEPR method will take the midpoint of the local edge of the source image as the center, and rotate the edge of the source image every 2°, the range of the rotating degree is set between $[-20,20]$, so it would obtain 21 rotating edges, they are drawn by the blue curve in Fig. 3a. The translation vector is calculated according to the midpoint of the segment of the source image edge and the segment of the target image edge. The 21 candidate image edges are translated to the edge of the target image and then sampled. As shown in Fig. 3b, in order to reduce the amount of calculation, when acquiring the edge sample points of the source image and the target image, one point is sampled every fixed number of pixels, and the sum of the distances between the corresponding sample points of the source edge and the target edge is calculated as the dissimilarity, and the minimum dissimilarity between the local edge of the source image and the local edge of the candidate image is used to evaluate whether the local edges of the two oracle bone fragment images can be rejoined. The matching length of two edges is determined by the number of sampling points and the number of pixels between adjacent sampling points, it is generally less than the length of the edges that can be rejoined, the local edge of the source image is equivalent to a sliding window, which is used to match all the local edges of the source image with all the local edges of the target image, and find the position of the smallest distance between the sampling points of the local edges of the two images.

As shown in formula (1), $S_j$ denotes the sampling point at the edge of the source image, j denotes the subscript of the first matching sampling point in the source image edge coordinate sequence, $D_i$ denotes the sampling point at the edge of the target image, and i denotes the subscript of the first matching sample point in the target image edge coordinate sequence. $S_{di}$ denotes the sum of the distance between the sample points of the source image and the target image edge. If the smallest distance between the edge of the candidate image and the edge of the target image is less than the threshold $T_d$, the local edges of the two images are matching at this location.

### 3.1.2 Edge Equal Distance Rejoining Method

Since the edges of the image with the same number of pixels may have different lengths, the EEDR method is proposed. As shown in Fig. 3c, when the candidate local matching edge of the source image is rotated and translated to the target image edge, the intersections of the image edge and the circles with the same center and equal distance increasing radius are used as the sampling points, and the sum of the distances between sample points on the edge of the target image and the source image is used as dissimilarity to evaluate whether the two images can be rejoined, the image edge matching length is determined by the number of sampling points and the distance between two adjacent sampling points.

As shown in formula (2), $S_{Rj}$ and $D_{Ri}$ respectively denotes the sampling points of the source image and the target image edges, $R_j$ denotes the subscript of the first matching sampling point in the source image edge coordinate list, and $R_i$ denotes the subscript of the first matching sampling point in the target image edge coordinate list, $S_{dRi}$ denotes the sum of the distances between corresponding sampling points on the edge of the two oracle bone fragment images calculated by the EEDR method, and $k$ represents the number of sampling points. Among the two methods, the EEPR method has a small amount of calculation. Because the EEDR method can skip the missing edge points, and its adaptability is stronger, in the ZLC oracle bone fragment image set, this method finds one pair of matching oracle bone fragment images, their codes are 797 and 799, respectively, as shown in Fig. 3d and Fig. 3e.

$$S_{di} = \sum_{t=0}^{t=k} \mathrm{dist}\left(S_{j+t}, D_{i+t}\right) < T_d \tag{1}$$

$$S_{dRi} = \sum_{t=0}^{t=k} \mathrm{dist}\left(S_{Rj+t}, D_{Ri+t}\right) < T_d \tag{2}$$

Different scale of oracle bone fragment image need be considered, the resolution of the captured image is usually 300 dots per inch (dpi), 400 dpi or 600 dpi, in order

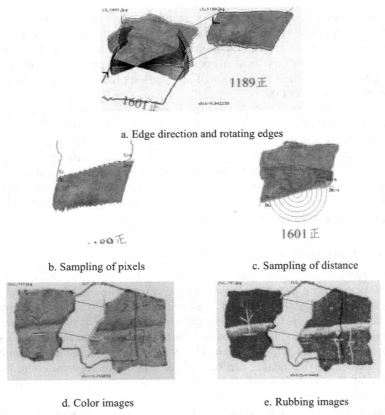

a. Edge direction and rotating edges

b. Sampling of pixels      c. Sampling of distance

d. Color images      e. Rubbing images

**Fig. 3.** Edge coordinate matching algorithm

to normalize the texture of the source and target image into the same scale space, we transform the image that has a high resolution into a low resolution. For example, the resolution of image $a$ is 300 dpi, and the resolution of image $b$ is 600 dpi, we transform the resolution of image $b$ into 300 dpi, so image $a$ and image $b$ would have the same resolution, and image $a$ keep its original size, and image $b$ would be set to half of its original size.

## 3.2 Two-Class Model

As shown in the Fig. 4, this paper proposes a deep learning model for rejoining oracle bone fragment images, which includes two parts: EEDR method and ResNet improved by MSP. There are three steps to rejoin the images of oracle bone fragment: (1) Using the EEDR method to find out the matching edge coordinates of two oracle bone fragment images. (2) Rejoining the images who's edge coordinates are matching into a whole image, and cutting the target area image at the matching position, extracting the target image texture similarity feature by improved residual network. (3) Establishing a two-class classification model to evaluate whether the two fragments are rejoinable or not in terms of texture based on target area image's feature. Its activation function is softmax, its kernel weights are initialized by the glorot uniform initializer, the adaptive moment estimation algorithm is used to optimize the model. As shown in Fig. 4a, the target area in the red box is located by EEDR method, and it is used to crop the TAI, (see Fig. 4b) we use the ResNet50 improved by MSP to extract maximum texture similarity feature from the target area image, and use the FCN to train the target area image set and judge whether the two fragment images can be rejoined or not and to give the classification probability.

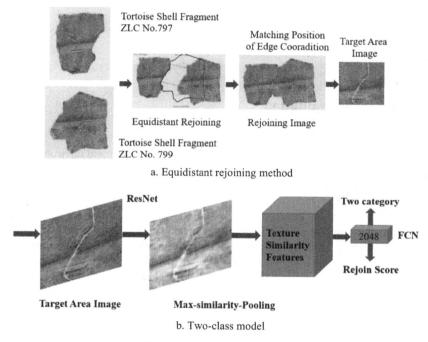

a. Equidistant rejoining method

b. Two-class model

**Fig. 4.** Deep learning model

## 3.3 Maximum Similarity Pooling

Maximum similarity pooling is proposed to calculate the texture similarity features of target area image [23, 24]. After detecting the matching position of the oracle bone images' edges, and cropping the target area image, we would use ResNet to get the convolution residual matrix size of $4 \times 4 \times 2048$, and the maximum similarity pooling is proposed to compute the maximum internal texture similarity of the convolution residual image, the result matrix is size of $2 \times 2 \times 2048$, and by the operation of maximum similarity pooling, the result matrix would has the similarity relationship and the position information of the pixels in the slip window (Fig. 5), it could increase the discrimination of the convolution feature. Pixel $P_0$ denotes one pixel in the pooling slip window size of $2 \times 2$, and so do $P_1, P_2, P_3$. $\sigma_{01}$ denotes absolute value of the subtraction between $P_0$ and $P_1$, similarly $\sigma_{02}$, $\sigma_{03}$, $\sigma_{12}$, $\sigma_{13}$ and $\sigma_{23}$. The similarity $S_{ij}$ is calculated by formula (3), **a** denotes the harmonized parameter, x denotes product of **a** and $\sigma_{ij}$, the maximum of $S_{ij}$ calculated in the slip window is treated as the maximum similarity pooling value.

$$S_{ij} = e^{(-1/(\mathbf{a} \times \sigma_{ij}))} \tag{3}$$

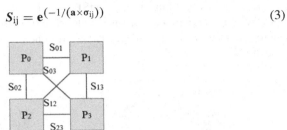

**Fig. 5.** Maximum similarity pooling

## 4  Performance Evaluation

### 4.1  Experiment Dataset

The experiment uses ubuntu operation system, pycharm development environment, tensorflow 2.1 framework and opencv3.4 image processing function library. This paper gives a positive and negative sample image set of target area images of oracle bone fragments, the image set includes about 110,000 unrejoinable image samples achieved from the Chinese calendar Tibetan oracle bone fragment image set (ZLC image set) by the EEDR method, and about 20,000 rejoinable image samples achieved by cropping the target area image from BingBian and HuaDong oracle bone fragment image sets, etc. The experiment tests a variety of two classification methods, the training set and the validation set accounted for 80% and 20% of the dataset respectively. In Fig. 6, four rejoinable images size of 121 × 121 are shown in the first row, and four unrejoinable images size of 121 × 121 are shown in the second row. When training each model, according to the input image size of ResNet50, the images are reset to be size of 64 × 64 or 224 * 224, each model is trained for twenty epochs to be convergent.

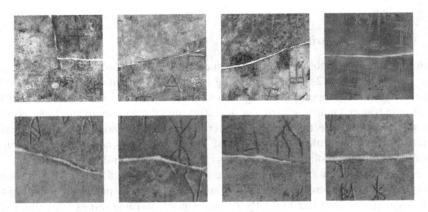

**Fig. 6.** Rejoinable and unrejoinable images

## 4.2  Performance of Different Methods

The performance of different methods test on the train dataset is shown in Table 1, the methods include AlexNet, VGG19, ResNet50, InceptionV3 and MobileNet. The deep rejoining model has the accuracy as 99.56%, it is comparable to other models, and its loss is 0.0023, which is less than other models, but the time it cost is neither higher nor lower than other methods. Test on the validation dataset (see Table 2), the model's accuracy is 99.81 and its loss is 0.0078, among all the models the deep rejoining model has the best performance.

**Table 1.**  Training accuracy, loss and time (ms/step)

| Methods | Accuarcy | Loss | Time |
|---|---|---|---|
| AlexNet | 83.39% | 0.4489 | 55 |
| VGG19 | 83.49% | 0.4480 | 582 |
| ResNet50 | 99.63% | 0.0126 | 362 |
| InceptionV3 | 99.68% | 0.0112 | 196 |
| MobileNet | 99.68% | 0.0108 | 173 |
| DRM | 99.56% | 0.0023 | 300 |

The ZLC image set which has 1920 images and 12 pairs of matching images is used to test the EEDR method and deep rejoining model. Test on the ZLC image set of oracle bones fragments, the EEDR method could find all the 12 pairs of matching images, but it have found more incorrect matching results. See Table 3, the performance of DRM test on the ZLC image set, the deep rejoining model performs best, and it has searched 11 oracle bone fragments image pairs, and the average confidence of the correct classification is 94.23%, and it is higher than AlexNet, VGG19, ResNet50 and InceptionV3, even it is not higher than MobileNet, but it shows a comparable precision with MobileNet.

See Table 2, because ResNet50 is improved as the two-class model in the DRM, its maximum pooling layer is replaced by the maximum similarity pooling layer, so the

**Table 2.**  The validation accuracy and loss

| Methods | Accuracy | Loss |
|---|---|---|
| AlexNet | 83.69% | 0.4447 |
| VGG19 | 83.38% | 0.4499 |
| ResNet50 | 95.66% | 3.2104 |
| InceptionV3 | 62.39% | 2.0513 |
| MobileNet | 90.90% | 0.1598 |
| DRM | 99.81% | 0.0078 |

accuracy of the DRM is 4% more than ResNet50, the DRM has a smaller loss among the deep learning models, and it has found more matching images in the practical rejoining job within a higher probability.

**Table 3.** Performance of practical rejoining job

| Methods | Pairs | Confidence |
|---------|-------|------------|
| AlexNet | 11 | 83.76% |
| VGG19 | 11 | 83.34% |
| ResNet50 | 10 | 89.07% |
| InceptionV3 | 8 | 66.29% |
| MobileNet | 11 | 96.86% |
| DRM | 11 | 94.23% |

### 4.3   Practical Rejoining Job

In the practical rejoining job, the oracle bone fragments include shells and bones. Then the model works on the image set of oracle bones fragments in Lvshun Museum, which has 2211 images, the model searches 14 pairs of oracle bone fragment images that can be rejoined and these pairs of oracle bone fragments have not been rejoined by oracle bone expert before. We show the number of the 14 pairs of fragments' images (see Table 4), and as can been seen in Fig. 7, Fig. 7a, Fig. 7b and Fig. 7c are three pairs of bones from the LvShun Museum, their numbers are 36 and 71, 884 and 340, 1577 and 1457 respectively, and Fig. 7d, Fig. 7e and Fig. 7f are three pairs of shells from the LvShun Museum, their numbers are 1617 and 1330, 1189 and 1601, 1316 and 443 respectively. The experiment result demonstrates that the model is not only suitable for rejoining bone fragments images, but also suitable for rejoining shell fragments images, at the same time, it shows that the model is more adaptable than the traditional algorithms, because they have not search matching oracle bone fragments images yet.

The EEDR algorithm could search the matching location to the 14 pairs of oracle bone fragment images, but it searched about 500 more disrejoinable image pairs. In order to evaluate the texture similarity of the fragment image pairs and improve the rejoining accuracy, we train the deep learning models such as AlexNet, VGG19, ResNet50, InceptionV3 and MobileNet on the dataset of rejoinable and disrejoinable image to predict the rejoinable conference of target area image. On the image set of oracle bones fragments in Lvshun Museum, our method can correctly judge whether the target area image of the 14 pairs of oracle bone fragment image is rejoinable, and the rejoinable confidence of correct classification is 92.1%, but AlexNet, VGG19 and MobileNet has given wrong judgement that the 14 target area images' texture is rejoinable or not, InceptionV3 and ResNet50 has respectively given 5 and 2 pairs of oracle bone images pairs, which is correctly judged.

**Table 4.** Rejoinable oracle bone fragments searched in Lvshun image set

| Image pairs | | Image pairs | |
|---|---|---|---|
| 36 | 71 | 1189 | 1601 |
| 120 | 1308 | 1199 | 611 |
| 324 | 1115 | 1316 | 443 |
| 526 | 1171 | 1546 | 1229 |
| 629 | 765 | 1577 | 1457 |
| 803 | 859 | 1610 | 1612 |
| 884 | 340 | 1617 | 1330 |

**Table 5.** The number of correct rejoinable image pairs searched by different models

| Model | AlexNet | VGG19 | ResNet50 | InceptionV3 | MobileNet | DRM |
|---|---|---|---|---|---|---|
| Numbers | 0 | 0 | 2 | 5 | 0 | 14 |
| Confidence | – | – | 89.67% | 79.62% | – | 92.10% |

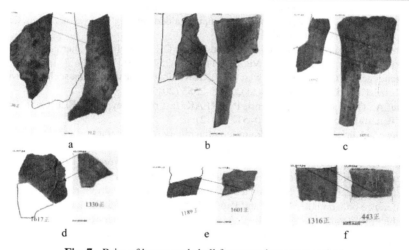

**Fig. 7.** Pairs of bones and shell fragment images searched

## 5 Conclusions

The deep rejoining model can be used in the practical job to rejoin the oracle bone fragment image, and it has a state-of-the-art performance, and it suitable for rejoining images of oracle bone fragments, ceramic fragments, bamboo slip fragments, ancient books and calligraphy fragments, etc., and also suitable for rejoining images of banknotes and invoice fragments in the financial field. But when the image include the fracture of the oracle bone in the third dimension, the EEDR method would find an incorrect boundary of the fragment's image, the DRM would not work well. So the future job is to improve the model's effectiveness and increase the accuracy and robustness of rejoining fragment images.

**Acknowledgements.** This work has been supported by the National Natural Science Foundation of China (62106007, 61806007), Department of Science and Technology of Henan Province (212102310549) and Anyang Normal University Science and Technology Research Project (2021C01GX012).

# References

1. Chou, H., Opstad, D.: Computer matching of oracle bone fragments: a preliminary report on a new research method. Archaeology **26**(33), 176–181 (1973)
2. Tong, E., Zhang, S., Cheng, J.: Preliminary report on the use of computers to rejoin fragments of Shang Daibujia. J. Sichuan Univ. (Nat. Sci. Edn.) **2**, 57–65 (1975)
3. Zhang, C., Wang, A.: A computer-aided oracle bone inscription rubbing conjugation method. Electron. Design Eng. **20**(17), 1–3 (2012)
4. Liu, Y., Wang, T., Wang, J.: The application of the technique of 2D fragments stitching based on outline feature in rejoining oracle bones. In: International Conference on Multimedia Information Networking and Security, pp. 964–968 (2010)
5. Wang, A., Liu, G., Ge, W., et al.: Oracle computer-aided conjugation system design. Comput. Eng. Appl. **46**(21), 59–62 (2010)
6. Tublee, E., Rabaud, V., Konolige, K., Bradski, G.: ORB: an efficient alternative to SIFT or SURF. IEEE Int. Conf. Comput. Vis. **58**(11), 2564–2571 (2011)
7. Leutenegger, S., Chli, M.Y., Siegwart, R.: BRISK: binary robust invariant scalable keypoints. IEEE Int. Conf. Comput. Vis. **58**(11), 2548–2555 (2012)
8. Alahi, A., Ortiz, R., Vandergheynst, P.: FREAK: fast retina keypoint. IEEE Conf. Comput. Vis. Pattern Recogn. **157**(10), 510–517 (2012)
9. Zhang, Z., Yang, D., Lian, M.: Circumferential binary feature extraction and matching search algorithms. IEEE Signal Process. Lett. **25**(7), 1074–1078 (2018)
10. Zhang, H., Xue, J., Dana, K.: Deep TEN: texture encoding network. In: IEEE Conference on Computer Vision and Pattern Recognition, pp. 2896–2905 (2017)
11. Xue, J., Zhang, H., Dana, K.: Deep texture manifold for ground terrain recognition. In: IEEE Conference on Computer Vision and Pattern Recognition, pp. 558–567 (2018)
12. Girshick, R., Donahue, J., Darrell, T., Malik, J.: Rich feature hierarchies for accurate object detection and semantic segmentation Tech report. In: IEEE International Conference on Computer Vision, pp. 580–587 (2014)
13. Girshick, R.: Fast R-CNN. In: IEEE International Conference on Computer Vision, pp. 1440–1448 (2015)
14. Ren, S., He, K., Girshick, R., Sun, J.: Faster R-CNN: towards real-time object detection with region proposal networks. IEEE Trans. Pattern Anal. Mach. Intell. **39**(6), 1137–1149 (2017)
15. He, K., Gkioxari, G., Dollar, P., Girshick, R.: Mask R-CNN. IEEE Trans. Pattern Anal. Mach. Intell. **42**(2), 386–397 (2020)
16. Szegedy, C., Liu, W., Jia, Y., et al.: A going deeper with convolutions. In: IEEE Conference on Computer Vision and Pattern Recognition, pp. 1–9 (2015)
17. Szegedy, C., Vanhoucke, V., Ioffe, S., et al.: Rethinking the inception architecture for computer vision. In: IEEE Conference on Computer Vision and Pattern Recognition, pp. 2818–2826 (2016)

18. Szegedy, C., Ioffe, S., Vanhoucke, V., Alemi, A.: Inception–V4, inception – ResNet and the impact of residual connections on learning. In: The 31th AAAI Conference on Artificial Intelligence, pp. 4278–4284 (2016)
19. Redmon, J., Divvala, S., Girshick, R., Farhadi, A.: You only look once: unified, real-time object detection. In: IEEE Conference on Computer Vision and Pattern Recognition, pp. 779–788 (2016)
20. Ruiz, L., Gama, F., Marques, A.G., Ribeiro, A.: Invariance-preserving localized activation functions for graph neural networks. IEEE Trans. Signal Process. **68**, 127–141 (2020)
21. Cao, W., Yan, Z., He, Z., et al.: A comprehensive survey on geometric neural networks. IEEE Access **8**, 35929–35949 (2020)
22. Lin, Y.: Exploiting Information Science Technology to Rejoin An-yang Oracle bones/Shells, pp. 32–41. Tsinghua University, Taiwan (2006)
23. Zhang, Z., Yang, D.: Internal and external similarity aggregation stereo matching algorithm. In: The 11th International Conference on Digital Image Processing, vol. 11179, p. 62 (2019)
24. Mei, X., Sun, X., Dong, W., Wang, H., et al.: Segment-tree based cost aggregation for stereo matching. In: IEEE Conference on Computer Vision and Pattern Recognition, pp. 313–320 (2013)

# Spatial Spectral Joint Correction Network for Hyperspectral and Multispectral Image Fusion

Tingting Wang, Yang Xu[✉], Zebin Wu, and Zhihui Wei

School of Computer Science and Engineering,
Nanjing University of Science and Technology, Nanjing, China
{wangtiting,xuyangth90,wuzb,gswei}@njust.edu.cn

**Abstract.** Hyperspectral and multispectral image (HS-MSI) fusion aims to generate a high spatial resolution hyperspectral image (HR-HSI), using the complementarity and redundancy of the low spatial resolution hyperspectral image (LR-HSI) and the high spatial resolution multispectral image (HS-MSI). Previous works usually assume that the spatial down-sampling operator between HR-HSI and LR-HSI, and the spectral response function between HR-HSI and HR-MSI are known, which is infeasible in many cases. In this paper, we propose a coarse-to-fine HS-MSI fusion network, which does not require the prior on the mapping relationship between HR-HSI and LRI or MSI. Besides, the result is improved by iterating the proposed structure. Our model is composed of three blocks: degradation block, error map fusion block and reconstruction block. The degradation block is designed to simulate the spatial and spectral down-sampling process of hyperspectral images. Then, error maps in space and spectral domain are acquired by subtracting the degradation results from the inputs. The error map fusion block fuses those errors to obtain specific error maps corresponding to initialize HSI. In the case that the learned degradation process could represent the real mapping function, this block ensures to generate accurate errors between degraded images and the ground truth. The reconstruction block uses the fused maps to correct HSI, and finally produce high-precision hyperspectral images. Experiment results on CAVE and Harvard dataset indicate that the proposed method achieves good performance both visually and quantitatively compared with some SOTA methods.

**Keywords:** Hyperspectral image · Image fusion · Deep learning · Degradation model

This work was supported in part by the National Natural Science Foundation of China (61772274, 62071233, 61671243, 61976117), the Jiangsu Provincial Natural Science Foundation of China (BK20211570, BK20180018, BK20191409), the Fundamental Research Funds for the Central Universities (30917015104, 30919011103, 30919011402, 30921011209), and in part by the China Postdoctoral Science Foundation under Grant 2017M611814, 2018T110502.

C. Wallraven et al. (Eds.): ACPR 2021, LNCS 13189, pp. 16–27, 2022.
https://doi.org/10.1007/978-3-031-02444-3_2

# 1  Introduction

With the steady development of sensor technology, the quantity and expression form of information are gradually enriched. Hyperspectral remote sensing image is mainly formed by acquiring electromagnetic waves of different wavelengths which are reflected from the ground objects after processing. Thus, the hyperspectral image generally consists of tens to hundreds of wavelengths and contains rich spectral information. Using different feature signals in hyperspectral images, many computer vision tasks such as detection [11,16] and segmentation [13] can be implemented. However, due to the limitation of existing optical remote sensing systems, it is difficult to guarantee both the spectral resolution and spatial resolution of HSI. High precision HR-HSI can provide high-quality data for subsequent more complex hyperspectral image processing tasks, and it can be produced by making full use of the MSI or HSI which can be captured by existing imaging equipment. Therefore, researchers have proposed a variety of hyperspectral image fusion methods to generate accurate HR HSI.

When composed of a single band, the multispectral image is reduced to a panchromatic image [10]. Consequently, the comprehensive evaluation of HS-MS fusion can be incorporated into the system of pan-sharpening, and the methods of HS-MS fusion and pan-sharpening are convergent. Most recent HS-MS fusion methods are based on image prior models, which formulate the fusion problem as an optimization problem constrained by HRI priors. In addition, some methods exploit the low-rank and sparse properties of HSI. These methods use matrix factorization or tensor factorization to characterize HSI and address the corresponding image fusion problem.

As recent years, deep learning (DL) in inverse problem reconstruction has gradually attracted wide attention from researchers with the continuous development of neural networks. Using back propagation of neural networks and optimization algorithms, the optimization problem can be solved effectively and achieve excellent reconstruction results. Compared with conventional fusion methods, DL-based ones need fewer assumptions on the prior knowledge from the to-be-recovered HR-HSI and the network can be trained directly on a set of training data. Although the network architecture itself needs to be handcrafted, properly designed network architectures have been shown to solve many problems and achieve high performance because of the robust feature extraction capabilities of convolutional networks [6]. Hence, based on CNN and the generation mechanism, we propose a spatial-spectral joint correction HS-MS fusion network (SSJCN). The implementation of the method revolves around the following points:

1. Improving the resolution accuracy of the fused images by concatenating the degradation models and the reconstruction models.
2. The error map between the degraded image and the input data maintains the high-frequency information of the input to ensure that the network does not lose detail information during forward propagation.

The rest of this article is organized as follows. In Sect. 2, we present some existing methods of hyperspectral fusion. In Sect. 3, we introduce the detailed implementation of the proposed model. Experimental results on two publicly available datasets and comparisons with other methods are reported in Sect. 4. Lastly, this paper ends with the summary of Sect. 5.

## 2   Related Work

### 2.1   Traditional Methods

Generally, the traditional approach is based on artificial priori assumptions. There are several pan-sharpening methods often assume that the spatial details of panchromatic and multispectral images are similar [9]. While some methods, such as [3,7], use sparse matrix decomposition to learn the spectral dictionary of LR-HSI, and then use the spectral dictionary and the coefficients learned from HR-MSI to construct HR-HSI. In [3], W. Dong et al. take the spatial structure into account to make full use of the priors. Also, tensor factorization-based methods have made great strides in hyperspectral image fusion problems, which treat HR-HSI as a three-dimensional tensor [8]. Although these methods are constantly evolving and have yielded positive results, the methods based on handcrafted priors are not flexible enough to adapt to different hyperspectral image structures because HR-HSI acquired from real scenes are highly diverse in both spatial and spectral terms.

### 2.2   Deep Learning Methods

Unlike traditional methods, deep learning-based fusion methods do not require building a specific priori model. Chao Dong [2] et al. proposed a three-layer super resolution model of convolutional neural networks (SRCNN) to learn the inherently unique feature relationships between LRI and HRI. SRCNN first demonstrates that the traditional sparse coding-based approach can be reformulated as a deep convolutional neural network, but the method does not consider the self-similarity of the data. Shuang Xu [15] et al. designed a multiscale fusion network (HAM-MFN), where the HSI was upscale 4 times and fused with MS images at each scale with the net going deeper. As existing imaging equipment cannot directly obtain HR-HSI, some methods use up-sampled LR-HSI or HR-MSI to simulate the target image. Based on that, Han et al. proposed spatial and spectral fusion CNN [4]. Even though this algorithm achieved better performance than state-of-the-art methods, the up-sampled images not only increased the number of pixels but also the computational complexity. Then in [5], a multi-scale spatial and spectral fusion architecture (MS-SSFNet) is proposed in order to reducing the computational complexity and alleviating the vanishing gradients problem.

## 3    Proposed Method

### 3.1    Problem Formulation

Given two input images: HR-MSI $X \in R^{c \times W \times H}$, and LR-HSI $Y \in R^{C \times w \times h}$ ($c \ll C$, $w \ll W$, $h \ll H$) where $C$, $W$ and $H$ represents the numbers of spectral bands, image width and height respectively. The purpose of hyperspectral image fusion is to produce a potential HR-HSI $Z \in R^{W \times H \times C}$ from the observed images. Usually, we describe the relationship between $Z$ and $X$, $Y$ in the following equation.

$$X = Z \times_3 P \tag{1}$$

$$Y = Z \times_1 S_1 \times_2 S_2 \tag{2}$$

Equation (1) indicates how to obtain HR-MSI X with the spectral response operator $P \in^{C \times c}$ ($c < C$). $S_1 \in^{W \times w}$ and $S_2 \in^{H \times h}$ in Eq. (2) is for blurring HR-HSI $Z$ (usually using Gaussian filtering) and $S$ denotes the spatial down-sampling operator. That is, $X$ is a down-sampling of $Z$ in the spectral dimension while the LR-HSI $Y$ is generated by down-sampling the HR-HSI. The proposed model estimates $Z$ using an end-to-end mapping function $f(\bullet)$ with the network parameters as

$$\hat{Z} = f_\theta(X, Y), \theta = \{w_1, \ldots, w_l; b_1, \ldots, b_l\} \tag{3}$$

where $\hat{Z}$ is the reconstructed HSI by the fusion network and $w_l$ and $b_l$ represent the weight and bias of the $l$th layer.

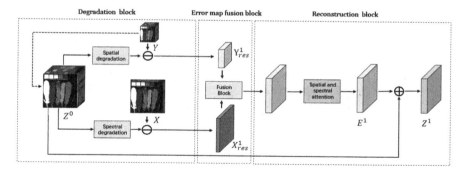

**Fig. 1.** The structure of the degradation block, the error map fusion block and the reconstruction block.

### 3.2    Degradation Block

Our network includes two inputs: LR-HSI $Y$ and HR-MSI $X$. Since the HR-MSI is spectral down-sampled, it has more spatial information than LR-HSI. Correspondingly, the LR-HSI preserves more spectral information than the HR-MSI. In order to simulate the degradation model using the convolutional network, we upscale LR-HSI by bicubic interpolation to obtain input data of the same size as the HR-HSI. The result of the up-sampling is denoted by $Z^0$, which can be considered as a rough estimate of HR-HSI.

At first, we feed $Z^0$ into the network and let it pass through the spectral and spatial degradation blocks respectively, which can be expressed as

$$\hat{X}^1 = D_{spe}\left(Z^0\right) \tag{4}$$

$$\hat{Y}^1 = D_{spa}\left(Z^0\right) \tag{5}$$

Many algorithms consider the spectrum down-sampling operator $P$ in Eq. (1) as a matrix and then HR-MSI can be calculated by simple matrix multiplication. We apply the $D_{spe}(\bullet)$ for modelling the HR-HSI spectral degradation mechanism, which is composed of a convolutional layer and an activation function layer. While the operator $B$ and $S$ in Eq. (2) have usually been implemented with convolution and pooling. The function $D_{spa}(\cdot)$ has the same structure as $D_{spe}(\bullet)$ and represents the non-linear mapping between LR-HSI and HR-HSI. Secondly, the spatial and spectral residuals of $Z^0$ are obtained by differencing the degradation results obtained in the first step with the observed data, which can be written as

$$X_{res}^1 = X - \hat{X}^1 \tag{6}$$

$$Y_{res}^1 = Y - \hat{Y}^1 \tag{7}$$

Finally, $X_{res}^1$ and $Y_{res}^1$ are used as the input of the error map feature extraction block to estimate residual map $E^1$ between $Z^0$ and $Z$. The implementation detail is described in Sect. 3.3.

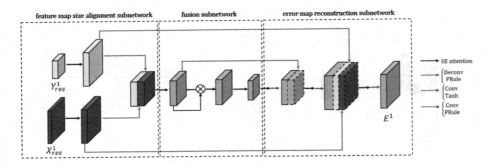

**Fig. 2.** The specific structure of the error map fusion block.

## 3.3   Error Map Fusion Block

In this section, we will specify the network structure of the error map fusion block like the Fig. 2. The $X_{res}^1$ and $Y_{res}^1$ outputted from the degradation block are used to produce the particular error map corresponding to $Z^0$. Degraded images $\hat{X}^1$ and $\hat{Y}^1$ retain the effective low-level semantic information of the $Z^0$ during the forward propagation of the network. Thus, residual data $X_{res}^1$ and

$Y_{res}^1$ are more accurate for the correction of $Z^0$. The error map fusion process can be expressed as

$$Z^0 = \Phi(X_{res}^1 , Y_{res}^1) \tag{8}$$

**Feature Map Size Alignment Subnetwork.** The size of LR-HSI $\hat{Y}^1$ is smaller than the HR-MSI $\hat{X}^1$ as it is spatially down-sampled. To maintain the consistency of the feature size between the extracted features and the fusion results, we up-sample the $Y_{res}^1$ using deconvolution while the learnable CNN can improve the up-sampling results for each channel. And then passed it through a down-sampling layer for initial feature extraction. Meanwhile, the $X_{res}^1$ is passed through a low-level feature extraction block consisting of one convolution layer and one PRelu layer. After that, it was also seed to a down-sampling layer.

**Fusion Subnetwork.** The features extracted from $X_{res}^1$ and $Y_{res}^1$ are concatenated along the spectral dimension. The fusion subnet consists of two convolution layers with separate activation functions. We incorporate a channel attention mechanism to the results of the first fusion layer to better preserve the spectral structure and reduce redundant information. The feature map is down-sampled again after this subnetwork. At this time, we have obtained the feature maps containing the spatial and spectral information simultaneously, which will be used to reconstruct the residual map of $Z^0$ by the subsequent up-sampling network.

**Error Map Reconstruction Subnetwork.** The error map reconstruction subnetwork is composed of two sets of network structures, each comprising successive convolutional, deconvolution layers and activation functions. In an effort to take advantage of the complementary nature of the higher-level and lower-level features, jump connections are added to the features after each deconvolution. The last concatenated feature maps are then convolved in two layers to obtain the final result. In this way, the error feature map $\hat{E}^1$ is acquired from this subnetwork. $\hat{E}^1$ contains high frequency information proposed from $X_{res}^1$ and $Y_{res}^1$, and used to rebuild the final result.

### 3.4  Reconstruction Block

The reconstruction block refines the $Z^0$ with the error map $\hat{E}^1$ outputted after the first two blocks. In order to make the error maps obtained in the previous part better modify the initial hyperspectral image, we apply spatial and spectral attention model to the maps. And then $\hat{E}^1$ are added to the $Z^0$ as shown by the skip connection in Fig. 1 to produce the reconstructed hyperspectral image $Z^1$, which can be written as

$$Z^1 = Z^0 + \hat{E}^1 \tag{9}$$

To improve the accuracy of $Z^1$, we refine it by one more degradation and reconstruction operation and the implementation process is the same as the three blocks above. The whole process is shown in the Fig. 3, and the final output is expressed as

$$Z^2 \;=\; Z^1 + \hat{E}^2 \;=\; Z^1 + \Phi\left(X_{res}^2,\; Y_{res}^2\right) = Z^1 + \Phi\left(D_{spe}\left(Z^1\right),\; D_{spa}\left(Z^1\right)\right) \quad (10)$$

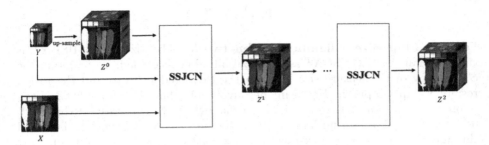

**Fig. 3.** The overall structure of the proposed spatial spectral joint correction network.

### 3.5 Loss Function

In our model, we reconstruct the HR-HSI by learning the mapping function $f_\theta(X, Y)$. The parameters $\theta$ are optimized by minimizing the loss between the outputs and the observed images. We choose the L1 norm function as the loss function for it is simple to implement and achieves good results in image super-resolution [17]. Thus, the loss function defined as

$$l\left(\theta\right) = \|Z - Z^2\| = \|f_\theta(X, Y) - Z^2\| \quad (11)$$

$X$ and $Y$ represent known LR-HSI and HR-MSI, which are obtained from the spatial and spectral down-sampling of the true value $Z$ respectively.

## 4    Experiments and Analysis

### 4.1    Data and Experimental Setup

We conducted experiments on CAVE and Harvard dataset. The CAVE dataset consists of HR-HSI captured under 32 indoor scenes with manipulated illumination. Each HR-HSI is 512*512*31 in size, where 512 is the spatial size of the image and 31 is the number of channels in the image, representing the reflectance of the material in the scene at different spectra. The Harvard database contains 50 images taken under daylight illumination, and 27 images under artificial or mixed lighting. In this experiment we use 50 images under daylight illumination. The first 20 of these HSIs are assigned as the training set, the middle 5 are used as the validation set, and the last 25 HSIs are used for testing.

We compare the proposed method with HySure [12], DHSIS [1] and DBIN [14]. HySure formulates the fusion problem as a convex optimization problem, which is solved by the split augmented Lagrange algorithm (SALSA). DHSIS optimizes the modeling results using the prior information extracted from the convolutional network, while DBIN is a network structure built entirely from convolutional layers. Figure 4 shows the output images obtained by the several methods and corresponding error maps.

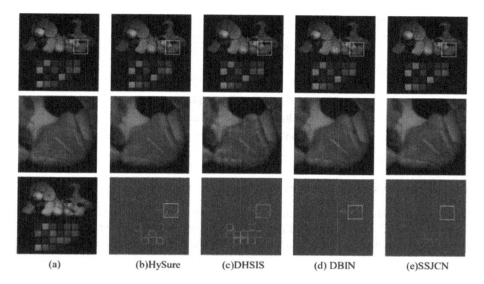

|   (a)   |   (b)HySure   |   (c)DHSIS   |   (d) DBIN   |   (e)SSJCN   |

**Fig. 4.** The results from *stuffed toys* at band 20 in the CAVE dataset. (a) the ground truth at band 20 and the HR-MSI. (b–d) reconstructed images and the corresponding error maps after image enhancement while light color represents the error.

## 4.2   Comparison with Other Methods on CAVE

We take the HSIs from the database as the ground truths. We first blur the ground truths with a Gaussian filter and then down-sample the blurred image by a factor of $1/4$. The result of the down-sampling is the simulated LR-HSI. While HR-MSI is generated by multiplying the HS-HSI and the spectral response matrix, and the total number of channels for the HR-MSI is 3. As an image of size $512 * 512$ is a heavy burden for reading data with CPU and training with GPU, we take $8 * 8$ blocks of images from the training set and use the extracted blocks for training.

The test set is being processed in the same way as the training set and the final restored images are obtained by patching the resulting images together in sequence. To better discern the difference, the image enhancement process was implemented on the error maps. The second row in Fig. 4 is a local enlargement of the results obtained by the different methods in the first row, where the results obtained by DHSIS have a clear rectangular block distortion. Although HySure and DBIN maintain the overall structure of the image, obviously results obtained by our proposed method have the least error with the original image. And also, according to the results shown in Table 1, the performance of the proposed method on CAVE dataset was best than those of other methods.

**Table 1.** Average performance of the compared methods of CAVE dataset.

|        | PSNR    | SSIM   | SAM    | EGRAS  |
|--------|---------|--------|--------|--------|
|        | +∞      | 1      | 0      | 0      |
| HySure | 40.5841 | 0.9779 | 6.2523 | 2.5095 |
| DHSIS  | 45.1842 | 0.9903 | 3.3527 | 1.3427 |
| DBIN   | 47.2403 | 0.9933 | 3.2230 | 1.1669 |
| **SSJCN** | **48.5434** | **0.9937** | **3.0916** | **1.0165** |

## 4.3   Comparison with Other Methods on Harvard

The images in the Harvard data are processed in the same way as the CAVE data. Figure 5 shows the reconstructed results and the corresponding error maps, again with image enhancement for ease of observation. Combining Fig. 5 and Table 2 we can clearly see that our proposed method yields the lowest error results.

**Table 2.** Average performance of the compared methods of Harvard dataset.

|        | PSNR    | SSIM   | SAM    | EGRAS  |
|--------|---------|--------|--------|--------|
|        | +∞      | 1      | 0      | 0      |
| HySure | 44.5991 | 0.9788 | 3.9709 | 2.8675 |
| DHSIS  | 45.7591 | 0.9812 | 3.7445 | 3.1335 |
| DBIN   | 46.1493 | 0.9839 | 3.6503 | 2.9645 |
| **SSJCN** | **47.1581** | **0.9847** | **3.3153** | **2.1151** |

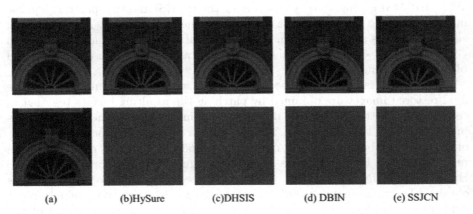

(a)          (b)HySure          (c)DHSIS          (d) DBIN          (e) SSJCN

**Fig. 5.** The results at band 20 of the selected part in the Harvard dataset. (a) the ground truth at band 20 and the HR-MSI. (b–d) reconstructed images and the corresponding error maps after image enhancement while light color represents the error. (Color figure online)

## 4.4    Effectiveness of Degradation Block

As mentioned in the previous section, we hold the opinion that learning the degradation model and error maps to improve the accuracy of the fusion results. Therefore, in this section we demonstrate the effectiveness of the degradation model of the proposed end-to-end model. Take CAVE dataset as an illustration, the results are shown in Fig. 6. Although the output image after RB (1) of Fig. 3 is visually close to the original image, we can see a considerable amount of rectangular deformation in the error image in the Fig. 6, which is reflected in the LR HSI acquired from the degradation of DB (2). It can be inferred that the degradation model in this experiment effectively preserves the details and structural information of the degraded images, which helps to improve the network results. Moreover, we can also observe that the estimation error map outputted from DB (2) is very close to the error between the results reconstructed after RB (1) and the true value, which indicates that the correction map is effective. Besides, performing two iterations on the input data further improves quality assessment values, and the comparison results showed on Table 3.

**Table 3.** The proposed methods with different iteration numbers of CAVE dataset.

|            | PSNR      | SSIM     | SAM     | EGRAS   |
|------------|-----------|----------|---------|---------|
|            | $+\infty$ | 1        | 0       | 0       |
| SSJCN (1)  | 47.1570   | 0.9928   | 3.2652  | 1.1584  |
| SSJCN (2)  | 48.5434   | 0.9937   | 3.0916  | 1.0165  |

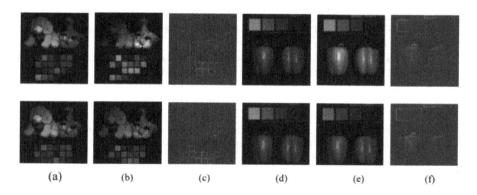

(a)          (b)          (c)          (d)          (e)          (f)

**Fig. 6.** The results from *stuffed toys* and *real and fake apples* at band 30. (a, d) first row: original RGB image, second row: the HR MSI obtained after DB (2). (b, e) original LR HSI and the LR HSI obtained after DB (2). (c, f) first row: the error map between the reconstructed result after RB (1) and the true value, second row: the estimated error map in DB2.

## 5    Conclusion

In this article, a spatial-spectral joint correction network is proposed for HS-MS fusion. SSJCN consists of degradation blocks, error map fusion blocks and the reconstruction blocks, which are used to simulate the degradation mechanism and make corrections to the initialized data respectively. The parameters of network are optimized by minimizing the loss between the outputs and the ground truth. The comparison results between the proposed method and other SOTA methods demonstrate the effectiveness of the proposed method.

## References

1. Dian, R., Li, S., Guo, A., Fang, L.: Deep hyperspectral image sharpening. IEEE Trans. Neural Netw. Learn. Syst. **29**(11), 5345–5355 (2018)
2. Dong, C., Loy, C.C., He, K., Tang, X.: Learning a deep convolutional network for image super-resolution. In: Fleet, D., Pajdla, T., Schiele, B., Tuytelaars, T. (eds.) ECCV 2014. LNCS, vol. 8692, pp. 184–199. Springer, Cham (2014). https://doi.org/10.1007/978-3-319-10593-2_13
3. Dong, W., et al.: Hyperspectral image super-resolution via non-negative structured sparse representation. IEEE Trans. Image Process. **25**(5), 2337–2352 (2016)
4. Han, X.H., Shi, B., Zheng, Y.: SSF-CNN: spatial and spectral fusion with CNN for hyperspectral image super-resolution. In: 2018 25th IEEE International Conference on Image Processing (ICIP) (2018)
5. Han, X.H., Zheng, Y., Chen, Y.W.: Multi-level and multi-scale spatial and spectral fusion CNN for hyperspectral image super-resolution. In: Proceedings of the IEEE/CVF International Conference on Computer Vision (ICCV) Workshops (2019)
6. He, K., Zhang, X., Ren, S., Sun, J.: Deep residual learning for image recognition. In: Proceedings of the IEEE Conference on Computer Vision and Pattern Recognition (CVPR) (2016)
7. Kwon, H., Tai, Y.W.: RGB-guided hyperspectral image upsampling. In: Proceedings of the IEEE International Conference on Computer Vision (ICCV) (2015)
8. Li, S., Dian, R., Fang, L., Bioucas-Dias, J.M.: Fusing hyperspectral and multispectral images via coupled sparse tensor factorization. IEEE Trans. Image Process. **27**(8), 4118–4130 (2018)
9. Liu, P., Xiao, L., Li, T.: A variational pan-sharpening method based on spatial fractional-order geometry and spectral-spatial low-rank priors. IEEE Trans. Geosci. Remote Sens. **56**(3), 1788–1802 (2018)
10. Loncan, L., et al.: Hyperspectral pansharpening: a review. IEEE Geosci. Remote Sens. Mag. **3**(3), 27–46 (2015)
11. Marinelli, D., Bovolo, F., Bruzzone, L.: A novel change detection method for multitemporal hyperspectral images based on binary hyperspectral change vectors. IEEE Trans. Geosci. Remote Sens. **57**(7), 4913–4928 (2019)
12. Simões, M., Bioucas-Dias, J., Almeida, L.B., Chanussot, J.: A convex formulation for hyperspectral image superresolution via subspace-based regularization. IEEE Trans. Geosci. Remote Sens. **53**(6), 3373–3388 (2015)
13. Saravanakumar, V., Ealai Rengasari, N.: A survey of hyperspectral image segmentation techniques for multiband reduction. Aust. J. Basic Appl. Sci. **15**, 446–451 (2019)

14. Wang, W., Zeng, W., Huang, Y., Ding, X., Paisley, J.: Deep blind hyperspectral image fusion. In: Proceedings of the IEEE/CVF International Conference on Computer Vision (ICCV) (2019)
15. Xu, S., Amira, O., Liu, J., Zhang, C.X., Zhang, J., Li, G.: HAM-MFN: hyperspectral and multispectral image multiscale fusion network with rap loss. IEEE Trans. Geosci. Remote Sens. **58**(7), 4618–4628 (2020)
16. Yan, H., Zhang, Y., Wei, W., Zhang, L., Li, Y.: Salient object detection in hyperspectral imagery using spectral gradient contrast. In: 2016 IEEE International Geoscience and Remote Sensing Symposium (IGARSS) (2016)
17. Zhao, H., Gallo, O., Frosio, I., Kautz, J.: Loss functions for image restoration with neural networks. IEEE Trans. Comput. Imaging **3**(1), 47–57 (2017)

# Learning Theory and Optimization

# q-Softplus Function: Extensions of Activation Function and Loss Function by Using q-Space

Motoshi Abe$^{(\boxtimes)}$ and Takio Kurita

Hiroshima University, Higashi-Hiroshima, Japan
i13abemotoshi@gmail.com, tkurita@hiroshima-u.ac.jp

**Abstract.** In recent years, the performance of machine learning algorithms has been rapidly improved because of the progress of deep learning. To approximate any non-linear function, almost all models of deep learning use the non-linear activation function. Rectified linear units (ReLU) function is most commonly used. The continuous version of the ReLU function is the softplus function and it is derived by the integration of the sigmoid function. Since a sigmoid function is based on Gaussian distribution, the softplus activation function is also based on Gaussian distribution. In machine learning and statistics, most techniques assume the Gaussian distribution because Gaussian distribution is easy to handle in mathematical theory. For example, the exponential family is often assumed in information geometry which connects various branches of mathematical science in dealing with uncertainty and information based on unifying geometric concepts. The q-space is defined to extend this limitation of information geometry. On the q-space, q-multiplication, q-division, q-exponential, and q-logarithm are defined with hyperparameter $q$ as a natural extension of multiplication and division, etc. in general space. In this paper, we propose to extend the activation function and the loss function by using q-space. By this extension, we can introduce hyperparameter $q$ to control the shape of the function and the standard softplus function can be recovered by setting the hyperparameter $q = 1$. The effectiveness of the proposed q-softplus function, we have performed experiments in which the q-softplus function is used for the activation function of a convolutional neural network instead of the ReLU function and the loss function of metric learning Siamese and Triplet instead of max function.

**Keywords:** q-Space · Activation function · q-Softplus

## 1 Introduction

In recent years, the performance of the machine learning algorithms has been rapidly improved. Many techniques of machine learning are proposed such as support vector machine [24], neural network [4], convolutional neural network [6], and so on. Since these models can approximate any non-linear function, they are effective for classification [11,13,20,21], person recognition [7,10], object detection [25], and so on.

© Springer Nature Switzerland AG 2022
C. Wallraven et al. (Eds.): ACPR 2021, LNCS 13189, pp. 31–44, 2022.
https://doi.org/10.1007/978-3-031-02444-3_3

To approximate any non-linear function, almost all models of deep learning use the non-linear activation function. Rectified linear units (ReLU) function is most commonly used as non-linear activation function of the hidden layers in the deep learning models. Sigmoid function or softmax function is often used as a non-linear activation function in the output layer of the deep learning models.

The continuous version of the ReLU function is softplus function and it is derived by the integration of the sigmoid function. The sigmoid function and softmax function are defined by using exponential function and have a close relation with Gaussian distribution. It means that the input of the sigmoid or softmax function is assumed to be a Gaussian distribution. Exponential linear units (ELU) [19], Sigmoid-weighted linear unit (SiLU) [9], swish [18], and mish [16] have been proposed as extension of ReLU function. The such activation functions are derived from ReLU function or sigmoid function.

In machine learning and statistics, most techniques assume the Gaussian distribution for prior distribution or conditional distribution because Gaussian distribution is easy to handle in mathematical theory. For example, the exponential family is often assumed in information geometry which connects various branches of mathematical science in dealing with uncertainty and information based on unifying geometric concepts. In information geometry, it is famous that the exponential family is flat under the e-connection. The Gaussian distribution is a kind of the exponential family.

However, some famous probability distributions, such t-distribution, is not exponential family. As an extension of information geometry, $q$-space is defined [22]. On the $q$-space, $q$-multiplication, $q$-division, $q$-exponential, and $q$-logarithm are defined with hyperparameter $q$ as a natural extension of multiplication and division, etc. in general space. In the $q$-space, the $q$-Gaussian distribution is derived by the maximization of the Tsallis entropy under appropriate constraints. The $q$-Gaussian distribution includes Gaussian distribution and t-distribution that can be represented by setting the hyperparameter $q$ to $q = 1$ for Gaussian distribution and $q = 2.0$ for t-distribution. Since the $q$-Gaussian distribution can be written by scalar parameter, we can handle some probability distributions as flat in $q$-space.

The authors proposed to used $q$-Gaussian distribution for dimensionality reduction technique. The t-Distributed Stochastic Neighbor Embedding (t-SNE) [15] and the parametric t-SNE [14] are extended by using the $q$-Gaussian distribution instead of t-distribution as the probability distribution on low-dimensional space. They are named $q$-SNE [1] and the parametric $q$-SNE [17].

In this paper, we propose to define the activation function and the loss function by using the $q$-exponential and $q$-logarithm of $q$-space. Especially we define $q$-softplus function as an extension of the softplus function. By this extension, we can introduce hyperparameter $q$ to control the shape of the function. For example, we can recover the standard softplus function or the shifted ReLU function by changing the hyperparameter $q$ of the $q$-softplus function. To make the origin of the proposed $q$-softplus function the same as the one of the ReLU function, we also defined the shifted $q$-softplus function.

To show the effectiveness of the proposed shifted *q*-softplus function, we have performed experiments in which the shifted *q*-softplus function is used as the activation function in a convolutional neural network instead of the standard ReLU function. Also, we have performed experiments in which the *q*-softplus function is used for loss function of metric learning Siamese [5, 8, 10] and Triplet [12, 23] instead of the max function. Through the experiments, the proposed *q*-softplus function shows better results on CIFAR10, CIFAR100, STL10, and TinyImageNet datasets.

## 2   Related Work

### 2.1   *q*-Space

Information geometry is an interdisciplinary field that applies the techniques of differential geometry to study probability theory and statistics [3]. It studies statistical manifolds, which are Riemannian manifolds whose points correspond to probability distributions. Tanaka [22] extended the information geometry developed on the exponential family to *q*-Gaussian distribution.

To do so, it is necessary to extend the standard multiplication, division, exponential, and logarithm to *q*-multiplication, *q*-division, *q*-exponential, and *q*-logarithm in [22]. Then we can consider a space in which these *q*-arithmetic operations are defined. In this paper, we call this space *q*-space.

In *q*-space, the *q*-multiplication and *q*-division of two functions $f$ and $g$ are respectively defined as

$$f \otimes_q g = \left( f^{1-q} + g^{1-q} - 1 \right)^{\frac{1}{1-q}} , \tag{1}$$

and

$$f \oslash_q g = \left( f^{1-q} - g^{1-q} + 1 \right)^{\frac{1}{1-q}} , \tag{2}$$

where $q$ is a hyperparameter.

Similarly the *q*-exponential and *q*-logarithm are defined as

$$exp_q(x) = \left( 1 + (1-q)\,x \right)^{\frac{1}{1-q}} , \tag{3}$$

and

$$log_q(x) = \frac{1}{1-q} \left( x^{1-q} - 1 \right) . \tag{4}$$

These *q*-arithmetic operations converge to the standard multiplication and division when $q \to 1$. In the *q*-space, the *q*-Gaussian distribution is derived by the maximization of the Tsallis entropy under appropriate constraints. The *q*-Gaussian distribution includes Gaussian distribution and t-distribution. Since the *q*-Gaussian distribution can be written with a scalar parameter $q$, we can handle a set of probability distributions as flat in *q*-space.

## 2.2 Activation Function

In a neural network, we use an activation function to approximate non-linear function. The ReLU function is famous and is mostly used in deep neural networks. The ReLU function is defined as

$$ReLU(x) = max(0, x). \tag{5}$$

The main reason why the ReLU function is used in deep neural network is that the ReLU function can prevent the vanishing gradient problem. The ReLU function is very simple and works well in deep neural networks. This function is also called the plus function.

The softplus function is a continuous version of the ReLU function and is defined as

$$Softplus(x) = \log{(1 + \exp{x})}. \tag{6}$$

The first derivative of this function is continuous around at 0.0 while one of the ReLU function is not. The softplus function is also derivation as integral of a sigmoid function.

Recently many activation functions have been proposed for deep neural networks [9,16,18,19]. Almost all of such activation functions are defined based on the ReLU function or sigmoid function or a combination of the ReLU function and sigmoid function.

These functions are also used to define loss function. For example, the max (ReLU) function or softplus function is used as contrastive loss or triplet loss uses in metric learning.

## 2.3 Metric Learning

The Siamese network and Triplet network have been proposed and often used for metric learning.

The Siamese network consists of two networks which have the shared weights and can learn metrics between two outputs. In the training, the two samples are fed to each network and the shared weights of the network are modified so that the two outputs of the network are closer together when the two samples belong to the same class, and so that the two outputs are farther apart when they belong to different classes.

Let $\{(\boldsymbol{x}_i, y_i)|i = 1 \ldots N\}$ be a set of training samples, where $\boldsymbol{x}_i$ is an image and $y_i$ is a class label of i-th sample. The loss function of the Siamese network is defined as

$$L_{siamese} = \frac{1}{2}t_{ij}d_{ij}^2 + \frac{1}{2}(1 - t_{ij})max(m - d_{ij}, 0)^2, \tag{7}$$

$$d_{ij} = \|f(\boldsymbol{x}_i; \theta) - f(\boldsymbol{x}_j; \theta)\|^2 \tag{8}$$

where $t_{ij}$ is the binary indicator which shows whether the i-th and j-th samples are the same class or not, $f$ is a function corresponding to the network, $\theta$ is a set of shared weights of the network. This $\theta$ is learned by minimizing this loss $L_{siamese}$. The Siamese loss is called the contrastive loss. It is noticed that the max (ReLU) function is used in this loss. It is possible to use the softplus function instead of the max function.

The Triplet network consists of three networks with the shared weights and learns metrics between three outputs. In the training, the three samples are fed to each network. One sample is called an anchor. The sample that is the same class with the anchor is called a positive sample and the sample that is a different class from the anchor is called a negative sample. For the positive sample, the networks is trained such that the two outputs of anchor and positive are closer together. For the negative sample, the networks is trained such that the two outputs of anchor and negative become away from each other.

Let $x_a$, $x_p$, and $x_n$ be the anchor, the positive, and the negative sample respectively. The loss function of the Triplet network is defined as

$$L_{triplet} = max(d_{ap} - d_{an} + m, 0), \tag{9}$$

where $m$ is a margin, $d_{ij}$ is a distance same as the contrastive loss. It is noticed that the max (ReLU) function is also used in this loss. We can use the softplus function instead of the max function. Since the max or softplus function is linear when $x >> 0$, they are effect to move the sample farther away. This is very important for metric learning.

# 3  *q*-Softplus Function and Shifted *q*-Softplus Function

The $q$-Space is defined to extend information geometry developed for exponential family. By using $q$-space, we can consider the natural extended world. In this paper, we proposed an extension of the standard activation functions or the loss functions by using $q$-space. Since $q$-exponential and $q$-logarithm express the various shape of a graph by setting a hyperparameter $q$, we can control the shape of the activation function or the loss function by selecting the better parameter $q$ in the $q$-space. In particular, in this paper, we proposed the $q$-softplus function as an extension of the softplus function.

## 3.1  *q*-Softplus Function

The $q$-softplus function is defined as

$$
\begin{aligned}
qsoftplus(x) &= log_q(1 + exp_q x) \\
&= \frac{1}{1-q}\left(\left(1 + max\left(1 + (1-q)\,x, 0\right)^{\frac{1}{1-q}}\right)^{1-q} - 1\right). \tag{10}
\end{aligned}
$$

When $q \to 1$, $q$-softplus function close to the original softplus function. Figure 1 (A) shows the shape of the $q$-softplus function compared with the max (ReLU) function and the softplus function. When $q = 0.999$ ($q$ close to 1), $q$-softplus

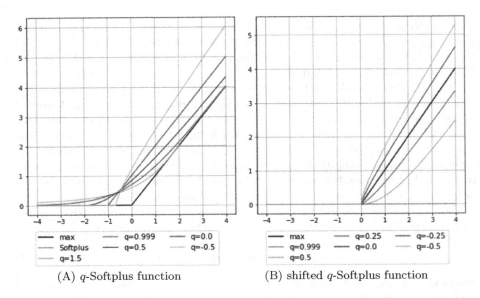

(A) $q$-Softplus function          (B) shifted $q$-Softplus function

**Fig. 1.** This figure shows the graph of the activation functions. In (A), it shows the max (ReLU) function, softplus function and $q$-softplus function with difference hyperparamete $q$. When $q = 0.999$, $q$ close to 1, the $q$-softplus function overlaps the softplus function. In (B), it shows the max (ReLU) function and shifted $q$-softplus function with difference hyperparamete $q$. When $q = 0.0$, the $q$-softplus function overlaps the max function.

function overlapped with the softplus function. Moreover, when $q = 0.0$, $q$-softplus function becomes the shifted max function. From Fig. 1 (A), it is noticed that the $q$-softplus function can represent the various shapes including the max (ReLU) function and the softplus function. When $1 + (1 - q)\, x > 0$ the first derivative of x is as follows,

$$\frac{dqsoftplus(x)}{dx} = \left(1 + (1 + (1-q)x)^{\frac{1}{1-q}}\right)^{-q} (1 + (1-q)x)^{\frac{q}{1-q}}$$
$$= (1 + exp_q x)^{-q} (exp_q x)^q,\tag{11}$$

other wise is 0. When $q \to 1$, Eq. 11 closes to first derivation of softplus function.

## 3.2   Shifted $q$-Softplus Function

The $q$-softplus function becomes shifted max function when $q = 0.0$. To make $q$-softplus with $q = 0.0$ the same as the max function, we propose to shift $q$-softplus function by introducing sift term. We call this function the shifted $q$-softplus

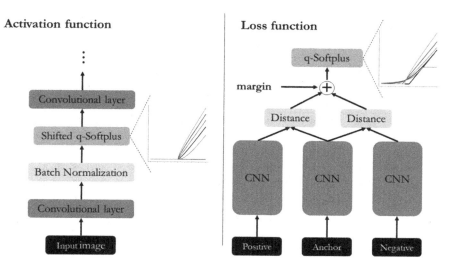

**Fig. 2.** This figure shows network architecture where $q$-softplus or shifted $q$-softplus function is used. As an activation function, the shifted $q$-softplus is replaced from ReLU function. As a loss function of triplet loss, the $q$-softplus function is replaced from max function.

function Then the shifted $q$-softplus function is defined as

$$sqsoftplus(x) = log_q(1 + exp_q(x - \frac{1}{1-q}))$$

$$= \frac{1}{1-q}\left(\left(1 + max\left(1 + (1-q)(x - \frac{1}{1-q}), 0\right)^{\frac{1}{1-q}}\right)^{1-q} - 1\right). \tag{12}$$

When $q = 0.0$, the shifted $q$-softplus function becomes the same as the max function. Figure 1 (B) shows the shapes of the shifted $q$-softplus function. It is noticed that the shifted $q$-softplus function can represent the various shapes including the max function from this figure.

### 3.3   Loss Function for Metric Learning

The loss function of the Siamese network or the Triplet network, the max or softplus function is important to move the sample farther away because the max or softplus function is linear when $x >> 0$. We also propose a new loss function called $q$-contrastive loss and $q$-triplet loss by using $q$-softplus. The $q$-contrastive loss is defined as

$$L_{qsiamese} = \frac{1}{2}t_{ij}d_{ij}^2 + \frac{1}{2}(1 - t_{ij})qsoftplus(m - d_{ij}, 0)^2. \tag{13}$$

**Table 1.** This table shows classification accuracy on CIFAR10, CIFAR100, STL10 and Tiny ImageNet. The hyperparameters $q$ of all activation function on VGG11 are same. The accuracy shows percentage for train and test sample respectively.

| | CIFAR10 | | | | CIFAR100 | | | |
|---|---|---|---|---|---|---|---|---|
| | VGG without BN | | VGG with BN | | VGG without BN | | VGG with BN | |
| | Train | Test | Train | Test | Train | Test | Train | Test |
| ReLU | 100 | 87.74 | 100 | 89.00 | 99.98 | 62.65 | 99.98 | 64.91 |
| $q = -0.5$ | 10 | 10 | 100 | 88.39 | 1 | 1 | 99.97 | 61.52 |
| $q = -0.25$ | 100 | 86.56 | 100 | 88.85 | 99.98 | 57.98 | 99.98 | 63.99 |
| $q = -0.1$ | 100 | 87.56 | 100 | 88.80 | 99.98 | 61.33 | 99.98 | 65.31 |
| $q = 0.0$ | 100 | 87.74 | 100 | 89.00 | 99.98 | 62.65 | 99.98 | 64.91 |
| $q = 0.1$ | 100 | **88.20** | 100 | 88.98 | 99.98 | 62.93 | 99.98 | **65.48** |
| $q = 0.2$ | 100 | 87.62 | 100 | **89.09** | 99.98 | **63.18** | 99.98 | 65.07 |
| $q = 0.25$ | 100 | 87.75 | 100 | 88.95 | 99.98 | 62.45 | 99.98 | 64.63 |
| $q = 0.5$ | 10 | 10 | 100 | 84.98 | 1 | 1 | 99.98 | 53.62 |

| | STL10 | | | | TinyImageNet | | | |
|---|---|---|---|---|---|---|---|---|
| | VGG without BN | | VGG with BN | | VGG without BN | | VGG with BN | |
| | Train | Test | Train | Test | Train | Test | Train | Test |
| ReLU | 100 | 91.76 | 100 | 92.68 | 85.18 | 52.50 | 92.03 | 56.10 |
| $q = -0.5$ | 10 | 10 | 100 | 87.55 | 0.5 | 0.5 | 72.46 | 50.98 |
| $q = -0.25$ | 100 | 89.75 | 100 | 91.11 | 62.04 | 47.69 | 86.29 | 54.36 |
| $q = -0.1$ | 100 | 91.45 | 100 | 92.08 | 78.62 | 51.50 | 90.40 | 56.09 |
| $q = 0.0$ | 100 | 91.76 | 100 | 92.68 | 85.18 | 52.50 | 92.03 | 56.10 |
| $q = 0.1$ | 100 | 91.34 | 100 | 92.59 | 88.86 | **53.24** | 92.39 | 56.60 |
| $q = 0.2$ | 100 | 90.60 | 100 | 92.34 | 89.97 | 52.94 | 92.19 | 56.33 |
| $q = 0.25$ | 100 | 89.85 | 100 | 91.90 | 90.20 | 52.73 | 92.14 | **56.87** |
| $q = 0.5$ | 10 | 10 | 25.32 | 18.23 | 0.5 | 0.5 | 62.35 | 49.13 |

Similarly, the $q$-triplet loss is defined as

$$L_{triplet} = qsoftplus(d_{ap} - d_{an} + m, 0). \qquad (14)$$

By using the $q$-softplus function, we can control the effect of moving the sample farther away. Since the first derivative of the $q$-softplus function is continuous at 0, it can move the sample more farther away than the given margin. We can also use the shifted $q$-softplus function in loss function. Since the shifted $q$-softplus function has distorted linear shapes, we can control the effect of loss.

Figure 2 shows the example of the network architecture where the $q$-softplus function or the shifted $q$-softplus function is used. In this figure, the example of the triplet loss is shown.

**Table 2.** This table shows test classification accuracy on CIFAR10, CIFAR100, STL10 and Tiny ImageNet by using optuna. The hyperparameters $q$ of shifted $q$-softplus function found by optuna are shown in Table 3. The accuracy shows percentage.

| | CIFAR10 | | CIFAR100 | |
|---|---|---|---|---|
| | VGG without BN | VGG with BN | VGG without BN | VGG with BN |
| ReLU | 87.74 | 89.00 | 62.65 | 64.91 |
| q-softplus | **88.34** | **89.23** | **63.58** | **65.57** |

| | STL10 | | TinyImageNet | |
|---|---|---|---|---|
| | VGG without BN | VGG with BN | VGG without BN | VGG with BN |
| ReLU | 91.76 | 92.68 | 52.50 | 56.10 |
| q-softplus | **91.81** | **92.80** | **53.33** | **56.97** |

**Table 3.** This table shows the found hyperparameter $q$ of each shifted $q$-softplus function on VGG11 by using optuna. VGG11 has 10 $q$-softplus activation functions. The qk denotes the k-th shifted $q$-softplus function from first layer.

| | CIFAR10 | | CIFAR100 | |
|---|---|---|---|---|
| | VGG without BN | VGG with BN | VGG without BN | VGG with BN |
| q0 | 0.015 | 0.118 | 0.105 | 0.012 |
| q1 | 0.198 | 0.039 | 0.107 | 0.162 |
| q2 | 0.075 | 0.086 | 0.007 | 0.249 |
| q3 | 0.184 | 0.246 | 0.048 | 0.158 |
| q4 | 0.241 | 0.067 | 0.106 | 0.023 |
| q5 | 0.227 | 0.067 | 0.143 | 0.042 |
| q6 | 0.201 | 0.145 | 0.204 | 0.113 |
| q7 | 0.155 | 0.162 | 0.073 | 0.166 |
| q8 | 0.034 | 0.057 | 0.058 | 0.249 |
| q9 | 0.151 | 0.035 | 0.003 | 0.064 |

| | STL10 | | TinyImageNet | |
|---|---|---|---|---|
| | VGG without BN | VGG with BN | VGG without BN | VGG with BN |
| q0 | 0.073 | 0.086 | 0.096 | 0.030 |
| q1 | 0.057 | 0.040 | 0.004 | 0.003 |
| q2 | 0.147 | 0.074 | 0.088 | 0.093 |
| q3 | 0.062 | 0.078 | 0.000 | 0.008 |
| q4 | 0.052 | 0.159 | 0.005 | 0.109 |
| q5 | 0.001 | 0.130 | 0.159 | 0.001 |
| q6 | 0.057 | 0.111 | 0.004 | 0.001 |
| q7 | 0.004 | 0.144 | 0.010 | 0.205 |
| q8 | 0.071 | 0.174 | 0.094 | 0.005 |
| q9 | 0.035 | 0.034 | 0.001 | 0.001 |

# 4 Experiments

## 4.1 Experimental Dataset

To confirm the effectiveness of the proposed $q$-softplus based activation function and loss function, we have performed experiments using MNIST, FashionMNIST, CIFAR10, CIFAR100, STL10, and Tiny ImageNet datasets.

**Table 4.** This table shows classification accuracy of test sample by Siamese network on MNIST, FashionMNIST and CIFAR10. The accuracy shows percentage for train and test sample respectively by k-nn.

| | MNIST | | | | | | FashionMNIST | | | | | |
|---|---|---|---|---|---|---|---|---|---|---|---|---|
| | q-softplus | | q-softplus with m-1 | | sq-softplus | | q-softplus | | q-softplus with m-1 | | sq-softplus | |
| | Train | Test | Train | Test | Train | Test | Train | Test | Train | Test | Train | Test |
| max | 99.99 | 99.37 | 99.99 | 98.37 | 99.99 | 99.37 | 99.83 | 91.29 | 99.37 | 91.26 | 99.83 | 91.29 |
| $q = -0.5$ | 99.99 | **99.41** | 99.99 | **99.42** | 99.99 | **99.43** | 99.84 | 91.08 | 99.82 | 91.33 | 99.83 | **91.53** |
| $q = -0.25$ | 99.99 | 99.39 | 99.99 | 99.41 | 99.99 | 99.41 | 99.86 | 90.95 | 99.83 | 91.27 | 99.81 | 91.29 |
| $q = 0.0$ | 99.99 | 99.41 | 99.99 | 99.37 | 99.99 | 99.37 | 99.86 | 90.91 | 99.83 | 91.29 | 99.83 | 91.29 |
| $q = 0.25$ | 99.99 | 99.36 | 99.99 | 99.35 | 99.99 | 99.33 | 99.86 | **91.29** | 99.79 | **91.36** | 99.25 | 91.28 |
| $q = 0.5$ | 99.99 | 99.38 | 99.99 | 99.36 | 99.99 | 99.29 | 99.86 | 91.26 | 99.72 | 91.25 | 95.83 | 90.30 |
| $q = 0.75$ | 99.99 | 99.35 | 99.99 | 99.30 | 99.82 | 98.99 | 99.85 | 91.22 | 99.56 | 91.30 | 75.37 | 65.81 |
| $q = 1.5$ | 74.76 | 64.74 | 74.76 | 64.74 | – | – | 76.96 | 67.54 | 77.03 | 67.64 | – | – |

| | CIFAR10 | | | | | |
|---|---|---|---|---|---|---|
| | q-softplus | | q-softplus with m-1 | | sq-softplus | |
| | Train | Test | Train | Test | Train | Test |
| max | 91.32 | 78.91 | 83.35 | 72.85 | 99.83 | 91.29 |
| $q = -0.5$ | 92.07 | **79.27** | 91.59 | **79.84** | 92.06 | **79.81** |
| $q = -0.25$ | 91.67 | 78.87 | 91.67 | 79.29 | 91.78 | 79.35 |
| $q = 0.0$ | 91.32 | 78.91 | 91.32 | 78.91 | 91.32 | 78.91 |
| $q = 0.25$ | 91.16 | 78.33 | 90.45 | 78.30 | 89.56 | 77.80 |
| $q = 0.5$ | 90.72 | 77.93 | 89.08 | 77.43 | 78.81 | 66.58 |
| $q = 0.75$ | 90.30 | 78.25 | 87.19 | 75.90 | 10 | 10 |
| $q = 1.5$ | 89.43 | 77.69 | 80.76 | 68.89 | – | – |

The MNIST has grey images of 10 class hand-written digits. The size of each image is $28 \times 28$ pixels. The number of training samples is 60,000 and the number of test samples is 10,000. The FashionMNIST has grey images of 10 classes of fashion items. The size of each image is $28 \times 28$ pixels. The number of training samples is 60,000 and the number of test samples is 10,000. The CIFAR10 has colored images of 10 class objects. The size of each image is $32 \times 32$ pixels. The number of training samples is 50,000 and the number of test samples is 10,000. The CIFAR100 has colored images of 100 class objects. The size of each image is $32 \times 32$ pixels. The number of training samples is 50,000 and the number of test samples is 10,000. The STL10 has colored images of 10 class objects. The size of each image is $96 \times 96$ pixels. The number of training samples is 500 and the number of test samples is 800. The TinyImageNet has colored images of 200 objects. The size of each image is $64 \times 64$ pixels. The number of training samples is 100,000 and the number of test samples is 10,000.

**Table 5.** This table shows classification accuracy of test sample by Triplet network on MNIST, FashionMNIST and CIFAR10. The accuracy shows percentage for train and test sample respectively by k-nn.

| | MNIST | | | | | | FashionMNIST | | | | | |
|---|---|---|---|---|---|---|---|---|---|---|---|---|
| | q-softplus | | q-softplus with m-1 | | sq-softplus | | q-softplus | | q-softplus with m-1 | | sq-softplus | |
| | Train | Test | Train | Test | Train | Test | Train | Test | Train | Test | Train | Test |
| max | 99.84 | 99.42 | 99.78 | 98.38 | 99.84 | 99.42 | 98.06 | 91.69 | 97.97 | 91.62 | 98.06 | 91.69 |
| $q = -0.5$ | 99.87 | **99.43** | 99.84 | **99.42** | 99.85 | **99.45** | 97.57 | 91.48 | 97.52 | 91.55 | 97.35 | 91.51 |
| $q = -0.25$ | 99.88 | 99.42 | 99.84 | 99.41 | 99.85 | 99.41 | 97.98 | 91.60 | 97.88 | 91.48 | 98.04 | 91.65 |
| $q = 0.0$ | 99.87 | 99.41 | 99.84 | 99.42 | 99.84 | 99.42 | 98.07 | 91.53 | 98.06 | 91.69 | 98.06 | 91.69 |
| $q = 0.25$ | 99.88 | 99.41 | 99.84 | 99.42 | 99.82 | 99.39 | 98.33 | **91.69** | 98.31 | **91.75** | 98.20 | 91.57 |
| $q = 0.5$ | 99.87 | 99.39 | 99.84 | 99.36 | 99.76 | 99.35 | 98.39 | 91.63 | 98.37 | 91.71 | 98.09 | 91.57 |
| $q = 0.75$ | 99.87 | 99.42 | 99.83 | 99.36 | 99.31 | 98.92 | 98.52 | 91.65 | 98.39 | 91.65 | 94.52 | 90.24 |
| $q = 1.5$ | 77.00 | 68.05 | 45.58 | 23.53 | – | – | 76.53 | 67.10 | 76.53 | 67.10 | – | – |

| | CIFAR10 | | | | | |
|---|---|---|---|---|---|---|
| | q-softplus | | q-softplus with m-1 | | sq-softplus | |
| | Train | Test | Train | Test | Train | Test |
| max | 86.47 | 75.36 | 86.47 | 75.36 | 86.47 | 75.36 |
| $q = -0.5$ | 80.34 | 69.44 | 83.35 | 72.75 | 81.17 | 69.99 |
| $q = -0.25$ | 81.12 | 70.06 | 84.81 | 74.02 | 84.11 | 73.19 |
| $q = 0.0$ | 81.79 | 70.47 | 86.47 | 75.36 | 86.47 | 75.36 |
| $q = 0.25$ | 82.59 | 71.44 | 86.97 | 75.43 | 89.27 | **77.69** |
| $q = 0.5$ | 83.96 | 72.88 | 86.80 | **75.46** | 88.24 | 77.05 |
| $q = 0.75$ | 83.83 | 72.37 | 86.66 | 75.15 | 10 | 10 |
| $q = 1.5$ | 35.00 | 15.31 | 82.12 | 71.10 | – | – |

## 4.2   Shifted *q*-Softplus as an Activation Function

To confirm the effectiveness to use the shifted *q*-softplus function as an activation function, we have performed experiments in which the shifted *q*-softplus function in CNN is used instead of the ReLU function. The classification accuracy is measured for the datasets CIFAR10, CIFAR100, STL10, and Tiny ImageNet. VGG11 [20] is used as the CNN model and the effect of Batch Normalization (BN) is also investigated. Stochastic gradient descent (SGD) with a momentum of 0.9 is used for optimization. The learning rate is at first set to 0.01 and is multiplied by 0.1 at 20 and 40 epochs. The parameter of the weight decay is set to 0.0001. The batch size is set to 100 training samples and the training is done for 100 epochs.

Table 1 shows the classification accuracy for different *q*. The score is calculated as the average of 5 trials with a different random seed. From this table, the shifted *q*-softplus function gives better classification accuracy than the ReLU function. From this table we can notice that the best hyperparameter *q* is around 0.2. When the hyperparameter *q* is positive, namely $q > 0.0$, the shape of the shifted *q*-softplus function becomes lower than the ReLU function. This means that better classification accuracy is obtained when the outputs of each layer are smaller than the outputs of the ReLU function.

We have also performed experiments to find the best hyperparameter $q$ of the shifted $q$-softplus function for each dataset by using optuna [2]. The optuna is developed for python language to find the best hyperparameter of the machine learning models. The objective function to find the best hyperparameter $q$ is the validation loss. We used 0.1% of training dataset as the validation samples. The trials of finding phase is set to 30.

The results of test accuracy for each dataset are shown in Table 2. Again, the values in the table are the averages of 5 trials with a different random seed. The best hyperparameters $q$ of the shifted $q$-softplus function for each dataset are shown in Table 3. It is noticed that the best hyperparameter $q$ is larger than 0.0 and smaller than 0.2 for almost all cases.

### 4.3   $q$-Softplus as an Loss Function of Metric Learning

To confirm the effectiveness of the $q$-softplus function as loss function, we have performed experiments in which the $q$-softplus function is used to define the loss function of the Siamese network and the Triplet network instead of the max function. We call these loss functions $q$-contrastive loss and $q$-triplet loss. MNIST, FashionMNIST, and CIFAR10 datasets are used in the experiments. The simple CNN with 2 convolutional layers and 3 fully connected layers is used for MNIST and FashionMNIST datasets. The ReLU function is used as the activation function in the hidden layers of the network. On the other hand, VGG11 with batch normalize is used for CIFAR10 dataset. The dimension of the final output is 10 for all datasets. Stochastic gradient descent (SGD) with a momentum of 0.9 is used for optimization. The learning rate is at first set to 0.01 and is multiplied by 0.1 at 20 and 40 epochs. The parameter of the weight decay is set to 0.0001. The batch size is to 100 samples and the training is done for 100 epochs. The margin in the loss function is determined by preliminary experiments.

The goodness of the feature vectors obtained by the trained network is evaluated by measuring the classification accuracy obtained by using k nearest neighbor (k-nn) in the 10-dimensional feature space. In the following experiment, k is set to 5 for k-nn. Since the $q$-softplus function becomes shifted max function when $q = 0.0$, we also included experiments with margin - 1.

Table 4 shows the classification accuracy obtained by the Siamese network and Table 5 shows the classification accuracy obtained by Triplet network. The score is the average of 5 trials with a different random seed.

It is noticed that the $q$-softplus function gives better classification accuracy than the max function. The best hyperparameter $q$ is around $-0.5$. Since the shape of the $q$-softplus function becomes higher than the max function when $q < 0.0$, to make the output larger is probably better to move the sample farther away.

# 5   Conclusion

In this paper, we proposed the $q$-softplus function and the shifted $q$-softplus function as an extension of the softplus function. Through the experiments of the classification task, we confirmed that the network in which the shifted $q$-softplus function is used as activation function in the hidden layers gives the better classification accuracy than the network using the ReLU function. Also, we found that the best $q$ in the shifted $q$-softplus function is around 0.2. This results suggest that better classification accuracy is obtained when the outputs of each layer are smaller than the outputs of the ReLU function. Through the experiments of metric learning, we confirmed that the $q$-softplus function can improve the contrastive loss of the Siamese network and the triplet loss of the Triplet network. For the metric learning, the best $q$ is around $-0.5$. This results suggest that better features can be obtained when the outputs are larger than the output of the max function.

**Acknowledgment.** This research was motivated from the insightful book by Prof. Masaru Tanaka at Fukuoka University. This work was partly supported by JSPS KAKENHI Grant Number 21K12049.

# References

1. Abe, M., Miyao, J., Kurita, T.: q-SNE: visualizing data using q-Gaussian distributed stochastic neighbor embedding. arXiv preprint arXiv:2012.00999 (2020)
2. Akiba, T., Sano, S., Yanase, T., Ohta, T., Koyama, M.: Optuna: a next-generation hyperparameter optimization framework. In: Proceedings of the 25rd ACM SIGKDD International Conference on Knowledge Discovery and Data Mining (2019)
3. Amari, S.: Differential-Geometrical Methods in Statistics, vol. 28. Lecture Notes in Statistics. Springer, New York (1985). https://doi.org/10.1007/978-1-4612-5056-2
4. Anthony, M., Bartlett, P.L.: Neural Network Learning: Theoretical Foundations. Cambridge University Press, Cambridge (2009)
5. Bromley, J., Guyon, I., LeCun, Y., Säckinger, E., Shah, R.: Signature verification using a "Siamese" time delay neural network. In: Advances in Neural Information Processing Systems, pp. 737–744 (1994)
6. Canziani, A., Paszke, A., Culurciello, E.: An analysis of deep neural network models for practical applications. arXiv preprint arXiv:1605.07678 (2016)
7. Chen, W., Chen, X., Zhang, J., Huang, K.: Beyond triplet loss: a deep quadruplet network for person re-identification. In: Proceedings of the IEEE Conference on Computer Vision and Pattern Recognition, pp. 403–412 (2017)
8. Chopra, S., Hadsell, R., LeCun, Y., et al.: Learning a similarity metric discriminatively, with application to face verification. In: CVPR (1), pp. 539–546 (2005)
9. Elfwing, S., Uchibe, E., Doya, K.: Sigmoid-weighted linear units for neural network function approximation in reinforcement learning. Neural Netw. **107**, 3–11 (2018)
10. Hadsell, R., Chopra, S., LeCun, Y.: Dimensionality reduction by learning an invariant mapping. In: 2006 IEEE Computer Society Conference on Computer Vision and Pattern Recognition (CVPR 2006), vol. 2, pp. 1735–1742. IEEE (2006)

11. He, K., Zhang, X., Ren, S., Sun, J.: Delving deep into rectifiers: surpassing human-level performance on imagenet classification. In: Proceedings of the IEEE International Conference on Computer Vision, pp. 1026–1034 (2015)
12. Hoffer, E., Ailon, N.: Deep metric learning using triplet network. In: Feragen, A., Pelillo, M., Loog, M. (eds.) SIMBAD 2015. LNCS, vol. 9370, pp. 84–92. Springer, Cham (2015). https://doi.org/10.1007/978-3-319-24261-3_7
13. Krizhevsky, A., Sutskever, I., Hinton, G.E.: ImageNet classification with deep convolutional neural networks. Adv. Neural. Inf. Process. Syst. **25**, 1097–1105 (2012)
14. van der Maaten, L.: Learning a parametric embedding by preserving local structure. In: van Dyk, D., Welling, M. (eds.) Proceedings of the Twelfth International Conference on Artificial Intelligence and Statistics. Proceedings of Machine Learning Research, vol. 5, pp. 384–391. PMLR, Hilton Clearwater Beach Resort, Clearwater Beach, Florida USA, 16–18 April 2009. http://proceedings.mlr.press/v5/maaten09a.html
15. van der Maaten, L., Hinton, G.: Visualizing data using t-SNE. J. Mach. Learn. Res. **9**(86), 2579–2605 (2008). http://jmlr.org/papers/v9/vandermaaten08a.html
16. Misra, D.: Mish: a self regularized non-monotonic activation function. arXiv preprint arXiv:1908.08681 (2019)
17. Motoshi Abe, J.M., Kurita, T.: Parametric q-Gaussian distributed stochastic neighbor embedding with convolutional neural network. In: Proceedings of International Joint Conference on Neural Network (IJCNN) (accepted) (2021)
18. Ramachandran, P., Zoph, B., Le, Q.V.: Searching for activation functions. arXiv preprint arXiv:1710.05941 (2017)
19. Shah, A., Kadam, E., Shah, H., Shinde, S., Shingade, S.: Deep residual networks with exponential linear unit. In: Proceedings of the Third International Symposium on Computer Vision and the Internet, pp. 59–65 (2016)
20. Simonyan, K., Zisserman, A.: Very deep convolutional networks for large-scale image recognition. arXiv preprint arXiv:1409.1556 (2014)
21. Szegedy, C., et al.: Going deeper with convolutions. In: Proceedings of the IEEE Conference on Computer Vision and Pattern Recognition, pp. 1–9 (2015)
22. Tanaka, M.: Geometry of Entropy. Series on Stochastic Models in Informatics and Data Science. Corona Publishing Co., LTD. (2019). (in Japanese)
23. Wang, J., et al.: Learning fine-grained image similarity with deep ranking. In: Proceedings of the IEEE Conference on Computer Vision and Pattern Recognition, pp. 1386–1393 (2014)
24. Wang, L.: Support Vector Machines: Theory and Applications, vol. 177. Springer, Heidelberg (2005). https://doi.org/10.1007/b95439
25. Zhou, B., Khosla, A., Lapedriza, A., Oliva, A., Torralba, A.: Object detectors emerge in deep scene CNNs. arXiv preprint arXiv:1412.6856 (2014)

# Super-Class Mixup for Adjusting Training Data

Shungo Fujii(✉), Naoki Okamoto, Toshiki Seo, Tsubasa Hirakawa,
Takayoshi Yamashita, and Hironobu Fujiyoshi

Chubu University, 1200 Matsumotocho, Kasugai, Aichi, Japan
{drvfs2759,naok,seotoshiki,hirakawa}@mprg.cs.chubu.ac.jp,
{takayoshi,fujiyoshi}@isc.chubu.ac.jp

**Abstract.** Mixup is one of data augmentation methods for image recognition task, which generate data by mixing two images. Mixup randomly samples two images from training data without considering the similarity of these data and classes. This random sampling generates mixed samples with low similarities, which makes a network training difficult and complicated. In this paper, we propose a mixup considering super-class. Super-class is a superordinate categorization of object classes. The proposed method tends to generate mixed samples with the almost same mixing ratio in the case of the same super-class. In contrast, given two images having different super-classes, we generate samples largely containing one image's data. Consequently, a network can train the features between similar object classes. Furthermore, we apply the proposed method into a mutual learning framework, which would improve the network output used for mutual learning. The experimental results demonstrate that the proposed method improves the recognition accuracy on a single model training and mutual training. And, we analyze the attention maps of networks and show that the proposed method also improves the highlighted region and makes a network correctly focuses on the target object.

**Keywords:** Mixup · Super-class · Data augmentation

## 1 Introduction

Data augmentation is a fundamental method for computer vision tasks, which increases the number of training data and data variations. The classical data augmentation approach is a simple image processing such as transition, resizing, adding noise, and contrast adjustment. Due to the recent development of deep learning-based methods and the requirements of a large number of training samples for enough network training, efficient data augmentation methods have been proposed [1,2,4,11,16,17,19]. To generate more efficient training samples, augmentation methods that uses multiple samples have been proposed [16,17]. Among them, the mixup [17] samples two images from training data and generate a mixed image. The mixup can make the diversity of training samples and improves the image recognition performance.

© Springer Nature Switzerland AG 2022
C. Wallraven et al. (Eds.): ACPR 2021, LNCS 13189, pp. 45–58, 2022.
https://doi.org/10.1007/978-3-031-02444-3_4

However, the mixup does not consider the similarity between mixed images. The mixup randomly samples two images from a training set and mixes them with a certain mixing ratio determined under the same conditions for all images. Although we can make a diverse training samples, this diversity affect negative influence on the network training. For example, in case that we use general object recognition dataset such as CIFAR [10] and ImageNet [3] datasets that have wide variety of object classes, random sampling tends to choose images with lower similarity, e.g., plants and fish, rather than those with higher similarity, e.g., different kinds of flowers. In addition to the effect of random sampling, the mixup decides the mixing ratio by using Beta distribution with a single fixed parameter $\alpha$. In other words, the mixup make mixed samples with the same manner for either lower or higher similarity image pairs. Generating intermediate samples for the higher similarity image pair would effective for learning the relationship between object classes. Meanwhile, the intermediate samples for lower similarity pair would impede to learn such relationship.

In this paper, we propose a super-class mixup, which adjust the mixed images by considering the similarity of object classes. Super-class is a class that classifies each object class by a superordinate object category, which can be defined by WordNet [12], a conceptual dictionary that represents the relationships between things. The proposed method actively generates a mixed image that equally contains the features of both images in case of that these images are categorized in the same super-class. On the other hand, if the super-classes of the images are different, we assume that the images have a low similarity and the proposed method generates a mixed image emphasizing the features of one of them. By using the proposed method, we can focus on learning features between similar classes. Furthermore, we apply the proposed method into the deep mutual learning (DML) [18]. DML uses multiple network and transferring the knowledge, i.e., classification probability obtained from network, as a soft target. Because the proposed method makes a network learn the relationship between object classes, we can improve the soft target from the other network and classification performance. The experimental results show that the proposed method improves the recognition accuracy for training a single model and mutual training. And, we further discuss the effect of the proposed method by using attention maps.

The contributions of this paper are as follows:

- We propose a super-class mixup that considers the similarity between object classes. The proposed method decides the similarity by following the super-class defined by WordNet. The proposed method can learn the relationship of features between similar classes and improve the classification performance.
- The proposed method is useful not only for a single network model training but also for mutual learning framework that uses multiple networks. We can improve the classification probability of the network considering the relationship between classes. The network output is used for the mutual learning as a soft target, which results in the improvement of the classification performance.

– We qualitatively analyze attention maps used for visual explanation. The results show that the proposed method improves the attention maps to capture the target object region.

## 2   Related Work

### 2.1   Data Augmentation

Data augmentation increase the number of training samples and data variation. It is a fundamental approach to improve recognition accuracy and to prevent overfitting to the training data and is widely used for various computer vision tasks. The classical augmentation is a simple image processing such as transition, resizing, adding noise, and contrast adjustment. In recent years, due to the requirements of the large number of training samples for training deep learning-based method, several augmentation approaches have been proposed. Reinforcement learning has been introduced to decide appropriate augmentation [2]. And, augmentation based on mask processing is also developed [1,4,11,19]. This approach removes the part of an image and use it for training, which is efficient for occlusion and image noise. Cutout [4] is one of mask processing-based augmentation, which removes the part of an image. This is simple and close to the classical image processing approach, but it is effective for improving recognition performance.

Among them, augmentation that uses multiple images to generate a augmented sample is simple and effective approach [16,17] and widely used in an image recognition task. Mixup [17] is a method of mixing two images and their corresponding labels to generate new mixed data. The mixed image is generated by mixing the entire image with pixel by pixel, and the mixing label represents the mixing ratio of each image. The mixing ratio is decide by the Beta distribution. During the training, the parameter of Beta distribution is fixed, that is, we mix samples with the same conditions even if the object classes of selected two samples are similar or different. This might affect the negative influence on the network training. Our method considers the similarity between the selected images and decide the mixing rate.

### 2.2   Knowledge Distillation and Mutual Learning

For improving accuracy and shrink the model size retaining the classification accuracy, transferring knowledge from the other network have been developed [6,8,13,18]. This approach trains a network by using the other network output, i.e., classification probability, as an additional supervised label. This additional label is called as a soft-target. This can be categorized into to two approaches. One is the knowledge distillation (KD) [6,8], which uses two networks. One is a teacher network that is relatively larger pre-trained network model and the other is a smaller student network. KD uses the network output of the teacher network as a soft-target and train a student network in addition to the correct label (hard-target), which improve the performance of the student network.

The other is the deep mutual learning (DML) [18], which is derived from KD. The DML does not use pre-trained model. Instead, each network transfer their knowledge (classification probabilities) as a soft-target mutually. Also, the DML uses the hard-target to train each network. As a result, the DML outperforms the accuracy compared with a single network model training.

The soft-target is depending on the network model. In the above mentioned two approaches, KD might be able to transfer reasonable knowledge because KD uses the pre-trained model as the teacher network. Meanwhile, since DML does not use pre-trained model, the network output at the beginning of training is improper. Using such inappropriate soft-target affects the output of networks and the network performance. In this paper, we apply the proposed method for DML framework. By using the proposed method, network learns the relationship between classes and soft-target, which results in the improvement of accuracy.

## 3    Proposed Method

We propose a super-class mixup, which adjusts mixed data by considering super-classes that classify object classes in higher categories.

### 3.1    Preliminaries

Let $D = \{(x_i, y_i)\}_{i=1}^n$ be a set of training data, where $x_i$ is a training sample and $y_i$ is the corresponding one-hot encoded label. And, $n$ is the number of training samples. Given the dataset $D$, we first draw two sets of sample and the label $(x_i, y_i)$ and $(x_j, y_j)$ from $D$ as

$$(x_i, y_i) \sim p(D). \tag{1}$$

Then, mixup [17] generate a augmented sample and label $(\tilde{x}, \tilde{y})$ by mixing two samples, which is defined by

$$\tilde{x} = \lambda x_i + (1 - \lambda)x_j \tag{2}$$
$$\tilde{y} = \lambda y_i + (1 - \lambda)y_j, \tag{3}$$

where $\lambda$ is a mixing ratio which decide the proportion to mix samples.

The mixup probabilistically samples $\lambda$ from the Beta distribution as

$$\lambda \sim \text{Beta}(\alpha, \alpha), \tag{4}$$

where $\alpha$ is a parameter for the Beta distribution and it adjusts the selection tendency of the mixing ratio. The mixup uses a single fixed value for $\alpha$ throughout the network training[1]. In case of $\alpha \in (0.0, 1.0)$, we tends to select larger or smaller values of $\lambda$. This means that the mixup generates a mixed image emphasizing the features of one of them. In contrast, using larger $\alpha$ than 1.0, $\lambda$ around 0.5 is highly selected, which means that the mixup generates a mixed image that equally contains the features of both images, And, $\alpha = 1.0$ uniformly samples $\lambda$.

---

[1] In [17], $\alpha \in [0.1, 0.4]$ is used for their experiments. In this paper, we discuss the other values of $\alpha$ and the effects of these values in our experiments.

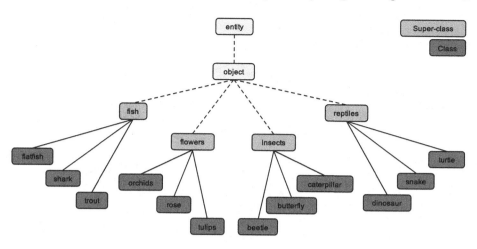

**Fig. 1.** Example of class structure in WordNet.

## 3.2   Super-Class Mixup

As mentioned above, the mixup uses a fixed parameter $\alpha$ throughout the training. However, depending on the similarity between two mixed images and the object classes, appropriate mixing ratio would be different. For the higher similarity image pair, generating intermediate samples would effective for learning the relationship between object classes. The intermediate samples for lower similarity pair would impede to learn such relationship. To overcome the problem and learn the relationship between object classes, we propose a super-class mixup.

Super-class mixup adjusts the mixing ratio considering the similarity of object class between mixed data. As the similarity, we adopt a super-class. The super-class is a class that classifies each object class in a higher category, and it is defined according to WordNet [12] that is a conceptual dictionary. Figure 1 shows an example of class structure in WordNet. We can see that each object class is categorized into the similar object class.

Figure 2 shows the overview of the proposed method. In these figures, "orchids" and "tulips" are the same super-class and "trout" is the different super-class. In this case, the proposed method mixes "orchids" and "tulips" class samples with the almost equal proportions. On the other hands, in the case of "tulip" class and "trout" classes, we generate a sample with the mixing ratio of one class is higher than the other.

Figure 3 shows an example of mixed images generated by the proposed method. Since the super-classes of the "orchids" and the "tulips" are the same, the proposed method selects 0.5 as the intermediate mixing ratio. On the other hand, the super-classes of "tulips" and "trout" are different, so the ratio of 0.9 is selected to increase the ratio of "tulips", or 0.1 to increase the ratio of "trout".

Let $S = \{s_1, \ldots, s_m\}$ is a set of super-class, where $m$ is the number of super-classes. We first prepare the training set with super-class $D_{sc} = \{(x_i, y_i, s_i)\}_{i=1}^{n}$,

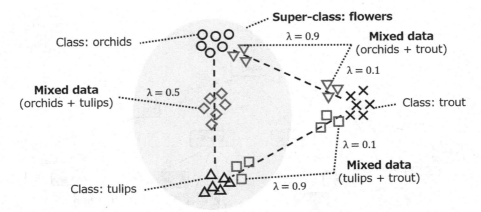

**Fig. 2.** Overview of adjusting mixed data with super-classes.

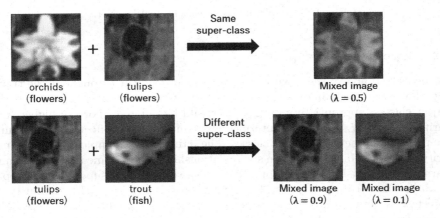

**Fig. 3.** Example of mixed images generated by the proposed method.

where $s_i$ is the super-class for $i$-th training sample. In the proposed method, we randomly choose two training samples from $D_{sc}$ as

$$(x_i, y_i, s_i) \sim p(D_{sc}). \tag{5}$$

Given $(x_i, y_i, s_i)$ and $(x_j, y_j, s_j)$, the super-class mixup generates a sample and the label as with the Eqs. (2) and (3). Here, we decides the mixing ratio $\lambda$ based on the super-class $s_i$ and $s_j$. In this paper, we propose two approaches for $\lambda(s_i, s_j)$ to select the mixing ratio: i) sampling from predetermined values and ii) sampling from the Beta distribution.

**Sampling from Predetermined Values.** In this approach, we decide the mixing ratio explicitly. The proposed method samples $\lambda$ from predetermined values, which is defined by

$$\lambda \sim p(\Lambda), \tag{6}$$

where $\Lambda$ is a set of predetermined mixing ratio. Based on the super-class, $\Lambda$ is selected as follows:

$$\Lambda = \begin{cases} \{0.4, 0.5, 0.6\} & (s_i = s_j) \\ \{0.8, 0.9, 1.0\} & (s_i \neq s_j). \end{cases} \tag{7}$$

**Sampling from Beta Distribution.** In this approach, we sample $\lambda$ from the Beta distribution as

$$\lambda \sim \text{Beta}\left(\alpha(s_i, s_j), \alpha(s_i, s_j)\right). \tag{8}$$

The parameter of the Beta distribution $\alpha(s_i, s_j)$ is decided by $s_i$ and $s_j$, which is defined by

$$\alpha(s_i, s_j) = \begin{cases} 8.0 & (s_i = s_j) \\ 0.2 & (s_i \neq s_j). \end{cases} \tag{9}$$

### 3.3   Training a Single Model

In training a single model, we input mixed data using the proposed method and output the prediction probabilities for each class. In other words, it is trained in the same way as the conventional mixup. Since the proposed method trains based on the similarity between the classes defined in WordNet, we can expect to improve the recognition accuracy.

### 3.4   Training Multiple Models by Deep Mutual Learning

Deep mutual learning [18] improves the recognition accuracy by using the same input data for multiple models and make their output close to each other. Each model in DML uses the other network output as a label, called as soft-target, in addition to a regular network training with class label, called as hard-target. The loss for hard-target is a cross-entropy loss and the loss for soft-target is calculated by Kullback-Leibler (KL) divergence. The loss function of DML $L_{\Theta_k}$ is the sum of the two loss values, which is defined as follows:

$$L_{\Theta_k} = L_{C_k} + \frac{1}{K-1} \sum_{l=1, l \neq k}^{K} D_{KL}(p_l || p_k), \tag{10}$$

where $L_{C_k}$ is the cross-entropy loss function for hard-target, $K$ is the number of models, $D_{KL}$ is the KL-divergence, and $p$ is the prediction probability of each model.

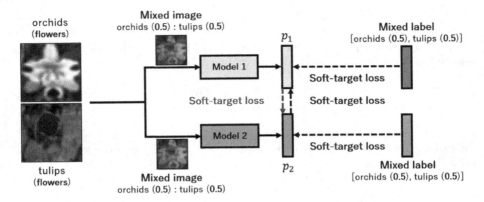

**Fig. 4.** Overview of the proposed method in DML framework. This shows the case that the super-classes of mixed samples are the same.

Because the prediction probability from a network depends on the model parameters, the network does not always output the desirable prediction probability that we intend. In case that we use a conventional mixup for the DML framework, the mixup generates intermediate mixed data with lower similarity samples because the mixup does not consider the similarity. Such mixed samples causes the complication of network training and decrease the consistency of predicted probability of each object classes. Consequently, the gap of probabilities between each network becomes large.

We apply the proposed method for DML. Because the super-class mixup generates an intended data with the desirable label, we can suppress the generation of such undesirable mixed data. This enables us to train networks efficiently. Figure 4 shows the overview of the proposed method in DML. During the training, we use the same data for the input of multiple networks and the networks predicts object classes. By using the network output, we train the networks so that the output from each network becomes close to each other.

## 4    Experiment

In this section, we show the results of our evaluation experiments. Specifically, we compare the effectiveness of the proposed method with the conventional method in a single model network training and DML. Then, we further analyse the attention maps as a visual explanation obtained from networks. Finally, we show that the proposed method is equally effective in CutMix.

### 4.1    Experimental Settings

**Dataset.** We use the CIFAR-100 [10] and ImageNet [3] datasets as benchmark dataset.

**Table 1.** Recognition accuracy in CIFAR-100 [%].

| Method | | Single | DML | |
|---|---|---|---|---|
| | | | Model 1 | Model 2 |
| Vanilla | | 69.64 | 71.51 | 71.46 |
| Mixup ($\alpha = 1.0$) | | 70.83 | 71.37 | 71.08 |
| Intermediate mixing ratio | Predetermined | 61.81 | 61.16 | 61.54 |
| | mixup ($\alpha = 8.0$) | 64.17 | 62.73 | 62.26 |
| Unbalanced mixing ratio | Predetermined | 70.98 | 72.06 | 71.80 |
| | mixup ($\alpha = 0.2$) | 71.39 | 72.20 | 72.32 |
| Ours | Predetermined | 71.32 | 72.23 | 71.93 |
| | Beta dist. | **71.68** | **73.28** | **73.01** |

**Table 2.** Recognition accuracy in ImageNet [%].

| Method | | Single | DML | |
|---|---|---|---|---|
| | | | Model 1 | Model 2 |
| Vanilla | | 73.04 | 73.55 | 73.39 |
| Mixup ($\alpha = 0.2$) | | 73.20 | **73.85** | 73.56 |
| Ours | Predetermined | 72.02 | 73.00 | 73.15 |
| | Beta dist. | **73.41** | 73.73 | **73.92** |

**Network Models.** We use ResNet [7] as the network model. For CIFAR-100 dataset, we use ResNet-20, -32, -44, -56, and -110. For ImageNet dataset, we use ResNet-34.

To visualize attention maps of trained network model, we adopt an attention branch network (ABN) [5]. ABN consists of the backbone network, that extracts features from an image and predicts classification result, and attention branch, that visualizes compute and output attention map. We used ResNet-32 as the backbone network of ABN and CIFAR-100 dataset.

For training each network, we set the mini-batch size as 128 for both dataset. The number of training epochs are 200 for CIFAR-100 and 90 for ImageNet, respectively.

## 4.2 Comparison of Recognition Accuracy for Each Dataset

Here, we compare the performance on CIFAR-100 and ImageNet dataset. As network model, we use ResNet-32 [7] for CIFAR-100 and ResNet-34 for ImageNet. Also, as a comparative methods, we evaluate the performance of a mixup using an intermediate or unbalanced mixing ratio regardless of the super-class. In the case of the predetermined, we randomly select 0.4, 0.5, or 0.6 as the intermediate mixing ratio when the super-classes are the same, or 0.8, 0.9, or 1.0 as the

**Table 3.** Variation of recognition accuracy with model size (Single model) [%].

| Method | | ResNet-20 | ResNet-32 | ResNet-44 | ResNet-56 | ResNet-110 |
|---|---|---|---|---|---|---|
| Vanilla | | 68.38 | 69.64 | 70.88 | 71.99 | 73.65 |
| Mixup ($\alpha = 1.0$) | | 68.59 | 70.83 | 72.57 | 73.12 | **74.19** |
| Ours | Predetermined | 69.22 | 71.32 | 71.96 | 72.40 | 73.73 |
| | Beta dist. | **69.73** | **71.68** | **73.01** | **73.49** | 74.15 |

**Table 4.** Variation of recognition accuracy with model size (DML) [%]. M1 and M2 in the table are the first and second model of DML, respectively.

| Method | | ResNet-20 | | ResNet-32 | | ResNet-44 | | ResNet-56 | | ResNet-110 | |
|---|---|---|---|---|---|---|---|---|---|---|---|
| | | M1 | M2 | M1 | M2 | M1 | M2 | M1 | M2 | M1 | M2 |
| Vanilla | | 70.11 | 70.35 | 71.51 | 71.46 | 73.07 | 72.93 | 73.70 | 73.91 | 74.95 | 74.79 |
| Mixup ($\alpha = 1.0$) | | 69.40 | 69.68 | 71.37 | 71.08 | 72.10 | 72.03 | 73.77 | 73.51 | **75.56** | **75.33** |
| Ours | Predetermined | 69.74 | 70.02 | 72.23 | 71.93 | 72.35 | 72.51 | 73.07 | 72.85 | 73.79 | 73.42 |
| | Beta dist. | **71.24** | **71.19** | **73.28** | **73.01** | **73.77** | **73.58** | **74.54** | **74.06** | 75.02 | 75.17 |

unbalanced mixing ratio when the super-classes are different. In the case of the beta distribution, we set the hyper-parameter $\alpha$ to 8.0 when the super-classes are the same, and set 0.2 when the super-classes are different. The value of $\alpha$ in conventional mixup is 1.0 for CIFAR-100 and 0.2 for ImageNet.

Table 1 shows the recognition accuracy of each method in CIFAR-100, and Table 2 shows the recognition accuracy in ImageNet. From Table 1, the proposed method achieves the highest accuracy in CIFAR-100 for both single model and DML, which is further improved by using beta distribution. Table 2 also shows that the proposed method has the highest accuracy in ImageNet for a single model, and it slightly outperforms the conventional method in DML overall. Therefore, the proposed method is effective for single model and DML. In addition, the results indicates that it is important to include a few data that is mixed with different super-class.

### 4.3 Comparison of Recognition Accuracy for Different Model Sizes

We compare the recognition accuracy of different models in CIFAR-100. We use ResNet-20, 32, 44, 56, and 110. The settings for each parameter are the same as in Sect. 4.2.

Table 3 and Table 4 show the recognition accuracy of each model in single model and DML. From these Tables, the proposed method achieves the highest accuracy for all the models except ResNet-110 in single model and DML. We believe that ResNet-110 can sufficiently improve the generalization performance using mixed data with high diversity by the conventional method. Therefore, the proposed method is effective for lightweight training models.

**Table 5.** Recognition accuracy of ABN on CIFAR-100 dataset [%].

| Method | Single | DML | |
|---|---|---|---|
| | | Model 1 | Model 2 |
| Vanilla | 71.79 | 74.25 | 74.12 |
| Mixup ($\alpha = 1.0$) | 71.70 | 71.48 | 71.45 |
| Ours (Beta dist.) | **73.26** | **74.71** | **74.94** |

**Table 6.** Recognition accuracy of CutMix on CIFAR-100 dataset [%].

| Method | | Single | DML | |
|---|---|---|---|---|
| | | | Model 1 | Model 2 |
| Vanilla | | 69.64 | 71.51 | 71.46 |
| CutMix ($\alpha = 1.0$) | | 70.57 | 72.26 | 71.92 |
| Ours | Predetermined | 72.29 | 73.82 | 73.68 |
| | Beta dist. | **73.11** | **74.61** | **74.43** |

## 4.4 Qualitative Evaluation of Attention Map

Next, we qualitatively analyse the attention maps obtained from each network. As mentioned in Sect. 4.1, we use ABN [5] with ResNet-32 backbone as a network model and train the ABN with CIFAR-100 dataset.

Table 5 shows the accuracy of ABN for each methods. In the both of single model training and DML, our method outperforms the other methods. This results show that our method is also effective for the other network model excepting for ResNet.

Figure 5 shows examples of the attention maps obtained from each method. In the top of Fig. 5, the target object of the input image is "boy" in the left part of the image. On the other hand, the attention maps of conventional mixup is widely distributed and does not focuses on the target object correctly. Also, the proposed method focuses around the shoulder although the conventional methods highlights the other regions. In the bottom of Fig. 5, the target object is "apple." The conventional mixup highlights background regions. The proposed method focuses on the three apples correctly. Therefore, the proposed method can capture the features of the recognition target more accurately while considering a wide range of important information.

## 4.5 Comparison of Recognition Accuracy in CutMix

Finally, we show the effectiveness of the proposed method in CutMix [16], a derivative of mixup. We compare the recognition accuracy on CIFAR-100. We use ResNet-32. The settings for each parameter are the same as in Sect. 4.2.

Table 6 shows the recognition accuracy. From Table 6, the proposed method has the highest accuracy in single model and DML. Therefore, the proposed

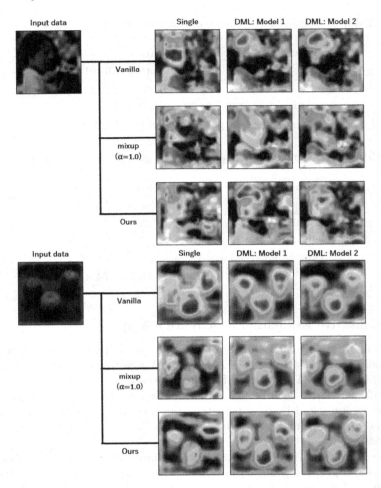

**Fig. 5.** Examples of attention maps for each method.

method is also effective in improving the recognition accuracy in CutMix. This result suggests that the proposed method may be applied to various data augmentation methods for mixing data. Currently, we are considering using the proposed method in combination with other state-of-the-art data expansion methods (Manifold Mixup [15], SaliencyMix [14], and Puzzle Mix [9]).

## 5    Conclusion

In this paper, we proposed super-class mixup, a effective data augmentation method considering super-class. The proposed method adjusts the mixed ratio by the similarity between the object classes. The experimental results with CIFAR-100 and ImageNet datasets show that our method improved the recognition accuracy on a single network model training and deep mutual learning framework. Moreover, we analyzed the attention maps as a visual explanation. As a result, our method improves the highlighted region to the target object correctly.

Our future work includes detailed analysis with respect to the obtained feature spaces, the effect for the improvement of the mis-classified samples. Also, we further extend the proposed method to dynamically decide the parameters during training phase and we will combine the existing another data augmentation methods.

# References

1. Chen, P., Liu, S., Zhao, H., Jia, J.: Gridmask data augmentation. arXiv preprint arXiv:2001.04086 (2020)
2. Cubuk, E.D., Zoph, B., Mane, D., Vasudevan, V., Le, Q.V.: AutoAugment: learning augmentation strategies from data. In: Proceedings of the IEEE Conference on Computer Vision and Pattern Recognition (CVPR) (2019)
3. Deng, J., Dong, W., Socher, R., Li, L.J., Li, K., Fei-Fei, L.: ImageNet: a large-scale hierarchical image database. In: Proceedings of the IEEE Conference on Computer Vision and Pattern Recognition (CVPR) (2009)
4. Devries, T., Taylor, G.W.: Improved regularization of convolutional neural networks with cutout. arXiv preprint arXiv:1708.04552 (2017)
5. Fukui, H., Hirakawa, T., Yamashita, T., Fujiyoshi, H.: Attention branch network: learning of attention mechanism for visual explanation. In: Proceedings of the IEEE Conference on Computer Vision and Pattern Recognition (CVPR) (2019)
6. Furlanello, T., Lipton, Z., Tschannen, M., Itti, L., Anandkumar, A.: Born again neural networks. In: Proceedings of the International Conference on Machine Learning (ICML). Proceedings of Machine Learning Research, vol. 80, pp. 1607–1616 (2018)
7. He, K., Zhang, X., Ren, S., Sun, J.: Deep residual learning for image recognition. In: Proceedings of the IEEE Conference on Computer Vision and Pattern Recognition (CVPR) (2016)
8. Hinton, G.E., Vinyals, O., Dean, J.: Distilling the knowledge in a neural network. In: Proceedings of NIPS workshop on Deep Learning and Representation Learning (2014)
9. Kim, J.H., Choo, W., Song, H.O.: Puzzle mix: exploiting saliency and local statistics for optimal mixup. In: Proceedings of the International Conference on Machine Learning (ICML) (2020)
10. Krizhevsky, A., Hinton, G., et al.: Learning multiple layers of features from tiny images, Technical report. University of Tront (2009)
11. Kumar Singh, K., Jae Lee, Y.: Hide-and-seek: forcing a network to be meticulous for weakly-supervised object and action localization. In: Proceedings of the IEEE International Conference on Computer Vision (ICCV) (2017)
12. Miller, G.A.: WordNet: a lexical database for English. Commun. ACM **38**(11), 39–41 (1995)
13. Mirzadeh, S.I., Farajtabar, M., Li, A., Levine, N., Matsukawa, A., Ghasemzadeh, H.: Improved knowledge distillation via teacher assistant. Proc. AAAI Conf. Artif. Intell. **34**(04), 5191–5198 (2020)

14. Uddin, A.F.M.S., Monira, M.S., Shin, W., Chung, T., Bae, S.H.: SaliencyMix: a saliency guided data augmentation strategy for better regularization. In: International Conference on Learning Representations (2021)

15. Verma, V., et al.: Manifold mixup: better representations by interpolating hidden states. In: Proceedings of the International Conference on Machine Learning (ICML). Proceedings of Machine Learning Research, vol. 97, pp. 6438–6447 (2019)

16. Yun, S., Han, D., Oh, S.J., Chun, S., Choe, J., Yoo, Y.: CutMix: regularization strategy to train strong classifiers with localizable features. In: Proceedings of the IEEE International Conference on Computer Vision (ICCV) (2019)

17. Zhang, H., Cisse, M., Dauphin, Y.N., Lopez-Paz, D.: Mixup: beyond empirical risk minimization. In: International Conference on Learning Representations (2018)

18. Zhang, Y., Xiang, T., Hospedales, T.M., Lu, H.: Deep mutual learning. In: Proceedings of the IEEE Conference on Computer Vision and Pattern Recognition (CVPR) (2018)

19. Zhong, Z., Zheng, L., Kang, G., Li, S., Yang, Y.: Random erasing data augmentation. In: Proceedings of the AAAI Conference on Artificial Intelligence (AAAI) (2020)

# Drop "Noise" Edge: An Approximation of the Bayesian GNNs

Xiaoling Zhou🅳 and Ou Wu$^{(\boxtimes)}$🅳

National Center for Applied Mathematics, Tianjin University, Tianjin 300072, China
{xiaolingzhou,wuou}@tju.edu.cn

**Abstract.** Graph neural networks (GNNs) have proven to be powerful tools for graph analysis. The key idea is to recursively propagate and gather information along the edges of a given graph. Although they have been successful, they are still limited by over-smoothing and noise in the graph. Over-smoothing means that the representation of each node will converge to the similar value as the number of layers increases. "Noise" edges refer to edges with no positive effect on graph representation in this study. To solve the above problems, we propose DropNEdge (Drop "Noise" Edge), which filters useless edges based on two indicators, namely, feature gain and signal-to-noise ratio. DropNEdge can alleviate over-smoothing and remove "noise" edges in the graph effectively. It does not require any changes to the network's structure, and it is widely adapted to various GNNs. We also show that the use of DropNEdge in GNNs can be interpreted as an approximation of the Bayesian GNNs. Thus, the models' uncertainty can be obtained.

**Keywords:** Drop "Noise" Edge · Over-smoothing · Bayesian GNNs

## 1 Introduction

Graph neural networks (GNNs) and their many variants have achieved success in graph representation learning by extracting high-level features of nodes from their topological neighborhoods. However, several studies have shown that the performances of GNNs decrease significantly with the increase in the number of neural network layers [15,16]. The reason is that the nodes' characteristics will converge to similar values with the continuous aggregation of information. Some existing methods (DropEdge [2], Dropout [3]) solve over-smoothing by dropping some information in the graph randomly. Although these methods are efficient, they cannot guarantee that the dropped information is harmful or beneficial. Hence, they can only bring sub-optimal effect.

In addition, the effect of GNNs is affected by noise edges [1,17]. Many graphs in real world have noise edges which requires GNNs to have the ability to identify

Supported by ZJFund 2019KB0AB03, NSFC 62076178, TJ-NSF (19JCZDJC31300, 19ZXAZNGX00050).

C. Wallraven et al. (Eds.): ACPR 2021, LNCS 13189, pp. 59–72, 2022.
https://doi.org/10.1007/978-3-031-02444-3_5

and remove noise edges. The recursive aggregation mode of GNNs makes it susceptible to the influence of surrounding nodes. Therefore, finding a principled way to decide what information not to aggregate will have a positive effect on GNNs' performance. Topological denoising [1] is an effective solution to solve this problem by removing noise edges. We can trim off the edges with no positive impact on the task to avoid GNNs from aggregating unnecessary information.

In this paper, we propose DropNEdge (Drop "Noise" Edge), which takes the structure and content information of a graph as input and deletes edges with no or little positive effect on the final task based on the node's signal-to-noise ratio and feature gain. The differences between our method and DropEdge are detailed as follows. First, DropNEdge treats the edges unequally and deletes edges based on the graph's information, which is a more reasonable and effective method to solve the limitations of GNNs. Second, deleting edges from the above two aspects can ensure that the dropped edges have no or little positive effect on the final task. Therefore, it can not only alleviate over-smoothing, but also remove "noise" edges. DropNEdge is widely adapted to most GNNs and does not need to change the networks' structure. Because DropNEdge changes the topology of the graph, it can be used as a graphical data enhancement method.

Considering that Dropout can be used as a Bayesian approximation for general neural networks, we prove that DropNEdge can be used as a Bayesian approximation for GNNs. If we use DropNEdge during the training and test phase, then the models' uncertainty can be obtained.

The main contributions of our work are presented as follows:

- We propose DropNEdge, which is a plug-and-play layer that is widely adapted to various GNNs. It can effectively alleviate the over-smoothing phenomenon and remove "noise" edges in the graph.
- We show that the use of DropNEdge in GNNs is an approximation of the Bayesian GNNs. In this way, the uncertainty of GNNs can be obtained.

## 2   Related Work

Deep stacking of layers usually results in a significant decrease in the performance of GNNs, such as GCN [13] and GAT [14]. Chen et al. [5] measured and alleviated the over-smoothing problem of GNNs from a topological perspective. Hou et al. [6] proposed two over-smoothing indicators to measure the quantity and quality of information obtained from graphic data and designed a new GNN model called CS-GNN. To prevent node embeddings from being too similar, PairNorm [7] was proposed which is a normalization layer based on the analysis of graph convolution operations. DropEdge [2] also effectively relieves the over-smoothing phenomenon by randomly removing a given percentage of edges in the graph.

Another limitation is the noise in the graph. A large number of papers show that GNNs are not robust to noise. Recently, graph sampling has been investigated in GNNs for the rapid calculation and to improve the generalization ability of GNNs, including neighbor-level [8], node-level [9] and edge-level sampling methods [10]. Unlike these methods that randomly sample edges during the training phase, PTDNet [4] uses a parametric network to actively remove "noise" edges for specific tasks. Moreover, it has been proved that the graph data enhancement strategy can effectively improve the robustness of GNNs [17].

Bayesian network is a hot topic which is critical for many machine learning systems. Since exact Bayesian inference is intractable, many approximation methods have been proposed such as Laplace approximation [20], Markov chain Monte Carlo (MCMC) [21], stochastic gradient MCMC [22], and variational inference methods [23]. Bernoulli Dropout and its extensions are commonly used in practice because they are fast in calculation and easy to be implemented. Bayesian neural networks also have some applications in GNNs. Zhang et al. [19] proposed a Bayesian graph convolutional neural networks for semi-supervised classification. Hasanzadeh et al. [25] proposed a unified framework for adaptive connection sampling in GNNs. And GNNs training with adaptive connection sampling is shown to be equivalent to an efficient approximation of training Bayesian GNNs.

## 3 Notations

Let $\mathcal{G} = (\mathcal{V}, \mathcal{E})$ represent the input graph of size $N$ with nodes $v_i \in \mathcal{V}$ and edges $(v_i, v_j) \in \mathcal{E}$. The node features are denoted as $\boldsymbol{X} = \{x_1, x_2, \cdots, x_N\} \in R^{N \times C}$ and the adjacent matrix is defined as $\mathcal{A} \in \mathcal{R}^{N \times N}$ which associates each edge $(v_i, v_j)$ with its element $\mathcal{A}_{ij}$. The node degrees are given by $d = \{d_1, d_2, \cdots, d_N\}$ where $d_i$ computes the sum of edge weights connected to node $i$. $\mathcal{N}_{v_i} = \{v_j : (v_i, v_j) \in \mathcal{E}\}$ denotes the set of neighbors of node $v_i$.

## 4 Methodology

### 4.1 Drop "Noise" Edge

The GNNs are superior to the existing Euclidean-based methods because they obtain a wealth of information from the nodes' neighbors. Therefore, the performance improvement brought by graphic data is highly related to the quantity and quality of domain information [11]. DropEdge [2] randomly drops edges in the graph. Although it is efficient, it does not consider the influence of adjacent nodes' information on the current node. Therefore, it can not determine whether the deleted information is beneficial or harmful to the task. Compared with DropEdge, DropNEdge treats the edges as unequal based on the influence of adjacent nodes' information on the current node and deletes edges with no or little positive impact on the final task. We use signal-to-noise ratio and feature gain indexes to measure the influence of adjacent nodes on the current node.

**Feature Gain.** Feature gain is used to measure the information gain of adjacent nodes' information relative to the current node. Considering that Kullback-Leibler (KL) divergence can measure the amount of information lost when an approximate distribution is adopted, it is used to calculate the information gain of the current node from its adjacent nodes [6]. The definition of KL divergence is stated as follows.

**Definition 1.** $C(K)$ *refers to the probability density function (PDF) of $\tilde{c}_{v_i}^k$, which is the ground truth and can be estimated by non-parametric methods with a set of samples. Each sample point is sampled with probability $|\mathcal{N}_{v_i}|/2|\mathcal{E}|$. $S(k)$ is the PDF of $\sum_{v_j \in N_{v_i}} a_{i,j}^{(k)} \cdot \tilde{c}_{v_j}^k$, which can be estimated with a set of samples $\{\sum_{v_j \in N_{v_i}} a_{i,j}^{(k)} \cdot \tilde{c}_{v_j}^k\}$. Each point is also sampled with probability $|\mathcal{N}_{v_i}|/2|\mathcal{E}|$ [6]. The information gain can be computed by KL divergence [12] as:*

$$D_{KL}\left(S^{(k)}||C^{(k)}\right) = \int_{x_k} S^{(k)}(x) \cdot log\frac{S^{(k)}(x)}{C^{(k)}(x)}dx. \tag{1}$$

In the actual calculation, the true and simulated distributions of the data are unknown. Thus, we use the feature gain to approximate KL divergence which measures the feature difference between the current node and its adjacent nodes. The definition of feature gain of node $v$ is

$$FG_v = \frac{1}{|\mathcal{N}_v|} \sum_{v' \in \mathcal{N}_v} ||x_v - x_{v'}||^2, \tag{2}$$

where $|\mathcal{N}_v|$ is the number of adjacent nodes of node $v$, and $x_v$ is the representation of node $v$. Moreover, the feature gain has the following relationship with KL divergence.

**Theorem 1.** *For a node $v$ with feature $x_v$ in space $[0,1]^d$, the information gain of the node from the surrounding $D_{KL}(S||C)$ is positively related to its feature gain $FG_v$; (i.e., $D_{KL}(S||C) \sim FG_v$). In particular, $D_{KL}(S||C) = 0$, when $FG_v = 0$.*

Thus, we know that the information gain is positively correlated to the feature gain. That is, the greater the feature gain means that the node can obtain more information from adjacent nodes. Therefore, we should first deal with nodes with less information gain. If the feature similarity of the nodes on both sides of a edge exceeds a given threshold, the edge should be dropped. In this way, edges with a significant impact on the task can be retained. The proof process of Theorem 1 is shown as follows.

*Proof.* For $D_{KL}(S||C)$, since the PDFs of $C$ and $S$ are unknown, a non-parametric way is used to estimate the PDFs of $C$ and $S$. Specifically, the feature space $X = [0,1]^d$ is divided uniformly into $r^d$ bins $\{H_1, H_2, \cdots, H_{r^d}\}$, whose length is $1/r$ and dimension is $d$. To simplify the use of notations, $|H_i|_C$ and $|H_i|_S$ are used to denote the number of samples that are in bin $H_i$. Thus, we yield

$$D_{KL}(S\|C) \approx D_{KL}(\hat{S}\|\hat{C})$$

$$= \sum_{i=1}^{r^d} \frac{|H_i|_S}{2|\mathcal{E}|} \cdot \log \frac{\frac{|H_i|_S}{2|\mathcal{E}|}}{\frac{|H_i|_C}{2|\mathcal{E}|}}$$

$$= \frac{1}{2|\mathcal{E}|} \cdot \sum_{i=1}^{r^d} |H_i|_S \cdot \log \frac{|H_i|_S}{|H_i|_C}$$

$$= \frac{1}{2|\mathcal{E}|} \cdot \left( \sum_{i=1}^{r^d} |H_i|_S \cdot \log |H_i|_S - \sum_{i=1}^{r^d} |H_i|_S \cdot \log |H_i|_C \right)$$

$$= \frac{1}{2|\mathcal{E}|} \cdot \left( \sum_{i=1}^{r^d} |H_i|_S \cdot \log |H_i|_S - \sum_{i=1}^{r^d} |H_i|_S \cdot \log \left( |H_i|_S + \Delta_i \right) \right), \quad (3)$$

where $\Delta_i = |H_i|_C - |H_i|_S$. Regard $\Delta_i$ as an independent variable, we consider the term $\sum_{i=1}^{r^d} |H_i|_S \cdot \log \left( |H_i|_S + \Delta_i \right)$ with second-order Taylor approximation at point 0 as

$$\sum_{i=1}^{r^d} |H_i|_S \cdot \log \left( |H_i|_S + \Delta_i \right) \approx \sum_{i=1}^{r^d} |H_i|_S \cdot \left( \log |H_i|_S + \frac{\ln 2}{|H_i|_S} \cdot \Delta_i - \frac{\ln 2}{2 \left( |H_i|_S \right)^2} \cdot \Delta_i^2 \right). \quad (4)$$

Note that the number of samples for the context and the surrounding are the same, where we have

$$\sum_{i=1}^{r^d} |H_i|_C = \sum_{i=1}^{r^d} |H_i|_S = 2 \cdot |\mathcal{E}|. \quad (5)$$

Thus, we obtain $\sum_{i=1}^{r^d} \Delta_i = 0$. Therefore, $D_{KL}(\hat{S}\|\hat{C})$ can be written as

$$D_{KL}(S\|C) \approx D_{KL}\left( \hat{S}\|\hat{C} \right)$$

$$= \frac{1}{2|\mathcal{E}|} \cdot \left( \sum_{i=1}^{r^d} |H_i|_S \cdot \log |H_i|_S - \sum_{i=1}^{r^d} |H_i|_S \cdot \log \left( |H_i|_S + \Delta_i \right) \right)$$

$$\approx \frac{1}{2|\mathcal{E}|} \cdot \left( \sum_{i=1}^{r^d} |H_i|_S \cdot \left( -\frac{\ln 2}{|H_i|_S} \cdot \Delta_i + \frac{\ln 2}{2 \left( |H_i|_S \right)^2} \cdot \Delta_i^2 \right) \right)$$

$$= \frac{1}{2|\mathcal{E}|} \cdot \sum_{i=1}^{r^d} \left( \frac{\ln 2}{2|H_i|_S} \cdot \Delta_i^2 - \ln 2 \cdot \Delta_i \right)$$

$$= \frac{\ln 2}{4|\mathcal{E}|} \cdot \sum_{i=1}^{r^d} \frac{\Delta_i^2}{|H_i|_S}. \quad (6)$$

If we regard $|H_i|_S$ as constant, we have: if $\Delta_i^2$ is large, then the information gain $D_{KL}(S||C)$ tends to be large. The above proof process is borrowed from Reference [6].

Considering the case of a node and its adjacent nodes, the samples of $C$ are equal to $x_v$ and the samples of $S$ are sampled from $\{x_{v'} : v' \in \mathcal{N}_v\}$. For the distribution of the difference between the surrounding and the context, we consider $x_{v'}$ as noises on the "expected" signal and $x_v$ is the "observed" signal. Then the difference between $C$ and $S$ is $\frac{1}{|\mathcal{N}_v|} \sum_{v' \in \mathcal{N}_v} ||x_v - x_{v'}||^2$, which is also the definition of $FG_v$. Thus, we obtain

$$\sum_{i=1}^{r^d} \Delta_i^2 \sim FG_v. \tag{7}$$

Therefore,

$$D_{KL}(S||C) = \frac{\ln 2}{4|\mathcal{E}|} \sum_{i=1}^{r^d} \frac{\Delta_i^2}{|H_i|_S} \sim FG_v. \tag{8}$$

And if $FG_v = 0$, the feature vectors of the current node and its adjacent nodes are the same. Thus, $D_{KL}(S||C) = 0$.                                    □

**Signal-to-Noise Ratio.** The reason for over-smoothing of GNNs is the low signal-to-noise ratio of received information. When aggregations among samples in different categories are excessive, the node representations in different classes will be similar. Thus, we assume that the aggregation of nodes among different categories is harmful, thereby bringing noise of information, and the aggregation of nodes in the same category brings useful signal. Here the signal-to-noise ratio is defined as

$$In_v = \frac{ds_v}{dh_v}, \tag{9}$$

where $ds_v$ and $dh_v$ represent the sum of edge weights connected to homogeneous and heterogeneous nodes of node $v$, respectively. Therefore, for a node with a small signal-to-noise ratio, we will drop the edges connected to heterogeneous nodes until the signal-to-noise ratio of the node is bigger than the given threshold.

**Algorithm of DropNEdge.** The specific approach of DropNEdge is shown in Algorithm 1. In this algorithm, if the ratio of deleted "noise" edges $r_1$ is set to 0, DropNEdge can be reduced to DropEdge.

## 4.2   Connection with Bayesian GNNs

Considering that Dropout can be an approximation of the Bayesian neural networks [18]; hence, we show that DropNEdge can be an approximation of Bayesian GNNs. We target the inference of the joint posterior of the random graph parameters, the weights in the GNN and the nodes' labels. Given that we are usually not directly interested in inferring the graph parameters, posterior estimates of the labels are obtained by marginalization [13]. The goal is to compute the posterior probability of labels, which is

$$p\left(Z \mid Y, X, \mathcal{G}_{obs}\right) = \int p(Z \mid W, \mathcal{G}, X)p(W \mid Y, X, \mathcal{G})p(\mathcal{G} \mid \lambda)p\left(\lambda \mid \mathcal{G}_{obs}\right) dW d\mathcal{G} d\lambda \qquad (10)$$

where $W$ is a random variable that represents the weights of the Bayesian GNN over graph $\mathcal{G}$, and $\lambda$ characterizes a family of random graphs. This integral is intractable, we can adopt a number of strategies, including variational

---

**Algorithm 1:** Drop "Noise" Edge.

---

**Input**: The adjacency matrix $\mathcal{A}$, the number of edges $|\mathcal{E}|$, the ratio of deleted "noise" edges $r_1$, the ratio of randomly deleted edges $r_2$, the signal-to-noise ratio threshold $\delta_1$, the feature similarity threshold $\delta_2$, the ratio $q$ which controls the proportion of edges deleted according to the two indexes.

**Output**: The adjacency matrix $\mathcal{A}'$.

1  Initialization: $N_1 = 0$ , $N_2 = 0$, $\mathcal{A}' = \mathcal{A}$ ;
2  Randomly set $|\mathcal{E}| \times r_2$ elements with value 1 in $\mathcal{A}'$ to 0;
3  Calculate $In_v$ and $FG_v$ of each node;
4  Re-sort the nodes according to the two indexes' values from small to large to form nodes_1 and nodes_2 lists;
5  **while** $N_1 < |\mathcal{E}| \times r_1 q$ **do**
6       **for** *node in nodes_1* **do**
7           **for** *_node in $\mathcal{N}_{node}$* **do**
8               **while** $In_{node} < \delta_1$ **do**
9                   **if** *node and _node in different class* **then**
10                      $\mathcal{A}'[node, \_node] = 0$;
11                      $N_1 += 1$ ;
12                      Update $In_{node}$;
13                  **end**
14              **end**
15          **end**
16      **end**
17 **end**
18 **while** $N_2 < |\mathcal{E}| \times r_1 (1 - q)$ **do**
19      **for** *node in nodes_2* **do**
20          **for** *_node in $\mathcal{N}_{node}$* **do**
21              **if** *feature_similarity [node, _node]* $> \delta_2$ **then**
22                  $\mathcal{A}'[node, \_node] = 0$;
23                  $N_2 += 1$ ;
24              **end**
25          **end**
26      **end**
27 **end**
28 **Return**: The adjacency matrix $\mathcal{A}'$

---

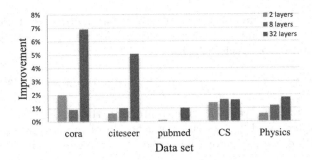

**Fig. 1.** The average absolute improvement by DropNEdge.

methods [24] and Markov Chain Monte Carlo (MCMC) [21], to approximate it. A Monte Carlo approximation of it is [13]

$$p\left(\boldsymbol{Z}|\boldsymbol{Y},\boldsymbol{X},\mathcal{G}_{obs}\right) \approx \frac{1}{V}\sum_{v}^{V}\frac{1}{N_G S}\sum_{i=1}^{N_G}\sum_{s=1}^{S}p\left(\boldsymbol{Z}|W_{s,i,v},\mathcal{G}_{i,v},\boldsymbol{X}\right). \qquad (11)$$

In the approximation, $V$ samples $\lambda_v$ are drawn from $p(\lambda|\mathcal{G}_{obs})$, $N_G$ graphs $\mathcal{G}_{i,v}$ are sampled from $p(\mathcal{G}|\lambda_v)$, $S$ weight matrices $W_{s,i,v}$ are sampled from $p(W|\boldsymbol{Y},\boldsymbol{X},\mathcal{G}_{i,v})$ in the Bayesian GNNs that correspond to the graph $\mathcal{G}_{i,v}$ [19]. The sampled $w_{s,i,v}$ and $G_{i,v}$ can be obtained from GNNs with DropNEdge. Thus, if we turn on DropNEdge during the training and test phase, the model's uncertainty can be obtained.

## 5   Experiments

### 5.1   Performance Comparison

We compare the performances of the four GNN models with DropNEdge (DNE) and DropEdge (DE). The results are shown in Table 1. The performances of the

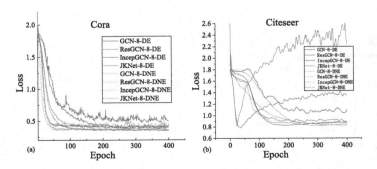

**Fig. 2.** (a) and (b) show the validation loss of different backbones with DropNEdge or DropEdge on Cora and Citeseer data sets.

**Table 1.** Accuracies of models with DropNEdge or DropEdge.

| Dataset | Backbone | 2 layers | | 8 layers | | 32 layers | |
|---|---|---|---|---|---|---|---|
| | | DropEdge | DNE | DropEdge | DNE | DropEdge | DNE |
| Cora | GCN | 0.865 | 0.867 | 0.858 | **0.873** | 0.746 | 0.796 |
| | JKNet | – | – | 0.878 | **0.886** | 0.876 | 0.878 |
| | IncepGCN | – | – | 0.882 | **0.887** | 0.877 | 0.886 |
| | ResGCN | – | – | 0.869 | **0.877** | 0.868 | 0.876 |
| Citeseer | GCN | 0.787 | 0.793 | 0.772 | **0.802** | 0.614 | 0.799 |
| | JKNet | – | – | 0.802 | **0.810** | 0.800 | 0.803 |
| | IncepGCN | – | – | 0.805 | 0.801 | 0.803 | **0.815** |
| | ResGCN | – | – | 0.788 | **0.790** | 0.779 | 0.781 |
| Pubmed | GCN | 0.912 | **0.913** | 0.909 | 0.909 | 0.862 | 0.901 |
| | JKNet | – | – | 0.912 | 0.912 | 0.913 | **0.914** |
| | IncepGCN | – | – | **0.915** | **0.915** | 0.905 | 0.905 |
| | ResGCN | – | – | 0.905 | 0.905 | **0.911** | **0.911** |
| Coauthor CS | GCN | 0.926 | **0.934** | 0.907 | 0.930 | 0.904 | 0.926 |
| | JKNet | – | – | 0.918 | **0.926** | 0.904 | 0.904 |
| | IncepGCN | – | – | 0.904 | **0.936** | 0.920 | 0.932 |
| | ResGCN | – | – | 0.898 | 0.900 | 0.896 | **0.926** |
| Coauthor physics | GCN | 0.954 | **0.965** | 0.940 | 0.950 | 0.932 | 0.946 |
| | JKNet | – | – | 0.941 | **0.955** | 0.936 | 0.950 |
| | IncepGCN | – | – | 0.936 | **0.956** | 0.936 | 0.953 |
| | ResGCN | – | – | 0.930 | **0.933** | 0.894 | 0.920 |

four models have been improved in most cases by DropNEdge. The improvement is more clearly depicted in Fig. 1, which counts the average improvement of different number of layers brought by DropNEdge. For example, on Cora data set, DropNEdge brings 6.9% average improvement to the models with 32 layers.

The results of models with and without DropNEdge are shown in Table 2. The effects of all models with DropNEdge have been consistently improved compared with models without DropNEdge. Thus the effect of DropNEdge is demonstrated. Figure 2 (a) and (b) show the comparison of the verification loss of models with DropNEdge or DropEdge which indicate that models with DropNEdge converge faster, and their losses are smaller.

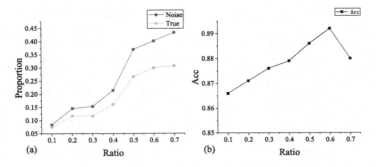

**Fig. 3.** The effect of removing noise edges.

**Table 2.** Accuracies of models with and without DropNEdge. "OOM" represents out of memory.

| Dataset | Backbone | 2 layers | | 8 layers | | 32 layers | |
|---|---|---|---|---|---|---|---|
| | | Original | DNE | Original | DNE | Original | DNE |
| Cora | GCN | 0.861 | 0.867 | 0.787 | **0.873** | 0.716 | 0.796 |
| | JKNet | – | – | 0.867 | **0.886** | 0.871 | 0.878 |
| | IncepGCN | – | – | 0.867 | **0.887** | 0.874 | 0.886 |
| | ResGCN | – | – | 0.854 | **0.877** | 0.851 | 0.876 |
| Citeseer | GCN | 0.759 | 0.793 | 0.746 | **0.802** | 0.592 | 0.799 |
| | JKNet | – | – | 0.792 | **0.810** | 0.717 | 0.803 |
| | IncepGCN | – | – | 0.796 | 0.801 | 0.726 | **0.815** |
| | ResGCN | – | – | 0.778 | **0.790** | 0.744 | 0.781 |
| Pubmed | GCN | 0.912 | **0.913** | 0.901 | 0.909 | 0.846 | 0.901 |
| | JKNet | – | – | 0.906 | 0.912 | 0.892 | **0.914** |
| | IncepGCN | – | – | 0.902 | **0.915** | OOM | 0.905 |
| | ResGCN | – | – | 0.896 | 0.905 | 0.902 | **0.911** |
| Coauthor CS | GCN | 0.885 | **0.934** | 0.885 | 0.930 | 0.846 | 0.926 |
| | JKNet | – | – | 0.901 | **0.926** | 0.863 | 0.904 |
| | IncepGCN | – | – | 0.930 | **0.936** | 0.897 | 0.932 |
| | ResGCN | – | – | 0.857 | 0.900 | 0.863 | **0.926** |
| Coauthor physics | GCN | 0.918 | **0.965** | 0.875 | 0.950 | 0.791 | 0.946 |
| | JKNet | – | – | 0.902 | **0.955** | 0.921 | 0.950 |
| | IncepGCN | – | – | 0.844 | **0.956** | OOM | 0.953 |
| | ResGCN | – | – | 0.847 | **0.933** | 0.910 | 0.920 |

The superiority of DropNEdge lies in the following reasons: (1) DropNEdge avoids excessive aggregation of node information by dropping "noise" edges, which alleviates the over-smoothing phenomenon effectively. (2) It can remove "noise" edges and retain meaningful edges which prevents the transmission of harmful information. (3) DropNEdge can be used as a graphical data enhancement method.

## 5.2   Remove "Noise" Edges

We randomly add a given proportion of edges to the graph of Cora data set which is set to 0.3 in this experiment. The added edges are considered to be "noise" edges. We change the ratio of deleted "noise" edges $r_1$. Subsequently, the proportions of deleted added edges to total added edges ($r_N$) and deleted non-added edges to the real edges ($r_T$) in the graph are counted. The model used is GCN-8 and the results are shown in Fig. 3 (a) and (b). From Fig. 3 (a), we can see that DropNEdge can remove "noise" edges because $r_N$ is always greater than $r_T$ no matter what the ratio $r_1$ is. Figure 3 (b) shows that the model's accuracy also increases as $r_1$ increases. However, when too many edges are deleted, the meaningful aggregation of information will also decrease. Thus, the accuracy of the model decreases.

## 5.3   Suppress Over-Smoothing

When the top-level output of GNNs converges to a subspace and becomes irrelevant to the input as the depth increases, over-smoothing phenomenon occurs. Considering that the convergent subspace cannot be derived explicitly, we measure the degree of smoothing by calculating the difference between the output of the current layer and the previous layer. Euclidean distance is used to calculate the difference. The smaller the distance, the more severe the over-smoothing. This experiment is carried out on GCN-8 with Cora data set whose results are shown in Fig. 4.

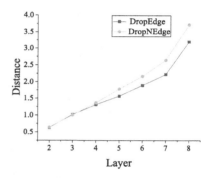

**Fig. 4.** The effect comparison between DropEdge and DropNEdge of suppressing over-smoothing.

DropNEdge is better than DropEdge in suppressing over-smoothing. As the number of layers increases, the distances between layers in models with DropEdge and DropNEdge both increase. Furthermore, the distance's increasing speed of the model with DropNEdge is faster than that of the model with DropEdge.

## 5.4   Layer Independent DropNEdge

The DropNEdge mentioned above is that all layers share the same perturbation adjacency matrix. In fact, we can perform it for each individual layer. Different layers can have different adjacent matrices. This layer-independent (LI) version brings more randomness and distortion of the original data. We experimentally compare its performance with the shared DropNEdge's performance on Cora data set. The model used is GCN-8 and the comparisons of the verification loss and training loss between shared and independent DropNEdge are shown in Fig. 5 (a). Although hierarchical DropNEdge may achieve better results, we still prefer to use shared DropNEdge which can not only reduce the risk of overfitting, but also reduce the computational complexity.

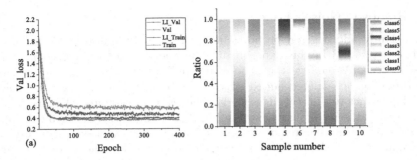

**Fig. 5.** (a) shows the comparison of the training and verification loss between Drop-NEdge and LI DropNEdge. (b) shows the uncertainty of model with DropNEdge.

## 5.5   Model Uncertainty

To obtain the model's uncertainty, we turn on DropNEdge during the training and test phase and set the ratio of deleted "noise" edges to 0.3. The experiment is carried out on GCN-8 with Cora data set. After the model predicts multiple times, different predictions may be produced for a sample. Figure 5 (b) shows the ratio of different labels obtained in 10 predictions for 10 samples. For example, for sample one, 40% of the ten predictions are class 0 and 60% of the predictions are class 3. Thus, the confidence of the predictions can be obtained by using DropNEdge. For high-confidence samples, that is, samples with consistent results after multiple predictions, the model's predictions can be used directly. If the model's predictions of some samples change greatly, other models should be further used or they should be artificially determined to get more reasonable predictions.

## 6   Conclusion

This paper proposes DropNEdge, a novel and effective method to alleviate the over-smoothing phenomenon and remove "noise" edges in graphs. It mainly considers two indicators based on the graph's information, namely, feature gain and signal-to-noise ratio. By using DropNEdge, the over-smoothing of GNNs is alleviated and the "noise" edges with no positive impact on the final task can be removed, thereby improving the performance of GNNs. DropNEdge does not need to change the network's structure and is widely adapted to various GNNs.

## References

1. Dongsheng, L., et al.: Learning to drop: robust graph neural network via topological denoising. In: Proceedings of the 14th ACM International Conference on Web Search and Data Mining (WSDM 2021), pp. 779–787. Association for Computing Machinery, Online (2021) . https://doi.org/10.1145/3437963.3441734

2. Yu, R., Wenbing, H., Tingyang, X., Junzhou, H.: DropEdge: towards deep graph convolutional networks on node classification. In: Proceedings of the 8th International Conference on Learning Representations (ICLR 2020), International Conference on Learning Representations, Addis Ababa (2020) . https://openreview.net/forum?id=Hkx1qkrKPr

3. Nitish, S., Geoffrey, H., Alex, K., Ilya, S.: Dropout: a simple way to prevent neural networks from overfitting. J. Mach. Learn. Res. 15(1), 1929–1958 (2014)

4. Qimai, Li., Zhichao, H., Xiao-Ming, W.: Deeper insights into graph convolutional networks for semi-supervised learning. In: The Thirty-Second AAAI Conference on Artificial Intelligence (AAAI-18), pp. 3538–3545. AAAI press, Louisiana (2018). https://arxiv.org/abs/1801.07606

5. Deli, C., Yankai, L., Wei, L., Peng, L., Jie, Z., Xu, S.: Measuring and relieving the over-smoothing problem for graph neural networks from the topological view. In: The Thirty-Fourth AAAI Conference on Artificial Intelligence (AAAI-20), pp. 3438–3445. AAAI press, New York (2020) . https://doi.org/10.1609/aaai.v34i04.5747

6. Yifan, H., et al.: Measuring and improving the use of graph information in graph neural network. In: The Eighth International Conference on Learning Representations (ICLR 2020), Addis Ababa (2020) . https://openreview.net/forum?id=rkeIIkHKvS

7. Lingxiao, Z., Leman, A.: PairNorm: tackling oversmoothing in GNNs. In: Proceedings of the 8th International Conference on Learning Representations (ICLR 2020), Addis Ababa (2020) . https://arxiv.org/abs/1909.12223

8. William, L. H., Rex, Y., Jure, L.: Inductive representation learning on large graphs. In: Proceedings of the 31st Annual Conference on Neural Information Processing Systems (NIPS 2017), pp. 1025–1035. Neural Information Processing Systems Foundation, California (2017). https://arxiv.org/abs/1706.02216

9. Jie, C., Tengfei, M., Cao, X.: FastGCN: fast learning with graph convolutional networks via importance sampling. In: Proceedings of the 6th International Conference on Learning Representations (ICLR 2018), Vancouver (2018). https://arxiv.org/abs/1801.10247

10. Santo, F.: Community detection in graphs. Phys. Rep. 486, 75–174 (2010)

11. Jie, Z., et al.: Graph neural networks: a review of methods and applications. arXiv:1812.08434 (2021)

12. Kullback, S., Leibler, R.A.: On information and sufficiency. Ann. Math. Stat. 22(1), 79–86 (1951)

13. Kipf, T.N., Welling, M.: Semi-supervised classification with graph convolutional networks. In: Proceedings of the 5th International Conference on Learning Representations (ICLR 2017), Toulon (2017). https://openreview.net/pdf?id=SJU4ayYgl

14. Petar, V., Guillem, C., Arantxa, C., Adriana, R., Pietro, L., Yoshua, B.: Graph attention networks. In: Proceedings of the 6th International Conference on Learning Representations (ICLR 2018), Vancouver (2018) . https://arxiv.org/abs/1710.10903

15. Chaoqi, Y., Ruijie, W., Shuochao, Y., Shengzhong, L., Tarek, A.: Revisiting oversmoothing in deep GCNs. arXiv:2003.13663 (2020)

16. Chen, C., Yusu, W.: A note on over-smoothing for graph neural networks. In: The Thirty-seventh International Conference on Machine Learning (ICML 2020), International Machine Learning Society, Online (2020) . https://arxiv.org/abs/2006.13318

17. James, F., Sivasankaran, R.: How robust are graph neural networks to structural noise? arXiv:1912.10206 (2019)
18. Yarin, G., Zoubin, G.: Dropout as a Bayesian approximation: representing model uncertainty in deep learning. In: The Thirty-Third International Conference on Machine Learning (ICML 2016), International Machine Learning Society, New York (2016) . https://arxiv.org/abs/1506.02142v1
19. Yingxue, Z., Soumyasundar, P., Mark, C., Deniz, Ü.: Bayesian graph convolutional neural networks for semi-supervised classification. In: The Thirty-Third AAAI Conference on Artificial Intelligence (AAAI 2019), pp. 5829–5836. AAAI Press, Hawaii (2019). https://arxiv.org/abs/1811.11103
20. David, J.C.M.: Bayesian Methods for Adaptive Models. California Institute of Technology, California (1992)
21. Radford, M.N.: Bayesian Learning for Neural Networks. Springer, New York (1996)
22. Welling, M., Yee, W.T.: Bayesian learning via stochastic gradient Langevin dynamics. In: Proceedings of the 28th International Conference on Machine Learning (ICML 2011), pp. 681–688. Association for Computing Machinery, Washington (2011). https://dl.acm.org/doi/10.5555/3104482.3104568
23. David, M.B., Alp, K., Jon, D.M.: Variational inference: a review for statisticians. J. Am. Stat. Assoc. **112**(518), 859–877 (2017)
24. Matthew, D.H., David, M.B., Chong, W., John, P.: Stochastic variational inference. J. Mach. Learn. Res. **14**(4), 1303–1347 (2013)
25. Arman, H., et al.: Bayesian graph neural networks with adaptive connection sampling. arXiv:2006.04064 (2020). https://arxiv.org/abs/2006.04064

# Fast Proximal Policy Optimization

Weiqi Zhao, Haobo Jiang, and Jin Xie[✉]

PCA Lab, Key Lab of Intelligent Perception and Systems for High-Dimensional Information of Ministry of Education, Nanjing University of Science and Technology, Nanjing, China
{zwq626,jiang.hao.bo,csjxie}@njust.edu.cn

**Abstract.** Proximal policy optimization (PPO) is one of the most promising deep reinforcement learning methods and has achieved remarkable success in a variety of challenging control tasks. However, its overall updating gradient of a batch of samples may mislead the optimization of some sub-samples. It potentially reduces the sample efficiency and degrades the final decision performance. Although the minimum operation of PPO can relieve it, its slow *escape speed* makes it difficult to escape the wrong optimization range within the limited epochs of the minibatch update. In this paper, we propose a novel fast version of PPO named fast-PPO that replaces the original minimum operation with two accelerating operations called *linear-pulling* and *quadratic-pulling*, respectively. Both of them can increase the updating weight of the gradient for the misled samples so that the gradient of the overall object follows their expected optimization direction. Extensive experiments on classic discrete control tasks and MuJoCo based continuous control tasks verify the effectiveness of our proposed fast PPO.

**Keywords:** Proximal Policy Optimization · Escape speed · Accelerating operations

## 1 Introduction

In recent years, deep reinforcement learning (DRL) has achieved great development and obtained impressive successes in different fields, such as competitive games (Doom [13], Atari 2600 [17,18], game Go [21], etc.), robot navigation [6,14,15] and control tasks [2,4,5,8,10,16]. Given a control problem formulated as a Markov Decision Problem (MDP), it is dedicated to learning an optimal policy that can obtain the highest cumulative rewards through extensive trial and error. In general, model-free DRL mainly contains the value function based method [11] and the policy gradient method [9], where the former indirectly learns the policy via learning an optimal action-value function while the latter directly optimizes the expected return by searching in the parameterized policy space. Compared to the value function based method, the policy gradient method presents a significant advantage on the complex continuous control problems and thus obtains more and more attention.

The trust region policy optimization (TRPO) method [19] is one of the widely studied policy gradient methods. It aims to safely perform policy updating with guaranteed

This work was supported by Shanghai Automotive Industry Science and Technology Development Foundation (No. 1917).

monotonic performance improvement by optimizing a surrogate object function (low bound of the original object) constrained by the divergence between the old policy distribution and the updated one. Although TRPO has a complete theoretical guarantee about monotonicity, its complicated second-order approximation for the constraint largely reduces its computation efficiency and hinders its applications in large-scale tasks. To relieve it, the Proximal Policy Optimization (PPO) [20] proposes a likelihood ratio based constraint for parameter updating, which is able to retain the stable optimization and sample efficiency of TRPO while only requires computationally efficient first-order optimization. In detail, the probability ratio between the old and new policy distributions is clipped within manually defined constant bounds (clipping range) so that it can remove the updating incentive for moving the likelihood ratio outside of the defined clipping bounds.

However, as demonstrated in [25], with the improper initialization, PPO may not perform sufficient exploration in its environment and thus suffers from the local optima. To handle it, Wang *et al.* proposes a trust-region guided PPO algorithm (TRGPPO), which can improve the exploration ability and achieve higher performance compared to the original PPO method through adaptively tuning its clipping range within the trust region. Furthermore, Wang *et al.* [24] finds that PPO could neither restrict the likelihood ratio within the clipping range strictly nor enforce the KL divergence lower than the specified bound. Therefore, PPO-RB [24] is proposed to replace the original flat clipping function with a rollback function (straight-reversed slope) which can weaken the incentive, driven by the overall function, of exceeding the clipping bounds. In addition, Zhu *et al.* [27] proposes a smoothed PPO variant that combines original PPO with PPO-RB to further improve the stability and sample efficiency of PPO-RB. Moreover, trust region-based PPO (TR-PPO) [24] substitutes the probability ratio based clipping function with the trust region based one, which is justified that such variant can sufficiently bound the KL divergence.

Although the variants of PPO discussed above can obtain great performance gain, all of them just focus on safe constraints on the likelihood ratio between the old and new policies, while neglecting the issue that the overall optimization gradient of a batch of samples may mislead the optimization for some sub-sample, named *negative optimization*. Intuitively, *negative optimization* means that the updated policy network may reduce the decision probability of the action that has the positive advantage value. Although the minimum operation of PPO can relieve it, it's still difficult to escape the wrong optimization within the finite epochs. To improve the *escape speed*, the weight of such samples in the overall object's gradient should be increased. To this end, we propose an improved PPO called Fast Proximal Policy Optimization algorithm (FPPO) to decrease the number of samples suffering from *negative optimization* after the finite updating epochs. Specifically, we first replace the minimum operation with an accelerating operation called *linear-pulling* which multiplies the objective function by an accelerating factor so that the weight of the misled examples can be increased in the linear sense. To adjust the accelerating factor adaptively, we propose another accelerating operation named *quadratic-pulling*, where the acceleration grows when the ratio goes away from the boundary. We theoretically prove that both of the proposed accelerating variants can improve the *escape speed* of PPO. Also, extensive experiment results further demonstrate their effectiveness.

## 2 Related Work

Policy gradient algorithm [12,22] is one of the popular studying directions in reinforcement learning. By parameterizing the policy network, it aims to update its network parameters following the gradient-direction of performance improvement. However, during the optimization process, selecting a proper updating step size is an important but challenging problem. Kakade *et al.* firstly proposed that it is better to update the policy within a region in the policy space. Inspired by the theory about the restricted region, the trust region policy optimization (TRPO) [19] proposed to enforce a hard constraint of KL divergence onto the surrogate objective function. Also, Wu *et al.* [26] proposed to use Kronecker-Factored trust regions to optimize the policy. To optimize the computational complexity of TRPO, the Proximal Policy Optimization algorithm (PPO) [20], a first-order algorithm, was proposed. It adopts a clipping mechanism to restrict the likelihood ratio between the old policy and the new one.

Despite the huge success that PPO had achieved in a range of challenging tasks, the original method still has some flaws that affect its performance. Wang *et al.* [25] proved that the clipping mechanism with a constant clipping range might fail in the case that the policy is initialized from a bad one. Thus, they proposed to adaptively adjust the clipping range of PPO to get sufficient exploration. Furthermore, Wang *et al.* [24] found that PPO can neither restrict the ratio within the clipping range strictly nor restrict strictly the policy within the trust region. To address it, they proposed two improvements: replace the flat constraint with a rollback operation, use the KL divergence bound as the clipping range. Moreover, [3,7] also empirically analyzed the implementation details and the code-level optimization of PPO. They argued that the practical success of PPO might be owed to the tricks adopted in the code.

All of the improved methods above neglect the *negative optimization* caused by improper gradient-direction of the overall object. Instead, our method is devoted to handling such issues and the proposed variant is proved to be able to effectively escape the *negative optimization*, which can potentially improve its sample efficiency as well as the final performance. We proposed two *accelerating operations* to improve the *escape speed* and justify them theoretically.

## 3 Preliminaries

We consider a finite Markov Decision Process (MDP) described by the tuple $(\mathcal{S}, \mathcal{A}, \mathcal{R}, \mathcal{T}, \gamma)$, where $\mathcal{S}$ and $\mathcal{A}$ denote the state and action spaces; $\mathcal{T}: \mathcal{S} \times \mathcal{A} \times \mathcal{S} \to \mathbb{R}$ is the transition probability distribution; $\mathcal{R} : \mathcal{S} \to \mathbb{R}$ is the reward function; $\gamma \in (0, 1)$ is the discount factor. In a finite MDP, the agent takes an action $\mathbf{a}_t \in \mathcal{A}$ in a state $\mathbf{s}_t \in \mathcal{S}$ and then gets a reward $r_t = \mathcal{R}(\mathbf{s}_{t+1})$ and the next state $\mathbf{s}_{t+1} \in \mathcal{S}$. The policy $\pi$ maps each state $\mathbf{s} \in \mathcal{S}$ to a distribution over $\mathcal{A}$ and our goal is to find an optimal policy that can achieve the maximum accumulated rewards.

In policy gradient methods [19, 22], the policy $\pi$ is usually represented by a policy network $\pi_\theta$ where $\theta$ denotes the network parameters. Then, the policy gradient algorithm aims to find the optimal parameter $\theta^*$ with the gradient ascent so that the object function $J(\theta)$ defined as below can be maximized:

$$J(\theta) = \mathbb{E}_{\pi_\theta} [Q^{\pi_\theta}(\mathbf{s}, \mathbf{a})], \tag{1}$$

where the state-action value function $Q^\pi(\mathbf{s}, \mathbf{a})$ denotes the expected value of accumulated rewards that an agent can obtain after performing an action $\mathbf{a}$ in the state $\mathbf{s}$ following a policy $\pi_\theta$:

$$Q^{\pi_\theta}(\mathbf{s}, \mathbf{a}) = \mathbb{E}_{\pi_\theta} \left[ \sum_{t=0}^{\infty} \gamma^t r_t \mid s_0 = \mathbf{s}, a_0 = \mathbf{a} \right]. \tag{2}$$

The parameter $\theta$ is updated along the gradient of the objective function as below:

$$\nabla_\theta J(\theta) = \mathbb{E}_{\pi_\theta} [\nabla_\theta \log \pi_\theta (Q^{\pi_\theta}(\mathbf{s}, \mathbf{a}) - b(\mathbf{s}))], \tag{3}$$

where $b(\mathbf{s}) : \mathcal{S} \rightarrow \mathbb{R}$ is a baseline which can reduce variance without changing the expected value of the gradient. The baseline is usually set to a state function $V^{\pi_\theta}(\mathbf{s}) = \mathbb{E}_{\pi_\theta} [\sum_{t=0}^{\infty} \gamma^t r_t \mid s_0 = \mathbf{s}]$. Next, we denote a advantage function $A^{\pi_\theta}(\mathbf{s}, \mathbf{a}) = Q^{\pi_\theta}(\mathbf{s}, \mathbf{a}) - V^{\pi_\theta}(\mathbf{s})$ and the policy gradient can be rewritten as:

$$\begin{aligned} \nabla_\theta J(\theta) &= \mathbb{E}_{\pi_\theta} [\nabla_\theta \log \pi_\theta (Q^{\pi_\theta}(\mathbf{s}, \mathbf{a}) - V^{\pi_\theta}(\mathbf{s}))] \\ &= \mathbb{E}_{\pi_\theta} [\nabla_\theta \log \pi_\theta (A^{\pi_\theta}(\mathbf{s}, \mathbf{a}))]. \end{aligned} \tag{4}$$

### 3.1  Trust Region Policy Optimization

Trust region policy optimization (TRPO) exploits the lower bound of the original optimization target as its objective function (i.e., surrogate objective), which is subjected to a constraint on the KL-divergence between the current policy distribution $\pi_\theta(\cdot \mid \mathbf{s}_t)$ and the old one $\pi_{\theta_{old}}(\cdot \mid \mathbf{s}_t)$. For simplicity, we denote $A_t$ as the advantage value at sample $(\mathbf{s}_t, \mathbf{a}_t)$, i.e., $A_t \triangleq A^{\pi_\theta}(\mathbf{s}_t, \mathbf{a}_t)$ and denote $r_t(\theta)$ as the likelihood ratio of sample $(\mathbf{s}_t, \mathbf{a}_t)$ between the current and the old policies, i.e., $r_t(\theta) \triangleq \frac{\pi_\theta(\mathbf{a}_t \mid \mathbf{s}_t)}{\pi_{\theta_{old}}(\mathbf{a}_t \mid \mathbf{s}_t)}$. Then, the optimization object of TRPO can be written as below:

$$\max_\theta \mathbb{E}_{\pi_\theta} [r_t(\theta) A_t] \tag{5}$$

$$\text{subject to} \quad \mathbb{E}_{\pi_\theta} [\text{KL} [\pi_{\theta_{old}}(\cdot \mid \mathbf{s}_t), \pi_\theta(\cdot \mid \mathbf{s}_t)]] \leqslant \sigma \tag{6}$$

where the hyper-parameter $\sigma$ constrains the KL-divergence between the current and old policies. Although the constraint on updating step above can effectively improve the optimization stability of TRPO, its second-order optimization usually has high computational complexity which is inefficient for large-scale applications, such as the tasks with the high-dimensional sensory input.

## 3.2 Proximal Policy Optimization

In order to handle the inefficient second-order optimization issue in TRPO, the Proximal Policy Optimization (PPO) algorithm [20] is proposed to directly clip the likelihood ratio $r_t(\theta)$ between the current and the old policies for robust policy optimization. Notably, such clipping operation retains the monotonicity of TRPO as well as just requires the first-order computation. Specifically, the objective function of PPO is defined as:

$$L^{\text{CLIP}}(\theta) = \mathbb{E}_{\pi_\theta}\left[\min(r_t(\theta)A_t, \mathcal{F}^{\text{CLIP}}(r_t(\theta), \epsilon)A_t\right], \tag{7}$$

where the clipping function $\mathcal{F}^{\text{CLIP}}(r_t(\theta), \epsilon) = \text{clip}(r_t(\theta), 1 - \epsilon, 1 + \epsilon)$, which remove the incentive that the ratio moves out of the clipping range $[1 - \epsilon, 1 + \epsilon]$, and the hyper-parameter $\epsilon \in (0, 1)$. The minimum operation is to guarantee that the final objective is a lower bound on the unclipped objective [20].

As demonstrated in Sect. 4.1, although the minimum operation in PPO can relieve the *negative optimization* problem to some extent, there are still some samples that suffer from the *negative optimization* after finite epochs of minibatch updates. Please refer to Sect. 4.1 for more details.

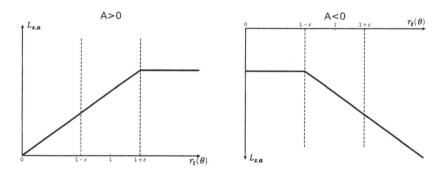

**Fig. 1.** Plots show how the slope of the surrogate function $L^{\text{CLIP}}$ varies with different $r_t(\theta)$, for positive advantages (left) and negative advantages (right). We can see that it loses gradient when $A_t > 0$, $r_t(\theta) > 1 + \epsilon$ or $A_t < 0$, $r_t(\theta) < 1 - \epsilon$. However it does not suffer from this issue when $A_t > 0$, $r_t(\theta) < 1 - \epsilon$ or $A_t < 0$, $r_t(\theta) > 1 + \epsilon$ because of the minimum operation.

## 4    Method

### 4.1    Sample Efficiency of PPO

As we can see in Fig. 1, $r_t(\theta)$ may be lower than $1 - \epsilon$ when $A_t > 0$. That is to say, the probability of an action a whose advantage value is positive decreases, called *negative optimization*. The diversity between the overall gradient of a batch of samples and that of a single sample lead to this case in practice. Without the minimum operation, the gradient of such examples will be zero so that their gradient can never be updated. The minimum operation in PPO can help those examples to regain their original gradients.

However, such examples can hardly escape from *negative optimization* in finite epochs by minimum operation. This will significantly hinder the sample efficiency of PPO. To address this issue, we propose to increase the weight of such examples to correct the fused gradient so that the examples could escape from *negative optimization* in the remaining epochs. For example, the angle between $g_1$ and $g$ (the left one of Fig. 2) is greater than 90° in the beginning while the corresponding example enjoys positive optimization again after increasing its gradient.

In original PPO, the ratio could be driven to go farther away from the bound in the case that *negative optimization* has already occurred. Formally, we give a theorem as follows.

**Theorem 1.** *Suppose there is a parameter $\theta_0$ that $r_t(\theta_0)$ satisfies the condition of negative optimization. Let $\theta_1^{PPO} = \theta_0 + \delta \nabla \hat{L}^{PPO}(\theta_0)$, where $\delta$ is the step size and $\nabla \hat{L}^{PPO}(\theta_0)$ is the gradient of $\hat{L}^{PPO}(\theta)$ at $\theta_0$. On the condition that*

$$\langle \nabla \hat{L}^{PPO}(\theta_0), \nabla r_t(\theta_0) \rangle A_t < 0, \tag{8}$$

*there exists such $\delta^* > 0$ that we have following property for any $\delta \in (0, \delta^*)$*

$$\left| r_t(\theta_1) - 1 \right| < \left| r_t(\theta_0) - 1 \right| < \epsilon. \tag{9}$$

Following [24], we give an formal proof as follows:

*Proof.* Let $\psi(\delta) = r_t(\theta_0 + \delta \nabla \hat{L}^{PPO}(\theta_0))$, then we can get the gradient:

$$\psi'(0) = \langle \nabla \hat{L}^{PPO}(\theta_0), \nabla r_t(\theta_0) \rangle \tag{10}$$

We have $\psi'(0) < 0$ when $r_t(\theta_0) < 1 - \epsilon$ and $A_t > 0$. Thus there is $\delta^* > 0$ such that for any $\delta \in (0, \delta^*)$, we have:

$$\psi(\delta) < \psi(0) \tag{11}$$

Then

$$r_t(\theta_1) < r_t(\theta_0) \leq 1 - \epsilon \tag{12}$$

That is

$$\left| r_t(\theta_1) - 1 \right| < \left| r_t(\theta_0) - 1 \right| \tag{13}$$

$\square$

The condition (8) will be triggered when the gradient-direction of the overall objective $\hat{L}^{PPO}(\theta_0)$ and that of $r_t(\theta_0) A_t$ is significantly different. This condition is possibly caused by the highly differentiated gradient-directions of a minibatch of samples.

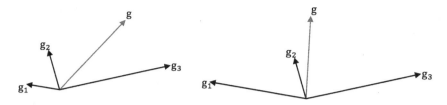

**Fig. 2.** g is the fused gradient, and $g_1$ is the gradient of a sample that owns a positive advantage but suffers from *negative optimization* in the left figure. We can correct the fused gradient by increasing the gradient of the negatively optimized samples. If the correction mechanism is effective enough, all examples will enjoy proper optimization gradients just as depicted in the right figure.

## 4.2 Fast Proximal Policy Optimization with Linear-Pulling

To better explain our method, we rewrite the Eq. 7 as the following:

$$L(\theta) = \mathbb{E}_{\pi_\theta} [\min (r_t(\theta)A_t, \mathcal{F}(r_t(\theta), \epsilon)A_t)] \tag{14}$$

where $\mathcal{F}$ is a clipping function to restrict the update step size of the policy. In PPO, $\mathcal{F} = \text{clip}(r_t(\theta), 1 - \epsilon, 1 + \epsilon)$. To enforce the gradient of the overall object across a batch of samples to correct, we can increase the weight of the examples suffering from *negative optimization*. Specifically, $\mathcal{F}$ multiplies by a factor greater than one in the case that $A_t > 0, r_t(\theta) < 1 - \epsilon$ or $A_t < 0, r_t(\theta) > 1 + \epsilon$. Our mechanism is to pull the ratio into the clipping range with a linear function, we called this operation *linear-pulling*. Then we get a new clipping function which is defined as

$$\mathcal{F}^{\text{FPPO-LP}} = \begin{cases} \alpha r_t(\theta) + (1 - \alpha)(1 - \epsilon), & A_t > 0 \text{ and } r_t(\theta) < 1 - \epsilon \\ \alpha r_t(\theta) + (1 - \alpha)(1 + \epsilon), & A_t < 0 \text{ and } r_t(\theta) > 1 + \epsilon \\ \text{CLIP}(r_t(\theta)), & \text{otherwise} \end{cases} \tag{15}$$

where the hyper-parameter $\alpha \in [1, +\infty)$ is to decide the force of acceleration. Figure 3 plots $L^{\text{FPPO-LP}}(\theta)$ as function of the ratio $r_t(\theta)$. As the figure depicted, when $r_t(\theta)$ is out of the clipping range, the slope of the side that suffers from *negative optimization* becomes larger. By correcting the overall object's gradient, *linear-pulling* could more forcefully keep the ratio $r_t(\theta)$ within the clipping range compared to the minimum operation in PPO. Formally, we have the following theorem.

**Theorem 2.** *Suppose there is a parameter* $\theta_0$, $\theta_1^{PPO} = \theta_0 + \delta \nabla \hat{L}^{PPO}(\theta_0)$, *and* $\theta_1^{FPPO\text{-}LP} = \theta_0 + \delta \nabla \hat{L}^{FPPO\text{-}LP}(\theta_0)$. *The set of indexes of the samples suffering from negative optimization is denoted as* $\Omega = \{t | 1 \leq t \leq T, |r_t(\theta_0) - 1| \geq \epsilon$ *and* $r_t(\theta_0)A_t \leq r_t(\theta_{old})A_t\}$. *If* $t \in \Omega$ *and* $r_t(\theta_0)$ *satisfies such condition that* $\sum_{t' \in \Omega} \langle \nabla r_t(\theta_0), \nabla r_{t'}(\theta_0) \rangle A_t A_{t'} > 0$, *then there exists some* $\delta^* > 0$ *such that for any* $\delta \in (0, \delta^*)$, *we have*

$$\left| r_t(\theta_1^{FPPO\text{-}LP}) - 1 \right| < \left| r_t(\theta_1^{PPO}) - 1 \right|. \tag{16}$$

*Proof.* Let $\psi(\delta) = r_t(\theta_0 + \delta\nabla\hat{L}^{\text{FPPO-LP}}(\theta_0)) - r_t(\theta_0 + \delta\nabla\hat{L}^{\text{PPO}}(\theta_0))$. We can get the gradient:

$$
\begin{aligned}
\psi'(0) &= \nabla r_t^\top(\theta_0)\left(\nabla\hat{L}^{\text{FPPO-LP}}(\theta_0) - \nabla\hat{L}^{\text{PPO}}(\theta_0)\right) \\
&= (\alpha - 1)\sum_{t'\in\Omega}\langle\nabla r_t(\theta_0), \nabla r_{t'}(\theta_0)\rangle A_{t'}
\end{aligned}
\tag{17}
$$

We have $\psi'(0) > 0$ in the case where $r_t(\theta_0) \le 1 - \epsilon$ and $A_t > 0$. Thus there exists $\delta^* > 0$ such that for any $\delta \in (0, \delta^*)$

$$
\phi(\delta) > \phi(0)
\tag{18}
$$

Then we have

$$
r_t(\theta_1^{\text{FPPO-LP}}) > r_t(\theta_1^{\text{PPO}})
\tag{19}
$$

That is

$$
\left|r_t(\theta_1^{\text{FPPO-LP}}) - 1\right| < \left|r_t(\theta_1^{\text{PPO}}) - 1\right|
\tag{20}
$$

Similarly, we can also get $\left|r_t(\theta_1^{\text{FPPO-LP}}) - 1\right| < \left|r_t(\theta_1^{\text{PPO}}) - 1\right|$ in the case where $r_t(\theta_0) \ge 1 + \epsilon$ and $A_t < 0$. $\square$

This theorem proves that *linear-pulling* can prevent the out-of-the-range ratios from going farther beyond the clipping range more forcefully. In other words, the *escape speed* is increased. Ideally, we can tune $\alpha$ to guarantee the new policy within the clipping range more effectively.

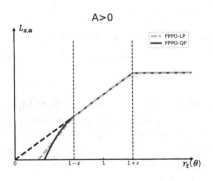 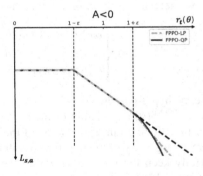

**Fig. 3.** Plots show the surrogate function $L_{\text{s,a}}$ as a function of $r_t(\theta)$ (the probability ratio), for positive advantages (left) and negative advantages (right). We can see that the slope of FPPO (both FPPO-LP and FPPO-QP) becomes larger than PPO when $A_t > 0$, $r_t(\theta) < 1 + \epsilon$ or $A_t < 0$, $r_t(\theta) > 1 + \epsilon$. The red dotted line corresponds to *linear-pulling* and the blue line corresponds to *quadratic-pulling*. (Color figure online)

### 4.3    Fast Proximal Policy Optimization with Quadratic-Pulling

In FPPO-LP, the accelerating factor $\alpha$ is a fixed parameter, however, the updating epochs of batch samples are finite, the examples suffering from *negative optimization* cannot escape within a few epochs if the ratio is too far away from the bound. Thus it is more reasonable that the farther the ratio goes away from the clipping range, the larger the parameter $\alpha$ in FPPO-LP should be set. Inspired by the motivation above, we have the following differential equation:

$$
\mathcal{F}'(r_t(\theta)) = \begin{cases} k(1 - \epsilon - r_t(\theta)) + 1, & A_t > 0 \text{ and } r_t(\theta) < 1 - \epsilon \\ k(r_t(\theta) - 1 - \epsilon) + 1, & A_t < 0 \text{ and } r_t(\theta) > 1 + \epsilon \\ \nabla \text{CLIP}(r_t(\theta)), & \text{otherwise} \end{cases} \tag{21}
$$

where $k$ is a hyper-parameter to control the change of slope. By solving differential equation Eq. 21, we obtain the *quadratic-pulling* operation:

$$
\mathcal{F}^{\text{FPPO-QP}} = \begin{cases} k(1 - \epsilon - r_t(\theta))^2 + r_t(\theta), & A_t > 0 \text{ and } r_t(\theta) < 1 - \epsilon \\ k(r_t(\theta) - 1 - \epsilon)^2 + r_t(\theta), & A_t < 0 \text{ and } r_t(\theta) > 1 + \epsilon \\ \text{CLIP}(r_t(\theta)), & \text{otherwise} \end{cases} \tag{22}
$$

where the value of $k$ is half of that in Eq. 21. Similarly, FPPO-QP has the same property as Theorem 2. Formally, we give the proof as following:

*Proof.* Let $\psi(\delta) = r_t(\theta_0 + \delta \nabla \hat{L}^{\text{FPPO-QP}}(\theta_0)) - r_t(\theta_0 + \delta \nabla \hat{L}^{\text{PPO}}\theta_0)$. When $r_t(\theta_0) < 1 - \epsilon$ and $A_t > 0$, We can get the gradient:

$$
\begin{aligned} \psi'(0) &= \nabla r_t^\top(\theta_0) \left( \nabla \hat{L}^{\text{FPPO-QP}}(\theta_0) - \nabla \hat{L}^{\text{PPO}}(\theta_0) \right) \\ &= 2k \left( 1 - \epsilon - r_t(\theta_0) \right) \sum_{t' \in \Omega} \langle \nabla r_t(\theta_0), \nabla r_{t'}(\theta_0) \rangle A_{t'} \end{aligned} \tag{23}
$$

We have $\psi'(0) > 0$, thus there exists $\delta^* > 0$ such that for any $\delta \in (0, \delta^*)$

$$
\psi(\delta) > \psi(0) \tag{24}
$$

Then we have

$$
\left| r_t(\theta_1^{\text{FPPO-QP}}) - 1 \right| < \left| r_t(\theta_1^{\text{PPO}}) - 1 \right| \tag{25}
$$

Similarly, we can also get $\left| r_t(\theta_1^{\text{FPPO-QP}}) - 1 \right| < \left| r_t(\theta_1^{\text{PPO}}) - 1 \right|$ in the case where $r_t(\theta_0) > 1 + \epsilon$ and $A_t < 0$. □

Theoretically, *quadratic-pulling* can guarantee that the slope of the surrogate objective function be tuned feasibly.

## 5   Experiments

In this section, we firstly present the performance of our algorithm in contrast with other policy gradient methods and then show the results of our ablation study.

The following algorithms are evaluated. (a) PPO: the version with clipping mechanism, we use the author recommended hyper-parameter $\epsilon = 0.2$ [20]. (b) TR-PPO: the ratio is clipped when the updated policy is out of the trust region [24]. The hyper-parameter $\delta = 0.035$. (c) PPO-RB: PPO with the rollback operation [24]. The rollback coefficient $\alpha = 0.3$ (d) FPPO-LP: fast PPO with linear-pulling. We choose $\alpha$ as recommended in Table 2. (e) FPPO-QP: fast PPO with quadratic-pulling. We use $k$ as recommended in Table 2.

**Table 1.** Max average return over 5 trials of 100 thousand timesteps (classic discrete tasks) or 1 million steps (MuJoCo tasks).

|  | Task | FPPO-LP | FPPO-QP | PPO | TR-PPO | PPO-RB |
|---|---|---|---|---|---|---|
| Discrete tasks | CartPole | **200.0 ± 0.03** | **200.0 ± 0.01** | **200.0** | 192.7 | **200.0** |
|  | Acrobot | $-84.2 \pm 1.2$ | $\mathbf{-82.0 \pm 0.7}$ | $-88.7$ | $-86.8$ | $-89.2$ |
|  | MountainCar | $\mathbf{-130.6 \pm 0.9}$ | $-131.0 \pm 1.4$ | $-143.3$ | $-140.2$ | $-146.2$ |
| Continuous tasks | Walker2d | **4030.4 ± 122.8** | 3893.4 ± 145.8 | 3368.5 | 3279.8 | 2858.4 |
|  | Ant | 2778.8 ± 183.7 | **3323.6 ± 200.5** | 2024.3 | 2013.0 | 2640.1 |
|  | Reacher | $\mathbf{-6.1 \pm 0.28}$ | $-6.5 \pm 0.29$ | $-7.6$ | $-6.0$ | $-7.8$ |
|  | Hopper | 2726.1 ± 118.4 | **2908.8 ± 116.0** | 2364.2 | 2341.8 | 1997.7 |
|  | HalfCheetah | 4107.0 ± 105.8 | **4478.3 ± 175.0** | 4141.7 | 3455.8 | 3420.1 |
|  | Swimmer | 113.6 ± 1.6 | **115.5 ± 1.9** | 100.2 | 108.9 | 99.8 |

### 5.1   Classic Discrete Control Tasks

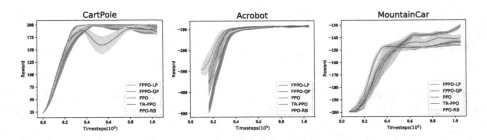

**Fig. 4.** Learning curves for the classic discrete control tasks.

We first conducted experiments on 3 classic discrete control tasks implemented in OpenAI Gym [1]. Figure 4 plots the performance during $10^5$ training timesteps and Table 1 shows the maximum average return over 5 trials of 100 thousand timesteps. For Cart-Pole, all the tested algorithms obtain the highest score in finite timesteps except for TR-PPO, and notably, FPPO-QP hits the highest score faster than other methods. For Acrobot and MountainCar, FPPO performs better than its competitors.

However, the improvements of FFPO in comparison with PPO are not so prominent, especially in the first two tasks. The main reason is that the exploration space is very small compared with continuous tasks so that different policy gradient methods have similar performance. Actually, value-based methods tend to perform better in such tasks. In addition, we notice that MountainCar is a sparse reward task, and thus the methods may be trapped in local optima if the *escape speed* is too low. Because of the *accelerating operations*, Both FPPO-LP and FPPO-QP obtain higher *escape speed* so that more prominent performance could be achieved.

## 5.2 Benchmark Tasks

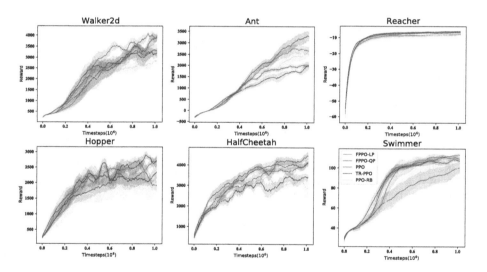

**Fig. 5.** Learning curves for the Mujoco continuous control tasks. The lines represent the average rewards over 5 random seeds and the shaded region represents the mean ± half of std. Curves are smoothed to get visual clarity.

In order to verify the effectiveness of our method, we evaluate PPO and its variants on continuous control benchmark tasks implemented in OpenAI Gym [1], simulated by MuJoCo [23]. 6 benchmark tasks are chosen to be tested on: Walker2d-v2, Ant-v2, Reacher-v2, Hopper-v2, HalfCheetah-v2, and Swimmer-v2. All tasks will run with $10^6$ timesteps over 5 random seeds.

The mean of the reward and the standard deviation are plotted in the figure. As our results suggest, FPPO performs better than other algorithms in all 6 tasks. It is worth

noting that FPPO is particularly prominent on Hopper, Ant, and Walker2d. Walker2d
has the largest sizes of action and observation spaces, which needs higher sample efficiency. The prominent performance on such a task proves the significance of high
*escape speed*.

## 5.3    Ablation Study

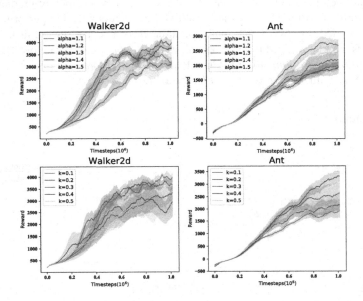

**Fig. 6.** Max average return over 5 trials of 1 million steps with different $\alpha$ and different $k$. The
ranges of $\alpha$ and $k$ are $[1.1, 1.5]$ and $[0.1, 0.5]$ respectively. And the intervals of two hyper-
parameters are both $0.1$.

**Table 2.** Used values for 6 different MuJoCo tasks respectively.

|          | CartPole | Acrobot | MountainCar | Hopper | Walker2d | HalfCheetah | Reacher | Swimmer | Ant |
|----------|----------|---------|-------------|--------|----------|-------------|---------|---------|-----|
| $\alpha$ | 1.3      | 1.3     | 1.3         | 1.3    | 1.3      | 1.3         | 1.1     | 1.1     | 1.3 |
| $k$      | 0.4      | 0.4     | 0.4         | 0.2    | 0.1      | 0.4         | 0.4     | 0.1     | 0.4 |

In this experiment we vary the hyper-parameter $\alpha$ to drop in the range $[1.1, 1.5]$, and
the interval is set to $0.1$. The hyper-parameter $k$ varies from $0$ to $0.5$, and the interval
is $0.1$. The benchmarks we tested on are Walker2d and Ant, which own huge action
spaces and observation spaces. From Fig. 6, we can observe that the performance of
the algorithm varies with the change of $\alpha$ and $k$, which proves that the accelerating
operation is essential. Furthermore, it is not true that the larger $\alpha$ and $k$ are, the better
performance will be achieved. Actually, the ratio may exceed the upper bound after a
few epochs, although it is used to be lower than the lower bound. Thus just as depicted
in Table 2, there exists the best value for $\alpha$ and $k$ respectively.

# 6 Conclusion

Although PPO and its various variants have achieved impressive performance, these methods have failed to make a difference in improving the *escape speed*. However, the low *escape speed* may result in the loss of the sample efficiency as well as the degradation of the performance. Based on this observation, we proposed two different acceleration tricks to correct the gradient of the overall object across a batch of samples in few epochs. Both these two techniques significantly improve speed of escaping *negative optimization* and the sample efficiency. Extensive results prove the effectiveness of our method.

In conclusion, our results highlight the necessity to improve the *escape speed*, leading to the improvement in sample efficiency and performance of the policy. To our knowledge, this is the first work to focus on *negative optimization* and *escape speed*. We found that it is essential to increase the gradient of the samples trapped in *negative optimization*. We propose to study more on the *negative optimization* and exploit more methods to increase the escape speed.

# References

1. Brockman, G., et al.: OpenAI Gym (2016)
2. Duan, Y., Chen, X., Houthooft, R., Schulman, J., Abbeel, P.: Benchmarking deep reinforcement learning for continuous control. In: International Conference on Machine Learning, pp. 1329–1338. PMLR (2016)
3. Engstrom, L., et al.: Implementation matters in deep policy gradients: a case study on PPO and TRPO. arXiv preprint arXiv:2005.12729 (2020)
4. Fujimoto, S., Hoof, H., Meger, D.: Addressing function approximation error in actor-critic methods. In: International Conference on Machine Learning, pp. 1587–1596. PMLR (2018)
5. Haarnoja, T., Zhou, A., Abbeel, P., Levine, S.: Soft actor-critic: off-policy maximum entropy deep reinforcement learning with a stochastic actor. In: International Conference on Machine Learning, pp. 1861–1870. PMLR (2018)
6. Hu, Y., Wang, W., Liu, H., Liu, L.: Reinforcement learning tracking control for robotic manipulator with kernel-based dynamic model. IEEE Trans. Neural Netw. Learn. Syst. **31**(9), 3570–3578 (2019)
7. Ilyas, A., et al.: Are deep policy gradient algorithms truly policy gradient algorithms? (2018)
8. Jiang, H., Qian, J., Xie, J., Yang, J.: Planning with learned dynamic model for unsupervised point cloud registration (2021)
9. Jiang, H., Qian, J., Xie, J., Yang, J.: Episode-experience replay based tree-backup method for off-policy actor-critic algorithm. In: Lai, J.-H., et al. (eds.) PRCV 2018. LNCS, vol. 11256, pp. 562–573. Springer, Cham (2018). https://doi.org/10.1007/978-3-030-03398-9_48
10. Jiang, H., Shen, Y., Xie, J., Li, J., Qian, J., Yang, J.: Sampling network guided cross-entropy method for unsupervised point cloud registration. arXiv preprint arXiv:2109.06619 (2021)
11. Jiang, H., Xie, J., Yang, J.: Action candidate based clipped double q-learning for discrete and continuous action tasks. In: Proceedings of the AAAI Conference on Artificial Intelligence, vol. 35, pp. 7979–7986 (2021)
12. Kakade, S.M.: A natural policy gradient. In: Advances in Neural Information Processing Systems, vol. 14 (2001)
13. Kempka, M., Wydmuch, M., Runc, G., Toczek, J., Jaśkowski, W.: ViZDoom: a doom-based AI research platform for visual reinforcement learning. In: 2016 IEEE Conference on Computational Intelligence and Games (CIG), pp. 1–8. IEEE (2016)

14. Levine, S., Finn, C., Darrell, T., Abbeel, P.: End-to-end training of deep visuomotor policies. J. Mach. Learn. Res. **17**(1), 1334–1373 (2016)
15. Li, T., Geyer, H., Atkeson, C.G., Rai, A.: Using deep reinforcement learning to learn high-level policies on the ATRIAS biped. In: 2019 International Conference on Robotics and Automation (ICRA), pp. 263–269. IEEE (2019)
16. Lillicrap, T.P., et al.: Continuous control with deep reinforcement learning. arXiv preprint arXiv:1509.02971 (2015)
17. Mnih, V., et al.: Playing Atari with deep reinforcement learning. arXiv preprint arXiv:1312.5602 (2013)
18. Mnih, V., et al.: Human-level control through deep reinforcement learning. nature **518**(7540), 529–533 (2015)
19. Schulman, J., Levine, S., Abbeel, P., Jordan, M., Moritz, P.: Trust region policy optimization. In: International Conference on Machine Learning, pp. 1889–1897. PMLR (2015)
20. Schulman, J., Wolski, F., Dhariwal, P., Radford, A., Klimov, O.: Proximal policy optimization algorithms. arXiv preprint arXiv:1707.06347 (2017)
21. Silver, D., et al.: Mastering the game of go with deep neural networks and tree search. nature **529**(7587), 484–489 (2016)
22. Sutton, R.S., McAllester, D.A., Singh, S.P., Mansour, Y., et al.: Policy gradient methods for reinforcement learning with function approximation. In: NIPS, vol. 99, pp. 1057–1063. Citeseer (1999)
23. Todorov, E., Erez, T., Tassa, Y.: MuJoCo: a physics engine for model-based control. In: 2012 IEEE/RSJ International Conference on Intelligent Robots and Systems, pp. 5026–5033. IEEE (2012)
24. Wang, Y., He, H., Tan, X.: Truly proximal policy optimization. In: Uncertainty in Artificial Intelligence, pp. 113–122. PMLR (2020)
25. Wang, Y., He, H., Tan, X., Gan, Y.: Trust region-guided proximal policy optimization. arXiv preprint arXiv:1901.10314 (2019)
26. Wu, Y., Mansimov, E., Liao, S., Grosse, R., Ba, J.: Scalable trust-region method for deep reinforcement learning using Kronecker-factored approximation. arXiv preprint arXiv:1708.05144 (2017)
27. Zhu, W., Rosendo, A.: Proximal policy optimization smoothed algorithm. arXiv preprint arXiv:2012.02439 (2020)

# Low-Rank Correlation Analysis for Discriminative Subspace Learning

Jiacan Zheng[1], Zhihui Lai[1,2(✉)], Jianglin Lu[1], and Jie Zhou[1]

[1] Computer Vision Institute, College of Computer Science and Software Engineering, Shenzhen University, Shenzhen 518060, China
lai_zhi_hui@163.com
[2] Shenzhen Institute of Artificial Intelligence and Robotics for Society, Shenzhen, China

**Abstract.** Linear dimensionality reduction is a commonly used technique to solve the curse of dimensionality problem in pattern recognition. However, learning a discriminative subspace without label is still a challenging problem, especially when the high-dimensional data is grossly corrupted. To address this problem, we propose an unsupervised dimensionality reduction method called Low-Rank Correlation Analysis (LRCA). The proposed model integrates the low-rank representation and the linear embedding together with a seamless formulation. As such, the robustness and discriminative ability of the learned subspace can be effectively promoted together. An iterative algorithm equipped with alternating direction method of multiplier (ADMM) and eigendecomposition is designed to solve the optimization problem. Experiments show that our method is more discriminative and robust than some existing methods.

**Keywords:** Dimensionality reduction · Low-rank representation · Dictionary learning

## 1 Introduction

Many real-world data, such as face image, natural language and text, usually have very high dimensionality. To avoid the curse of dimensionality problem, a commonly used technique is linear dimensionality reduction, which aims to project the original high-dimensional data to a low-dimensional subspace with some desired intrinsic structure preservation. As stated in [2], a compact and discriminative embedding is vitally crucial for pattern recognition.

Principal Component Analysis (PCA) [23] is the most classical subspace learning method, which can preserve the global structure. Besides, some manifold-learning-based methods, such as Locality Preserving Projections (LPP) [11] and Neighborhood Preserving Embedding (NPE) [10], are recently proposed to learn a subspace with local geometric structure preservation. However, these unsupervised dimensionality reduction methods only assume that the data lies

C. Wallraven et al. (Eds.): ACPR 2021, LNCS 13189, pp. 87–100, 2022.
https://doi.org/10.1007/978-3-031-02444-3_7

on a single low-dimensional subspace or manifold [16]. Therefore, they cannot well capture the global class-special structure for multi-class data, which greatly degrades the discriminative ability of the learned subspace.

The key to improve the discriminative ability is to preserve the multi-subspace structure of original data [15,22]. As studied in [24], many real-world data can be seen as lying near multiple subspaces with each subspace corresponding to one class, e.g. face image [1]. Such a discriminative structure is crucial for data clustering, as studied in Sparse Subspace Clustering (SCC) [7] and Low-Rank Representation (LRR) [17].

Recently, some innovative works further demonstrate the great potential of the multi-subspace structure prior in representation learning. In [12,13,20,29], a deep convolutional auto-encoder is first initialized to learn a compact representation, and then the multi-subspace structure is enforced into the deep feature space, resulting the so-call self-expression layer. Besides, a recent work [28] shows that the objective of maximal coding rate reduction (MCR$^2$) will lead to the multiple orthogonal subspaces structure, which is significantly more robust than maximal cross-entropy in deep learning. Moreover, in [5,25], MCR$^2$ is further considered as the first principle of deep networks, for the unrolling algorithm to optimize MCR$^2$ is actually a modern residual network.

Motivated by these encouraging researches, this paper focus on enforcing the multi-subspace structure into the linear embedding space to improve the discriminative ability. To this end, we propose a novel dimensionality reduction method called Low-Rank Correlation Analysis (LRCA). The main contributions of this paper are listed as follows.

- We design a seamless formulation to optimize LRR and the linear embedding of data jointly. As such, the discriminative multi-subspace structure uncovered by LRR can be enforced into the embedding space.
- An iterative algorithm is designed to solve the proposed joint model. Technically, the designed algorithm optimizes the objective function by alternating direction method of multiplier (ADMM) and eigendecomposition iteratively.
- Theoretically, we prove the convergence of the designed algorithm. Experiments on several real-world datasets show that the proposed LRCA is more discriminative and robust than some existing methods.

## 2   Related Work

In this paper, the column-centered data matrix is denoted by $\mathbf{X} \in \mathbb{R}^{d \times n}$ where each column $\mathbf{x}_i$ is a $d$-dimensional sample. The projection matrix is denoted by $\mathbf{P} \in \mathbb{R}^{d \times k}$. The trace function of a square matrix is defined by $\mathrm{tr}(\cdot)$ and the inner product of two matrices is denoted by $\langle \cdot, \cdot \rangle$.

### 2.1   Canonical Correlation Analysis

Canonical correlation analysis (CCA) [9] is the analog to PCA for two data matrices. The correlation coefficients of two random variables $\mathbf{x}, \mathbf{y}$ is defined as follows:

$$\text{Corr}(\mathbf{x}, \mathbf{y}) = \frac{\mathbb{E}[(\mathbf{x} - \mathbb{E}(\mathbf{x}))(\mathbf{y} - \mathbb{E}(\mathbf{y}))]}{\sqrt{\text{var}(\mathbf{x})\text{var}(\mathbf{y})}}. \tag{1}$$

Now suppose that we have two data matrices, denoted by $\mathbf{X}$ and $\mathbf{Y}$, with centered columns. To find a most correlated latent subspace, CCA maximizes the empirical correlation criterion between two projected data matrices $\mathbf{P}^T\mathbf{X}$ and $\mathbf{Q}^T\mathbf{Y}$, which can be mathematically expressed as:

$$\max_{\mathbf{P},\mathbf{Q}} \frac{\langle \mathbf{P}^T\mathbf{X}, \mathbf{Q}^T\mathbf{Y} \rangle}{\sqrt{\langle \mathbf{P}^T\mathbf{X}, \mathbf{P}^T\mathbf{X} \rangle \langle \mathbf{Q}^T\mathbf{Y}, \mathbf{Q}^T\mathbf{Y} \rangle}}, \tag{2}$$

where the denominator is used to control the variance of $\mathbf{P}^T\mathbf{X}$ and $\mathbf{Q}^T\mathbf{Y}$.

### 2.2 Low-Rank Representation

LRR [16] aims to uncover the latent multi-subspace structure of data by optimizing a low-rank coefficient matrix $\mathbf{Z}$, leading to the following problem:

$$\min_{\mathbf{Z}} \text{ rank}(\mathbf{Z}), \quad \text{s.t. } \mathbf{X} = \mathbf{X}\mathbf{Z}. \tag{3}$$

Considering the NP-hard property of rank minimization problem and the existing outliers, LRR practically solves the following relaxed convex optimization model:

$$\min_{\mathbf{Z}} \ \|\mathbf{E}\|_{2,1} + \lambda\|\mathbf{Z}\|_*, \quad \text{s.t. } \mathbf{X} = \mathbf{X}\mathbf{Z} + \mathbf{E}, \tag{4}$$

where $\lambda \geq 0$ is a balance parameter, $\|\cdot\|_*$ represents the nuclear norm and $\|\cdot\|_{2,1}$ denotes the $\ell_{2,1}$-norm. The relaxed convex model (4) can be efficiently solved by ADMM. Such a low-rank coefficient matrix $\mathbf{Z}$ can well describe the class-special structure and thus is expected to be enforced into the embedding space.

## 3   Low-Rank Correlation Analysis

Many multi-class data can be modeled as samples drawn from multiple subspaces with each subspace corresponding to one class. However, most existing unsupervised dimensionality reduction methods assume that the data lies on a single subspace or manifold, therefore they fail to capture the global class-special structure, which greatly degrades the discriminative ability.

Motivated by this observation, our key insight is to enforce the multi-subspace structure into the embedding space $\mathbb{R}^k$. To this end, we first utilize LRR for robust subspace segmentation. Then, we propose a novel correlation criterion to establish the connection between the low rank coefficient matrix $\mathbf{Z}$ and the linear embedding $\mathbf{P}^T\mathbf{X}$.

**Correlation Criterion:** Suppose we have an over-complete dictionary $\mathbf{D} \in \mathbb{R}^{k \times n}$ with each column $\mathbf{d}_i$ being an atomic vector in embedding space $\mathbb{R}^k$, we then construct the so-called self-expressive data matrix $\mathbf{DZ}$. As the coefficient matrix $\mathbf{Z}$ captures the multi-subspace structure of the original data, self-expressive data matrix $\mathbf{DZ}$ then have the potential to preserve such a structure into the embedding space. Similar to CCA (2), we naturally maximize the correlation criterion between the linear embedding $\mathbf{P}^T\mathbf{X}$ and the self-expressive data matrix $\mathbf{DZ}$ to find a latent correlated subspace:

$$\text{Corr}(\mathbf{D}, \mathbf{P}) = \frac{\langle \mathbf{DZ}, \mathbf{P}^T\mathbf{X} \rangle}{\sqrt{\langle \mathbf{DZ}, \mathbf{DZ} \rangle \langle \mathbf{P}^T\mathbf{X}, \mathbf{P}^T\mathbf{X} \rangle}}. \tag{5}$$

To optimize a compact and discriminative embedding, we need to impose some regularizations into the over-complete dictionary $\mathbf{D}$ and the projection matrix $\mathbf{P}$. However, correlation criterion (5) does not facilitate the use of regularization due to the existence of the denominator. Therefore, we have to transform this formulation.

**Regularization:** For the projection matrix $\mathbf{P}$, parsimony have been widely used as a guiding principle. Therefore, the formulation (5) should equip with a regularization $\mathcal{R}(\mathbf{P})$. Motivated by MMC [14] where a penalty term is used to replace the denominator of the classical Fisher's criterion, we redefine a modified correlation criterion as follows:

$$\mathcal{J}(\mathbf{D}, \mathbf{P}) = 2\langle \mathbf{DZ}, \mathbf{P}^T\mathbf{X} \rangle - \text{tr}(\mathbf{P}^T\mathbf{XX}^T\mathbf{P}) - \alpha\mathcal{R}(\mathbf{P}), \tag{6}$$

where $\alpha \geq 0$ is a balance parameter. As we can see, $\mathcal{J}(\mathbf{D}, \mathbf{P})$ uses the penalty term $\text{tr}(\mathbf{P}^T\mathbf{XX}^T\mathbf{P})$ to control the variance of $\mathbf{P}^T\mathbf{X}$. In our model, we only consider a simple regularization $\mathcal{R}(\mathbf{P}) = \|\mathbf{P}\|_F^2$. Now the correlation criterion (5) becomes:

$$\max_{\mathbf{D}, \mathbf{P}} \frac{\mathcal{J}(\mathbf{D}, \mathbf{P})}{\sqrt{\text{tr}(\mathbf{D\Omega D}^T)}}, \tag{7}$$

where $\mathbf{\Omega} = \mathbf{ZZ}^T$.

For the over-complete dictionary $\mathbf{D}$, the atomic vectors $\mathbf{d}_i$ corresponding to the same subspace should be kept as compact as possible in the embedding space. Therefore, we need to optimize a locality-preserving dictionary $\mathbf{D}$:

$$\min_{\mathbf{D}} \sum_j \sum_i \|\mathbf{d}_i - \mathbf{d}_j\|_2^2 \mathbf{W}_{ij} \Leftrightarrow \min_{\mathbf{D}} \text{tr}(\mathbf{DLD}^T), \tag{8}$$

where $\mathbf{W}$ is an affinity matrix and $\mathbf{L}$ is the corresponding Laplacian matrix. Note that, $\mathbf{W}$ can be simply constructed from the low rank coefficient matrix $\mathbf{Z}$ as follows:

$$\mathbf{W}_{ij} = \begin{cases} 1 & \text{if } \mathbf{x}_i \in C_t(\mathbf{x}_j) \text{ or } \mathbf{x}_j \in C_t(\mathbf{x}_i) \\ 0 & \text{otherwise,} \end{cases} \tag{9}$$

where $C_t(\mathbf{x}_i)$ is the set of $t$ nearest data points of $\mathbf{x}_i$ computed by $|\mathbf{Z}|$. By replace $\Omega$ in (7) with the Laplacian matrix $\mathbf{L}$, we then derive the following problem:

$$\max_{\mathbf{D},\mathbf{P}} \frac{\mathcal{J}(\mathbf{D},\mathbf{P})}{\sqrt{\mathrm{tr}(\mathbf{DLD}^T)}}. \tag{10}$$

To facilitate optimization, by fixing the denominator of (10), we can optimize the constraint correlation criterion as follows:

$$\max_{\mathbf{D},\mathbf{P}} \mathcal{J}(\mathbf{D},\mathbf{P})$$
$$\text{s.t. } \mathbf{DLD}^T = \mathbf{I_k}. \tag{11}$$

**LRCA Model:** Combining the model (4) with the model (11), a two-step model can be directly developed to learn a discriminative subspace. However, in such two-step scheme, the coefficient matrix $\mathbf{Z}$ is learned from (4) independently, and thus cannot be adaptive during the iterative process. To address this drawback, we design a joint formulation, called Low-Rank Correlation Analysis (LRCA), as follows:

$$\min_{\mathbf{E},\mathbf{Z},\mathbf{D},\mathbf{P}} \|\mathbf{E}\|_{2,1} + \lambda\|\mathbf{Z}\|_* - \gamma\mathcal{J}(\mathbf{D},\mathbf{P})$$
$$\text{s.t. } \mathbf{X} = \mathbf{XZ} + \mathbf{E}, \ \mathbf{DLD}^T = \mathbf{I_k}, \tag{12}$$

where $\gamma \geq 0$ is a trade-off parameter.

The proposed LRCA integrates the robust subspace segmentation (4) and the constraint correlation criterion (11) together with a seamless framework. As a result, the robustness and discriminative ability can be greatly improved.

## 4  Optimization and Convergence

Since the proposed LRCA contains four matrix variables, we design an algorithm to iteratively optimize variable pairs $(\mathbf{E}, \mathbf{Z})$ and $(\mathbf{D}, \mathbf{P})$ one by one.

**Low-Rank Representation Step:** Fixed $(\mathbf{D}, \mathbf{P})$, with some simple transformation on (12), we can easily obtain the following equivalent problem:

$$\min_{\mathbf{E},\mathbf{Z}} \|\mathbf{E}\|_{2,1} + \lambda\|\mathbf{Z}\|_* - 2\gamma\langle\mathbf{Z},\mathbf{M}\rangle$$
$$\text{s.t. } \mathbf{X} = \mathbf{XZ} + \mathbf{E}, \tag{13}$$

where $\mathbf{M} = \mathbf{D}^T\mathbf{P}^T\mathbf{X}$ is a constant matrix. Now we present how to solve this modified LRR problem by alternating direction method of multiplier (ADMM) algorithm. First, by introducing an auxiliary variable $\mathbf{J}$, we convert (13) to the following equivalent problem:

$$\min_{\mathbf{E},\mathbf{Z},\mathbf{J}} \|\mathbf{E}\|_{2,1} + \lambda\|\mathbf{J}\|_* - 2\gamma\langle\mathbf{Z},\mathbf{M}\rangle$$
$$\text{s.t. } \mathbf{X} = \mathbf{XZ} + \mathbf{E}, \ \mathbf{Z} = \mathbf{J}, \tag{14}$$

---

**Algorithm 1:** SOLVING SUBPROBLEM (13) BY ADMM.

**Input:** Data matrix $\mathbf{X}$, matrix $\mathbf{M}$, parameter $\lambda, \gamma, \mu$
**Output:** Low rank coefficient matrix $\mathbf{Z}$

1 Initialize $\mathbf{Z} = \mathbf{J} = \mathbf{0}, \mathbf{Y}_1 = \mathbf{0}, \mathbf{Y}_2 = \mathbf{0}$
2 **while** *no converged* **do**
3     Update $\mathbf{J}$ by $\mathbf{J} = \arg\min \frac{\lambda}{\mu}\|\mathbf{J}\|_* + \frac{1}{2}\|\mathbf{J} - (\mathbf{Z} + \mathbf{Y}_2/\mu)\|_F^2$.
4     Update $\mathbf{Z}$ by $\mathbf{Z} = (\mathbf{X}^T\mathbf{X} + \mathbf{I})^{-1}[\mathbf{X}^T\mathbf{X} - \mathbf{X}^T\mathbf{E} + \mathbf{J} + (\mathbf{X}^T\mathbf{Y}_1 - \mathbf{Y}_2)/\mu + 2\gamma\mathbf{M}]$.
5     Update $\mathbf{E}$ by $\mathbf{E} = \arg\min \frac{1}{2}\|\mathbf{E} - (\mathbf{X} - \mathbf{X}\mathbf{Z} + \mathbf{Y}_1/\mu)\|_F^2 + \frac{1}{\mu}\|\mathbf{E}\|_{2,1}$.
6     Update $\mathbf{Y}_1, \mathbf{Y}_2$ by $\mathbf{Y}_1 = \mathbf{Y}_1 + \mu(\mathbf{X} - \mathbf{X}\mathbf{Z} - \mathbf{E})$ and $\mathbf{Y}_2 = \mathbf{Y}_2 + \mu(\mathbf{Z} - \mathbf{J})$.
7     Check the convergence conditions $\|\mathbf{X} - \mathbf{X}\mathbf{Z} - \mathbf{E}\|_\infty < \epsilon$ and $\|\mathbf{Z} - \mathbf{J}\|_\infty < \epsilon$.

---

**Algorithm 2:** LOW RANK CORRELATION ANALYSIS.

**Input:** Data matrix $\mathbf{X}$, parameter $\lambda, \gamma, \alpha$, iteration times $T$
**Output:** Dictionary $\mathbf{D}$, Projection matrix $\mathbf{P}$

1 Initialize coefficient matrix $\mathbf{Z}$ by LRR
2 **for** $i = 1 : T$ **do**
3     Update $\mathbf{D}$ by (20).
4     Update $\mathbf{P}$ by (18).
5     Compute $\mathbf{M} = \mathbf{D}^T\mathbf{P}^T\mathbf{X}$.
6     Update $(\mathbf{Z}, \mathbf{E})$ by Algorithm 1.

---

which can be solved by minimizing the augmented Lagrangian function as follows:

$$\mathcal{L} = \|\mathbf{E}\|_{2,1} + \lambda\|\mathbf{J}\|_* - 2\gamma\langle\mathbf{Z}, \mathbf{M}\rangle + \mathrm{tr}\left[\mathbf{Y}_1^T(\mathbf{X} - \mathbf{X}\mathbf{Z} - \mathbf{E})\right]$$
$$+ \mathrm{tr}\left[\mathbf{Y}_2^T(\mathbf{Z} - \mathbf{J})\right] + \frac{\mu}{2}\left(\|\mathbf{X} - \mathbf{X}\mathbf{Z} - \mathbf{E}\|_F^2 + \|\mathbf{Z} - \mathbf{J}\|_F^2\right), \quad (15)$$

where $\mathbf{Y}_1$ and $\mathbf{Y}_2$ are Lagrange multipliers and $\mu > 0$ is a penalty parameter. The detailed ADMM algorithm is presented in Algorithm 1.

**Maximal Correlation Step:** Fixed $(\mathbf{Z}, \mathbf{E})$, by discarding some constant terms in (12), the optimization problem becomes:

$$\max_{\mathbf{D}, \mathbf{P}} 2\langle\mathbf{D}\mathbf{Z}, \mathbf{P}^T\mathbf{X}\rangle - \mathrm{tr}(\mathbf{P}^T\mathbf{X}\mathbf{X}^T\mathbf{P}) - \alpha\|\mathbf{P}\|_F^2$$
$$\text{s.t. } \mathbf{D}\mathbf{L}\mathbf{D}^T = \mathbf{I_k}. \quad (16)$$

Fortunately, problem (16) have a close form of solution by eigendecomposition. Mathematically, fixed $\mathbf{D}$, we can derive a equivalent regression formulation as follows:

$$\min_{\mathbf{P}} \|\mathbf{D}\mathbf{Z} - \mathbf{P}^T\mathbf{X}\|_F^2 + \alpha\|\mathbf{P}\|_F^2. \quad (17)$$

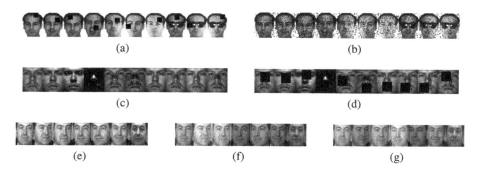

(a)                                         (b)

(c)                                         (d)

(e)                    (f)                    (g)

**Fig. 1.** The corrupted image samples of different datasets. AR dataset corrupted by (a) $10 \times 10$ block, (b) 10% salt-and-pepper noise. Extended Yale B dataset corrupted by (c) $0 \times 0$ block and (d) $20 \times 20$ block. FERET dataset corrupted by gray image with intensity in (e) $[0, 0]$, (f) $[0, 100]$ and (g) $[0, 200]$.

Setting the partial derivative of the objective function in (17) with respect to $\mathbf{P}$ equal to zero gives the optimal solution of $\mathbf{P}$:

$$\mathbf{P} = (\mathbf{XX}^T + \alpha \mathbf{I})^{-1}\mathbf{XZ}^T\mathbf{D}^T. \tag{18}$$

Then, by substituting (18) back into (16), we derive the following trace maximization problem for $\mathbf{D}$:

$$\max_{\mathbf{D}} \; \text{tr}[\mathbf{DZX}^T(\mathbf{XX}^T + \alpha \mathbf{I})^{-1}\mathbf{XZ}^T\mathbf{D}^T]$$
$$\text{s.t. } \mathbf{DLD}^T = \mathbf{I_k}. \tag{19}$$

The optimal solution of (19) is given from solving the generalized eigen equation as follows:

$$[\mathbf{ZX}^T(\mathbf{XX}^T + \alpha \mathbf{I})^{-1}\mathbf{XZ}^T]\,\mathbf{v} = \eta\,\mathbf{Lv}, \tag{20}$$

where $\eta$ is the eigenvalue and $\mathbf{v}$ is the corresponding eigenvector. Then, we can obtain the optimal solution of $\mathbf{D}^*$ with the $i$-th row being the eigenvectors corresponding to the $i$-th largest eigenvalues. Substituting the optimal $\mathbf{D}^*$ into (17) further gives the optimal solution of $\mathbf{P}^*$.

Overall, the total scheme is easy to implement. We describe the iterative process in Algorithm 2. Since the designed algorithm is an iterative method, we also give the Theorem 1 for its convergence.

**Theorem 1.** *The Algorithm 2 monotonically decreases the objective function value of (12) in each iteration and gives a local optimal solution.*

*Proof.* Boyd *et al.* [3] have comprehensively proven the convergence of the ADMM algorithm. Since the subproblem (13) is a convex optimization problem with two block variables and a linear constraint, as a direct result, the proposed Algorithm 1 will approach an optimal value of the objective function

(13). Besides, for the subproblem (16), the close form (18) and (20) give its optimal solution. Therefore, the total objective function of (12) will be decreased in each iteration. As the objective function (12) is bounded, the iterative scheme in Algorithm 2 will finally converge to a local optimal solution.

## 5 Experiments

We evaluate the robustness and discriminative ability of the proposed LRCA on three standard face datasets, e.g., AR, FERET and Extended Yale B datasets, where each face subject correspond to a subspace. Some most related methods are selected for comparison, such as PCA [23] and JSPCA [27], manifold-learning-based methods (NPE [10], LPP [11], OLPP [4]), and some low-rank methods LRR-Graph embedding [26], LRLE [6].

**Table 1.** The performance (recognition accuracy (%), dimension) of different algorithms on AR dataset different kinds of noise.

| Method | $AR$ | | $AR_{10\times10}$ | | $AR_{20\times20}$ | | $AR_{\text{salt-and-pepper}}$ | |
|---|---|---|---|---|---|---|---|---|
| | $T=5$ | $T=7$ | $T=5$ | $T=7$ | $T=5$ | $T=7$ | $T=5$ | $T=7$ |
| PCA | 85.83 | 87.59 | 63.48 | 67.49 | 36.67 | 38.44 | 77.54 | 82.92 |
| | (90) | (100) | (100) | (100) | (100) | (100) | (83) | (96) |
| JSPCA | 80.78 | 85.54 | 60.14 | 65.05 | 29.90 | 33.64 | 75.67 | 81.16 |
| | (100) | (100) | (100) | (100) | (100) | (100) | (100) | (100) |
| LPP | 88.11 | 91.54 | 61.13 | 66.72 | 34.37 | 40.03 | 73.22 | 80.42 |
| | (100) | (100) | (100) | (100) | (98) | (100) | (43) | (68) |
| OLPP | 78.67 | 84.24 | 53.08 | 59.81 | 25.81 | 30.95 | 66.89 | 75.81 |
| | (100) | (98) | (100) | (100) | (100) | (99) | (51) | (84) |
| NPE | 93.50 | 96.25 | 77.24 | 83.60 | 46.51 | 52.65 | 65.00 | 79.35 |
| | (90) | (96) | (99) | (96) | (100) | (100) | (32) | (44) |
| LRLE | 84.36 | 88.21 | 66.99 | 70.75 | 34.99 | 38.74 | 78.63 | 83.78 |
| | (100) | (100) | (100) | (100) | (100) | (100) | (81) | (98) |
| LRR-Graph | 91.27 | 93.70 | 65.26 | 70.69 | 44.68 | 48.99 | 76.92 | 83.79 |
| | (100) | (100) | (100) | (100) | (100) | (100) | (47) | (55) |
| **LRCA** | **95.82** | **97.52** | **83.56** | **90.63** | **53.88** | **62.87** | **88.52** | **92.70** |
| | **(99)** | **(100)** | **(98)** | **(100)** | **(100)** | **(100)** | **(54)** | **(55)** |

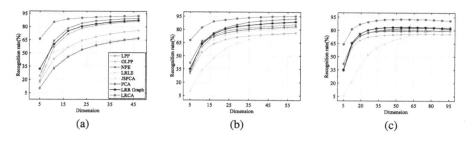

**Fig. 2.** Recognition on the (a) Extended Yale B (T = 30) (b) AR (T = 5) and (c) AR (10% salt-and-pepper noise, T = 7).

## 5.1  Datasets

The AR dataset [19] contains 2400 face images of 120 people. To test the robustness, all the face images are randomly corrupted by $10 \times 10$ block, $20 \times 20$ block occlusion and 10% salt-and-pepper noise, respectively.

The Extended Yale B dataset [8] contains 64 frontal face images per subject taken under different illumination conditions. Face images from 38 subjects are included, all the face images are randomly corrupted by $10 \times 10$ block and $20 \times 20$ block occlusion, respectively.

The FERET dataset [21] contains the 200 classes while there are only 7 samples for each person. All the face images are corrupted by gray image with random intensity generated from uniform distribution in [0, 100] and [0, 200], respectively.

Figure 1 show some sample images of these datasets.

**Table 2.** The performance (recognition accuracy (%), dimension) of different algorithms on FERET dataset with different intensity gray occlusion.

| Intensity | PCA | JSPCA | LPP | OLPP | NPE | LRLE | LRR-Graph | **LRCA** |
|---|---|---|---|---|---|---|---|---|
| [0, 0] | 53.87 | 56.23 | 55.05 | 54.50 | 51.90 | 53.10 | 61.23 | **61.70** |
| | (100) | (89) | (100) | (99) | (78) | (100) | (100) | **(70)** |
| [0, 100] | 29.55 | 30.35 | 53.33 | 49.53 | 51.88 | 29.38 | 55.87 | **61.43** |
| | (100) | (85) | (100) | (99) | (52) | (90) | (94) | **(70)** |
| [0, 200] | 21.83 | 21.63 | 55.13 | 52.17 | 55.48 | 21.45 | 52.70 | **59.07** |
| | (91 | (97) | (98) | (100) | (66) | (100) | (98) | **(63)** |

**Table 3.** The performance (recognition accuracy (%), dimension) of different algorithms on Extended Yale B dataset with different sizes of block occlusion.

| Block size (T) | PCA | JSPCA | LPP | OLPP | NPE | LRLE | LRR-Graph | **LRCA** |
|---|---|---|---|---|---|---|---|---|
| $0 \times 0$ (10) | 55.40 | 53.18 | 74.96 | 54.62 | 82.44 | 55.15 | 79.17 | **83.03** |
| | (100) | (63) | (100) | (100) | (97) | (100) | (100) | **(100)** |
| $10 \times 10$ (10) | 37.23 | 37.73 | 44.77 | 32.99 | 53.63 | 36.89 | 52.88 | **58.20** |
| | (100) | (100) | (100) | (100) | (100) | (100) | (97) | **(100)** |
| $20 \times 20$ (10) | 15.23 | 17.06 | 18.22 | 14.19 | 21.14 | 14.65 | 20.26 | **26.71** |
| | (100) | (60) | (100) | (100) | (97) | (100) | (100) | **(100)** |
| $0 \times 0$ (20) | 66.75 | 65.32 | 85.66 | 73.36 | **89.35** | 66.78 | 86.92 | 89.32 |
| | (100) | (64) | (100) | (100) | **(100)** | (100) | (100) | (100) |
| $10 \times 10$ (20) | 46.84 | 47.80 | 59.63 | 48.41 | 70.60 | 46.88 | 64.10 | **73.55** |
| | (100) | (64) | (100) | (100) | (100) | (100) | (100) | **(100)** |
| $20 \times 20$ (20) | 20.39 | 23.21 | 26.50 | 21.14 | 28.76 | 19.66 | 28.61 | **36.02** |
| | (100) | (60) | (100) | (100) | (100) | (100) | (100) | **(100)** |
| $0 \times 0$ (30) | 74.61 | 73.00 | 89.37 | 81.93 | 91.84 | 74.50 | 90.43 | **93.10** |
| | (100) | (64) | (100) | (100) | (100) | (100) | (100) | **(100)** |
| $10 \times 10$ (30) | 53.86 | 55.34 | 67.86 | 58.08 | 79.05 | 54.51 | 71.33 | **83.80** |
| | (100) | (100) | (100) | (100) | (100) | (100) | (100) | **(100)** |
| $20 \times 20$ (30) | 23.73 | 27.33 | 32.03 | 24.95 | 33.84 | 22.76 | 33.53 | **41.43** |
| | (99) | (60) | (100) | (100) | (100) | (100) | (100) | **(100)** |

## 5.2 Experimental Settings

We randomly select $T$ training samples per class and the rest samples for test. According to the different sizes of each dataset, we choose $T$ for the AR, FERET and Extended Yale B datasets as $T = 5, 7$, $T = 4$ and $T = 10, 20, 30$, respectively. For simplicity, we directly set the balance parameter $\gamma = 1$ for the proposed LRCA. The dimensions of the low-dimensional subspace ranged from 1 to 100. The nearest neighbor classifier (1NN) with Euclidean distance is used to compute the average recognition rates of the learned representation on the test set. All algorithms are independently run 10 times on each dataset to provide reliable experimental results, and the average recognition rate is computed and reported.

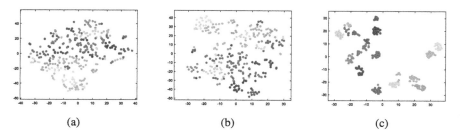

**Fig. 3.** t-SNE representation of the first 20 dimensions obtained by (a) PCA, (b) LPP and (c) LRCA on AR dataset with $10 \times 10$ block (T = 7).

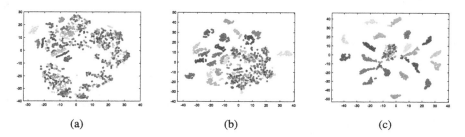

**Fig. 4.** t-SNE representation of the first 40 dimensions obtained by (a) PCA, (b) LPP and (c) LRCA on Extended Yale B dataset (T = 30).

### 5.3   Results and Discussions

Tables 1, 2 and 3 report the average recognition rate and the corresponding dimension of these datasets. As can be seen, LRCA achieves the best recognition rate in most cases. The key reason is that LRCA can uncover the multi-subspace structure, thus the face representation learned by the proposed LRCA is more discriminative.

LRCA is also significantly robust for different kinds of noises. When the datasets are corrupted by block occlusion, salt-and-pepper noise and illumination variation, the recognition rate of LRCA is higher than other methods. The key reason is that the proposed LRCA imposes the global low rank constraint on coefficient matrix, therefore, some corrupted data can be automatically corrected.

LRCA derives a more compact face representation. As can be seen in Fig. 2, the recognition rate curve of LRCA is steeper than the others, which means LRCA can learn a sufficiently discriminative face representation with relatively low dimensionality.

### 5.4   Visualization of Discriminative Ability

Figure 3 and Fig. 4 display the t-SNE representation [18] learned by PCA, LPP and LRCA, where each color denotes a subject of face images. Specifically, for

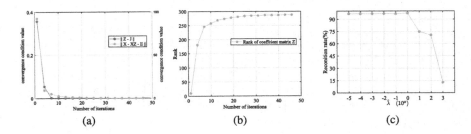

**Fig. 5.** The variation of (a) two convergence conditions of ADMM Algorithm 1, (b) the corresponding coefficient matrix **Z**'s rank on Extend Yale B dataset. (c) Recognition rates versus the value of parameter $\hat{\lambda}$ on AR dataset.

corrupted AR dataset, we first project 15 subjects of face images to the first 20-dimensional subspace, and then visualize them on 2-dimensional spaces by t-SNE algorithm. For the Extended Yale B dataset, we project 20 subjects of face images to the first 40-dimensional subspace and then perform t-SNE algorithm. As can be seen, the face images of different classes are well separated and the intra-class distances are simultaneously compressed by the proposed LRCA. Therefore, LRCA can intuitively derive a more compact and discriminative face representation.

### 5.5   Convergence and Parameter Sensitivity Study

As the designed Algorithm 1 is convergent, we explore the convergence speed and the parameter sensitivity. Figure 5(a) and 5(b) show the convergent properties of the Algorithm 1 and the corresponding rank of the coefficient matrix **Z** on Extended Yale B dataset, respectively. As can be seen, the convergence speed of ADMM Algorithm 1 is very fast.

We set parameter $\lambda$ as $\lambda = \hat{\lambda}E_\lambda$ to control the low rank property, in which $E_\lambda = \sum_{i=1}^{n} \|\mathbf{x}_i\|_2/n$ is used to eliminate influence of dimension. From Fig. 5(c), when $\hat{\lambda} > 1$, the recognition rate declined rapidly. The reason is that the rank of the coefficient matrix **Z** is too low to capture the multi-subspace structure.

## 6   Conclusion

In this paper, we propose a novel unsupervised dimensionality reduction method. Since the proposed LRCA utilize LRR for robust subspace segmentation and preserve such a class-special structure, the robustness and discriminative ability of the embedding space can be greatly improved together. We design an iterative algorithm with convergence guarantee to optimize the objective function by using ADMM and eigendecomposition alternatively. Extensive experiments show the superior robustness and discriminative ability of the proposed LRCA.

**Acknowledgement.** This work was supported in part by the Natural Science Foundation of China under Grant 61976145, Grant 62076164 and Grant 61802267, in part by the Guangdong Basic and Applied Basic Research Foundation (No. 2021A1515011861), and in part by the Shenzhen Municipal Science and Technology Innovation Council under Grants JCYJ20180305124834854 and JCYJ20190813100801664.

# References

1. Basri, R., Jacobs, D.W.: Lambertian reflectance and linear subspaces. IEEE Trans. Pattern Anal. Mach. Intell. **25**(2), 218–233 (2003)
2. Bengio, Y., Courville, A., Vincent, P.: Representation learning: a review and new perspectives. IEEE Trans. Pattern Anal. Mach. Intell. **35**(8), 1798–1828 (2013). https://doi.org/10.1109/TPAMI.2013.50
3. Boyd, S.P., Parikh, N., Chu, E., Peleato, B., Eckstein, J.: Distributed optimization and statistical learning via the alternating direction method of multipliers. Found. Trends Mach. Learn. **3**(1), 1–122 (2011)
4. Cai, D., He, X., Han, J., Zhang, H.: Orthogonal Laplacianfaces for face recognition. IEEE Trans. Image Process. **15**(11), 3608–3614 (2006)
5. Chan, K.H.R., Yu, Y., You, C., Qi, H., Wright, J., Ma, Y.: Deep networks from the principle of rate reduction. arXiv preprint arXiv:2010.14765 (2020)
6. Chen, Y., Lai, Z., Wong, W.K., Shen, L., Hu, Q.: Low-rank linear embedding for image recognition. IEEE Trans. Multimedia **20**(12), 3212–3222 (2018)
7. Elhamifar, E., Vidal, R.: Sparse subspace clustering: algorithm, theory, and applications. IEEE Trans. Pattern Anal. Mach. Intell. **35**(11), 2765–2781 (2013)
8. Georghiades, A.S., Belhumeur, P.N., Kriegman, D.J.: From few to many: illumination cone models for face recognition under variable lighting and pose. IEEE Trans. Pattern Anal. Mach. Intell. **23**(6), 643–660 (2001)
9. Härdle, W.K., Simar, L.: Canonical Correlation Analysis, pp. 443–454. Springer, Heidelberg (2015)
10. He, X., Cai, D., Yan, S., Zhang, H.J.: Neighborhood preserving embedding. In: IEEE International Conference on Computer Vision, vol. 2, pp. 1208–1213 (2005)
11. He, X., Niyogi, P.: Locality preserving projections. IEEE Trans. Knowl. Data Eng., 153–160 (2003)
12. Ji, P., Zhang, T., Li, H., Salzmann, M., Reid, I.D.: Deep subspace clustering networks. In: Conference on Neural Information Processing Systems, pp. 24–33 (2017)
13. Kheirandishfard, M., Zohrizadeh, F., Kamangar, F.: Deep low-rank subspace clustering. In: IEEE Conference on Computer Vision and Pattern Recognition Workshops, pp. 3776–3781. IEEE (2020)
14. Li, H., Jiang, T., Zhang, K.: Efficient and robust feature extraction by maximum margin criterion. In: Conference and Workshop on Neural Information Processing Systems, pp. 97–104. MIT Press (2003)
15. Li, J., Wu, Y., Zhao, J., Lu, K.: Low-rank discriminant embedding for multiview learning. IEEE Trans. Cybern. **47**(11), 3516–3529 (2017)
16. Liu, G., Lin, Z., Yan, S., Sun, J., Yu, Y., Ma, Y.: Robust recovery of subspace structures by low-rank representation. IEEE Trans. Pattern Anal. Mach. Intell. **35**(1), 171–184 (2013)
17. Liu, G., Lin, Z., Yu, Y.: Robust subspace segmentation by low-rank representation. In: International Conference on Machine Learning, pp. 663–670. Omnipress (2010)
18. van der Maaten, L., Hinton, G.: Visualizing data using t-SNE. J. Mach. Learn. Res. **9**(86), 2579–2605 (2008)

19. Martinez, A., Benavente, R.: The AR face database. CVC Technical Report 24 (1998)
20. Peng, X., Xiao, S., Feng, J., Yau, W., Yi, Z.: Deep subspace clustering with sparsity prior. In: International Joint Conferences on Artificial Intelligence, pp. 1925–1931. IJCAI/AAAI Press (2016)
21. Phillips, P.J., Moon, H., Rizvi, S.A., Rauss, P.J.: The FERET evaluation methodology for face-recognition algorithms. IEEE Trans. Pattern Anal. Mach. Intell. **22**(10), 1090–1104 (2000)
22. Sørensen, M., Sidiropoulos, N.D.: Multi-set low-rank factorizations with shared and unshared components. IEEE Trans. Sig. Process. **68**, 5122–5137 (2020)
23. Turk, M., Pentland, A.: Eigenfaces for recognition. J. Cogn. Neurosci. **3**(1), 71–86 (1991)
24. Vidal, R., Ma, Y., Sastry, S.: Generalized principal component analysis (GPCA). IEEE Trans. Pattern Anal. Mach. Intell. **27**(12), 1945–1959 (2005)
25. Wu, Z., Baek, C., You, C., Ma, Y.: Incremental learning via rate reduction. CoRR abs/2011.14593 (2020)
26. Yan, S., Xu, D., Zhang, B., Zhang, H., Yang, Q., Lin, S.: Graph embedding and extensions: a general framework for dimensionality reduction. IEEE Trans. Pattern Anal. Mach. Intell. **29**(1), 40–51 (2007)
27. Yi, S., Lai, Z., He, Z., Cheung, Y., Liu, Y.: Joint sparse principal component analysis. Pattern Recogn. **61**, 524–536 (2017)
28. Yu, Y., Chan, K.H.R., You, C., Song, C., Ma, Y.: Learning diverse and discriminative representations via the principle of maximal coding rate reduction. CoRR abs/2006.08558 (2020)
29. Zhang, J., et al.: Self-supervised convolutional subspace clustering network. In: IEEE Conference on Computer Vision and Pattern Recognition, pp. 5473–5482. Computer Vision Foundation/IEEE (2019)

# Rapid and High-Purity Seed Grading Based on Pruned Deep Convolutional Neural Network

Huanyu Li[1](✉), Cuicao Zhang[1], Chunlei Li[1](✉), Zhoufeng Liu[1], Yan Dong[1], and Shuili Tang[2]

[1] Zhongyuan University of Technology, Zhengzhou 450007, China
{lihuanyu,lichunlei1979}@zut.edu.cn
[2] Hi-Tech Heavy Industry Co., Ltd., Zhengzhou, China

**Abstract.** The crop seed grading method based on deep learning has achieved ideal recognition results. However, an effective deep neural network model for seed grading usually needs a relatively high computational complexity, memory space, or inference time, which critically hampers the utilization of complex CNNs on devices with limited computational resources. For this reason, a method of combining layer pruning and filter pruning is proposed to realize fast and high-purity seed grading. First, we propose an effective approach based on feature representation to eliminate redundant convolutional layers, which greatly reduces the model's consumption of device storage resources. Then, the filter-level pruning based on the Taylor expansion criterion is introduced to further eliminate the redundant information existing in the convolutional layer. Finally, an effective and practical knowledge distillation technology (MEAL V2) is adopted to transfer knowledge of well-performing models, to compensate for the information loss caused by the pruning of the network. Experiments on red kidney bean datasets demonstrate that the method is effective and feasible. We proposed the Vgg_Beannet, which can achieve 4× inference acceleration while the accuracy is only reduced by 0.13% when the filter is pruned by 90%. Moreover, we also compared some handcrafted lightweight architectures such as MobileNetv2, MixNet, etc. The results show that the pruned network outperforms the above network in inference time (2.07 ms vs. 7.83 ms, 22.23 ms) and accuracy (96.33% vs. 95.94%, 94.89%).

**Keywords:** Seed grading · Deep learning · Neural network pruning · Knowledge distillation

## 1 Introduction

In the processing industry, the purity of seeds is an important evaluation criterion of quality rating. The seed grading can improve the seed quality, save the sowing quantity and cereals, advantageous to achieving sowing mechanization and precision sowing, and it can bring significant social benefits. Traditional seed

C. Wallraven et al. (Eds.): ACPR 2021, LNCS 13189, pp. 101–115, 2022.
https://doi.org/10.1007/978-3-031-02444-3_8

defect detection methods generally rely on manual detection, which is inefficient and subjective. Therefore, an objective and automated seed grading method is required.

To solve this problem, researchers have applied machine vision technology to detect seed quality [1–3]. Features, such as histogram of oriented gradient (HOG), color, texture, Gabor etc., can be extracted from images of seeds, and then, the various effective classifiers are employed to identify the defects of the seed, such as support vector machine (SVM), decision tree (DT) etc. However, because of the diversity and fine-grained recognition of defective seeds, these methods based on manual feature extraction are difficult to distinguish fine-grained difference, resulting in low classification accuracy and lack of self-adaptivity.

Recently, some researchers also adopted deep learning technology in crop identification tasks and achieved good performance [4–6]. The deep network model represented by a convolutional neural network (CNN) significantly improves the accuracy of traditional detection and recognition problem by automatically learning a hierarchical feature representation from raw data. Heo et al. [4] used CNN to filter weed seeds from high-quality seeds, Uzal et al. [5] adopted CNN to estimate the number of soybean seeds. However, the accuracy of the above crop classification methods based on deep learning depends on the model depth. However, with the rise of network depth and width, the time complexity and spatial complexity of the depth model will increase, which will suffer from slow inference speed, especially the seed sorting system with high throughput. Moreover, the massive researches indicate that the existing DNN models have numerous parameter redundancy, which consumes massive computing and storage resources.

Due to the limited computing resource platform such as FPGA, GPU, MCU, etc. Deep model compression provides an effective solution for reducing the model size and lowering the computation overheads, such as network structure search (NAS) [7], weight quantization [8], knowledge distillation [9,19], and network pruning [11,12]. NAS requires massive computing resources and brings a set of new hyperparameter problems. Quantization reduces the bit-width of parameters, thus decreases memory footprint, but requires specialized hardware instructions to achieve latency reduction [13]. Network pruning has the advantages of simple operation, efficient implementation, can reduce network complexity and solve over-fitting problems, and has shown broad prospects in various emerging applications.

Neural network pruning can realize the pruning of weights, filters, and convolutional layers. The fine-grained pruning at the weight level is flexible, but it needs specialized software or hardware to achieve the practical effect. The coarse-grained pruning based on the filter not only owns high flexibility but also does not need the corresponding cooperation of software and hardware, however, it has certain limitations in reducing latency. The pruning model obtained by layer pruning owns less runtime memory usage and inference time because fewer layers mean fewer data moving in memory, thereby improving computational efficiency.

In this study, a mixed pruning strategy, which takes both layer pruning and channel pruning into consideration, is proposed to achieve model compression and improve the inference speed of the algorithm. First, we designed a set of linear classifiers to explore the roles and dynamics of intermediate layers and combined with feature visualization analysis to remove the redundant convolution layer. Then, we adopted the criterion based on Taylor expansion to approximate the change in the loss function if removing the least important parameters and then directly prunes those corresponding to the almost flat gradient of the loss function. Finally, a multi-teacher integrated knowledge distillation technology [10] is introduced to transfer knowledge to the pruning network to compensate for the accuracy loss caused by pruning. Overall, our contributions are three-fold as follows:

1) We proposed a mixed pruning strategy based on feature representation and Taylor expansion to achieve fast and high-purity seed grading.
2) A simple and effective multi-teacher integrated knowledge distillation method (i.e., meal V2) is introduced to transfer the knowledge of CNN with high accuracy to the pruned network to recover its predictive accuracy.
3) Experiments are conducted on our constructed red kidney bean datasets, and the results show this method greatly improves the inference speed, memory consumption, and computation cost with almost no loss of accuracy.

## 2   Proposed Method

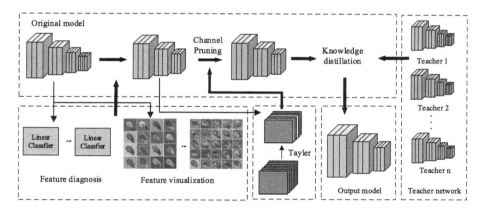

**Fig. 1.** The structure flow chart of the proposed method.

Automatic seed grading based on deep learning provides an effective solution for improving seed quality. However, high computational complexity, memory space and inference time of the deep learning model limit its deployment on resource-constrained edge devices. We proposed a mixed pruning strategy based on feature representation and Taylor expansion to achieve fast and high-purity seed grading, as shown in Fig. 1. In the stage of layer pruning, we designed a set of linear classifiers for feature diagnosis and combined feature visualization technology to remove redundant convolutional layers. In the filter pruning stage, a highly efficient method based on the Taylor expansion criterion is employed, which adopts the first derivative as the criterion to measure the importance of filters and eliminate redundant filters. Finally, multi-teacher integrated knowledge distillation technology is utilized to transfer knowledge to the pruning network to compensate for the accuracy loss caused by pruning. And the proposed method is specifically described as follows.

### 2.1  Network Structure and Feature Diagnosis

***A. Network Structure.*** Vggnet [14] is a very deep convolutional network and has good generalization ability to a wide range of complex pattern recognition tasks. Moreover, compared with some complex networks, it has the advantages of simple structure, fast inference speed, and easy deployment, so it is still heavily used for real-world applications in both academia and industry. In this paper, an improved VggBN-16 [15] network is selected as the feature extraction network, its structure is shown in Fig. 2.

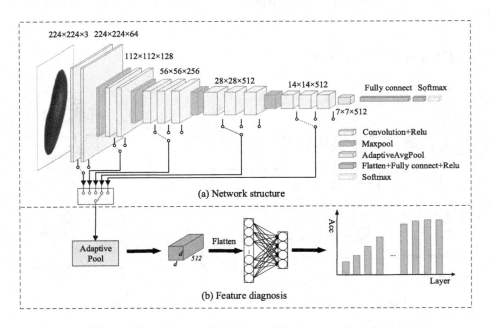

**Fig. 2.** The structure flow chart of the proposed method.

***B. Feature Diagnosis.*** CNN (including VggBN-16) containing both feature extractor and classifier, learns reasonable feature representations specific to the current task with corresponding training data. While the features from the last convolutional layer of a CNN tend to provide the best discriminative power, features from intermediate layers also contain important information related to the tasks and can be utilized to analyze the behaviors of the corresponding CNN. At the same time, with the increase of network depth, the computational cost of this method will increase dramatically and the test accuracy will be affected. Therefore, we trained a set of linear classifiers on features extracted at different layers within the network and visualized the outputs to explore the roles and dynamics of intermediate layers, then determined the optimal number of network layers.

As shown in Fig. 2, since each layer has a different output feature shape, we adopted adaptive average pool to simplify the method and unified the embedding length so that each layer can produce roughly the same output size, the pooling is done as follows:

$$d_i = round\left(\sqrt{\tfrac{N}{n_i}}\right) \tag{1}$$

$$E_i = AdaptiveAvgPool\left(M_i, d_i\right) \tag{2}$$

where $N$ is the embedding length, $i$ ($1 \le i \le L$) is the convolution layer index, $n_i$ is the number of filters in the $i$-th convolutional layer, $M_i$ is layer $i$'s ($1 \le i \le L$) output map. AdaptiveAvgpool reduces $M_i$ to embedding $E_i \in R^{n \times d \times d}$. Then, the output $E_i$ of each layer is flattened to $z_i$ as the input of the fully connected network. Finally, we train a set of linear classifiers $F_i(z_i)$ to predict the correct class $y$ using only the specific intermediate result:

$$z_i = flatten\left(E_i\right) \tag{3}$$

$$y_i = F_i\left(z_i\right) = softmax\left(w_i z_i + b_i\right) \tag{4}$$

where $w_i$ and $b_i$ respectively represent the weight and bias of the $i$-th linear classifier. During training, we will freeze the parameters of the original network model, finetune the auxiliary classifier through backpropagation, and finally determine the feature extraction ability of the convolutional layer.

Combining the feature visualization technology, we found that the shallow network has good feature extraction capabilities. Through the experimental results, the layer with less contribution in the deep model is eliminated, and the compression of the convolutional layer of the model is realized, which speeds up the reasoning of the model.

## 2.2  Taylor Expansion Criterion-Based Channel Pruning

Through feature visualization, we also found that some feature maps are similar to each other, which proves that the neural network structure still has some redundant information, so we can prune the convolution network model to remove redundant information, thus enhancing the inference speed. And the Tayler expansion based network pruning methods [15] have been widely used to condense the structure of the CNN and then make a balance between the generalization and compact network because it does not lack basic theoretical guidance or bring a new set of hyperparameter problems. It regards channel pruning as an optimization problem, i.e., minimizing the difference between the cost functions before and after pruning.

Raw data were processed to generate training samples

$$\mathcal{W} = \left\{ \left(w_1^1, b_1^1\right), \left(w_1^2, b_1^2\right), \cdots, \left(w_L^{C_l}, b_L^{C_l}\right) \right\}$$

where $w_i^l(i = 1, 2, \cdots, L)$ is the weight parameter, $C_l$ is the number of channels. $\mathcal{L}(\mathcal{D} \mid \mathcal{W})$ represents the cost function, which is the optimization objective of this study. In the process of channel pruning, a subset $\mathcal{W}'$ is refined from original parameters $\mathcal{W}$ by using the following combinatorial optimization:

$$\min_{\mathcal{W}'} |\mathcal{L}(\mathcal{D} \mid \mathcal{W}') - \mathcal{L}(\mathcal{D} \mid \mathcal{W})| \quad s.t. \|\mathcal{W}'\|_0 \le B \tag{5}$$

the norm $l_0$ in $\|\mathcal{W}'\|_0$ limits the number of nonzero parameters $B$. If $\mathcal{L}(\mathcal{D} \mid \mathcal{W}') \approx \mathcal{L}(\mathcal{D} \mid \mathcal{W})$, it is easy to reach the global minimum of Eq.(5). After pruning a specific parameter, the change in the loss function is approximated by

$$|\Delta\mathcal{L}(h_i)| = |\mathcal{L}(\mathcal{D}, h_i = 0) - \mathcal{L}(\mathcal{D}, h_i)| \tag{6}$$

where $\mathcal{L}(\mathcal{D}, h_i = 0)$ is the cost after pruning, $\mathcal{L}(\mathcal{D}, h_i)$ is the cost without pruning, $h_i$ is the eigenvalue of parameter $i$ output. Using a first-order Taylor polynomial $\mathcal{L}(\mathcal{D}, h_i = 0)$ is approximated by [15]

$$\mathcal{L}(\mathcal{D}, h_i = 0) = \mathcal{L}(\mathcal{D}, h_i) - \frac{\delta\mathcal{L}}{\delta h_i} h_i + R_1(h_i = 0) \tag{7}$$

where $R_1(h_i = 0)$ is expressed as:

$$R_1(h_i = 0) = \frac{\delta^2\mathcal{L}}{\delta(h_i^2 = \xi)} \frac{h_i^2}{2} \tag{8}$$

where $\xi$ is a value in the range of 0 and $h_i$. If the influence caused by removing the high-order term can be ignored, substituting Eq.(7) into Eq.(6).

$$\theta_{\text{TE}}(h_i) = |\Delta\mathcal{L}(h_i)| = \left|\mathcal{L}(\mathcal{D}, h_i) - \frac{\delta\mathcal{L}}{\delta h_i} h_i - \mathcal{L}(\mathcal{D}, h_i)\right| = \left|\frac{\delta\mathcal{L}}{\delta h_i} h_i\right| \tag{9}$$

Based on this definition, the parameters having an almost flat gradient of the cost should be pruned, and then $\theta_{\text{TE}}$ is computed for a feature map by [15].

## 2.3   Knowledge Distillation of Multi-model Ensemble

After the mixed pruning of channel and layer, we have obtained networks with a more compact architecture. However, in the process of network pruning, some useful information may be lost, which leads to the performance degradation of the model. To compensate for the performance loss, we introduced a simple and effective knowledge distillation technology (Meal v2) to transfer knowledge from the original model and some CNNs with high accuracy to the pruned model for boosting its performance.

The method adopted the similarity loss and discriminator only on the final outputs and used the average of SoftMax probabilities from all teacher ensembles as the stronger supervision for distillation [10]. The realization process is shown in Fig. 3, which mainly consists of three parts: teacher ensemble, KL divergence loss, and the discriminator.

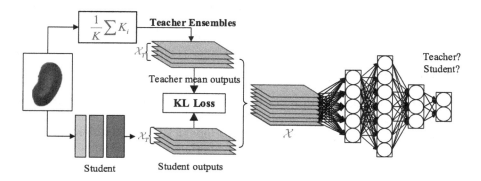

**Fig. 3.** The realization process of knowledge distillation based on Meal v2 [10].

***A. Teachers Ensemble.*** We chosen some models that perform well in the seed dataset as the teacher network and adopted the average of softmax probabilities of these pre-trained teachers as an ensemble. Assuming $\mathcal{T}_\theta$ as a teacher network, the output ensemble probability $\hat{p}_e^{\mathcal{T}_\theta}$ can be described as:

$$\hat{p}_e^{\mathcal{T}_\theta}(X) = \frac{1}{k} \sum_{t=1}^{k} \mathbf{p}_t^{\mathcal{T}_\theta}(X) \tag{10}$$

where $\mathbf{p}_t^{\mathcal{T}_\theta}$ represents the $t$-th teacher's softmax prediction. $X$ is the input image and $k$ is the number of total teachers [10].

***B. KL Divergence.*** It is used to measure the similarity of two probability distributions. We trained the student network $\mathcal{S}_\theta$ by minimizing between its output $\hat{p}^{\mathcal{S}_\theta}(x_i)$ and the ensembled soft labels $\hat{p}_e^{\mathcal{T}_\theta}(x_i)$ generated by the teacher ensemble. In practice, we can simply minimize the equivalent cross-entropy loss as follows [10]:

$$\mathcal{L}_{\mathrm{CE}}(\mathcal{S}_\theta) = -\frac{1}{n} \sum_{i=1}^{n} \mathbf{p}_t^{\mathcal{T}_\theta}(x_i) \log \mathbf{p}^{\mathcal{S}_\theta}(x_i) \tag{11}$$

where $n$ is the number of samples.

***C. Discriminator.*** The discriminator is a binary classifier, which is used to determine whether the input features come from the teacher set or the student network. It consists of a sigmoid function following the binary cross-entropy loss [10]. The loss can be formulated as:

$$\mathcal{L}_\mathcal{D} = -\frac{1}{N} \sum_{i=1}^{N} \left[ \mathbf{y}_i \cdot \log \hat{\mathbf{p}}_i^\mathcal{D} + (1 - \mathbf{y}_i) \cdot \log \left(1 - \hat{\mathbf{p}}_i^\mathcal{D}\right) \right] \tag{12}$$

$$\mathbf{p}^{\mathcal{D}}(x; \theta) = \sigma \left( f_\theta \left( \{x_T, x_S\} \right) \right) \tag{13}$$

where $y_i \in \{0, 1\}$ is the binary label for the input features $x_i$, and $\hat{\mathbf{p}}_i^{\mathcal{D}}$ is the corresponding probability vector. $\mathbf{p}^{\mathcal{D}}(x; \theta)$ is a *sigmoid* function is used to model the individual teacher or student probability. $f_\theta$ is a three-FC-layer subnetwork and $\theta$ is its parameter, $\sigma(*)$ is the logistic function. The final loss function is:

$$\mathcal{L}_{LOSS} = \mathcal{L}_{\mathcal{D}} + \mathcal{L}_{CE} \tag{14}$$

Finally, the loss is minimized by backpropagation.

## 3   Experiments

In this section, we demonstrate our experiments as follows. Part 1 introduces the dataset used in the experiments. Part 2 indicates training details and the performance metrics we used such as Acc, Flops, F1_scores, interference time, and parameters. At last, Part 3 presents the experimental results and discussions.

### 3.1   Red Kidney Bean Dataset

In the training stage, as the deep convolutional network described, a large amount of data is required. However, there is currently no suitable seed database, so the seed images used in our method were acquired by the sorting machine in the actual seed harvest process using a highspeed camera in a real environment. According to the requirements for the quality grading of red kidney beans by enterprises, the sample images of red kidney beans were divided into four categories: plump beans (1661), peeled beans (509), dried beans (1173), and broken beans (488), which were randomly assigned to the training set, verification set and test set at a ratio of 3:1:1, typical images are shown in Fig. 4.

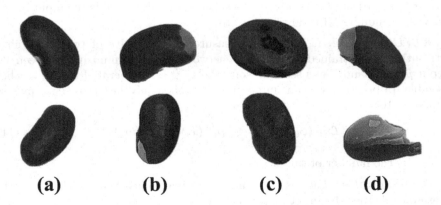

**Fig. 4.** Red kidney bean dataset. (a) plump beans (b) peeled beans (c) dried beans (d) broken beans. (Color figure online)

## 3.2    Training Details and Evaluation Metric

All experiments were performed on a 64-bit Linux-based operation system, Ubuntu 18.04. The software is mainly based on the deep learning architecture of Pytorch and python development environment Spyder. The hardware is based on an NVIDIA 1080 TI GPU, with CUDA10.1 accelerating calculation.

The size of the input image is $224 \times 224$, and use small batch stochastic gradient descent (SGD) to train the network, the initial learning rate is 0.001, the Batch_size is 16, the epoch is 100. In the number of steps at 1/2 and 3/4, the learning rate is adjusted to 1/10 of the original, the momentum parameter is set to 0.9, and the weight decay parameter is set to 0.0001. Besides, every iteration, each of the input batch-size images through some transformations, such as Flip horizontally or vertically etc.

The number of parameters and required Float Points Operations (denoted as FLOPs) are employed to evaluate the model size and computational requirement, which are widely used protocols. To evaluate the seed grading task performance, we also provide the accuracy, F1_score models, and inference time on Quadro m5000 GPU for an image.

**Table 1.** Performance of some popular CNN in red kidney bean test set.

| Model | Params (M) | FLOPs | Time (ms) | Acc (%) | F1_score (%) |
|---|---|---|---|---|---|
| Alexnet [16] | 57.02 | 711.46M | 2.31 | 88.60 | 88.22 |
| Resnet50 [17] | 23.52 | 4.12G | 10.44 | 95.54 | 95.54 |
| DenseNet121 [18] | 6.96 | 2.88G | 22.71 | 95.67 | 95.67 |
| Googlenet [19] | 5.60 | 1.51G | 10.89 | 96.85 | 96.87 |
| VggBN-16 | 14.82 | 15.41G | 9.53 | 96.59 | 96.58 |

## 3.3    Experimental Results and Analysis

**Selection of Pruning Model.** In this study, we first compared the performance of some popular CNNs in the red kidney bean test set. It mainly includes VggBN-16, Alexnet [16], ResNet50 [17], DenseNet121 [18], and GoogleNet [19]. Experimental results of Table 1 show that VggBN-16 and GoogleNet can achieve higher accuracy (96.59%, 96.85%) and f1-score (96.69% and 96.87%). In addition, although VggBN-16 has more parameters and computation, it has a faster inference speed than other networks (excluding Alexnet). The main reasons for this problem are as follows: 1) The complicated multi-branch designs make the model difficult to implement and customize, slow down the inference and reduce the memory utilization. 2) Some components (e.g., depthwise Conv in Xception and MobileNets and channel shuffle in ShuffleNets) increase the memory access cost and lack supports of various devices. Therefore, we will further compress the VggBN-16 to make it easy to be deployed on edge devices to achieve fast and high-purity seed grading.

**Feature Map Visualization and Feature Diagnosis.** CNN is an end-to-end architecture. The recognition result can be automatically obtained by feeding only the pictures to be recognized to the network. The intermediate process is usually a black box and not interpretable. We used visualization technology to extract the output feature maps of each layer in the network. To facilitate observation, we selected seeds with obvious damage. We showed the output feature map of the active layer from layer 3 to layer 13 in Fig. 5. It could be seen that the layer retained the original image color, shape, and texture feature information. In addition, we can observe that the features extracted by the network become more abstract as the depth of the layer increases.

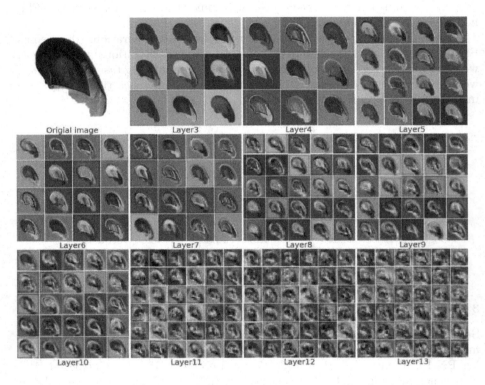

**Fig. 5.** The visualization results of the feature map in a pseudocolor image.

Meantime, we trained a set of linear classifiers on features extracted at different layers within the network to explore the roles and dynamics of intermediate layers, then determine the optimal number of network layers. As shown in Fig. 6, The recognition accuracy of CNN is gradually improved with the increase of network depth, and after the tenth layer, its performance is not significantly improved. Combined with the above analysis results of feature visualization, we think that the shape, texture, and color feature information extracted from the first ten layers of the network can achieve better results, and if the network is too deep, the computational cost of the network will increase dramatically and the test accuracy will be affected. Therefore, we try to change the VggBN-16 network structure to further optimize the performance of seed sorting. Ultimately, we only keep the convolution structure of the first ten layers of VggBN-16 and name it Vgg_BeanNet. The F1_score after finetuning is 96.47%, as shown in Table 2.

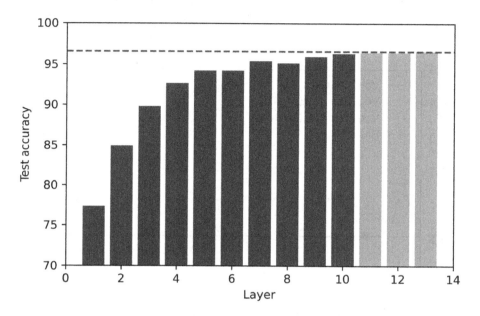

**Fig. 6.** Visualization of feature diagnosis.

**Table 2.** Performance comparison between VggBN-16, Vgg_BeanNet and network after pruning

| Model (Filter pruning ratio) | Params (M) | FLOPs | Time (ms) | Acc (%) | F1_score (%) |
|---|---|---|---|---|---|
| VggBN-16 (Baseline) | 14.82 | 15.39G | 9.53 | 96.59 | 96.58 |
| Vgg_BeanNet | 7.74 | 14.02G | 8.43 | 96.47 | 96.47 ($\downarrow$0.11) |
| Vgg_BeanNet (66.67%) | 0.81 | 1.98G | 2.25 | 96.99 | 97.00 ($\uparrow$0.42) |
| Vgg_BeanNet (90.48%) | 0.07 | 210.92M | 2.07 | 95.93 | 95.97 ($\downarrow$0.61) |

**Channel Pruning and Knowledge Distillation.** From the visualization results of the output feature map of each convolutional layer of the VggBN-16 model, it can be found that there are many similar feature maps, which indicates that there is still redundant information of the parameters stored in the high-dimensional tensors, so we use the channel pruning method based on Taylor to further compress the Vgg_BeanNet. The relationship between pruning rate and model precision is shown in Fig. 7. The results show that the model still has good performance when the pruning rate is less than 70%. Sometimes the performance of the pruning model (66.67% filter pruning) is even higher than that of the original model, which may be due to overfitting caused by too many parameters, and network pruning is essentially a problem of searching the optimal network structure. When the pruning rate is more than 70%, the accuracy of the Vgg_BeanNet is significantly reduced, but the compression effect of the model is better. Specifically, we also report the test results of filter pruning rate of 66.67% and 90.48% in Table 2.

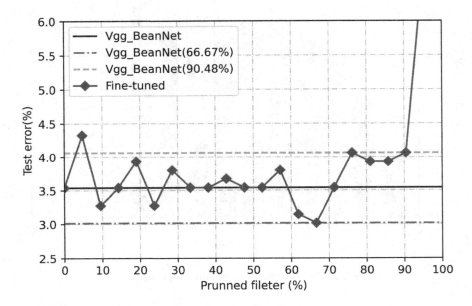

**Fig. 7.** The effect of pruning varying percentages of channels.

Meantime, we adopt knowledge distillation technology to improve the recognition accuracy of the Vgg_BeanNet (90.48%). From the above experimental results, we can see that GoogleNet and Vgg_Beannet (66.67%) have achieved good recognition accuracy of 96.85%, and 96.99% respectively. Therefore, we construct a multi-teacher model to guide students to learn the feature information of the teacher model and narrow the gap between them. Table 3 compares the performance improvement of the Mealv2 method and KD [9] on the Vgg_BeanNet (90.48%) and Alexnet networks. From the experimental results, we can find that both methods are significantly improved and Mealv2 obtains better results.

**Table 3.** Accuracy comparison before and after knowledge distillation experiment

| Model (Filter pruning ratio) | Time (ms) | Scrach | Fitune | KD [9] | Mealv2 |
|---|---|---|---|---|---|
| Vgg_BeanNet (90.48%) | 2.07 | 95.67 | 95.97 | 96.07 | 96.33 |
| Alexnet | 2.31 | 88.60 | – | 93.05 | 94.62 |

**Performance Comparison of Lightweight Network.** In addition, we also compared with typical handcrafted lightweight networks (Mobilenetv2 [20], ShffleNetv2 [21], GhostNet [22], and Mixnet [23]). As shown in Table 4, in the case of similar computational complexity, the pruned network also gets the best classification accuracy (96.33%) and inference speed (2.07 ms), this also shows that the proposed method does not rely too much on expert experience and is highly efficient under actual deployment conditions.

**Table 4.** Performance comparison before and after knowledge distillation experiment

| Model (Filter pruning ratio) | Params (M) | FLOPs | Time (ms) | Acc (%) | F1_score (%) |
|---|---|---|---|---|---|
| Mobilenetv2 [20] | 2.23 | 318.96M | 7.83 | 95.94 | 95.93 |
| ShuffleNetv2 [21] | 1.26 | 149.58M | 10.01 | 94.10 | 94.07 |
| GhostNet [22] | 3.91 | 149.4M | 15.56 | 94.36 | 94.28 |
| MixNet [23] | 3.48 | 357.63M | 22.23 | 94.89 | 94.88 |
| Vgg_BeanNet (90.48%) | 0.07 | 210.92M | 2.07 | 96.33 | 96.33 |

# 4    Conclusions

To solve the problem of a large number of parameters and low efficiency of a deep learning model for seed sorting, this paper propose a mixed pruning strategy based on feature representation and Taylor expansion to achieve fast and high-purity seed grading. Moreover, we introduce a simple and effective knowledge distillation technology to transfer the knowledge of CNNs with high accuracy to the pruned network to recover its predictive accuracy. The experimental results verify the reliability of the scheme on red kidney bean data sets, which not only ensures the accuracy of classification but also reduces the volume of the network model. Meantime, experiments on Quadro m5000 GPU verify that the compressed model has better performance and inference speed on mobile devices than some cleverly designed lightweight CNN networks such as mobilenetv2 and shufflenetv2, etc.

**Acknowledgement.** This work was supported by NSFC (U1804157, No. 61772576, No. 62072489), Henan science and technology innovation team (CXTD2017091), IRT-STHN (21IRTSTHN013), ZhongYuan Science and Technology Innovation Leading Talent Program (214200510013). Program for Interdisciplinary Direction Team in Zhongyuan University of Technology.

# References

1. Sofu, M.M., Er, O., Kayacan, M.C., et al.: Design of an automatic apple sorting system using machine vision. Comput. Electron. Agric. **127**, 395–405 (2016)
2. Altuntaş, Y., Kocamaz, A.F., Cengiz, R., Esmeray, M.: Classification of haploid and diploid maize seeds by using image processing techniques and support vector machines. In: 2018 26th Signal Processing and Communications Applications Conference (SIU), pp. 1–4 (2018). https://doi.org/10.1109/SIU.2018.8404800
3. Choudhary, R., Paliwal, J., Jayas, D.S.: Classification of cereal grains using wavelet, morphological, colour, and textural features of non-touching kernel images. Biosys. Eng. **99**(3), 330–337 (2008)
4. Jin, H.Y., Jin, K.S., Dayeon, K., et al.: Super-high-purity seed sorter using low-latency image-recognition based on deep learning. IEEE Robot. Autom. Lett. **3**, 3035–3042 (2018)
5. Uzal, L.C., Grinblat, G.L., Namías, R., et al.: Seed-per-pod estimation for plant breeding using deep learning. Comput. Electron. Agric. **14**, 196–204 (2018)
6. Li, C., Li, H., Liu, Z., Li, B., Huang, Y.: SeedSortNet: a rapid and highly efficient lightweight CNN based on visual attention for seed sorting. PeerJ Comput. Sci. **7**, e639 (2021). https://doi.org/10.7717/peerj-cs.639
7. Liu, H., Simonyan, K., Yang, Y.: DARTS: differentiable architecture search. arXiv preprint arXiv:1806.09055 (2018)
8. Wang, K., Liu, Z., Lin, Y., Lin, J., Han, S.: HAQ: hardware-aware automated quantization with mixed precision. In: 2019 IEEE/CVF Conference on Computer Vision and Pattern Recognition (CVPR), pp. 8604–8612 (2019)
9. Hinton, G., Vinyals, O., Dean, J.: Distilling the knowledge in a neural network. arXiv preprint arXiv:1503.02531 (2015)
10. Shen, Z., Savvides, M.: MEAL V2: boosting Vanilla ResNet-50 to 80%+ top-1 accuracy on ImageNet without tricks. arXiv preprint arXiv:2009.08453 (2020)
11. Wang, Z., Liu, X., Huang, L., et al.: Model pruning based on quantified similarity of feature maps. arXiv preprint arXiv:2105.06052 (2021)
12. Molchanov, P., Tyree, S., Karras, T., et al.: Pruning convolutional neural networks for resource efficient inference. arXiv preprint arXiv:1611.06440 (2016)
13. Elkerdawy, S., Elhoushi, M., Singh, A., et al.: To filter prune, or to layer prune, that is the question. In: Proceedings of the Asian Conference on Computer Vision (2020)
14. Simonyan, K., Zisserman, A.: Very deep convolutional networks for large-scale image recognition. arXiv preprint arXiv:1409.1556 (2014)
15. Zhang, T.: A systematic DNN weight pruning framework using alternating direction method of multipliers. In: Ferrari, V., Hebert, M., Sminchisescu, C., Weiss, Y. (eds.) ECCV 2018. LNCS, vol. 11212, pp. 191–207. Springer, Cham (2018). https://doi.org/10.1007/978-3-030-01237-3_12
16. Smirnov, E.A., Timoshenko, D.M., Andrianov, S.N.: Comparison of regularization methods for ImageNet classification with deep convolutional neural networks. AASRI Procedia **6**, 89–94 (2014)
17. He, K., Zhang, X., Ren, S., et al.: Deep residual learning for image recognition. In: Proceedings of the IEEE Conference on Computer Vision and Pattern Recognition, pp. 770–778 (2016)
18. Huang, G., Liu, Z., Van Der Maaten, L., et al.: Densely connected convolutional networks. In: Proceedings of the IEEE Conference on Computer Vision and Pattern Recognition, pp. 4700–4708 (2017)

19. Szegedy, C., Liu, W., Jia, Y., et al.: Going deeper with convolutions. In: Proceedings of the IEEE Conference on Computer Vision and Pattern Recognition, pp. 1–9 (2019)
20. Sandler, M., Howard, A., Zhu, M., et al.: MobileNetV 2: inverted residuals and linear bottlenecks. In: Proceedings of the IEEE Conference on Computer Vision and Pattern Recognition, pp. 4510–4520 (2018)
21. Ma, N., Zhang, X., Zheng, H.-T., Sun, J.: ShuffleNet V2: practical guidelines for efficient CNN architecture design. In: Ferrari, V., Hebert, M., Sminchisescu, C., Weiss, Y. (eds.) Computer Vision – ECCV 2018. LNCS, vol. 11218, pp. 122–138. Springer, Cham (2018). https://doi.org/10.1007/978-3-030-01264-9_8
22. Han, K., Wang, Y., Tian, Q., et al.: GhostNet: more features from cheap operations. In: Proceedings of the IEEE/CVF Conference on Computer Vision and Pattern Recognition, pp. 1580–1589 (2020)
23. Tan, M., Le, Q.V.: MixConv: mixed depthwise convolutional kernels. CoRR, abs/1907.09595 (2019)

# Estimating the Level of Inference Using an Order-Mimic Agent

Haram Joo[1]🆔, Inhyeok Jeong[2]🆔, and Sang Wan Lee[1(✉)]🆔

[1] Department of Bio and Brain Engineering, Korea Advanced Institute of Science
and Technology, Daejeon, South Korea
{haramjoo,sangwan}@kaist.ac.kr
[2] School of Freshman, Korea Advanced Institute of Science and Technology,
Daejeon, South Korea
jih7368@kaist.ac.kr
http://aibrain.kaist.ac.kr

**Abstract.** Multi-agent reinforcement learning (RL) considers problems
of learning policies and predicting values through interactions with multiple opponents. To make the solutions feasible, one assumes single-type
opponents. However, this may not hold in most real-world situations.
Interactions with a mixture of different types of agents make it extremely
hard to learn. This study examines the hypothesis that when the potential types of agents are unknown, the level of agent inference can act as
a proxy for characterizing the opponents. We present a computational
framework to estimate the level of agent's inference using a deterministic
and stochastic order-mimic agent. We then propose a calibration method
for unbiased estimation, which offsets the adverse effect of order-mimic
agents on the environment's order estimation. Finally, to generalize the
method to a wide range of contexts, we proposed iterative inference level
estimation. We demonstrate the feasibility of the proposed method in
computer simulations with agents mimicking agents' behavior with various inference levels. Our framework can estimate the learning capacity
of various algorithms and humans; therefore it can be used to design
high-level inference models that can effectively handle the complexity of
multi-agent learning problems.

**Keywords:** Multi-agent reinforcement learning · Keynesian beauty
contest · Level of inference

## 1 Introduction

The problem of reinforcement learning (RL) is defined based on the Markov
decision process (MDP). The basic idea is to capture the most important features that predict future rewards [1]. In traditional RL, the agent interacts with
the environment, or only one opponent exists and is thought of as part of the

© Springer Nature Switzerland AG 2022
C. Wallraven et al. (Eds.): ACPR 2021, LNCS 13189, pp. 116–126, 2022.
https://doi.org/10.1007/978-3-031-02444-3_9

environment [2–4]. Recently, multi-agent reinforcement learning (MARL) concerns the learning problem in which one agent interacts with other opponents [5–9]. It is difficult to deal with a mixture of different types of agents, so it is generally assumed that the opponents are single-type. However, this may not generalize to real-world situations. It will be effective if we can estimate the level of inference and use it to understand the behavior of others.

In this study, we propose a method to estimate an agent's level of inference. In doing so, we defined an order-mimic agent, and combined it with the Keynesian beauty contest environment, a generic task for evaluating the ability to infer public perception [10–14], as a multi-agent simulation scenario. Simulations demonstrated the validity of the proposed method. To the best of our knowledge, this is the first study to open up the possibility of estimating the level of inference of humans and algorithms.

## 2   Keynesian Beauty Contest

Keynesian beauty contest was designed by Keynes [15] to explain stock market price fluctuations. To be precise, we quote the description of the Keynesian beauty contest from his book:

> It is not a case of choosing those [faces] that, to the best of one's judgment, are really the prettiest, nor even those that average opinion genuinely thinks the prettiest. We have reached the third degree where we devote our intelligences to anticipating what average opinion expects the average opinion to be. And there are some, I believe, who practice the fourth, fifth and higher degrees [15].

This implies that participants want to choose a face they think other people will choose a lot, and this is affected by their level of inference. The Keynesian contest can be also used to simulate a stock market choice between what is considered an asset's fundamental value and the value it expects to appreciate by other investors.

Nagel [16] has formulated the Keynesian beauty contest mathematically to use it in a multi-agent simulation scenario. Each participant chooses a number from 0 to 100. The winner of $p$-beauty contest is the one who picks a number close to $p$ times the average number chosen by all participants. In this study, the same reward was given to all winners, regardless of the number of winners. To implement a task with a high degree of freedom, the choice was defined in *(python)float64* range.

## 3    Method

### 3.1    Order-Mimic Agent

If all agents in Keynesian beauty contest randomly pick a number, the average of all submitted numbers is 50. If the level-1 participant know $p = 2/3$, it will choose $50 * 2/3 = 33.33$. Similarly, the level-2 participant will choose $50 * 4/9 = 22.22$ by assuming opponents are level-1. The level-k assume opponents are level-(k-1), and the Keynesian beauty contest used in our study repeats multiple rounds, so it can be expanded as follows:

$$a_t^{(1)} = \overline{x_{t-1}} \times p$$

$$a_t^{(2)} = \overline{x_{t-1}} \times p^2$$

$$...$$

$$a_t^{(k)} = \overline{x_{t-1}} \times p^k \tag{1}$$

where $a_t^{(i)}$ refers to the level-i participant's action in the current round, and $\overline{x_{t-1}}$ represents the average of all submitted numbers in the previous round.

Equation (1) assumes that the participant knows $p$. Therefore, we generalize the formula with the information available in the actual contest only:

$$a_t^{(k)} = \overline{x_{t-1}} \times (\frac{a_{t-1}^*}{\overline{x_{t-1}}})^k, \tag{2}$$

where $a_{t-1}^*$ refers to the number that was associated with the reward in the previous round. In this study, the agent following Eq. (2) is named as order-k mimic agent, $M_k$. For example, the order-3 mimic agent, $M_3$, chooses $\overline{x_{t-1}} \times (\frac{a_{t-1}^*}{\overline{x_{t-1}}})^3$ as the action every round. All order-mimic agents' first round actions are chosen randomly.

### 3.2    Inference Level Estimation Method

The order-k agent assumes that opponents are order-(k-1) agents and chooses the best action. Therefore, if the order-k agent and the order-(k-1) agent confront in a non-probabilistic environment, theoretically the order-k agent will always win. This means that if the order-k agent performs the task where order-(k-1) agents are dominant, the order-k agent can obtain a higher reward.

The proposed algorithm makes the best use of this characteristic. If a population of target agents of which we want to estimate the order is dominant, we can compute the order by using the order-mimic agent. The order of the target agent can be estimated by averaging the number of rewards that order-mimic agents earned:

$$ORD(T) = \frac{\sum_{A_i \neq T} ORD(A_i) R_i}{\sum_{A_i \neq T} R_i} - 1 \tag{3}$$

where $T$ refers to the target agent, and $A_i$, $R_i$ represents the i-th agent and its cumulative reward. Rewards are accumulated each round until convergence. $ORD(x)$ stands for the order of agent x. For example, the order of the order-mimic agent is $ORD(M_k) = k$.

All agents except target agents, $\sum_{A_i \neq T}$, are order-mimic agents. By calculating the average based on the reward ratio of the order-mimic agent, we can approximate the order that performs best in a given environment. Furthermore, subtracting one from this value is the order of target agents.

While Eq. (3) is potentially a good order estimator, it does not take into account the effect of order-mimic agents on the environment's order, which is used to estimate the order of target agent. To tackle this issue, we propose a method for order calibration:

$$y = \frac{n_t y' + \sum_{A_i \neq T} ORD(A_i)}{n_t + n_m}$$

$$y' = \frac{(n_t + n_m)y - \sum_{A_i \neq T} ORD(A_i)}{n_t} \tag{4}$$

where $y$ refers to the previously estimated order by Eq. (3), $ORD(T)$, and $y'$ represents the calibrated order.

In the default setting, order-mimic agents are used one by one from order-1 to order-$n_m$, so Eq. (4) can be organized as follows:

$$y' = \frac{(n_t + n_m)y - \frac{n_m(n_m+1)}{2}}{n_t}$$

$$y' = \frac{2(n_t + n_m)y - n_m(n_m + 1)}{2n_t} \tag{5}$$

Additionally, in $n_t \gg n_m$ environment where the target agent is highly dominant, we can confirm that $y' \approx y$.

$$y' = (1 + \frac{n_m}{n_t})y - \frac{n_m^2}{2n_t} - \frac{n_m}{2n_t} \approx y$$

Using Eq. (3) and Eq. (5), we propose the inference level estimation algorithm:

---

**Algorithm 3.1:** INFERENCELEVELESTIMATIONALGORITHM$(T, n_t, n_m, p)$

---

INPUT $T$ : Target agent
         $n_t$ : Number of target agents
         $n_m$ : Number of order-mimic agents
         $p$ : Keynesian beauty contest hyperparameter
OUTPUT $y'$ : Esimated (calibrated) order of target agent
$A, a \leftarrow InitializeAgent(T, n_t, n_m)$
$R, r \leftarrow InitializeReward(n_t, n_m)$
$C \leftarrow CreateContest(A, p)$
**while** *TRUE*
        $\begin{cases} a \leftarrow A(a, r) \\ r \leftarrow C(a) \\ \textbf{if } \sum r = n_t + n_m \\ \quad \textbf{then } break \\ R \leftarrow R + r \end{cases}$
   **do**
$y \leftarrow \frac{\sum_{A_i \neq T} ORD(A_i)R_i}{\sum_{A_i \neq T} R_i} - 1$
$y' \leftarrow \frac{2(n_t + n_m)y - n_m(n_m + 1)}{2n_t}$
**return** $(y')$

---

## 4 Result and Discussion

### 4.1 Performance and Efficiency of the Proposed Method

First, we ran in the situation with $n_m = 5$ and $p = 2/3$ while varying the $n_t$ from 5 to 100. Order-mimic agents were used one each from order-1 mimic to order-5 mimic. Figure 1 shows the results when using an order-1 mimic agent and order-2 mimic agent as target agents. We applied noise to target agents (range of $\times 0.95$ to $\times 1.05$). Note that y is the order without calibration, and y' is the calibrated order. As shown in Fig. 1, the error of y decreases as the number of target agents increases. Because, y does not take into account the changing of the environment's order due to order-mimic agents, as $n_t$ increases, the order of the target agent and the order of the environment become similar.

Next, to simulate a stochastic environment, we implemented the order-1.5 mimic agent. The order-1.5 mimic agent has a 50% chance to act as an order-1 mimic agent and a 50% chance to act as an order-2 mimic agent. The order-2.5 mimic agent can be defined in the same way.

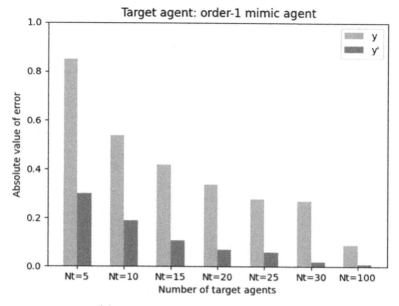

(a) $T$=order-1 mimic agent, $n_m$=5, $p$=2/3

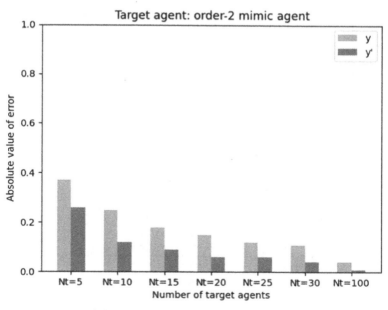

(b) $T$=order-2 mimic agent, $n_m$=5, $p$=2/3

**Fig. 1.** Absolute value of error of two methods in the $p$-beauty contest. Silver bar (y) represents the uncalibrated method, and gold bar (y') represents the calibrated method. Order-mimic agents are used one each from order-1 mimic to order-$n_m$ mimic. The noise was applied in the range of ×0.95 to ×1.05.

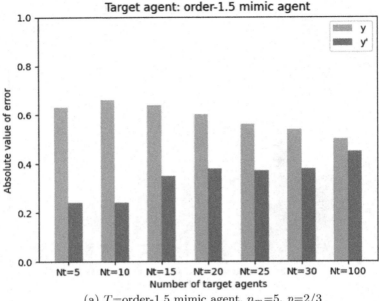

(a) $T$=order-1.5 mimic agent, $n_m$=5, $p$=2/3

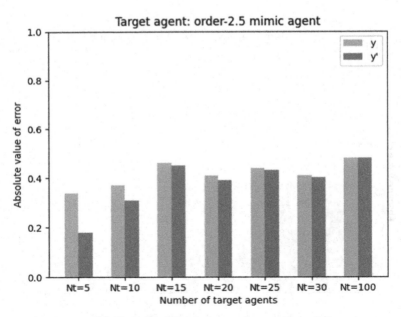

(b) $T$=order-2.5 mimic agent, $n_m$=5, $p$=2/3

**Fig. 2.** Absolute value of error when target agent is stochastic. Silver bar (y) represents the uncalibrated method, and gold bar (y') represents the calibrated method. Order-mimic agents are used one each from order-1 mimic to order-$n_m$ mimic. The noise was applied in the range of $\times 0.95$ to $\times 1.05$.

Figure 2 shows the results when using an order-1.5 mimic agent and order-2.5 mimic agent as target agents in $n_m = 5$ and $p = 2/3$. When the target agent is stochastic, the error is larger than the case with the deterministic target agent. Despite stochastic settings, the calibrated method outperforms the original version.

**Table 1.** Sum of error absolute values.

| Nt | 5 | 10 | 15 | 20 | 25 | 30 | 100 |
|---|---|---|---|---|---|---|---|
| y | 2.19 | 1.82 | 1.70 | 1.50 | 1.40 | 1.33 | 1.11 |
| y' | 0.98 | 0.86 | 1.00 | 0.90 | 0.92 | 0.84 | 0.95 |

Table 1 represents the sum of error absolute values for the four cases executed above, from order-1 mimic agent to order-2.5 mimic agent. The error of y decreases as the number of target agents increases, but the error of y' is less affected by $n_t$. This is because y' cancels out the adverse effect of order-mimic agents on the environment's order. Another important implication is that we do not necessarily have to simulate in huge $n_t$ to get smaller errors. Note that the calibrated method always performs better than the original method.

### 4.2   Iterative Inference Level Estimation

Theoretically, the proposed method requires that the order of target agent should be less than the order of the highest order-mimic agent minus one. This is because the proposed method is based on the idea that an order-mimic agent, close to the target agent's order plus one, obtains a larger amount of reward where the target agent is dominant.

To investigate the effect of the measurable range on estimation performance, we ran the simulation where $n_t = 25$, $p = 2/3$, and order-5 mimic agent as target agent. As shown in Fig. 3, the estimation error increases when the target agent's order is out of the measurable range ($n_m = 4$ and $n_m = 5$). As long as it remains within the measurable range, the error appears to be small regardless of $n_m$.

The fact that the true order of an arbitrary agent is not known may impede the ability of estimation. However, this issue can be solved by the following iterative inference level estimation, which uses the results in Fig. 3:

(1) Start with small $n_m$ and gradually increase to large $n_m$ (not necessarily in increments of one), if values are similar in several consecutive intervals, it can be considered as the order of the target agent.
    or
(2) The order of the target agent can be obtained by simulating only once with a sufficiently large $n_m$.

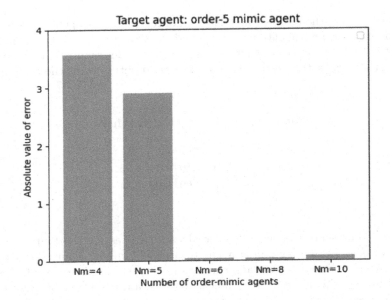

**Fig. 3.** The range of inference level of the proposed method. The y-axis represents the absolute value of error of calibrated method. The measurable range of the proposed method is 0 to highest order-mimic agent's order minus one. Order-mimic agents are used one each from order-1 mimic to order-$n_m$ mimic. $T =$ order-5 mimic agent, $n_t = 25$, $p = 2/3$, and the noise was applied in the range of $\times 0.95$ to $\times 1.05$.

## 5    Conclusion

In this study, we proposed a method to estimate the level of arbitrary agent's inference. For this, we defined a deterministic and stochastic order-mimic agent. We also propose a calibration method for unbiased estimation, which offsets the adverse effect of order-mimic agents on the environment's order estimation. Simulation results show that the unbiased estimation outperforms the basic method regardless of the number of target agents. We also analyzed the measurable range of the proposed method, and confirmed that the estimation error is small as long as the target agent's order is within the measurable range. Finally, to generalize the method to a wide range of contexts, we proposed iterative inference level estimation.

In future research, it is possible to design an agent that better deals with opponents by using their level of inference. It would also be interesting to examine the relationship between the level of inference and task performance of various algorithms and humans. These will contribute to the development of high-level inference models.

**Acknowledgements.** This work was supported by Institute for Information & communications Technology Planning & Evaluation (IITP) grant funded by the Korea government (MSIT) (No. 2019-0-01371, Development of brain-inspired AI with human-like intelligence), the National Research Foundation of Korea (NRF) grant funded by the Korea government (MSIT) (NRF-2019M3E5D2A01066267), Samsung Research Funding Center of Samsung Electronics under Project Number SRFC-TC1603-52, Institute of Information & communications Technology Planning & Evaluation (IITP) grant funded by the Korea government (MSIT) (No. 2021-0-02068, Artificial Intelligence Innovation Hub), Electronics and Telecommunications Research Institute (ETRI) grant funded by the Korean government [21ZS1100, Core Technology Research for Self-Improving Integrated Artificial Intelligence System].

# References

1. Sutton, R.S., Barto, A.G.: Reinforcement Learning: An Introduction. MIT Press, MA (2018)
2. Tsitsiklis, J.N., van Roy, B.: An analysis of temporal-difference learning with function approximation. IEEE Trans. Autom. Control **42**, 674–690 (1997). https://doi.org/10.1109/9.580874
3. Sutton, R.S., McAllester, D.A., Singh, S.P., Mansour, Y., et al.: Policy gradient methods for reinforcement learning with function approximation. In: NIPS, pp. 1057–1063 (1999)
4. Kakade, S.: A natural policy gradient. In: Advances in Neural Information Processing Systems (2002)
5. Tampuu, A., et al.: Multiagent cooperation and competition with deep reinforcement learning. PLoS ONE **12**, 1–12 (2017). https://doi.org/10.1371/journal.pone.0172395
6. Garant, D., da Silva, B.C., Lesser, V., Zhang, C.: Accelerating multi-agent reinforcement learning with dynamic co-learning. Technical report (2015)
7. Leibo, J.Z., Zambaldi, V., Lanctot, M., Marecki, J., Graepel, T.: Multi-agent reinforcement learning in sequential social dilemmas. In: Proceedings of the International Joint Conference on Autonomous Agents and Multiagent Systems, AAMAS, vol. 1, pp. 464–473 (2017)
8. Harper, M., Knight, V., Jones, M., Koutsovoulos, G., Glynatsi, N.E., Campbell, O.: Reinforcement learning produces dominant strategies for the Iterated Prisoner's Dilemma. PLoS ONE **12**, e0188046 (2017). https://doi.org/10.1371/JOURNAL.PONE.0188046
9. Cao, K., Lazaridou, A., Lanctot, M., Leibo, J.Z., Tuyls, K., Clark, S.: Emergent communication through negotiation. In: 6th International Conference on Learning Representations, ICLR 2018 - Conference Track Proceedings, pp. 1–15 (2018)
10. Crawford, V.P.: Boundedly rational versus optimization-based models of strategic thinking and learning in games. Voprosy Ekonomiki **2014**, 27–44 (2014). https://doi.org/10.32609/0042-8736-2014-5-27-44
11. García-Schmidt, M., Woodford, M.: Are low interest rates deflationary? A paradox of perfect-foresight analysis. Am. Econ. Rev. **109**, 86–120 (2019). https://doi.org/10.1257/aer.20170110
12. Cornand, C., dos Santos Ferreira, R.: Cooperation in a differentiated duopoly when information is dispersed: a beauty contest game with endogenous concern for coordination. Math. Soc. Sci. **106**, 101–111 (2020). https://doi.org/10.1016/J.MATHSOCSCI.2020.02.003
13. Coricelli, G., Nagel, R.: Neural correlates of depth of strategic reasoning in medial prefrontal cortex. Proc. Natl. Acad. Sci. U.S.A. **106**, 9163–9168 (2009). https://doi.org/10.1073/pnas.0807721106

14. Pantelis, P.C., Kennedy, D.P.: Autism does not limit strategic thinking in the "beauty contest" game. Cognition **160**, 91–97 (2017). https://doi.org/10.1016/j.cognition.2016.12.015
15. Keynes, J.M.: The General Theory of Employment, Interest, and Money. Palgrave Macmillan, London (1936)
16. Nagel, R.: Unraveling in guessing games: an experimental study. Am. Econ. Rev. **85**, 1313–1326 (1995)

# Predicting Decision-Making in the Future: Human Versus Machine

Hoe Sung Ryu[1] , Uijong Ju[2] , and Christian Wallraven[1,3](✉)

[1] Department of Artificial Intelligence, Korea University, Seoul, Korea
{hoesungryu,wallraven}@korea.ac.kr
[2] Department of Information Display, Kyung Hee University, Seoul, Korea
juuijong@khu.ac.kr
[3] Department of Brain and Cognitive Engineering, Korea University, Seoul, Korea

**Abstract.** Deep neural networks (DNNs) have become remarkably successful in data prediction, and have even been used to predict future actions based on limited input. This raises the question: do these systems actually "understand" the event similar to humans? Here, we address this issue using videos taken from an accident situation in a driving simulation. In this situation, drivers had to choose between crashing into a suddenly-appeared obstacle or steering their car off a previously indicated cliff. We compared how well humans and a DNN predicted this decision as a function of time before the event. The DNN outperformed humans for early time-points, but had an equal performance for later time-points. Interestingly, spatio-temporal image manipulations and Grad-CAM visualizations uncovered some expected behavior, but also highlighted potential differences in temporal processing for the DNN.

**Keywords:** Deep learning · Video prediction · Humans versus machines · Decision-making · Video analysis

## 1 Introduction

The ability to predict, anticipate and reason about future events is the essence of intelligence [17] and one of the main goals of decision-making systems [11]. In general, predicting human behavior in future situations is of course an extremely hard task in an unconstrained setting. Given additional information about the context and the type of behavior to be predicted, however, behavior forecasting becomes a more tractable problem.

Recently, deep neural networks (DNNs) have dramatically improved the state-of-the-art in speech recognition, visual object recognition, object detection, and many other domains [15]. Although DNNs yield excellent performance in such applications, it is often difficult to get insights into how and why a certain classification result has been made. To address this issue, Explainable Artificial Intelligence (XAI) proposes to make a shift towards more transparent AI [1]. As part of this shift, research has focused on comparing DNN performance in

C. Wallraven et al. (Eds.): ACPR 2021, LNCS 13189, pp. 127–141, 2022.
https://doi.org/10.1007/978-3-031-02444-3_10

a task with human performance to better understand the underlying decision-making capacities of DNNs [31]. Here it becomes important to look closely at the metric with which performance is measured - for example, if humans and DNNs have the same, high accuracy in identifying COVID-19 chest radiographs, this does not mean that DNNs use the same image-related cues to solve the task [9]. Therefore, [23] proposed to use metrics *beyond accuracy* to understand more deeply how DNNs and humans differ. Methods from XAI, such as feature visualization, for example, can help to understand which visual input is important for the network in making a certain decision [9].

Examples of behavior prediction that have been tackled with DNNs recently include, for example, predicting a future action by observing only a few portions of an action in progress [27], anticipating the next word in textual data given context [21], or predicting human driving behavior before dangerous situations occur [22]. Hence, DNNs seem to be capable of analyzing the spatio-temporal contents of an event to predict an outcome - the important question, then, becomes, do these networks actually "understand" the event similar to humans, or do they use spurious, high-dimensional correlations to form their prediction [9]?

In the present work, we take an accident situation during driving as a challenging context for studying this question. To explain the situation, imagine you are driving and there is a fork ahead; a prior warning sign alerted you that one of the directions of the fork will lead to a cliff, which will fatally crash the car. The other direction seems safe to drive, until, suddenly an obstacle appears on this direction of the fork, blocking the safe path. How do you react to this sudden change of circumstance? Understanding and modeling human behavior and its underlying factors in such situations can teach us a lot about decision-making under pressure and with high-risk stakes and has many important application areas.

Since it is impossible to study such a situation in the real world, a recent study by [18] employed virtual reality (VR) to investigate exactly this event. In this experiment, participants were trained to navigate a driving course that contained multiple, warning-indicated forks. The aforementioned accident situation was inserted only during the final test-run to see how participants would react to the sudden appearance of the obstacle (turn left and crash into the obstacle, or turn right and crash the car fatally off the cliff). From this study, here, we take the in-car videos that lead up to that final decision and segment them into time periods for predicting the turn direction. Importantly, the resulting short video segments were analyzed by *both* human participants and a DNN to predict the final decision. Using this strategy, we can compare human and DNN performance in predicting decision-making, but also look closer into the decision features of the DNN, using the tools of explainable AI.

# 2 Related Work

## 2.1 Predicting the "Future"

There has been growing interest in predicting the future through DNNs where machines have to react to human actions as early as possible such as autonomous driving, human-robotic interaction. In general, anticipating actions before these begin is a challenging problem, as this requires extensive contextual knowledge.

To solve this problem, approaches have used predefined target classes and a few portions of an action from short video segments leading up to an event (e.g., [27] for predicting the future motion of a person). Similarly, in the field of natural language processing, [21] proposed a method of predicting what a person will say next from given contextual data.

Other methods for human trajectory prediction, include, for example, [4, 34] trying to predict pedestrian trajectories from 3D coordinates obtained from stereo cameras and LIDAR sensors using deep learning-based models. Although adding information from various sensors improved the prediction performance, obtaining such data is still a challenging problem in general, leading to image-only approaches such as [25].

## 2.2 Comparisons of Humans and DNNs

In order to better peek into the black box of DNNs, comparing performance between humans and DNNs has become an important research topic. Focusing on the human visual system, research has discussed human-machine comparisons at a conceptual level [7,16,20]. Indeed, these works show that deep learning systems not only solve image classification, but also reproduce certain aspects of human perception and cognition. This even goes as far as being able to reproduce phenomena of human vision, such as illusions [14] or crowding [33].

In addition, several studies have been conducted trying to impart more higher-level decision-making skills into DNNs: in [3], for example, ResNet models were able to solve abstract visual reasoning problems (IQ test) significantly better than humans - it is highly unlikely, however, that the model's knowledge representation matches that of humans, as the resulting networks were not able to learn visual relationships efficiently and robustly [12] - see also the many examples of adversarial attacks [2].

In other studies, input stimuli are manipulated or degraded to determine important visual features for human or machine decision-making. In [13], for example, twelve different types of image degradation were tested to compare error-patterns between humans and DNNs in classification. The authors found that the human visual system seemed to be more robust for image manipulations, but it DNNs trained directly on the degraded images were able to outperform humans. Similarly, based on adversarial perturbations, [7,26] indicate that DNNs may have the potential ability to provide predictions and explanations of cognitive phenomena.

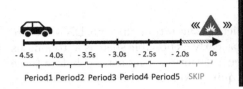

(a) Flow chart of the segmentation    (b) Final frame in the segmented video

**Fig. 1.** (a) Segmentation setup and (b) screenshot from experiment video

Overall, the field therefore seems to have quite heterogenous results when trying to compare human and machine performance with some studies finding commonalities and others finding critical differences. Here, we try to add to this general topic by comparing human and DNN performance in predicting a decision in a critical accident situation and analyzing the critical DNN features for prediction using similar tools.

## 3    Method

### 3.1    Experiment Setup

**Data:** To compare the prediction of decision-making between humans and DNNs, we used the original, in-car videos from [18] - both humans and DNNs received the same data and the same task for a fair comparison. First, we trimmed the total of $n_{\text{total}} = 74$ videos from all participants to 2 to 4.5 s before the final decision - hence, the actual decision in which the car turned left or right was not part of the video. Let $D$ denote our set of trimmed videos. Second, we partitioned $D$ into five non-overlapping subsets $D_p \subset \{D_1, D_2, D_3, D_4, D_5\}$ with each $D_p$ being a 0.5 s-long video, containing 16 frames at 480 px × 720 px (width × height). For each video, this yields a total of 5 time segments such that, for example, $D_5$ indicates the final segment running from $-2.5$ s to $-2.0$ s, where 0 s would indicate the actual time of the decision. In addition, each of the $D_p$ is labelled either as fall ($n_{\text{fall}} = 23$) and collision ($n_{\text{collide}} = 51$). Given the human decision proportions in this accident situation (most people chose to collide with the obstacle, rather than to crash their car off the cliff), this results in an imbalanced, binary dataset with label ratios of $\approx 31\%$ versus $\approx 69\%$, respectively.

### 3.2    Behavioral Experiment

**Participants:** A total of 29 participants (18 females, mean age 24.69 ± 3.11 (SD)) were recruited from the student population of Korea University. All participants had normal or corrected-to-normal vision and possessed a driver's license.

The experiment adhered to the tenets of the Declaration of Helsinki and was approved by the Institutional Review Board of Korea University with IRB number KUIRB-2018-0096-02s.

**Experimental Procedure:** As for the experimental procedure, participants were tested in a small, enclosed room with no distractions. Upon entering the room, the procedure of the experiment was explained to them - in particular, that the video clips were part of a longer video sequence leading up to a final decision by a driver whether to collide with the trees or to fall down the cliff. Participants were not informed that the decision ratio of the dataset was imbalanced. The whole experiment was conducted on a laptop running at 480 px × 720 px resolution - participants sat a distance of ≈60 cm, with video segments subtending a visual angle of ≈30°. The behavioral experiment was created in PsychoPy (v3.0) [24].

Each experiment had a sequence of $370 = 5 \times 74$ trials, in which participants were asked to determine whether the car was going to collide or fall. In each trial, a short video segment $D_p$ was randomly chosen and repeatedly shown to the participant until they felt they knew the answer, at which time they were to press the space bar. There was no time limit set by the experimenter, nor were participants explicitly instructed to respond as quickly or as accurately as possible. After the space bar was pressed, the time from start of the segment to the key press was recorded as response time, the video segment stopped looping and disappeared, and a text appeared in the center of the screen: "Which direction will the car go: collide or fall?". Participants were to press the right arrow button for a collision and the left arrow button for a fall decision. All

**Table 1.** ResNet(2+1)D architecture in our experiments. Convolutional residual blocks are shown illustrated in brackets, next to the number of times each block is repeated in the stack.

| Layer name | Filter shape | Repeats |
|---|---|---|
| conv1 | 7 × 7 × 7×, 64, stride 1 | 1 |
| conv2_x | 3 × 3 × 3 max pool stride 2 | 2 |
| | $\begin{bmatrix} 3 \times 3 \times 3,\ 64 \\ 3 \times 3 \times 3,\ 64 \end{bmatrix}$ | |
| conv3_x | $\begin{bmatrix} 3 \times 3 \times 3,\ 64 \\ 3 \times 3 \times 3,\ 64 \end{bmatrix}$ | 2 |
| conv4_x | $\begin{bmatrix} 3 \times 3 \times 3,\ 64 \\ 3 \times 3 \times 3,\ 64 \end{bmatrix}$ | 2 |
| conv5_x | $\begin{bmatrix} 3 \times 3 \times 3,\ 64 \\ 3 \times 3 \times 3,\ 64 \end{bmatrix}$ | 2 |

Average Pooling, $512-d$ FC, Sigmoid

video segments were pseudo-randomly chosen and shown only once. Dependent variables were response time and response.

## 3.3   Computational Experiment

**ResNet(2+1)D Architecture:** A popular architecture in action recognition consists of a 3D convolutional neural network (CNN), which extends the typical 2D filters of image-based CNNs to 3D convolutional filters. This approach therefore directly extracts spatio-temporal features from videos by creating hierarchical representations and was shown to perform well on large-scale video datasets (e.g., [6]). In our experiments, we use a similar ResNet(2+1)D architecture [32] in which the 3D filters are factorized into 2D spatial convolutions and a 1D temporal convolution, which improves optimization.

In ResNet(2+1)D, the input tensor $D_p$ ($p \in \{1, 2, 3, 4, 5\}$) is $5D$ and has size $B \times F \times C \times W \times H$, where $B$ is the number of mini-batch, $F$ is the number of frames of each video, $C$ is RGB channel, and $W$ and $H$ are the width and height of the frame, respectively.

Our Network takes 16 clips consisting of RGB frames with the size of 112 px $\times$ 112 px as an input. Each input frame is channel-normalized with mean (0.43216, 0.394666, 0.37645) and SD (0.22803, 0.22145, 0.216989). Downsampling of the inputs is performed by conv1, conv3_1, conv4_1, and conv5_1. Conv1 is implemented by convolutional striding of $1 \times 2 \times 2$, and the remaining convolutions are implemented by striding of $2 \times 2 \times 2$. Since our overall sample size is small, a fine-tuning strategy with a pre-trained network was used. Its earlier layers remain fixed during training on our data with only the later layers of the network being optimized for prediction. In our experiments, the ResNet(2+1)D model is pre-trained on the Kinetics dataset [32] and fine-tuned on layers conv_5 upwards.

To illustrate the importance of the temporal context, we further experiment with three additional settings: models trained on 8 frame clips (sampled uniformly from each segment) or 2 frame clips (using only the first or the last two consecutive frames in the segment).

During training, batch normalization is applied to all convolutional layers. We deploy the Adamax optimizer with a mini-batch size of 16. Learning rates are updated by using a one-cycle scheduler [30] that starts with a small learning rate of 1e−4, which is increased after each mini-batch until the maximum learning rate of 8e−3. All processing was done on an Intel Xeon (Gold 5120 @2.20 GHz) CPU and two NVIDIA V100 GPUs using Pytorch version 1.4.0.

**Performance Measures:** For the experiment, we repeated a 5-fold cross-validation process 20 times, which created 100 folds in total. In every batch per epoch, we balanced the label of the training data set to 1 : 1 using sampling with replacement - this was not applied to the test set.

## 4    Experimental Results

### 4.1    Comparison of Humans and DNN

We compared the ResNet(2+1)D prediction results to human performance on the exact same video sequences. As Fig. 2 shows, the model achieves higher recognition rates compared to human participants until Period 3, whereas results seemed more similar to humans in periods 4 and 5.

A two-way analysis of variance (ANOVA) with factors of group (human or DNN) and time periods (5 periods) showed significant differences among groups ($F(1, 48) = 13.8882$, $p < .001$), time periods $F(4, 192) = 107.2769882$, $p < .001$) and the interaction between group and time periods ($F(4, 192) = 21.6405$, $p < .001$) - see Table 2.

Since the interaction was significant, we next performed multiple pairwise comparisons on all possible combinations. To correct for multiple comparisons, we applied a Bonferroni correction, correcting our alpha-level to 0.005 (=0.05/10). Results overall showed no significant differences in period 5 ($p = 0.5853$) between human and ResNet(2+1)D, but significant differences from period 1 to 4 - see Table 3.

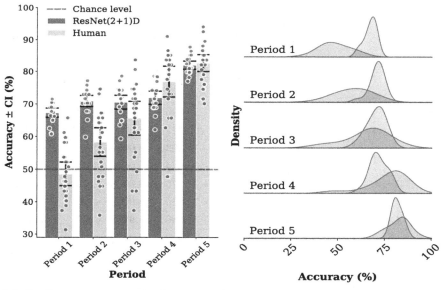

(a) Prediction accuracy for humans vs DNN

(b) Kernel density estimate plot

**Fig. 2.** Performance comparison of humans and ResNet(2+1)D. The margin of error was calculated at a confidence level of 95%. Gaussian kernels were used to estimate kernel density and bandwidth calculated by Scott's rule from [28].

**Table 2.** Two-way ANOVA of performance comparing humans and ResNet

| Factor | Num DF | Den DF | F-statistic | p-value | $\eta^2$ |
|---|---|---|---|---|---|
| Group | 1 | 47 | 13.1187 | <.001 | 0.2182 |
| Time | 4 | 188 | 164.2998 | <.001 | 0.7775 |
| Interaction | 4 | 188 | 35.9250 | <.001 | 0.4332 |

## 4.2   Discriminative Features - Grad-CAM Attention Map

In the previous analysis, we compared only the performance of humans versus machines. Here, we employ the popular Grad-CAM method [29] from explainability research to detect the most important spatial (and temporal) information for the prediction. The output of Grad-CAM is a heatmap visualization for a given class label and provides a localization map that highlights important regions in the image.

**Table 3.** Results of post-hoc multiple comparisons

| Contrast | Time | A | B | T | dof | p-adjust | cohen |
|---|---|---|---|---|---|---|---|
| Group | – | Human | ResNet | −4.2540 | 34.1198 | <.001 | −1.0528 |
| Time | – | Period1 | Period2 | −7.7186 | 48.0000 | <.001 | −0.6803 |
| Time | – | Period1 | Period3 | −7.2275 | 48.0000 | <.001 | −1.0843 |
| Time | – | Period1 | Period4 | −8.6652 | 48.0000 | <.001 | −1.8413 |
| Time | – | Period1 | Period5 | −14.7811 | 48.0000 | <.001 | −3.0093 |
| Time | – | Period2 | Period3 | −3.6096 | 48.0000 | <.001 | −0.4241 |
| Time | – | Period2 | Period4 | −6.8742 | 48.0000 | <.001 | −1.2161 |
| Time | – | Period2 | Period5 | −13.3034 | 48.0000 | <.001 | −2.4194 |
| Time | – | Period3 | Period4 | −5.9944 | 48.0000 | <.001 | −0.7870 |
| Time | – | Period3 | Period5 | −11.3766 | 48.0000 | <.001 | −1.9326 |
| Time | – | Period4 | Period5 | −7.0810 | 48.0000 | <.001 | −1.0476 |
| Time * Group | Period1 | Human | ResNet | −11.2901 | 38.9798 | <.001 | −2.8579 |
| Time * Group | Period2 | Human | ResNet | −6.3592 | 39.4529 | <.001 | −1.6135 |
| Time * Group | Period3 | Human | ResNet | −2.0353 | 40.1793 | 0.0484 | −0.5183 |
| Time * Group | Period4 | Human | ResNet | 2.2670 | 40.9008 | 0.0287 | 0.5795 |
| Time * Group | Period5 | Human | ResNet | 0.5498 | 42.6486 | 0.5853 | 0.1119 |

As shown in Fig. 3(a), (b) for an example segment of Period 5, both attention maps focus on the central, steering wheel part. Beyond this, however, there are crucial differences in the resulting attention map depending on the condition. In the collision condition (Fig. 3(a)), the network fixates areas nearby the tree in every frame of the period. In contrast, the model concentrates on both tree and cliff in the fall condition (Fig. 3(b)), but as time progresses, the concentration on the cliff becomes more prominent.

The visualizations for the earliest Period 1 showed that the network focuses on the steering wheel and hill ridges in the collision condition and on similar areas on both trees and cliffs in fall conditions (cf. Fig. 3(c), (d)).

These qualitative differences were highly consistent in all input videos, indicating that the DNN is paying attention to meaningful - and expected - visual features for making the prediction.

## 4.3    Effect of Spatial Degradation

We next test the generalizability and robustness of the model by degrading the visual input. We first add spatial Gaussian noise to an image during testing either in the top 60% or the bottom 40% of the image.

Performance in the two conditions for all periods is shown in Fig. 5(a). Overall, bottom blurring has virtually no effect on performance, whereas top blurring significantly reduces performance in the initial period, and especially in the final period (performance in Period 5: 72.76% for top-blurring versus 81.85% for bottom blurring and 81.97% for unblurred images). Hence, as one would expect from the attention-map analysis in Fig. 3, top-blurring considerably reduces the networks ability for predicting decision-making.

Figure 4 compares the attention maps of the non-blurred with the two blurred conditions to confirm the accuracy results. Indeed, when blurring the top part, almost all activation focuses on the bottom, non-blurred input, virtually disregarding the important features outside the car. Perhaps the remaining focus on the steering wheel may lead to the above-chance prediction performance that could still be observed. As one would expect, blurring the bottom part of the image has virtually no effect on the attention map, barring a slight decrease of focus on the steering wheel (see Fig. 4(c)).

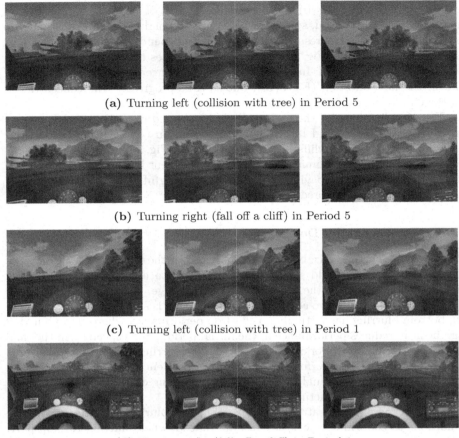

(a) Turning left (collision with tree) in Period 5

(b) Turning right (fall off a cliff) in Period 5

(c) Turning left (collision with tree) in Period 1

(d) Turning right (fall off a cliff) in Period 1

**Fig. 3.** Attention maps from Grad-CAM at equally sampled time points (left = start; right = end) for Periods 1 and 5. In Period 5, which is the closest period to the final decision, the DNN focuses on tree or cliff. In the earlier Period 1, the DNN puts more focus on the steering wheel or the ridge of the hill.

## 4.4    Temporal Analysis

In general, continuous sequences of frames in the video are known to be critical for understanding events (see, for example, [8] for a detailed study on the dynamics of facial expressions). To determine the importance of different temporal aspects, we next present experiments that modified the number of input frames or changed the temporal order of frames.

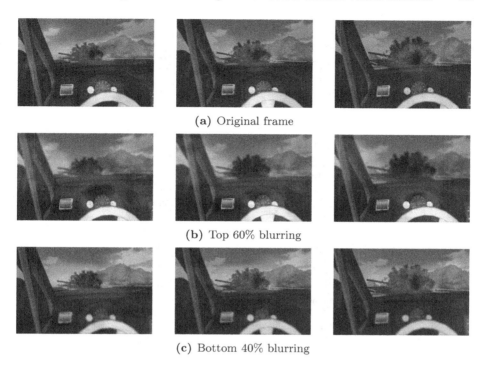

(a) Original frame

(b) Top 60% blurring

(c) Bottom 40% blurring

**Fig. 4.** Effect of spatially-selective blurring on discriminative features. From left to right: start frame to end frame of Period 5. The top row shows discriminative features for the original sequence. Blurring effects are shown applied to the top 60% of the original frame (middle row), or the bottom 40% (bottom row).

**Changing Number of Frames:** Reducing the number of input frames from 16 frames to 8 frames showed only minor decreases in performance (Fig. 5(b)). A further reduction from the original 16 frames to only 2 frames (Fig. 5(c)) showed varying results: original performance levels could only be obtained with the last 2 frames of the segment, whereas using the first 2 frames of the Period resulted in an overall drop in performance, especially towards the final Period. Interestingly, for Period 4, prediction accuracy for the final 2 frames outperformed those obtained by all 16 frames, reaching almost peak accuracy.

Overall, these results seem to suggest that prediction seems to rely on the final, few frames of each period with limited advantages of adding further frames for temporal context.

**Changing Temporal Order:** Given prior results from human studies on the importance of the direction of time and the preservation of temporal structure in general [8], we next reversed time or shuffled the frames. As Fig. 5(d) shows, this has very little effect on performance, indicating that temporal structure itself bears little importance for the model.

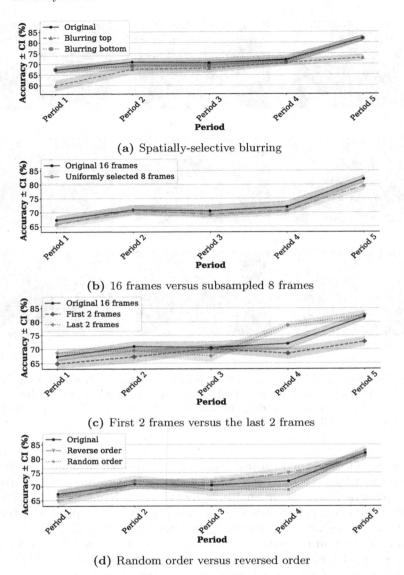

(a) Spatially-selective blurring

(b) 16 frames versus subsampled 8 frames

(c) First 2 frames versus the last 2 frames

(d) Random order versus reversed order

**Fig. 5.** Prediction accuracy for manipulations in space (blurring (a)) and time (16 vs 8 frames (b), first vs last frames (c), shuffling and time-reversal (d)).

## 5    Conclusion

In this paper, we investigated the difference between humans and a DNN in predicting the final decision in an accident situation. Our results showed that both humans and DNNs increased in accuracy as the time period approached the actual decision - a result in line with expectations, as both the path of the car and the steering movements may "settle" on their final direction at that point. We also found that the DNN made more accurate judgments compared to the human at early time points. Grad-CAM analysis further showed that its attended features are meaningful in terms of semantic content: interestingly, for the early time period, in which the DNN outperforms humans, its focus is on a wider view of the scene (including the ridge of hill) as well as the steering wheel, whereas in later time periods it focuses on closer things (tree or cliff). In future work, we will compare these computational attention maps to those obtained with further human experiments, using, for example, eye-tracking.

Moreover, several analyses were conducted to dive deeper into the underlying spatial and temporal features that may give rise to the prediction accuracy. In terms of spatial features, blurring showed that the outside, top view drove most of the recognition performance, which matches with expectations. In terms of temporal features, we found that the number of input frames does affect performance to some degree, but also showed that even two frames - when properly selected - still yield high performance. Again, it remains to be seen whether human performance would be similar with the same kind of input reduction.

Although most of the analyses so far would match with qualitative expectations about the important features for predictions, our analysis of time reversal and shuffling indicates no adverse effects of these manipulations. This is perhaps somewhat surprising given ample evidence in the human literature that time structure is crucially important in event analysis [8,19]. Here, human experiments would most likely yield quite reduced performance, indicating that especially the learned *temporal* representation of DNNs may be different to those of humans. Further experiments will be necessary with different pre-training schemes and "deeper" visual hierarchies (vision transformers [10]) to investigate in more detail to what degree human and DNNs representations are similar.

We would like to end on the general note that comparing data from human and computational experiments is bound to be complex: the DNN was specifically trained on a decision that was tested later, hence, there was no notion of task generalizability; similarly, humans will attach "meaning" to the outcome of the decision, with the left/right choice carrying consequences that are implicitly understood - such semantic grounding is so far missing from the DNN representation. It will be interesting to see how the current trend of research towards "foundation models" [5] will create frameworks that are capable of producing more human-level, semantically-rich, and generalizable task solutions.

**Acknowledgements.** This work was supported by the National Research Foundation of Korea under Grant NRF-2017M3C7A1041824 and by two Institutes of Information and Communications Technology Planning and Evaluation (IITP) grants funded by the Korean government (MSIT): Development of BCI based Brain and Cognitive Computing Technology for Recognizing User's Intentions using Deep Learning (2017-0-00451), and Artificial Intelligence Graduate School Program (Korea University) (2019-0-00079).

# References

1. Adadi, A., Berrada, M.: Peeking inside the black-box: a survey on explainable artificial intelligence (XAI). IEEE Access **6**, 52138–52160 (2018)
2. Akhtar, N., Mian, A.: Threat of adversarial attacks on deep learning in computer vision: a survey. IEEE Access **6**, 14410–14430 (2018)
3. Barrett, D., Hill, F., Santoro, A., Morcos, A., Lillicrap, T.: Measuring abstract reasoning in neural networks. In: International Conference on Machine Learning, pp. 511–520. PMLR (2018)
4. Bhattacharyya, A., Fritz, M., Schiele, B.: Long-term on-board prediction of people in traffic scenes under uncertainty. In: Proceedings of the IEEE Conference on Computer Vision and Pattern Recognition, pp. 4194–4202 (2018)
5. Bommasani, R., et al.: On the opportunities and risks of foundation models (2021)
6. Carreira, J., Zisserman, A.: Quo Vadis, action recognition. A new model and the kinetics dataset. CoRR, abs/1705.07750 2(3) (2017)
7. Cichy, R.M., Kaiser, D.: Deep neural networks as scientific models. Trends Cogn. Sci. **23**(4), 305–317 (2019)
8. Cunningham, D.W., Wallraven, C.: Dynamic information for the recognition of conversational expressions. J. Vis. **9**(13), 7 (2009)
9. DeGrave, A.J., Janizek, J.D., Lee, S.I.: AI for radiographic COVID-19 detection selects shortcuts over signal. medRxiv (2020)
10. Dosovitskiy, A., et al.: An image is worth $16 \times 16$ words: transformers for image recognition at scale. arXiv preprint arXiv:2010.11929 (2020)
11. Edwards, W.: The theory of decision making. Psychol. Bull. **51**(4), 380 (1954)
12. Funke, C.M., Borowski, J., Stosio, K., Brendel, W., Wallis, T.S., Bethge, M.: Five points to check when comparing visual perception in humans and machines. J. Vis. **21**(3), 16 (2021)
13. Geirhos, R., Temme, C.R.M., Rauber, J., Schütt, H.H., Bethge, M., Wichmann, F.A.: Generalisation in humans and deep neural networks. arXiv preprint arXiv:1808.08750 (2018)
14. Gomez-Villa, A., Martin, A., Vazquez-Corral, J., Bertalmío, M.: Convolutional neural networks can be deceived by visual illusions. In: Proceedings of the IEEE/CVF Conference on Computer Vision and Pattern Recognition, pp. 12309–12317 (2019)
15. Goodfellow, I., Bengio, Y., Courville, A., Bengio, Y.: Deep Learning, vol. 1. MIT Press, Cambridge (2016)
16. Han, Y., Roig, G., Geiger, G., Poggio, T.: Scale and translation-invariance for novel objects in human vision. Sci. Rep. **10**(1), 1–13 (2020)
17. Hawkins, J., Blakeslee, S.: On Intelligence. Macmillan (2004)
18. Ju, U., Chuang, L.L., Wallraven, C.: Acoustic cues increase situational awareness in accident situations: a VR car-driving study. IEEE Trans. Intell. Transp. Syst. **23**, 3281–3291 (2020)
19. Liu, Y., Dolan, R.J., Kurth-Nelson, Z., Behrens, T.E.: Human replay spontaneously reorganizes experience. Cell **178**(3), 640–652 (2019)
20. Majaj, N.J., Pelli, D.G.: Deep learning-using machine learning to study biological vision. J. Vis. **18**(13), 2 (2018)
21. Mikolov, T., Karafiát, M., Burget, L., Černocký, J., Khudanpur, S.: Recurrent neural network based language model. In: 11th Annual Conference of the International Speech Communication Association (2010)

22. Ontanón, S., Lee, Y.C., Snodgrass, S., Winston, F.K., Gonzalez, A.J.: Learning to predict driver behavior from observation. In: 2017 AAAI Spring Symposium Series (2017)
23. Oprea, S., et al.: A review on deep learning techniques for video prediction. IEEE Trans. Pattern Anal. Mach. Intell. (2020)
24. Peirce, J.: PsychoPy2: experiments in behavior made easy. Behav. Res. Meth. **51**(1), 195–203 (2019)
25. Poibrenski, A., Klusch, M., Vozniak, I., Müller, C.: Multimodal multi-pedestrian path prediction for autonomous cars. ACM SIGAPP Appl. Comput. Rev. **20**(4), 5–17 (2021)
26. Ritter, S., Barrett, D.G., Santoro, A., Botvinick, M.M.: Cognitive psychology for deep neural networks: a shape bias case study. In: International Conference on Machine Learning, pp. 2940–2949. PMLR (2017)
27. Rodriguez, C., Fernando, B., Li, H.: Action anticipation by predicting future dynamic images. In: Leal-Taixé, L., Roth, S. (eds.) ECCV 2018. LNCS, vol. 11131, pp. 89–105. Springer, Cham (2019). https://doi.org/10.1007/978-3-030-11015-4_10
28. Scott, D.W.: Multivariate Density Estimation: Theory, Practice, and Visualization. Wiley (2015)
29. Selvaraju, R.R., Cogswell, M., Das, A., Vedantam, R., Parikh, D., Batra, D.: Grad-CAM: visual explanations from deep networks via gradient-based localization. In: Proceedings of the IEEE International Conference on Computer Vision, pp. 618–626 (2017)
30. Smith, L.N.: Cyclical learning rates for training neural networks. In: 2017 IEEE Winter Conference on Applications of Computer Vision (WACV), pp. 464–472. IEEE (2017)
31. Tan, M., Le, Q.: EfficientNet: rethinking model scaling for convolutional neural networks. In: International Conference on Machine Learning, pp. 6105–6114. PMLR (2019)
32. Tran, D., Wang, H., Torresani, L., Ray, J., LeCun, Y., Paluri, M.: A closer look at spatiotemporal convolutions for action recognition. In: Proceedings of the IEEE Conference on Computer Vision and Pattern Recognition, pp. 6450–6459 (2018)
33. Volokitin, A., Roig, G., Poggio, T.: Do deep neural networks suffer from crowding? arXiv preprint arXiv:1706.08616 (2017)
34. Zhang, Z., Gao, J., Mao, J., Liu, Y., Anguelov, D., Li, C.: STINet: spatio-temporal-interactive network for pedestrian detection and trajectory prediction. In: Proceedings of the IEEE/CVF Conference on Computer Vision and Pattern Recognition, pp. 11346–11355 (2020)

# Least Privilege Learning for Attribute Obfuscation

Glen Brown$^{(\boxtimes)}$ , Jesus Martinez-del-Rincon , and Paul Miller

Centre for Secure Information Technologies, Queen's University Belfast, Belfast, UK
{gbrown29,j.martinez-del-rincon,p.miller}@qub.ac.uk
https://www.qub.ac.uk/ecit/CSIT

**Abstract.** As machine learning systems become ever more prevalent in everyday life, the need to secure such systems is becoming a critically important area in cybersecurity research. In this work, we address the "feature misuse" attack vector, where the features output by a model are abused to perform a function that they were not originally designed for, such as determining a person's gender in a facial verification system. To mitigate this, we take the security concept of "least privilege", where a system can only access resources it explicitly needs to complete its task, and apply it to training deep neural networks. This "least privilege learning" ensures features do not contain information regarding protected attributes that are superfluous to the primary task, reducing the potential attack surface for feature misuse and reducing undesired information leakage. In this paper, we present two main contributions. Firstly, a novel training paradigm that enables least privilege learning by obfuscating protected attributes in verification and re-identification scenarios. Secondly, a comprehensive evaluation framework for models trained with least privilege learning, encompassing multiple datasets and three application settings: verification, re-identification, and attribute prediction.

**Keywords:** Least privilege learning · Attribute obfuscation · Machine learning feature misuse · Adversarial learning · Protecting deep learning models

## 1 Introduction

Security of machine learning is emerging as a new frontier for cybersecurity. Since Goodmann et al.'s seminal paper [15], adversarial learning has been an area of much research activity. When considering the security of machine learning, one needs to consider the confidentiality, integrity and availability challenges posed by each phase of the machine learning cycle. Of particular interest is the training phase, which is one of the most critical steps, since it establishes the baseline behaviour of the application. This is the area that is most likely to present unique security challenges, as learning is at the core of the machine learning process.

The training stage consists of running the model iteratively with a baseline data set for which the desired output is known. With each iteration, the

© Springer Nature Switzerland AG 2022
C. Wallraven et al. (Eds.): ACPR 2021, LNCS 13189, pp. 142–156, 2022.
https://doi.org/10.1007/978-3-031-02444-3_11

model parameters are adjusted to achieve more accurate performance, and this is repeated until an optimal or acceptable level of accuracy is achieved. It is critical that the training data set is of high quality, as any inaccuracies or inconsistencies can lead to the model behaving incorrectly. A typical example of a biometric access control system which utilises facial analysis involves a user with an identifying card. The card stores (or can be used to retrieve) a previously generated feature vector which encodes the properties of the user's face. On presentation of the card to the system, a camera takes a new image and encodes it as a new feature vector. If the distance between the new and stored feature vectors is below a pre-determined threshold, they are deemed to match and access is granted. Otherwise, access is denied.

However the performance of the training task should not be the only goal, since features generated by a model can be used, without further training, for inference purposes other than that which they were intended. For example, a biometric face recognition system developed for access control, may contain a model whose features can be used to recognise a person's gender, age or ethnic group. Facial biometric systems are becoming ever more prevalent, so potential avenues of abuse against such systems need to be investigated.

Feature misuse is the attack which we address in this paper. To do so we introduce the concept here of least privileged learning. Along with Need to Know, Least Privilege is one of the underlying principles of security which states that an entity should only be given access to a specific resource that is needed to perform a task. In the context of learning, we can apply least privilege to ensure that a model, or its features, can only be used for that purpose for which it was designed and nothing else. Hence, in the biometric access control example we want to ensure that the features learnt for verifying an identity cannot be used to determine a person's gender for example. To achieve this we propose the use of a second unlearning task in which the system is trained to become ignorant of the attribute of interest, in this case gender. To accomplish this, we construct a novel training paradigm that can obfuscate attributes in facial biometric systems, as well as a comprehensive framework for evaluating systems that utilise least privilege learning.

## 2   Related Work

Different training paradigms have been proposed to mitigate the encoding of unwanted attributes into models. One approach is to alter the input data. Authors in [12] use a style transfer system to remove features from the images which are correlated with demographic attributes, producing "neutral" faces. Authors in [6] also use a style transfer technique, but instead use a data augmentation procedure to increase the demographic diversity of the training data by transforming images into other demographics.

Another approach alters the training paradigm. [18] demonstrated an *Adversarial Debiasing* model on word embeddings using an adversarial training scenario [7], combining a *predictor* which learns the primary task, and an *adversary* which attempts to predict the protected attribute. The loss across the full model is formulated in such a way that updates made to the *predictor* are prevented from decreasing the *adversary's* loss, thereby removing bias encoded in the *predictor's* output. Similarly, Authors in [13] use a *gradient reversal layer* in a multitask-training model based on [5] which updates the weights of the model in opposition to the secondary task, namely protected attribute prediction. Research in [1] introduced a Joint Learning and Unlearning (JLU) framework utilising a confusion loss (inspired by [17]) where they successfully trained a gender-blind age classifier. The confusion loss computes the cross-entropy between the model output and a uniform distribution, moving the model towards a state of randomness with respect to protected attribute prediction. While our work is related, we apply the general method in conjunction with metric learning and a different training paradigm to facial verification and/or re-identification tasks across several standard "in-the-wild" datasets, as opposed to the attribute discrimination tasks in the original paper.

## 3    Method

The basis of our least privilege learning framework takes inspiration from both Domain-Adversarial Neural Networks (DANN) [5] and Generative Adversarial Networks (GAN) [7], while using a confusion loss as in [1]. We start with a Multi-Task Learning model with the two tasks being *verification* and *attribute discrimination* (Sect. 3.1). Then, we utilise a penalising loss function, also known as a confusion loss (Sect. 3.3), and a two-stage training step (Sect. 3.2) to correctly back-propagate the penalised gradients, while still allowing effective learning. With this process, the model can learn a suitable representation of the latent space with which Verification/Re-identification is possible while not leaking information about the protected attribute in the resulting embedding vectors.

### 3.1    Multi-task Learning

The basic model architecture consists of a central CNN Backbone $F$ which functions as a deep *feature extractor*, and a separate Multilayer Perceptron $P$ called the *Attribute Prediction Branch (APB)* which takes the generated features $x'$ as inputs and discriminates the value of the protected attribute. This results in the model having two outputs: the generated features $x'$ that are used for verification and the predicted attribute values $\hat{a}$. Different loss values are derived from the separate outputs, corresponding to a particular task. The loss $L_F$ derives from the extracted features $x'$ when trained using Metric Learning for the verification/re-identification task. Whereas $L_A$ is the penalisation loss, derived from the predicted attribute values $\hat{a}$ and the ground-truth values $a$. The precise definitions of $L_F$ and $L_A$ can be found in Sect. 3.3.

Given $L_F$ and $L_A$ likely have different numerical properties such as scale, stability, etc., it's necessary to weight $L_F$ and $L_A$ when summing them together to produce the overall loss $L$. To do this, like in [5], we use the regularisation hyper-parameter $\lambda$ as shown in Eq. 1. Naturally, when $\lambda = 0$ the training is no longer multi-task as $L = L_F$. We use this as a baseline for both verification/re-identification and attribute discrimination performance.

$$L = (1 - \lambda)L_F + \lambda L_A \tag{1}$$

## 3.2   Two-Stage Adversarial Training

As stated above (Sect. 3.1) we use a multi-task learning model with a penalised loss $L_A$ on the attribute prediction branch. However, this by itself is insufficient for the model to learn an effective embedding space while encoding no information about the protected attribute: preliminary experiments trained in a straightforward multi-task scenario failed with regards to obfuscation. The reason is that during back-propagation, the weights of the APB $P$ will simply be updated to produce near-random output regardless of input due to the effect of $L_A$. Therefore the gradients penalising the encoding of the protected attribute, back-propagated into the CNN Backbone $F$, will be relatively insignificant and attribute obfuscation will not take place.

To ensure the penalised gradients from $L_A$ are adequately back-propagated throughout the entire model, we employ a two-stage training step as shown in Fig. 1, with the full algorithm in Algorithm 1. This is somewhat analogous to the training of the *discriminator* and *generator* in GAN [7] based architectures.

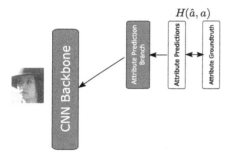 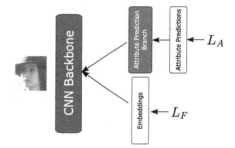

(a) Stage 1 Back-prop: APB is trained using predicted and ground-truth attribute values with $H(\hat{a}, a)$. The CNN Backbone is not optimized.

(b) Stage 2 Back-prop: The CNN Backbone is trained with $L_A$ and $L_F$ (Sec. 3.3), weighted according to Eq. 1. The APB is not optimised.

**Fig. 1.** Two-stage training step

**Stage 1.** The Attribute Prediction Branch (APB) $P$ of the Multitask model is trained using the cross-entropy between predicted and ground-truth attribute values ($H(\hat{a}, a)$, see Eq. 2) to correctly discriminate the attribute. During back-prop only the APB's parameters are updated while keeping the CNN Backbone's weights frozen. See Fig. 1a.

$$H(\hat{a}, a) = -\sum_{x \in \mathcal{X}} \hat{a}(x) \log a(x) \tag{2}$$

**Stage 2.** The CNN Backbone is trained with respect to $L_F$ and $L_A$ in a multitask scenario. Importantly, the gradients are derived with respect to the parameters in the CNN backbone $F$ only: the APB $P$ is not updated during this stage. See Fig. 1b.

---

**Algorithm 1:** Two-Stage Adversarial Training

---

**Data:** $F$: CNN Backbone Model, $P$: Attribute Prediction Branch, $\lambda$, $x$: images, $y$: identity labels, $a$: attribute labels, $\theta_F$: $F$'s weights, $\theta_A$: $A$'s weights

**Result:** Updated $\theta_F$, $\theta_A$

1 **for** *epochs* **do**
2     **for** $x_b, y_b, a_b \in (x, y, a)$ **do**
       // Stage 1
3        $\hat{a}_b \longleftarrow P(F(x^b))$
4        $\min H(\hat{a}_b, a_b)$, updating $\theta_A$ only;
       // Stage 2
5        $x'_b \longleftarrow F(x_b)$
6        $\hat{a}_b \longleftarrow P(x'_b)$
7        $L \longleftarrow (1 - \lambda)L_F(x'_b, y_b) + \lambda L_A(\hat{a}_b, a_b)$
8        $\min L$, updating $\theta_F$ only
9     **end for**
10 **end for**

---

### 3.3 Losses

**Semi-Hard Online Mined Triplet Loss.** For $L_F$ we use the Semi-Hard Online Mined Triplet Loss described in [14]. Equation 3 shows the formulation of the triplet loss where $a$, $p$, and $n$ are the *anchor*, *positive* and *negative* exemplars of the triplet respectively. $d(x_i, y_i) = ||\mathbf{x}_i - \mathbf{y}_i||_2$ and $\alpha$ is the margin (we set it to 1.0).

$$L_T(a, p, n) = \max\{d(a_i, p_i) - d(a_i, n_i) + \alpha, 0\} \tag{3}$$

If all possible valid triplets are generated, there will be many that are trivial: where $L_T(a, p, n) = 0$. Therefore the selection of valid triplets is a critical component for efficient training. At run-time, *hard* triplets where $L_T(a, p, n) > 0$ are "mined" from the minibatch. In this particular variation, priority is given to mining hard triplets which satisfy the condition $d(a_i, p_i) < d(a_i, n_i)$. These are known as the *semi-hard* triplets, as the *negative* sits within the margin $\alpha$, as opposed to being closer to the *anchor* that the *positive*. It's reported in [14] that simply selecting the hardest triplets can lead to bad local minima early in training, whereas selecting these less hard triplets helps avoid that issue.

**KL-Divergence with Discrete Uniform Target Distribution.** The purpose of the loss $L_A$ is to obfuscate the attribute so that no information about the attribute may be extracted from the embeddings produced by the *feature* *extractor* part of the multi-task model. More concretely, when we train the CNN Backbone $F$ we desire the output of the APB $P$ to be random (where each predicted value is equally likely regardless of input), indicating that a discriminatory representation cannot be found.

For this reason the loss we use is a variation of the KL-Divergence shown in Eq. 4 which is a measure of relative entropy between a probability distribution $Q$ to another probability distribution $P$ (with both $P$ and $Q$ defined on the same probability space $\mathcal{X}$).

We set $P$ to be the discrete uniform distribution $\mathcal{U}\{0, C\}$ where $C$ is the number of discrete classes the attribute may take, with the probability of each value simply being $C^{-1}$. $Q$ is set to the predicted attribute probabilities $\hat{a}$ (see Eq. 5). Given that all values in $\mathcal{U}\{0, C\}$ have an equal probability, we can further simplify this using the scalar value $C^{-1}$ as shown in Eq. 6. Optimising this loss means the attribute predictions $\hat{a}$ move closer to a random distribution.

Using this penalising loss, in conjunction with an accurate APB $P$ in the multi-task model (Sect. 3.1) and the two-stage training step (Sect. 3.2), we try to force the CNN Backbone $F$ to produce embeddings which an otherwise effective attribute discriminating model cannot discriminate. This indicates no information regarding the protected attribute is encoded the in feature vectors.

$$D_{KL}(P||Q) = \sum_{x \in \mathcal{X}} P(x) \log \frac{P(x)}{Q(x)} \tag{4}$$

$$L_A = D_{KL}(\mathcal{U}\{0, C\}||\hat{a}) \tag{5}$$

$$= \sum_{\hat{a}^i \in \hat{a}} C^{-1}(\log C^{-1} - \log \hat{a}^i) \tag{6}$$

## 4    Experimental Design

### 4.1    Models

In these experiments the CNN backbone $F_\lambda$, as in [14], is based on Resnet50 [8]. The Attribute Prediction Branch $P_\lambda$ of the Multi-Task model, as well as the Attribute Extraction Models (AEMs) $A_\lambda^{\mathcal{P}}$, used to simulate a malicious attribute extraction and in testing attribute obfuscation performance (Sect. 4.3), are Multilayer Perceptrons with 3 Fully Connected Layers of lengths 128, 32, and $C$, where $C$ is the number of classes the protected attribute may take on. Since gender is used in this work as a binary attribute, $C = 2$. The output feature vectors from $F_\lambda$ are of length 512.

### 4.2    Datasets

We train and evaluate on VGGFace2 [4] and CelebA [10]. VGGFace2 comprises 3.31 million facial images of 9131 subjects, split into two designated partitions: *train* (8631 identities, 3138924 images) and *test* (500 identities, 169177 images).

VGGFace2 only comes with annotations for pose and age. Additional attributes were obtained from [16]. VGGFace2's gender split is 59% Male to 41% Female. Whenever VGGFace2's *train* set is used for training a model, 5% of identities are randomly selected and held out as a validation set. CelebA consists of 202599 facial images of 10177 identities, split into three designated partitions: *train* (8192 identities, 162770 images), *validation* (985 identities, 19967 images), and *test* (1000 identities, 19962 images). The images in CelebA are also annotated with 45 attributes. The gender split in CelebA is 42% Male, 58% Female. Both datasets were pre-processed using MTCNN [19] for facial alignment.

### 4.3   Testing Methodology

**Verification Performance.** We assess this by running a verification scenario using the embeddings produced by the *feature extractor* portion $F_\lambda$ of the multi-task model, where $\lambda$ is the value of $\lambda$ during the original multi-task training (see Sect. 3.1). Evaluation takes place on a dataset's designated *test* partition. Positive pairs of images (where images belong to the same identity) are selected from the dataset, along with an equal number of non-matching images pairs (where the pair of images belong to different identities). As many unique, positive pair combinations are selected as possible, up to a limit of 1000000. This results in a balanced verification dataset of up to 2000000 matching and non-matching pairs. These image pairs are then processed by the *feature extractor* to obtain embedding pairs.

10-fold Cross-validation is used to evaluate verification performance on the embedding pairs from the testing split as described above, with 90% of pairs per fold used to calculate a optimum threshold distance using Receiver Operating Characteristic (ROC) Curves. The final 10% of embedding pairs per fold are thresholded accordingly to produce matching/non-matching label predictions for those pairs. The predicted and ground-truth labels are then used to calculate relevant metrics for that fold. The final results are the metrics averaged over all 10 folds. In addition to ROC-AUC (ROC-Area Under Curve) and accuracy, we also report False Acceptance Rate (FAR) and False Rejection Rate (FRR) as given in Eq. 7, where $TP$, $FN$, $TN$, $FP$ are true-positives, false-negatives, true-negatives, and false-positives respectively.

$$FAR = \frac{FR}{FP + TN}$$

$$FRR = \frac{FN}{FN + TP} \tag{7}$$

**Re-identification Performance.** Using a particular dataset's designated test partition, we construct a *gallery* by randomly sampling a single image per identity in the dataset. All other images from all identities are added the *probe* set. Images are passed through the *feature extractor* $F_\lambda$ to obtain embeddings $x'_\lambda$, and distances between each probe embedding and all gallery embeddings are calculated and ranked. The results are averaged over all probe samples and cumulative accuracy per rank is reported.

**Attribute Obfuscation Performance.** For a protected attribute to be obfuscated, it means there is no information in the output embedding vectors that can be used to discriminate the attribute. To determine obfuscation performance, we run multiple attack scenarios with varying prior-information conditions. The metric we are primarily concerned with is "Balanced Accuracy" [3], where the accuracy is weighted per sample according to the inverse support of the attribute's label. Therefore, for any binary attribute a balanced accuracy value of 0.5 equates with randomised output, even on unbalanced data.

*Full Technical Knowledge:* The attacker has full knowledge of the models (but not the trained models themselves) and datasets used, including the corresponding attribute label for each stolen embedding. In this scenario, the attacker trains a separate model called an *Attribute Extraction Model (AEM)* using the stolen embeddings $x'_\lambda$ originating from a feature model $F_\lambda$. This kind of attack would produce a feature-abusing model that can be used when further embeddings are exfiltrated without the corresponding attribute labels. One real-world situation that could enable such an attack would be the case of unsecured cloud-based storage that supports a facial verification system, containing both input (images) and output (embedding) files.

A successful attack is when the trained AEM has sufficient discriminating power to accurately predict the attribute label from the embeddings. Therefore, a successful defence would be where an AEM fails to learn such a mapping, indicating that there's insufficient latent information regarding the attribute encoded in the embeddings. Training involves predicting the attribute $\hat{a}$, and updating the AEM's weights to minimise the cross-entropy loss $H(\hat{a}, a)$ (Eq. 2).

We evaluate the AEM's performance on same and cross-dataset scenarios to help rule out results caused by overfitting to the training dataset. Concretely, each feature extractor $F_\lambda$ is trained on VGGFace2's *train* set (162770 samples, 8631 identities) as part of a multi-task training scenario (see Sect. 3.1). For each $F_\lambda$, we train an AEM using embeddings generated from the same VGGFace2 *train* set $A_\lambda^V$. Training lasts for 10 epochs. For each $A_\lambda^V$ (where $V$ indicates the AEM was trained on embeddings from VGGFace2), we evaluate attribute discrimination performance using both VGGFace2's *test* set (169177 samples, 500 identities), and CelebA's *test* set (19,967 samples, 1000 identities). This results in 2 sets of results per $F_\lambda$

*Partial Technical Knowledge:* In this scenario, the attacker has access to the trained model $F$ as well as stolen embeddings $x'$ generated by $F$. They do not however know the attribute labels for each embedding, nor have access to the original dataset. This makes the attack in the Full Knowledge scenario impossible as supervised learning utilising the stolen embeddings $x'$ and attribute labels $a$ cannot be done. To get around this, the attacker uses their own annotated dataset $\mathcal{D}$ and the model $F$ to generate new embeddings $x'^{\mathcal{D}}$. Now, as in the Full Knowledge scenario, they can train an AEM $A^{\mathcal{D}}$ using $x'^{\mathcal{D}}$ and $a^{\mathcal{D}}$ in a supervised manner, which can then be used to discriminate the gender of the original stolen embeddings $x'$. With the rise of publicly available, pre-trained models this scenario may become commonplace as facial embedding models get reused across many systems. This scenario also applies to cloud computing providers which provide such models as-a-service.

To reiterate, each model $F_\lambda$ is trained on VGGFace2's *train* set. For this scenario, we use CelebA (denoted with $C$) as our "external" dataset. Using $F_\lambda$ we generate embeddings $x'^C_\lambda$ from CelebA's *train* partition, which along with $a^C$ we use to train an AEM $A^C_\lambda$. As above, we then evaluate $A^C_\lambda$'s discriminative performance on both VGGFace2 and CelebA's respective *test* partitions, giving two sets of results per $F_\lambda$.

*Zero Technical Knowledge:* In this scenario, the attacker has no prior technical knowledge: the only asset they have are the stolen embeddings $x'$. In the specific case of a binary gender attribute, given the intrinsic role gender plays in facial recognition [2] an attacker could reasonably assume that gender-based clusters exists in the embedding space. Therefore, they perform unsupervised clustering on the embeddings to assign each embedding to 1 of 2 clusters. Afterwards, using publicly available information (such as the rough demographic makeup of employees) or a reasonable guess (certain industries such as construction or the military are gender imbalanced in general), they can assign an attribute label to each cluster.

To evaluate this scenario, we generate embeddings $x'_\lambda$ from each trained CNN Backbone $F_\lambda$. We reduce $x'_\lambda$ to 2 Dimensions $x''_\lambda$ using t-SNE [11] (with perplexity = 50) and finally cluster $x''_\lambda$ with a Gaussian Mixture Model (GMM). As the goal of this attack is to simply cluster and assign attribute labels to the stolen embeddings $x'$, and there is no danger of overfitting to the attribute labels during training as they are never used in this scenario, we train the GMM and evaluate on the same data: embeddings generated by $F_\lambda$ from VGGFace2 and CelebA's test sets, producing two sets of results for each $F_\lambda$ model. Note that due to the computational complexity of t-SNE, the number of images taken from each dataset are limited to a randomly sampled 10000.

### 4.4  Hyper-parameters

As the results in this work will primarily be judged relative to our own baseline ($\lambda = 0$, see Eq. 1), for computational efficiency we are limiting any hyper-parameter searching to $\lambda$ itself. We initially test 12 values of $\lambda$: 0, 0.0001, 0.001, 0.01, 0.1, 0.3, 0.5, 0.7, 0.9, 0.99, 0.999 and 0.9999. This choice reflects a good range of values with more precision nearer the equilibrium point while still checking many orders of magnitude. Additional values of $\lambda$ were tested (0.75, 0.8, 0.85) after the initial 12 values, with the aim to find a balance between verification and attribute obfuscation performance. The optimizers used are all Adam [9] with learning rate 0.01, $\beta_1 = 0.9$, and $\beta_2 = 0.999$. The Multi-Task Models (consisting of $F_\lambda$ and $P_\lambda$) and the AEMs $A^\mathcal{D}_\lambda$ are trained for 30 and 10 epochs respectively.

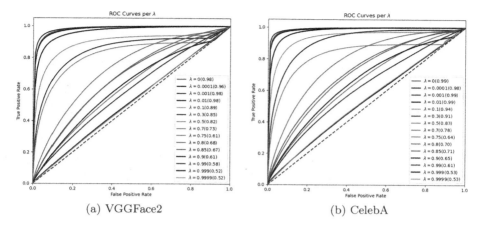

(a) VGGFace2                                    (b) CelebA

**Fig. 2.** Verification scenario results - receiver operating characteristics (ROC) curves per $\lambda$ value. ROC-AUC in parentheses.

# 5    Results

*Verification Performance:* we can clearly see in Fig. 2 and Table 1 that as $\lambda$ increases, it becomes increasingly difficult to use the embeddings produced by the corresponding CNN Backbone $F_\lambda$ for verification. $\lambda < 0.1$ has a near-negligible

**Table 1.** Verification Scenario Results. Embeddings generated from dataset $\mathcal{D}$'s *test* partition by appropriate $F_\lambda$.

| $\lambda$ | VGGFace2 | | | | CelebA | | | |
|---|---|---|---|---|---|---|---|---|
| | AUC | Accuracy | FAR | FRR | AUC | Accuracy | FAR | FRR |
| 0 | 0.982 | 0.936 | 0.064 | 0.064 | 0.990 | 0.955 | 0.045 | 0.045 |
| 0.0001 | 0.964 | 0.906 | 0.094 | 0.094 | 0.978 | 0.927 | 0.073 | 0.073 |
| 0.001 | 0.986 | 0.945 | 0.055 | 0.055 | 0.992 | 0.961 | 0.039 | 0.039 |
| 0.01 | 0.981 | 0.932 | 0.068 | 0.068 | 0.988 | 0.951 | 0.049 | 0.049 |
| 0.1 | 0.894 | 0.846 | 0.154 | 0.154 | 0.937 | 0.884 | 0.116 | 0.116 |
| 0.3 | 0.847 | 0.797 | 0.203 | 0.203 | 0.912 | 0.838 | 0.162 | 0.162 |
| 0.5 | 0.818 | 0.776 | 0.224 | 0.224 | 0.830 | 0.792 | 0.208 | 0.208 |
| 0.7 | 0.730 | 0.675 | 0.325 | 0.325 | 0.781 | 0.715 | 0.285 | 0.285 |
| 0.75 | 0.612 | 0.579 | 0.421 | 0.421 | 0.645 | 0.603 | 0.397 | 0.397 |
| 0.8 | 0.675 | 0.628 | 0.372 | 0.372 | 0.702 | 0.649 | 0.351 | 0.351 |
| 0.85 | 0.668 | 0.628 | 0.372 | 0.372 | 0.714 | 0.658 | 0.342 | 0.342 |
| 0.9 | 0.612 | 0.589 | 0.411 | 0.411 | 0.651 | 0.616 | 0.384 | 0.384 |
| 0.99 | 0.584 | 0.558 | 0.442 | 0.442 | 0.611 | 0.582 | 0.418 | 0.418 |
| 0.999 | 0.520 | 0.514 | 0.486 | 0.486 | 0.531 | 0.523 | 0.477 | 0.477 |
| 0.9999 | 0.516 | 0.510 | 0.490 | 0.490 | 0.534 | 0.526 | 0.474 | 0.474 |

effect whereas $\lambda > 0.9$ approaches near-random outputs. This matches our intuition given the adversarial nature of the multi-task learning (Sect. 3.1), and indicates that selecting an appropriate $\lambda$ depends on the characteristics of the task at hand. For example, if accurate verification is the top priority then $\lambda$ must be constrained appropriately, whereas if avoiding feature-abuse is paramount then a sacrifice in verification performance may be acceptable. Performance when evaluating on CelebA is slightly better ( 1–5% higher accuracy) across all values of $\lambda$. Considering CelebA is "wider" with many identities and fewer images each (19867 samples for 1000 identities in the test set) while VGGFace2 is "deeper" with fewer identities and more images per identity (169177 samples for 500 identities), this makes sense as we expect the intra-identity variation in VGGFace2 to be higher than in CelebA, making verification more difficult.

**Table 2.** 10-Identity Re-Identification Scenario. Gallery and Probe constructed from dataset $\mathcal{D}$'s *test* partition, with embeddings generated by appropriate $F_\lambda$.

| $\lambda$ | VGGFace2 | | | CelebA | | |
|---|---|---|---|---|---|---|
| | Rank 1 | Rank 3 | Rank 5 | Rank 1 | Rank 3 | Rank 5 |
| 0 | 0.937 | 0.997 | 0.999 | 0.846 | 0.979 | 1.000 |
| 0.0001 | 0.870 | 0.993 | 0.997 | 0.709 | 0.850 | 0.949 |
| 0.001 | 0.951 | 0.997 | 1.000 | 0.816 | 0.970 | 0.987 |
| 0.01 | 0.929 | 0.997 | 0.999 | 0.774 | 0.868 | 0.949 |
| 0.1 | 0.751 | 0.962 | 0.984 | 0.547 | 0.825 | 0.953 |
| 0.3 | 0.676 | 0.938 | 0.962 | 0.534 | 0.765 | 0.808 |
| 0.5 | 0.614 | 0.868 | 0.922 | 0.551 | 0.752 | 0.897 |
| 0.7 | 0.279 | 0.600 | 0.799 | 0.346 | 0.581 | 0.722 |
| 0.75 | 0.196 | 0.442 | 0.606 | 0.205 | 0.457 | 0.658 |
| 0.8 | 0.192 | 0.515 | 0.765 | 0.278 | 0.607 | 0.692 |
| 0.85 | 0.233 | 0.569 | 0.746 | 0.278 | 0.526 | 0.714 |
| 0.9 | 0.156 | 0.439 | 0.648 | 0.209 | 0.491 | 0.701 |
| 0.99 | 0.126 | 0.349 | 0.588 | 0.269 | 0.509 | 0.654 |
| 0.999 | 0.119 | 0.342 | 0.534 | 0.150 | 0.342 | 0.551 |
| 0.9999 | 0.127 | 0.323 | 0.514 | 0.167 | 0.376 | 0.577 |

*Re-identification Performance:* The 10-identity scenario in Table 2 shows that performance degrades quickly after $\lambda$ exceeds the equilibrium point of 0.5 and becomes almost random beyond 0.99, indicating that re-identification is more sensitive to our method than verification. That this is the case implies the least privilege learning is operating strongly on the local scale, as "neighbouring" identities in the embedding space begin to overlap significantly with sufficient values of $\lambda$.

**Table 3.** Attribute Extraction Attack Results. Full and Zero Knowledge Scenarios. Values are "Balanced Accuracy". 0.5 corresponds to perfect *obfuscation*. 2nd row indicates the evaluation dataset.

| $\lambda$ | Full knowledge | | Partial knowledge | | Zero knowledge | |
|---|---|---|---|---|---|---|
| | VGGFace2 | CelebA | VGGFace2 | CelebA | VGGFace2 | CelebA |
| 0 | 0.781 | 0.986 | 0.779 | 0.985 | 0.932 | 0.878 |
| 0.0001 | 0.786 | 0.985 | 0.786 | 0.984 | 0.978 | 0.977 |
| 0.001 | 0.779 | 0.985 | 0.783 | 0.985 | 0.958 | 0.969 |
| 0.01 | 0.782 | 0.983 | 0.785 | 0.983 | 0.920 | 0.934 |
| 0.1 | 0.785 | 0.973 | 0.789 | 0.972 | 0.932 | 0.891 |
| 0.3 | 0.756 | 0.948 | 0.725 | 0.881 | 0.903 | 0.729 |
| 0.5 | 0.742 | 0.931 | 0.721 | 0.907 | 0.889 | 0.912 |
| 0.7 | 0.695 | 0.866 | 0.662 | 0.809 | 0.815 | 0.825 |
| 0.75 | 0.503 | 0.513 | 0.445 | 0.501 | 0.511 | 0.554 |
| 0.8 | 0.609 | 0.701 | 0.592 | 0.669 | 0.539 | 0.525 |
| 0.85 | 0.613 | 0.753 | 0.607 | 0.738 | 0.579 | 0.545 |
| 0.9 | 0.498 | 0.500 | 0.444 | 0.500 | 0.574 | 0.546 |
| 0.99 | 0.497 | 0.500 | 0.444 | 0.500 | 0.516 | 0.528 |
| 0.999 | 0.497 | 0.500 | 0.448 | 0.504 | 0.529 | 0.506 |
| 0.9999 | 0.497 | 0.500 | 0.444 | 0.500 | 0.522 | 0.524 |

*Attribute Obfuscation (Full Knowledge):* The attribute discrimination performance of the AEMs $A_\lambda^V$ have no significant deterioration until $\lambda >= 0.3$, after which performance declines until the attributes are sufficiently obfuscated at $\lambda = 0.75$ and $\lambda >= 0.9$. See Table 3. This being the case when evaluating on both VGGFace2 and CelebA illustrates the cross-dataset viability of our method.

*Attribute Obfuscation (Partial Knowledge):* The performance of the AEMs $A_\lambda^C$ in this scenario aligns closely with the performance of the Full Knowledge AEMs $A_\lambda^V$, with obfuscation occurring at the same values: $\lambda = 0.75$ and $\lambda >= 0.9$. That the two scenarios give similar results indicate that $\lambda$ is the dominant factor, with the specific embeddings $x'_D$ the AEMs are trained with playing a lesser role in discrimination performance.

*Attribute Obfuscation (Zero Knowledge):* The results in Table 3 show that extracting a binary gender attribute from embeddings intended for facial verification can be quite straightforward, even under unsupervised approaches with little knowledge held by the attacker. Thus, segmenting an embedding space into two clusters can result in a balanced accuracy of over 95% when $\lambda$ is sufficiently small. The discriminative performance drops significantly when $\lambda > 0.5$, with the attribute being obfuscated at $\lambda >= 0.75$ so mitigating against this attack is slightly easier than the Full and Partial Knowledge scenarios, but is in no way trivial. Figure 3 visualises the results. We can see that at $\lambda = 0$ the embeddings are distinctly clustered by gender. At $\lambda = 0.7$, the clusters have begun to merge and the gender attribute has become more diffuse, before the total obfuscation shown at $\lambda = 0.9$.

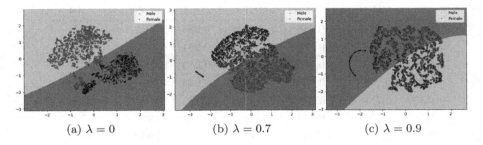

(a) $\lambda = 0$          (b) $\lambda = 0.7$          (c) $\lambda = 0.9$

**Fig. 3.** Visualisation of Zero Technical Knowledge attack results. Embeddings generated from VGGFace2's test set. Background colours indicate GMM Decision boundary for each cluster.

## 6    Conclusion

In this paper we propose a novel training paradigm to obfuscate protected attributes in verification and re-identification systems, enabling least privilege learning in the interest of stopping feature abuse. It achieves this by applying the KL-Divergence with Discrete Uniform Target Distribution loss to the protected attribute, in conjunction with a Two-Stage Adversarial Training procedure in a Multi-Task Learning scenario. In terms of obfuscating protected attributes, we succeed at reducing the amount of extractable latent information regarding the attribute in the resulting feature vectors to near zero, given sufficiently large values of $\lambda$. While the main learning task performance may suffer, an effective balance between verification/re-identification and attribute obfuscation is possible in the range of $\lambda \in [0.75, 0.9]$.

We have also proposed a comprehensive evaluation framework combining 2 different datasets and 3 application settings: verification, re-identification, and attribute prediction across multiple scenarios with various levels of attacker knowledge, that allows us to clearly measure the (often competing) performance requirements of a least privilege learning model. This could be used as a comprehensive testbench for future works.

As future work we will focus on maintaining the obfuscation performance of the proposed method, while minimising the sacrifice in identity discriminating power. Further, the application of least privilege learning would be most powerful if successfully applied to multiple attributes simultaneously.

# References

1. Alvi, M., Zisserman, A., Nellåker, C.: Turning a blind eye: explicit removal of biases and variation from deep neural network embeddings. In: Leal-Taixé, L., Roth, S. (eds.) ECCV 2018. LNCS, vol. 11129, pp. 556–572. Springer, Cham (2019). https://doi.org/10.1007/978-3-030-11009-3_34
2. Baudouin, J.Y., Tiberghien, G.: Gender is a dimension of face recognition. J. Exp. Psychol. Learn. Mem. Cogn. **28**(2), 362–365 (2002)
3. Brodersen, K.H., Ong, C.S., Stephan, K.E., Buhmann, J.M.: The balanced accuracy and its posterior distribution. In: 2010 20th International Conference on Pattern Recognition, pp. 3121–3124 (August 2010)
4. Cao, Q., Shen, L., Xie, W., Parkhi, O.M., Zisserman, A.: VGGFace2: a dataset for recognising faces across pose and age. arXiv:1710.08092 [cs] (May 2018)
5. Ganin, Y.: Domain-adversarial training of neural networks. In: Csurka, G. (ed.) Domain Adaptation in Computer Vision Applications. ACVPR, pp. 189–209. Springer, Cham (2017). https://doi.org/10.1007/978-3-319-58347-1_10
6. Georgopoulos, M., Oldfield, J., Nicolaou, M.A., Panagakis, Y., Pantic, M.: Mitigating demographic bias in facial datasets with style-based multi-attribute transfer. Int. J. Comput. Vis. **129**(7), 2288–2307 (2021). https://doi.org/10.1007/s11263-021-01448-w
7. Goodfellow, I., et al.: Generative adversarial nets. In: Ghahramani, Z., Welling, M., Cortes, C., Lawrence, N.D., Weinberger, K.Q. (eds.) Advances in Neural Information Processing Systems 27, pp. 2672–2680 (2014)
8. He, K., Zhang, X., Ren, S., Sun, J.: Deep residual learning for image recognition. In: 2016 IEEE Conference on Computer Vision and Pattern Recognition (CVPR), pp. 770–778 (June 2016)
9. Kingma, D.P., Ba, J.: Adam: a method for stochastic optimization. arXiv:1412.6980 [cs] (January 2017)
10. Liu, Z., Luo, P., Wang, X., Tang, X.: Deep learning face attributes in the wild. arXiv:1411.7766 [cs] (September 2015)
11. van der Maaten, L., Hinton, G.: Visualizing data using t-SNE. J. Mach. Learn. Res. **9**(86), 2579–2605 (2008)
12. Quadrianto, N., Sharmanska, V., Thomas, O.: Discovering fair representations in the data domain. In: 2019 IEEE/CVF Conference on Computer Vision and Pattern Recognition (CVPR), Long Beach, CA, USA, pp. 8219–8228 (June 2019)
13. Raff, E., Sylvester, J.: Gradient reversal against discrimination. arXiv:1807.00392 [cs, stat] (July 2018)
14. Schroff, F., Kalenichenko, D., Philbin, J.: FaceNet: a unified embedding for face recognition and clustering. In: 2015 IEEE Conference on Computer Vision and Pattern Recognition (CVPR), pp. 815–823 (June 2015)
15. Szegedy, C., et al.: Intriguing properties of neural networks. arXiv:1312.6199 [cs] (February 2014)
16. Terhörst, P., Fährmann, D., Kolf, J.N., Damer, N., Kirchbuchner, F., Kuijper, A.: MAAD-Face: a massively annotated attribute dataset for face images. arXiv:2012.01030 [cs] (December 2020)
17. Tzeng, E., Hoffman, J., Darrell, T., Saenko, K.: Simultaneous deep transfer across domains and tasks. In: 2015 IEEE International Conference on Computer Vision (ICCV), pp. 4068–4076 (December 2015)

18. Zhang, B.H., Lemoine, B., Mitchell, M.: Mitigating unwanted biases with adversarial learning. In: Proceedings of the 2018 AAAI/ACM Conference on AI, Ethics, and Society, AIES 2018, New York, NY, USA, pp. 335–340 (December 2018)
19. Zhang, K., Zhang, Z., Li, Z., Qiao, Y.: Joint face detection and alignment using multitask cascaded convolutional networks. IEEE Sig. Process. Lett. **23**(10), 1499–1503 (2016)

# Applications, Medical and Robotics

# Hierarchical Attentive Upsampling on Input Signals for Remote Heart Rate Estimation

Pengfei Zhang, Xiang Li, Jianjun Qian$^{(\boxtimes)}$, Zhong Jin, and Jian Yang

Key Lab of Intelligent Perception and Systems for High-Dimensional Information
of Ministry of Education, School of Computer Science and Engineering,
Nanjing University of Science and Technology, Nanjing, China
{zhangpengfei,xiang.li.implus,csjqian}@njust.edu.cn

**Abstract.** Heart Rate (HR) is one of the most important indicators reflecting the physiological state of the human body, and more researches have begun to focus on remote HR measurement in order to meet the challenging but practical non-contact requirements. Existing remote HR estimation methods rely on the high-resolution input signals constructed from low-resolution Spatial-Temporal Map (STMap) of facial sequences, but most of them use simple linear projection, which are difficult to capture the complex temporal and spatial relationships in between weak raw signals. To address this problem, we propose a Hierarchical Attentive Upsampling Module (HAUM) to obtain rich and discriminating input signals from STMap for accurate HR estimation. Our approach includes two parts: (1) a Hierarchical Upsampling Strategy (HUS) for progressively enriching the spatial-temporal information, and (2) an Attentive Space Module (ASM) to focus the model on more discriminating HR signal regions with clearer periodicity. The experiments performed on two public datasets VIPL-HR and MAHNOB-HCI show that the proposed approach achieves the state-of-the-art performance.

**Keywords:** Remote heart rate estimation · Spatial-Temporal map · Hierarchical attentive upsampling module

## 1 Introduction

Heart rate (HR) reflects the physiological information directly and is closely related to cardiovascular diseases [1,9]. The traditional HR measurement techniques are based on the Electrocardiography (ECG) and Photoplethysmography (PPG), which are generally applied to professional medical diagnosis, such as wearable devices. However, these contact measurements are poorly performed for daily monitoring, especially under long-term human-computer interaction (HCI) situations.

This work was supported by the National Science Fund of China under Grant Nos. 61876083.

Due to these realistic demands, one of the measurement techniques based on remote Photoplethysmography (rPPG) has been developed rapidly [2,16,24,34]. It has been proved that the measurement of HR can be realised by extracting subtle color variations of facial skin from a distance of several meters using cameras [30]. These researches aspire to get more accurate HR predicted results, in order to monitor the HR information at home and office by using abundant computing resources.

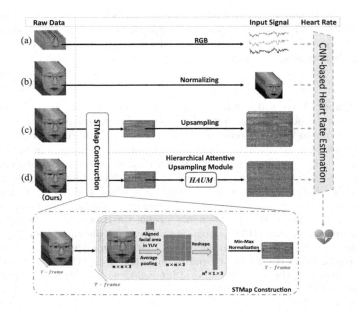

**Fig. 1.** Existing works ((a), (b), (c)) *vs.* our method (d) for obtaining discriminating high-resolution input signals. The construction of STMap is also illustrated in the dotted frame. (Color figure online)

Under the popular framework of Convolution Neural Network (CNN) [4,27], most existing works based on rPPG focus on how to construct high-quality or high-resolution input signals with more discriminating spatial and temporal information, as shown in the Fig. 1. Similarly with the traditional methods [16,24,30], [6] (Fig. 1(a)) records the pixel intensity averages of the Red, Green and Blue (RGB) channels over the face region as the input signals, which, however, is too simple to capture the critical information. More other works [2,29,34] (Fig. 1(b)) normalize the face sequences into smaller size, where the excessively dense sampling of the face image will bring more noises into the signal representation. Figure 1(c) [19] illustrates a more reasonable approach named Spatial-Temporal Map (STMap) to represent input signals. With the appropriate face region allocation, the STMap preserves color statistical information while suppressing irrelevant noises, which effectively avoid the drawbacks of the aforementioned approaches. As depicted in the bottom of the Fig. 1, the face video is compressed into STMap via space region division and time sequence concatenation. In addition, by means of linear color space transformation and average pooling of the face region, it also constructs color features with higher correlation between heart rhythm and pixel intensity.

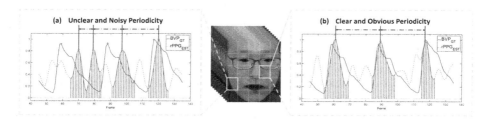

**Fig. 2.** Illustration of rPPG signal estimated from different face regions. Due to the uneven distribution of capillaries in skin regions, the contribution of each region to the rPPG estimation is not consistent. $\mathbf{BVP}_{GT}$: the Ground-truth Blood Volume Pulse. $\mathbf{rPPG}_{EST}$: the Estimated rPPG signal generated by [3].

However, the STMap-based method simply uses linear upsampling to construct the high-resolution input signal from the low-resolution STMap, making it difficult to extract the informative and complex spatial-temporal relationship. Moreover, as illustrated in Fig. 2, the rPPG signals estimated from various regions usually lack consistency due to the uneven distribution of micro-vessel density, leading to many ineffective areas with considerable noises. Therefore, the suppression of these noisy regions is very important for HR estimation considering the inconsistent contribution of each skin region.

To address these problems, we propose a Hierarchical Attentive Upsampling Module (HAUM) (see Fig. 1(d)), which consists of a Hierarchical Upsampling Strategy (HUS) and an Attentive Space Module (ASM), to obtain informative and discriminating high-resolution input signals. The Hierarchical Upsampling Strategy uses a multi-level approach to generate high-resolution input signal and extract complicated spatial-temporal information from the low-resolution STMap. The Attentive Space Module selects the regions with higher correlation with the target HR signals, aiming at reducing the influence of the noisy areas on the HR estimation.

In summary, our contributions include: (1) To the best of our knowledge, our work is the first to explore the discriminating features from the perspective of the original high-resolution input signal in an end-to-end fashion, greatly enhancing the low-resolution STMap. (2) We propose a novel Hierarchical Attentive Upsampling Module (HAUM), which can produce richer and discriminating input signal, especially highlight the regions with stronger heart rhythm signal. (3) Our method achieves state-of-the-art performance in most of the significant metrics on the public VIPL-HR dataset [19]. E.g., the mean absolute error between the estimated result and the ground-truth improves from 5.02 bpm to 4.67 bpm, which is 0.35 bpm superior than previous best record.

## 2   Related Work

**rPPG-Based Remote HR Estimation.** The rPPG-based remote HR estimation is founded on the fact that blood circulation causes periodic blood volume fluctuations in the micro-vascular tissue bed beneath the skin, which is induced by heartbeat, and then leads to the miniature variations in skin color. Although these subtle variations are not visible to the human eyes intuitively, they can be captured by the camera.

An early study proposed by Verkruysse [30] only used the green channel as the HR feature and analyzed its implicit physiological information. However, limited by its less-information, the methods after that usually used the average intensity of all facial skin pixels as the original features, such as Chrominance-based rPPG (CHROM) [3], Independent Component Analysis (ICA) [23], Plane-orthogonal-to-skin (POS) [31]. However, due to the difference in the density of facial capillaries, the signals in different facial regions may be distorted. There are also works [25,33] that only select a single face region, which may ignore the correlation between the regions. In recent years, a great deal of methods that use deep learning techniques to estimate HR are proposed, including [2]. These works use 2D CNN to extract spatial features from each frame of video, but do not take the relevance of temporal dimension into consideration. Another type of methods use 3D CNN to directly process the video sequences end-to-end [29,34]. They pay well attention to the features in temporal dimension, but these dense sampling approaches may easily introduce irrelevant noises caused by illumination and motion-induced artifacts.

**Representation of Input Signal.** How to represent HR signal is the most important component of the HR estimation. The earlier methods use the facial pixel intensity averages of the RGB channels as the input signals [23,24,30], and the green channel is widely used because of it featuring the strongest pulsatile signal [16,30]. However, the signal generated in this way is less informative and does not take the physiological differences of face regions into consideration. Later, [29,34] estimate rPPG signals from the video sequences, which are not robust enough since this intensive sampling method for direct processing of the face images is susceptible to complex scenarios, even if normalizing images to smaller size. [20] introduces a novel representation called STMap, which represents its physiological features by regional division with pixel intensity averaging and temporal concatenation with continuous video sequences. The methods mentioned above mainly focus on how to characterize the input signals, while our method pays more attention to make the input signals more discriminating.

**Selection of Space Region.** Theoretically, all skin areas exposed to light are employable to estimate HR. While, in practice, only the part of the face regions has a high correlation with physiological features such as HR. In the past few years, several works have discussed the influence of different face regions on the quality of rPPG signals [11,12,14]. Moreover, there are also works [2,17,22,34] proposed from the perspective of spatial dimension to improve the accuracy of HR estimation. [17] focuses on the super resolution of the original face image for recovering physiological information. While, [2, 34] rely on the skin segmentation implemented by attention mechanism to select region of interest (ROI). Similarly, [22] advocates a spatial attention mechanism to the feature extraction network of ResNet [4], where the attention weights concentrate on both temporal and spatial dimensions of high-level convolutional features. Different from the above approaches, in our method, the selection of the skin area is performed on the initial STMap, which greatly reduces the risks of introducing more spatial noises into the subsequent network.

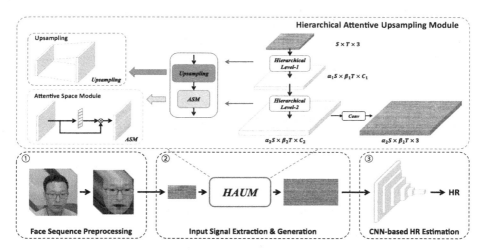

**Fig. 3.** The overview of our approach about rPPG-based remote heart rate estimation with Hierarchical Attentive Upsampling Module (HAUM).

## 3   Method

### 3.1   The Framework of HR Estimation

As depicted in Fig. 3, our approach is composed of three steps. The first step is the preprocessing of the video sequences. As described in [11, 14], the only useful information for HR estimation is heart-induced variation of skin color. Given the likely weakness of such signal compared with noises and artifacts, it is essential to select maximal pulsatile ROI. Consequently, we remove irrelevant pixels such as background, etc. based on facial landmarks.

Secondly, we generate initial low-resolution STMap, and then, apply the Hierarchical Attentive Upsampling Module (HAUM) to STMap on the purpose of constructing richer and discriminating input signals. The HAUM is made up of Hierarchical Upsampling Strategy (HUS) and Attentive Space Module (ASM) as illustrated in the top of Fig. 3. The details of HAUM will be explained in the following subsections.

In the third step, the popular framework of CNN is employed to estimate HR of each video sequence with the corresponding input signal, as commonly practiced in [6, 20].

## 3.2   Hierarchical Upsampling Strategy

With regards to the estimation HR from face video sequence, constructing effective representation of input signals is the majority component of the task. As mentioned in Sect. 2, previous HR measurement methods use too simple or excessively noisy statistics, which are not beneficial for HR estimation task since these input signals can not reflect the discriminating physiological information. Moreover, the situation becomes even worse with respect to the cases of varying illuminations and motions.

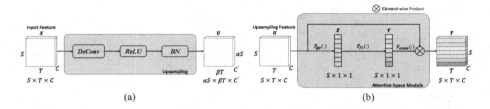

**Fig. 4.** (a)The Upsampling Layer. (b)The Attentive Space Module.

Compared with the previous work, the STMap proposed by Niu *et al.* [20] reasonably divides the skin region into an appropriate number of sub-regions, which can extract better statistical features of spatial-temporal signal. However, it applies the linear projection to the STMap for upsampling, which ignores the limitations of linear mapping in complex and varied scenarios.

**Non-linear Spatial-Temporal Upsampling.** For the sake of characterizing the more complex spatial-temporal data relationship of HR, and projecting the original color signal into a color space with stronger HR correlation, we use a non-linear spatial-temporal upsampling layer to construct the input feature. The upsampling layer is shown in Fig. 4(a). Specifically, for the input feature $\mathbf{X} \in \mathbb{R}^{S \times T \times C}$, where $S$, $T$, $C$ represent space, time and channel dimensions respectively, we expand its spatial and temporal dimensions via $\mathcal{F}_{up}(\cdot)$ and map it to the output feature $\mathbf{U} \in \mathbb{R}^{\alpha S \times \beta T \times C'}$:

$$\mathbf{U} = \mathcal{F}_{up}(\mathbf{X}) = \mathcal{B}\Big(\delta\big(DeConv(\mathbf{X})\big)\Big), \tag{1}$$

where $\mathcal{B}$ indicates the Batch Normalization [8], $\delta$ denotes the ReLU function [18], and $DeConv(\cdot)$ is a deconvolution layer with the $\times \alpha$ and $\times \beta$ expansion of space and time dimensions respectively. In addition, the channel dimension is changed from $C$ to $C'$ for the sake of diverse features. Although the non-linear spatial-temporal upsampling layer improves the discriminability of the input signal, the hierarchical upsampling representation can model complex spatial-temporal relationships more accurately.

**Hierarchical Upsampling.** Previous works [3,12,24] assume that the rPPG signal extracted from face can be treated as a linear combination of the RGB channel signals. However, its performance significantly degrades when in challenging conditions [5]. On the contrary, [21] proposes the physiological encoder to get physiological feature implemented by several convolution layers, which confirms the spatial-temporal complexity of physiological signal from the side. Considering the limitation to one single layer of non-linear upsampling, we adopt the Hierarchical Upsampling Strategy to enable the non-linear upsampling layer model higher correlated representation with remote HR signal. Specifically, we propose to construct the high-resolution input signals by progressively expanding the spatial and temporal dimensions of the low-resolution STMap, aiming at modelling the underlying complex spatial-temporal relationship.

As illustrated in Fig. 3, with respect to the low-resolution STMap, a hierarchical upsampling block (e.g., with two levels) is applied for obtaining the high-resolution input signals. Following the sequential upsampling modules, the dimension of the channel is restored back to 3 through a convolution layer.

### 3.3   Attentive Space Module

Due to physiological factors such as uneven distribution of micro-vessel density in facial skin tissues, as well as external environmental elements such as facial rigid motion and external light changes, the HR information reflected by different facial regions is not equally important.

As shown in Fig. 2, The rPPG signal generated from the left part (a) of the face is noisy and the periodicity is not significant. The skin in this area does not face the camera and the skin illumination changes may not be obvious. In contrast, the periodicity of the rPPG signal shows a more regular shape on the right region (b), thus it can potentially provide more accurate HR estimations.

Based on the above observations and inspired by recent attention modules [7,15], we propose an Attentive Space Module (ASM, see Fig. 4(b)) that aims to explicitly suppress the ineffective areas and leverage more information from the discriminating ones. Specifically, it consists of two parts: the Spatial Information *Aggregation* and *Selection.*

**Spatial Information Aggregation.**   As stated above, the purpose of our method is to select discriminating regions for HR estimation according to the distribution of physiological information in face. The basic idea is to integrate all the features of different spatial regions. Therefore, we first aggregate the global information of all features along different spatial regions by using the global average pooling $\mathcal{F}_{gp}(\cdot)$ over both time and channel dimensions. Specifically, the $s$-th element of $z \in \mathbb{R}^{S \times 1 \times 1}$ is calculated by shrinking $\mathbf{U} \in \mathbb{R}^{S \times T \times C}$ through dimensions $T \times C$:

$$z_s = \mathcal{F}_{gp}(u_s) = \frac{1}{T \times C} \sum_{i=1}^{T} \sum_{j=1}^{C} u_s(i,j). \tag{2}$$

**Spatial Information Selection.** By using the spatial information aggregated from different *time-channel* dimensions, we create a vector $v \in \mathbb{R}^{S \times 1}$ to selectively extract more remarkable features, which is achieved through two fully connected layers $\mathcal{F}_{fc}(\cdot)$. Thus, it can be written as:

$$v_s = \mathcal{F}_{fc}(z, W) = \sigma\big(W_2 \delta(W_1 z)\big). \tag{3}$$

Here, $\sigma$ denotes sigmoid activation, $\delta$ refers to ReLU function [18] and $W_1 \in \mathbb{R}^{\frac{s}{\gamma} \times s}$, $W_2 \in \mathbb{R}^{s \times \frac{s}{\gamma}}$. We also use a reduction ratio $\gamma$ to limit the complexity of the model and facilitate information interaction between features. Then, the vector $v$ is dimensionally expanded and calculated with $U$ via $\mathcal{F}_{scale}(\cdot)$, which denotes space-wise multiplication:

$$Y = \mathcal{F}_{scale}(v_s, u_s) = v_s \cdot u_s, \tag{4}$$

finally, we get the output feature $Y \in \mathbb{R}^{S \times T \times C}$ with the suppression of the noisy region and the prominent of the effective region.

**Discussion.** Although related, our ASM differs from the popular SE block [7] in both the *attentive targets and aggregated information*. While SE utilizes pure global spatial information to calibrate features in a channel-wise manner, our ASM makes use of both temporal and channel feature maps to selectively suppress or enhance signals from various regions, as illustrated in Fig. 6.

### 3.4 Implementation Details

Our HR estimation framework is based on the method of RhythmNet [20], but because the source code of RhythmNet is not publicly available, some details may be biased. Therefore, in this section, we mainly introduce some implementation details of STMap generation and subsequent deep convolutional networks.

**Facial Skin Segmentation.** First, we use SeetaFace[1] to detect the face region and get the facial landmarks of each frame, then perform median filtering on the sequence of each landmark to obtain stable and accurate face landmarks. After that, the face is aligned according to the eye center position of the landmarks, and the original image is cropped with the bounding box of $w \times 1.2\,h$, where $w$ is the horizontal distance between the left and right borders of the face contour, and $h$ is the vertical distance from the lower border to the mean value of the eyebrow landmarks. Finally, the skin area is segmented. For simplicity, we directly use landmarks to remove the pixels of irrelevant areas, such as background, eyes and mouth. Consequently, the rest area is highly correlated with HR information.

---

[1] https://github.com/seetaface/SeetaFaceEngine.

**Spatial-Temporal Map Generation.** After getting the the image with aligned face and segmented skin, we first convert the RGB color space of each frame to YUV color space, and then divide it into $S$ sub-regions. Next, we calculate the average value of the $C$ channel pixels of each sub-region, where only the pixels of skin are considered. By concatenating the features of the $T$-frame images, we can get an initial time series signal. After that, the min-max normalization is applied to the $S$-dimensional time series of the $C$ channels with scaling the value into $[0, 255]$, which can reduce the influence of inconsistent environmental illumination and amplify the weak signal to some extent. Finally, the STMap is constructed with a size of $S \times T \times C$.

**CNN-Based HR Estimation Network.** The backbone network we used is ResNet-18 [4]. Following [22], the CBAM [32] module is integrated into building blocks of ResNet-18. The final HR estimation is obtained by the last fully connected layer. For each long face video, we use a sliding window with a fixed number $T$ of frames to prepare a series of samples. During the training phase, each sample corresponds to a ground-truth HR. Whilst in the test phase, we average the estimated HR of all the samples from the same long video as the final predicted HR of the video. $L_1$ loss is used for measuring the gap between the estimated HR and the ground-truth one.

## 4   Experiment

### 4.1   Experiment Setup

**Databases.** Two popular public databases are adopted to verify the effectiveness of our method. Among them, VIPL-HR [19] is a large database for remote HR estimation. The database contains 9 scenarios of face videos for 107 subjects recorded by 3 different devices. The other database is MAHNOB-HCI [28], which contains 527 facial videos from 27 subjects. Following [20], we downsample the videos from 61 fps to 30.5 fps for efficiency. Moreover, the heart rate signal is measured by an ECG sensor. Following [16,34], we use the EXG2 channel[2] signal to generate the corresponding HR value. Specifically, we use $qrs\_detector$ function from the MNE package[3] to clean-up and calculate the HR based on the ECG sensor information provided. By referring to the previous work [2,34], we use only a 30-second (frames 306 to 2135) clip of each video in our experiments.

**Training Details.** For VIPL-HR and MAHNOB-HCI database, we use a sliding window of $T = 300$ frames, the interval of the sliding window being 0.5s, the number of face region division being $S = 25$. The estimated HR is obtained according to its frame rate. The data augmentation method uses the strategy proposed in [22] as well as the random mask strategy to simulate the situation of missing face detection. Random horizontal flip and random crop are also applied to the input signals before fed into the network. Our method is implemented

---

[2] The position of ECG sensor is upper left corner of chest and under clavicle bone.
[3] https://github.com/mne-tools/mne-python.

using the PyTorch[4] framework, where the training uses the Adam [10] optimizer with the initial learning rate of 0.001, the batch size of 64, the maximum epoch number of VIPL-HR database being 50, and MAHNOB-HCI being 100.

**Performance Metrics.** There are a variety of different data evaluation metrics used to validate the performance of HR estimation approaches [16,20]. Among them, we use six widely used metrics: the mean (Mean) and standard deviation (Std) of the error, the mean absolute error (MAE), the root mean squared HR error (RMSE), the mean of error rate percentage (MER), and Pearson's correlation coefficients $r$.

## 4.2   Ablation Study

In this section, we conduct several ablation experiments to get a better understanding of the proposed HAUM. All experiments are performed on the VIPL-HR database.

**Effectiveness of Attentive Space Module.** We examine the significance of using Attentive Space Module (ASM) under two-hierarchical-level setting. As illustrated in the Table 1, the usage of ASM leads to a clear performance improvement in every evaluation metric.

**Table 1.** The effect of ASM for HR estimation. "H-Level" denotes the total Hierarchical Levels applied in HAUM block.

| ASM | H-Level | MAE (bpm) | RMSE (bpm) | MER | $r$ |
|-----|---------|-----------|------------|-------|------|
| ✓ | 1 | 4.81 | 7.41 | 5.98% | 0.81 |
|   | 1 | 4.73 | 7.25 | 5.88% | 0.82 |
| ✓ | 2 | 4.77 | 7.33 | 5.90% | 0.81 |
|   | 2 | 4.67 | 7.10 | 5.84% | 0.82 |

**Table 2.** The HR estimation results by different reduction ratio $\gamma$ of ASM on the VIPL-HR database.

| Ratio $\gamma$ | MAE (bpm) | RMSE (bpm) | MER | $r$ |
|------|-----------|------------|-------|------|
| 2 | 5.03 | 7.89 | 6.28% | 0.78 |
| 4 | 4.89 | 7.62 | 6.12% | 0.79 |
| 8 | 4.88 | 7.43 | 6.04% | 0.81 |
| 16 | 4.67 | 7.10 | 5.84% | 0.82 |
| 32 | 4.85 | 7.51 | 6.06% | 0.80 |

---

[4] https://pytorch.org/.

**Settings for Attentive Space Module.** From Eq. (3), the reduction ratio $\gamma$ can potentially adjust the complexity of the module as it controls the hidden dimension of ASM. It would be reasonable to see how it affects the overall performance. Till this end, we conduct experiments with various reduction ratios, as shown in Table 2. It is observed that $\gamma = 16$ achieves best performance, therefore, due to its effectiveness, we apply the ASM in subsequent experiments.

**Settings for Hierarchical Upsampling Strategy.** In order to verify the effectiveness of the Hierarchical Upsampling Strategy (HUS), we study the effect of hierarchical levels by fixing the size of the output signal as $300 \times 600 \times 3$. It can be seen from Table 3 that the two-level is the best for HR estimation task.

### 4.3 Comparison with State-of-the-Arts

In this section, we compare our method with a variety of state-of-the-art approaches on two public datasets VIPL-HR [19] and MAHNOB-HCI [28]. For the sake of fairness, we use a five-fold subject-exclusive evaluation protocol to train the VIPL-HR database, and use the same train/test split as mentioned in [19]. The results of other methods are directly borrowed from [20]. All experimental results of the VIPL-HR database are shown in Table 4. Similarly, for the MAHNOB-HCI database, following [20,34], we use a three-fold subject-independent cross-validation protocol. The experimental results of this database are shown in Table 5. It can be seen from Table 4 that our method achieves superior results over most of the significant metrics. It reflects that the enhancement of input signals is very crucial for HR estimation task, whilst most existing works fail to pay much attention on it. By introducing the proposed HAUM for boosted input signals, we obtain the new state-of-the-art performance on the VIPL-HR database, reaching a lower $MAE$ of 4.67 and increasing the correlation $r$ from 0.79 to 0.82. Table 5 shows that our method can generalize to other database, with a consistent improvement over most evaluation metrics, compared with the previous state-of-the-art methods.

**Table 3.** The HR estimation results w.r.t. different number of the Hierarchical Levels (H-Level) on the VIPL-HR database.

| H-Level | MAE (bpm) | RMSE (bpm) | MER | $r$ |
|---------|-----------|------------|-------|------|
| 0 | 4.84 | 7.41 | 6.02% | 0.81 |
| 1 | 4.73 | 7.25 | 5.88% | 0.82 |
| 2 | 4.67 | 7.10 | 5.84% | 0.82 |
| 3 | 4.82 | 7.52 | 6.00% | 0.80 |

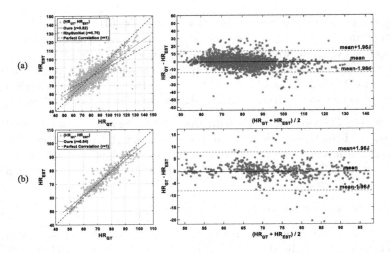

**Fig. 5.** The scatter plots and the Bland-Altman plot on the VIPL-HR (a) and MAHNOB-HCI (b) database. **HR**$_{GT}$: the Ground-truth HR. **HR**$_{EST}$: the Estimated HR by our method. The green dashed line in (a) is borrowed from the original paper [20]. The solid lines in the right plot represent the mean, and the dotted lines represent the 95% limits of agreement. (Color figure online)

### 4.4    Analysis

**HUS and ASM Improve Accuracy.** For the purpose of clearly illustrating the improvement of the data relevance of our method in HR estimation task, we draw scatter plots and the Bland-Altman plot on the VIPL-HR and MAHNOB-HCI database. The diagram is illustrated in Fig. 5. It can be observed that most of the estimated HRs are highly correlated with the ground-truth ones. Moreover, compared with RhythmNet, our method demonstrates a better linear correlation of data on the VIPL-HR database.

**Table 4.** Comparisons between state-of-the-art methods on VIPL-HR database. Best: bold; Second best: blue.

| Method | Mean (bpm) | Std (bpm) | MAE (bpm) | RMSE (bpm) | MER | $r$ |
|---|---|---|---|---|---|---|
| POS [31] | 7.87 | 15.3 | 11.5 | 17.2 | 18.5% | 0.30 |
| CHROM [3] | 7.63 | 15.1 | 11.4 | 16.9 | 17.8% | 0.28 |
| DeepPhy [2] | -2.60 | 13.6 | 11.0 | 13.8 | 13.6% | 0.11 |
| Niu2019 [22] | **−0.16** | 7.99 | 5.40 | 7.99 | 6.70% | 0.66 |
| RhythmNet [20] | 0.73 | 8.11 | 5.30 | 8.14 | 6.71% | 0.76 |
| CVD [21] | - | 7.92 | 5.02 | 7.97 | – | 0.79 |
| **ours** | 0.35 | **7.08** | **4.67** | **7.10** | **5.84%** | **0.82** |

**Table 5.** Comparisons between state-of-the-art methods on MAHNOB-HCI database. Best: **bold**; Second best: blue.

| Method | Mean (bpm) | Std (bpm) | MAE (bpm) | RMSE (bpm) | MER | $r$ |
|---|---|---|---|---|---|---|
| Poh2011 [23] | 2.04 | 13.5 | – | 13.6 | 13.2% | 0.36 |
| CHROM [3] | −2.89 | 13.67 | – | 10.7 | 12.9% | 0.82 |
| Li2014 [16] | −3.30 | 6.88 | – | 7.62 | 6.87% | 0.81 |
| rPPGNet [34] | – | 5.57 | 4.03 | 5.93 | – | 0.88 |
| RhythmNet [20] | 0.41 | 3.98 | – | 4.00 | 4.18% | 0.87 |
| Meta-rPPG [13] | – | 4.90 | 3.01 | – | – | 0.85 |
| Deep-HR [26] | 2.08 | **3.47** | – | **3.41** | **2.73%** | 0.92 |
| **ours** | **−0.14** | 3.96 | **2.68** | 3.98 | 3.70% | **0.94** |

**Visualization of ASM.** In order to prove the effectiveness of ASM, we visualize several face images. From the highlighted regions in the Fig. 6(a), we observe that the network tends to prefer larger skin areas when selecting effective face areas, regardless of the angle of the face. Furthermore, Fig. 6(b) also clearly shows the detailed rPPG signal estimated from different regions. We observe that the quality of rPPG signal is relatively consistent with the focus by ASM: the more periodic the signal area, the more attention the network tends to pay. Please note that in those regions containing background pixels (e.g., ②), only facial part is considered in our data-processing as mentioned in Sect. 3.4.

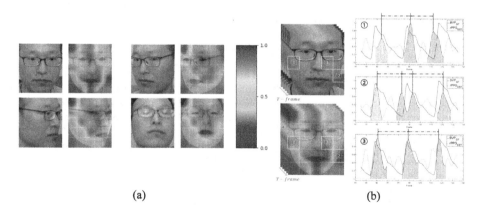

(a)                                                              (b)

**Fig. 6.** (a)Visualization of the discriminating face regions that the network focused on. (b)Illustration of rPPG estimated from different face regions.

## 5    Conclusion

In this paper, we propose a Hierarchical Attentive Upsampling Module (HAUM) for acquiring rich and discriminating input signals based on the Spatial-Temporal

Map for heart rate estimation. The Hierarchical Upsampling Strategy is used to progressively enrich the Spatial-Temporal information, and the Attentive Space Module is cascaded to select effective regions with clearer periodicity. The performances on two public datasets demonstrate the superiority of our approach.

# References

1. Brüser, C., Antink, C.H., Wartzek, T., Walter, M., Leonhardt, S.: Ambient and unobtrusive cardiorespiratory monitoring techniques. IEEE Rev. Biomed. Eng. **8**, 30–43 (2015)
2. Chen, W., McDuff, D.: DeepPhys: video-based physiological measurement using convolutional attention networks. In: Proceedings of IEEE ECCV, pp. 349–365 (2018)
3. De Haan, G., Jeanne, V.: Robust pulse rate from chrominance-based rPPG. IEEE Trans. Biomed. Eng. **60**(10), 2878–2886 (2013)
4. He, K., Zhang, X., Ren, S., Sun, J.: Deep residual learning for image recognition. In: Proceedings of IEEE CVPR, pp. 770–778 (2016)
5. Heusch, G., Anjos, A., Marcel, S.: A reproducible study on remote heart rate measurement. arXiv preprint arXiv:1709.00962 (2017)
6. Hsu, G.S., Ambikapathi, A., Chen, M.S.: Deep learning with time-frequency representation for pulse estimation from facial videos. In: 2017 IEEE International Joint Conference on Biometrics, pp. 383–389. IEEE (2017)
7. Hu, J., Shen, L., Sun, G.: Squeeze-and-excitation networks. In: Proceedings of IEEE CVPR, pp. 7132–7141 (2018)
8. Ioffe, S., Szegedy, C.: Batch normalization: accelerating deep network training by reducing internal covariate shift. arXiv preprint arXiv:1502.03167 (2015)
9. Jain, P.K., Tiwari, A.K.: Heart monitoring systems-a review. Comput. Biol. Med. **54**, 1–13 (2014)
10. Kingma, D.P., Ba, J.: Adam: a method for stochastic optimization. arXiv preprint arXiv:1412.6980 (2014)
11. Kwon, S., Kim, J., Lee, D., Park, K.: ROI analysis for remote photoplethysmography on facial video. In: 2015 37th Annual International Conference of the IEEE Engineering in Medicine and Biology Society, pp. 4938–4941. IEEE (2015)
12. Lam, A., Kuno, Y.: Robust heart rate measurement from video using select random patches. In: ICCV, pp. 3640–3648 (2015)
13. Lee, E., Chen, E., Lee, C.Y.: Meta-RPPG: remote heart rate estimation using a transductive meta-learner. In: Proceedings of IEEE ECCV (2020)
14. Lempe, G., Zaunseder, S., Wirthgen, T., Zipser, S., Malberg, H.: ROI selection for remote photoplethysmography. In: Meinzer, H.P., Deserno, T., Handels, H., Tolxdorff, T. (eds.) Bildverarbeitung für die Medizin 2013, pp. 99–103. Springer, Heidelberg (2013). https://doi.org/10.1007/978-3-642-36480-8_19
15. Li, X., Wang, W., Hu, X., Yang, J.: Selective kernel networks. In: Proceedings of IEEE CVPR, pp. 510–519 (2019)
16. Li, X., Chen, J., Zhao, G., Pietikainen, M.: Remote heart rate measurement from face videos under realistic situations. In: Proceedings of IEEE CVPR, pp. 4264–4271 (2014)
17. McDuff, D.: Deep super resolution for recovering physiological information from videos. In: CVPR Workshops, pp. 1367–1374 (2018)

18. Nair, V., Hinton, G.E.: Rectified linear units improve restricted Boltzmann machines. In: ICML (2010)
19. Niu, X., Han, H., Shan, S., Chen, X.: VIPL-HR: a multi-modal database for pulse estimation from less-constrained face video. In: Jawahar, C.V., Li, H., Mori, G., Schindler, K. (eds.) ACCV 2018. LNCS, vol. 11365, pp. 562–576. Springer, Cham (2019). https://doi.org/10.1007/978-3-030-20873-8_36
20. Niu, X., Shan, S., Han, H., Chen, X.: RhythmNet: end-to-end heart rate estimation from face via spatial-temporal representation. TIP **29**, 2409–2423 (2019)
21. Niu, X., Yu, Z., Han, H., Li, X., Shan, S., Zhao, G.: Video-based remote physiological measurement via cross-verified feature disentangling. In: Proceedings of IEEE ECCV (2020)
22. Niu, X., Zhao, X., Han, H., Das, A., Dantcheva, A., Shan, S., Chen, X.: Robust remote heart rate estimation from face utilizing spatial-temporal attention. In: 2019 14th IEEE International Conference on Automatic Face & Gesture Recognition, pp. 1–8. IEEE (2019)
23. Poh, M.Z., McDuff, D.J., Picard, R.W.: Advancements in noncontact, multiparameter physiological measurements using a webcam. IEEE Trans. Biomed. Eng. **58**(1), 7–11 (2010)
24. Poh, M.Z., McDuff, D.J., Picard, R.W.: Non-contact, automated cardiac pulse measurements using video imaging and blind source separation. Opt. Exp. **18**(10), 10762–10774 (2010)
25. Qiu, Y., Liu, Y., Arteaga-Falconi, J., Dong, H., El Saddik, A.: EVM-CNN: real-time contactless heart rate estimation from facial video. IEEE Trans. Multimed. **21**(7), 1778–1787 (2018)
26. Sabokrou, M., Pourreza, M., Li, X., Fathy, M., Zhao, G.: Deep-HR: fast heart rate estimation from face video under realistic conditions. arXiv preprint arXiv:2002.04821 (2020)
27. Simonyan, K., Zisserman, A.: Very deep convolutional networks for large-scale image recognition. arXiv preprint arXiv:1409.1556 (2014)
28. Soleymani, M., Lichtenauer, J., Pun, T., Pantic, M.: A multimodal database for affect recognition and implicit tagging. IEEE Trans. Affect. Comput. **3**(1), 42–55 (2011)
29. Tsou, Y.Y., Lee, Y.A., Hsu, C.T., Chang, S.H.: Siamese-rPPG network: remote photoplethysmography signal estimation from face videos. In: Proceedings of the 35th Annual ACM Symposium on Applied Computing, pp. 2066–2073 (2020)
30. Verkruysse, W., Svaasand, L.O., Nelson, J.S.: Remote plethysmographic imaging using ambient light. Opt. Express **16**(26), 21434–21445 (2008)
31. Wang, W., den Brinker, A.C., Stuijk, S., de Haan, G.: Algorithmic principles of remote PPG. IEEE Trans. Biomed. Eng. **64**(7), 1479–1491 (2016)
32. Woo, S., Park, J., Lee, J.Y., So Kweon, I.: CBAM: convolutional block attention module. In: Proceedings of IEEE ECCV, pp. 3–19 (2018)
33. Yan, Y., Ma, X., Yao, L., Ouyang, J.: Noncontact measurement of heart rate using facial video illuminated under natural light and signal weighted analysis. Bio-Med. Mater. Eng. **26**(s1), S903–S909 (2015)
34. Yu, Z., Peng, W., Li, X., Hong, X., Zhao, G.: Remote heart rate measurement from highly compressed facial videos: an end-to-end deep learning solution with video enhancement. In: ICCV, pp. 151–160 (2019)

# CASIA-onDo: A New Database for Online Handwritten Document Analysis

Yu-Ting Yang[1,2]([✉]) [ID], Yan-Ming Zhang[1] [ID], Xiao-Long Yun[1,2] [ID], Fei Yin[1] [ID], and Cheng-Lin Liu[1,2] [ID]

[1] National Laboratory of Pattern Recognition, Institute of Automation of Chinese Academy of Sciences, Beijing 100190, People's Republic of China
{yuting.yang,ymzhang,xiaolong.yun,fyin,liucl}@nlpr.ia.ac.cn
[2] School of Artificial Intelligence, University of Chinese Academy of Sciences, Beijing 100049, People's Republic of China

**Abstract.** In this paper we introduce an online handwritten document database (CASIA-onDo), serving as a standard database for the development and evaluation of methods in the field of online handwritten document layout analysis. It consists of 2,012 documents including a total of 841,159 online strokes. The database, covering Chinese and English languages, was produced by 200 writers. Six types of contents occur in the documents, namely text, formulas, diagrams, tables, figures, and lists. The distribution of different types is close to the actual situation. Benefiting from detailed annotations, CASIA-onDo can support different tasks of layout analysis under online or offline settings. Firstly, based on the semantic level annotation, it can be used for many classification tasks such as text/non-text classification, table/non-table classification, multi-class stroke classification and so on. Secondly, based on the instance level annotation, it can be used for segmentation tasks such as text line separation and formula segmentation. Thirdly, based on the various writing styles, it can be used for handwriting recognition and writer clustering tasks. In addition, we perform preliminary experiments to provide a benchmark on this database with a state-of-the-art method. More techniques can be evaluated on this challenging database in the future.

**Keywords:** Online handwritten document · Document layout analysis · Stroke classification · Database

## 1 Introduction

Nowadays, pen-based and touch-based interfaces are widely used, producing a large number of handwritten documents with mixed objects. Automatic understanding of online freehand documents, aiming to convert handwritten inputs into digital formats, has been an active and challenging research field. There are a great many difficult tasks in the process of document analysis. Firstly, different types of contents need to be separated by stroke classification. Secondly, different objects have to be extracted by instance segmentation. Thirdly, these

C. Wallraven et al. (Eds.): ACPR 2021, LNCS 13189, pp. 174–188, 2022.
https://doi.org/10.1007/978-3-031-02444-3_13

different instances can be fed to specialized recognition engines, including those for text lines, diagrams, formulas, and tables. The first two tasks are referred as document layout analysis and are the key for an automatic document processing system.

A standard database of online handwritten documents is important to facilitate research in the field. It should be well-constructed and large enough to provide reliable evaluation metrics for different tasks. Previously released online handwriting databases include text databases (UNIPEN [1], IRONOFF [2], IAMonDB [3], HANDS-Kondate [4], SCUT-COUCH [5] and CASIA-OLHWDB [6]), diagram databases (FC_A [7], FC_B [8], FC [9] and CASIA-OHFC [10]), math expression databases (CROHME [11–13]). Since these databases were designed for specific recognition tasks, they typically contain data of one type and thus cannot be used for document layout analysis. The only databases that cover entire document objects are Kondate [14] and IAMonDo [15]. However, Kondate and IAMonDo databases only have small number of documents and simple layout structures, and are also limited in content types and language types. Therefore, it is essential to have a more comprehensive database to foster the research of document layout analysis.

In this paper, we release the CASIA-onDo database, which is the largest online handwritten multi-contents document database so far, with detailed annotation information and complex structure. All this data will be freely public to the academic community and released with this paper.[1] The database consists of 2012 documents containing handwritten text, figures, diagrams, formulas, tables and lists arranged in an unconstrained way. The database is designed primarily for the development of algorithms for document layout analysis. Semantic level and instance level annotations are provided. With semantic level annotations, the database can be applied to semantic segmentation tasks such as multi-class stroke classification, text/non-text classification and table/non-table classification. With instance level annotations, it is suitable for instance segmentation tasks such as text line separation and formula segmentation. It is potentially useful for text recognition, formula recognition, table analysis and diagram recognition by adding corresponding annotations in the future. We also perform multiple semantic segmentation experiments on the new database based on EGAT [22] model, and provide initial experimental results as a baseline.

The rest of this paper is organized as follows. Section 2 reviews related works on handwritten document databases and methods on layout analysis research. Section 3 elaborates the design of the CASIA-onDo database. Section 4 presents the statistics and usage of the database. Section 5 presents our experimental results with a novel automatic stroke feature extraction method. Section 6 draws conclusions.

---

[1] http://www.nlpr.ia.ac.cn/databases/CASIA-onDo/index.html.

## 2   Related Work

This part mainly discusses databases and approaches for online handwritten document layout analysis, and so we summarize the related works from these two aspects.

Most previous databases of online handwriting focused on handwritten text only, such as UNIPEN [1], IRONOFF [2], CASIA-OLHWDB [6] and IAMonDB [3]. Databases containing different content types are Kondate [14] and IAMonDo [15]. IAMonDo is a collection of handwritten English online documents. It consists of 1000 documents, mixing text, diagrams, formulas, tables, figures and lists. Kondate is made up of 669 freehand Japanese online documents and contains text, formula, figure, ruled line and editing mask. Up to now, there is no database that contains Chinese documents. What'more, the layout and the contents in these databases are simple, for example, there is no in-line formulas and complex tables.

Tasks in document analysis are traditionally modeled as structured prediction problems, which can be divided into three mainstream branches: conditional random fields (CRF) [16,17], recurrent neural networks (RNN) [18,19], and graph neural networks (GNN) [21–23]. Among them, GNN is most powerful in modeling complex structure. Ye *et al.* [21,22] formulated stroke classification problem as node classification problem in the relational graph. For multi-class classification, EGAT [22] achieves 95.81% on IAMonDo database. Further, the promoted network [23] performed node clustering and node classification jointly to solve the text line grouping and stroke classification problem.

## 3   Database Design

### 3.1   Types of Contents

We suppose that the online handwritten documents are mainly created in the context of note taking in the class. Six different content types are considered when producing this database. Details can be seen from the following list:

**Text Block:** Text blocks are paragraphs or text lines composed of Chinese or English characters. Note that text placed in diagrams, lists and tables does NOT fall into this category.

**Formula:** Formulas are math expressions composed of numbers, variables, operators and functions. Formula may have 2-dimensional structures such as subscripts or superscripts, and can appear in text lines, in lists or in diagrams and can be on a single line or multiple lines.

**Diagram:** Diagrams are flowcharts composed of symbols, connecting lines and text. They are commonly used in documents to represent algorithms and workflows.

**Table:** Table consists of table lines and content in the table units. They can be regular or complex. Regular tables have aligned table lines, while complex tables may have invisible table lines or unaligned structures.

**List:** Lists are featured by a sign at the beginning of each term, for example numbers, letters, asterisk, etc. Items in a list can be placed horizontally or vertically.

**Figure:** Figures include objects such as circuit diagrams in Physics, line charts in mathematics, freehand sketches, etc.

## 3.2 Templates of Contents

To control the distribution of different types of contents, we make templates for contributors to copy.

Plenty of text paragraphs, lists, formulas, figures, tables and diagrams are collected from the Internet, and then mixed together to form templates. We made a total of 1000 templates.

Considering the real situation of notes in science and engineering, we insert a large number of formulas and tables into the templates. The figures are mainly obtained from the graphs that commonly appear in mathematics and physics, such as circuit diagrams and line charts. The list is used to simulate the options in multiple-choice questions.

When generating the templates, some criteria must be applied to guarantee the desired distribution, which are summarized as follow:

**Standardization.** The distribution of content types in the templates should meet with the reality as much as possible.

**Diversity.** The template should cover both Chinese and English and have different layouts. Each type should have various representations and scales.

**Complexity.** This is mainly reflected in the diverse layout, inline formula and tables without ruling.

More specifically, the quantitative rules which are applied during generation of one template are listed below:

- A template contains at least 3 content types.
- In all texts, the ratio of Chinese to English is 8:2.
- With equal probability, either a random table, or a random figure or a random list is added.
- With equal probability, the table is without ruling, with just horizontal ruling, or with a fully ruled grid.
- The list contains 2–7 items.
- All contents can be in random direction.

## 3.3 Data Acquisition

In order to cover diverse writing styles as far as possible, we asked 200 writers to copy the documents. Generally, each individual template was copied by 2 different writers, and each writer drew 10 different documents. While 12 sheets were copied by three writers, so there are 2012 documents in total. We compare the statistic of CASIA-onDo with aforementioned document databases in Table 1.

**Table 1.** Online handwritten document databases overview.

| Database | Classes | Partition | Writers | Templates | Documents | Strokes |
|----------|---------|-----------|---------|-----------|-----------|---------|
| Kondate [14] | 3 | Train | 67 | – | 210 | 41190 |
| | | Valid | | – | 100 | 18525 |
| | | Test | | – | 359 | 71846 |
| IAMonDo [15] | 5 | Train | 200 | 400 | 400 | 141421 |
| | | Valid | | 200 | 200 | 68725 |
| | | Test | | 212 | 212 | 70927 |
| CASIA-onDo | 6 | Train | 200 | 700 | 1400 | 588884 |
| | | Valid | | 100 | 200 | 81693 |
| | | Test | | 200 | 412 | 170582 |

We used Huawei tablets with stylus to collect the documents. It is accurate and can deliver time and pressure information besides the coordinates of the digital ink. Every stroke corresponds to a sequence of 5-dimensional points which contain the information of (x, y) coordinates, time, pressure and the state of pen tip.

In the instructions, the writers are allowed to rearrange the content and keep their own sketchy styles. There are no further constraints and supervision on how to create documents on them. This is done with the purpose of reflecting the workflow in a realistic context. Figure 1 shows how different writers copied the content of a template to the document.

### 3.4   Annotation

We provide two levels of annotations for each stroke: the semantic class and instance ID of its associate symbol. The contents of texts and formulas have not been provided.

For semantic annotation, we provide 11 semantic labels in total rather than 6 labels listed in Sect. 3.1, so as to facilitate multiple usage of the dataset. In particular, the formula class is divided into four subclasses: in-line formula, inter-line formula, in-list formula and in-diagram formula. The diagram class is divided into symbol within diagram, text within diagram, and formula within diagram. The table class is divided into table line and text within the table.

In annotating formulas, isolated numbers or variables (such as $8, a$) are not marked as formulas, while math expressions with 2-dim layout (such as $8^2, a_2$) and special mathematical symbols (such as $\pi, \sum, \infty$) are marked as formulas regardless of their length. In annotating lists, as long as there is a symbol in front of each item, regardless of the length and number, it is marked as a list. For easy viewing, each annotation is given a symbol as shown in Table 2. The colored annotation of document is shown in Fig. 2.

For instance level annotation, each text line is treated as an instance with a unique ID. For the remaining five categories, different entities have different IDs.

We choose the InkML (*Ink Markup Language*) [20] language to store the documents, which can represent information flexibly. This is mainly achieved

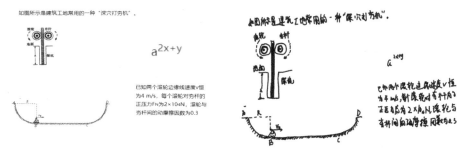

（a）A template given to writer A, and the document created by the writer.

（b）A template given to writer B, and the document created by the writer.

**Fig. 1.** Templates and corresponding handwritten documents.

**Table 2.** Annotations and corresponding symbols.

| Annotation | Symbol | Annotation | Symbol |
|---|---|---|---|
| TEXT | A | LINEOUT_MATH_EXPRESSION | G |
| LIST | B | LINEIN_MATH_EXPRESSION | H |
| LISTIN_MATH_EXPRESSION | C | TABLE | I |
| DIAGRAM | D | TABLEIN_TEXT | J |
| DIAGRAMIN_TEXT | E | FIGURE | K |
| DIAGRAMIN_MATH_EXPRESSION | F | | |

through two elements. The first one is the **trace** element. This XML tag represents a stroke $s$. It contains a stroke ID and a sequence of trajectory points with a variable-length $m$.

$$s = \{[x_1, y_1, p_1, s_1, t_1], [x_2, y_2, p_2, s_2, t_2], \cdots, [x_m, y_m, p_m, s_m, t_m]\}, \quad (1)$$

where $x_i$ and $y_i$ mean xy-coordinates, $p_i$ is the pressure on the pen tip, $s_i$ indicates the pen state (down or up) of the $i$-th point and $t_i$ is time. The second one is the **traceGroup** element, which records a collection of strokes belonging to the same category. The label exists in its child element **annotationXML** in the format of "label_id", where "label" represents which content type the group of strokes belong to, and "id" is used to distinguish different instances.

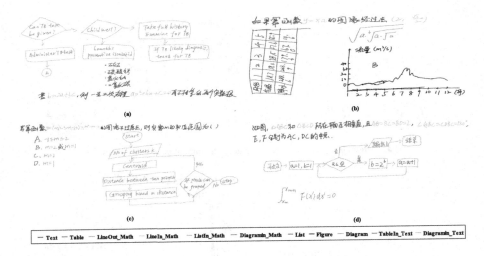

**Fig. 2.** Visualization of colored annotation.

# 4    Recommendations of Usage

The CASIA-onDo database has some favorable merits: (1) It records rich online information; (2) It involves various content types; (3) It has both semantic and instance level annotations; (4) The documents are stored writer by writer.

For using the database for research, we recommend standard partitioning into training, validation and test sets, and propose some research scenarios.

## 4.1    Data Structure and Statistics

The documents are randomly divided into three disjoint subsets–a training set, a validation set and a test set at the ratio of 7:1:2. Therefore, there are 1400/200/412 documents in the training/validation/test set, respectively. The statistics details of the CASIA-onDo dataset are shown in Table 3.

The database consists of 2,012 documents with 841159 individual online strokes. The entire database contains 5046 text lines, 1180 tables, 1254 lists, 745 diagrams, 1328 figures and 7406 formulas.

## 4.2    Research Scenarios

Based on the CASIA-onDo database, some typical research tasks of handwritten document analysis can be performed. Our recommendations are as follows.

1) *Stroke classification*: Our database is made up of a large number of strokes, grouped into six categories. For different levels of classification, user can use the annotations from Table 2 to generate appropriate labels neatly. The corresponding relationship between annotations and labels is shown in Table 4.

**Table 3.** Statistics of strokes and instances in the CASIA-onDo database.

| | Train | | Valid | | Test | |
|---|---|---|---|---|---|---|
| | Strokes | Instances | Strokes | Instances | Strokes | Instances |
| Text | 200924 | 3501 | 29452 | 531 | 56844 | 1014 |
| Formula | 58787 | 5154 | 7729 | 735 | 17677 | 1517 |
| Diagram | 66944 | 497 | 11672 | 88 | 22794 | 160 |
| Table | 144876 | 837 | 18049 | 113 | 38376 | 230 |
| Figure | 38518 | 937 | 4881 | 121 | 11397 | 270 |
| List | 78835 | 879 | 9910 | 116 | 23494 | 259 |
| Total | 588884 | 11805 | 81693 | 1704 | 170582 | 3450 |

2) *Text separation and formula segmentation*: Our database contains 5046 text lines and 7406 formulas in total. What's more, all the instances are separated in the ground-truth. It is convenient for training and evaluating text line segmentation and formula segmentation algorithms.

3) *Writer identification*: In our database, all the documents are stored in writer-specific files and each writer has 10 handwritten pages. We can perform experiments to judge whether two documents are from the same writer or not (writer verification) or classify a page to a nearest reference page of known writer (writer identification).

**Table 4.** Annotations according to different levels of classification.

| Task | Label | | | | | | | | | | |
|---|---|---|---|---|---|---|---|---|---|---|---|
| | Symbol | | | | | | | | | | |
| | A | B | C | D | E | F | G | H | I | J | K |
| Text/non-text | 1 | 1 | 0 | 0 | 1 | 0 | 0 | 0 | 0 | 1 | 0 |
| Table/non-table | 0 | 0 | 0 | 0 | 0 | 0 | 0 | 0 | 1 | 1 | 0 |
| Diagram/non-diagram | 0 | 0 | 0 | 1 | 1 | 1 | 0 | 0 | 0 | 0 | 0 |
| Formula/non-formula | 0 | 0 | 1 | 0 | 0 | 1 | 1 | 1 | 0 | 0 | 0 |
| List/non-list | 0 | 1 | 1 | 0 | 0 | 0 | 0 | 0 | 0 | 0 | 0 |
| Multi-class | 0 | 1 | 3 | 2 | 2 | 3 | 3 | 3 | 4 | 4 | 5 |

# 5    Experimental Evaluation

To validate the functionalities of our newly created CASIA-onDo database, we systematically evaluate a state-of-the-art method EGAT [22] based on both hand-crafted features and automatic features as baselines on different tasks from Table 4. Furthermore, we introduce a novel automatic stroke feature extraction method, which will be described in detail.

## 5.1   Stroke Classification Framework

EGAT [22] is a method that models the stroke classification problem as node classification in a document graph based on graph attention networks. It contains the following three modules:

**Graph Construction.** EGAT formalizes a document into a relational graph, in which nodes represent strokes and edges represent interaction between strokes. There are two kinds of contextual information in the graph, namely spatial context and temporal context. Spatially adjacent strokes are more likely to have the same labels. Intuitively, the spatial neighbors are found by selecting the nearest $k_s$ strokes in the document by $k$ nearest search. Temporal adjacent strokes captures the sequence of writing. Temporal neighbors are defined as the strokes whose temporal distance is less than $k_t$ from the current stroke. Here, both $k_s$ and $k_t$ are hyperparameters.

**Feature Extraction.** In the original EGAT, 13 contour-based shape features and 10 local context features are extracted from each stroke as node features, and 37 pairwise relation features are extracted from two connected nodes (strokes) as edge features. Since hand-crafted features may suffer from limited descriptive ability, in this work, we come up with an automatic stroke feature extraction method with three steps.

*Preprocessing.* Given a stroke in Eq. 1, to depict the direction of writing trajectory at each time step $i$, the original point $(x_i, y_i, s_i)$ is processed into a 9-dimensional vector by calculating the first- and second-order derivatives:

$$[x_i, y_i, \Delta x_i, \Delta y_i, \Delta' x_i, \Delta' y_i, s_i^1, s_i^2, s_i^3], \tag{2}$$

where $\Delta x_i = x_{i+1} - x_i$, $\Delta y_i = y_{i+1} - y_i$, $\Delta' x_i = x_{i+2} - x_i$, $\Delta' y_i = y_{i+2} - y_i$. The last three values $[s_i^1, s_i^2, s_i^3]$ is the one-hot encoding of the pen state $s_i$. $[1, 0, 0]$, $[0, 1, 0]$ and $[0, 0, 1]$ represent pen-down, ongoing and pen-up, respectively.

*Extracting Node Feature.* The stroke made up of encoded points is then input into a stroke feature extraction network based on LSTM. The architecture of the network is shown in Fig. 3. Multiple bi-directional LSTM layers are stacked and each layer has forward and backward units. The vectors from the last LSTM layer is passed through a max pooing layer and a fully connected layer.

*Extracting Edge Feature.* We design a method to capture the spatial relation between two strokes. The trajectories of two strokes are resampled to equal length adopting the equal interval interpolation method. Then the coordinates of sampling points between two strokes are subtracted as the original edge feature.

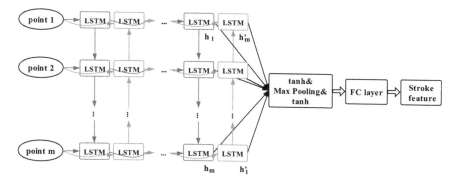

**Fig. 3.** Stacked BiLSTM for stroke feature extraction.

**Edge Graph Attention Network.** EGAT is a graph neural network which improves the classic graph attention network model [21] with a novel attention mechanism. Basically, EGAT consists of several stacked edge graph attention layers. A set of stroke and edge features and a set of edges are fed into the first layer. Then the representation of strokes is updated by exploiting temporal and spatial contextual information from the neighborhood by graph convolution with attention mechanisms. Please refer to the original paper [22] for more details.

## 5.2 Experimental Setup

In graph construction, $k_t$ and $k_s$ are both set to 8. For stroke feature extraction, the bi-directional LSTM consists of 3 layers. Each layer has 50 forward and 50 backward LSTM units, so the stroke feature is a 100-dimensional vector. Xavier Normalization is adopted to initialize the parameters. For edge feature extraction, the number of sampling points is 20, so the dimension of edge feature is 40. EGAT employs 3 stacked attention layers. The dimension in hidden layer is set to 32 and the dimension of the output features is equal to the number of categories. 8 attention heads are utilized for concatenation.

When using hand-crafted feature, we utilize Adam optimizer to train the model and batch size is set to 16. For the end-to-end model, the AdamW optimizer is chosen instead and batch size is 4. In both cases, the initial learning rate $\alpha$ is set to 0.001. The model is trained for at most 500 epochs, and early stopping is performed when validation loss does not decrease for ten consecutive epochs. We implement the method with the DGL library and its PyTorch backend. All experiments are conducted with a TITAN RTX GPU.

## 5.3   Evaluation Metrics

We evaluate EGAT on two-class classification and multi-class classification problems defined in Table 4. For two-class classification, the accuracy is defined as:

$$Accuracy = \frac{\sum_{i=1}^{N} \sum_{t=1}^{T_i} \sigma(\hat{y}_{it} = y_{it})}{\sum_{i=1}^{N} T_i} \tag{3}$$

where $N$ is the number of documents, $T_i$ represents the number of strokes in the $i$-th document, and $\hat{y}_{it}$ and $y_{it}$ are the corresponding prediction and groundtruth. For multi-class classification, the accuracy for each class $c$ is defined as:

$$Accuracy[c] = \frac{\sum_{i=1}^{N} \sum_{t=1}^{T_i} \sigma(y_{it} = c)\sigma(\hat{y}_{it} = y_{it})}{\sum_{i=1}^{N} \sum_{t=1}^{T_i} \sigma(y_{it} = c)} \tag{4}$$

## 5.4   Results and Analysis

1) *Quantitative Results*: Table 5 and Table 6 show two-class and multi-class stroke classification accuracy on CASIA-onDo, respectively. As it can be seen from the tables, multi-class classification is much harder than two-class classification. In addition, our proposed automatic features achieve better performance than hand-crafted features.

**Table 5.** Two-class stroke classification accuracy on CASIA-onDo (%).

| Task | Hand-crafted feature | | | Automatic feature | | |
|---|---|---|---|---|---|---|
| | Positive | Negative | Total | Positive | Negative | Total |
| Text/non-text classification | 98.53 | 88.28 | 96.12 | 98.55 | 90.76 | 96.72 |
| Table/non-table classification | 94.34 | 98.67 | 97.69 | 90.31 | 98.97 | 97.02 |
| Diagram/non-diagram classification | 92.34 | 99.29 | 98.36 | 96.94 | 98.91 | 98.65 |
| Formula/non-formula classification | 86.08 | 98.52 | 97.08 | 84.04 | 98.88 | 97.16 |
| List/non-list classification | 69.51 | 97.71 | 93.30 | 75.73 | 97.29 | 93.91 |

**Table 6.** Multi-class stroke classification accuracy on CASIA-onDo (%).

| Feature | Text | Formula | Diagram | Table | Figure | List | Total |
|---|---|---|---|---|---|---|---|
| Hand-crafted | 89.59 | 76.94 | 98.17 | 94.50 | 91.26 | 76.13 | 88.79 |
| Automatic | 93.04 | 89.43 | 96.07 | 94.35 | 91.17 | 68.55 | 89.87 |

|          | Text  | Formula | Diagram | Table | Figure | List  |
|----------|-------|---------|---------|-------|--------|-------|
| **Text**    | 93.04 | 0.16    | 0.21    | 1.04  | 0.20   | 3.92  |
| **Formula** | 7.42  | 89.43   | 0.08    | 0.54  | 0.43   | 2.09  |
| **Diagram** | 0.79  | 0.50    | 96.07   | 0.91  | 1.29   | 0.43  |
| **Table**   | 3.41  | 0.33    | 0.42    | 94.35 | 0.52   | 0.96  |
| **Figure**  | 2.75  | 1.03    | 1.86    | 2.06  | 91.17  | 1.13  |
| **List**    | 26.76 | 3.11    | 0.20    | 1.14  | 0.24   | 68.55 |

**Fig. 4.** The confusion matrix of end-to-end stroke classification result (%).

2) *Qualitative Results*: In Fig. 5, we show some visual results of end-to-end stroke classification on CASIA-onDo, where each color corresponds to a content type. According to statistics, most of the samples enjoy good results.

3) *Failure Analysis*: There are two difficulties of stroke classification on CASIA-onDo database, one is in-line formula, the other is list. In-line formulas are interspersed between text, which is common in class notes. It is easy to confuse the beginning and end of the formula with the surrounding text, resulting in errors. Lists, specially long ones, are also easily confused with text lines, indicating that the model does not learn the intrinsic feature of lists well. We show the confusion matrix in Fig. 4 and some failure cases in Fig. 6.

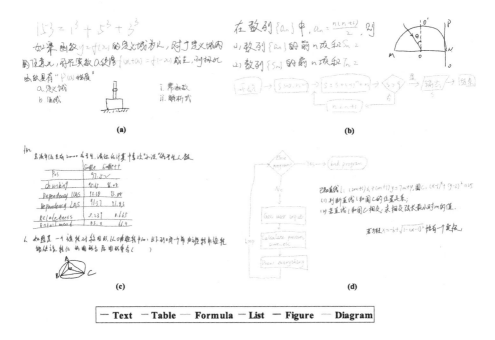

(a)                                          (b)

(c)                                          (d)

— Text  — Table  — Formula  — List  — Figure  — Diagram

**Fig. 5.** Visualization of multi-class stroke classification results.

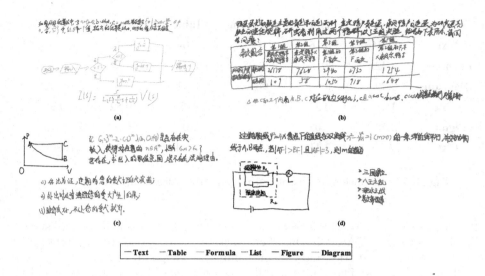

**Fig. 6.** Some typical examples of misclassification.

## 6    Conclusion and Outlook

This paper describes a database of online handwritten documents containing text blocks, diagrams, formulas, tables, figures and lists. The documents are written in an unconstrained manner and reflect documents generated in a realistic context. With 200 different writers, many different styles in writing and drawing are included. The distribution of the content types is kept stable over all individual documents. The database can serve as a basis for tasks such as document layout analysis, text line segmentation, formula detection, as well as handwriting recognition, etc.

We evaluate a document layout analysis method EGAT on CASIA-onDo. The results serve as a baseline for future methods to be developed on this database. To overcome the shortcomings of hand-crafted features, we propose an automatic feature extraction method and conduct contrast experiments to demonstrate the efficiency.

There are still many challenging problems need to be further explored, such as precise distinction between inline formula and text and distinction between list and text. These issues are of great research value and important application prospects.

**Acknowledgement.** This work has been supported by the National Key Research and Development Program under Grand No. 2020AAA0109700 and the National Natural Science Foundation of China (NSFC) under Grant No. 61773376.

# References

1. Guyon, I., Schomaker, L., Plamondon, R., et al.: UNIPEN project of on-line data exchange and recognizer benchmarks. In: 12th International Conference on Pattern Recognition, vol. 2, pp. 29–33. IEEE, New York (1994)
2. Viard-Gaudin, C., Lallican, P.M., Knerr, S., et al.: The IRESTE On/Off (IRONOFF) dual handwriting database. In: 5th International Conference on Document Analysis and Recognition, pp. 455–458. IEEE, New York (1999)
3. Liwicki, M., Bunke, H.: IAM-OnDB-an on-line English sentence database acquired from handwritten text on a whiteboard. In: 8th International Conference on Document Analysis and Recognition, pp. 956–961. IEEE, New York (2005)
4. Nakagawa, M., Onuma, M.: Online handwritten Japanese text recognition free from constrains on line direction and character orientation. In: 7-th International Conference on Document Analysis and Recognition, pp. 519–523. IEEE, New York (2003)
5. Jin, L., Gao, Y., Liu, G., et al.: SCUT-COUCH2009-a comprehensive online unconstrained Chinese handwriting database and benchmark evaluation. Int. J. Doc. Anal. Recogn. 14(1), 53–64 (2011)
6. Liu, C.L., Yin, F., Wang, D.H., et al.: CASIA online and offline Chinese handwriting databases. In: International Conference on Document Analysis and Recognition, pp. 37–41. IEEE (2011)
7. Awal, A.M., Feng, G., et al.: First experiments on a new online handwritten flowchart database. In: Document Recognition and Retrieval XVIII, vol. 7874, p. 78740A. International Society for Optics and Photonics, Bellingham (2011)
8. Bresler, M., Průša, D., Hlaváč, V.: Online recognition of sketched arrow-connected diagrams. Int. J. Doc. Anal. Recogn. (IJDAR) 19(3), 253–267 (2016). https://doi.org/10.1007/s10032-016-0269-z
9. Bresler, M., Van Phan, T., Prusa, D., et al.: Recognition system for on-line sketched diagrams. In: 14th International Conference on Frontiers in Handwriting Recognition, pp. 563–568. IEEE, New York (2014)
10. Yun, X.L., Zhang, Y.M., Yin, F., et al.: Instance GNN: a learning framework for joint symbol segmentation and recognition in online handwritten diagrams. IEEE Trans. Multimedia (2021)
11. Mouchère, H., Zanibbi, R., Garain, U., Viard-Gaudin, C.: Advancing the state of the art for handwritten math recognition: the CROHME competitions, 2011–2014. Int. J. Doc. Anal. Recogn. (IJDAR) 19(2), 173–189 (2016). https://doi.org/10.1007/s10032-016-0263-5
12. Mouchere, H., Viard-Gaudin, C., Zanibbi, R., et al.: ICFHR2014 competition on recognition of on-line handwritten mathematical expressions. In: 14th International Conference on Frontiers in Handwriting Recognition, pp. 791–796. IEEE, New York (2014)
13. Mouchère, H., Viard-Gaudin, C., Zanibbi, R., et al.: ICFHR2016 CROHME: competition on recognition of online handwritten mathematical expressions. In: 15th International Conference on Frontiers in Handwriting Recognition, pp. 607–612. IEEE, New York (2016)
14. Mochida, K., Nakagawa, M.: Separating figures, mathematical formulas and Japanese text from free handwriting in mixed online documents. Int. J. Pattern Recognit. Artif. Intell. 18(07), 1173–1187 (2004)

15. Indermühle, E., Liwicki, M., Bunke, H.: IAMonDo-database: an online handwritten document database with non-uniform contents. In: 9th International Workshop on Document Analysis Systems, pp. 97–104. Association for Computing Machinery, New York (2010)
16. Delaye, A., Liu, C.L.: Contextual text/non-text stroke classification in online handwritten notes with conditional random fields. Pattern Recogn. **47**(3), 959–968 (2014)
17. Ye, J.Y., Zhang, Y.M., Liu, C.L.: Joint training of conditional random fields and neural networks for stroke classification in online handwritten document. In: International Conference on Pattern Recognition, pp. 3264–3269. IEEE (2016)
18. Indermühle, E., Frinken, V., Bunke, H.: Mode detection in online handwritten documents using BLSTM neural networks. In: International Conference on Frontiers in Handwriting Recognition, pp. 302–307. IEEE (2012)
19. Van Phan, T., Nakagawa, M.: Combination of global and local contexts for text/non-text classification in heterogeneous online handwritten documents. Pattern Recognit. **51**, 112–124 (2016)
20. Watt, S.M., Underhill, T., Chee, Y.M., et al.: Ink markup language (InkML). W3C Proposed Recommendation, vol. 10 (2011)
21. Ye, J.Y., Zhang, Y.M., Yang, Q., et al.: Contextual stroke classification in online handwritten documents with graph attention networks. In: International Conference on Document Analysis and Recognition, pp. 993–998. IEEE, New York (2019)
22. Ye, J.Y., Zhang, Y.M., Yang, Q., et al.: Contextual stroke classification in online handwritten documents with edge graph attention networks. SN Comput. Sci. **1**, 1–13 (2020)
23. Ye, J.Y., Zhang, Y.M., Yang, Q., et al.: Joint stroke classification and text line grouping in online handwritten documents with edge pooling attention networks. Pattern Recognit. **114**, 107859 (2021)

# UnDeepLIO: Unsupervised Deep Lidar-Inertial Odometry

Yiming Tu[1,2] and Jin Xie[1,2(✉)]

[1] PCA Lab, Key Lab of Intelligent Perception and Systems for High-Dimensional, Information of Ministry of Education, Nanjing University of Science and Technology, Nanjing, China
{tymstudy,csjxie}@njust.edu.cn
[2] Jiangsu Key Lab of Image and Video Understanding for Social Security, School of Computer Science and Engineering, Nanjing University of Science and Technology, Nanjing, China

**Abstract.** Extensive research efforts have been dedicated to deep learning based odometry. Nonetheless, few efforts are made on the unsupervised deep lidar odometry. In this paper, we design a novel framework for unsupervised lidar odometry with the IMU, which is never used in other deep methods. First, a pair of siamese LSTMs are used to obtain the initial pose from the linear acceleration and angular velocity of IMU. With the initial pose, we perform the rigid transform on the current frame and align it to the last frame. Then we extract vertex and normal features from the transformed point clouds and its normals. Next a two-branch attention module is proposed to estimate residual rotation and translation from the extracted vertex and normal features, respectively. Finally, our model outputs the sum of initial and residual poses as the final pose. For unsupervised training, we introduce an unsupervised loss function which is employed on the voxelized point clouds. The proposed approach is evaluated on the KITTI odometry estimation benchmark and achieves comparable performances against other state-of-the-art methods.

**Keywords:** Unsupervised · Deep learning · Lidar-inertial odometry

## 1 Introduction

The task of odometry is to estimate 3D translation and orientation of autonomous vehicles which is one of key steps in SLAM. Autonomous vehicles usually collect information by perceiving the surrounding environment in real time and use on-board sensors such as lidar, Inertial Measurement Units (IMU), or camera to estimate their 3D translation and orientation. Lidar can provide high-precision 3D measurements but also has no requirement for light. The point clouds generated by the lidar can provide high-precision 3D measurements, but if

This work was supported by Shanghai Automotive Industry Science and Technology Development Foundation (No. 1917).

it has large translation or orientation in a short time, the continuously generated point clouds will only get few matching points, which will affect the accuracy of odometry. IMU has advantages of high output frequency and directly outputting the 6DOF information to predict the initial translation and orientation that the localization failure phenomenon can be reduced when lidar has large translation or orientation.

The traditional methods [1,18,19,23] are mainly based on the point registration and work well in ideal environments. However, due to the sparseness and irregularity of the point clouds, these methods are difficult to obtain enough matching points. Typically, ICP [1] and its variants [14,18] iteratively find matching points which depend on nearest-neighbor searching and optimize the translation and orientation by matching points. This optimization procedure is sensitive to noise and dynamic objects and prone to getting stuck into the local minima.

Thanks to the recent advances in deep learning, many approaches adopt deep neural networks for lidar odometry, which can achieve more promising performance compared to traditional methods. But most of them are supervised methods [10,12,13,20,21]. However, supervised methods require ground truth pose, which consumes a lot of manpower and material resources. Due to the scarcity of the ground truth, recent unsupervised methods are proposed [5,15,22], but some of them obtain unsatisfactory performance, and some need to consume a lot of video memory and time to train the network.

Two issues exist in these methods. First, these methods ignore IMU, which often bring fruitful clues for accurate lidar odometry. Second, those methods do not make full use of the normals, which only take the point clouds as the inputs. Normals of point clouds can indicate the relationship between a point and its surrounding points. And even if those approaches [12] who use normals as network input, they simply concatenate points and normals together and put them into network, but only orientation between two point clouds relates to normals, so normals should not be used to estimate translation.

To circumvent the dependence on expensive ground truth, we propose a novel framework termed as UnDeepLIO, which makes full use of the IMU and normals for more accurate odometry. We compare against various baselines using point clouds from the KITTI Vision Benchmark Suite [7] which collects point clouds using a 360° Velodyne laser scanner.

Our main contributions are as follows:

- We present a self-supervised learning-based approach for robot pose estimation. our method can outperform [5,15].
- We use IMU to assist odometry. Our IMU feature extraction module can be embedded in most network structures [5,12,15,21].
- Both points and its normals are used as network inputs. We use feature of points to estimate translation and feature of both of them to estimate orientation.

# 2   Related Work

## 2.1   Model-Based Odometry Estimation

Gauss-Newton iteration methods have a long-standing history in odometry task. Model-based methods solve odometry problems generally by using Newton's iteration method to adjust the transformation between frames so that the "gap" between frames keeps getting smaller. They can be categorized into two-frame methods [1,14,18] and multi-frame methods [19,23].

Point registration is the most common skill for two-frame methods, where ICP [1] and its variants [14,18] are typical examples. The ICP iteratively search key points and its correspondences to estimate the transformation between two point clouds until convergence. Moreover, most of these methods need multiple iterations with a large amount of calculation, which is difficult to meet the real-time requirements of the system.

Multi-frame algorithms [2,19,23] often relies on the two-frame based estimation. They improve the steps of selecting key points and finding matching points, and use additional mapping step to further optimize the pose estimation. Their calculation process is generally more complicated and runs at a lower frequency.

## 2.2   Learning-Based Odometry Estimation

In the last few years, the development of deep learning has greatly affected the most advanced odometry estimation. Learning-based model can provide a solution only needs uniformly down sampling the point clouds without manually selecting key points. They can be classified into supervised methods and unsupervised methods.

Supervised methods appear relatively early, Lo-net [12] maps the point clouds to 2D "image" by spherical projection. Wang *et al.* [21] adopt a dual-branch architecture to infer 3-D translation and orientation separately instead of a single network. Velas *et al.* [20] use point clouds to assist 3D motion estimation and regarded it as a classification problem. Differently, Li *et al.* [13] do not simply estimate 3D motion with fully connected layer but Singular Value Decomposition (SVD).

Unsupervised methods appear later. Cho *et al.* [5] first apply unsupervised approach on deep-learning-based LiDAR odometry which is an extension of their previous approach [4]. The inspiration of its loss function comes from point-to-plane ICP [14]. Then, Nubert *et al.* [15] report methods with similarly models and loss function, but they use different way to calculate normals of each point in point clouds and find matching points between two continuous point clouds.

# 3   Methods

## 3.1   Data Preprocess

**Data Input.** At every timestamp $k \in \mathbb{R}^+$, we can obtain one point clouds $P_k$ of $N * 3$ dimensions and between every two timestamps we can get $S$ frames IMU $I_{k,k+1}$ of $S * 6$ dimensions including 3D angular velocity and 3D linear acceleration. We take above data as the inputs.

**Vertex Map.** In order to circumvent the disordered nature of point clouds, we project the point clouds into the 2D image coordinate system according to the horizontal and vertical angle. We employ projection function $\Pi : \mathbb{R}^3 \mapsto \mathbb{R}^2$. Each 3D point $\boldsymbol{p} = (p_x, p_y, p_z)$ in a point clouds $P_k$ is mapped into the 2D image plane $(w, h)$ represented as

$$\begin{pmatrix} w \\ h \end{pmatrix} = \begin{pmatrix} (f_w - \arctan(\frac{p_y}{p_x}))/\eta_w \\ (f_h - \arcsin(\frac{p_z}{d}))/\eta_h \end{pmatrix},$$

$$H > h \geq 0, W > w \geq 0,$$

(1)

where depth is $d = \sqrt{p_x{}^2 + p_y{}^2 + p_z{}^2}$. $f_w$ and $f_h$ are the maximum horizontal and vertical angle. $H$ and $W$ are shape of vertex map. $f_h$ depends on the type of the lidar. $\eta_w$ and $\eta_h$ control the horizontal and vertical sampling density. If several 3D points correspond the same pixel values, we choose the point with minimum depth as the final result. If one pixel coordinate has no matching 3D points, the pixel value is set to $(0, 0, 0)$. We define the 2D image plane as vertex map $\boldsymbol{V}$.

**Normal Map.** The normal vector of one point includes its relevance about the surrounding points, so we compute a normal map $\boldsymbol{N}$ which consists of normals $\boldsymbol{n}$ and has the same shape as corresponding vertex map $\boldsymbol{V}$. We adopt similar operations with Cho et al. [5] and Li et al. [12] to calculate the normal vectors. Each normal vector $\boldsymbol{n}$ corresponds to a vertex $\boldsymbol{v}$ with the same image coordinate. Due to sparse and discontinuous characteristics of point clouds, we pay more attention on the vertex with small Euclidean distance from the surrounding pixel via a pre-defined weight, which can be expressed as $w_{a,b} = e^{\{-0.5|d(v_a)-d(v_b)|\}}$. Each normal vector $\boldsymbol{n}$ is represented as

$$\boldsymbol{n}_p = \sum_{i \in [0,3]} w_{p_i,p}(v_{p_i} - v_p) \times w_{p_{i+1},p}(v_{p_{i+1}} - v_p),$$

(2)

where $p_i$ represents points in 4 directions of the central vertex $p$ (0-up, 1-right, 2-down, 3-left).

## 3.2   Network Structure

**Network Input.** Our pipeline is shown in the Fig. 1. Each point clouds associates with a vertex/normal map of $(3, H, W)$ dimensions, so we concatenate the vertex/normal map of $k$ and $k + 1$ timestamp to get vertex/normal pair of $(2, 3, H, W)$ dimensions. We take a pair of vertex/normal maps and IMU between $k$ and $k+1$ timestamp as the inputs of our model, where the IMU consists of the linear acceleration and angular velocity both of $(S, 3)$ dimensions, and $S$ is the

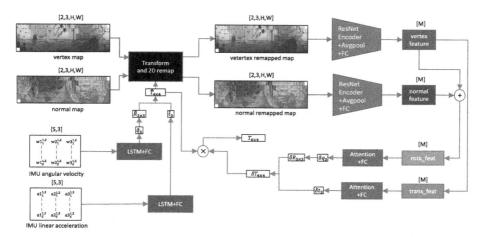

**Fig. 1.** The proposed network and our unsupervised training scheme. FC represents fully connected layer. $t$ means translation and $q$ means Euler angle of orientation. LSTM takes continuous frames of IMU as inputs and output initial relative pose $\hat{T}$. $\hat{T}$ are used to transform two maps of current frame to last frame. Then we send the remapped maps into ResNet Encoder, which outputs feature maps, including vertex and normal features. From the features, we propose an attention layer to estimate residual pose $\delta T$. The final output is their sum $T = \delta T \hat{T}$.

length of IMU sequence. Our model outputs relative pose $T_{k,k+1}$, where $R_{k,k+1}$ is orientation and $t_{k,k+1}$ is translation.

$$T_{k,k+1}^{4\times4} = \begin{bmatrix} R_{k,k+1}^{3\times3} & t_{k,k+1}^{3\times1} \\ 0 & 1 \end{bmatrix}, \tag{3}$$

**Estimating Initial Relative Pose from IMU.** Linear acceleration is used to estimate translation and angular velocity is used to estimate orientation. We employ LSTM on IMU to extract the features of IMU. Then the features are forwarded into the FC layer to estimate initial relative translation or orientation.

**Mapping the Point Clouds of Current Frame to the Last Frame.** Each vertex/normal pair consists of last and current frames. They are not in the same coordinate due to the transformation. The initial relative pose can map current frame in current coordinate to last coordinate, then we can obtain the remapped current map with the same size as the old one. The relationship between two maps are shown as formula (4). Take the $v_{k+1,p}^{k}$ for example, it is the mapped vertex at timestamp $k$ from timestamp $k+1$ via the initial pose.

$$v_{k+1,p}^{k} = R_{k,k+1} v_{k+1,p}^{k+1} + t_{k,k+1}, \tag{4}$$

$$n_{k+1,p}^{k} = R_{k,k+1} n_{k+1,p}^{k+1}. \tag{5}$$

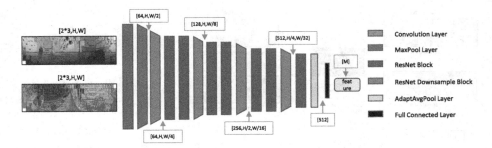

**Fig. 2.** The detail structure of ResNet Encoder + Avgpool + FC part.

**Estimating Residual Relative Pose from the Remapped Maps.** We use ResNet Encoder (see Fig. 2) as our map feature extractor. ResNet [8] is used in image recognition. Its input is the 2D images similar to us. Therefore, this structure can extract feature in our task as well. We send the remapping vertex/normal map pair into siamese ResNet Encoder, which outputs feature maps, including vertex and normal features. From the features, we propose an attention layer (by formula (6), $x$ is input) which is inspired by LSTM [9] to estimate residual pose $\delta T$ between last frame and the remapped current frame. Among them, vertex and normal features are combined to estimate orientation, but only vertex is used to estimate translation because the change of translation does not cause the change of normal vectors. Together with initial relative pose, we can get final relative pose $T$.

$$
\begin{aligned}
i &= \sigma(W_i x + b_i), \\
g &= tanh(W_g x + b_g), \\
o &= \sigma(W_o x + b_o), \\
out &= o * tanh(i * g).
\end{aligned}
\tag{6}
$$

### 3.3 Loss Function

For unsupervised training, we use a combination of geometric losses in our deep learning framework. Unlike Cho *et al.* [5] who use pixel locations as correspondence between two point clouds, we search correspondence on the whole point clouds. For speeding up calculation, we first calculate the normals $NP_i$ of whole point clouds $P_k$ by plane fitting $\Phi$ [17], and then remove its ground points by RANSAC [6], at last perform voxel grid filtering $\Downarrow$ (the arithmetic average of all points in voxel as its representation. The normal vectors of voxel are processed in the same way and standardized after downsample.) to downsample to about $K$ points (The precess is shown in Fig. 3). Given the predicted relative pose $T_{k,k+1}$, we apply it on preprocessed current point clouds $DP_{k+1}$ and its normals $NP_{k+1}$. For the correspondence search, we use KD-Tree [3] to find the nearest point in

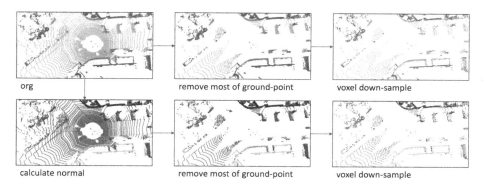

**Fig. 3.** Point downsample process, including point (up) and normal (down).

the last point clouds $DP_k$ of each point in the transformed current point clouds $\overline{DP}_{k+1}$.

$$DP_k = \Downarrow (\mathsf{RANSAC}(P_k)),$$
$$NP_k = \Downarrow (\mathsf{RANSAC}(\Phi(P_k))), \tag{7}$$

$$\overline{NP}_{k+1} = R_{k,k+1} NP_{k+1},$$
$$\overline{DP}_{k+1} = R_{k,k+1} DP_{k+1} + t_{k,k+1}. \tag{8}$$

**Point-to-Plane ICP Loss.** We use every point $\overline{dp}_{k+1}$ in current point clouds $\overline{DP}_{k+1}$, corresponding point of $dp_k$ and normal vector of $np_k$ in last point clouds $DP_k$ to compute the distance between point and its matching plane. The loss function $\mathcal{L}_{po2pl}$ is represented as

$$\mathcal{L}_{po2pl} = \sum_{\overline{dp}_{k+1} \in \overline{DP}_{k+1}} |(\overline{dp}_{k+1} - dp_k) \cdot np_k|_1, \tag{9}$$

where **.** denotes inner product.

**Plane-to-Plane ICP Loss.** Similarly to point-to-plane ICP, we use normal $\overline{np}_{k+1}$ of every point in $\overline{NP}_{k+1}$, corresponding normal vector of $np_k$ in $NP_k$ to compute the angle between a pair of matching plane. The loss function $\mathcal{L}_{pl2pl}$ is represented as

$$\mathcal{L}_{pl2pl} = \sum_{\overline{np}_{k+1} \in \overline{NP}_{k+1}} |\overline{np}_{k+1} - np_k|_2^2. \tag{10}$$

**Overall Loss.** Finally, the overall unsupervised loss is obtained as

$$\mathcal{L} = \alpha \mathcal{L}_{po2pl} + \lambda \mathcal{L}_{po2pl}, \tag{11}$$

where $\alpha$ and $\lambda$ are balancing factors.

# 4    Experiments

In this section, we first introduce implementation details of our model and benchmark dataset used in our experiments and the implementation details of the proposed model. Then, comparing to the existing lidar odometry methods, our model can obtain competitive results. Finally, we conduct ablation studies to verify the effectiveness of the innovative part of our model.

## 4.1    Implementation Details

The proposed network is implemented in PyTorch [16] and trained with a single NVIDIA Titan RTX GPU. We optimize the parameters with the Adam optimizer [11] whose hyperparameter values are $\beta_1 = 0.9$, $\beta_2 = 0.99$ and $w_{decay} = 10^{-5}$. We adopt step scheduler with a step size of 20 and $\gamma = 0.5$ to control the training procedure, the initial learning rate is $10^{-4}$ and the batch size is 20. The length $S$ of IMU sequence is 15. The maximum horizontal and vertical angle of vertex map are $f_w = 180°$ and $f_h = 23°$, and density of them are $\eta_w = \eta_h = 0.5$. The shapes of input maps are $H = 52$ and $W = 720$. The loss weight of formula (11) is set to be $\alpha = 1.0$ and $\lambda = 0.1$. The initial side length of voxel downsample is set to 0.3m, it is adjusted according to the number of points after downsample, if points are too many, we increase the side length, otherwise reduce. The adjustment size is 0.01m per time. The number of points after downsample is controlled within $K \pm 100$ and $K = 10240$.

## 4.2    Datasets

The KITTI odometry dataset [7] has 22 different sequences with images, 3D lidar point clouds, IMU and other data. Only sequences 00-10 have an official public ground truth. Among them, only sequence 03 does not provide IMU. Therefore, we do not use sequence 03 when there exists the IMU assist in our method.

## 4.3    Evaluation on the KITTI Dataset

We compare our method with the following methods which can be divided into two types. Model-based methods are: LOAM [23] and LeGO-LOAM [19]. Learning-based methods are: Nubert et al. [15], Cho et al. [5] and SelfVoxeLO [22].

In model-based methods, we show the lidar odometry results of them with mapping and without mapping.

In learning-based methods, we use two ways to divide the train and test set. First, we use sequences 00-08 for training and 09-10 for testing, as Cho et al. [5] and Nubert et al. [15] use Sequences 00-08 as their training set. We name it as "Ours-easy". Then, we use sequences 00-06 for training and 07-10 for testing, to compare with SelfVoxeLO which uses Sequences 00-06 as training set. We name it as "Ours-hard".

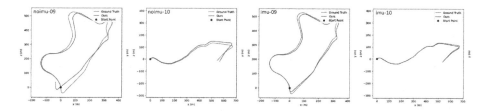

**Fig. 4.** 2D estimated trajectories of our method on sequence 09 and 10.

Table 1 contains the details of the results: $t_{rel}$ means average translational RMSE (%) on length of 100 m–800 m and $r_{rel}$ means average rotational RMSE (°/100 m) on length of 100 m–800 m. LeGO-LOAM is not always more precise by adding imu, traditional method is more sensitive to the accuracy of imu (In sequence 00, there exists some lack of IMU), which is most likely the reason for its accuracy drop. Even if the accuracy of the estimation is improved by the IMU, the effect is not obvious, especially after the mapping step. Our method gains a significant improvement by using IMU in test set, and has a certain advantage over traditional method without mapping, and is not much lower than with mapping. In the easy task (For trajectories results, see Fig. 4), our method without imu assist is also competitive compared to Cho *et al.* [5] and Nubert *et al.* [15] which also project the point clouds into the 2D image coordinate system. Our method can acquire a lot of improvements with imu. In the hard task, comparing to the most advanced method SelfVoxeLO [22] which uses 3D convolutions on voxels and consumes much video memory and training time, our method also can get comparable results with IMU. Since they did not publish the code, we are unable to conduct experiments on their method with imu.

### 4.4   Ablation Study

In order to prove the effectiveness of each proposed module, we conduct ablation experiments on KITTI, use sequences 00-08 as trainset and sequences 09-10 as testset.

**IMU.** As mentioned earlier, IMU can greatly improve the accuracy of odometry, but the role played by different IMU utilization methods is also different. If only use IMU to extract features through the network, and directly merge with the feature of the point clouds, the effect is limited (see Fig. 5). Our method uses IMU and LSTM network to estimate a relative initial pose, project vertex image and normal vector image of the original current frame, and then send the projection images into the point clouds feature extraction network, so that the IMU can not only have a direct connection with the final odometry estimate network, but also make the coordinate of two consecutive frames closer. The comparison is shown in Table 2.

**Table 1.** KITTI odometry evaluation.

| $t_{rel}(\%)$ | 00 | 01 | 02 | 03 | 04 | 05 | 06 | 07 | 08 | 09 | 10 | trainavg | testavg |
|---|---|---|---|---|---|---|---|---|---|---|---|---|---|
| LeGO-LOAM (w/ map)[19] | 1.44 | 21.12 | 2.69 | 1.73 | 1.70 | 0.98 | 0.87 | 0.77 | 1.35 | 1.46 | 1.84 | 3.27 | |
| LeGO-LOAM (w/ map)+imu | 7.24 | 20.07 | 2.56 | x | 1.68 | 0.82 | 0.86 | **0.67** | 1.29 | 1.49 | 1.75 | 3.84 | |
| LeGO-LOAM (w/o map) | 6.98 | 26.52 | 6.92 | 6.16 | 3.64 | 4.57 | 5.16 | 4.05 | 6.01 | 5.22 | 7.73 | 7.54 | |
| LeGO-LOAM (w/o map)+imu | 10.46 | 22.38 | 6.05 | x | 2.04 | 1.98 | 2.98 | 2.99 | 3.23 | 3.29 | 2.74 | 5.81 | |
| LOAM (w/ map)[23] | **1.10** | **2.79** | **1.54** | 1.13 | 1.45 | **0.75** | **0.72** | 0.69 | **1.18** | **1.20** | **1.51** | **1.28** | |
| LOAM (w/o map) | 15.99 | 3.43 | 9.40 | 18.18 | 9.59 | 9.16 | 8.91 | 10.87 | 12.72 | 8.10 | 12.67 | 10.82 | |
| Nubert et al.[15] | NA | NA | NA | NA | NA | NA | NA | NA | NA | 6.05 | 6.44 | 3.00 | 6.25 |
| Cho et al.[5] | NA | NA | NA | NA | NA | NA | NA | NA | NA | 4.87 | 5.02 | 3.68 | 4.95 |
| Ours-easy | **1.33** | **3.40** | 1.53 | 1.43 | 1.26 | 1.22 | 1.19 | **0.97** | 1.92 | 3.87 | 2.69 | 1.58 | 3.28 |
| Ours-easy+imu | 1.50 | 3.44 | **1.33** | x | **0.94** | **0.98** | **0.90** | 1.00 | **1.63** | **2.24** | **1.83** | **1.46** | **2.03** |
| SelfVoxelLO[22] | NA | NA | NA | NA | NA | NA | NA | **3.09** | **3.16** | 3.01 | 3.48 | 2.50 | **3.19** |
| Ours-hard | 1.58 | **3.42** | 2.27 | 2.53 | 0.96 | 1.36 | 0.99 | 6.58 | 6.89 | 5.77 | 5.82 | | |
| Ours-hard+imu | **1.15** | 3.58 | **1.40** | x | **0.89** | **1.12** | 1.03 | 4.58 | 3.18 | **2.66** | **2.84** | **1.53** | 3.32 |
| $r_{rel}(°/100\,\mathrm{m})$ | 00 | 01 | 02 | 03 | 04 | 05 | 06 | 07 | 08 | 09 | 10 | trainavg | testavg |
| LeGO-LOAM (w/ map) | 0.65 | 2.17 | 0.99 | 0.99 | 0.69 | 0.47 | 0.45 | 0.51 | 0.58 | 0.64 | 0.74 | 0.81 | |
| LeGO-LOAM (w/ map)+imu | 2.44 | 0.61 | 0.91 | x | 0.59 | **0.38** | 0.43 | 0.38 | 0.53 | 0.58 | 0.63 | 0.75 | |
| LeGO-LOAM (w/o map) | 3.27 | 4.61 | 3.10 | 3.42 | 2.98 | 2.38 | 2.24 | 2.41 | 2.85 | 2.61 | 4.03 | 3.08 | |
| LeGO-LOAM (w/o map)+imu | 3.72 | 1.79 | 2.12 | x | 0.88 | 0.88 | 1.24 | 1.64 | 1.23 | 1.75 | 1.57 | 1.68 | |
| LOAM (w/ map) | **0.53** | **0.55** | **0.55** | 0.65 | **0.50** | **0.38** | **0.39** | **0.50** | **0.44** | **0.48** | **0.57** | **0.50** | |
| LOAM (w/o map) | 6.25 | 0.93 | 3.68 | 9.91 | 4.57 | 4.10 | 4.63 | 6.76 | 5.77 | 4.30 | 8.79 | 5.43 | |
| Nubert et al. | NA | NA | NA | NA | NA | NA | NA | NA | NA | 2.15 | 3.00 | 1.38 | 2.58 |
| Cho et al. | NA | NA | NA | NA | NA | NA | NA | NA | NA | 1.95 | 1.83 | 0.87 | 1.89 |
| Ours-easy | **0.69** | **0.97** | 0.68 | 1.04 | **0.73** | 0.66 | 0.64 | 0.58 | **0.78** | 1.67 | 1.97 | 0.75 | 1.82 |
| Ours-easy+imu | 0.70 | 0.99 | **0.59** | x | 0.78 | **0.56** | **0.45** | 0.54 | **0.78** | 1.13 | 1.14 | 0.67 | **1.14** |
| SelfVoxelLO | NA | NA | NA | NA | NA | NA | NA | **1.81** | **1.14** | 1.14 | **1.11** | 1.11 | **1.30** |
| Ours-hard | 0.91 | 1.09 | 1.19 | 1.42 | **0.61** | 0.78 | 0.64 | 4.56 | 2.86 | 2.34 | 2.89 | 0.95 | 3.16 |
| Ours-hard+imu | **0.57** | **0.98** | **0.62** | x | 0.74 | **0.64** | **0.52** | 2.34 | 1.35 | **1.12** | 1.42 | **0.68** | 1.56 |

NA: The result of other papers do not provide.
x: Do not use this sequence in method.
Trainavg and testavg of traditional methods are the average results of all 00-10 sequences.

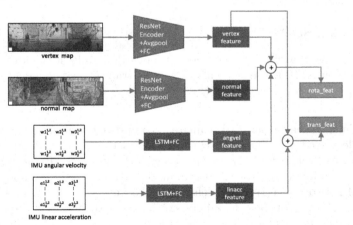

**Fig. 5.** Use IMU only as feature.

**Table 2.** Comparison among different ways to preprocess imu and whether using imu.

| $t_{rel}(\%)$ | 00 | 01 | 02 | 03 | 04 | 05 | 06 | 07 | 08 | 09 | 10 | trainavg | testavg |
|---|---|---|---|---|---|---|---|---|---|---|---|---|---|
| imu (w preprocess) | 1.50 | 3.44 | **1.33** | x | **0.94** | **0.98** | **0.90** | 1.00 | 1.63 | **2.24** | **1.83** | **1.58** | **2.03** |
| imu (w/o preprocess) | 1.35 | 3.56 | 1.57 | x | 1.07 | 1.21 | 1.03 | **0.90** | **1.59** | 2.46 | 1.87 | 1.66 | 2.17 |
| noimu | **1.33** | **3.40** | 1.53 | 1.43 | 1.26 | 1.22 | 1.19 | 0.97 | 1.92 | 3.87 | 2.69 | 1.89 | 3.28 |
| $r_{rel}(°/100\,m)$ | 00 | 01 | 02 | 03 | 04 | 05 | 06 | 07 | 08 | 09 | 10 | trainavg | testavg |
| imu (w preprocess) | 0.70 | **0.99** | **0.59** | x | 0.78 | **0.56** | **0.45** | **0.54** | 0.78 | **1.13** | **1.14** | **0.76** | **1.14** |
| imu (w/o preprocess) | **0.67** | 1.01 | 0.69 | x | **0.63** | 0.68 | 0.56 | 0.60 | **0.71** | **1.13** | 1.28 | 0.80 | 1.20 |
| noimu | 0.69 | 0.97 | 0.68 | 1.04 | 0.73 | 0.66 | 0.64 | 0.58 | 0.78 | 1.67 | 1.97 | 0.95 | 1.82 |

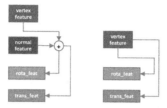

**Fig. 6.** The network structure of learning translation and rotation features from concatenated vetex and normal features simultaneously (left) and the network structure without the normal feature (right).

**Different Operations to Obtain the Rotation and Translation Features.**
The normal vector contains the relationship between a point and its surrounding points, and can be used as feature of pose estimation just like the point itself. Through the calculation formula of the normal vector, we can know that the change of the normal vector is only related to the orientation, and the translation will not bring about the change of the normal vector. Therefore, we only use the feature of the point to estimate the translation. We compare the original method with the two strategies of not using normal vectors as the network input and not distinguishing feature of the normals and points (see Fig. 6). The comparison is shown in Table 3.

**Attention.** After extracting the features of the vertex map and the normal map, we add an additional self-attention module to improve the accuracy of pose estimation. The attention module can self-learn the importance of features, and give higher weight to more important features. We verify its effectiveness by comparing the result of the model which replaces the self-attention module with a single FC layer with activation function (as formula (12)). The comparison is show in Table 4.

$$out = tanh(W_2(tanh(W_1x + b_1)) + b_2). \tag{12}$$

**Loss Function.** Cho *et al.* [5] adopt the strategy of using the points with the same pixel in last and current vertex map as the matching points. Although the

**Table 3.** Comparison among whether distinguishing features (dist) and whether using normal.

| $t_{rel}(\%)$ | 00 | 01 | 02 | 03 | 04 | 05 | 06 | 07 | 08 | 09 | 10 | trainavg | testavg |
|---|---|---|---|---|---|---|---|---|---|---|---|---|---|
| imu (w normal, w dist) | 1.50 | **3.44** | **1.33** | x | 0.94 | **0.98** | **0.90** | 1.00 | **1.63** | **2.24** | 1.83 | **1.58** | **2.03** |
| imu (w normal, w/o dist) | **1.45** | 3.68 | 2.03 | x | **0.72** | 1.11 | 1.15 | **0.68** | 1.67 | 3.44 | 1.86 | 1.78 | 2.65 |
| imu (w/o normal, w/o dist) | 2.54 | 3.81 | 4.13 | x | 0.95 | 1.77 | 0.99 | 1.25 | 1.93 | 2.72 | 2.21 | 2.23 | 2.47 |
| noimu (w normal, w dist) | **1.33** | **3.40** | **1.53** | **1.43** | 1.26 | 1.22 | 1.19 | **0.97** | 1.92 | **3.87** | **2.69** | **1.89** | **3.28** |
| noimu (w normal, w/o dist) | 1.49 | 3.95 | 2.49 | 2.27 | **0.88** | **1.19** | **0.90** | 1.47 | 2.02 | 4.93 | 4.34 | 2.36 | 4.64 |
| noimu (w/o normal, w/o dist) | 1.63 | 4.96 | 2.99 | 2.36 | 2.15 | 1.31 | 1.31 | 1.51 | **1.89** | 5.75 | 6.11 | 2.91 | 5.93 |

| $r_{rel}(°/100\,m)$ | 00 | 01 | 02 | 03 | 04 | 05 | 06 | 07 | 08 | 09 | 10 | trainavg | testavg |
|---|---|---|---|---|---|---|---|---|---|---|---|---|---|
| imu (w normal, w dist) | **0.70** | **0.99** | **0.59** | x | 0.78 | **0.56** | **0.45** | 0.54 | 0.78 | **1.13** | **1.14** | **0.76** | **1.14** |
| imu (w normal, w/o dist) | 0.65 | 1.04 | 0.96 | x | **0.53** | **0.56** | 0.58 | **0.46** | **0.64** | 1.45 | 1.15 | 0.80 | 1.30 |
| imu (w/o normal, w/o dist) | 1.31 | 1.05 | 1.60 | x | 0.52 | 0.88 | 0.48 | 0.87 | 0.93 | 1.15 | 1.21 | 1.00 | 1.18 |
| noimu (w normal, w dist) | **0.69** | **0.97** | **0.68** | **1.04** | 0.73 | **0.66** | **0.64** | **0.58** | **0.78** | 1.67 | 1.97 | **0.95** | **1.82** |
| noimu (w normal, w/o dist) | 0.88 | 1.24 | 1.20 | 1.38 | **0.66** | 0.70 | 0.58 | 1.03 | 0.95 | 1.92 | 2.06 | 1.15 | 1.99 |
| noimu (w/o normal, w/o dist) | 0.90 | 1.48 | 1.37 | 1.49 | 1.38 | 0.79 | 0.73 | 1.08 | 0.93 | 2.31 | 2.73 | 1.38 | 2.52 |

**Table 4.** Comparison among whether using attention module.

| $t_{rel}(\%)$ | 00 | 01 | 02 | 03 | 04 | 05 | 06 | 07 | 08 | 09 | 10 | trainavg | testavg |
|---|---|---|---|---|---|---|---|---|---|---|---|---|---|
| imu (w attention) | 1.50 | **3.44** | **1.33** | x | 0.94 | 0.98 | 0.90 | 1.00 | 1.63 | **2.24** | 1.83 | 1.58 | **2.03** |
| imu (w fc+activation) | **1.19** | 3.49 | 1.48 | x | **0.83** | **0.95** | **0.64** | **0.91** | **1.49** | 3.21 | **1.54** | **1.57** | 2.38 |
| noimu (w attention) | **1.33** | **3.40** | **1.53** | **1.43** | 1.26 | **1.22** | 1.19 | **0.97** | 1.92 | **3.87** | **2.69** | **1.89** | **3.28** |
| noimu (w fc+activation) | 1.65 | 3.59 | 1.67 | 1.88 | **0.87** | 1.34 | **1.10** | 1.23 | **1.76** | 6.64 | 3.25 | 2.27 | 4.95 |

| $r_{rel}(°/100\,m)$ | 00 | 01 | 02 | 03 | 04 | 05 | 06 | 07 | 08 | 09 | 10 | trainavg | testavg |
|---|---|---|---|---|---|---|---|---|---|---|---|---|---|
| imu (w attention) | 0.70 | 0.99 | **0.59** | x | **0.78** | 0.56 | 0.45 | **0.54** | 0.78 | **1.13** | 1.14 | **0.76** | 1.14 |
| imu (w fc+activation) | **0.62** | **0.97** | 0.64 | x | 1.02 | **0.54** | **0.42** | 0.55 | **0.70** | 1.20 | **1.07** | 0.77 | **1.13** |
| noimu (w attention) | **0.69** | **0.97** | 0.68 | **1.04** | 0.73 | **0.66** | 0.64 | **0.58** | **0.78** | 1.67 | 1.97 | **0.95** | **1.82** |
| noimu (w fc+activation) | 0.77 | 0.99 | **0.67** | 1.10 | **0.70** | 0.67 | **0.48** | 0.80 | 0.80 | 2.36 | 2.07 | 1.04 | 2.21 |

**Fig. 7.** Matching points search strategy of Cho *et al.*(pixel-to-pixel), our and Nubert *et al.*(point-to-point).

calculation speed is fast, the matching points found in this way are likely to be incorrect. Therefore, we and Nubert *et al.* [15] imitate ICP algorithm, using the nearest neighbor as the matching point(see Fig. 7). Although we use the same loss functions and the same matching point search strategy (nearest neighbor) as Nubert *et al.* [15], we search in the entire point clouds space, and maintain the number of points in search space not too large by removing most of the ground points and operating voxel grids downsample on point clouds. The number of points even is only 1/3 of the points sampled by the 2D projection which used in [15]. Table 5 shows the necessity of two loss parts and strategy of searching matching points in the entire point clouds.

**Table 5.** Comparison among different loss functions and matching point search strategy.

| $t_{rel}(\%)$ | 00 | 01 | 02 | 03 | 04 | 05 | 06 | 07 | 08 | 09 | 10 | trainavg | testavg |
|---|---|---|---|---|---|---|---|---|---|---|---|---|---|
| imu (w point-to-plane))+point-to-point | **1.50** | **3.44** | **1.33** | x | 0.94 | 0.98 | 0.90 | 1.00 | 1.63 | 2.24 | **1.83** | **1.58** | **2.03** |
| imu (w/o point-to-plane)+point-to-point | 2.27 | 4.33 | 2.24 | x | 1.59 | 1.70 | 1.26 | 1.29 | 1.87 | **2.04** | 2.07 | 2.07 | 2.06 |
| imu (w point-to-plane)+pixel-to-pixel | 2.14 | 4.36 | 2.29 | x | 1.65 | 1.66 | 1.17 | 1.36 | 1.73 | 2.95 | 2.28 | 2.16 | 2.61 |
| noimu (w point-to-plane)+point-to-point | **1.33** | **3.40** | **1.53** | 1.43 | 1.26 | 1.22 | 1.19 | **0.97** | 1.92 | 3.87 | **2.69** | **1.89** | **3.28** |
| noimu (w/o point-to-plane)+point-to-point | 1.46 | 3.44 | 1.67 | 1.91 | **0.92** | **1.00** | **1.11** | 1.36 | **1.81** | 4.72 | 2.78 | 2.02 | 3.75 |
| noimu (w point-to-plane))+pixel-to-pixel | 2.76 | 4.43 | 2.73 | 2.07 | 1.71 | 1.50 | 1.32 | 1.32 | 1.95 | **3.68** | 3.65 | 2.47 | 3.67 |

| $r_{rel}(°/100\,\mathrm{m})$ | 00 | 01 | 02 | 03 | 04 | 05 | 06 | 07 | 08 | 09 | 10 | trainavg | testavg |
|---|---|---|---|---|---|---|---|---|---|---|---|---|---|
| imu (w point-to-plane))+point-to-point | **0.70** | **0.99** | **0.59** | x | 0.78 | 0.56 | 0.45 | 0.54 | 0.78 | 1.13 | 1.14 | **0.76** | **1.14** |
| imu (w/o point-to-plane)+point-to-point | 1.01 | 1.12 | 0.98 | x | 0.96 | 0.82 | 0.62 | 0.78 | 0.86 | 1.14 | 1.19 | 0.95 | 1.16 |
| imu (w point-to-plane)+pixel-to-pixel | 0.96 | 1.11 | 0.96 | x | 0.98 | 0.83 | 0.58 | 0.83 | 0.87 | 1.52 | 1.27 | 0.99 | 1.39 |
| noimu (w point-to-plane)+point-to-point | **0.69** | **0.97** | **0.68** | 1.04 | 0.73 | 0.66 | 0.64 | **0.58** | 0.78 | 1.67 | 1.97 | **0.95** | 1.82 |
| noimu (w/o point-to-plane)+point-to-point | 0.73 | 0.99 | 0.70 | 1.34 | **0.69** | **0.58** | **0.49** | 0.85 | **0.76** | 1.85 | **1.84** | 0.98 | 1.85 |
| noimu (w point-to-plane))+pixel-to-pixel | 1.10 | 1.16 | 1.11 | 1.40 | 1.03 | 0.76 | 0.62 | 0.78 | 0.89 | **1.56** | 2.05 | 1.13 | **1.80** |

# 5   Conclusion

In this paper, we proposed UnDeepLIO, an unsupervised learning-based odometry network. Different from other unsupervised lidar odometry methods, we additionally used IMU to assist odometry task. There have been already many IMU and lidar fusion algorithms in the traditional field for odometry, and it has become a trend to use the information of both at the same time. Moreover, we conduct extensive experiments on kitti dataset and experiments verify that our method is competitive with the most advanced methods. In ablation study, we validated the effectiveness of each component of our model. In the future, we will study how to incorporate mapping steps into our network framework and conduct online tests.

# References

1. Arun, K.S., Huang, T.S., Blostein, S.D.: Least-squares fitting of two 3-D point sets. TPAMI **9**(5), 698–700 (1987)
2. Behley, J., Stachniss, C.: Efficient surfel-based SLAM using 3D laser range data in urban environments. In: Robotics: Science and Systems, vol. 2018 (2018)
3. Bentley, J.L.: Multidimensional binary search trees used for associative searching. Commun. ACM **18**(9), 509–517 (1975)
4. Cho, Y., Kim, G., Kim, A.: DeepLO: geometry-aware deep lidar odometry. arXiv preprint arXiv:1902.10562 (2019)
5. Cho, Y., Kim, G., Kim, A.: Unsupervised geometry-aware deep lidar odometry. In: ICRA, pp. 2145–2152. IEEE (2020)
6. Fischler, M.A., Bolles, R.C.: Random sample consensus: a paradigm for model fitting with applications to image analysis and automated cartography. Commun. ACM **24**(6), 381–395 (1981)
7. Geiger, A., Lenz, P., Urtasun, R.: Are we ready for autonomous driving? The KITTI vision benchmark suite. In: CVPR, pp. 3354–3361. IEEE (2012)
8. He, K., Zhang, X., Ren, S., Sun, J.: Deep residual learning for image recognition. In: CVPR, pp. 770–778 (2016)

9. Hochreiter, S., Schmidhuber, J.: Long short-term memory. Neural Comput. **9**(8), 1735–1780 (1997)

10. Javanmard-Gh, A., Iwaszczuk, D., Roth, S.: DeepLIO: deep LIDAR inertial sensor fusion for odometry estimation. ISPRS **1**, 47–54 (2021)

11. Kingma, D.P., Ba, J.: Adam: a method for stochastic optimization. In: ICLR (2015)

12. Li, Q., et al.: LO-Net: deep real-time lidar odometry. In: CVPR, pp. 8473–8482 (2019)

13. Li, Z., Wang, N.: DMLO: deep matching lidar odometry. In: IROS (2020)

14. Low, K.L.: Linear least-squares optimization for point-to-plane icp surface registration. University of North Carolina, Chapel Hill, vol. 4, no. 10, pp. 1–3 (2004)

15. Nubert, J., Khattak, S., Hutter, M.: Self-supervised learning of lidar odometry for robotic applications. In: ICRA (2021)

16. Paszke, A., et al.: PyTorch: an imperative style, high-performance deep learning library. In: NIPS (2019)

17. Pauly, M.: Point primitives for interactive modeling and processing of 3D geometry. Hartung-Gorre (2003)

18. Segal, A., Haehnel, D., Thrun, S.: Generalized-ICP. In: Robotics: Science and Systems, vol. 2, no. 4, p. 435 (2009)

19. Shan, T., Englot, B.: LeGO-LOAM: lightweight and ground-optimized lidar odometry and mapping on variable terrain. In: IROS, pp. 4758–4765. IEEE (2018)

20. Velas, M., Spanel, M., Hradis, M., Herout, A.: CNN for IMU assisted odometry estimation using velodyne LiDAR. In: ICARSC, pp. 71–77. IEEE (2018)

21. Wang, W., et al.: DeepPCO: end-to-end point cloud odometry through deep parallel neural network. In: IROS (2019)

22. Xu, Y., et al.: SelfVoxeLO: self-supervised LiDAR odometry with voxel-based deep neural networks. In: CoRL (2020)

23. Zhang, J., Singh, S.: LOAM: LiDAR odometry and mapping in real-time. In: Robotics: Science and Systems, vol. 2, no. 9 (2014)

# Exploiting Multi-scale Fusion, Spatial Attention and Patch Interaction Techniques for Text-Independent Writer Identification

Abhishek Srivastava[1](✉), Sukalpa Chanda[2], and Umapada Pal[1]

[1] Computer Vision and Pattern Recognition Unit, Indian Statistical Institute, Kolkata, India
abhisheksrivastava2397@gmail.com, umapada@isical.ac.in
[2] Department of Computer Science and Communication, Østfold University College, Halden, Norway

**Abstract.** Text independent writer identification is a challenging problem that differentiates between different handwriting styles to decide the author of the handwritten text. Earlier writer identification relied on handcrafted features to reveal pieces of differences between writers. Recent work with the advent of convolutional neural network, deep learning-based methods have evolved. In this paper, three different deep learning techniques - spatial attention mechanism, multi-scale feature fusion and patch-based CNN were proposed to effectively capture the difference between each writer's handwriting. Our methods are based on the hypothesis that handwritten text images have specific spatial regions which are more unique to a writer's style, multi-scale features propagate characteristic features with respect to individual writers and patch-based features give more general and robust representations that helps to discriminate handwriting from different writers. The proposed methods outperforms various state-of-the-art methodologies on word-level and page-level writer identification methods on three publicly available datasets - CVL, Firemaker, CERUG-EN datasets and give comparable performance on the IAM dataset.

**Keywords:** Convolutional neural network · Writer identification · MSRF-Net

## 1 Introduction

Handwriting of an individual is unique and this particular phenomenon has been utilized by forensic handwriting experts for many decades. Handwriting experts today are aided by computer programs which actually can identify an individual on the basis of his handwriting, this technique of identifying a writer from a document image using a software is termed as "Writer Identification". Over the last

© Springer Nature Switzerland AG 2022
C. Wallraven et al. (Eds.): ACPR 2021, LNCS 13189, pp. 203–217, 2022.
https://doi.org/10.1007/978-3-031-02444-3_15

two decades many work has been published on "Writer Identification". But text independent Writer Identification in a limited data scenario is still a challenging task. It has found various applications in forensic [17] and historical [1] document analysis. Before the advent of deep-learning techniques, handcrafted features like gradient, chain-code, allograph, texture etc., were mostly used for writer identification. These feature extraction techniques render discriminating features in predicting the identity of the writer. Deep-learned features have shown impressive performance in various types of image classification problem and "Writer Identification" is also not an exception. Deep learning-based methods in general demand a huge amount of annotated text for proper training. For an application like "Writer Identification" it might not be possible always to procure enough annotated data. Over the last few years, some deep-learning based methods [16], [11] have explored writer identification. To tackle these issues methods which require limited data for identification of the authors are required. Word level writer identification is challenging since very limited information about writer's pattern and technique is available to make a decision. Few deep learning based methodologies are available, for example, He et al. [6] proposed fragment based deep neural network to use convolution neural networks (CNN) for writer identification. CNN were able to learn high level features of the text block and recognize various discriminative features in the word image. CNN's have been previously used to capture local features at the sub-region and character level and combining them for writer identification. Attention based mechanisms are well suited to identify characteristic and discriminative region in an image and enhance the performance of visual recognition based systems. In case of text independent writer identification, the word image is constituted of various segments which capture the unique style of the person's handwriting. Previous deep learning methodologies fail to exploit the contribution of more informative regions of the text image. Recent advances in computer vision has generated interest in fusion of multi-scale features to obtain diverse and rich feature representations [26]. Various resolution scales in handwritten text capture different aspects of a writer's style and structure of his/her handwriting, exploiting multi scale features and their fusion for eventual classification that obtains higher accuracy.

We devise three deep learning techniques to address and exploit those above mentioned facts and compare them to study the impact of different deep learning techniques for writer identification at word and page level. The contributions of our work are as follows:

- We propose a Spatial Attention network (SA-Net) which incorporates spatial attention to enhance relevant and informative feature maps and suppress irrelevant features for effective writer identification performance. Another potential discriminative features in text images are multi-scale features.
- To achieve efficient multi-scale fusion, we customized the MSRF-Net [22] to a classification network suitable for writer identification.
- Inspired by He and Schomaker [6] we propose another patch based CNN named PatchNet which has separate pathways for each patch and uses a

Dual Patch Dense Feature Exchange (DPDFE) block to exchange information across various patches, and making separate writer identity prediction for each patch.
- We attained new benchmarks on CVL, Firemaker and CERUG-EN datasets on word-level and page-level writer identification tasks.

The structure of this paper is as follows. Section 2 provides an overview of related methods and strategies introduced over previous years. Section 3 introduces our proposed methodologies for text independent writer identification. The details of our experiment settings and datasets used are presented in Sect. 4. In Sect. 5 we report the results attained by our methods and their comparison with other state-of-the-art methods on word-level and page-level writer identification tasks, we conclude our paper in Sect. 6.

## 2   Related Work

The initial works in the field of writer identification were guided by handcrafted feature generation and later with the advent of deep-learning, deep-learning based writer identification methods were proposed. Before the deep-learning methods a wide variety of classifiers like SVM, K-NN, Neural Network were used along with different tools like PCA and LDA to magnify the discriminativeness of various hand crafted features. In the following two subsections we will have a brief discussion on handcrafted features for writer identification followed by deep-learning based approaches.

### 2.1   Hand Crafted Feature Based Writer Identification

Difference in visual shapes in handwritten characters has been exploited by considering Connected component contour shapes, textural and allograph level features in [2], Schomaker and Bulacu [19] proposed connected-component contours and its probability density function for writer identification. Bulacu et al. [2] exploited to identify the writer. He et al. [8] used Hidden Markov Tree (HMT) in wavelet domain for writer identification. Tan et al. [24] developed a Continuous Character Prototype Distribution feature extraction technique and made classification using Minimum Distance method. Jain and Doermann [9] used K adjacent segments (KAS) to model character contours. The KAS features were clustered using a technique called affinity propagation to build a codebook for the bag of features model. Jain and Doerman [10] captured shape and curvature using contour gradients and used psuedo alphabets as features. Then writer identification was performed using K-Nearest Neighbour classifier. He et al. [7] extracted features such as junction detection, final junction refinement quill and hinge and linked it with a learned codebook to increase performance. Chahi et al. [3] used connected components of the sub-images to extract features referred to as Cross multi-scale Locally encoded Gradient Patterns (CLGP). These CLGP histogram feature vectors were fed into a Nearest Neighbor classifier for writer identification.

## 2.2   Deep Learning Feature Based Writer Identification

Recently deep learning has drawn attention as convolutional neural networks(CNN) have proven effective in extracting discriminative features from handwritten texts. Initially, Fiel and Sablatnig [4] trained a CNN classifier and used the output of second last fully connected layer as features to perform nearest neighbour classification. Tang and Wu [25] performed data augmentation on handwritten documents to allow training of a deep CNN. The CNN is then used for feature extraction and Joint Bayesian technique is used for writer identification. DeepWriter [27] used multi-stream CNNs to learn diverse representation of text images. Rehman et al. [18] augmented text images using various techniques like contour, negatives and sharpness using text line images. Multiple patches were generated from the text images and fed into an architecture similar to AlexNet pretrained on Imagenet to generate features. These features were classified using a support vector machine classifier. Keglevic et al. [12] designed a triplet network to calculate similarity measure between different patches, and trained it by maximizing inter-class distance and minimizing intra-class distance. Global features of document is then calculated by aggregating vector of local image patch descriptors. Nguyen et al. [16] generated tuples of text images by randomly sampling characters as input for their CNNs. They trained CNNs to extract sub-region, character and global level features and effectively aggregated them to predict the identity of writer. He et al. [6] designed FragNet which first builds a global feature pyramid and then a local fragment pathway which leverages fragments of global feature pyramids to make separate writer identity prediction for each writer. Javidi and Jampour [11] quantified the thickness of handwritten documents using handwriting thickness descriptors(HTD). Resnet-18 was used to extract features from the text images and they were combined with HTDs for classification. In this work, we propose three different deep learning models which uses different architecture based components suitable for identifying and capturing various aspects of a writer's technique and style.

## 3   Methodology

In this section we discuss about our proposed approaches. We have developed the following methods.

1. We develop a spatial attention based mechanism for identifying various author specific features of the word image. The characteristic style and features of the word occupy a very limited region in the word image. Generating a spatial attention map can help enhancing the features exploited from such regions. This serves as the basis of our spatial attention network(SA-Net) for writer identification.
2. Multi-Scale features can capture information of varying spatial and receptive field sizes. The word images can have key discriminative features of diverse scale sizes which convey various characteristic features of writer. Thus, it is advantageous to design a writer identification system which effectively

leverage multi-scale features while predicting the identity of our writer. We convert our MSRF-Net [22] to MSRF(Multi-Scale Residual Fusion) Classification network to effectively fuse multi-scale features and leverage them into predicting the identity of the writer more accurately.

3. Inspired by FragNet [6] we develop a patch based convolutional neural network called PatchNet. We use a different stream for each patch used and densely exchange various patch features using our Dual Patch Dense Feature Exchange (DPDFE) blocks. Each local patch predictions are then averaged over to make our final writer identity prediction.

This section is structured as follows. In Sect. 3.1 we describe our spatial attention network(SA-Net), Sect. 3.2 describes how we amend our MSRF network to a classification network and exploit multi-scale features of word images to develop a more accurate system for writer identification. Finally, in Sect. 3.3 we describe our proposed Patch-Net.

### 3.1  Spatial Attention Network

In this section we introduce our spatial network for writer identification. Specific regions of word images have characteristic textural and shape information which is unique to a specific writer. Characters in the word images also have a unique style in the manner they are written. To allow the identification and recognition of these regions we develop a spatial attention mechanism. Let $I_w$ denote word images where ( $I_w \in R^{W \times H}$). The framework resembles a VGG-style network [21] where each $I_w$ is initially processed by a convolutional block. Each convolutional block has 2 consecutive convolutional layers with $3 \times 3$ kernel size followed by batch-normalization and ReLU activation. This is described in Eq. 1 where $X$ denotes the input tensor.

$$X_{conv} = ReLU(BN(Conv(Conv(X))))$$  (1)

The convolutional blocks are followed by a spatial attention unit (see Fig. 1). This block comprises of two convolutional layers followed by a sigmoid activation function which calculates attention coefficient for each spatial location in the feature maps (see Eq. 2). These attention maps are denoted as $A_{att}$. We multiply these attention maps described in Eq. 3 to suppress regions which are non relevant and enhance the spatial location of relevant and important feature maps.

$$A_{att} = \sigma(Conv(X_{conv}))$$  (2)

$$X_{spa} = X_{conv} \otimes A_{att}$$  (3)

$X_{spa}$ denotes the spatial attention enhanced feature maps which are then halved using max pooling. The number of feature maps in a convolutional and spatial attention unit are set to [64, 128, 256, 512] respectively. We use adaptive average pooling at the last layer and a fully connected layer to make the final prediction or writer identity. For page level prediction we make predictions for all word

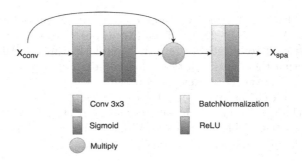

**Fig. 1.** Architecture of spatial attention unit employed in SA-Net

images in the page and average over them as described in Eq. 4, where N are the total word images in a page and $ID_{page}$ represents the identity of the writer.

$$ID_{page} = \frac{1}{N} \sum_{n=1}^{n=N} P(I_w^n) \tag{4}$$

## 3.2 MSRF Classification Network

Multi-scale feature exchange has been studied in past years in the field of computer vision. Fusion of multi-scale features result in diverse representations consequently generating richer and accurate feature maps. The word images are also structured such that different scale features capture varying writer characteristics. We use this motivation to convert our MSRF-Net [22] into a classification network (see Fig. 2). Dual scale dense fusion (DSDF) blocks used in MSRF-Net serves the purpose of fusion of two different scaled features. The dense nature of the blocks allows features of various receptive fields to be generated and the residual connections allow relevant high-level and low-level features to be maintained while making final predictions. We modify the MSRF-Sub-network to translate it into a classification head. Contrary to the MSRF sub-network which aimed to fuse and exchange multi-scale features across all scales, we ensure that all different scaled representations are able to flow in the last scale level of the classification network (see Fig. 3.2). To improve gradient flow, we allow last scale level of the MSRF classification network to make prediction before and after each DSDF block in the last scale level as shown in Fig. 2. We use an adaptive pooling module and a fully connected layer in succession to make predict writer of the word image. Finally we average over all the predictions of to make our final predictions as shown in Eq. 5, where $C$ represents the number of classification layers in the MSRF classification network and $ID_{word}$ represents the identity of the writer for the word image.

$$ID_{word} = \frac{1}{C} \sum_{k=1}^{k=C} P(I_w^k) \tag{5}$$

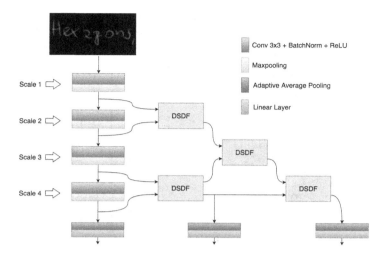

**Fig. 2.** Architecture of multi-scale residual fusion classification network

In order to make page level prediction, we again average over all word level predictions contained in the page as shown in Eq. 6.

$$ID_{page} = \frac{1}{N} \sum_{n=1}^{n=N} P(I_w^n) \qquad (6)$$

### 3.3 PatchNet

Inspired by FragNet [6] we develop a patch based classification network (see Fig. 4). The $\mathcal{I}_w$ is divided into patches of size $64 \times 64$. We generate 5 patches from the original $64 \times 128$ $\mathcal{I}_w$ and make different pathways for each patch. Each path has a initial convolutional unit of two successive convolutional layers, batch-normalization and ReLU activation. Which is followed by a maxpooling layer to reduce the spatial dimension by a factor of 2. To exchange information between two patches we design dual patch feature exchange (DPDFE) block. The entire convolutional unit, DPDFE blocks and max-pooling sequence is repeated 4 times to make patch level predictions. We also use a global prediction pathway which has a similar architecture as SA-Net without the spatial attention unit. Each patch level predictions and global prediction are averaged to make the final prediction. Page level predictions are made according to Eq. 7.

$$ID_{page} = \frac{1}{N} \sum_{n=1}^{n=N} P(I_w^n) \qquad (7)$$

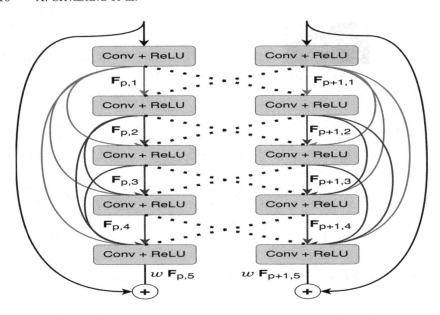

**Fig. 3.** Architecture of dual patch dense feature exchange block (dotted lines represent features incoming from parallel patch stream)

**Dual Patch Dense Feature Exchange Blocks.** In this section, we describe the structure of our dual patch dense feature exchange blocks. Let two successive patches be denoted by $\mathcal{I}_p$ and $\mathcal{I}_{p+1}$. The feature maps generated by convolutional unit of each patch stream be denoted by $M_{p,l}$, where $l$ denotes how many layers of DPDFE blocks the feature maps have been processed by and initially $l = 0$. The DPDFE blocks are residual dense blocks which takes feature maps of two different patches and process each of them using two different densely connected streams (see Fig. 3). Each stream has 5 densely connected convolutional layers, Let the output of each such layer be $F_{p,c}$ where $p$ denotes which patch is being processed and c denotes which convolutional layer has processed the feature maps in the dense stream. After each convolutional layer in the dense stream, the two different patch streams exchanges features as described in Eq. 8 ($M_{p,l}$ and $F_{p,0}$ are the same).

$$M_{p,l+1} = F_{p,c} \oplus F_{p,c-1} \oplus F_{p,c-2} \oplus \cdots \oplus F_{p+1,0} \tag{8}$$

We again scale the output features of DPDFE blocks by a factor of $w = 0.4$ to avoid instability [14,23] and add it back to the input of the respective DPDFE block as shown in Eq. 9.

$$M_{p,l+1} = w \times M_{p,l+1} + M_{p,l} \tag{9}$$

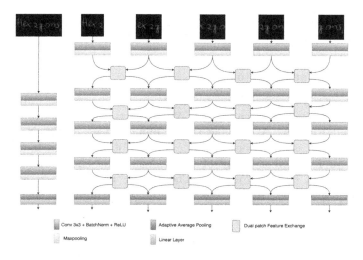

**Fig. 4.** Architecture of our proposed PatchNet

# 4    Experiments

In this section we describe the writer identification datasets used for our experiments. We also describe the implementation details of our three deep learning-based writer identification methods. We use the training and testing split used by He and Schomaker in FragNet [6]. It is ensured that each word image from each page either occurs in the training split or in the testing split, which makes the methods suitable for both word-level and page-level writer identification tasks.

## 4.1    Datasets

We benchmark our methods on four publicly available datasets namely: CERUG-EN [7], Firemaker [20], CVL [13] and IAM [15]

1. CERUG-EN [7] has 105 documents, predominantly from Chinese students. There are two paragraphs in English where one paragraph is used for training and another is used for testing. Since word images are not provided separately we use the roughly segmented word images provided by He and Schomaker in the publicly released code of FragNet.
2. Firemaker [20] has 250 different writers where each writer writes four pages. First page is used for training and the fourth page is used for testing.
3. CVL [13] has 310 writers. Each person has written five pages of text with 27 writers contributing seven pages. First three pages are used for training and the rest are used for testing.
4. IAM [15] has 610 different writers contributing varying amount of text. When more than one page is available for a writer, we choose one page for training and rest for testing. When only one page is available the lines

are divided into training and testing subsets. The word images are publicly available.

## 4.2   Implementation Details

We pre-process the images to $64 \times 128$ while maintaining aspect ratio. To avoid distortion white pixel padding is done. We use a batch size of 16 and train all methods for 50 epochs. We follow the training setting of FragNet to ensure fair and complete comparison. Adam optimizer is used with initial learning rate 0.0001 and a weight decay of $1e-4$. We decay the learning rate by a factor of 0.5 after every 10 epochs. The feature maps in each level of classification networks are [64, 128, 256, 512] for all 3 methods. The FLOPs of WordImgNet are 1.05G, whereas FLOPs of FragNet-64, FragNet-32, Frag-Net-16 are approximately 7.14G, 7.41G and 3.90G, respectively. The FLOPs of MSRF-Classification network, SA-Net and PatchNet, and ResNet18+HTDs are around 5.5G, 4.10G, and 7.65G respectively. The proposed models are available at https://github.com/NoviceMAn-prog/SA-Net-MSRF-CNet-and-PatchNet-for-Writer-Identification.

## 5   Results and Discussion

In this section we will compare our MSRF Classification Network, SA-Net and PatchNet with other published state-of-the-art methods on word-level and page-level writer identification task. It is worth mentioning here that there exists many deep-learning methods for writer identification, and even though those experiments were conducted on public datasets, lack of publicly available source code of those published methods creates hindrance towards a fair comparison. Additionally we chose methods that were designed for word level writer identification. Keeping those factors in mind, we could compare our methods with [6,11] as those methods have released their code. We train and test those methods using the same set of training and test images as we did for our proposed methods for an unbiased comparison. We establish new state-of-the-art writer identification results on three benchmark datasets - CVL, Firemaker and CERUG-EN datasets. Section 5.1 describes various other state-of-the-art deep learning methods we select for comparison with our methods on word-level and page-level writer identification tasks. In Sect. 5.1 we provide quantitative comparison of our methods with other baselines on word level writer identification tasks. Section 5.1 provides writer identification results on page level writer identification task.

### 5.1   Comparison with Other Published Methods

To provide exhaustive comparison of our methods with other baselines we select ResNet18 [5], ResNet18 conjugated with handwriting thickness descriptors(HTD) [11], WordImgNet [6] and FragNet-q [6] where q represents the $q \times q$ fragment size.

1. ResNet18 is a standard computer vision classification baseline.
2. FragNet is fragmentation based CNN with two streams. First global feature pyramid used for extraction of features. Second stream is a fragment pathway to process fragments of the original image and receive fragments from the global feature pyramid to make prediction. Each fragment has its own prediction and the final prediction is made by averaging over all local fragment predictions. We use FragNet-64, FragNet-32 and FragNet-16 for our experiments.
3. WordImgNet is designed such that the entire image is fed into a CNN framework identical to the fragment pathway to make a single global prediction.
4. ResNet18 + HTDs, ResNet18 captures high level features of the input text image. HTDs are spatial descriptor that analyze a writer's handwriting thickness depending upon factors like pressure of pen, unique style. The features extracted by ResNet18 are concatenated with HTDs which serves as additional discriminative features.

**Result on Word Level Writer Identification.** In this section we compare the Top-1 and Top-5 writer identification accuracy of our proposed methods with other state-of-the-art methods at word level. In Table 1 we present the detailed comparison of all methods on all four datasets. In CERUG-EN [7] we observe that SA-Net gives the best performance outperforming the previous state-of-the-art performer FragNet-64 by 4.7% accuracy in Top-1 and by 1.5% in Top-5. We can notice that along with SA-Net, MSRF Classification also beats FragNet-64 in performance in both Top-1 and Top-5 accuracy, PatchNet is comparable to it in performance. For Firemaker dataset, our SA-Net again gives the best performance gaining 3.2% and 0.8% in Top-1 and Top-5 accuracy over FragNet-64. MSRF-Net gives the second best performance gaining 2.2% and 0.8% in Top-1 and Top-5 accuracy over FragNet. In CVL dataset writer identification problem, MSRF Classification obtains the best performance achieving 91.4% Top-1 and 97.6% Top-5 accuracy outperforming FragNet-64 by 1.2% and 0.1% in Top-1 and Top-5 accuracy. SA-Net also performs better than FragNet-64 achieving 90.7% and 97.4% Top-1 and Top-5 accuracy. PatchNet gives a comparable 86.1% Top-1 and 96.3% Top-1 and Top-5 accuracy respectively. On the writer identification task on IAM dataset, FragNet-64 reports the best Top-1 accuracy of 85.1% while the best Top-5 accuracy is shared between FragNet-64 and MSRF Classification network, both achieving 95%. The superior performance of SA-Net on two datasets i.e. Firemaker and CERUG-EN shows the potential of spatial attention mechanism's ability to extract relevant differentiating elements of a writer's handwriting. The multi scale features obtained and fused in MSRF classification network obtains the highest Top-1 and Top-5 accuracy on CVL dataset. This displays the capacity of multi-scale features to identify the characteristics of writer's style in his handwriting. Although PatchNet outperforms previous state-of-the-art methods on only one dataset, it shows the potential of patch or fragment based networks for writer identification.

**Table 1.** Result comparison on word level writer identification

| Method | IAM | | CVL | | Firemaker | | CERUG-EN | |
|---|---|---|---|---|---|---|---|---|
| | Top-1 | Top-5 | Top-1 | Top-5 | Top-1 | Top-5 | Top-1 | Top-5 |
| ResNet18 [5] | 83.2 | 94.3 | 88.5 | 96.7 | 63.9 | 86.4 | 70.6 | 94.0 |
| ResNet18+HTD [11] | 76.9 | 91.6 | 85.1 | 95.6 | 60.7 | 82.6 | 70.1 | 91.8 |
| WordImgNet [6] | 81.8 | 94.1 | 88.6 | 96.8 | 67.9 | 88.1 | 77.3 | 96.4 |
| FragNet-16 [6] | 79.8 | 93.3 | 89.0 | 97.2 | 59.6 | 83.2 | 60.6 | 90.3 |
| FragNet-32 [6] | 83.6 | 94.8 | 89.0 | 97.3 | 65.0 | 86.8 | 62.3 | 90.1 |
| FragNet-64 [6] | **85.1** | **95.0** | 90.2 | 97.5 | 69.0 | 88.5 | 77.5 | 95.6 |
| Patch (proposed) | 80.2 | 93.5 | 86.1 | 96.2 | 62.4 | 84.9 | 77.1 | 96.5 |
| SA-Net (proposed) | 83.4 | 94.6 | 90.7 | 97.4 | **72.2** | **89.3** | **82.2** | **97.1** |
| MSRF-Net (proposed) | 84.6 | **95.0** | 91.4 | **97.6** | 71.2 | **89.3** | 79.6 | 96.8 |

**Table 2.** Result comparison on page level writer identification

| Method | IAM | | CVL | | Firemaker | | CERUG-EN | |
|---|---|---|---|---|---|---|---|---|
| | Top-1 | Top-5 | Top-1 | Top-5 | Top-1 | Top-5 | Top-1 | Top-5 |
| ResnNet18+HTD [11] | 95.2 | 98.0 | 98.3 | 98.3 | 98.0 | 99.2 | 98.0 | **100** |
| WordImgNet [6] | 95.8 | 98.0 | 98.8 | 99.4 | 97.6 | 98.8 | 97.1 | 100 |
| FragNet-16 [6] | 94.2 | 97.4 | 98.5 | 99.4 | 92.8 | 98.0 | 79.0 | 97.1 |
| FragNet-32 [6] | 95.3 | 98.0 | 98.6 | 99.4 | 96.0 | 99.2 | 84.7 | 97.1 |
| FragNet-64 [6] | **96.3** | 98.0 | 99.1 | 99.4 | 97.6 | **99.6** | 98.1 | **100** |
| Patch (proposed) | 93.6 | 96.9 | 99.0 | 99.3 | 95.6 | 98.4 | 98.1 | **100** |
| SA-Net (proposed) | 94.7 | **98.2** | **99.4** | 99.4 | **98.0** | **99.6** | **99.1** | **100** |
| MSRF-Net (proposed) | 94.8 | 98.1 | **99.4** | **99.6** | 97.2 | 99.2 | 98.1 | **100** |

**Result on Page Level Writer Identification.** In this section we provide the quantitative analysis of the comparison between our proposed methods and other state-of-the-art methods on page level writer identification. In the Firemaker dataset writer identification task, the proposed SA-Net outperforms FragNet-64 by 0.4% in Top-1 accuracy. SA-Net reports a Top-5 accuracy of 99.6% which is equal to the Top-5 accuracy to FragNet-64. SA-Net reports the highest Top-1 page level accuracy on CERUG-EN of 99.1%. Additionally, FragNet-64, PatchNet, SA-Net, MSRF classification network and ResNet18+HTDs all tie for the best Top-5 performance of 100% on CERUG-EN. MSRF-Net and SA-Net both outperforms FragNet-64 by 0.3% on Top-1 page level accuracy on the CVL dataset. MSRF-Net report the highest 99.6% Top-5 page level accuracy while FragNet-64 and SA-Net gives 99.4% Top-5 page level accuracy. For IAM dataset, FragNet-64 reports the highest 96.3% Top-1 page level accuracy. SA-Net and MSRF-Net reports the first and second best Top-5 accuracy of 98.2% and 98.1%, respectively. We notice that again SA-Net and MSRF-Net attains new benchmarks on IAM, CVL, Firemaker and CERUG-EN datasets, exhibiting the potential of amplified features on the basis of spatial attention and multi-scale features (Table 2).

# 6 Conclusion

In this paper we proposed three deep learning based solutions for text-independent writer identification. Our proposed SA-Net was able to identify and enhance the feature flow from spatial regions more relevant and significant in determining the identity of the writer. MSRF Classification network performed multi-scale feature fusion to gather more diverse representations consisting of features having varying receptive fields. The residual nature of the dual scale dense fusion (DSDF) blocks allow an effective combination of high- and low-level feature representations to be available at the disposal of final classification layer to make more accurate predictions. On the other-hand, PatchNet allows effective feature exchange between different patch streams to make more robust predictions. Our methods were able to outperform previous state-of-the-art methods for word-level and page-level writer identification on CVL, Firemaker and CERUG-EN datasets, while giving comparable performance on the IAM dataset. We show that developing deep learning based mechanisms exploiting spatially relevant regions and multi scale features is also a viable option to increase performance of writer identification systems.

**Acknowledgement.** This is a collaborative research work between Indian Statistical Institute, Kolkata, India and Østfold University College, Halden, Norway. The experiments in this paper were performed on a high performance computing platform "Experimental Infrastructure for Exploration of Exascale Computing" (eX3), which is funded by the Research Council of Norway.

# References

1. Brink, A., Smit, J., Bulacu, M., Schomaker, L.: Writer identification using directional ink-trace width measurements. Pattern Recogn. **45**(1), 162–171 (2012)
2. Bulacu, M., Schomaker, L.: Text-independent writer identification and verification using textural and allographic features. IEEE Trans. Pattern Anal. Mach. Intell. **29**(4), 701–717 (2007)
3. Chahi, A., Ruichek, Y., Touahni, R., et al.: Cross multi-scale locally encoded gradient patterns for off-line text-independent writer identification. Eng. Appl. Artif. Intell. **89**, 103459 (2020)
4. Fiel, S., Sablatnig, R.: Writer identification and retrieval using a convolutional neural network. In: Azzopardi, G., Petkov, N. (eds.) CAIP 2015. LNCS, vol. 9257, pp. 26–37. Springer, Cham (2015). https://doi.org/10.1007/978-3-319-23117-4_3
5. He, K., Zhang, X., Ren, S., Sun, J.: Deep residual learning for image recognition. In: Proceedings of the IEEE Conference on Computer Vision and Pattern Recognition, pp. 770–778 (2016)
6. He, S., Schomaker, L.: FragNet: writer identification using deep fragment networks. IEEE Trans. Inf. Forensics Secur. **15**, 3013–3022 (2020)

7. He, S., Wiering, M., Schomaker, L.: Junction detection in handwritten documents and its application to writer identification. Pattern Recogn. **48**(12), 4036–4048 (2015)
8. He, Z., You, X., Tang, Y.Y.: Writer identification of Chinese handwriting documents using hidden Markov tree model. Pattern Recogn. **41**(4), 1295–1307 (2008)
9. Jain, R., Doermann, D.: Offline writer identification using K-adjacent segments. In: 2011 International Conference on Document Analysis and Recognition, pp. 769–773. IEEE (2011)
10. Jain, R., Doermann, D.: Writer identification using an alphabet of contour gradient descriptors. In: 2013 12th International Conference on Document Analysis and Recognition, pp. 550–554. IEEE (2013)
11. Javidi, M., Jampour, M.: A deep learning framework for text-independent writer identification. Eng. Appl. Artif. Intell. **95**, 103912 (2020)
12. Keglevic, M., Fiel, S., Sablatnig, R.: Learning features for writer retrieval and identification using triplet CNNs. In: 2018 16th International Conference on Frontiers in Handwriting Recognition (ICFHR), pp. 211–216. IEEE (2018)
13. Kleber, F., Fiel, S., Diem, M., Sablatnig, R.: CVL-database: an off-line database for writer retrieval, writer identification and word spotting. In: 2013 12th International Conference on Document Analysis and Recognition, pp. 560–564. IEEE (2013)
14. Lim, B., Son, S., Kim, H., Nah, S., Mu Lee, K.: Enhanced deep residual networks for single image super-resolution. In: Proceedings of the IEEE Conference on Computer Vision and Pattern Recognition Workshops, pp. 136–144 (2017)
15. Marti, U.V., Bunke, H.: The IAM-database: an English sentence database for offline handwriting recognition. Int. J. Doc. Anal. Recogn. **5**(1), 39–46 (2002)
16. Nguyen, H.T., Nguyen, C.T., Ino, T., Indurkhya, B., Nakagawa, M.: Text-independent writer identification using convolutional neural network. Pattern Recogn. Lett. **121**, 104–112 (2019)
17. Pervouchine, V., Leedham, G.: Extraction and analysis of forensic document examiner features used for writer identification. Pattern Recogn. **40**(3), 1004–1013 (2007)
18. Rehman, A., Naz, S., Razzak, M.I., Hameed, I.A.: Automatic visual features for writer identification: a deep learning approach. IEEE Access **7**, 17149–17157 (2019)
19. Schomaker, L., Bulacu, M.: Automatic writer identification using connected-component contours and edge-based features of uppercase western script. IEEE Trans. Pattern Anal. Mach. Intell. **26**(6), 787–798 (2004)
20. Schomaker, L., Vuurpijl, L., Schomaker, L.: Forensic writer identification: a benchmark data set and a comparison of two systems (2000)
21. Simonyan, K., Zisserman, A.: Very deep convolutional networks for large-scale image recognition. arXiv preprint arXiv:1409.1556 (2014)
22. Srivastava, A., et al.: MSRF-Net: a multi-scale residual fusion network for biomedical image segmentation. arXiv preprint arXiv:2105.07451 (2021)
23. Szegedy, C., Ioffe, S., Vanhoucke, V., Alemi, A.: Inception-v4, inception-ResNet and the impact of residual connections on learning. In: Proceedings of AAAI Conference on Artificial Intelligence, vol. 31 (2017)
24. Tan, G.X., Viard-Gaudin, C., Kot, A.C.: Automatic writer identification framework for online handwritten documents using character prototypes. Pattern Recognit. **42**(12), 3313–3323 (2009)
25. Tang, Y., Wu, X.: Text-independent writer identification via CNN features and joint Bayesian. In: 2016 15th International Conference on Frontiers in Handwriting Recognition (ICFHR), pp. 566–571. IEEE (2016)

26. Wang, J., et al.: Deep high-resolution representation learning for visual recognition. IEEE Trans. Pattern Anal. Mach. Intell. **43**, 3349–3364 (2020)
27. Xing, L., Qiao, Y.: DeepWriter: a multi-stream deep CNN for text-independent writer identification. In: 2016 15th International Conference on Frontiers in Handwriting Recognition (ICFHR), pp. 584–589. IEEE (2016)

# DCT-DWT-FFT Based Method for Text Detection in Underwater Images

Ayan Banerjee[1], Palaiahnakote Shivakumara[2](✉), Soumyajit Pal[1], Umapada Pal[1], and Cheng-Lin Liu[3,4]

[1] Computer Vision and Pattern Recognition Unit, Indian Statistical Institute, Kolkata, India
ab2141@cse.jgec.ac.in, umapada@isical.ac.in
[2] Department of Computer System and Technology, Faculty of Computer Science and Information Technology, University of Malaya, Kuala Lumpur, Malaysia
shiva@um.edu.my
[3] National Laboratory of Pattern Recognition, Institute of Automation of Chinese Academy of Sciences, Beijing, China
liucl@nlpr.ia.ac.cn
[4] School of Artificial Intelligence, University of Chinese Academy of Sciences, Beijing, China

**Abstract.** Text detection in underwater images is an open challenge because of the distortions caused by refraction, absorption of light, particles, and variations depending on depth, color, and nature of water. Unlike existing methods aimed at text detection in natural scene images, in this paper, we have proposed a novel method for text detection in underwater images through a new enhancement model. Based on observations that fine details of text in image share with high energy, spatial resolution, and brightness, we consider Discrete Cosine Transform (DCT), Discrete Wavelet Transform (DWT), and Fast Fourier Transform (FFT) for image enhancement to highlight the text features. The enhanced image is fed to a modified Character Region Awareness for Text Detection (CRAFT) model to detect text in underwater images. To explore enhancement methods, we evaluate six combinations of image enhancement techniques, namely, DCT-DWT-FFT, DCT-FFT-DWT, DWT-DCT-FFT, DWT-FFT-DCT, FFT-DCT-DWT, FFT-DWT-DCT. Experimental results on our dataset of underwater images and benchmark datasets of natural scene text detection, namely, MSRA-TD500, ICDAR 2019 MLT, ICDAR 2019 ArT, Total-Text, CTW1500, and COCO Text show that the proposed method performs well for both underwater and natural scene images and outperforms the existing methods on all the datasets.

**Keywords:** Under water images · Text detection in underwater images · Image enhancement · Discrete cosine transform · Wavelet transform · Fourier transform · Modified Character Region Awareness for Text Detection (CRAFT)

## 1 Introduction

At present the tourism sector has been extended to perform activities, such as games, dining, marriage rituals, undersea, river, and water. Therefore, image indexing, retrieval, and

C. Wallraven et al. (Eds.): ACPR 2021, LNCS 13189, pp. 218–233, 2022.
https://doi.org/10.1007/978-3-031-02444-3_16

understanding of underwater images have received increasing attention from researchers in the field of image processing and computer vision [1, 2]. For example, in the case of scuba diving under the sea, text detection approach can be used to trace the swimmer by using text appeared on equipment and camera, such that we can prevent them to reaching dangerous area. At the same time, guide can control and monitor the swimmer and teach them different skills. In the similar way, text detection can be used to retrieve under water activities in the ocean. Therefore, text detection in underwater images is useful and significant in understanding underwater images and videos. Compared to text detection in natural scene images, detection in underwater images is more challenging due to various distortions caused by the refraction of light, the surface of water, depth of water, and particles in water. Many methods have been proposed for text detection in natural scene images [3, 4] but text detection in underwater images has received little attention. Existing natural scene text detection methods do not perform well on underwater images. In Fig. 1, the results of two state-of-the-art methods, ContourNet [3] and FDTA [4] are shown where it can be seen that tiny text lines in underwater images are missed despite their excellence performance on natural scene images. This is because underwater images lose quality due to distortion caused by the nature of water. On the other hand, the proposed method can detect such text properly in underwater as well as

Underwater            ICDAR 2019 MLT            ICDAR ArT 2019

(a)    ContourNet [3]

(b) FDTA [4]

(c) Proposed Method

**Fig. 1.** Example of text detection of proposed and existing methods for under water and natural scene images. Results of ContourNet, FDTA and the proposed method are shown in (a), (b) and (c), respectively.

natural scene images. This is the contribution of the proposed model compared to the state-of-the-art methods.

In order to address the challenges of underwater images, inspired by the work [5], which combine different frequency domain analysis methods to improve the image quality for face anti-spoofing detection, we explore different combinations of Discrete Cosine Transform (DCT), Discrete Wavelet Transform (DWT) and Fast Fourier Transform (FFT) to enhance the text details in underwater images. The intuition behind the idea is that the text pixels in any image share high energy, spatial resolution, and brightness compared to non-text pixels. It is noted that the energy can be achieved by DCT, the fine scaling can be achieved by DWT and the brightness is achieved by FFT. The combination of DCT-DWT-FFT produces six enhanced images. The enhanced images are supplied to modified Character Region Awareness for Text Detection (CRAFT) [6] in such a way that the model should work for both underwater and natural scene images.

In summary, the main contributions of the proposed method are as follows. (i) This is the first work addressing the challenges of text detection in underwater images. (ii) The combination of DCT-DWT-FFT is introduced for enhancing low contrast text information in underwater images. (iii) The proposed text detection method performs well on both underwater and natural scene images and outperforms state-of-the-art methods on multiple datasets.

## 2   Related Work

The existing methods on text detection in natural scene images can be categorized into top-down (regression based), bottom-up (segmentation based), and hybrid models for accurate text detection. We review the recent methods of the same.

The regression-based methods consider the whole text as an object for text detection. For instance, Cao et al. [4] proposed FDTA, which is fully convolutional scene text detection with text attention. Liu et al. [7] proposed GCCNet, which is a grouped channel composition network for scene text detection in natural scene images. The model optimizes anchor functions rather than a handcrafted feature for tackling the challenges of text detection. Shi et al. [8] explored iterative polynomial parameter regression for accurate arbitrarily shaped scene text detection. However, these methods are not robust for handling an arbitrarily shaped text.

To overcome the problem of arbitrarily-orientation and arbitrarily shaped text, the segmentation-based methods were developed. These methods used character and pixel information as local information for accurate text detection. For instance, Qin et al. [9] explored soft attention mechanism and dilated convolution for detecting arbitrarily shaped text in natural scene images. Baek et al. [6] developed a model called CRAFT, which is character region awareness for text detection in natural scene images. Dai et al. [10] proposed scale-aware data augmentation and shape similarity constant for accurate text detection in natural scene images. Hu et al. [11] proposed TATD, which is text contour attention for scene text detection in natural scene images. The model uses text center intensity maps and text kernel maps for accurate results. Liao et al. [12] proposed MaskTextSpotter, which is a trainable neural network for spotting text with arbitrary shapes. The model works based on developing sequence to sequence network. Deng et al. [13] developed a method called RFRN, which is recurrent features refinement network for accurate and efficient text detection in natural scene images. However, these methods are sensitive to distortion and complex background images.

To overcome the problems of regression and segmentation-based methods, hybrid methods were developed. These methods consider merits of regression and segmentation-based approaches to improve text detection performance. For example, Wang et al. [3] proposed ContourNet for detecting text in natural scene images that use advantages of both regressions-based models and segmentation-based models to tackle the challenge of arbitrarily shaped text detection. Liu et al. [14] proposed semi-supervised learning for text detection in natural scene images.

In summary, most of the models targeted the challenges of text detection in natural scene images but not other images, such as low light images, deformable text detection, tattoo text detection, and underwater images. However, there are methods [15–17] that consider the combination of enhancement and deep learning for low light images, deformable text detection from sports images based on episodic learning, and tattoo text detection based on deformable convolutional inception neural network. None of the existing methods consider underwater images for text detection. Hence, this work aims to develop an enhancement model for improving text detection in underwater and natural scene images.

## 3   Proposed Method

To detect text in underwater and natural scene images, it is observed that the properties of pixels, such as energy, fine scaling (spatial resolution), and brightness are common for all the text pixels regardless of image type and irrespective of qualities. Inspired by the method [5] where the combinations of DWT-LBP-FFT have been used for separating pixels affected by face attack from the actual pixels, we explore the combination in a different way for enhancing text pixels in the underwater images. In addition, it is noted that the proposed transforms involve combination of low and high pass filters to find fine details, namely edge information for reconstructing images. This observation motivated us to propose different combinations of above transforms such that the fine details in poor quality under water image caused by multiple adverse factors can be enhanced.

To explore the optimal configuration of image enhancement model, we evaluate different combinations of three image transform techniques: DCT, DWT, and FFT. The combinations of transforms results in six versions of enhanced images, namely, DCT-DWT-FFT, DCT-FFT-DWT, DWT-DCT-FFT, DWT-FFT-DCT, FFT-DCT-DWT, FFT-DWT-DCT. After image enhancement, we adopt the state-of-the-art text detection method, Character Region Awareness for Text Detection (CRAFT) [6], which works well for good quality images by studying character shape. We use the same to modify the model such that the modified model can withstand the challenges of text detection in underwater images by considering six enhanced images as input in this work. The schematic diagram of the proposed work is shown in Fig. 2.

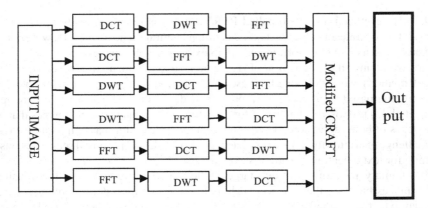

**Fig. 2.** The proposed block diagram for text detection in underwater images.

## 3.1 DCT-DFT-FFT Images for Enhancement

For the input image, the proposed method obtains IDCT, IDWT, and IFFT images. In order to take advantage of DCT, DWT, and FFT, the proposed approach performs the combination of DCT, DWT, and FFT bypassing reconstructed images. For example, the reconstructed image of DCT is supplied to DWT, the reconstructed image of DWT is supplied to FFT, which outputs the final reconstructed image of the first combination. The same process is continued to obtain all the six reconstructed images by the six combinations, namely, DCT-DWT-FFT, DCT-FFT-DWT, DWT-DCT-FFT, DWT-FFT-DCT, FFT-DCT-DWT, FFT-DWT-DCT. The calculations of DCT, DWT and FFT are obtained as defined in Eqs. (1)–(3), respectively.

$$G(r, s) = \beta_r \beta_s \sum_{x=0}^{P-1} \sum_{y=0}^{Q-1} g(x, y) cos\left[\frac{\pi(2x + 1)r}{2P}\right] cos\left[\frac{\pi(2y + 1)s}{2Q}\right], \quad (1)$$

$$g(x, y) = \frac{1}{\sqrt{PQ}} \sum_u \sum_v W_\delta(k_0, u, v)\delta_{k_0,u,v}(x, y)$$

$$+ \frac{1}{\sqrt{PQ}} \sum_{i=H,V,D} \sum_{k=k_0} \sum_u \sum_v W_\omega^i(k, u, v)\omega_{k,u,v}^i(x, y), \quad (2)$$

$$B_j = \sum_{u=0}^{U-1} e^{-i\frac{2\pi ju}{U}} b_u, \quad (3)$$

where, $\beta_r$ and $\beta_s$ represent the beta distribution of the pixel, P and Q are the spectrum intensity and spectrum density, respectively. On the other hand, $W_\delta$ is the wavelet transform function k, u, v represents the horizontal, vertical and diagonal transform, respectively. Last but not the least, $b_u$ depicts the pixel value before DFT. Fast Fourier Transform (FFT) is a fast way of computing Discrete Fourier Transform by taking 2-point and 4-point DFT and generalizing them to 8-point, 16-point, ..., $2^r$-point.

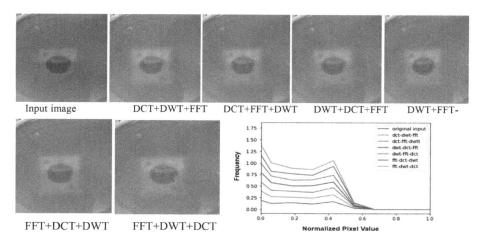

Input image    DCT+DWT+FFT    DCT+FFT+DWT    DWT+DCT+FFT    DWT+FFT-

FFT+DCT+DWT    FFT+DWT+DCT

**Fig. 3.** Six combinations of enhanced images and their pixel distributions.

The results of each combination can be seen in Fig. 3 for the input image, where it can be seen that the brightness increase for all the enhanced images. We believe that each combination helps us to enhance the fine details of text pixels in the underwater images. As a result, the contrast between text and non-text pixel increases. It is evident from the plots of six enhanced images shown in Fig. 3. Here, X-axis represents the normalized pixel value and Y-axis represents the pixel frequency downscaled by 100. Higher pixel frequency means high degree of enhancement which helps for better detection. It can be seen that the pixel frequency of six enhanced images increases compared to the values in the input image. This observation motivated us to explore CRAFT mode for text detection from the enhanced images. Therefore, we modify the CRAFT such that it accepts all the six enhanced images as input for accurate text detection irrespective of image type and quality.

### 3.2   Proposed Modified CRAFT for Text Detection in Underwater Images

It is noted that the existing CRAFT can address most of the challenges, such as arbitrarily shaped, arbitrarily-orientation, which are common in the case of underwater images. However, it works well for the images with good quality and contrast but not for the underwater image which generally suffers from poor quality. Therefore, we modify the CRAFT such that it performs well for underwater images by considering all the six enhanced images obtained from the previous section as input. The modified architecture can be seen in Fig. 4. The ResNet-50 has been used here as the foundation of CRAN. We use FPN to meld include maps produced by various phases of the backbone initializing from the top. Utilizing the melded highlight maps, the consideration module further upgrades its discriminative parts by creating comparing consideration loads. Then the improved element maps are used in the correction module and the acknowledgment organization to create the character groups. The proposed network is an end-to-end trainable and the acknowledgment network utilized is equivalent to the consideration-based encoder-decoder in [18].

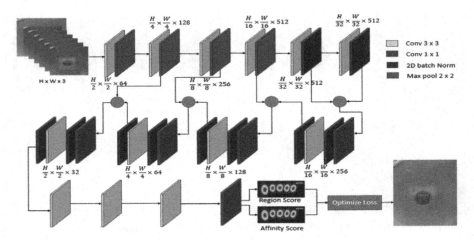

**Fig. 4.** Proposed modified CRAFT for text detection in under water image.

The 2D character detection module comprises a detection head, a component savvy duplication (i.e. element-wise multiplication) activity. Given the information highlight maps $I_{in}$, the consideration head produces the consideration map, *CM* through three convolution layers, every one of which is trailed by a cluster standardization (i.e. batch normalization) layer and a ReLU activation layer. Then, at that point the yield highlight maps $I_{out}$ can be registered as defined in Eq. (4).

$$I_{out} = I_{in} \otimes CM \qquad (4)$$

where $\otimes$ addresses component insightful augmentation. Note that *CM* has one channel and therefore, the proposed model broadcast it to a similar shape as $I_{in}$ to accomplish component astute augmentation. Even though our consideration module is exceptionally basic, it brings extensive improvement because of the oversight of the consideration map during preparation.

We use the correction module to amend the element guides of discretionary formed examples to customary ones. It comprises an amendment head organization and a sampler. In the first place, the correction head predicts the directions of K control focuses, then, at that point the sampler utilizes Thin-Plate-Spline (TPS) change to produce the redressed include maps. Unique concerning Aster that straightforwardly redresses the info pictures, we amend the upgraded highlight maps. As enough discriminative data is separated, we don't require as many convolution layers as Aster. The configuration of our modified CRAFT architecture is shown in Table 1.

**Table 1.** Configuration of the proposed modified CRAFT architecture

| Layer name | Configuration | Out size |
|---|---|---|
| Conv 1 | $7 \times 7$; $2 \times 2$; $2 \times 2$; 64, maxpool: $2 \times 2$; $2 \times 2$; $0 \times 0$ | $8 \times 16$ |
| Conv2 | $5 \times 5$; $1 \times 1$; $1 \times 1$; 128, maxpool: $2 \times 2$; $2 \times 2$; $0 \times 0$ | $4 \times 8$ |
| Conv3 | $3 \times 3$; $1 \times 1$; $\times 1$; 256, maxpool: $2 \times 2$; $2 \times 2$; $0 \times 0$ | $2 \times 4$ |
| Conv4 | $1 \times 1$; $1 \times 1$; $\times 1$; 512, maxpool: $2 \times 2$; $2 \times 2$; $0 \times 0$ | $1 \times 4$ |
| fc1 | 512 | 512 |
| fc2 | $K \times 3$ | $K \times 3$ |

During preparation, the consideration module and acknowledgment module are regulated. The entire framework can be prepared in a start to finish way, with the accompanying loss function as defined in Eq. (5).

$$L = \sum_{I \in textImage} \lambda \times L_{att} + L_{rec},  \qquad (5)$$

where, $L_{att}$ addresses the deviation between the anticipated consideration map and the ground truth, which is determined by the Smooth $L_1$ Loss as defined in Eq. (6).

$$Smooth_{L_1}(x) = \{-0.5a^2 if\ a < 1;$$
$$= \{|a| - 0.5\ otherwise  \qquad (6)$$

So, $L_{att}$ can be defined using Eq. (7).

$$L_{att} = Smooth_{L_1}\left(CM - CM^*\right),  \qquad (7)$$

where $CM$ is the anticipated consideration guide and $CM^*$ is the comparing ground truth. Moreover, $L_{rec}$ denotes the recognition loss, which can be formulated as defined in Eq. (8).

$$L_{rec} = -\frac{1}{N} \sum_{i=1}^{N} \log p(x_i | I, \emptyset),  \qquad (8)$$

where $x_1, x_2, \ldots\ldots\ldots, x_N$ is the ground truth record grouping, $\emptyset$ addresses all teachable boundaries of our organization, $I$ is the info picture. The hyper-boundary $\lambda$ is intended to balance two losses. Samples are chosen from SynthText and Synth90K is utilized during preparation. For tests from SynthText, we use jumping box comments of each character to create the ground reality of the consideration map. Since Synth90K doesn't provide character-level comments, we disregard $L_{att}$ for tests from Synth90k, i.e., the acknowledgment misfortune is utilized to upgrade the model. $\lambda$ is observationally set to 1000 in our tests.

The results of the proposed modified CRAFT and the existing CRAFT are shown in Fig. 5(a)–(b), where it can be seen that the proposed modified CRAFT detects all the text in all the three images including tiny and a big text as shown in Fig. 5(b), while the existing CRAFT misses' text in underwater images especially for tiny text as shown in Fig. 5(a). This shows that modifications to existing CRAFT are effective for accurate text detection in underwater images.

(a) The results of existing CRAFT model

(b) The results of the proposed modified CRAFT model

**Fig. 5.** Effectiveness of the proposed modified CRAFT for different water images.

## 4 Experimental Results

Creating a dataset for text detection in underwater images is not an easy task and at present there is no dataset for underwater images. Therefore, we created our own dataset by immersing objects containing text in the water at different levels. Both clear and polluted water are used for data collection. For making the dataset complex, we have added dust and mud into water. In addition, we used different objects, papers, bottles with labels, different covers of the packets for creating the dataset. The text in such images can have arbitrary-shaped characters, orientation, and dense text in addition to the adverse effect of water. We believe that the way we created the dataset matches with the real scenario of underwater images. Our dataset consists of 500 images with large variations.

To show that the proposed model works well for natural scene images, we consider six benchmark datasets as follows. **MSRA-TD500** [19]: This is to test the ability of multi-oriented and multi-lingual text detection. The dataset provides 300 images for training and 200 images for testing. **CTW1500** [19]: This is to test the curved text detection ability of the methods. It provides 1000 images for training and 500 images for testing. **Total-Text** [19]: This is also a curved text dataset with more variations in the images for evaluating the performance of the methods. It provides 1255 images for training and 300 for testing. **ICDAR 2017 MLT** [19]: This is to test the multi-lingual ability of the methods, which includes 9 different languages. It provides 7200 images for training images, 1800 images for validation, and 9000 images for testing. **ICDAR 2019 ArT dataset** [20]: This dataset combines the images of Total-Text, CTW1500, and Baidu Curved Scene Text. This is a huge dataset compared to all other datasets. In total, 10,166 images are there, and 5603 images are used for training and 4563 images for testing. **COCO-Text** [19]: This is not created to evaluate text detection methods; the images are collected with the intention of other objectives. As a result, one can expect large variations in the images compared to other benchmark datasets. It provides 43686 images for training, 20000 images for validation, and 900 images for testing.

To show the superiority of the proposed method over existing methods, we compared the results of the proposed method with the results of the SOTA methods [3, 4, 6, 8, 9, 14]. The reason to choose the above existing methods for comparison is that the objective of these methods is the same as the proposed work. In addition, the methods addressed the challenges that similar to text detection in underwater images. To test the above-mentioned existing methods on our underwater image dataset, we retrain the methods with training samples of respective datasets. The standard measures, namely, Precision (P), Recall (R), and F-Score (F) for evaluating the performance of the methods are used as defined in [3–8].

For experiments, we use 70:30 ratios for training and testing in the case of our underwater image dataset while for all other benchmark datasets, we use the number of training and testing samples according to the ratio provided in the respective datasets. However, the evaluation scheme followed in this study is the same for all the experiments.

## 4.1 Ablation Study

The key steps of the proposed method are the combination of DCT-DWT-FFT and modifications to the existing CRAFT to achieve the best text detection performance. To validate the contribution of each transform, enhanced images obtained by six combinations, and the effectiveness of the proposed modified CRAFT, the following experiments are conducted.

(i) The existing CRAFT without any modifications was applied on an underwater image dataset for calculating measures as reported in Table 2 and the results are considered as baseline results for comparing with other steps of the proposed method. In this experiment, the input underwater images are passed to the existing CRAFT for text detection. (ii)–(iv) The reconstructed images given by DCT, DWT, and FFT are fed to the proposed modified CRAFT for text detection. This is to test the contribution of DCT alone, DFT alone and FFT alone to achieve the best detection results by the proposed method. (v)–(x) Enhanced images given by each combination are supplied to proposed modified CRAFT for text detection. This is to test the effectiveness of each combination. (xi) The input images are passed to the proposed modified CRAFT without enhancement images. This is to test the contribution of the modifications done to the existing CRAFT. (xii) All the six enhanced images are fed to the proposed modified CRAFT for text detection in underwater images.

It is observed from Table 2 that the results of experiments from (ii)–(xi) show the Precision, Recall and F-Score of each experiment are improving compared to the baseline results of the experiment (i). Therefore, one can infer that the transforms, the combinations of different transforms, and modifications to the existing CRAFT are all effective and contribute equally to achieving the best results for text detection in underwater images by the proposed method as reported in Experiment (xii).

**Table 2.** Ablation Study using our underwater images dataset.

| # | Experiments | P | R | F |
|---|---|---|---|---|
| (i) | Baseline method: Existing CRAFT [6] | 60.3 | 61.8 | 60.1 |
| (ii) | DCT+ Proposed modified CRAFT | 62.7 | 62.2 | 62.3 |
| (iii) | DWT+ Proposed modified CRAFT | 64.3 | 65.8 | 65.1 |
| (iv) | FFT+ Proposed modified CRAFT | 66.7 | 66.2 | 66.3 |
| (v) | DCT-FFT-DWT+ Proposed modified CRAFT | 70.3 | 71.8 | 71.1 |
| (vi) | DWT-DCT-FFT+ Proposed modified CRAFT | 72.7 | 72.2 | 72.3 |
| (vii) | DWT-FFT-DCT+ Proposed modified CRAFT | 76.3 | 75.8 | 76.1 |
| (viii) | FFT-DCT-DWT+ Proposed modified CRAFT | 82.7 | 82.2 | 82.3 |
| (ix) | FFT-DWT-DCT+ Proposed modified CRAFT | 84.4 | 84.9 | 84.2 |
| (x) | DCT-DWT-FFT+ Proposed modified CRAFT | 86.8 | 86.3 | 86.4 |
| (xi) | Proposed modified CRAFT (without enhancement) | 87.2 | 87.1 | 87.1 |
| (xii) | Proposed method | **89.2** | **88.7** | **89.1** |

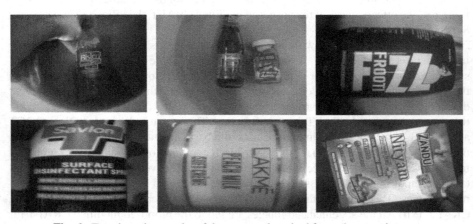

**Fig. 6.** Text detection results of the proposed method for underwater images.

## 4.2 Experiments on Our Underwater Images Dataset

Sample results of the proposed method for text detection in underwater images are shown in Fig. 6, where it can be seen that the proposed method is capable of detecting the different types of texts in the underwater images including tiny, dense, arbitrarily oriented text with complex background. Therefore, one can argue that the proposed model is robust to underwater images of different qualities. For quantitative results, to show that the enhancement step presented in Sect. 3.1 is effective in improving the text detection performance of the methods, we calculate the measures by feeding input image as input for the proposed and existing methods, which is called before enhancement experiments. Similarly, the measures are calculated by feeding six enhanced obtained by enhancement steps as input to the proposed and existing methods, which is called after enhancement experiments.

In the case of before-enhancement experiments, the input images are fed to the proposed modified CRAFT without enhanced images for text detection. For after-enhancement experiments, the six enhanced images are fed to the proposed modified CRAFT for text detection. It is observed from Table 3 that all the methods report better results in terms of Precision, Recall, and F-Score for after-enhancement compared to before-enhancement. This indicates that the enhancement step is effective and contributes to achieving better detection results for underwater images. In the same way, when we compare the results of the proposed and existing methods before and after enhancement, the proposed method is the best at Precision, Recall and F-Score compared to the existing methods. Therefore, one can conclude that the proposed method is capable of addressing the challenges of underwater images. On the other hand, since the existing methods were developed for detecting text in natural scene images, the existing methods are not effective for underwater images, which are affected by distortion caused by the depth of water, purity of water, light refraction, light absorption, and the objects like labels on the bottles, covers, papers, different objects etc.

**Table 3.** Performance of the proposed and existing methods on underwater images dataset

| Methods | Before enhancement | | | After enhancement | | |
|---|---|---|---|---|---|---|
| | P | R | F | P | R | F |
| ContourNet [3] | 69.7 | 65.9 | 67.8 | 71.7 | 67.9 | 69.8 |
| FDTA [4] | 77.9 | 80.1 | 79.4 | 79.9 | 82.1 | 81.4 |
| Qin et al. [9] | 84.7 | 83.2 | 84.2 | 85.7 | 84.2 | 85.2 |
| Shi et al.[8] | 83.9 | 84.3 | 84.1 | 84.9 | 85.3 | 85.1 |
| SemiText [14] | 84.2 | 85.5 | 84.7 | 85.2 | 86.5 | 85.7 |
| CRAFT [6] | 60.3 | 61.8 | 60.1 | 64.3 | 65.8 | 64.1 |
| Proposed | **89.2** | **88.7** | **89.1** | **91.2** | **90.7** | **91.1** |

## 4.3   Experiments on Benchmark Dataset of Natural Scene Images

To show that the proposed method has ability to detect text in natural scene images, the measures are calculated for the images of six standard natural scene text datasets, namely, MSRA-TD500, ICDAR 2019 MLT, CTW1500, Total-Text, ICDAR 2019 ArT, and COCO-Text. Sample results of the proposed method are shown in Fig. 7, where we can observe that the proposed method detects text well for all the images of different datasets. This shows that despite the proposed model is developed for text detection in underwater images, it detects text well for natural scene images and hence the proposed method is robust.

Quantitative results of the proposed and existing methods before, after-enhancement for all the aforementioned datasets are reported in Tables 4 and 5. Tables 4 and 5 show that all the methods including the proposed method report high results for after-enhancement (After) compared to before-enhancement (Before) in terms of all the three measures. Therefore, we can confirm that the proposed enhancement is useful for improving text detection performance even for natural scene images also. Similarly, the results of the proposed and existing methods after-enhancement show that the proposed method is better than existing methods. This indicates that the proposed method is independent of image type, text type, and image quality. It is evident from the results of the proposed method on all the datasets that the results are almost the same for all the datasets. This is the advantage of obtaining the enhanced images by the six combinations of DCT-DWT-FFT and modified CRAFT. The reason for the poor results of existing methods is that although the models are robust to low contrast, low resolution, and taking advantage of deep learning, the models are not consistent and stable when the images suffer from poor quality affected by multiple adverse factors of water images. Overall, the proposed enhancement is effective in improving the performance of text detection for both underwater and natural scene images. In addition, the proposed model is generic because it performs well for images of different complexities.

**Fig. 7.** Example of text detection of the proposed model for images of different benchmark natural scene text datasets.

Sometimes, when the text is too tiny and water contains more dust as shown in Fig. 8, the proposed model does not detect text, accurately. It can be seen from the examples shown in Fig. 8, where the proposed model misses text and does not fix proper bounding boxes for each text line in the images. Therefore, there is a scope for improving the proposed model further. In these cases, just enhancement using image information is not sufficient. We need to extract object information to define the context and then the context information can be used to enhance the whole region rather than focusing only on text information. Next, to improve the quality of the enhanced region, one can think of super-resolution concept, which enhances the fine details of the text.

**Table 4.** Text detection performance of the proposed and existing methods on MSRATD-500, ICDAR 2019 MLT and CTW1500.

| Methods | MSRA-TD500 | | | | | | ICDAR 2019 MLT | | | | | | CTW1500 | | | | | |
|---|---|---|---|---|---|---|---|---|---|---|---|---|---|---|---|---|---|---|
| | Before | | | After | | | Before | | | After | | | Before | | | After | | |
| | P | R | F | P | R | F | P | R | F | P | R | F | P | R | F | P | R | F |
| ContourNet [3] | 68.7 | 68.9 | 68.8 | 78.7 | 78.9 | 78.8 | 79.7 | 75.9 | 77.8 | 81.7 | 77.9 | 79.8 | 84.6 | 82.7 | 83.7 | 86.6 | 84.7 | 85.7 |
| FDTA [4] | 77.9 | 86.1 | 83.4 | 79.9 | 88.1 | 85.4 | 77.1 | 80.2 | 79.3 | 79.1 | 82.2 | 81.3 | 83.1 | 79.9 | 81.5 | 85.1 | 81.9 | 83.5 |
| Qin et al. [9] | 86.7 | 84.2 | 85.2 | 88.7 | 86.2 | 87.2 | 84.4 | 83.5 | 84.6 | 86.4 | 85.5 | 85.6 | 84.9 | 79.6 | 82.3 | 86.9 | 81.6 | 84.3 |
| Shi et al.[8] | 85.9 | 85.3 | 85.1 | 87.9 | 87.3 | 87.1 | 83.7 | 84.8 | 84.9 | 85.7 | 86.8 | 85.9 | 86.1 | 81.2 | 83.4 | 88.1 | 83.2 | 85.4 |
| SemiText [14] | 84.2 | 86.5 | 85.7 | 86.2 | 88.5 | 87.7 | 84.0 | 85.1 | 84.2 | 86.0 | 87.1 | 86.2 | 85.8 | 83.1 | 84.5 | 87.8 | 85.1 | 86.5 |
| CRAFT [6] | 80.3 | 81.8 | 80.1 | 82.3 | 83.8 | 82.1 | 80.8 | 81.8 | 81.2 | 82.8 | 83.8 | 83.2 | 80.8 | 81.8 | 81.2 | 82.8 | 83.8 | 83.2 |
| Proposed | **89.3** | **88.8** | **89.2** | **91.3** | **90.8** | **91.2** | **89.3** | **89.4** | **89.5** | **91.3** | **91.4** | **91.5** | **89.6** | **89.1** | **89.3** | **91.6** | **91.1** | **91.3** |

**Table 5.** Text detection performance of the proposed and existing methods on Total-Text, ICDAR 2019 ArT and COCO-text datasets.

| Methods | Total-text | | | | | | ICDAR 2019 ArT | | | | | | COCO-text | | | | | |
|---|---|---|---|---|---|---|---|---|---|---|---|---|---|---|---|---|---|---|
| | Before | | | After | | | Before | | | After | | | Before | | | After | | |
| | P | R | F | P | R | F | P | R | F | P | R | F | P | R | F | P | R | F |
| ContourNet [3] | 82.6 | 74.6 | 78.5 | 84.6 | 76.7 | 80.6 | 84.1 | 82.7 | 83.3 | 86.1 | 84.7 | 85.3 | 87.7 | 85.9 | 86.8 | 89.7 | 87.9 | 88.8 |
| FDTA [4] | 85.7 | 75.8 | 80.4 | 87.7 | 77.8 | 82.4 | 83.2 | 79.8 | 81.4 | 84.2 | 81.8 | 83.4 | 79.9 | 82.1 | 81.4 | 81.9 | 84.1 | 83.4 |
| Qin et al. [9] | 81.3 | 79.8 | 80.7 | 83.3 | 81.8 | 82.7 | 84.3 | 79.9 | 82.5 | 86.3 | 81.9 | 84.5 | 86.7 | 84.2 | 85.2 | 88.7 | 86.2 | 87.2 |
| Shi et al.[8] | 84.1 | 77.8 | 80.9 | 86.1 | 79.8 | 82.9 | 86.4 | 81.0 | 83.6 | 88.4 | 83.0 | 85.6 | 83.8 | 84.7 | 84.4 | 85.8 | 86.7 | 86.4 |
| SemiText [14] | 87.5 | 79.8 | 83.7 | 89.5 | 81.8 | 85.7 | 85.5 | 83.1 | 84.7 | 87.5 | 85.1 | 86.7 | 84.5 | 85.3 | 84.2 | 86.5 | 87.3 | 86.2 |
| CRAFT [6] | 81.8 | 82.8 | 82.2 | 83.8 | 84.8 | 84.2 | 80.3 | 81.8 | 80.1 | 82.3 | 83.8 | 82.1 | 81.8 | 82.8 | 82.2 | 83.8 | 84.8 | 84.2 |
| Proposed | **89.6** | **88.8** | **88.6** | **91.6** | **90.8** | **90.6** | **88.6** | **88.2** | **87.8** | **90.6** | **90.2** | **89.8** | **89.9** | **89.7** | **89.6** | **91.9** | **91.7** | **91.6** |

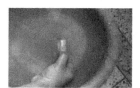  

**Fig. 8.** Limitation of the proposed model.

# 5   Conclusion

We have proposed a novel method for text detection in underwater images through a new enhancement approach and using modifications of existing CRAFT. The main objective of the proposed work is to address the challenges of text detection in underwater images and natural scene images. To the best of our knowledge, this is the first work of its kind, unlike existing methods that focus only on text detection in natural scene images. For the enhancement, the proposed approach explores the combination of DCT-DWT-FFT, which generates six enhanced images for each input image. For text detection results, we have modified the existing CRAFT to detect text in underwater images irrespective of image type, text type, and quality affected by multiple adverse factors, which consider nine enhanced images as input. Experimental results of the proposed and existing methods on the underwater image dataset and six standard natural scene text datasets show that the proposed model is superior to existing methods in terms of consistency, stable results, and robustness to different datasets.

**Acknowledgements.** The work of Cheng-Lin Liu was supported by the National Key Research and Development Program under Grant No. 2018AAA0100400 and the National Natural Science Foundation of China under Grant No. 61721004. This work also partially supported by TIH, ISI, Kolkata.

# References

1. Xue, M., et al.: Deep invariant texture features for water image classification. SN Appl. Sci. **2**(12), 1–19 (2020). https://doi.org/10.1007/s42452-020-03882-w
2. Kezebou, L., Oludare, V., Panetta, K., Againa, S.S.: Underwater object tracking benchmark and dataset. In: Proceedings of the HST (2019). https://doi.org/10.1109/HST47167.2019.9032954
3. Wang, Y., Xie, H., Zha, Z.J., Xing, M., Fu, Z., Zhang, Y.: ContourNet: Taking a further step toward accurate arbitrary-shaped scene text detection. In: Proceedings of the CVPR, pp. 11753–11762 (2020)
4. Cao, Y., Ma, S., Pan, H.: FDTA: Fully convolutional scene text detection with text attention. IEEE Access 155441–155449 (2020)
5. Zhang, W., Xiang, S.: Face anti-spoofing detection based on DWT-LBP-DCT features. Signal Process. Image Commun. (2020). https://doi.org/10.1016/j.image.2020.115990
6. Baek, Y., Lee, B., Han, D., Yun, S., Lee, H.: Character region awareness for text detection. In: Proceedings of the CVPR, pp. 9365–9374 (2019)
7. Liu, C., Yang, C., Hou, J.B., Wu, L.H., Zhu, X.B., Xiao, L.: GCCNet: Grouped channel composition network for scene text detection. Neurocomputing **454**, 135–151 (2021)
8. Shi, J., Chen, L., Su, F.: Accurate arbitrary-shaped scene text detection via iterative polynomial parameter regression. In: Ishikawa, H., Liu, C.-L., Pajdla, T., Shi, J. (eds.) ACCV 2020. LNCS, vol. 12624, pp. 241–256. Springer, Cham (2021). https://doi.org/10.1007/978-3-030-69535-4_15
9. Qin, X., Jiang, J., Yuan, C.A., Qiao, S., Fan, W.: Arbitrary shape natural scene text detection method based on soft attention mechanism and dilated convolution. IEEE Access 122685–122694 (2020)
10. Dai, P., Li, Y., Zhang, H., Li, J., Cao, X.: Accurate scene text detection via scale-aware data augmentation and shape similarity constraint. IEEE Trans. Multim. (2021). https://doi.org/10.1109/TMM.2021.3073575
11. Hu, Z., Wu, X., Wang, J.: TCATD: text contour attention for scene text detection. In: Proceedings of the ICPR, pp. 1083–1088 (2021)
12. Liao, M., Lyu, P., He, M., Yao, C., Wu, W., Bai, X.: Mask TextSpotter: an end-to-end trainable neural network for spotting text with arbitrary shapes. In: Ferrari, V., Hebert, M., Sminchisescu, C., Weiss, Y. (eds.) Computer Vision – ECCV 2018. LNCS, vol. 11218, pp. 71–88. Springer, Cham (2018). https://doi.org/10.1007/978-3-030-01264-9_5

13. Deng, G., Ming, Y., Xue, J.-H.: RFRN: A recurrent feature refinement network for accurate and efficient scene text detection. Neurocomputing **453**, 465–481 (2021)
14. Liu, J., Zhong, Q., Yuan, Y., Su, H., Du, B.: SemiText: scene text detection with semi-supervised learning. Neurocomputing **407**, 343–353 (2020)
15. Xue, M., et al.: Arbitrarily-oriented text detection in low light natural scene images. IEEE Trans. Multim. **23**, 2706–2720 (2020)
16. Chowdhury, P.N., et al.: A new episodic learning-based network for text detection on human body in sports images. IEEE Trans Circuits Syst. Video Technol. (2021). https://doi.org/10.1109/TCSVT.2021.3092713
17. Chowdhury, T., Shivakumara, P., Pal, U., Tong, L., Raghavendra, R., Chanda, S.: DCINN: deformable convolution and inception based neural network for tattoo text detection through skin region. In: Lladós, J., Lopresti, D., Uchida, S. (eds.) Document Analysis and Recognition – ICDAR 2021: 16th International Conference, Lausanne, Switzerland, September 5–10, 2021, Proceedings, Part II, pp. 335–350. Springer International Publishing, Cham (2021). https://doi.org/10.1007/978-3-030-86331-9_22
18. Zhou, X., et al.: East: an efficient and accurate scene text detector. In: Proceedings of the CVPR, pp. 2642–2651 (2017)
19. Roy, S., Shivakumara, P., Pal, U., Lu, T., Kumar, G.H.: Delaunay triangulation-based text detection from multi-view images of natural scene. Pattern Recogn. Lett. **129**, 92–100 (2020)
20. Chng, C.K., Liu, Y., Sun, Y., Ng, C.C., Luo, C., Ni, Z.: ICDAR2019 robust reading challenge on arbitrarily-shaped text-RRC-ArT. In: Proceedings of the ICDAR, pp. 1571–1576 (2019)

# Joint Dermatological Lesion Classification and Confidence Modeling with Uncertainty Estimation

Gun-Hee Lee[1], Han-Bin Ko[2], and Seong-Whan Lee[1(✉)]

[1] Korea University, Seoul, Republic of Korea
{gunhlee,sw.lee}@korea.ac.kr
[2] VUNO Inc., Seoul, Republic of Korea
hanbin.ko@vuno.co

**Abstract.** Deep learning has played a major role in the interpretation of dermoscopic images for detecting skin defects and abnormalities. However, current deep learning solutions for dermatological lesion analysis are typically limited in providing probabilistic predictions which highlights the importance of concerning uncertainties. This concept of uncertainty can provide a confidence level for each feature which prevents overconfident predictions with poor generalization on unseen data. In this paper, we propose an overall framework that jointly considers dermatological classification and uncertainty estimation together. The estimated confidence of each feature to avoid uncertain feature and undesirable shift, which are caused by environmental difference of input image, in the latent space is pooled from confidence network. Our qualitative results show that modeling uncertainties not only helps to quantify model confidence for each prediction but also helps classification layers to focus on confident features, therefore, improving the accuracy for dermatological lesion classification. We demonstrate the potential of the proposed approach in two state-of-the-art dermoscopic datasets (ISIC 2018 and ISIC 2019).

**Keywords:** Lesion classification · Automatic diagnosis · Uncertainty estimation · Confidence modeling

## 1 Introduction

Deep learning has remarkably developed and improved the ares of research, e.g. computer vision [26–30], natural language processing, data analysis, signal processing, etc. They even improve the state-of-the-art performances in skin lesion analysis, including lesion classification [17], localization [24], and segmentation

This work was supported by Institute of Information & communications Technology Planning & Evaluation (IITP) grant funded by the Korea government (MSIT) (No. 2019-0-00079, Artificial Intelligence Graduate School Program (Korea University)).

[23]. As classification of dermatological lesion received attention, the International Skin Imaging Collaboration (ISIC) [20] developed digital imaging standards for skin cancer imaging with creating a public archive containing revolutionary amount of publicly available collection of quality controlled dermoscopic images of skin lesions. The dermoscopic skin lesion dataset [8] which contains 129,450 images of skin lesion, brought a massive improvement in the field where many researchers competed to achieve state-of-the art performance. Convolutional Neural Networks (CNNs) have been widely used for melanoma classification [15,17] where the standard for training melanoma classification models was to tune a pretrained CNN and use ensembles. Along with the development of neural network, deep learning models started to achieve similar or better performance compared to expert dermatologists [17]. The accuracy measures are even now consistently improving with applying various methodologies from the computer vision fields such as data augmentation [18] or ensembles [19].

Although there have been many approaches, there are only few works on estimating the uncertainties of the model which is crucial for medical studies where the ground truth is uncertain by nature. Skin lesion datasets contain large variability which is concerned as high degree noise. These noises are mainly due to the image quality or other disturbing objects such as hair or lump, which distracts the model from letting out correct predictions. In addition, it is also very important to detect samples that deviate from the distribution of the training data. This is why modeling uncertainties along with results is crucial to help machine learning-based methods to interact with experts by showing how confident the model is for its prediction.

Using the obtained uncertainty to model the confidence of the predictions has been a long-standing challenge for computer vision. In this work, our idea started from this following aspect. When experts are asked to speak out the results for a medical image, they could give the result with confidence, or with ambiguity. They would list all the features which back up his or her theory, each with its own confidence level. Thus, if any feature is ambiguous, doctors will ignore the corresponding features and focus on the confident ones. This can go the same with the medical models. A good model will express the confidence for every features they give out. These can help the decision layers to know what features they need to focus on.

However, past models give a deterministic point representation for each dermoscopic image in the embedding space [15,17,18]. This can result in bringing sophisticated problems where each feature would be represented with overconfidence which lacks generalization on unseen data [13]. As some uncertain images contain ambiguous medical features, a large shift in the embedded points is inevitable leading to false classification.

To address the above problems, we propose an uncertainty-aware classification network, which jointly classifies dermatological lesion and models the confidence for its prediction. Our model addresses dermatological classification in a three-fold way: (1) The model encodes a probabilistic distribution in the latent space rather than just a point vector. (2) During the classification step,

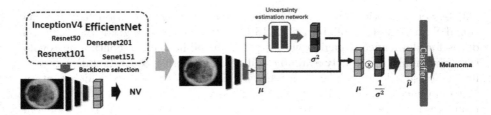

**Fig. 1.** The flow of dermatological image classification network with uncertainty estimation. We first choose the backbone structure from various kinds of base models. Our model estimates a probabilistic distribution of the latent features. We use the inverse of estimated variance as a weight for the features which can help the decision layers to focus on confident features

our model pays more attention to confident features while penalizing uncertain ones. (3) Along with the prediction, the model uses the estimated uncertainty value to model the confidence for the prediction. The overall framework of our method is shown in Fig. 1.

## 2   Related Work

**Dermoscopic Image Classification.** In this section, we briefly review the literature in model design for skin lesion classification. We focus on CNN models which are the state of the art in the image classification field. For past days, Resnet [1], Densenet [2] and Inception-v3 [3] architectures were widely used as a base model. [21] proposes a CNN model which performed on par with 145 dermatologists for melanoma classification. [22] uses the fusion of deep learning and handcrafted method for higher diagnostic accuracy on melanoma classification. On ISIC classification challenge showed a much wider range of architectures, including Squeeze-and-Excitation Networks [4], Dual Path Networks [5], PNAS-Net [7], EfficientNet [6], etc. As the CNN architecture has proved to achieve excellent performance on these tasks, [18] uses data augmentation, and [19] uses ensembles to further improve the accuracy. However, as mentioned in Sect. 1, all of the above models use deterministic embeddings, which predicts overconfident estimation of features even for the unseen or uncertain data.

**Uncertainty Learning in DNNs.** To improve the reliability of Deep Neural Networks (DNNs), uncertainty learning is receiving more attention in a lot of fields [11,12]. The concept of uncertainty is generally divided into two uncertainties, epistemic and aleatoric. Model uncertainty or Epistemic uncertainty refers to the uncertainty of model parameters given the training data. This uncertainty arises from the insufficient training data which lacks to correctly infer the underlying data-generating function. Data uncertainty or aleatoric uncertainty measures the noise inherent in the observation. Unlike epistemic uncertainty, aleatoric uncertainty arises due to the variables or measurement errors which cannot be decreased by obtaining more data. For computer vision tasks, uncertainties are mainly modeled with Bayesian analysis. The uncertainties are formed as a probabilistic distribution for the model parameters or model inputs. Since Bayesian inference is complex to apply directly to neural networks, approximation techniques such as Laplace approximation, Markov chain Monte Carlo methods, and variational inference methods are widely used. However, there is not much work for estimating the uncertainties in the medical domain compared to other tasks [12–14], especially for dermatological images. Also, adopting Bayesian analysis or approximations techniques to recent models is still complex. This is why we propose an non-complex way to estimate epistemic uncertainty which can be used along with any other existing models. We also investigate the usage of uncertainty in dermatological lesion classification where we can both improve the accuracy and model prediction confidence.

## 3    Method

This paper proposes a network for joint dermatological lesion classification and confidence modeling with uncertainty estimation. Our model as in Fig. 2 represents features as a probabilistic Gaussian distribution for the given lesion image. The mean of the distribution is the most likely feature value which is estimated by a base model. The variances for each latent feature are estimated by an additional uncertainty estimation network. We estimate the confidence as the inverse of the variance for each feature. The measured confidence is then pooled with every corresponding feature before it is passed to the decision layers. This way, the decision layers will focus more on the confident features and ignore the uncertain ones. In this section, we explain how we estimate the probabilistic Gaussian distribution for the latent features and use the inverse of the variance as a weight of each feature. Then, we finally will show how we use the measured uncertainty to model the confidence value of each predictions.

### 3.1    Mean Estimation

For the mean value of the distribution we first choose a backbone network and then estimate a deterministic feature by training the CNN model. Note that, backbone networks which are commonly used in other skin-analysis researches or competitions were selected for training. Given the input image, we apply a weighted cross entropy loss as follows:

$$L_{wce} = -\sum_{c=1}^{C} n_c t_c \log (p_c) . \tag{1}$$

The weight $n_c = (N/N_c)^k$ balances training for each class. Here, $N$ is the total number of the dataset, $N_c$ is the number of data for class $c$ and $k$ is the factor that controls the balance severity. Also, $C$ represents the total class number, $t_c$ to a one-hot code vector for the corresponding class $c$, and $p_c$ to the softmax value of the score for class $c$.

## 3.2 Variance Estimation

As mentioned earlier, our goal is to estimate a probabilistic Gaussian distribution for the latent representations which can be expressed as follows:

$$p(\mathbf{z}|\mathbf{x}) = \mathcal{N}(\mathbf{z}; \mu, \sigma^2), \tag{2}$$

where $\mu$ and $\sigma^2$ are D-dimensional vectors predicted by each network from the input image $x$. The $\mu$ value, which is estimated from the base network, should encode the most likely lesion features of the input image. The $\sigma$ value is estimated by an additional uncertainty estimation network which measures model's variance along each feature dimension.

An ideal embedding space $Z$ should only encode lesion-related features where each lesion category should have a unique embedding $\mathbf{z} \in Z$ that best represents the lesion class. An ideal model would focus to estimate the same $z$ for every image in the same lesion class. For the representation pair of images $(x_i, x_j)$, we estimate the likelihood $S(z_i, z_j)$ of them belonging to the same lesion class with also sharing the same Gaussian distribution: $p(\Delta z = 0)$, for two latent vectors $z_i \sim p(\mathbf{x}|\ \mathbf{z_i})$ and $z_j \sim p(\mathbf{x}|\ \mathbf{z_j})$. Specifically, the equation can be represented as follows:

$$S(z_i, z_j) = \int p(\mathbf{z}_i|\mathbf{x}_i) p(\mathbf{z}_j|\mathbf{x}_j) \delta(\mathbf{z}_i - \mathbf{z}_j) d\mathbf{z}_i d\mathbf{z}_j. \tag{3}$$

We consider an alternative vector $\Delta z = z_i - z_j$, instead of directly solving the integral, where $z_i \sim p(\mathbf{x}|\ \mathbf{z_i})$ and $z_j \sim p(\mathbf{x}|\ \mathbf{z_j})$. Then, $p(z_i = z_j)$ is equivalent to the density value of $p(\Delta z = 0)$. The $l^{th}$ component of $\Delta z$, $\Delta z^{(l)}$, can be represented as the subtraction of two Gaussian variables, which can be approximated as another normal distribution as follows:

$$\Delta z^{(l)} \sim N\left(\mu_i^{(l)} - \mu_j^{(l)}, \sigma_i^{2(l)} + \sigma_i^{2(l)}\right). \tag{4}$$

So then, we use log likelihood along with Gaussian approximation which solution is given as follows:

$$R(z_i, z_j) = \ln(S(z_i, z_j))$$
$$= -\frac{1}{2}\sum_{l=1}^{D}\left(\frac{\left(\mu_i^{(l)} - \mu_j^{(l)}\right)^2}{\sigma_i^{2(l)} + \sigma_j^{2(l)}} + \ln\left(\sigma_i^{2(l)} + \sigma_j^{2(l)}\right)\right) - \frac{D}{2}\log 2\pi, \tag{5}$$

where $D$ is the total number of dimensions for the latent vector. We use the above equation as a loss to train the uncertainty estimation network, which will ideally output the correct variance value for each latent feature.

## 3.3 Confidence Pooling

We use the estimated variance value as weights for each feature to make a new latent feature. We define confidence value $q_n$ as a normalized value in range of

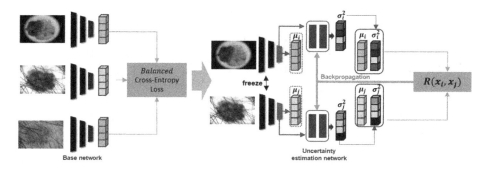

**Fig. 2.** The training procedure of our network. The base network is trained to estimate the $\mu$ value and the confidence network is trained to estimate the $\sigma^2$ value for the corresponding feature.

(0,1] for $c_n = 1/\sigma_n^2$, where $\sigma^2$ is the output of the uncertainty network and $n$ represents the $n^{th}$ dimension. Then we can obtain a new mean value for all $D$ dimensions as follows:

$$\hat{\mu}_n = \frac{q_n \mu_n}{\sum_j^D q_j}. \tag{6}$$

This metric $\hat{\mu}_j$ denotes the new mean value pooled by its own variance. The confidence pooling method helps classification layer to focus on confident features and ignore the uncertain ones. The concept of confidence pooling is different from attention mechanisms where attention mechanisms pay more attention to parts of the input while confidence pooling pays attention to the features with more confidence. This way, the network can be robust to noises or uncertainties in the input.

### 3.4 Confidence Modeling

We measure confidence of the feature by using the variance estimated from the above section. As we have the value of weights for the classification layer, the score value of each class can be approximated using linear combinations of Gaussian distributions assuming all features are independent. We can approximate a new Gaussian distribution as follows:

$$\mathbf{p}\left(c_i | \mathbf{x}\right) \sim \mathcal{N}\left(\Sigma_j^R a_j \mu_j, \Sigma_j^D a_j^2 \sigma_j^2\right), \tag{7}$$

where $a$ is the weights connected to the corresponding classification node. Note that if there are more than one fully connected layer, the same process are performed iteratively. We can use the variance measure to either reject the input or concern the reliability of the model's predictions. We also note that these measures act like confidence for the predictions.

### 3.5   Training

Our work focuses on estimating a probabilistic Gaussian distribution of the features instead of discrete features. In order to do so, we estimate the $\mu$ and $\sigma^2$ value for each corresponding feature. We can train the $\mu$ by training the base network as any other deterministic model does. We choose the backbone network and train the $\mu$ value with the image and corresponding label. Using the same bottleneck layer, which is the layer before concatenation of $\mu$, we use that layer as an input to the confidence network which will output initial variance value at first. This will be optimized along with the training process.

We use a two-stage training strategy. First, training the backbone network with training dataset using weighted cross-entropy loss. Second, given a pre-trained model $f$, we fix its parameters, take $\mu(x) = f(x)$, and optimize an additional uncertainty estimating network to estimate $\sigma(x)^2$. The uncertainty estimation network shares the corresponding layer in order to estimate the variance for each latent feature value. We form a loss function using the Eq. 5 for all genuine pairs $(x_i, x_j)$. Formally, the loss function to minimize is as follows:

$$L = \frac{1}{|P|} \sum_{(i,j) \in P}^{D} -R\left(z_i, z_j\right), \tag{8}$$

where $P$ is the set of all genuine pairs. In practice, the loss function is optimized within each mini-batch. Intuitively, this loss function can be known and understood as an alternative to maximize $p(z|x)$: if the latent distributions of all possible genuine pairs have a large overlap, the latent target $z$ should have a large likelihood for and corresponding input. Note that since the mean value is fixed, the optimization would not lead the $\mu$ values to collapse.

Among the two uncertainties introduced in Sect. 2, our work focuses on modeling epistemic uncertainty which is helpful to identify out-of-distribution images or noisy inputs.

## 4   Dataset and Experiment

Our work is evaluated on the publicly available ISIC 2018 [8] and ISIC 2019 [8–10]. ISIC 2018 or HAM10000 dataset contains 10,015 images with 7 classes, including melanoma (MEL), melanocytic nevus (NV), basal cell carcinoma (BCC), Actinic keratosis (AK), benign keratosis (BK), dermatofibroma (DF) and vascular lesion (VS). The largest category, melanocytic nevus has 6,705 images while the smallest category, dermatofibroma only has 115 images. All of the images were preprocessed in order to normalize their intensity.

We also carried out an experiment on the ISIC 2019 set, which comprises of 25,331 dermoscopic images. The following dataset contains 8 classes, including melanoma, melanocytic nevus, basal cell carcinoma, actinic keratosis, benign keratosis, dermatofibroma, vascular lesion and squamous cell carcinoma (SCC). We do not augment the training set with external data, and we randomly split the available data into training (80%) and test (20%) sets. We use 5-fold cross validation for evaluation.

**Table 1.** Results for ISIC 2018 with each backbone network. After we tested on various base models, we added the uncertainty estimation network for confidence pooling (CP). Then again, we measured the performance on F1, accuracy (ACC), balanced accuracy (BACC), and mean AUC.

| Model | F1 | ACC. | BACC. | Mean AUC |
|---|---|---|---|---|
| ResNet50 | 63.5% | 83.3% | 67.5% | 89.6% |
| ResNet101 | 63.3% | 84.6% | 67.5% | 88.9% |
| Densenet121 | 64.1% | 85.0% | 67.0% | 87.6% |
| Densenet201 | 64.5% | 86.5% | 68.7% | 88.6% |
| se-Resnext50 | 65.2% | 87.1% | 70.4% | 90.3% |
| se-Resnext101 | 66.5% | 88.7% | 69.9% | 86.3% |
| Senet154 | 66.3% | 86.2% | 68.1% | 87.2% |
| EfficientNetb3 | 68.2% | 89.8% | 73.4% | 93.7% |
| EfficientNetb4 | 69.0% | 90.7% | 74.2% | 94.1% |
| ResNet50+CP | 65.4% | 85.5% | 71.1% | 92.1% |
| ResNet101+CP | 65.1% | 86.2% | 71.2% | 90.6% |
| Densenet121+CP | 66.5% | 87.1% | 71.9% | 89.0% |
| Densenet201+CP | 66.9% | 88.2% | 72.2% | 89.1% |
| se-Resnext50+CP | 67.0% | 89.5% | 73.1% | 92.1% |
| se-Resnext101+CP | 68.1% | 90.9% | 74.0% | 89.9% |
| Senet154+CP | 66.5% | 86.5% | 70.2% | 87.0% |
| EfficientNetb3+CP | 70.1% | 91.1% | 77.0% | 95.5% |
| EfficientNetb4+CP | 71.2% | 92.3% | 78.7% | 95.7% |

### 4.1 Implementation Details

We conduct various experiments with different deep architectures, including ResNet50, ResNet101, Densenet121, Densenet201, se-Resnext50, se-Resnext101, Senet154, EfficientNetb3 and EfficientNetb4. Before training the network, we resize the input image differently for each backbone network. We mainly resize the image to $256 \times 256$ pixels and use normalization within the range of $[0, 1]$. For base model training, we choose Adam optimization [25] with a batch-size of 32 as the model parameter. We initialize the learning rate at 0.01 and decay it by 0.1 every 50 epochs. The uncertainty estimation network is composed of two fully connected layers with 1,024 dimensions. We use Adam optimization with a batch size of 32 with the learning rate of 0.005. We decay the learning rate by 0.1 every 100 epochs. Our algorithm runs on two NVIDIA TITAN Xp GPUs with 12 GB of VRam.

**Table 2.** Results for ISIC 2019 with each backbone network. We tested on two settings, with and without uncertainty estimation, which is used for confidence pooling. We measure performance on F1, accuracy, balanced accuracy, and mean AUC.

| Model | F1 | ACC. | BACC. | Mean AUC |
|---|---|---|---|---|
| Densenet201 | 59.5% | 72.5% | 65.7% | 88.6% |
| se-Resnext101 | 60.5% | 72.7% | 64.9% | 86.3% |
| Senet154 | 61.3% | 68.2% | 63.1% | 86.2% |
| EfficientNetb4 | 63.0% | 75.8% | 71.1% | 89.1% |
| Densenet201+CP | 62.9% | 74.2% | 69.2% | 89.7% |
| se-Resnext101+CP | 63.1% | 75.9% | 70.0% | 89.9% |
| Senet154+CP | 65.5% | 71.3% | 68.5% | 88.8% |
| EfficientNetb4+CP | 67.2% | 79.0% | 75.5% | 91.9% |

**Table 3.** Results for each class on EfficientNetb4 with uncertainty estimation. We compare the results between two models with and without uncertainty estimation. We evaluate all categories with sensitivity, specificity and accuracy. Note that accuracy here is not the precision.

| | Sensitivity | Specificity | ACC. | Sensitivity (ours) | Specificity (ours) | ACC. (ours) |
|---|---|---|---|---|---|---|
| Mel | 0.76 | 0.91 | 0.89 | 0.80 | 0.92 | 0.90 |
| NV | 0.81 | 0.95 | 0.88 | 0.82 | 0.97 | 0.90 |
| BCC | 0.77 | 0.96 | 0.94 | 0.85 | 0.96 | 0.95 |
| AK | 0.70 | 0.96 | 0.95 | 0.70 | 0.97 | 0.96 |
| BK | 0.56 | 0.98 | 0.94 | 0.62 | 0.98 | 0.94 |
| DF | 0.68 | 0.99 | 0.98 | 0.78 | 0.99 | 0.99 |
| VS | 0.76 | 0.98 | 0.98 | 0.80 | 0.98 | 0.98 |
| SCC | 0.66 | 0.97 | 0.96 | 0.67 | 0.98 | 0.97 |

## 5    Results

We evaluated the proposed model on a test set of dermoscopy images and quantified its performance using various metrics regarding the class-specific sensitivity (SE) and specificity (SP), and the overall balanced accuracy (BACC). The balanced multi-class accuracy is defined as the measure of accuracy of each category weighted by the category prevalence. Specifically, it can be interpreted as the arithmetic mean of the (true positives/positives) across each categories of diseases. Note that this metric is semantically similar to the average recall score. The Area Under the Curve (AUC) for each class was also computed. We carried an experiment on only using base architectures, however, we can easily add the uncertainty estimating network to any other existing models.

### 5.1    ISIC 2018

Table 1 shows the performance for each network with and without uncertainty information on ISIC 2018 test set. We tested our confidence network with using

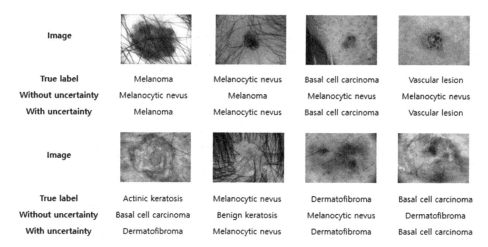

**Fig. 3.** Ablation study on confidence pooling. Image used for the second row are the images which are selected for high uncertainty. We sorted test images for each category with their confidence value and selected images within 10% low confidence.

**Table 4.** Experiments using EfficientNetb4 to investigate the benefit of rejecting uncertain inputs based on the uncertainty measure. Here, we sort out images with the highest uncertainty for each category in the test set of ISIC 2019.

| Rejection ratio | F1 | ACC | BACC |
|---|---|---|---|
| Ours [0%] | 67.2% | 79.0% | 75.5% |
| Ours [5%] | 71.1% | 86.9% | 82.1% |
| Ours [10%] | 74.2% | 89.2% | 85.3% |
| Ours [20%] | 75.5% | 90.7% | 86.7% |

various backbone architectures; ResNet, Densenet, se-Resnext, Senet, and EfficientNet. Note that we chose the backbone architectures which are frequently used for the competitions. As shown in Table 1, we could clearly see that concerning uncertainties actually improves the performances of all metrics for almost all architectures. The accuracy had about 2% improvement while the balanced accuracy had improvement about 4%. This shows that by pooling the confidence to the latent features, the additional uncertainty information actually assists the decision layers to focus more on confident features, therefore bringing improvements to the model.

## 5.2   ISIC 2019

We perform more experiments on ISIC 2019 dataset [16] due to its diverse and more advanced data compared to ISIC 2018. Table 2 shows the performance with each backbone network with and without uncertainty information on ISIC 2019 validation set. Again, we use the architectures which are frequently used in competitions along with models which performed relatively good in Sect. 5.1. Similar to the experiment we did before, additional uncertainty information helped to improve all metrics for most models. As a result, we can be assured that estimating uncertainty and using it for classification level actually improves results by helping the decision layers to avoid uncertain features for dermatological image classification tasks.

To take a closer look, Table 3 shows the sensitivity, specificity, accuracy, and AUC for each category using EfficentNetb4 as the backbone structure. Since melanocytic nevus has bigger proportions in the dataset, it achieves higher performance. Moreover, adding uncertainty information to the decision layers again further improves all four metrics especially sensitivity, which is very important for medical predictions. Also, as shown in Fig. 3, we show the effect on applying uncertainties by showing some examples with high uncertainty. The images in the second row are modeled with very low prediction confidence. Note that these low prediction confidence can be due to the hair, color distribution or some other uncertain features which shift the features from its category's cluster. While other deterministic base models tend to misclassify these uncertain images, we can see that most uncertain data are correctly classified by the assist of confidence measures.

**Rejecting Data on Test Set.** The measured confidence for each feature can be efficiently used in the process of computer-aided diagnosis which would help the interaction between the doctor and machine. As mentioned in Sect. 1, it would be best if the model can share its opinion with the level of confidence for the prediction. Since our model can additionally model confidence as in Sect. 3.4, we can think of a way to reject the input with high uncertainty. For experiment, we collected the confidence of the prediction for each category. The prediction confidence for each corresponding input is sorted which then we eliminate 0%, 5%, 10%, 20% of test samples with eliminating the lowest confidence from the measurement. We use the F1 score, accuracy and balanced accuracy for performance analysis. The metrics improved on the test set as we increased the amount of rejection as in Table 4. This is quite an increase, demonstrating the potential of this strategy to improve the robustness of the model. Without any Bayesian techniques or inference, our method can be easily applied to any base models in the needs of modeling confidence. Note that, in the real world, a doctor would set a threshold of this confidence level to automatically reject inputs.

## 6    Conclusion

This paper proposes a dermatological lesion classification network with uncertainty estimation. Our qualitative experiments show that these measures of uncertainty can not only be used for modeling confidence for the output but also increase the performance for classification tasks. We evaluated our method on the ISIC datasets and show that our strategy has the potential of having wide applications either to improve the performance of the model. Moreover, the obtained uncertainty can be used to reject inputs with low confidence or actively ask and interact with the expert, as well as to provide more insightful information in the diagnosis process.

# References

1. He, K., Zhang, X., Ren, S., Sun, J.: Deep residual learning for image recognition. In: Proceedings of the IEEE Conference on Computer Vision and Pattern Recognition (CVPR), pp. 770–778, June 2016
2. Huang, G., Liu, Z., Van Der Maaten, L., Weinberger, K.Q.: Densely connected convolutional networks. In: Proceedings of the IEEE Conference on Computer Vision and Pattern Recognition (CVPR), pp. 4700–4708, July 2017
3. Szegedy, C., Vanhoucke, V., Ioffe, S., Shlens, J., Wojna, Z.: Rethinking the inception architecture for computer vision. In: Proceedings of the IEEE Conference on Computer Vision and Pattern Recognition (CVPR), pp. 2818–2826, June 2016
4. Hu, J., Shen, L., Sun, G.: Squeeze-and-excitation networks. In: Proceedings of the IEEE Conference on Computer Vision and Pattern Recognition (CVPR), pp. 7132–7141, June 2018
5. Chen, Y., Li, J., Xiao, H., Jin, X., Yan, S., Feng, J.: Dual path networks. In: Advances in neural information processing systems (NeurIPS), pp. 4470–4478, December 2017
6. Tan, M., Le, Q.: EfficientNet: rethinking model scaling for convolutional neural networks. In: Proceedings of International Conference on Machine Learning (ICML), pp. 6105–6114, June 2019
7. Liu, C., et al.: Progressive neural architecture search. In: Proceedings of the European Conference on Computer Vision (ECCV), pp. 19–34, September 2018
8. Tschandl, P., Rosendahl, C., Kittler, H.: The HAM10000 dataset, a large collection of multi-source dermatoscopic images of common pigmented skin lesions. Sci. Data 5(1), 1–9 (2018)
9. Codella, N.C., et al.: Skin lesion analysis toward melanoma detection: a challenge at the 2017 International Symposium on Biomedical Imaging (ISBI), hosted by the International Skin Imaging Collaboration (ISIC). arXiv:1710.05006 (2017)
10. Combalia, M., et al.: BCN20000: dermoscopic lesions in the wild. arXiv:1908.02288 (2019)
11. Kendall, A., Gal, Y.: What uncertainties do we need in Bayesian deep learning for computer vision? In: Proceedings of Advances in Neural Information Processing Systems (NeurIPS), pp. 5580–5590, December 2017
12. Gal, Y., Ghahramani, Z.: Bayesian convolutional neural networks with Bernoulli approximate variational inference. In: Proceedings of the International Conference on Learning Representations (ICLR) Workshop Track, May 2016
13. Ghesu, F.C., et al.: Quantifying and leveraging classification uncertainty for chest radiograph assessment. In: Shen, D., et al. (eds.) MICCAI 2019. LNCS, vol. 11769, pp. 676–684. Springer, Cham (2019). https://doi.org/10.1007/978-3-030-32226-7_75
14. Lakshiminarayanan, B., Pritzel, A., Blundell, C.: Simple and scalable predictive uncertainty estimation using deep ensembles. In: Proceedings of the Advances in Neural Information Processing Systems (NeurIPS), pp. 6405–6416, December 2017

15. Yoon, C., Hamarneh, G., Garbi, R.: Generalizable feature learning in the presence of data bias and domain class imbalance with application to skin lesion classification. In: Shen, D., et al. (eds.) MICCAI 2019. LNCS, vol. 11767, pp. 365–373. Springer, Cham (2019). https://doi.org/10.1007/978-3-030-32251-9_40

16. Codella, N., et al.: Skin lesion analysis toward melanoma detection 2018: a challenge hosted by the International Skin Imaging Collaboration (ISIC). arXiv:1902.03368 (2019)

17. Esteva, A., et al.: Dermatologist-level classification of skin cancer with deep neural networks. Nature **562**(7639), 115–118 (2017)

18. Perez, F., Vasconcelos, C., Avila, S., Valle, E.: Data augmentation for skin lesion analysis. In: Stoyanov, D., et al. (eds.) CARE/CLIP/OR 2.0/ISIC -2018. LNCS, vol. 11041, pp. 303–311. Springer, Cham (2018). https://doi.org/10.1007/978-3-030-01201-4_33

19. Matsunaga, K., Hamada, A., Minagawa, A., Koga, H.: Image classification of melanoma, nevus and seborrheic keratosis by deep neural network ensemble. arXiv:1703.03108 (2017)

20. The international skin imaging collaboration. https://www.isic-archive.com/

21. Liu, X., et al.: A comparison of deep learning performance against health-care professionals in detecting diseases from medical imaging: a systematic review and meta-analysis. Lancet Digital Health **1**(6), 271–297 (2019)

22. Hagerty, J.R., et al.: Deep learning and handcrafted method fusion: higher diagnostic accuracy for melanoma dermoscopy images. IEEE J. Biomed. Health Inform. **23**(4), 1385–1391 (2019)

23. Jungo, A., Reyes, M.: Assessing reliability and challenges of uncertainty estimations for medical image segmentation. In: Shen, D., et al. (eds.) MICCAI 2019. LNCS, vol. 11765, pp. 48–56. Springer, Cham (2019). https://doi.org/10.1007/978-3-030-32245-8_6

24. Ibtehaz, N., Rahman, M.: MultiResUNet: rethinking the U-Net architecture for multimodal biomedical image segmentation. Neural Netw. **121**, 74–87 (2020)

25. Kingma, D.P., Ba, J.: Adam: a method for stochastic optimization. In: Proceedings of the International Conference on Learning Representations (ICLR), May 2015

26. Yang, H.-D., Lee, S.-W.: Reconstruction of 3D human body pose from stereo image sequences based on top-down learning. Pattern Recogn. **40**(11), 3120–3131 (2007)

27. Roh, M.-C., Kim, T.-Y., Park, J., Lee, S.-W.: Accurate object contour tracking based on boundary edge selection. Pattern Recogn. **40**(3), 931–943 (2007)

28. Bülthoff, H.H., Wallraven, C., Lee, S.-W., Poggio, T.A. (eds.): BMCV 2002. LNCS, vol. 2525. Springer, Heidelberg (2002). https://doi.org/10.1007/3-540-36181-2

29. Ahmad, M., Lee, S.-W.: Human action recognition using multi-view image sequences features. In: Proceedings of the 7th IEEE International Conference on Automatic Face and Gesture Recognition, pp. 523–528, April 2006

30. Lee, S.-W., Song, H.-H.: A new recurrent neural-network architecture for visual pattern recognition. IEEE Trans. Neural Netw. **8**(2), 331–340 (1997)

# Resting-State Electroencephalography (EEG)-Based Diagnosis System for Drug-Naive Female Major Depressive Disorder Patients

Miseon Shim[1], Seung-Hwan Lee[2,3](✉), and Han-Jeong Hwang[1,4](✉)

[1] Department of Electronics and Information Engineering, Korea University, Sejong, Republic of Korea
hwanghj@korea.ac.kr
[2] Psychiatry Department, Ilsan Paik Hospital, Inje University, Goyang, Republic of Korea
lshpss@hanmail.net
[3] Clinical Emotion and Cognition Research Laboratory, Goyang, Republic of Korea
[4] Interdisciplinary Graduate Program for Artificial Intelligence Smart Convergence Technology, Korea University, Sejong, Republic of Korea

**Abstract.** A resting-state EEG-based computer-aided diagnosis (CAD) system could assist the accurate diagnosis of major depressive disorder (MDD) patients. The purpose of this study is to develop a resting-state EEG-based CAD system for diagnosis of drug-naive female MDD patients. To this end, eyes-closed resting-state EEG data were recorded from 30 female MDD patients and sex-matched 30 healthy controls. Three types of features were extracted, i.e., power spectral density (PSD), phase locking values (PLV) and network indices (strength, clustering coefficient, and path length). The classification performances of each feature set were evaluated using a support vector machine with leave-one-out cross-validation. The best classification performance was achieved when using PLV features (accuracy – 85.00%). In our future studies, we will attempt to develop a practically useful CAD system for MDD patients by applying channel selection approach.

**Keywords:** Major depressive disorder (MDD) · Computer-aided diagnosis (CAD) system · Machine-learning · Resting-state electroencephalography (EEG) · Functional connectivity

## 1 Introduction

Major depressive disorder (MDD) is a serious mental disease suffered from depressed mood, and they are characterized by loss of interest or pleasure, insomnia, concentration difficulties, and fatigue [1, 2]. Clinical symptoms of MDD patients could be alleviated by early diagnosis and treatment in a timely manner, but it often failed due to several reasons such as ignorance of depression symptoms and comorbid symptoms with other mental disorders [3, 4]. In order to assist accurate diagnosis of MDD patients, recent studies have tried to develop computer-aided diagnosis (CAD) systems based on machine-learning methods using object physiological biomarkers [3, 4].

© Springer Nature Switzerland AG 2022
C. Wallraven et al. (Eds.): ACPR 2021, LNCS 13189, pp. 247–253, 2022.
https://doi.org/10.1007/978-3-031-02444-3_18

Resting-state electroencephalography (EEG) is widely used to develop a CAD system for MDD patients because the altered functional characteristics of MDD patients have been well-revealed by resting-state EEG-based biomarkers [5, 6]. Indeed, previous EEG studies showed reasonable diagnostic performances (>80%) for MDD patients [3, 4]. However, most of them did not consider not only gender- but also drugs-effects when computing resting-state EEG-based biomarkers [7–10]. Since both gender- and drugs-effects disturb to extract the patients' physiological traits, both effects should be cautiously handled to develop an accurate diagnostic system.

In the present study, we developed a robust resting-state EEG-based CAD system by controlling the effects of both gender and drugs. To this end, we recruited the drug-naive female MDD patients and gender-matched healthy controls (HC). Then, three types of features were computed (e.g., power spectral density (PSD), functional connectivity (phase locking value, PLV), and network indices), and the classification performances were evaluated using support-vector machine (SVM) with leave-one-out cross-validation (LOOCV). Furthermore, we investigated the neurophysiological traits of MDD patients based on the selected features when achieving the best classification performance.

## 2   Methods

### 2.1   Participants

Thirty MDD patients and 30 HC were recruited for this study from the Psychiatry Department of Inje University Ilsan Paik Hospital. The patients' diagnosis was based on the Diagnostic and Statistical Manual of Mental Disorders, 4th edition (DSM-IV) Axis I Psychiatric Disorders by a board-certified psychiatrist. Patients were excluded if they accorded with the following criteria: 1) abnormality of the central nervous system, 2) medical histories of alcohol or drug abuse, 3) mental retardation, 4) history of head injuries with loss of consciousness and experience with electrical therapy (e.g. electroconvulsive therapy, ECT), and 5) psychotic symptoms lasting for at least 24 h. Depression and anxiety symptoms of MDD patients were estimated by clinical experts based on the Hamilton Depression Rating Scale (HAM-D) and Hamilton Anxiety Rating Scale (HAM-A), respectively. HC were recruited from the local community through local newspapers and posters. Individuals without any psychiatric medical history were recruited for HC. If HC took or have taken any kinds of psychotropic medication, they were excluded in the study. All participants provided written informed consent, and the study protocol was approved by the Institutional Review Board of Inje University Ilsan Paik Hospital (2016-08-017 and 2015-04-316) (Table 1).

**Table 1.** Demographic data of drug-naive female major depressive disorder (MDD) patients and healthy controls (HC). All participants are female. The $p$-value indicates statistical differences between two groups using independent $t$-test.

| | MDD | HC | $p$-value |
|---|---|---|---|
| Cases ($N$) | 30 | 30 | |
| Age (years) | 49.17 ± 10.52 | 52.97 ± 7.29 | 0.121 |
| Education | 12.8 ± 2.84 | 13.62 ± 2.52 | 0.243 |
| HAM-D | 26.90 ± 7.40 | | |
| HAM-A | 25.50 ± 5.35 | | |

Abbreviations: HAM-D – Hamilton Depression Rating Scale; HAM-A – Hamilton Anxiety Rating Scale

## 2.2 EEG Recording and Preprocessing

Resting-state EEG data were recorded with a band-pass filter of 1–100 Hz for 5 min during eyes closed (sampling rate: 1000 Hz), for which 64 Ag/AgCl scalp electrodes were evenly mounted on the scalp according to the extended International 10–20 system (NeuroScan SynAmps2 (Compumedics USA, El Paso, TX, USA); references: M1 and M2). Eye movement artifacts were removed using established mathematical procedures based on regression approach [11], and other gross artifacts were rejected by visual inspection. Then, EEG data were band-pass filtered between 1 and 55 Hz and were epoched as a length of 5 s, and epochs were rejected if they contained significant physiological artifacts (±100 μV) at any electrodes [12]. Only artifacts-free epochs were used to exract features, and the number of used epcohs in each group were 54.86 ± 10.49 for MDD patients and 57.92 ± 10.38 for HC ($p = 0.149$), repectively.

## 2.3 Feature Extraction

PSDs were computed by a complex Morlet-wavelet method implemented in Fieldtrip toolbox [13]. The Morlet-wavelet transform with a sinusoidal wave modified by a Gaussian shape was applied to each channel. The PSDs of each channel were independently quantified in seven frequency bands (delta [1–4 Hz], theta [4–8 Hz], low-alpha [8–10 Hz], high-alpha [10–12 Hz], low-beta [12–22 Hz], high-beta [22–30 Hz], and gamma [30–55 Hz]), respectively, thereby producing 434 PSD features.

PLVs were computed not only for extracting classification features as a functional connectivity measure, but also for performing network analysis. In this study, Hilbert Transform based PLV were computed for each of seven frequency bands as in the PSD estimation [14]. PLVs were computed between all possible pairs of 62 channels at each time point, and a PLV matrix was quantified by averaging over time. The range of PLVs is from 0 to 1; a high PLV means that the connection strength between two brain areas is stronger than other pairs of brain areas and vice versa. 1,891 PLV values for each frequency band were extracted as classification features; a total of 13,237 PLV values for each subject.

Weighted network indices were computed based on graph theory. To this end, an adjacency PLV matrix, without any distortion, was used as an input data to minimize information loss. Weighted network indices were evaluated at two levels as global- and nodal-level, respectively, based on graph theory. For global-level network indices that take account of the whole-brain structure, the following three indices were computed: i) strength, ii) clustering coefficient, and iii) path length. In addition, both strength and clustering coefficient were calculated at each sensor to compute nodal-level network indices which evaluate local characteristics of brain regions. Please see the added references about each network index for details. All network measures were computed using Brain connectivity Toolbox (BCT, http://www.brain-connectivity-toolbox.net) based on Matlab [15]. 889 network features were estimated (21 global-level features + 868 nodal-level features).

## 2.4 Classification

Three different types of feature sets were independently tested for classification, i.e., PSDs, PLVs, and network indices. In order to reduce the computational cost and avoid the overfitting of a classifier caused by the use of a large number of features, feature selection based on Fisher score method was performed. A higher Fisher score for each feature represents the better discrimination capability between the two groups (MDD patients vs. HC). The features with relatively higher Fisher scores were used sequentially from 1 to 20 (number of features) for classification [16]. The classification accuracy was evaluated using a linear SVM classifier with a LOOCV method for each feature set. To evaluate group differences of selected features used when achieving best classification performance, independent $t$-test was performed for each feature set with adjusted $p$-values using the false discovery rate (FDR) method.

## 3 Results

### 3.1 Classification

Table 2 presents the best classification accuracies, specificities, and sensitivities for three different feature sets with the number of selected features used for classifying two groups. A maximum classification accuracy of 85.00% was achieved when using the five PLV features, and its sensitivity and specificity were 86.67% and 83.33%, respectively. For the network feature set, the best classification accuracy of 76.67% was obtained when using eighteen features, and sensitivity and specificity were 86.67% and 66.67%, respectively. The PSD feature set showed relatively poor classificaiton classification accuracy 51.67% when using two features (Fig. 1).

**Table 2.** Best classification accuracies, sensitivities, and specificities (unit: %) and the number of selected features used when achieving the best classification performance for each feature set.

|         | Accuracy | Sensitivity | Specificity | n  |
|---------|----------|-------------|-------------|----|
| **PLVs**    | **85.00**    | **86.67**       | **83.33**       | **5**  |
| Network | 76.67    | 86.67       | 66.67       | 18 |
| PSDs    | 51.67    | 73.33       | 30.00       | 2  |

Abbreviations: PLVs – phase-locking values; PSDs – power spectrum densities; n – number of selected features

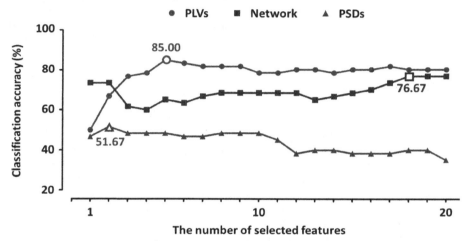

**Fig. 1.** Classification accuracies of three different features (e.g., PLVs, network indices, and PSDs) with respect to the number of selected features. Empty symbols indicate the best classification accuracy for each feature set.

## 3.2 Spatial Distribution of Importance Features

The spatial characteristics of selected features could provide physiological information to assist the pathophysiological interpretation of MDD patients. Thus, we discovered the spatial characteristics of the most selected PLV features within cross-validation used when achieving the best classification performance. Five PLV features in theta, high-alpha, and high-beta frequency bands were selected (Fig. 2), and MDD patients showed significantly reduced PLVs in five pairs compared to HC (FDR corrected $p < 0.05$); in particular, theta PLVs were mostly selected for attaining a high classification accuracy.

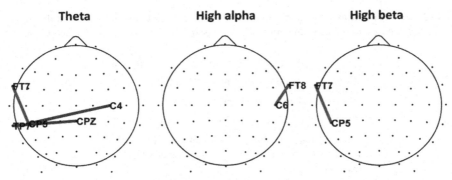

**Fig. 2.** Spatial distribution of the selected PLV features in three frequency bands (theta, high alpha, and high beta bands), which were used to obtain the best classification performance. Major depressive disorder (MDD) patients show significantly reduced PLVs in three frequency bands compared to healthy controls (independent $t$-test with false discovery rate (FDR) adjusted $p <$ 0.05).

## 4    Conclusion

In the presen tstudy, we developed a resting-state EEG-based CAD system for drug-naive female MDD patients using a machine-learning algorithm and evaluated the classification performances using three different features (PSDs, PLVs, and network). The best classification performance of 85.00% was obtained when using PLV features. Moreover, the five selected PLVs, which used when obtaining best classification performance, were siginificantly reduced in MDD patients as compared to HC. Even though this study achieved the high classification performance to diagnose MDD patients using EEG-based features, it is insufficient for practical purpose due to low efficacy and high cost requiring when computing a large number of diagnostic features. Thus, as our further study, we will develop a practically useful CAD system of MDD patients by applying a channel selection approach.

**Acknowledgements.** This work was supported by the Institute for Information & Communications Technology Planning & Evaluation (IITP) grant funded by the Korean government (No. 2017-0-00451; Development of BCI based Brain and Cognitive Computing Technology for Recognizing User's Intentions using Deep Learning), by the Basic Research Program through the National Research Foundation of Korea (NRF) funded by the MSIT (NRF-2020R1A4A1017775 and NRF-2019R1I1A1A01063313), by the Korea Medical Device Development Fund grant funded by the Korea government (the Ministry of Science and ICT, the Ministry of Trade, Industry and Energy, the Ministry of Health &Welfare, the Ministry of Food and Drug Safety) (1711138348, KMDF_PR_20200901_0169), and by the Brain Research Program through the National Research Foundation of Korea(NRF) funded by the Ministry of Science, ICT & Future Planning (NRF-2015M3C7A1028252).

## References

1. Ohayon, M.M., Hong, S.-C.: Prevalence of major depressive disorder in the general population of South Korea. J. Psychiatr. Res. **40**, 30–36 (2006)

2. Whiteford, H.A., et al.: Global burden of disease attributable to mental and substance use disorders: findings from the Global Burden of Disease Study 2010. The Lancet **382**, 1575–1586 (2013)
3. Acharya, U.R., Sudarshan, V.K., Adeli, H., Santhosh, J., Koh, J.E., Adeli, A.: Computer-aided diagnosis of depression using EEG signals. Eur. Neurol. **73**, 329–336 (2015)
4. Mahato, S., Paul, S.: Electroencephalogram (EEG) signal analysis for diagnosis of major depressive disorder (MDD): a review. In: Nath, V., Mandal, J.K. (eds.) Nanoelectronics, Circuits and Communication Systems. LNEE, vol. 511, pp. 323–335. Springer, Singapore (2019). https://doi.org/10.1007/978-981-13-0776-8_30
5. de Aguiar Neto, F.S., Rosa, J.L.G.: Depression biomarkers using non-invasive EEG: a review. Neurosci. Biobehav. Rev. **105**, 83–93 (2019)
6. Mohammadi, M., et al.: Data mining EEG signals in depression for their diagnostic value. BMC Med. Inform. Decis. Mak. **15**, 108 (2015)
7. Baskaran, A., Milev, R., McIntyre, R.S.: The neurobiology of the EEG biomarker as a predictor of treatment response in depression. Neuropharmacology **63**, 507–513 (2012)
8. Mumtaz, W., Xia, L., Ali, S.S.A., Yasin, M.A.M., Hussain, M., Malik, A.S.: Electroencephalogram (EEG)-based computer-aided technique to diagnose major depressive disorder (MDD). Biomed. Signal Process. Control **31**, 108–115 (2017)
9. Olbrich, S., Arns, M.: EEG biomarkers in major depressive disorder: discriminative power and prediction of treatment response. Int. Rev. Psychiatry **25**, 604–618 (2013)
10. Subasi, A.: EEG signal classification using wavelet feature extraction and a mixture of expert model. Expert Syst. Appl. **32**, 1084–1093 (2007)
11. Semlitsch, H.V., Anderer, P., Schuster, P., Presslich, O.: A solution for reliable and valid reduction of ocular artifacts, applied to the P300 ERP. Psychophysiology **23**, 695–703 (1986)
12. Kim, J.-Y., Son, J.-B., Leem, H.-S., Lee, S.-H.: Psychophysiological alteration after virtual reality experiences using smartphone-assisted head mount displays: an EEG-based source localization study. Appl. Sci. **9**, 2501 (2019)
13. Oostenveld, R., Fries, P., Maris, E., Schoffelen, J.-M.: FieldTrip: open source software for advanced analysis of MEG, EEG, and invasive electrophysiological data. Comput. Intell. Neurosci. **2011** (2011)
14. Lachaux, J.P., Rodriguez, E., Martinerie, J., Varela, F.J.: Measuring phase synchrony in brain signals. Hum. Brain Mapp. **8**, 194–208 (1999)
15. Rubinov, M., Sporns, O.: Complex network measures of brain connectivity: uses and interpretations. Neuroimage **52**, 1059–1069 (2010)
16. Shim, M., Hwang, H.-J., Kim, D.-W., Lee, S.-H., Im, C.-H.: Machine-learning-based diagnosis of schizophrenia using combined sensor-level and source-level EEG features. Schizophr. Res. **176**, 314–319 (2016)

# Paperswithtopic: Topic Identification from Paper Title Only

Daehyun Cho[1] and Christian Wallraven[1,2]

[1] Department of Artificial Intelligence, Korea University, Seoul, Korea
{1phantasmas,wallraven}@korea.ac.kr
[2] Department of Brain and Cognitive Engineering, Korea University, Seoul, Korea

**Abstract.** The deep learning field is growing rapidly as witnessed by the exponential growth of papers submitted to journals, conferences, and pre-print servers. To cope with the sheer number of papers, several text mining tools from natural language processing (NLP) have been proposed that enable researchers to keep track of recent findings. In this context, our paper makes two main contributions: first, we collected and annotated a dataset of papers paired by title and sub-field from the field of artificial intelligence (AI), and, second, we present results on how to predict a paper's AI sub-field from a given paper title only. Importantly, for the latter, short-text classification task we compare several algorithms from conventional machine learning all the way up to recent, larger transformer architectures. Finally, for the transformer models, we also present gradient-based, attention visualizations to further explain the model's classification process. All code can be found online (Code available here: https://github.com/1pha/paperswithtopic).

**Keywords:** Natural language processing · Sequence classification · Deep learning · Model comparison

## 1 Introduction

The field of artificial intelligence (AI) has undergone a rapid expansion over the past decades, fuelled especially by the advent of deep learning (DL) techniques in 2012 [1]. As exemplary statistics, around 370,000 papers from the United States and another 320,000 papers from China alone were published in the field of AI between 1997 and 2017 [2]. Publication growth has been largely exponential over the past few years, which has increased the need for researchers and users in AI for text-mining tools that help to search, organize, and summarize the "flood" of papers published every month. Popular bibliography tools have started to assist people through recommendation and ordering functions, including Mendeley [3] and EndNote [4], for example. However, these applications currently still use "standard" keyword association models [5], and hence may have trouble in customizing recommendations and sorting according to specific user requirements. With the advent of more powerful natural language processing (NLP) tools over

C. Wallraven et al. (Eds.): ACPR 2021, LNCS 13189, pp. 254–267, 2022.
https://doi.org/10.1007/978-3-031-02444-3_19

the past decade, additional methods for paper recommendation or summarization have been introduced, such as semantic-scholar [6], which uses a series of NLP models to summarize a given paper into one sentence.

In the present work, we aim to add to this field of recommendation and summarization systems by presenting a framework that is able to predict a paper's sub-field (in AI) from its title alone. One of the most popular resources for AI researchers is the pre-print service arXiv,[1] at which AI-related papers can be "published" without peer-review. For predicting research fields, a dataset based on arXiv papers from various domains such as physics, computer-science, or chemistry [7] has already been created - this dataset, however, only contains these broad research domains, and does not indicate sub-fields, such as natural-language-processing or computer-vision for AI, for example. Such a more detailed classification, however, is crucial for a better organizing of papers - especially those that do not contain keywords, or non-curated, noisy keywords.

In order to address this issue, here we first present a dataset that pairs current papers in the field of AI with their corresponding sub-field. We then show results from a series of algorithms that try to predict the sub-field from the paper's title - these algorithms range from conventional machine learning methods all the way up to recent, deep-learning-based transformer models, thus setting benchmarks for this task. Using methods from explainable AI, we also show how the latter, transformer-based models arrive at their decision.

## 2 Related Work

The basic task for addressing the title-to-sub-field classification problem is called "short sequence classification" - one of the most fundamental tasks in the NLP field [8]. In the following, we review methods for this task ranging from conventional machine learning models to current transformer-based architectures.

### 2.1 Conventional Machine Learning Methods

Initial learning-based text classification methods first found wide adoption with the introduction of the *Naive Bayes* [9] model, still one of the most commonly-used spam mail classification methods [10]. Although this model treats words as individually-independent, it still demonstrates high performance in short text classification tasks. However, without sophisticated preprocessing algorithms, the naive bayes classifier cannot handle multi-label tasks easily. The NLP field then introduced tree-based classifiers, such as *decision trees* or ensemble versions as *random forests* for such classification tasks - however, to sometimes mixed results that did not surpass existing machine learning models [11]. Since tree models are powerful at pruning tabular data, informative features with many different unique words may cause these models to still pay attention to

---

[1] https://arxiv.org/.

uninformative features in order to keep the representation rich enough. Several approaches addressed this problem [12], usually by boosting the ensembling of individual weak tree classifiers, such as *XGBoost* [13], or *LightGBM* [14].

## 2.2   Recurrent Networks

Among methods based on neural networks (NN), one of the earliest approaches to sequence classification is the *recurrent neural network* [15,16] (RNN) framework, in which sequential data is fed into a neural network with the goal of predicting a future state or sequence. Given that text forms a natural sequence (of letters, words, and/or sentences), RNNs were quickly adopted for text classification [17] once large-enough corpora and powerful GPU processing became available. A critical issue with standard RNN models is that their gradients vanish in long sequences, which prompted the development of the *long-short term memory* (LSTM) [18] architecture. Although the gates introduced in the LSTM framework managed to deal with the vanishing gradient problem, the framework overall suffered from exceedingly high computational cost due to the large amount of matrix multiplications per sequence. To reduce these computational costs, derivatives of the LSTM model, such as *gated recurrent unit* (GRU) [19] were introduced. Overall, recurrent models already increased accuracy by a significant margin compared to conventional machine learning algorithms.

## 2.3   Attention-Based Models

A further development in sequence processing and in NLP in general came from the development of the *attention mechanism*, which was first introduced into one of the recurrent network models *seq2seq* [20] - a model that is still widely used in machine translation tasks in NLP. The main idea of this mechanism is to find the relationship between an input sequence with a hidden vector. Through this attentional connection, models became better able at capturing relations between sequences at even longer distances and better fidelity.

Perhaps one of the most significant developments in NLP in recent years was made by the introduction of the *transformer* architecture - a further development of the attention mechanism [21]. This model and its subsequent derivatives have become the de-facto benchmark for nearly all language-related tasks over the past years. Derivatives of the original transformer architecture include Google BERT [22], Open-AI GPT [23] (now in its third, to date largest iteration), and ELECTRA [24]. Similarly to the early issues of LSTM, however, the attention mechanism inside the transformer architecture has in principle quadratic sequence length complexity - an issue that was addressed in updated architectures, such as Performer [25] based on a kernel method, for example. Similarly, ALBERT [26] tried to reduce the computational cost by using extensive weight sharing and factorized embedding parametrization.

## 2.4  Recommendation Systems for Paper Management

As our application domain is similar to recommendation systems, we will briefly review some relevant methods for these systems as well: these often use methods based on collaborative filtering, sometimes adding content-based filtering or graph-based methods [27]. The core idea here is to translate the interaction between user and item into a pivot table matrix. Similarities between users or items based on this matrix are then found by using cosine similarity or matrix factorization methods to derive embedding vectors. A common issue with these approaches is the "cold-start problem": new users or items lack interaction with others, which makes it hard to retrieve their embedding vectors. Deep learning methods that are not based on user information may be able to find such representations better. Services that are make use of such methods are Mendeley [5], arxiv-sanity, or semantic-scholar - the latter being based on the recent, state-of-the-art GPT-3 transformer model [6,23].

A scientific dataset that was created for a short sentence classification task similar to the one we deal with, is PubMed 200k [28]. This is a collection of sentences labeled according to the section they belong to, such as 'Results' or 'Methods', and has been used with different NLP models - it does not, however, give any insights about the specific paper topic they belong to.

# 3  Methods

The bulk of the experimental work was implemented with Python and the PyTorch deep learning framework [29]. Most of the conventional machine learning models were implemented through scikit-learn [30], with recent transformer models using the huggingface library [31]. Experiment maintenance and logging made use of wandb.ai [32].[2]

In the following, we describe the overall pipeline from data collection, preprocessing, model implementation, hyper-parameter optimization, to result collection. Overall classification performance was measured using the area under the receiver operating curve (AUROC, [33]).

## 3.1  Dataset

One of the most popular resources for AI researchers is paperswithcode.[3] This site allows researchers to see state-of-the-art models based on different tasks. From their publicly-available database, we collected the meta-data resulting in 49,980 available papers. The full meta-data, including abstracts or publication date, was saved in .json format, and the paper title paired with corresponding sub-field category labels were saved in .csv format in a pivot table scheme. There were a total of sixteen imbalanced labels: adversarial, audio, computer-code, computer-vision, graphs, knowledge-base, medical, methodology, miscellaneous, music, natural-language-processing, playing-games, reasoning, robots,

---

[2] Wandb project link: https://wandb.ai/1pha/paperswithtopic.
[3] Paperswithcode: https://paperswithcode.com/.

and speech. Since the label methodology introduced a large amount of skew into the distribution, we excluded this label from the training phase, resulting in a total of 15 labels. From this dataset, we split stratified train, validation and test sets with a 90/5/5 ratio, resulting in 34,572 papers for training and 1,921 papers for validation and test set, respectively.

## 3.2   Preprocessing

Preprocessing the input into a correct, machine-learning suitable format is one of the most important parts of any NLP pipeline. Typical boilerplate pipelines include removing extra whitespaces and special characters, as well as lowercasing, which we followed in this order. Pipelines also often include removing numbers or expanding contractions (i.e. I'll to I will) - here, we want to keep the numbers as they may be important predicting factors (e.g., GPT-"3"); in contrast, contractions rarely happen in paper titles, which is why we skipped these two preprocessing stages. Moreover, lemmatization is often done to improve generalization, but again, titles do not tend to include much tense shifting, hence this step was also not included. Finally, the pre-processed titles were tokenized into an index and filled by <pad> for sequences shorter than the designated maximum sequence length (in our case set to 64 characters; sequences longer than the 64 characters would get truncated, but the paperswithcode dataset did not contain any title longer than 50 characters). For deep learning models, these sequences are usually further embedded into vectors, in order to represent words with contextual information. This procedure can be done via embedding matrices included inside the deep learning methods, or via libraries that assist with this process such as FastText [34] or Word2Vec [35] - these approaches will be discussed more in Sect. 4.2.

## 3.3   Conventional Machine Learning Models

We implemented the following conventional machine learning models: Gaussian naive Bayes, complement naive Bayes, extra tree classifier, random forest classifier, k-nearest neighbor classifier, AdaBoost classifier, LightGBM, and XGBoost. Hyper-parameters for all models were used with their default values as implemented in scikit-learn.

Since our task is a multi-label classification task with some instances having multiple labels, which some methods cannot handle properly, models were fitted with each label sequentially, hence treating labels as individually independently distributed.

## 3.4   Recurrent Neural Network Models

For standard RNN models, we used a "vanilla" RNN [15], as well as LSTM [18] and its derivate GRU [19]. All RNNs used binary cross-entropy loss for each label and then used a mean loss across all labels for each batch. We employed the Adam optimizer with a learning rate of $10^{-4}$ and default update parameters of $\beta_1 = 0.9$ and $\beta_2 = 0.999$. Early stopping was used on the validation set with a patience of 15 epochs.

Variations to these RNN models [36] can be done by stacking more layers into the network or by increasing the embedding dimensions, which may affect performance. We therefore performed an additional grid search on these two parameters.

### 3.5   Transformer Models

A number of high-performance transformer variations came out starting with BERT [22]. Here, we compared BERT [22], ELECTRA models [24] starting with default parameters of a single layer of 8 attention heads, and a hidden dimension of 128. Furthermore, for the ELECTRA model we performed a grid search on modulating the number of layers and number of heads.

### 3.6   Word Embeddings

For both the RNNs and the Transformer models, we also tested three different ways to embed/process the tokenized inputs: first, we created a trainable lookup table for each token, such that the matrix has its shape of (# of tokens, # of dimensions). This is an end-to-end process in that a single model learns embeddings and classification. For our second and third method, we used the two embedding methods of word2vec and FastText. These methods learn to embed the tokens into a vector first, with the neural networks getting trained on the classification task on these vectors. This can be regarded as two-stage model with the optimizer, however, not being able to affect the embedding itself.

### 3.7   Pooling Method

For transformer methods, researchers typically use the last hidden state of the transformer outputs to classify sequences (last token pooling in Table 4). The Huggingface API, however, also supports sequence classification models for each transformer architecture that can use the *first* hidden states for classification. For this, the first hidden state is internally pooled as a process of point-wise feedforward action - similar to the attention calculation proposed in [21]. For the BERT and ELECTRA models, we therefore also compared the first and last token pooling classification results.

### 3.8   Visualization

It is possible for transformer models to retrieve an "attention score" that illustrates the relation between sequences. The standard Bahdanau attention mechanism [21] yields an attention matrix consisting of a set of scores for each sequence (normalized to 1). This matrix encodes which relations between sequences affect the final output as they receive point-wise feedforward from the final output. This method works well for seq2seq models [20], but not directly for transformer architectures, as these have multiple layers each with multiple heads. Preliminary research [37,38] has shown that a resulting attention matrix in the latest transformer architectures only indirectly visualizes their predictions (it can still be used, however, to follow the training process [39,40]).

Here, we tried to find a visualization of the models based on the idea of Gradient-weighted Class Activation Mapping (Grad-CAM) [41] instead, which uses the gradient to locate inputs (originally pixels) important for the models' decision. The main logic here is to retrieve the gradient of the target layer during optimization, convert it to a mean averaged kernel and to overlay this kernel with the original image to highlight the "important" input. For this, we retrieved the gradients that were backward-passed from the embedding matrix to the tokenized input in our transformer architectures (using the trainable lookup embedding), and normalized the result using the $L2$-norm for each sequence to get an attention/importance score.

# 4    Results

## 4.1    Conventional Machine Learning Models

Table 1 shows the AUROC for the conventional machine learning models. Extra Tree and K-Nearest Neighbour had low performance close to chance (AUROC = 0.5 equals a random guess). It is especially interesting in this context that both naive Bayes models did not result in significant performance increases given their general use as spam-filters. We assume that these models are more vulnerable to unseen words (e.g. "flickering" which did not appear in the training set) due to their naive multiplication of word probabilities. Beyond the Extra Tree model, other tree-based models, however, showed higher performance. Nonetheless, these performance levels seem not sufficient enough for use in practical applications.

**Table 1.** AUROC comparison between machine learning models, using tokenized input. Error indicates Standard Error of the Mean (SEM) across 10 folds.

| Types | Models | AUROC |
|---|---|---|
| Machine learning | Extra Tree | 52.4 ± 0.02 |
| | Complement Naive Bayes | 52.5 ± 0.12 |
| | Naive Bayes | 52.9 ± 0.05 |
| | K-Nearest Neighbour | 53.2 ± 0.03 |
| | Random Forest | 56.4 ± 0.05 |
| | AdaBoost | 59.8 ± 0.06 |
| | LightGBM | 63.9 ± 0.08 |
| | XGBoost | 66.8 ± 0.09 |

## 4.2   Recurrent Neural Network Models

Using a single layer LSTM and GRU models already outperformed all conventional methods (cf. first column in Table 2 versus Table 1). Improvements across number of layers or architectures, however, was less visible. Adding more layers to the "vanilla" RNN resulted in a clear decrease in performance for all values of the hidden dimension, most likely due to the issue of vanishing gradients which resulted in unstable optimization. For the other two RNNs, however, stacking more layers either kept performance or resulted in lower overall performance. Best performance for both LSTM and GRU models was obtained with the maximum amount of hidden dimensions and single layer. Performance for the GRU model seemed to be more stable as the number of layer increased compared to the LSTM model that decreased performance with increasing number of layers.

**Table 2.** Grid search result for hyper-parameters for recurrent neural networks (AUROC): #H = hidden size; #L = the number of layers. Bolded values indicate best performance for each model.

| Model | #H | #L | | | |
|-------|-----|------|------|------|------|
| | | 1 | 2 | 3 | 4 |
| RNN | 128 | 61.7 | 56.0 | 59.7 | 55.3 |
| | 256 | 54.1 | **62.8** | 54.1 | 49.8 |
| | 512 | 52.8 | 51.0 | 50.7 | 50.4 |
| LSTM | 128 | 85.9 | 85.1 | 83.3 | 82.9 |
| | 256 | 86.8 | 85.7 | 85.2 | 85.4 |
| | 512 | **90.4** | 89.4 | 87.5 | 75.8 |
| GRU | 128 | 85.4 | 87.1 | 88.0 | 87.7 |
| | 256 | 90.2 | 88.8 | 89.0 | 88.2 |
| | 512 | **92.2** | 88.9 | 89.2 | 88.0 |

## 4.3   Transformer Models

Table 3 shows the results of the grid search for the ELECTRA model that predicts with the result from first token pooling. Performance in all cases is high around 0.9 (except for one optimization failure shown in italics in Table 3). The number of attention heads has limited influence across all parameters in most cases. However, the model fails to train with more layers with small hidden dimension even with large number of multiple heads. The size of the hidden state, however, results in a slight improvement across architectures and other hyper-parameters, with the best results reaching around 93.7 for the medium hidden dimensionality.

**Table 3.** Grid search result over number of layers, heads and hidden dimension for the ELECTRA Transformer Model pooled with first sequence label: #L = the number of layers; #A = the number of attention heads; #H = hidden size.

| Model | #L | #A | #H | | |
|---|---|---|---|---|---|
| | | | 128 | 256 | 512 |
| ELECTRA | 1 | 8 | 93.0 | 93.1 | 92.7 |
| | | 16 | 93.1 | 93.1 | **93.6** |
| | | 32 | 93.6 | 93.4 | 93.6 |
| | 2 | 8 | 91.5 | 92.9 | 88.4 |
| | | 16 | 92.5 | 93.7 | 90.8 |
| | | 32 | 92.6 | **93.8** | 92.6 |
| | 3 | 8 | *53.7* | 93.2 | 81.3 |
| | | 16 | *53.1* | **93.7** | 87.5 |
| | | 32 | 91.2 | 93.1 | 92.2 |
| | 4 | 8 | *52.6* | 93.5 | 74.4 |
| | | 16 | *50.3* | 93.3 | 84.4 |
| | | 32 | *53.7* | **93.7** | 89.9 |

## 4.4 Comparison of Deep Learning Models; Effects of Embedding and Token Pooling

Table 4 shows the AUROC results for the different RNNs, Transformer Models (for the two different pooling methods), and the effect of the tokenization embedding method. To make recurrent network models comparable to transformer models, we used 2 layers for recurrent network models while transformer models used a single layer with 8 attention heads. In the recurrent network and last token pooling transformer models, word2vec and FastText method surpassed the lookup matrix in all number of hidden dimensions, while first token pooling model showed high performance when lookup table matrix was used. Increasing the embedding dimension enhanced the result in most recurrent networks. On the other hand, transformer models with last token pooling often failed to optimize as the embedding size increased. There was also a performance drop with the increment of embedding dimension in first token pooling but not as much as last token pooling. Comparing this to the base BERT [22] model that uses embedding dimension of 768 and shows high performance in general NLP tasks, we suppose that these effects are due to the small size of vocabulary and input of relatively short sequences in our application domain. We could also observe that first token pooling, in overall, slightly outperforms last token pooling.

## 4.5 Visualization

Results of the gradient-based visualization are demonstrated in Figs. 1 for four different examples.

**Table 4.** AUROC comparison between deep learning models, using different embedding methods and embedding dimensionalities as well as different token pooling methods. Last and first token pooling refers to which token was pooled to determine the logits. Best results for each method are bolded, failed optimizations are shown in italics: #E = embedding size.

| Types | Models | #E | AUROC | | |
|-------|--------|-----|--------|--------|----------|
| | | | Lookup | Word2Vec | FastText |
| Recurrent networks | RNN | 128 | 55.1 | 60.7 | 55.9 |
| | | 256 | 59.3 | 55.5 | 53.4 |
| | | 512 | 65.7 | **66.9** | 62.9 |
| | LSTM | 128 | 79.1 | 83.8 | **89.7** |
| | | 256 | 88.5 | 89.9 | 89.3 |
| | | 512 | 86.0 | 89.0 | 87.1 |
| | GRU | 128 | 88.3 | 88.0 | 77.5 |
| | | 256 | 88.2 | 88.4 | 74.0 |
| | | 512 | 86.6 | 89.1 | **88.6** |
| Last token pooling | BERT | 128 | 88.9 | 92.3 | 91.8 |
| | | 256 | 82.8 | 90.2 | **92.0** |
| | | 512 | *56.7* | 80.7 | *54.3* |
| | ELECTRA | 128 | 91.3 | 92.1 | **92.4** |
| | | 256 | 90.8 | 92.3 | 91.9 |
| | | 512 | *50.0* | *50.0* | *50.0* |
| First token pooling | BERT | 128 | **92.8** | 91.8 | 91.2 |
| | | 256 | 91.9 | 91.8 | 91.2 |
| | | 512 | 91.6 | 89.9 | 90.0 |
| | ELECTRA | 128 | **93.0** | 91.7 | 91.7 |
| | | 256 | 92.6 | 92.3 | 91.8 |
| | | 512 | 92.7 | 89.9 | 89.6 |

The first figure is the result for the paper title of "Neural Machine Translation by Jointly Learning to Align and Translate", which our model correctly predicts as natural-language-processing. Figure 1a clearly highlights "translation" as the most important word for that decision. Other words (including prepositions or words that do not directly correlate with the prediction - at least from human intuition) have comparatively small values. Figure 1b and Fig. 1c depict additional, successful cases in which the attention seems to rest on well-matching words.

In contrast, Fig. 1d illustrates a failure case for the first category prediction for a paper with the title of "Faster R-CNN towards real-time object detection with region proposal networks"— this was mis-classified as belonging to the robots category. Here, the gradient-based visualization highlights the

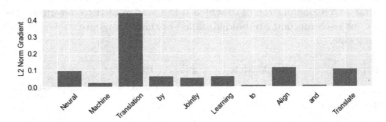

(a) Model top-3 predictions: natural-language-processing, medical, speech. The top-1 prediction and true paper topic align.

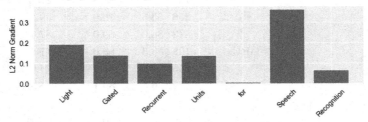

(b) Model top-3 predictions: speech, natural-language-processing, time-series. Correct top-1 prediction, but note that the following predictions fit as well.

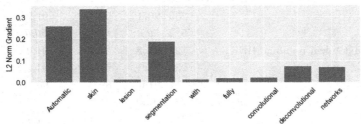

(c) Model top-3 predictions: medical, computer-vision, robots. Correct for top-1 and top-2 predictions.

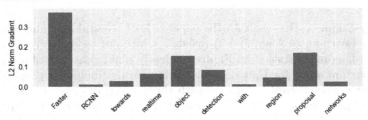

(d) Model top-3 predictions: robots, computer-vision, medical. Top-1 prediction is not correct, top-2 is.

**Fig. 1.** Gradient-based visualization of the output

word "Faster", as well as "object", which may have given rise to that wrong classification. Interestingly, the (correct) category of computer-vision, was the next-highest choice for the model, indicating that a Top-N accuracy evaluation method might result in even better scores for the transformer models.

## 5   Discussion and Conclusion

The main contribution of our work presented here was to compare different NLP models for a short-sequence-classification task in which a paper topic was to be predicted from its title. Based on our initial dataset on AI-topics, we found that current deep learning models fared best with a AUROC of 93.8 on the held-out test set, indicating excellent performance for this task domain. Less deep RNN models still achieved passable performance with a GRU, RNN reaching up to 92.2 with a large number of hidden states, yet at only one layer. Conventional machine learning models failed to reach satisfactory results indicating the superiority of sequence-based models in current NLP tasks even for—relatively—small datasets.

We also performed grid-search on a number of hyper-parameters of NN models and compared different tokenization and pooling methods for pre-processing and classification. Here, results showed that the number of hidden dimensions and also the embedding dimensionality need to be matched to the size of the dataset (in our case, towards the smaller end). Further experiments will need to be done with larger datasets to trace these performance patterns as the sample size increases.

In the future, we would like to extend our approach also to a wider range of scientific topics, expanding our dataset further. Similarly, additional features could be taken into account, such as authors, conferences, abstracts, keywords, or arXiv URLs. From a methodological point of view, we need to compare our results also to the popular topic modeling methods, such as Latent Dirichlet Allocation (LDA) [42] or Latent Semantic Analysis (LSA) [43], which would make our analysis more complete. Additional extensions from the NN perspective concern methods that explicitly use weakly-labeled data ([7] such as present in the categories of arXiv) or self-supervised improvements.

**Acknowledgments.** This work was partly supported by Institute of Information & Communications Technology Planning & Evaluation (IITP) grants funded by the Korean government (MSIT) (No. 2019-0-00079, Department of Artificial Intelligence, Korea University; No. 2021-0-02068-001, Artificial Intelligence Innovation Hub).

## References

1. Krizhevsky, A., Sutskever, I., Hinton, G.E.: ImageNet classification with deep convolutional neural networks. In: NeurIPS, vol. 25, pp. 1097–1105 (2012)
2. Liu, S.: Number of papers published in the field of artificial intelligence (AI) worldwide from 1997 to 2017, by country. https://www.statista.com/statistics/941037/ai-paper-publications-worldwide-by-country/

3. Zaugg, H., West, R.E., Tateishi, I., Randall, D.L.: Mendeley: creating communities of scholarly inquiry through research collaboration. TechTrends **55**(1), 32–36 (2011). https://doi.org/10.1007/s11528-011-0467-y
4. Hupe, M.: Endnote X9. J. Electron. Resour. Med. Libr. **16**(3–4), 117–119 (2019)
5. Mendeley: Mendeley MREC recommendation system (2021). https://github.com/Mendeley/mrec
6. Cachola, I., Lo, K., Cohan, A., Weld, D.S.: TLDR: extreme summarization of scientific documents (2020)
7. Clement, C.B., Bierbaum, M., O'Keeffe, K.P., Alemi, A.A.: On the use of arXiv as a dataset (2019)
8. Goldberg, Y.: Neural Network Methods for Natural Language Processing. Synthesis Lectures on Human Language Technologies, vol. 10, no. 1, pp. 1–309 (2017)
9. Lewis, D.D.: Naive (Bayes) at forty: the independence assumption in information retrieval. In: Nédellec, C., Rouveirol, C. (eds.) ECML 1998. LNCS, vol. 1398, pp. 4–15. Springer, Heidelberg (1998). https://doi.org/10.1007/BFb0026666
10. Metsis, V., Androutsopoulos, I., Paliouras, G.: Spam filtering with naive Bayes-which naive Bayes? In: CEAS, Mountain View, CA, vol. 17, pp. 28–69 (2006)
11. Baoxun, X., Guo, X., Ye, Y., Cheng, J.: An improved random forest classifier for text categorization. JCP **7**(12), 2913–2920 (2012)
12. Islam, M.Z., Liu, J., Li, J., Liu, L., Kang, W.: A semantics aware random forest for text classification. Association for Computing Machinery, New York (2019)
13. Chen, T., Guestrin, C.: XGBoost: a scalable tree boosting system. In: SIGKDD, pp. 785–794 (2016)
14. Ke, G., et al.: LightGBM: a highly efficient gradient boosting decision tree. In: NeurIPS, vol. 30, pp. 3146–3154 (2017)
15. Rumelhart, D.E., Hinton, G.E., Williams, R.J.: Learning internal representations by error propagation. Technical report, California Univ. San Diego La Jolla. Inst. for Cognitive Science (1985)
16. Jordan, M.I.: Serial order: a parallel distributed processing approach. Technical report, June 1985–March 1986 (1986). https://www.osti.gov/biblio/6910294
17. Guo, L., Zhang, D., Wang, L., Wang, H., Cui, B.: CRAN: a hybrid CNN-RNN attention-based model for text classification. In: Trujillo, J.C., et al. (eds.) ER 2018. LNCS, vol. 11157, pp. 571–585. Springer, Cham (2018). https://doi.org/10.1007/978-3-030-00847-5_42
18. Hochreiter, S., Schmidhuber, J.: Long short-term memory. Neural Comput. **9**(8), 1735–1780 (1997)
19. Cho, K., van Merrienboer, B., Gülçehre, Ç., Bougares, F., Schwenk, H., Bengio, Y.: Learning phrase representations using RNN encoder-decoder for statistical machine translation. CoRR
20. Bahdanau, D., Cho, K., Bengio, Y.: Neural machine translation by jointly learning to align and translate. In: ICLR (2015). http://arxiv.org/abs/1409.0473
21. Vaswani, A., et al.: Attention is all you need. CoRR arXiv:1706.03762 (2017)
22. Devlin, J., Chang, M.W., Lee, K., Toutanova, K.: BERT: pre-training of deep bidirectional transformers for language understanding. CoRR arXiv:1810.04805 (2018)
23. Brown, T.B., et al.: Language models are few-shot learners. CoRR arXiv:2005.14165 (2020)
24. Clark, K., Luong, M.T., Le, Q.V., Manning, C.D.: ELECTRA: pre-training text encoders as discriminators rather than generators. CoRR arXiv:2003.10555 (2020)
25. Choromanski, K., et al.: Rethinking attention with performers. CoRR arXiv:2009.14794 (2020)

26. Lan, Z., Chen, M., Goodman, S., Gimpel, K., Sharma, P., Soricut, R.: ALBERT: A lite BERT for self-supervised learning of language representations. CoRR arXiv:1909.11942 (2019)

27. Bai, X., Wang, M., Lee, I., Yang, Z., Kong, X., Xia, F.: Scientific paper recommendation: a survey. IEEE Access **7**, 9324–9339 (2019)

28. Dernoncourt, F., Lee, J.Y.: Pubmed 200k RCT: a dataset for sequential sentence classification in medical abstracts. CoRR arXiv:1710.06071 (2017)

29. Paszke, A., et al.: PyTorch: an imperative style, high-performance deep learning library. In: Wallach, H., Larochelle, H., Beygelzimer, A., d'Alché-Buc, F., Fox, E., Garnett, R. (eds.) NeurIPS, vol. 32, pp. 8024–8035. Curran Associates Inc. (2019). http://papers.neurips.cc/paper/9015-pytorch-an-imperative-style-high-performance-deep-learning-library.pdf

30. Pedregosa, F., et al.: Scikit-learn: machine learning in Python. J. Mach. Learn. Res. **12**, 2825–2830 (2011)

31. Wolf, T., et al.: HuggingFace's transformers: state-of-the-art natural language processing. CoRR arXiv:1910.03771 (2019)

32. Biewald, L.: Experiment tracking with weights and biases (2020). https://www.wandb.com/

33. Hanley, J.A., McNeil, B.J.: The meaning and use of the area under a receiver operating characteristic (ROC) curve. Radiology **143**(1), 29–36 (1982)

34. Joulin, A., Grave, E., Bojanowski, P., Douze, M., Jégou, H., Mikolov, T.: FastText.zip: compressing text classification models. CoRR arXiv:1612.03651 (2016)

35. Mikolov, T., Chen, K., Corrado, G., Dean, J.: Efficient estimation of word representations in vector space. In: Bengio, Y., LeCun, Y. (eds.) ICLR (2013). http://arxiv.org/abs/1301.3781

36. Jozefowicz, R., Zaremba, W., Sutskever, I.: An empirical exploration of recurrent network architectures. In: ICML, pp. 2342–2350. PMLR (2015)

37. Brunner, G., Liu, Y., Pascual, D., Richter, O., Wattenhofer, R.: On the validity of self-attention as explanation in transformer models. CoRR arXiv:1908.04211 (2019)

38. Jain, S., Wallace, B.C.: Attention is not explanation. CoRR arXiv:1902.10186 (2019)

39. Wiegreffe, S., Pinter, Y.: Attention is not explanation. CoRR arXiv:1908.04626 (2019)

40. Clark, K., Khandelwal, U., Levy, O., Manning, C.D.: What does BERT look at? An analysis of BERT's attention. CoRR arXiv:1906.04341 (2019)

41. Selvaraju, R.R., Cogswell, M., Das, A., Vedantam, R., Parikh, D., Batra, D.: GradCAM: visual explanations from deep networks via gradient-based localization. In: Proceedings of the IEEE International Conference on Computer Vision, pp. 618–626 (2017)

42. Jelodar, H., et al.: Latent Dirichlet allocation (LDA) and topic modeling: models, applications, a survey. Multimedia Tools Appl. **78**(11), 15169–15211 (2019)

43. Dumais, S.T.: Latent semantic analysis. Ann. Rev. Inf. Sci. Technol. **38**(1), 188–230 (2004)

# Subject-Independent Motor Imagery EEG Classification Based on Graph Convolutional Network

Juho Lee, Jin Woo Choi, and Sungho Jo[✉]

School of Computing, Korea Advanced Institute of Science and Technology (KAIST),
Daejeon 34141, South Korea
{leejh1021,rayoakmont,shjo}@kaist.ac.kr

**Abstract.** Electroencephalogram (EEG) motor imagery (MI) has attracted much attention in brain-computer interfaces (BCIs) as it directly encodes human intentions. However, the variability of EEG-based brain signals between individuals requires current BCI systems to undergo calibration procedures before its usage. In this paper, we propose a model that targets minimizing such procedures by improving inter-subject classification performance. The purpose of our proposed method is to extract features using previously studied convolution-based deep learning structures while utilizing a graph structure to analyze inter-subject relationships with multiple subjects. By utilizing not only features but also the relationship between subject-specific features, it becomes possible to make predictions focusing on subjects with high similarity. Therefore, even new users not seen during the training process are predicted relatively efficiently. To validate our method, we evaluated our model with the public dataset BCI Competition IV IIa. The results in our study suggest that our proposed method improved the cross-subject classification accuracy by combining it with the previous deep learning model and induced a balanced prediction for the classes. Our study has shown the potential to develop MI-based BCI applications that do not require user calibration by training the model with pre-existing datasets.

**Keywords:** Brain-computer interfaces (BCIs) · Graph convolutional network (GCN) · Deep learning (DL) · Electroencephalography (EEG) · Motor imagery (MI) · Subject-independent

## 1 Introduction

Brain-computer interface (BCI) systems provide a communication path that can interact with external devices by classifying the user's brain neural activity patterns [1–3]. One of the non-invasive ways to record brain activity is through electroencephalogram (EEG), which utilizes multiple electrodes placed on a specific scalp area. EEG signals have been widely used in BCI applications as they can record brain activity relatively easily and inexpensively compared to other neural acquisition techniques [4–8].

© Springer Nature Switzerland AG 2022
C. Wallraven et al. (Eds.): ACPR 2021, LNCS 13189, pp. 268–281, 2022.
https://doi.org/10.1007/978-3-031-02444-3_20

So far, EEG-based BCI applications have been developed using neurophysiological patterns, including steady-state visual evoked potential (SSVEP), event-related potential (ERP), movement-related cortical potentials (MRCPs), and motor imagery (MI) [9–12]. Among these BCI studies, MI, which classifies EEG signals based on the imagination of body movement, has recently attracted much attention. MI EEG signal can be elicited in a specific pattern when a subject imagines performing a specific movement, such as moving of hand or foot. Several studies have researched MI-based EEG patterns in advance, as it is a signal that both healthy and disabled people can control without external stimulation.

Recently, with the success of machine learning and deep learning in computer vision [13] and speech recognition [14], many studies have been conducted to apply them to the EEG classification task. For instance, Ang et al. and Pfurtscheller et al. applied machine learning techniques using power spectral density (PSD) measures from MI EEG to classify participants' intentions [15,16]. However, machine learning has a limitation in that it relies on the hand-crafted features of human experts. Therefore, to overcome the limitations of machine learning, deep learning-based methods have been proposed, and significant improvements have been made. In particular, convolutional neural network (CNN) has been widely applied to MI classification tasks because they effectively extract temporal and spatial features from EEG signals [17,18].

In general, human EEG signals change according to the difference in each individual's mental state, resulting in large variability on inter-subject relations [19,20]. Existing machine learning and deep learning methods have been successful in MI classification, but many have poor performance when there is insufficient data on new users. Therefore, most MI task methods, including the studies mentioned above, require the calibration process to be performed using sufficient data from new users. However, the calibration process is time-consuming and inconvenient [21]. This is a significant obstacle in the practical application of the BCI system, and research to eliminate or minimize the calibration process is necessary.

In this paper, we focus on improving subject-independent classification accuracy to take a step closer to BCI systems that do not require calibration from the user. Thus, the proposed model in our study performs the relation-based prediction by defining the relationship between multiple subjects through a graph structure. This approach enables efficient prediction even for new users by focusing on subjects with high similarity. The main contributions are as follows.

- In order to improve the inter-subject classification performance, we developed a method applicable to the existing deep learning-based MI classification model.
- We applied the proposed method to the previously studied MI classification model and analyzed the performance with and without our method.

## 2   Related Work

Most of the existing methods for the MI EEG task have been developed based on the intra-subject situation requiring calibration time [22,23]. In previous studies, researchers have employed techniques based on machine learning using hand-crafted features. As one of several methods, common spatial pattern (CSP) is a method for maximizing the variance difference between different classes [24, 25]. In particular, filter bank CSP (FBCSP), an algorithm based on CSP method, is one of the widely used methods in MI-based BCI [26]. These features are fed to classifiers such as support vector machine (SVM) [27] and Random Forest [28] to generate predictions.

Existing machine learning methods classified EEG MI data with good performance. However, such methods have limitations on achieving higher accuracy as it relies heavily on handcrafted features created by human experts. Deep learning methods such as CNN overcome these limitations through automated feature extraction. For example, Schirrmeister et al. [17] outperformed the existing FBCSP [26] algorithm by using CNN.

MI classification methods mentioned above are intra-subject-based methods that require a calibration process. However, the calibration process is time-consuming and inconvenient to acquire data [21]. Recently, several methods have been proposed to reduce the calibration time in the MI-based BCI system. For example, Tang et al. [29] suggested a method using the adversarial domain adaptation technology and reduced the inconvenience of the calibration process by using only unlabeled data of new users. An et al. [30] applied the attention module to the few-shot relation network structure [31] and reduced the calibration time by using only a few seconds of data from new users.

Wang et al. [32] tried to solve the lack of data in the target domain in computer vision by utilizing multi-source domain adaptation. We applied this study to improve inter-subject classification performance in BCI applications. We defined the relationship between each EEG feature of subjects as a graph structure and utilized the relationship information for prediction using a graph convolution network [33]. In addition, it was implemented as a model suitable for classifying EEG signals by designing a structure to extract temporal and spatial characteristics of EEG signals effectively.

## 3    Method

### 3.1    Definition and Notation

Before a detailed description of the proposed model, we first describe the definitions and notations.

Data of a single subject is defined with $\{(X_i, y_i), i = 1, 2, ..., l\}$, where $l$ denotes the number of motor imagery EEG trials, $X_i \in \mathbb{R}^{E \times T}$ denotes EEG signals from a single trial with dimensions $E$, the number of electrodes, by $T$, the number of time points sampled, $y$ corresponds to a label defined by $y \in \{1, 2, ..., C\}$, and $C$ is the number of classes.

### 3.2    Network Architecture

Figure 1 shows the overall architecture of the proposed model. The description of the architecture is divided into Feature extraction, Prototype update, Graph construction, Prediction, and Model inference. In the feature extraction part, the raw EEG signals of subjects from $S_1$ to $S_n$ are passed through the feature extractor and are converted into fixed-dimensional feature embeddings. The extracted features are used in two different ways: as updating elements for prototypes representing features per class for each subject, and as queries used for classification. While prototypes are used to learn similarities between classes and subjects using graph structure, the feature embeddings are also concatenated as a query sample and are predicted through the graph convolutional network to classify into labels. As the query is predicted by considering the relationships between all subjects and classes, subject-independent prediction is taken in consideration within the model.

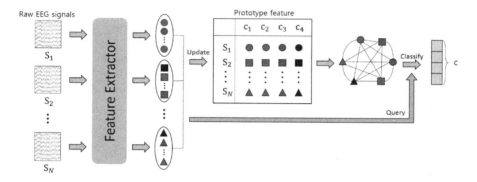

**Fig. 1.** An overview of the proposed model. From left to right, raw EEG signals, feature extractor, extracted features, prototype features, prototype graph, and prediction probability are shown. $S_1, S_2, \ldots, S_n$ denote subjects, and $c_1, c_2, c_3, c_4$ denote classes.

**Feature Extraction.** The raw EEG signal is first band-pass filtered from 4 to 38 Hz, the range of motor imagery frequency, and then cropped to fixed window size. A feature extractor $f(\cdot)$ serves to convert EEG signals into features and is designed by modifying the representative MI classifier model. The feature extractor can be flexibly replaced, and in this paper, we designed the feature extractor by modifying the architectures of Shallownet [17], and EEGnet [18], which were used as comparison groups. In the case of Shallownet, features are extracted using temporal and spatial convolution and square and logarithm activation functions. EEGnet extract features using depth-wise separable convolution and Elu activation function. The detailed structure is in Table 1 and Table 2.

**Prototype Update.** For every mini-batch, sampled EEG feature embeddings are used to estimate prototypes representing each subject and class label. The estimated prototype $\hat{p}_{S_n,c}$ is measured as the average value of the corresponding features (Subject $S_n$, class $c$) for each mini-batch. The prototype features $p_{S_n,c}$ are updated while accommodating some of the estimated prototypes as follows:

$$p_{S_n,c} = \beta p_{S_n,c} + (1-\beta)\hat{p}_{S_n,c} \qquad n = 1, 2, ..., N \qquad (1)$$

**Table 1.** Details of the Shallownet feature extractor. Parameters contain the kernel size, the number of the feature map, and the type of layer.

| Layers | Output size | Parameters |
|---|---|---|
| Input | $1 \times 22 \times 1000$ | – |
| Temporal conv | $40 \times 22 \times 976$ | $(1 \times 22)$, 40, conv |
| Spatial conv | $40 \times 1 \times 976$ | $(22 \times 1)$, 40, conv |
| Batch norm | $40 \times 1 \times 976$ | – |
| Square activation | $40 \times 1 \times 976$ | – |
| Average pooling | $40 \times 1 \times 61$ | $(1 \times 75)$, stride 15, avg pool |
| Logarithm activation | $40 \times 1 \times 61$ | – |
| Dropout | $40 \times 1 \times 61$ | Rate = 0.5 |
| Global average pooling | $40 \times 1 \times 1$ | $(1 \times 61)$, avg pool |

**Table 2.** Details of the EEGnet feature extractor. Parameters contain the kernel size, the number of the feature map, and the type of layer.

| Layers | Output size | Parameters |
|---|---|---|
| Input | $1 \times 22 \times 1000$ | – |
| Conv | $8 \times 22 \times 1000$ | $(1 \times 125)$, 8, conv, pad = same |
| Batch norm | $8 \times 22 \times 1000$ | – |
| Depth-wise conv | $16 \times 1 \times 1000$ | $(22 \times 1)$, 16, depth-wise conv |
| Batch norm | $16 \times 1 \times 1000$ | – |
| Elu activation | $16 \times 1 \times 1000$ | – |
| Max pooling | $16 \times 1 \times 250$ | $(1 \times 4)$, max pool |
| Dropout | $16 \times 1 \times 250$ | rate = 0.5 |
| Separable conv | $16 \times 1 \times 250$ | $(1 \times 16)$, 16, separable conv, pad = same |
| Batch norm | $16 \times 1 \times 250$ | – |
| Max pooling | $16 \times 1 \times 31$ | $(1 \times 8)$, max pool |
| Dropout | $16 \times 1 \times 31$ | rate = 0.5 |
| Flatten | 496 | – |

$\beta$ is an exponential decay rate that determines the update rate, and $N$ is the number of train subjects.

**Graph Construction.** One of our important purposes is to make good predictions on a sampled query sample. In order to use the relationship between each subject and class for query sample prediction, prototype features were utilized to construct a graph $G_p$. To be specific, the graph is composed of a prototype feature matrix $M \in \mathbb{R}^{NC \times d}$ and a prototype adjacency matrix $A \in \mathbb{R}^{NC \times NC}$, where C is the number of classes and d is the size of a single feature. Each feature of the feature matrix constitutes as a vertex of the graph, and the adjacency matrix represents all edges between the vertices. The prototype feature matrix $M$ is produced by concatenating the prototype features $p_{S_n,c}$ calculated in Eq. 1.

The prototype adjacency matrix represents the relationship between each vertex. As the distance between vertices increases, the element value of $A$ should decrease. Specifically, all elements of $A$ are computed as Gaussian kernel values of two pairs of vertex features:

$$A_{i,j} = exp\left(-\frac{\|M_i - M_j\|_2^2}{2\sigma^2}\right) \tag{2}$$

$\sigma$ is a parameter that controls the sparsity of $A$ and is set to 0.005 in this paper.

**Prediction.** In this step, predictions are performed on the query samples and prototype features for each batch $B$. To begin with, an expanded graph $\bar{G}$ is constructed by adding query samples to the prototype graph $G_p$. The expanded feature matrix $\bar{M} \in \mathbb{R}^{(NC+|B|)\times d}$ of $\bar{G}$ is created by concatenating the features of query samples into the prototype feature matrix of $G_p$.

To obtain the expanded adjacency matrix $\bar{A} \in \mathbb{R}^{(NC+|B|)\times(NC+|B|)}$ of the $\bar{G}$, adjacency matrix $A'$ between the prototypes and query samples is measured. $A'$ is computed using a Gaussian kernel as before when calculating $A$:

$$A'_{i,j} = exp\left(-\frac{\|M_i - f(q_j)\|_2^2}{2\sigma^2}\right) \tag{3}$$

Finally, the $\bar{A}$ is calculated by connecting $A$ and $A'$ with the identity matrix $I$. The reason for using $I$ is that the similarity between a query and another query is uncertain. $\bar{A}$ is obtained as:

$$\bar{A} = \begin{bmatrix} A & A' \\ A'^T & I \end{bmatrix} \tag{4}$$

After the expanded graph $\bar{G}$ is completed, it is fed to graph convolutional network to generate predicted values. Specifically, the graph convolutional network receives the expanded feature matrix and expanded adjacency matrix of $\bar{G}$ and outputs the classification prediction probability. The architecture of a graph convolutional network is shown in Table 3.

**Table 3.** Details of the graph convolutional network. Parameters contain the output feature size and the type of layer.

| Layers | Type of input | Output size | Parameters |
|---|---|---|---|
| Input | feature, adj matrix | $(NC+|B|) \times d$, $(NC+|B|) \times (NC+|B|)$ | – |
| Graph conv | feature, adj matrix | $(NC+|B|) \times d$ | $d$, GCN |
| Relu activation | gcn feature | $(NC+|B|) \times d$ | – |
| Dropout | gcn feature | $(NC+|B|) \times d$ | rate = 0.5 |
| Classifier | gcn feature, adj matrix | $(NC+|B|) \times C$ | $C$, GCN |

**Model Inference.** During the testing process, no more prototype updates are performed, and only the feature extraction and query sample prediction phase are used. Specifically, after the training process is over, the feature extractor, the graph convolutional network, the prototype feature matrix $M$, and the prototype adjacency matrix $A$ are stored prior to testing. As a testing procedure, the Prediction phase is performed using the test data as query data. The process includes creating an expanded feature matrix and an expanded adjacency matrix as described in the Prediction phase, and going through graph convolutional network to output the classification probability of test samples.

### 3.3   Model Optimization

During training, the proposed model is optimized by four losses. The total loss function can be expressed as:

$$L = \lambda_1 L_{global} + \lambda_2 L_{local} + L_{proto} + L_{query} \tag{5}$$

where $\lambda_1$ and $\lambda_2$ are trade-off parameters between $L_{global}$ and $L_{local}$.

$L_{global}$ serves to reinforce the invariance of features, and the higher the $\lambda_1$, the stronger the influence of $L_{global}$. $L_{local}$ plays a role in improving the feature compactness of each class, and the higher the $\lambda_2$, the stronger the influence of $L_{local}$. $L_{proto}$ and $L_{query}$ are classification losses that allow features to be distinguished by category.

**Global Relation Alignment Loss.** In the training process, the relative position of feature embeddings should be constrained, excluding the effort to extract subject-independent features. This loss aims to align the features of subjects at the global level. By setting the similarity of all element pair combinations of the adjacency matrix A to loss, the similarity between all subjects and classes is maintained consistently.

$$L_{global} = \frac{1}{N^4} \sum_{i,j,m,n=1}^{N} \|A_{i,j} - A_{m,n}\|_F \tag{6}$$

where $|\cdot|_F$ denotes the Frobenius norm.

**Local Relation Alignment Loss.** The $L_{local}$ aims to align the features of subjects at the local level. It is calculated as the average of the $l2$ distance between all query samples and their corresponding prototype features. By minimizing the $l2$ distance, the compressibility of the feature is improved.

**Prototype Classification Loss.** The $L_{proto}$ is a loss to increase the distinguishability of prototype features. A cross-entropy loss was employed to calculate the difference between the label and the predicted probability. $L_{proto}$ is calculated as the average of the cross-entropy loss of the true value and the predicted probability in the prototype features.

**Query Classification Loss.** The $L_{query}$ is a loss to increase the distinguishability of query features. Like $L_{proto}$, it is calculated as the average of the cross-entropy loss of the true value and the predicted probability in the query samples.

# 4 Experiments and Results

## 4.1 Datasets

To evaluate the proposed method, one of the public datasets of the MI task, BCI Competition IV IIa [34], was used. The dataset contains nine subjects, where each subject performed imagination of four different body movements (left hand, right hand, both feet, and tongue). The EEG signal was measured using a 22 Ag/AgCl electrode with a sampling frequency 250 Hz. The dataset was divided into two sessions, and each session was measured on a different day. A single session included 72 trials per each MI task. Overall, there are a total of 288 trials of EEG data per session.

## 4.2 Experiment Settings

To demonstrate the advantages of the proposed model, Shallownet [17], and EEGnet [18] which are two popular models for MI classification, were used. Shallownet is a CNN-based deep learning model designed to extract discriminative oscillatory EEG features. EEGnet is a compressed CNN framework designed to be applied to various BCI paradigms, including MI. For a fair comparison, both models were implemented with the optimal set of hyperparameters recommended in the original paper, and conditions such as data preprocessing process and GPU device were set the same.

The experiment is performed with a leave-one(subject)-out cross-validation (LOSO-CV) protocol. For example in [34], when the test set is the data of $subject_1$, the train and validation set consists of the remaining subjects ($subject_2$ to $subject_9$) excluding $subject_1$.

The proposed method was implemented using the Pytorch framework, and the training process was implemented using the NVIDIA GeForce GTX 1080 Ti with 11GB memory. The loss function was optimized using the Adam optimizer for Shallownet and EEGnet with learning rates of $2 \times 10^{-4}$, $1 \times 10^{-3}$ respectively. Batch size was set to 32, $\lambda_1$ was set to 20, $\lambda_2$ was set to 0.01. The EEG data was cropped with 4 s sliding window, 0.5 s stride before being fed to the model. Moreover, the early stopping technique [35] was used to prevent overfitting. So, if there was more than the minimum epoch and the validation loss did not decrease for 20 epochs, training was terminated early. The minimum epochs of Shallownet and EEGnet were set to 200 and 800, respectively.

## 4.3 Experimental Results

**Classification Performance.** For Shallownet and EEGnet, we evaluated the version with and without our method. Accuracy and F1-score were used to evaluate the performance of the All considered algorithm. We reported the experimental results of 'Shallownet without our method' and 'Shallownet with our method' in Table 4, and the experimental results of 'EEGnet without our method' and 'EEGnet with our method' were reported in Table 5. As seen on the tables, performance improvements were observed in both models when using along with our method.

**Table 4.** Comparison of classification performance (average accuracy ± standard deviation and average F1-score ± standard deviation) in % with and without our method in Shallownet

| Method | Avg accuracy ± Std | Avg F1-score ± Std |
| --- | --- | --- |
| Shallownet | 42.86 ± 12.24 | 37.96 ± 15.13 |
| Shallownet w/ours | **44.33 ± 15.07** | **39.95 ± 17.34** |

**Table 5.** Comparison of classification performance (average accuracy ± standard deviation and average F1-score ± standard deviation) in % with and without our method in EEGnet

| Method | Avg accuracy ± Std | Avg F1-score ± Std |
| --- | --- | --- |
| EEGnet | 42.59 ± 16.30 | 38.61 ± 17.42 |
| EEGnet w/ours | **44.40 ± 16.02** | **40.83 ± 18.82** |

Figure 2 shows the accuracy with and without our model as a scatter plot. The diagonal dash line corresponding to $y = x$ indicates a boundary line with the same accuracy regardless of applying our model. Based on the diagonal dash line, the upper dots correspond to the subject with improved performance by

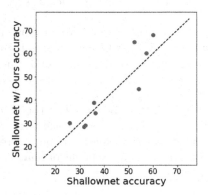 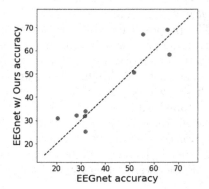

**Fig. 2.** Scatter plots for the baseline model and the model combining our method with the baseline. The left plot is the comparison result when combined with Shallownet, and the right plot is the comparison result when combined with EEGnet.

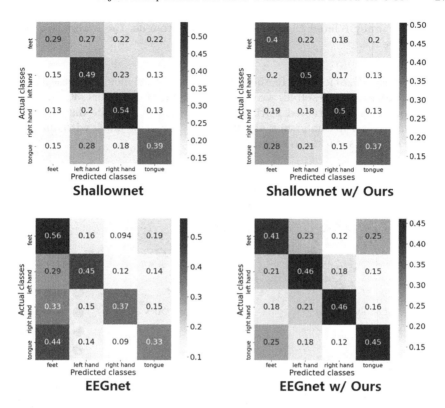

**Fig. 3.** Confusion matrices for the baseline model and the model combining our method with the baseline. The plots on the left are the results for the baseline model, and the plots on the right are the results for the model combining our method with the baseline. And the upper plots are the results for Shallownet, and the below plots are the results for EEGnet.

combining our model, and the lower dots correspond to the subject with reduced performance. As seen on the figure, accuracy was enhanced from five and six subjects out of nine total for Shallownet and EEGnet, respectively, when using along with our method.

**Efficiency Analysis.** Figure 3 shows the confusion matrix with and without our model using Shallownet and EEGnet. The values on the diagonal of the confusion matrix are correctly predicted samples in the MI classification task. As seen from the figure, the diagonal values of the confusion matrix were balanced when our method was applied to the model, indicating the balance of classification accuracy between classes. As for Shallownet, relatively great improvements were observed for accurately classifying feet class. And in EEGnet, by using our model, the prediction biased to the feet class was changed in a balanced way, and the accuracy related to the right hand and tongue, the lowest two classes, was improved.

**Feature Visualization.** To further investigate how balancing accuracy between different classes were resulted, we employed t-SNE embeddings [36] to visualize the distribution of extracted features. As shown in Fig. 4, the distributions by class became clear in Shallownet and EEGnet when using along with our method for $subject_1$ and $subject_8$, respectively.

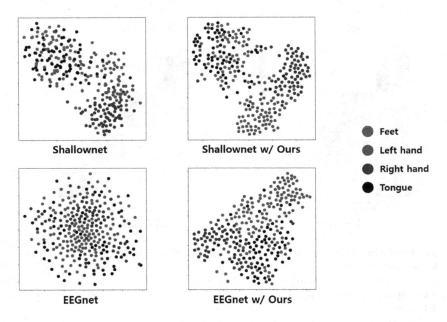

**Fig. 4.** Examples of t-SNE visualization for the baseline model and the model combining our method with the baseline. The upper plots are the results of $subject_1$ for Shallownet, and the plots below are the results of $subject_8$ for EEGnet.

## 5    Discussion and Conclusion

This paper proposed a framework that can improve the prediction probability for new users not seen in the training process. The proposed method was applied to the existing deep learning models for MI classification to improve subject-independent classification accuracy. Thus, we used relationship information between multiple subjects for training and prediction through a graph convolutional network. The public dataset BCI Competition IV IIa was used to validate the inter-subject classification performance of our method. As a result, the average classification performance was enhanced by applying our method to two types of MI classification deep learning models.

Most previous deep learning-based studies have only used features of EEG signals for training. However, we performed efficient prediction on new users while utilizing not only EEG features but also relationship information between subject-specific features for learning. The relationship between subjects was defined using the graph structure, and this relationship was used for training and prediction through a graph convolutional network.

The effectiveness of our method is clearly shown through the confusion matrixes and t-SNE plots. The existing deep learning-based MI classification model used in the experiments showed biased results in inter-subject classification. For example, Shallownet output biased results to all classes except feet class, whereas EEGnet output biased results to feet class. However, after applying our method, all classes were predicted in a balanced way. The t-SNE plots are also relatively well aligned for each class after applying our method.

In this work, we have proven through experiments that we can make more efficient predictions in inter-subject tasks by using our method. In addition, the proposed method has the potential to be applied to various deep learning-based MI classification models. This study provides insight to develop BCI applications that work well in the real world without a calibration process for new users.

**Acknowledgment.** This work was supported by the Institute of Information and Communications Technology Planning and Evaluation (IITP) grant funded by the Korea government (MSIT) (No. 2017-0-00432) and the Defense Challengeable Future Technology Program of Agency for Defense Development, Republic of Korea.

# References

1. Sawangjai, P., Hompoonsup, S., Leelaarporn, P., Kongwudhikunakorn, S., Wilaiprasitporn, T.: Consumer grade EEG measuring sensors as research tools: a review. IEEE Sens. J. **20**(8), 3996–4024 (2019)
2. Choi, J.W., Huh, S., Jo, S.: Improving performance in motor imagery BCI-based control applications via virtually embodied feedback. Comput. Biol. Med. **127**, 104079 (2020)
3. Kim, B.H., Jo, S., Choi, S.: ALIS: learning affective causality behind daily activities from a wearable life-log system. IEEE Trans. Cybern. (2021)
4. Kaongoen, N., Choi, J., Jo, S.: Speech-imagery-based brain-computer interface system using ear-EEG. J. Neural Eng. **18**(1), 016023 (2021)
5. Gao, Z., et al.: EEG-based spatio-temporal convolutional neural network for driver fatigue evaluation. IEEE Trans. Neural Netw. Learn. Syst. **30**(9), 2755–2763 (2019)
6. Vidyaratne, L.S., Iftekharuddin, K.M.: Real-time epileptic seizure detection using EEG. IEEE Trans. Neural Syst. Rehabil. Eng. **25**(11), 2146–2156 (2017)
7. Chakladar, D.D., Dey, S., Roy, P.P., Iwamura, M.: EEG-based cognitive state assessment using deep ensemble model and filter bank common spatial pattern. In: 2020 25th International Conference on Pattern Recognition (ICPR), pp. 4107–4114. IEEE (2021)
8. Chakladar, D.D., Dey, S., Roy, P.P., Dogra, D.P.: EEG-based mental workload estimation using deep BLSTM-LSTM network and evolutionary algorithm. Biomed. Signal Process. Control **60**, 101989 (2020)

9. Autthasan, P., et al.: A single-channel consumer-grade EEG device for brain-computer interface: enhancing detection of SSVEP and its amplitude modulation. IEEE Sens. J. **20**(6), 3366–3378 (2019)

10. Zou, Y., Nathan, V., Jafari, R.: Automatic identification of artifact-related independent components for artifact removal in EEG recordings. IEEE J. Biomed. Health Inform. **20**(1), 73–81 (2014)

11. Jeong, J.-H., Kwak, N.-S., Guan, C., Lee, S.-W.: Decoding movement-related cortical potentials based on subject-dependent and section-wise spectral filtering. IEEE Trans. Neural Syst. Rehabil. Eng. **28**(3), 687–698 (2020)

12. Choi, J.W., Kim, B.H., Huh, S., Jo, S.: Observing actions through immersive virtual reality enhances motor imagery training. IEEE Trans. Neural Syst. Rehabil. Eng. **28**(7), 1614–1622 (2020)

13. Krizhevsky, A., Sutskever, I., Hinton, G.E.: ImageNet classification with deep convolutional neural networks. In: Advances in Neural Information Processing Systems, vol. 25, pp. 1097–1105 (2012)

14. Amodei, D., et al.: Deep speech 2: end-to-end speech recognition in English and Mandarin. In: International Conference on Machine Learning, pp. 173–182. PMLR (2016)

15. Ang, K.K., Guan, C.: EEG-based strategies to detect motor imagery for control and rehabilitation. IEEE Trans. Neural Syst. Rehabil. Eng. **25**(4), 392–401 (2016)

16. Pfurtscheller, G., Neuper, C.: Motor imagery and direct brain-computer communication. Proc. IEEE **89**(7), 1123–1134 (2001)

17. Schirrmeister, R.T., et al.: Deep learning with convolutional neural networks for EEG decoding and visualization. Hum. Brain Mapp. **38**(11), 5391–5420 (2017)

18. Lawhern, V.J., Solon, A.J., Waytowich, N.R., Gordon, S.M., Hung, C.P., Lance, B.J.: EEGNet: a compact convolutional neural network for EEG-based brain-computer interfaces. J. Neural Eng. **15**(5), 056013 (2018)

19. Kim, B.H., Jo, S.: Deep physiological affect network for the recognition of human emotions. IEEE Trans. Affect. Comput. **11**(2), 230–243 (2018)

20. Lotte, F.: Signal processing approaches to minimize or suppress calibration time in oscillatory activity-based brain-computer interfaces. Proc. IEEE **103**(6), 871–890 (2015)

21. Lotte, F., Congedo, M., Lécuyer, A., Lamarche, F., Arnaldi, B.: A review of classification algorithms for EEG-based brain-computer interfaces. J. Neural Eng. **4**(2), R1 (2007)

22. Blankertz, B., Kawanabe, M., Tomioka, R., Hohlefeld, F.U., Nikulin, V.V., Müller, K.-R.: Invariant common spatial patterns: alleviating nonstationarities in brain-computer interfacing. In: NIPS, pp. 113–120 (2007)

23. Wang, H., Zheng, W.: Local temporal common spatial patterns for robust single-trial EEG classification. IEEE Trans. Neural Syst. Rehabil. Eng. **16**(2), 131–139 (2008)

24. Ramoser, H., Muller-Gerking, J., Pfurtscheller, G.: Optimal spatial filtering of single trial EEG during imagined hand movement. IEEE Trans. Rehabil. Eng. **8**(4), 441–446 (2000)

25. Blankertz, B., Dornhege, G., Krauledat, M., Müller, K.-R., Curio, G.: The non-invasive berlin brain-computer interface: fast acquisition of effective performance in untrained subjects. Neuroimage **37**(2), 539–550 (2007)

26. Ang, K.K., Chin, Z.Y., Wang, C., Guan, C., Zhang, H.: Filter bank common spatial pattern algorithm on BCI competition IV datasets 2a and 2b. Front. Neurosci. **6**, 39 (2012)

27. Bishop, C.M.: Pattern recognition. In: Machine learning, vol. 128, no. 9 (2006)
28. Fraiwan, L., Lweesy, K., Khasawneh, N., Wenz, H., Dickhaus, H.: Automated sleep stage identification system based on time-frequency analysis of a single EEG channel and random forest classifier. Comput. Methods Programs Biomed. **108**(1), 10–19 (2012)
29. Tang, X., Zhang, X.: Conditional adversarial domain adaptation neural network for motor imagery EEG decoding. Entropy **22**(1), 96 (2020)
30. An, S., Kim, S., Chikontwe, P., Park, S.H.: Few-shot relation learning with attention for EEG-based motor imagery classification. In: 2020 IEEE/RSJ International Conference on Intelligent Robots and Systems (IROS), pp. 10933–10938. IEEE (2020)
31. Sung, F., Yang, Y., Zhang, L., Xiang, T., Torr, P.H., Hospedales, T.M.: Learning to compare: relation network for few-shot learning. In: Proceedings of the IEEE Conference on Computer Vision and Pattern Recognition, pp. 1199–1208 (2018)
32. Wang, H., Xu, M., Ni, B., Zhang, W.: Learning to combine: knowledge aggregation for multi-source domain adaptation. In: Vedaldi, A., Bischof, H., Brox, T., Frahm, J.-M. (eds.) ECCV 2020. LNCS, vol. 12353, pp. 727–744. Springer, Cham (2020). https://doi.org/10.1007/978-3-030-58598-3_43
33. Kipf, T.N., Welling, M.: Semi-supervised classification with graph convolutional networks. arXiv preprint arXiv:1609.02907 (2016)
34. Brunner, C., Leeb, R., Müller-Putz, G., Schlögl, A., Pfurtscheller, G.: BCI competition 2008-Graz data set A, vol. 16, pp. 1–6. Institute for Knowledge Discovery (Laboratory of Brain-Computer Interfaces), Graz University of Technology (2008)
35. Caruana, R., Lawrence, S., Giles, L.: Overfitting in neural nets: backpropagation, conjugate gradient, and early stopping. In: Advances in Neural Information Processing Systems, pp. 402–408 (2001)
36. Donahue, J., et al.: DeCAF: a deep convolutional activation feature for generic visual recognition. In: International Conference on Machine Learning, pp. 647–655. PMLR (2014)

# Multimodal Co-training for Fake News Identification Using Attention-aware Fusion

Sreyasee Das Bhattacharjee[(✉)] and Junsong Yuan[(✉)]

State University of New York at Buffalo, Buffalo, USA
{sreyasee,jsyuan}@buffalo.edu

**Abstract.** Rapid dissemination of fake news to purportedly mislead the large population of online information sharing platforms is a societal problem receiving increasing attention. A critical challenge in this scenario is that a multimodal information content, e.g., supporting text with photos, shared online, is frequently created with an aim to attract attention of the readers. While 'fakeness' does not exclusively synonymize 'falsity' in general, the objective behind creating such content may vary widely. It may be for depicting additional information to clarify. However, very frequently it may also be for propagating fabricated or biased information to purposefully mislead, or for intentionally manipulating the image to fool the audience. Therefore, our objective in this work is evaluating the veracity of a news content by addressing a two-fold task: (1) if the image or the text component of the content is fabricated and (2) if there are inconsistencies between image and text component of the content, which may prove the image to be out of context. We propose an effective attention-aware joint representation learning framework that learns the comprehensive fine-grained data pattern by correlating each word in the text component to each potential object region in the image component. By designing a novel multimodal co-training mechanism leveraging the class label information within a contrastive loss-based optimization, the proposed method exhibits a significant promise in identifying cross-modal inconsistencies. The consistent out-performances over other state-of-the-art works (both in terms of accuracy and F1-score) in two large-scale datasets, which cover different types of fake news characteristics (defining the information veracity at various layers of details like 'false', 'false connection', 'misleading', and 'manipulative' contents), topics, and domains demonstrate the feasibility of our approach.

**Keywords:** Fake news detection · Rumor · Multimodal classification · Co-training · Attention · Feature fusion

## 1 Introduction

The task of Fake news detection is to identify deceptive digital news content in the web-based platforms. With an abundance of information available from

© Springer Nature Switzerland AG 2022
C. Wallraven et al. (Eds.): ACPR 2021, LNCS 13189, pp. 282–296, 2022.
https://doi.org/10.1007/978-3-031-02444-3_21

**Fig. 1.** Examples of some real instances of Fake News articles which use Multimodal content to dupe readers. In (a)I, (b)I, (a)II, and (b)II, images were purposely manipulated to describe a fake article. The instances in (a)III and (b)III represent some out of context images, so the images do not accurately support their text descriptions.

competing resources, it is often difficult for users to gauge the veracity of an online news content in a timely manner. While, per Gallup poll'20[1], only 40% of the Americans trust their mass media resources to report the news 'fully, accurately and fairly', a critical bias towards Internet based resources (like blogs and social media) still prevails. Such alternative digital information resources leave the readers more susceptible to incomplete and deceptive information [1].

Figure 1 shows some instances ((a)I, (a)II, (b)I, and (b)II) of fake news, where image components were purportedly forged/morphed to support fake news contents. Unlike these standard methods for misrepresentations, to obfuscate the usual fact checking software, recent trends have been using out of context images as shown in the right column images ((a)III, (b)III), where a manipulative correlation is generated between two components to propagate disinformation. So for this type of fake-news contents, relevance of the text topic of the news content with its image component is not pertinent. Therefore, our objective in this work is evaluating the veracity of a news content by addressing a two-fold task: (1) if the image or the text component of the content is fabricated and (2) if there are inconsistencies between image and text component of the content, which may prove the image to be out of context.

A good set of works have leveraged traditional machine learning methods as well as recent deep learning models [10,23,24,29], most of which rely on textual content or other metadata (like news source, emotional features, number of likes, etc.) including content creator's profile information. While a few recent works have proposed multimodal methods to address the task of fake news detection [11,13,15,30], majority of these methods just combine different mode-specific feature vectors (visual, textual features, and semantic information),

---

[1] https://news.gallup.com/poll/321116/americans-remain-distrustful-mass-media.aspx.

derived from some independently customized pre-trained models. Therefore, the mutual relation between these mode-specific representations and how they may jointly describe the veracity trait of a news content, are still under-explored.

We argue that grounding the text component to different semantic areas in the image component of a multimodal news content is crucial for evaluating the veracity of its information. Additionally, to gauge the quality of the visual component, interaction between different object regions and relative position information within its visual component often play a critical role. Finally, in order to 'bridge the gap' between the complementary modes, it is important to identify the hard positives, which may be leveraged to enhance the contrastive characteristics of the learned joint representation, so the clusters of points belonging to the same class are pulled together in the learned embedding space, while simultaneously pushing apart clusters of samples from different classes. To this end, the contributions of this work include the followings:

1. To ensure a more accurate evaluation of the quality of the visual and text component of a news content, the proposed method learns the localized data patterns by leveraging self- and cross-modal attentions at multiple layers of details. This enables capturing the correlation of each word to each potential object region within the image component, within the learned initial joint representation, while ascertaining an enhanced decision interpretability in parallel.

2. To analyze the cross-modal inconsistencies, the initial joint representation is further finetuned by a multimodal co-training scheme that leverages the label information within a formulation of the supervised contrastive learning framework, to explicitly capture the complementary category relevant information and their mutual interaction observed within the different mode representations of the same data source.

3. The proposed method is extensively evaluated on two benchmark datasets (Twitter Dataset, as part of MediaEval [4], which was released for evaluating methods for detecting fake multimedia content in social media and the large scale Fakeddit Dataset [21] that has samples from up to six different categories of information disorder) and it consistently outperforms other state-of-the-art approaches both in terms of accuracy and F1-score.

The rest of the paper is organized as follows: Sect. 2 briefly describes related works. The proposed method is explained in Sect. 3. Sections 4 and 5 respectively present the experimental results and conclusion.

## 2   Related Works

The existing set of literature addressing the task of Fake news recognition may be split into two groups: uni-mode methods [3,20] and multimodal methods

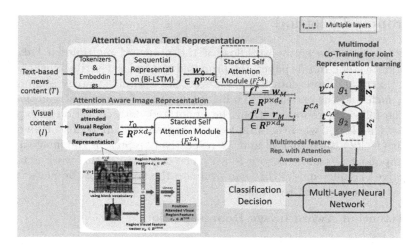

**Fig. 2.** The Proposed Method Overview is shown in (a) and the *Position attended Visual Region Feature Representation* scheme is illustrated in (b).

[15,30,32]. Many early works utilizing only the text-based features, retrieve linguistic features (like special characters, emojis) [3,20] or language stylistic features (like assertive verbs, discourse markers) [22] to assess the credibility of the news content. Researchers have also explored the role of profile information [9,24], emotions [8], social context features [13], and source credibility [6] to evaluate the factual quality of the post. In a recent work, Lago et al. [19] have evaluated different methods for identifying manipulated images.

Recent studies have shown that analyzing the accompanying visual component may improve the fake-news detection task [13,21,26,30]. Singhal et al. [26] propose a multimodal fake news detection framework that employs a language transformer and visual module warmed up by the pre-trained CNNs to derive mode-specific features, which are later concatenated to obtain a learned multimodal feature descriptor. Wang et al. [30] propose an adversarial network utilizing a two-stream event invariant feature extractors ( text-based CNN for text mode and VGG-19 based network for visual mode). Both descriptors learned independently using the samples' mode-specific representations are just concatenated for designing a single feature vector. Similarly, Nakamura et al. [21] utilize a two-stream network for processing textual (using bidirectional BERT model) and visual (using ResNet50 model) information. Authors analyze three fixed feature fusion techniques (maximum, average, and concatenate) for their performance in fake news detection task. Another set of works also leverage textual, visual and metadata [5,13,18]. However, the relation between these mode-specific representations and how they may jointly interact to evaluate the veracity trait of a news content are still not sufficiently investigated, which form the foundation of our method.

# 3    Proposed Method

Figure 2 presents the entire workflow of the proposed multimodal Fake-news recognition system. In this paper, the proposed method is described for two-mode (image, text) data representations. However, the learning strategy is completely generic, such that the extension to a higher number of modes is straightforward.

In the following representation, the annotated data collection is expressed as: $\mathcal{D} = \{(\mathbf{s}^j, l^j)\}_j$, where a sample $\mathbf{s}^j$ is represented in terms of an image-text pair $(I^j, T^j)$, such that $I^j$ and $T^j$ respectively represent the image and the text component $\mathbf{s}^j$ from category $l^j \in \mathcal{C}$. The objective of this work is to learn an effective classifier model that can evaluate the veracity of the news content passed as a query during test time.

## 3.1    Attention Aware Image Representation

While usually for the representation task, the entire image is considered as a single quantity, which is processed using a CNN [12], for a richer and more detailed understanding of the image, in this work, we aim to divide the image into semantically meaningful regions to derive a region-level representation.

*Region Visual Features:* Given a multimedia data content $(I, T)$ as a sample, its image component $I$ is represented in terms of $n$ candidate interest regions $\{v_k\}_{k=1}^n$ called 'proposals', generated by Selective Search [27]. Each region depicts a potential object region within the image $I$ and is represented in terms of a CNN vector, i.e. $I = \{\mathbf{v}_k\}_{k=1}^n$, where $\mathbf{v}_k \in \mathbb{R}^{2048}$ is the CNN feature vector representing the $k^{th}$ region $v_k$ within $I$. In our experiments, image region representation was extracted from VGG-19 model pre-trained on ImageNet [25], which was dimension reduced using Principal Component Analysis (PCA) to a 2048 dimension feature [14].

*Region Positional Features:* Intuitively, the position information of the image regions and their relative placements in the whole image are very important. Motivated by this thought, we combine the position information within the learning procedure to capture more accurate and fine-grained image spatial layout information. For any given multimedia data content $(I, T)$, its image component $I$ is first resized to a pre-defined size $W \times H$. Then we adopt the position representation approach by Wang et al. [31] to equally split into $B \times B$ blocks. This collection of split blocks forms the position vocabulary to represent the positional information of every region within $I$. The position of each split block represented by the one-hot vector of dimension $B^2$, indicating its index in the position vocabulary. Finally, the $L$ dimensional region position vector for each $v_k$ defined by an embedding vector $\mathbf{e}_k$, is defined as $\mathbf{e}_k[l] = OV(b_l, v_k) \times f(b_l, v_k)$ where $f(b_l, v_k)$ computes the spatial proximity between the region $v_k$ and the $l^{th}$ max overlapping block $b_l$ $(1 \leq l \leq L)$ and $OV(b_l, v_k)$ computes their normalized pairwise overlap ratio. In order to capture the spatial information of each region and preserve the locality within the derived embedding vector (i.e. the neighboring position embeddings should be similar), we encode the normalized position information of $v_k$ as: $\mathbf{p}_k = [N(x_k), N(y_k), N(w_k), N(h_k)]$, where $(x_k, y_k, w_k, h_k)$ denotes the (x-location, y-location, width, height) of $v_k$ and $N(.)$ normalizes the input within a range of 0 and 1. The spatial proximity between $b_l$ and $v_k$ is computed as $f(b_l, v_k) = e^{-\frac{||\mathbf{p}_k - \mathbf{p}_l||}{2\sigma^2}}$, where $\mathbf{p}_l$ represents the normalized position information of the position vocabulary box $b_l$ and $\sigma \in \mathbb{R}$ is a scalar, set as the average distance between all the position embeddings. The region position vector $\mathbf{e}_k$ is concatenated with the region visual feature $\mathbf{v}_k$ and pass through a linear layer to obtain the final $d_v$ dimensional *Position attended Visual Region Feature* vector $\mathbf{c}_k \in \mathbb{R}^{d_v}$ ($d_v = 768$). The process is illustrated in Fig. 2.

**Image Representation:** The collection of $\{\mathbf{c}_k\}_{k=1}^n$ describes potential object regions within the image $I$ and passed through a feature representation module of $F_v^{SA}$, comprising of a stack of $M$ self attention layer based units, to derive an attention aware final image representation vector $\mathbf{f}^I$. More precisely, given the initial region-based representation of $I$ as $\mathbf{r}_0 = [\mathbf{c}_1, \mathbf{c}_2, ...\mathbf{c}_n]$, the $m^{th}$-layer processing of $F_v^{SA}$, which takes $\mathbf{r}_0 \in \mathbb{R}^{n \times d_v}$ as input at the layer $m = 0$, is performed as $\mathbf{r}_{m+1} = linear\left(Softmax(\frac{\mathbf{r}_m \mathbf{r}_m^T}{\sqrt{d_v}})\mathbf{r}_m\right)$. The final $M^{th}$ layer output $\mathbf{r}_M = F_v^{SA}(\mathbf{r}_0, M) \in \mathbb{R}^{n \times d_v}$, is used to represent the image component $I$ and we set $\mathbf{f}^I = \mathbf{r}_M$.

## 3.2 Attention Aware Text Representation

The proposed textual embedding processing module maps each word to a high dimensional vector space. Each input text component $T$ is considered as a sequence of $p$ words, i.e. $T = \{\omega_1, \omega_2, ..., \omega_p\}$. We employ the pretrained model BERT [7] to obtain the fixed word embedding vector of size $d_w$. To capture the contextual information of each word, we employ Bi-LSTM following the embedding layer, which has a forward hidden state $\overrightarrow{\mathbf{h}_w} \in \mathbb{R}^{d_w^{hid}}$ and the backward hidden state $\overleftarrow{\mathbf{h}_w} \in \mathbb{R}^{d_w^{hid}}$, where $d_w^{hid}$ is the number of hidden units. For each $\omega_i$, we concatenate both its forward and the backward hidden state representation to derive the final word representation vector $\mathbf{h}_i = [\overrightarrow{\mathbf{h}_w}, \overleftarrow{\mathbf{h}_w}] \in \mathbb{R}^{2d_w^{hid}}$ ($d_w^{hid} = 384$). Therefore, the text component $T$ is represented in terms of a sequence of word descriptors $\mathbf{w}_0 = [\mathbf{h}_1, \mathbf{h}_2, ...\mathbf{h}_p]$, where $\mathbf{h}_i \in \mathbb{R}^{d_t}$ with $d_t = 2d_w^{hid} = 768$. Similar to the image representation technique, the proposed attention aware text representation module of $F_t^{SA}$ is also comprised of a stack of self attention layer based units followed by a linear layer, which takes $\mathbf{w}_0$ as input at layer $m = 0$ to learn an attention aware text representative. The output of the $m^{th}$ layer in $F_t^{SA}$ is taken as an input to its $(m + 1)^{th}$ layer, which is computed as $\mathbf{w}_{m+1} = linear\left(Softmax(\frac{\mathbf{w}_m \mathbf{w}_m^T}{\sqrt{d_t}})\mathbf{w}_m\right)$. The output of the last layer (we have considered a stack of $M$ self attention layers for both visual and text representations), computed as $\mathbf{w}_M = F_t^{SA}(\mathbf{w}_0, M) \in \mathbb{R}^{p \times d_t}$, is used as the attention aware text representative for $T$ and we set $\mathbf{f}^{Txt} = \mathbf{w}_M$.

## 3.3   Multimodal Feature Representation with Attention Aware Fusion

For the fake news recognition task, the content is primarily described using two-mode representation: visual and text. Therefore, to obtain an effective multimodal representation of the content, it is important to integrate two mode-specific representations in such way that would preserve a detailed understanding of its text component and the relevance of the visual information accompanying the text. Therefore, directly concatenating the mode-specific features [21] may not be the most effective information fusion approach for this application setting. In this work, we propose a multimodal fusion method that leverages cross-modal attention information to fuse these two mode-specific features $\mathbf{f}^I$ and $\mathbf{f}^{Txt}$. The proposed fusion module $F^{CA}$, consists of a stack of $M$ multimodal attention layers (i.e. the key and value pair represents one mode and the query represents another mode) which merges two parallel and independent attention submodules to jointly learn two sophisticated multimodal attention enhanced visual and text representations denoted by $\mathbf{v}_M^{text}$ and $\mathbf{t}_M^{vis}$ respectively. At the $0^{th}$ layer of $F^{CA}$, $\mathbf{f}^I$ and $\mathbf{f}^{Txt}$ respectively represent visual and text-based representation of the given multimodal sample $(I, T)$ i.e., $\mathbf{v}_0^{text} = \mathbf{f}^I \in \mathbb{R}^{n \times d_v}$ and $\mathbf{t}_0^{vis} = \mathbf{f}^{Txt} \in \mathbb{R}^{p \times d_t}$. Also, the entire $M$-layer non-linear multimodal fusion module can be represented as $(\mathbf{v}_M^{text}, \mathbf{t}_M^{vis}) = F^{CA}(\mathbf{f}^I, \mathbf{f}^{Txt})$. At any intermediate $m^{th}$ layer of $F^{CA}$, the attention enhanced joint embeddings are simultaneously updated as:

$$\mathbf{v}_{m+1}^{text} = linear\left( Softmax\left(\frac{\mathbf{VT}_m(\mathbf{VT}_m)^T}{\sqrt{d_v}}\right)\mathbf{VT}_m \right) \tag{1}$$

$$\mathbf{t}_{m+1}^{vis} = linear\left( Softmax\left(\frac{\mathbf{TV}_m(\mathbf{TV}_m)^T}{\sqrt{d_t}}\right)\mathbf{TV}_m \right) \tag{2}$$

where we have $\mathbf{VT}_m = linear(Softmax(\frac{\mathbf{v}_m^{text}(\mathbf{t}_m^{vis})^T}{\sqrt{d_v}})\mathbf{t}_m^{vis})$ and similarly compute $\mathbf{TV}_m = linear(Softmax(\frac{\mathbf{t}_m^{vis}(\mathbf{v}_m^{text})^T}{\sqrt{d_t}})\mathbf{v}_m^{text})$. In fact, for any intermediate $m^{th}$ layer, the $\mathbf{VT}_m$ (and $\mathbf{TV}_m$) is the multimodal scaled dot product attention that derives the semantic (and visual) context for a *multimodal attention enhanced visual* (and *text*) *feature* $\mathbf{v}_{m+1}^{text} \in \mathbb{R}^{n \times d_t}$ (and $\mathbf{t}_{m+1}^{vis} \in \mathbb{R}^{p \times d_v}$).

Finally, both $\mathbf{v}_M^{text}$ and $\mathbf{t}_M^{vis}$ are average pooled along their respective first dimension, to obtain an aggregated *multimodal attention enhanced visual* representation $\mathbf{v}^{CA} = MeanPool(\mathbf{v}_M^{text}) \in \mathbb{R}^{d_t}$ and an aggregated *multimodal attention enhanced text* representation $\mathbf{t}^{CA} = MeanPool(\mathbf{t}_M^{vis}) \in \mathbb{R}^{d_v}$. The function $MeanPool(.)$ is the average pooling function along the first dimension of its argument.

### 3.4    Multimodal Co-training for Joint Representation Learning

Each sample $(\mathbf{s}^j, l^j) \in \mathcal{D}$ is now represented using two views, $\mathbf{s}^j = \{\mathbf{v}^{CA,j}, \mathbf{t}^{CA,j}\}$, where $\mathbf{v}^{CA,j}$ refers to the *multimodal attention enhanced visual* feature space representation of $I^j$ (the image component of $\mathbf{s}^j$) and $\mathbf{t}^{CA,j}$ refers to the *multimodal attention enhanced text* feature space representation of $T^j$ (the text component of $\mathbf{s}^j$). To further highlight the cross-modal consistency utilizing the label information, the objective of multimodal co-training is to learn two functions $g_1$ and $g_2$, where $\mathbf{z}_1^j = g_1(\mathbf{v}^{CA,j})$ and $\mathbf{z}_2^j = g_2(\mathbf{t}^{CA,j})$, so that both $\mathbf{z}_1^j$ and $\mathbf{z}_2^j$ would emit higher similarity scores with the elements of a hard positive set $\mathcal{P}^j$ while simultaneously enhancing their differences with the elements of the negative set $\mathcal{N}^j$.

We propose to co-train these models ($g_1$ and $g_2$) by retrieving the hard positives from the other view representation. The function $g_1$ is updated with a supervised contrastive loss [16] computed using a random batch of samples $\mathcal{B} \subset \mathcal{D}$:

$$\mathcal{L}_1 = -\sum_{i \in \mathcal{B}} \mathbb{E}\left[log\frac{\sum_{p \in \mathcal{P}_i^j} exp(\mathbf{z}_1^j \cdot \mathbf{z}_1^p/\tau)}{\sum_{p \in \mathcal{P}_1^j} exp(\mathbf{z}_1^j \cdot \mathbf{z}_1^p/\tau) + \sum_{n \in \mathcal{N}_1^j} exp(\mathbf{z}_1^j \cdot \mathbf{z}_1^n/\tau)}\right] \tag{3}$$

where the numerator is defined as a sum of 'similarity' between $\mathbf{z}_1^j$ (i.e. the $g_1$ transformed output of $\mathbf{v}^{CA,j}$) and a positive set $\mathcal{P}_1^j$, constructed by identifying the most similar samples using its corresponding *multimodal attention enhanced text* feature $\mathbf{t}^{CA,j}$. The term $\tau \in \mathbb{R}^+$ is scaler temperature parameter. By leveraging the label information in a supervised scenario, the structure of $\mathcal{P}_1^j$ is defined as follows:

$$\mathcal{P}_1^j = \{A^{vis}(I^j, a), I^k | k \in Nbr_K(\mathbf{z}_2^j \cdot \mathbf{z}_2^i), \forall(\mathbf{s}^i, l^i) \in \mathcal{D} \setminus \{(\mathbf{s}^j, l^j)\}, l^k == l^j, a \in \mathcal{A}^{vis}\} \tag{4}$$

where $A^{vis}(I^j, a)$ obtains the augmented version of $I^j$, parameterized by $a$ sampled from a pre-defined set of augmentation transformations in $\mathcal{A}^{vis}$, $Nbr_K(x, .)$ identifies the indices of top $K$ similar samples to $x$ and $\mathbf{z}_2^j \cdot \mathbf{z}_2^i$ computes the similarity between $\mathbf{z}_2^j$ and $\mathbf{z}_2^i$. Hence the $\mathcal{P}_1^j$ consists of top-K similar samples to $\mathbf{s}^j$ retrieved using their $g_2$ transformed *multimodal attention enhanced text* feature space representation plus the $j^{th}$ sample's own augmentations, and $\mathcal{N}_1^j$ represents the complement of $\mathcal{P}_1^j$ that does not include samples with the same annotation $l^j$ and their augmentations.

Similarly the function $g_2$ is updated with a similar supervised contrastive loss computed using a random batch of samples $\mathcal{B} \subset \mathcal{D}$:

$$\mathcal{L}_2 = -\sum_{i \in \mathcal{B}} \mathbb{E}\left[log\frac{\sum_{p \in \mathcal{P}_i^j} exp(\mathbf{z}_2^j \cdot \mathbf{z}_2^p/\tau)}{\sum_{p \in \mathcal{P}_2^j} exp(\mathbf{z}_2^j \cdot \mathbf{z}_2^p/\tau) + \sum_{n \in \mathcal{N}_2^j} exp(\mathbf{z}_2^j \cdot \mathbf{z}_2^n/\tau)}\right] \tag{5}$$

where the numerator is defined as a sum of 'similarity' between $\mathbf{z}_2^j$ (i.e. the $g_2$ transformed output of $\mathbf{t}^{CA,j}$) and a positive set $\mathcal{P}_2^j$, constructed by identifying the most similar samples using its corresponding *multimodal attention enhanced visual* feature $\mathbf{v}^{CA,j}$. The structure of $\mathcal{P}_2^j$ is similarly defined as:

$$\mathcal{P}_2^j = \{A^{text}(T^j, a), T^k | k \in Nbr_K(\mathbf{z}_1^j \cdot \mathbf{z}_1^i), \forall(\mathbf{s}^i, l^i) \in \mathcal{D} \setminus \{(\mathbf{s}^j, l^j)\}, l^k == l^j, a \in \mathcal{A}^{text}\} \tag{6}$$

where $A^{text}(T^j, a)$ obtains the augmented version of $T^j$, parameterized by $a$ sampled from a pre-defined set of augmentation transformations in $\mathcal{A}^{text}$ and $\mathcal{N}_2^j$ represents the complement of $\mathcal{P}_2^j$ that does not include samples with the same annotation $l^j$ and their augmentations. Both models $g_1()$ and $g_2()$ are initialized independently by learning in the uni-mode environments and then co-training process proceeds by alternatively optimizing $\mathcal{L}_1$ (Eq. 3) and $\mathcal{L}_2$ (Eq. 5). In all our experiments, we have used $K = 5$. More about these implementation details will be discussed in Sect. 4.2.

### 3.5    Fake News Classification

After the functions $g_1$ and $g_2$ are learned, $\mathbf{s}^j$ is represented using its joint multimodel representation $\mathbf{z}^{j,Merged} = [\mathbf{z}_1^j, \mathbf{z}_2^j]$ and is fed into a stack of Fully Connected (FC) layers for classification. In order to address the issue of overfitting, dropout-based regularization is employed, which randomly chooses a percentage $\kappa$ of hidden units during the updating step. A scaled version of the learned weight ($wt_{sc} = \kappa \cdot wt$) without applying the dropout, is used at the inference step. The standard back propagation algorithm is employed to update FC layer weight parameters. The activation of the last FC layer is fed into a softmax layer to obtain the probabilistic class membership scores.

| Image | Text | Ground Truth label | Image-mode Classifier Prediction | Text-mode Classifier Prediction | Multi-mode Classifier Prediction |
|---|---|---|---|---|---|
| 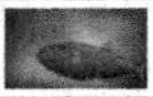 | "a fish in the new England aquarium" | True | True | True | True |
| | "other discussions" | False Connection | True | True | False Connection |
|  | "'cutest baby cow ive seen in my head all day and just enjoy destiny for what it is'" | Misleading Content | Manipulated Content | True | False Connection |
|  | "three corgis larping at the beach" | True | True | Manipulated Content | True |

**Fig. 3.** Example results of the proposed method in 6-way classification task of Fakeddit Dataset [21]

**Table 1.** Results in Twitter dataset [4]

| Method | Accuracy | Real news F1-score | Fake news F1-score |
|---|---|---|---|
| Text-mode Classifier | 0.62 | 0.61 | 0.64 |
| Visual-mode Classifier | 0.64 | 0.67 | 0.63 |
| Neural Talk [28] | 0.61 | 0.63 | 0.59 |
| VQA [2] | 0.63 | 0.61 | 0.65 |
| EANN [30] | 0.65 | 0.62 | 0.66 |
| att-RNN [13] | 0.66 | 0.68 | 0.65 |
| MVAE [15] | 0.75 | 0.76 | 0.73 |
| Spotfake [26] | 0.77 | 0.70 | 0.82 |
| Proposed Method | **0.82** | **0.80** | **0.85** |

## 4    Experiments

In this section, we will discuss the experimental details and the performance of the proposed method using state-of-the-art datasets.

### 4.1    Dataset Description

While publicly available dataset to evaluate the multimodal fake news detection techniques are relatively rare, in this paper, we use two datasets, which are comprised of multimodal social media contents, which have been popularly used in the research community: (1) Twitter Dataset, as part of MediaEval [4], which was released for evaluating methods for detecting fake multimedia content in social media; (2) the large scale Fakeddit Dataset [21] that was collected using pushshift API to capture samples from up to six different categories of information disorder. Each sample in the Twitter dataset is represented using a short Twitter message along with the visual and social context information. It has around 17,000 unique tweets discussed on different events and the authors provide the development/test dataset splits with no overlap of events. The development set has 9,000 fake news contents and 6,000 real news contents. The test set has 2,000 tweets. We use the training collection to build the model and the test collection is used for evaluation. The Fakeddit dataset has 1,000,000 samples from up to 6 different categories. Authors provide the ground truth labels for binary fake/real classification as well as more fine-grained categorization of 3 and 6 classes, respectively. While several metadata attributes are also available, which includes up- and down-votes of postings, the number of comments, up- and down-vote score for each comment, to ensure generalization across different data platforms, the proposed method in this work uses only the post content (text and visual) to analyze its veracity. For our experiments we adopt a similar pre-processing technique as in [21] to remove samples which may not have provided information using both modes ( text and image) and use the remaining

$560, 622$ samples for training, $58, 972$ for validation, and $58, 954$ of the Fakeddit dataset for testing. Each subreddit is labeled with one 2-way, 3-way, and 6-way label. This helps in both high-level and fine-grained fake news classification tasks. The 2-way classification determines whether a sample is fake or true. The 3-way classification determines whether a sample is completely true, the sample is fake and contains text that is true (i.e. direct quotes from propaganda posters), or the sample is fake with false text. The 6-way classification labels are : True, Satire/Parody, Misleading Content, Imposter Content, False Content, and Manipulated Content.

## 4.2   Implementation Details

For each sample, the text component and their respective images are pre-processed to ensure a uniform size specification. For the text mode, the input length is fixed as 20 tokens, which was decided based on the average length of the text data components in both the datasets. For the image mode, all the images are resized to $224 \times 224 \times 3$. Each image is split into $16 \times 16$ blocks (i.e. $B = 16$) and we set $L = 15$. We have chosen $M = 2$ layers in *Attention Aware Image Description* module $F_v^{SA}$, the *Attention Aware Text Description* module $F_t^{SA}$, and also in *Multimodal Feature Representation with Attention Aware Fusion* module $F^{CA}$. The final *Fake News Classifier* is trained with Adam optimizer($LR = 10^{-5}$) [17] and batch size 128. At the initialization stage of multimodal co-training, both $g_1$ (and $g_2$) are initialized independently by identifying the $\mathcal{P}_1^j$ (and $\mathcal{P}_2^j$) and $\mathcal{N}_1^j$ (and $\mathcal{N}_2^j$) using the existing $\mathbf{z}_1^j$ (and $\mathbf{z}_2^j$). Then during alteration, each model ($g_1$ and $g_2$) is trained for 50 epochs using the positive sets from the other view. For optimization, we use Adam with $10^{-3}$ learning rate and $10^{-5}$ weight decay. For the visual data augmentation to build $\mathcal{A}^{vis}$, we apply nine crops (center crop plus four corners, with horizontal flipping)) to the visual component of each sample. For the text data augmentation to build $\mathcal{A}^{text}$, we apply 2 Synonym Replacements, 2 Random Insertions, 2 Random Deletions, and 3 Random Swaps to the text component of each sample.

## 4.3   Results

Table 1 compares the performance of the proposed method against several state-of-the-art algorithms in Twitter dataset using Accuracy, Precision, Recall, and F1 scores (harmonic mean of Precision and Recall). While the proposed multimodal approach demonstrates a significantly improved performance compared to the existing methods in the uni-mode environment, visual feature reports a more reliable performance compared to its text-based counterpart. For the Visual mode classifier, we use the attention aware image representation technique described in Sect. 3.1 and derive a uni-mode implementation of a supervised contrastive loss based learning. More specifically, in the uni-mode environment, the positive set (Eq. 4) is identified by the existing function $\mathbf{g}_1$ (instead of $\mathbf{g}_2$ in the multimodal environment) for computing the loss value (Eq. 3). For the text-based classifier also, we adopt a similar approach and leverage the positive set (Eq. 6)identified by the existing function $\mathbf{g}_2$ for computing the loss value (Eq. 5).

**Table 2.** Results in Fakeddit dataset [21]

| Method | 2-way | | 3-way | | 6-way | |
|---|---|---|---|---|---|---|
| | Validation accuracy | Test accuracy | Validation accuracy | Test accuracy | Validation accuracy | Test accuracy |
| Text-mode Classifier [21] | 0.87 | 0.86 | 0.86 | 0.86 | 0.76 | 0.77 |
| Image-mode Classifier [21] | 0.74 | 0.74 | 0.73 | 0.73 | 0.64 | 0.65 |
| Multimode Classifier [21] | 0.87 | 0.87 | 0.84 | 0.84 | 0.81 | 0.82 |
| Text-mode Classifier [18] | 0.88 | 0.88 | – | – | – | – |
| Image-mode (Inception V3) Classifier [18] | 0.81 | 0.82 | – | – | – | – |
| Multimode Classifier [18] | 0.91 | 0.91 | – | – | – | – |
| Proposed Method (Text mode) | 0.92 | 0.91 | 0.87 | 0.85 | 0.81 | 0.80 |
| Proposed Method (Image mode) | 0.78 | 0.76 | 0.75 | 0.74 | 0.69 | 0.68 |
| Proposed Multimode Classifier | **0.94** | **0.93** | **0.90** | **0.89** | **0.85** | **0.85** |

The proposed method is also compared against several state-of-the-art methods including Visual Question Answering (VQA) [2], Neural Talk [28], Event Adversarial Neural Network (EANN) [30] att-RNN [13] and Multimodal Variational Autoencoder (MVAE) [15]. To ensure a fair comparison, we adopt the approach followed by Khatar et al. [15] and build similar architectures for Visual Question Answering (VQA) [2], Neural Talk [28]. The table compares the performance with their two mode frameworks, which do not utilize the social context information. We note that among the other multimodal models, while Spotfake and MVAE show improved performance, att-RNN reports better performance compared to EANN specifically in detecting the real-news sub-collection and thereby demonstrates effectiveness of attention mechanism. As observed in the table, by a hierarchical analysis of the local semantics within/across different modes and a novel co-training mechanism leveraging the supervised contrastive loss in a multimodal environment, the proposed method shows a significantly better performance compared to MVAE by reporting around 6% improvement in accuracy and 9% improvement in F1-score.

The performance of the proposed method using Fakeddit dataset [21] is detailed in Table 2, where the evaluation is performed in multiple steps and the results are reported in both uni-mode and multimode environments. Armin et al. [18] report the performance only using the 2-way annotations of the dataset. As mentioned by the authors of [18], different visual encoders (including VGG-19) were evaluated and Inception-v3 provided the best results for their framework. Therefore, Armin et al. [18] report their best performance using Inception-v3. While leveraging a more discriminative encoder may be a tool for improving the performance for any methods including ours, the objective in this work was to analyze the effectiveness of the proposed multimodal analytical framework, without relying on any specific encoder to boost up the performance. VGG-19 is one of the most popular visual encoders employed by different models developed for this problem scenario, we have used it in our work. By comparing Row 3 with 4, Row 6 with 7, and Row 9 with 10 of Table 2, we observe that the text-mode representation of the news content is most effective in isolation. Also, the uni-mode classifiers (both text and visual) designed in this work, significantly outperform their respective configurations reported by [21] and [18]. Finally the performance of the proposed multimodal classifier that leverages self- and cross-modal attentions at multiple layers of details and learns a discriminative joint representation via multimodal co-training, demonstrates a significant promise in improving the overall identification performance. By observing the accuracy scores reported in Row 11 and comparing them against its corresponding baselines in Row 5 and 8, we find that the proposed method achieves 2–5% improvements in accuracy score across various testing environments (2-, 3-, and 6-way). In fact, in the more complex 3- and 6-way problem settings, the proposed method enhances the performance by respectively reporting a more reliable 89% (compared to 84% as reported by [21]) and 85% (compared to 82% as reported by [21]) accuracy scores in the test subcollections. This analysis thus clearly proves beneficial and highlights the intrinsic multimodal nature of the problem setting. Some example results are shown in Fig. 3.

## 5   Conclusion

In this paper we propose a novel multimodal fake-news identification model. To capture a detailed relationship across multiple visual regions and also their correlation with the text component of the input news content, its image component is represented using a set of features describing its potential object regions and its text component as a sequence of words. A pair of mode-specific independent branches of self-attention layers, followed by an attention aware cross-model fusion module learns an initial joint representation by specifically highlighting the correlation between each word and each image region. The proposed multimodal co-training scheme employs an effective formulation of the supervised contrastive loss based optimization process, which utilizes the complementary category relevant information from different mode-specific data representations to derive an enhanced joint descriptor with improved discriminative capacity. Experiments were performed on two large scale public datasets witt news articles with varied characteristics. The consistently improved performances across various experiment settings clearly demonstrate the feasibility of our approach over existing methods. In future we would also like to leverage the access to other metadata (e.g. publishing resource, pattern of responses from viewers, which may be beneficial to evaluate the veracity of content more accurately.

# References

1. Allcott, H., Gentzkow, M.: Social media and fake news in the 2016 election. J. Econ. Perspect. **31**(2), 211–36 (2017)
2. Antol, S., et al.: VQA: visual question answering. In: Proceedings of the IEEE International Conference on Computer Vision, pp. 2425–2433 (2015)
3. Bhattacharjee, S.D., Talukder, A., Balantrapu, B.V.: Active learning based news veracity detection with feature weighting and deep-shallow fusion. In: 2017 IEEE International Conference on Big Data (Big Data), pp. 556–565. IEEE (2017)
4. Boididou, C., et al.: Verifying multimedia use at mediaeval (2016)
5. Cui, L., Wang, S., Lee, D.: Same: sentiment-aware multi-modal embedding for detecting fake news. In: Proceedings of the 2019 IEEE/ACM International Conference on Advances in Social Networks Analysis and Mining, pp. 41–48 (2019)
6. Davidson, T., Warmsley, D., Macy, M., Weber, I.: Automated hate speech detection and the problem of offensive language. In: Proceedings of the International AAAI Conference on Web and Social Media, vol. 11 (2017)
7. Devlin, J., Chang, M.W., Lee, K., Toutanova, K.: BERT: pre-training of deep bidirectional transformers for language understanding. arXiv preprint arXiv:1810.04805 (2018)
8. Ghanem, B., Rosso, P., Rangel, F.: An emotional analysis of false information in social media and news articles. ACM Trans. Internet Technol. (TOIT) **20**(2), 1–18 (2020)
9. Giachanou, A., Ríssola, E.A., Ghanem, B., Crestani, F., Rosso, P.: The role of personality and linguistic patterns in discriminating between fake news spreaders and fact checkers. In: Métais, E., Meziane, F., Horacek, H., Cimiano, P. (eds.) NLDB 2020. LNCS, vol. 12089, pp. 181–192. Springer, Cham (2020). https://doi.org/10.1007/978-3-030-51310-8_17
10. Giachanou, A., Rosso, P., Crestani, F.: Leveraging emotional signals for credibility detection. In: Proceedings of the 42nd International ACM SIGIR Conference on Research and Development in Information Retrieval, pp. 877–880 (2019)
11. Giachanou, A., Zhang, G., Rosso, P.: Multimodal fake news detection with textual, visual and semantic information. In: Sojka, P., Kopeček, I., Pala, K., Horák, A. (eds.) TSD 2020. LNCS (LNAI), vol. 12284, pp. 30–38. Springer, Cham (2020). https://doi.org/10.1007/978-3-030-58323-1_3
12. Hoffer, E., Ailon, N.: Deep metric learning using triplet network. In: Feragen, A., Pelillo, M., Loog, M. (eds.) SIMBAD 2015. LNCS, vol. 9370, pp. 84–92. Springer, Cham (2015). https://doi.org/10.1007/978-3-319-24261-3_7
13. Jin, Z., Cao, J., Guo, H., Zhang, Y., Luo, J.: Multimodal fusion with recurrent neural networks for rumor detection on microblogs. In: Proceedings of the 25th ACM international conference on Multimedia, pp. 795–816 (2017)
14. Kambhatla, N., Leen, T.K.: Dimension reduction by local principal component analysis. Neural Comput. **9**(7), 1493–1516 (1997)
15. Khattar, D., Goud, J.S., Gupta, M., Varma, V.: MVAE: multimodal variational autoencoder for fake news detection. In: The World Wide Web Conference, pp. 2915–2921 (2019)
16. Khosla, P., et al.: Supervised contrastive learning. arXiv preprint arXiv:2004.11362 (2020)
17. Kingma, D.P., Ba, J.: Adam: a method for stochastic optimization. arXiv preprint arXiv:1412.6980 (2014)

18. Kirchknopf, A., Slijepcevic, D., Zeppelzauer, M.: Multimodal detection of information disorder from social media. arXiv preprint arXiv:2105.15165 (2021)

19. Lago, F., Phan, Q.T., Boato, G.: Visual and textual analysis for image trustworthiness assessment within online news. In: Security and Communication Networks 2019 (2019)

20. Ma, J., Gao, W., Wong, K.F.: Rumor detection on twitter with tree-structured recursive neural networks. Association for Computational Linguistics (2018)

21. Nakamura, K., Levy, S., Wang, W.Y.: r/fakeddit: a new multimodal benchmark dataset for fine-grained fake news detection. arXiv preprint arXiv:1911.03854 (2019)

22. Popat, K., Mukherjee, S., Strötgen, J., Weikum, G.: Credibility assessment of textual claims on the web. In: Proceedings of the 25th ACM International on Conference on Information and Knowledge Management, pp. 2173–2178 (2016)

23. Popat, K., Mukherjee, S., Yates, A., Weikum, G.: Declare: debunking fake news and false claims using evidence-aware deep learning. arXiv preprint arXiv:1809.06416 (2018)

24. Shu, K., Wang, S., Liu, H.: Understanding user profiles on social media for fake news detection. In: 2018 IEEE Conference on Multimedia Information Processing and Retrieval (MIPR), pp. 430–435. IEEE (2018)

25. Simonyan, K., Zisserman, A.: Very deep convolutional networks for large-scale image recognition. arXiv preprint arXiv:1409.1556 (2014)

26. Singhal, S., Shah, R.R., Chakraborty, T., Kumaraguru, P., Satoh, S.: SpotFake: a multi-modal framework for fake news detection. In: 2019 IEEE Fifth International Conference on Multimedia Big Data (BigMM), pp. 39–47. IEEE (2019)

27. Uijlings, J.R.R., van de Sande, K.E.A., Gevers, T., Smeulders, A.W.M.: Selective search for object recognition. Int. J. Comput. Vision **104**(2), 154–171 (2013)

28. Vinyals, O., Toshev, A., Bengio, S., Erhan, D.: Show and tell: a neural image caption generator. In: Proceedings of the IEEE Conference on Computer Vision and Pattern Recognition, pp. 3156–3164 (2015)

29. Wang, W.Y.: "Liar, liar pants on fire": a new benchmark dataset for fake news detection. arXiv preprint arXiv:1705.00648 (2017)

30. Wang, Y., et al.: EANN: event adversarial neural networks for multi-modal fake news detection. In: Proceedings of the 24th ACM SIGKDD International Conference on Knowledge Discovery & Data Mining, pp. 849–857 (2018)

31. Wang, Y., et al.: Position focused attention network for image-text matching. arXiv preprint arXiv:1907.09748 (2019)

32. Zlatkova, D., Nakov, P., Koychev, I.: Fact-checking meets fauxtography: verifying claims about images. arXiv preprint arXiv:1908.11722 (2019)

# Gaussian Distribution Prior Based Multi-view Self-supervised Learning for Serous Retinal Detachment Segmentation

Sha Xie[1], Yuhan Zhang[1], Mingchao Li[1], Zexuan Ji[1], Songtao Yuan[2], and Qiang Chen[1(✉)]

[1] Nanjing University of Science and Technology, Nanjing, China
Chen2qiang@njust.edu.cn
[2] The First Affiliated Hospital with Nanjing Medical University, Nanjing, China

**Abstract.** Assessment of serous retinal detachment (SRD) plays an important role in the diagnosis of central serous chorioretinopathy (CSC). In this paper, we propose an unsupervised method, called *G*aussian distribution prior based *M*ulti-view *S*elf-supervised *L*earning (G-MSL), for the segmentation of SRD, in spectral domain optical coherence tomography (SD-OCT) images. We firstly count the Gaussian distribution prior for each targeted retinal layer from normal SD-OCT images. Then the Gaussian distribution prior-based fitting detects the abnormal pixels belonging to SRD in each targeted retinal layer. The generated coarse SRD region masks are used for self-supervised learning to optimize the SRD regions. The fully connected conditional random field is applied to obtain the SRD segmentation results. To improve the robustness of the proposed method for 3D SD-OCT volumes, we repeatedly carry out the above-mentioned operations from another view. The final segmentation results are obtained by getting the union of the results of multiple views. Experimental results on 20 subjects with CSC demonstrate that the proposed method can achieve the average dice similarity coefficient of 91.69%. G-MSL shows enough potential for the improvements of the clinical CSC evaluation and achieves higher segmentation accuracy than the existing supervised deep learning methods when the training set is not very large.

**Keywords:** Anomaly detection · Self-supervised learning · Gaussian distribution prior · Serous retinal detachment segmentation · SD-OCT

## 1 Introduction

Serous retinal detachment (SRD), such as pigment epithelial detachment (PED) and neurosensory retinal detachment (NRD) as shown in Fig. 1, is a prominent characteristic of central serous chorioretinopathy (CSC). CSC is a common retina disease characterized

This study was supported in part by National Natural Science Foundation of China (62172223, 61671242), in part by Key R&D Program of Jiangsu Science and Technology Department (BE2018131) and the Fundamental Research Funds for the Central Universities (30921013105).

C. Wallraven et al. (Eds.): ACPR 2021, LNCS 13189, pp. 297–306, 2022.
https://doi.org/10.1007/978-3-031-02444-3_22

by decompensation of the retinal pigment epithelium (RPE) and has a relative high recurrence rate. Some people are left with permanent vision loss due to progressive and irreversible photoreceptor damage or RPE atrophy [1]. Quantitative assessment of SRD is fundamental for diagnosis and treatment of CSC. Therefore, automatic segmentation for SRD in spectral domain optical coherence tomography (SD-OCT) is essential for clinical application.

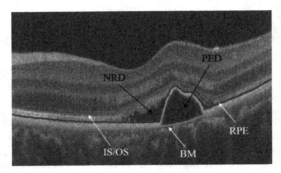

**Fig. 1.** SD-OCT B-scan with NRD and PED.

Several image processing methods and machine learning methods have been applied for the retinal fluid in OCT images: (1) For the image processing methods, Wu et al. [2] detected and segmented the fluid-associated abnormalities by using thickness map prior and a fuzzy level set method. Ji et al. [3] constructed an aggregate generalized Laplacian of Gaussian method based on Hessian to achieve fluid segmentation into small blob candidate regions. Sun et al. [4] presented a novel automatic segmentation approach based on two-stage clustering and an improved 3D level set method to quantify NRD regions in SD-OCT images. (2) For the machine learning methods, Sun et al. [5] proposed a framework for serous PED segmentation that combined AdaBoost classification and a shape-constrained graph cut. Roy et al. [6] proposed ReLayNet for OCT fluid segmentation by U-Net as a framework. Gao et al. [7] proposed an image-to-image double-branched and area-constraint fully convolutional networks (DA-FCN) for segmenting subretinal fluid. Bekalo et al. [8] presented a fully three-dimensional method to segment the retinal layers and NRD associated subretinal fluid using graph search and graph cut. Yang et al. [9] proposed a residual multiple pyramid pooling network (RMPPNet) to segment NRD in SD-OCT images. Gao et al. [10] proposed a method for automatic fluid segmentation on the basis of improved U-Net++.

Most image processing methods are ineffective for complex retinopathy and are not as robust as deep learning methods. However, supervised deep learning methods require a long processing time to manually annotate abnormal regions. In addition, most methods can only segment NRD or PED. To improve the segmentation performance and avoid the manual annotation, we proposed an automated and unsupervised framework for SRD segmentation in SD-OCT images, called Gaussian distribution prior based *M*ulti-view *S*elf-supervised *L*earning (G-MSL), and the segmentation results demonstrate the efficiency and feasibility of the proposed framework.

The contributions of this work are summarized as follows. (1) An anomaly detection strategy based on Gaussian distribution prior is proposed to obtain the pseudo labels, which avoids manual labeling and achieves unsupervised segmentation. (2) A multi-view strategy is utilized for SRD segmentation to make full use of the three-dimensional information. (3) Our unsupervised method achieves higher segmentation accuracy than the existing supervised deep learning methods when the training set is not very large.

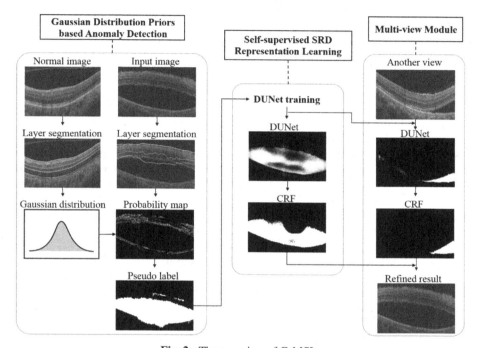

**Fig. 2.** The overview of G-MSL.

## 2 Method

### 2.1 Dataset

In this study, a data set of 20 SD-OCT volumes from 20 cases diagnosed with CSC were acquired (13 cases with only NRD, 3 cases with only PED, and 4 cases with both NRD and PED) by a RTVue XR Avanti OCTA device with center wavelength of 840 nm (Optovue, CA). Each full scan generates a SD-OCT cube (640 × 400 × 400 voxels) containing the corresponding trim size of 2 mm × 6 mm × 6 mm in the axial, horizontal and vertical directions respectively. Each slice along with vertical direction with size of 640 × 400 is referred to a B-scan. The ground truth of NRD and PED in all B-scans is manually delineated by ophthalmologists. To balance the positive and negative samples in the stage of unsupervised learning, we eliminate the B-scans without any SRD.

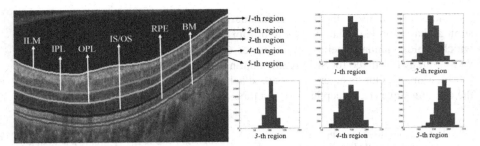

**Fig. 3.** A normal SD-OCT B-scan for visualization of six layer surfaces and the intensity distribution of the five layer regions.

## 2.2 Model

The proposed G-MSL consists of Gaussian distribution prior based anomaly detection, self-supervised learning and multi-view module (Fig. 2). The first module is utilized to segment the retinal intensity abnormalities based on the obtained layer segmentation results and Gaussian distribution prior. Then, the self-supervised module utilizes the pseudo label generated by the first module and DUNet [11] to make the proposed framework unsupervised and robust. The fully connected conditional random field (CRF) [12] is used to improve the results of DUNet. The last module tries to get more refined segmentation results by combining the results of multiple views.

**Gaussian Distribution Prior Based Anomaly Detection**
According to the statistics analysis of 80 normal SD-OCT cubes, the intensity distribution of normal SD-OCT retinal images follows a Gaussian distribution, as shown in Fig. 3. The most obvious feature of SRD is that their intensity is much lower than the normal pixels. Besides, NRD is between Inner segment/Outer segment (IS/OS) and RPE, and PED is between RPE and Bruch's membrance (BM). Thus, we detect the abnormal pixels by using the structural texture and intensity information of retinal layers, where the retinal layers were segmented with the robust deep learning model [13].

The detailed anomaly detection algorithm based on Gaussian distribution prior is as follows:

- Apply the layer segmentation algorithm proposed by Zhang et.al [13] to obtain six-layer segmentation results of Internal limiting membrane (ILM), Inner plexiform layer (IPL), Outer plexiform layer (OPL), IS/OS, RPE and BM on another data set which includes 80 normal SD-OCT retinal cubes (3200 B-scan images).
- Calculate the intensity mean $\mu_i$ and standard deviation $\sigma_i$ of the $i$-th layer region. $\mu = [137.26\ 111.83\ 101.54\ 146.97\ 174.81]$, $\sigma = [8.69\ 6.50\ 5.02\ 10.40\ 9.46]$.
- Given a pixel $x_i \in \mathcal{R}_i$, where $\mathcal{R}_i$ is the pixel set of $i$-th layer region, we perform the Gaussian fitting according to $\mu_i \in \mu$ and $\sigma_i \in \sigma$ on our data set of 20 cubes with CSC:

$$f(x_i) = \frac{1}{\sqrt{2\pi}\sigma_i}\exp(-\frac{(x_i - \mu_i)^2}{2\sigma_i{}^2}) \tag{1}$$

- The smaller the function value of the pixel, the higher the probability that its intensity value is not in the intensity distribution, the greater the abnormal probability of the pixel. In addition, we ignore the pixels whose intensity values are higher than the intensity mean.
- Set threshold T to convert the probability maps into binary images. Due to the influence of noise, vessels or other lesions, it is finally verified through experiments that the pseudo label segmentation results are best when T is set to 1e-4.

### Self-supervised Learning SRD Representation Learning

Although the relatively good segmentation results can be obtained by using only the first module, there are mistakes when SRDs have high intensity or backgrounds have low intensity. The model that only relies on intensity feature will not be robust. Therefore, we use the segmentation results of the first module as the pseudo label for neural network training, so that the network can learn the high-level SRD representations automatically. Here, we apply the deformable U-Net (DUNet) with the obtained pseudo label to perform self-supervised learning. The size of input to DUNet is 640 × 400.

DUNet integrates the advantages of the deformable unit and U-Net architecture. In each encoding and decoding phase, deformable convolutional blocks are used to model serous retinal detachment of various shapes and scales through learning local, dense and adaptive receptive fields. With this architecture, DUNet can learn discriminative features and generate the precise serous retinal detachment segmentation results. Besides, we use the fully connected CRF to further improve the DUNet segmentation results. It is a graph-based method that utilizes spatial information by capturing the correlation between image pixels, so as to identify misclassified regions and obtain more accurate segmentation boundaries.

### Multi-view Module

This module is designed towards the refinement of the under-segmentation. Through DUNet and CRF, most B-scans have achieved excellent segmentation results. However, some B-scans have obvious under-segmentation because of dark background and blurry boundaries. Therefore, we make full use of the three-dimensional information of the lesions, and the images sliced in horizontal direction with size of 640 × 400, shown in Fig. 4(c), are tested on the self-supervised module. The final segmentation results of the whole SD-OCT cubes are obtained by getting the union of the segmentation results of the vertical and horizontal views.

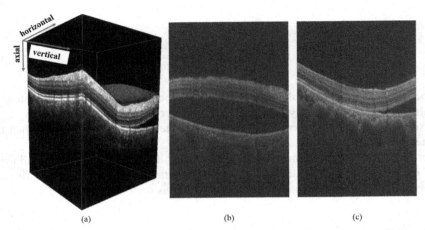

(a)                          (b)                          (c)

**Fig. 4.** (a) A full SD-OCT cube. The cube contains 640(axial) × 400(horizontal) × 400(vertical) voxels with the corresponding trim size of 2 mm × 6 mm × 6 mm. (b) The last image sliced in vertical direction with the size of 640 × 400. (c) The first image sliced in horizontal direction with the size of 640 × 400.

## 3   Experiment

### 3.1   Evaluation Metrics

The proposed algorithm uses the dice similarity coefficient (DSC), Precision and Recall as the evaluation metrics:

$$DSC = 2(|A \cap B|)/(|A| + |B|) \tag{2}$$

$$Precision = TP/(TP + FP) \tag{3}$$

$$Recall = TP/(TP + FN) \tag{4}$$

where A is the automated segmentation result, and B is the ground truth. TP, FP, and FN are the true positive, false positive, and false negative, respectively.

### 3.2   Ablation Study

In order to evaluate the performance of each module, we show the representatively qualitative and quantitative results of the ablation experiment in Fig. 5 and Table 1. The results of DUNet are obtained by applying the DUNet with the obtained pseudo label. The results of CRF are obtained by applying the CRF based on the results of DUNet. And the results of multi-view are obtained by applying the multi-view module based on the results of CRF. It can be seen that the final multi-view results are more similar to ground truth visually and the segmentation results of each module are gradually improved, which indicates that every module of the algorithm is necessary.

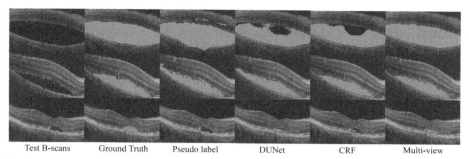

| Test B-scans | Ground Truth | Pseudo label | DUNet | CRF | Multi-view |

**Fig. 5.** Qualitative comparisons of the ablation experiment. The segmentation regions are marked with green. (Color figure online)

The pseudo labels are obtained based on anomaly detection by only considering the intensity information. Therefore, there are over-segmentation in the low-intensity background or the shadow region below retinal vessels, and under-segmentation in the high-intensity SRD regions. DUNet can improve segmentation accuracy and make the model more robust by learning other features of SRD automatically, such as contour. The fully connected CRF mainly reduces the over-segmentation. On the contrary, the multi-view module mainly reduces the under-segmentation by getting the union of the results of multiple views.

**Table 1.** Quantitative comparisons of the ablation experiment (unit: %).

|              | DSC (mean ± std)  | Precision (mean ± std) | Recall (mean ± std) |
|--------------|-------------------|------------------------|---------------------|
| Pseudo label | 86.09 ± 29.35     | 86.52 ± 28.25          | 85.66 ± 27.09       |
| DUNet        | 88.67 ± 22.01     | 89.31 ± 24.15          | 88.04 ± 16.86       |
| CRF          | 90.80 ± 27.26     | **95.35 ± 25.44**      | 86.67 ± 25.73       |
| Multi-view   | **91.69 ± 24.81** | 94.84 ± 23.12          | **88.74 ± 22.69**   |

### 3.3   Comparison with the State-of-the-Art Methods

Our proposed G-MSL model is compared with the state-of-the-art deep learning based segmentation models, BRU-Net [14], Deeplabv3+ [15], ReLayNet [6], U-Net [16], UNet++ [17], UNet 3+ [18] and DUNet [11]. The segmentation results of the comparative methods are obtained by a four-fold cross validation at a volume level.

For qualitative evaluation, the representative segmentation results are shown in Fig. 6 from different CSC cases. The first three rows in Fig. 6 are the results with only NRD. The segmentation results of the comparative methods have the obvious under-segmentation, as shown in the first row. Our method has two ways to reduce the under-segmentation. First, we apply the layer segmentation to detect the retinal intensity abnormalities based on Gaussian distribution prior. Second, we apply multi-view instead of single view to obtain better integral results. Besides, as shown in the third row, the segmentation results of the comparative methods include obvious false positive regions below the BM layer, which have a similar intensity profile to the fluid region. Those false positives can be suppressed by the layer segmentation in our approach.

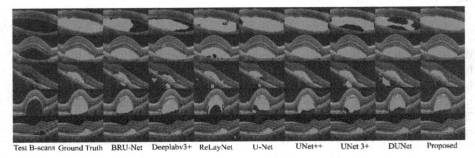

Test B-scans  Ground Truth  BRU-Net  Deeplabv3+  ReLayNet  U-Net  UNet++  UNet 3+  DUNet  Proposed

**Fig. 6.** Qualitative comparison of different methods. The segmentation regions are marked with green. (Color figure online)

The fourth row of Fig. 6 is the result with only PED. There are obvious under-segmentation because of the indistinct BM layer, while our approach can tackle this problem by retinal anomaly detection. And the last row is the result with both NRD and PED. It shows that all the comparative methods cannot distinguish between NRD and PED accurately. Our method achieves good agreement with the ground truth.

Table 2 summarizes the quantitative evaluation of DSC, Precision and Recall. Our method achieves the best DSC compared to other approaches, which indicates that

**Table 2.** Quantitative comparisons of different methods (unit: %).

| Method | DSC (mean ± std) | Precision (mean ± std) | Recall (mean ± std) |
|---|---|---|---|
| BRU-Net [14] | 86.48 ± 16.81 | 94.68 ± 16.54 | 79.59 ± 19.53 |
| Deeplabv3+ [15] | 84.46 ± 31.83 | 90.51 ± 31.67 | 79.17 ± 31.27 |
| ReLayNet [6] | 84.01 ± 13.86 | 87.36 ± 16.10 | 80.92 ± 13.27 |
| U-Net [16] | 85.16 ± 14.32 | 86.62 ± 12.22 | 83.74 ± 16.46 |
| UNet++ [17] | 84.41 ± 19.99 | 80.39 ± 22.02 | **88.86 ± 9.32** |
| UNet 3+ [18] | 86.39 ± 13.48 | 84.99 ± 17.31 | 87.85 ± 10.89 |
| DUNet [11] | 88.97 ± 9.75 | 91.21 ± 13.48 | 86.85 ± 8.38 |
| G-MSL | **91.69 ± 24.81** | **94.84 ± 23.12** | 88.74 ± 22.69 |

because our proposed G-MSL makes full use of the normal retinal structure and intensity prior based on anomaly detection and the disease information based on self-supervised learning, our unsupervised method can achieve better segmentation accuracy than the supervised methods when the training images are not too many.

## 4  Conclusion

Serous retinal detachment segmentation for SD-OCT images is a fundamental task, which can assist ophthalmologists in the diagnosis and treatment of CSC. However, it is difficult to accurately segment serous retinal detachment with severe lesions. In this paper, we propose a Gaussian distribution prior based multi-view self-supervised model to segment NRD and PED, which achieves higher segmentation accuracy than the state-of-the-art segmentation methods. The proposed model is flexible to be extended to perform the segmentation tasks of other lesions with obvious intensity abnormality.

## References

1. Semeraro, F., Morescalchi, F., Russo, A., et al.: Central serous chorioretinopathy: pathogenesis and management. Clin. Ophthalmol. **13**, 2341–2352 (2019)
2. Wu, M., Fan, W., Chen, Q., et al.: Three-dimensional continuous max flow optimization-based serous retinal detachment segmentation in SD-OCT for central serous chorioretinopathy. Biomed. Opt. Exp. **8**(9), 4257 (2017)
3. Ji, Z., et al.: Beyond retinal layers: a large blob detection for subretinal fluid segmentation in SD-OCT images. In: Frangi, A.F., Schnabel, J.A., Davatzikos, C., Alberola-López, C., Fichtinger, G. (eds.) MICCAI 2018. LNCS, vol. 11071, pp. 372–380. Springer, Cham (2018). https://doi.org/10.1007/978-3-030-00934-2_42
4. Sun, Y., Niu, S., Dong, J., Chen, Y.: 3D level set method via local structure similarity factor for automatic neurosensory retinal detachment segmentation in retinal SD-OCT images. In: Knight, K., Zhang, C., Holmes, G., Zhang, M.-L. (eds.) ICAI 2019. CCIS, vol. 1001, pp. 83–92. Springer, Singapore (2019). https://doi.org/10.1007/978-981-32-9298-7_7
5. Sun, Z., Chen, H., Shi, F., et al.: An automated framework for 3D serous pigment epithelium detachment segmentation in SD-OCT images. Sci. Rep. **6**(1), 21739 (2016)
6. Roy, A.G., Conjeti, S., Karri, S.P.K., et al.: ReLayNet: retinal layer and fluid segmentation of macular optical coherence tomography using fully convolutional networks. Biomed. Opt. Express **8**(8), 3627–3642 (2017)
7. Gao, K., Niu, S., Ji, Z., et al.: Double-branched and area-constraint fully convolutional networks for automated serous retinal detachment segmentation in SD-OCT images. Comput. Methods Programs Biomed. **176**, 69–80 (2019)
8. Bekalo, L., Niu, S., He, X.J., et al.: Automated 3-D retinal layer segmentation from SD-OCT images with neurosensory retinal detachment. IEEE Access **7**, 14894–14907 (2019)
9. Yang, J., Ji, Z., Niu, S., et al.: RMPPNet: residual multiple pyramid pooling network for subretinal fluid segmentation in SD-OCT images. OSA Continuum **3**(7), 1751 (2020)
10. Gao, Z., Wang, X., Li, Y.: Automatic segmentation of macular edema in retinal OCT images using improved U-Net++. Appl. Sci. **10**(16), 5701 (2020)
11. Jin, Q., Meng, Z., Pham, T.D., et al.: DUNet: a deformable network for retinal vessel segmentation. Knowl.-Based Syst. **178**, 149–162 (2019)
12. Krähenbühl, P., Koltun, V.: Efficient inference in fully connected CRFs with Gaussian edge potentials. Adv. Neural. Inf. Process. Syst. **24**, 109–117 (2011)

13. Zhang, Y., et al.: Robust layer segmentation against complex retinal abnormalities for en face OCTA generation. In: Martel, A.L., et al. (eds.) MICCAI 2020. LNCS, vol. 12265, pp. 647–655. Springer, Cham (2020). https://doi.org/10.1007/978-3-030-59722-1_62

14. Apostolopoulos, S., De Zanet, S., Ciller, C., Wolf, S., Sznitman, R.: Pathological OCT retinal layer segmentation using branch residual U-shape networks. In: Descoteaux, M., Maier-Hein, L., Franz, A., Jannin, P., Collins, D.L., Duchesne, S. (eds.) MICCAI 2017. LNCS, vol. 10435, pp. 294–301. Springer, Cham (2017). https://doi.org/10.1007/978-3-319-66179-7_34

15. Chen, L.-C., Zhu, Y., Papandreou, G., Schroff, F., Adam, H.: Encoder-decoder with atrous separable convolution for semantic image segmentation. In: Ferrari, V., Hebert, M., Sminchisescu, C., Weiss, Y. (eds.) ECCV 2018. LNCS, vol. 11211, pp. 833–851. Springer, Cham (2018). https://doi.org/10.1007/978-3-030-01234-2_49

16. Ronneberger, O., Fischer, P., Brox, T.: U-Net: convolutional networks for biomedical image segmentation. In: Navab, N., Hornegger, J., Wells, W.M., Frangi, A.F. (eds.) MICCAI 2015. LNCS, vol. 9351, pp. 234–241. Springer, Cham (2015). https://doi.org/10.1007/978-3-319-24574-4_28

17. Zhou, Z., Rahman Siddiquee, M.M., Tajbakhsh, N., Liang, J.: UNet++: a nested U-Net architecture for medical image segmentation. In: Stoyanov, D., et al. (eds.) DLMIA/ML-CDS -2018. LNCS, vol. 11045, pp. 3–11. Springer, Cham (2018). https://doi.org/10.1007/978-3-030-00889-5_1

18. Huang, H., Lin, L., Tong, R., et al.: UNet 3+: a full-scale connected UNet for medical image segmentation. In: IEEE International Conference on Acoustics, Speech and Signal Processing (ICASSP), pp. 1055–1059 (2020)

# Learning Symbol Relation Tree for Online Handwritten Mathematical Expression Recognition

Thanh-Nghia Truong[1]([✉]) [ID], Hung Tuan Nguyen[2] [ID], Cuong Tuan Nguyen[1] [ID], and Masaki Nakagawa[1] [ID]

[1] Department of Computer and Information Sciences, Tokyo University of Agriculture and Technology, 2-24-16 Naka-cho, Koganei-shi, Tokyo 184-8588, Japan
Thanhnghiadk@gmail.com, fx4102@go.tuat.ac.jp,
nakagawa@cc.tuat.ac.jp
[2] Institute of Global Innovation Research, Tokyo University of Agriculture and Technology, 2-24-16 Naka-cho, Koganei-shi, Tokyo 184-8588, Japan

**Abstract.** This paper proposes a method for recognizing online handwritten mathematical expressions (OnHME) by building a symbol relation tree (SRT) directly from a sequence of strokes. The recognition system has two parts: a temporal classifier and a tree connector. The temporal classifier uses global context to produce a sequence of symbols and spatial relations between symbols from an OnHME pattern. It is a bidirectional recurrent neural network trained from multiple derived paths of SRTs. The tree connector splits the sequence into several sub-SRTs and connects them to form the SRT by looking up the best combination among those sub-SRTs. Besides, we adopt a tree sorting method to deal with various stroke orders. Recognition experiments indicate that the proposed OnHME recognition system is competitive to other methods. The recognition system achieves 44.12% and 41.76% expression recognition rates on the Competition on Recognition of Online Handwritten Mathematical Expressions (CROHME) 2014 and 2016 testing sets, respectively.

**Keywords:** Online recognition · Handwritten mathematical expression · Symbol relation tree · BLSTM · CTC

## 1 Introduction

Mathematical expressions play an essential role in scientific documents since they are indispensable for describing problems, theories, and solutions in math, physics, and many other fields. Due to the rapid emergence of pen-based or touch-based input devices such as digital pens, tablets, and smartphones, people have begun to use handwriting interfaces as an input method. Although the input method is natural and convenient, it is useful if handwritten mathematical expressions (HMEs) are correctly recognized.

There are two approaches to recognize handwriting based on the type of input patterns. The first approach uses the real-time sequences of pen-tip, or finger-top coordinates, collected from modern electronic devices, termed as online input. The other

© Springer Nature Switzerland AG 2022
C. Wallraven et al. (Eds.): ACPR 2021, LNCS 13189, pp. 307–321, 2022.
https://doi.org/10.1007/978-3-031-02444-3_23

approach processes handwritten images captured from a scanner or a camera termed as offline input. Offline recognition has the problem of segmentation, but it is free from various stroke orders or duplicated strokes. Online input allows touching strokes to be separated from time sequence information, but it is troubled by writing order variation and stroke duplication.

The problem of HME recognition has been studied for decades. Several grammar-based, tree-based, graph-based, or Deep Neural Network (DNN) based approaches have been applied to settle HME recognition [1–4]. Generally, three subtasks are involved in both online and offline HME recognition [5, 6]: (1) symbol segmentation to group strokes belonging to the same symbol; (2) symbol recognition to classify the segmented symbol; (3) structural analysis to identify spatial relations between symbols to produce a mathematical interpretation with the help of grammars.

The traditional approach is mainly grammar-driven methods. Generally, these methods predict a set of symbol hypotheses and select the best one using a structural analysis algorithm. Nonetheless, they achieve low recognition rates [5, 6] because of two main reasons. First, they depend on predefined rules and handcrafted features, which are less robust for various handwriting styles. Second, their isolated subtasks perform poorly without sharing global context. The tree-based and graph-based approaches show their advantages in representing the structures of HMEs. These approaches use a tree [3] or a graph [7] to describe the 2D structure of an HME. However, they are still limited with low HME recognition rates because they also depend on the performance of their isolated subtasks.

The DNN-based approach has recently been successfully used to parse the structures directly from HME training samples. It deals with HME recognition as an input-to-sequence problem [4] where input can be either an HME image (OffHME) or an online HME (OnHME) pattern. This approach is flexible and archives good performance because it uses a shared context to learn HME recognition. However, it requires a large number of training data to improve the generalization of the DNN-based model. Moreover, DNNs have difficulty extracting the 2D structure of HMEs using the 1D structure of LaTeX sequences [3]. Furthermore, the approach has weak grammar constraints, so that it might generate wrong candidates.

In this work, we focus on OnHME recognition from a new perspective. It is treated as a problem of deriving a symbol relation tree (SRT) from an input OnHME with a temporal classifier. The temporal classifier recognizes an input to produce an output sequence of symbols and spatial relations between the recognized symbols. We first obtain sub-SRTs from the output sequence and then reconstruct the final SRT representing the input OnHME from these sub-SRTs. The SRT reconstruction method includes a tree-based symbol level sorting, which solves the problem of writing order variation. With this approach, we make the model learn from the 2D structure of the OnHME patterns.

In summary, we make the following contributions:

1. We propose a temporal classifier for OnHME patterns to generate both symbols and relations directly. It helps the model encode a better context for recognizing symbols and predicting the relations between them.
2. We propose an OnHME recognition method based on an SRT that is the output of the temporal classifier.

The rest of the paper is organized as follows. Section 2 provides an overview of the state-of-the-art. Section 3 declares our method proposed in this paper. Section 4 describes our dataset and experiments. Section 4.2 highlights the results of the experiments. Section 5 draws the conclusion and future works.

## 2  Related Works

In this section, we briefly summarize some methods closely related to our method. These methods follow two main steps for symbol recognition and structural analysis.

### 2.1  Structural Approach for OnHME Recognition

The problem of OnHME recognition, as well as OffHME recognition, has been studied for decades [8] from the early top-down methods [9], bottom-up methods [10], and their variations [5, 6]. The most common approach to represent an OnHME is to use predefined grammar. Yamamoto et al. used Probabilistic Context-Free Grammars [11], MacLean and Labahn developed a method using relational grammars and fuzzy sets [12]. Grammars show their strength in representing the semantic structure of HME [5, 6]. However, the grammars need to be carefully designed to avoid the lack of generality and extensibility. Moreover, the results of symbol segmentation, symbol recognition, and spatial relation classification also affect the result of the grammar-based approach.

Another approach by Zhang et al. used Stroke Label Graph (SLG) to represent an OnHME in which nodes represent strokes whereas labels on the edges encode either segmentation or layout information [7]. They used a tree-based model and a sequential model to learn the stroke-level structure of OnHMEs [3]. The recognition result is obtained by combining the results from different paths to rebuild a math expression. Learning from stroke-level, however, incurs limited precision and recall of both the symbol classification and spatial relations.

### 2.2  Learning Spatial Relations

The structural analysis task aims to learn syntactic models that represent spatial relations between the mathematical symbols. Many approaches used a tree-based model in their HME recognition systems [11, 13, 14] to represent the 2D spatial relations of an HME. However, they depend on symbol recognition performance and need to process a large number of hypotheses for spatial relation. Moreover, the approach lacks the global context to classify the spatial relations since they are independently solved with other HME recognition tasks.

The spatial relations could also be learned directly from sequential features [7] or tree-based features [3]. This approach benefits from the global context of the sequence or the tree structure. However, their performance is low since learning spatial relations at the stroke level is difficult for the recognizer.

### 2.3   Global Context for Improving HME Recognition

The task of symbol recognition aims at segmenting all symbols in an OnHME and then recognizing the symbols. Generally, many works combined online features extracted from pen traces and offline features from the rendered image of an OnHME [15, 16]. Deep learning-based methods are frequently used to encode DNN-based features for symbol recognition [17].

Graves et al. [20] showed a crucial drawback of isolated classification methods compared with sequence classification. The isolated classification methods use only the context information from the current isolated symbol to classify the label. Many other works [6, 15] also demonstrated that isolated symbol recognition faces difficulty in discriminating symbols of similar shapes such as (X, x, \times), (O, o, 0), without using context.

On the other hand, deep learning-based methods are frequently used to solve HME recognition tasks in recent years. Zhelezniakov et al. used a Bidirectional Long Short-Term Memory (BLSTM) to segment and classify symbols in an HME [18]. For a sequence of symbols in an HME, the BLSTM encodes the global information of the context using the preceding states and succeeding states of a sequential input, and Connectionist Temporal Classification (CTC) optimizes the alignment and classification. Nguyen et al. improved the symbol recognition in an HME using a deep BLSTM-CTC model to encode global context information [17]. They encoded bidirectional context for symbol classification to solve the problem of recognizing ambiguous symbols. However, the global context is not shared with other HME recognition tasks, such as relation classification.

## 3   Our Approach

In this section, we propose a symbol-relation temporal classifier and how we prepare data for training the temporal classifier. Then, we propose an OnHME recognition system using the temporal classifier to generate and then reconstruct an SRT to represent an input OnHME pattern.

### 3.1   Symbol-Relation Temporal Classifier

OnHME can be represented at the symbol level as an SRT. Each node represents a symbol in an SRT, while a label on each edge indicates the relation between symbols. An SRT represents the placement of symbols on baselines (writing lines) and the spatial arrangement of the baselines [3]. The SRT of the whole structure of the HME could be represented by derived paths of consecutive symbols and spatial relations from the SRT.

We propose a sequential model for recognizing both symbols and spatial relations in an OnHME. The model receives an input of an extracted feature sequence, consisting of both written strokes and off-strokes (pen movements between strokes), and generates an output sequence of symbols and spatial relations between two consecutive symbols. The output sequence can be considered as a derived path. Assuming that the sequential order of symbols and input strokes is consistent (i.e., there are no delayed strokes), symbols

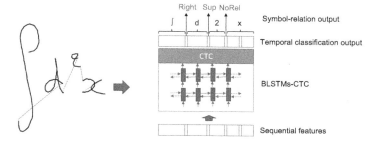

**Fig. 1.** BLSTM for symbol segmentation, recognition, and relation classification.

are separated by the off-strokes between them, and they are bound to the corresponding strokes and off-strokes.

We apply a deep BLSTM for symbol classification to encode the global context, as shown in Fig. 1. It combines multiple BLSTM layers that process the input in both forward and backward directions. The forward and backward context by the two LSTM layers is combined and feed to the next BLSTM layer in the networks. The deep BLSTM stacks multiple levels of BLSTMs to learn high-level features. After the output gate of the final BLSTM layer, we use a CTC layer to generate symbol segmentation and relation classification results.

From the sequential model, segmentation is performed by finding the off-strokes with a high probability of relations. For an OnHME, let $S$ is a sequence of $n$ strokes of the HME as $S = (s_0, \ldots, s_{n-1})$ and $O$ is a sequence of $(n-1)$ off-strokes as $O = (o_1, \ldots, o_{n-1})$ where $o_i$ is an off-stroke between two strokes $s_{i-1}$ and $s_i$. The $i^{th}$ off-stroke $o_i$ is a relation or '**blank**' if it is between two strokes inside a symbol. The relation having the highest probability at the $i^{th}$ off-stroke is considered as the relation between the $(i-1)^{th}$ and $i^{th}$ symbols, as shown in Eq. (1):

$$Rel(o_i) = \begin{cases} argmax(P_{rel}(o_i|\varphi_{HME})) & \text{if } max(P_{rel}(o_i|\varphi_{HME})) \geq P_{\textbf{blank}} \\ \textbf{blank} & \text{if } max(P_{rel}(o_i|\varphi_{HME})) < P_{\textbf{blank}} \end{cases} \quad (1)$$

where:

- $Rel(o_i)$ is the predicted relation of the $i^{th}$ off-stroke.
- $P_{rel}(o_i|\varphi_{HME})$ is the probability of the relation "rel" at $o_i$ given the BLSTM context $\varphi_{HME}$, by parsing $S$ with the symbol-relation temporal classifier.
- $P_{\textbf{blank}}$ is the probability of $o_i$ being '**blank**' produced by the classifier.

Symbol recognition is performed by taking the maximum probability of symbols between two relation outputs. The symbol recognition for a list of $t$ consecutive strokes $(s_i, \ldots, s_{i+t})$ is computed as in Eq. (2):

$$Symbol\left(s_{\overline{i,i+1}}\right) = argmax\left(P_{symbol}\left(o_{\overline{i,i+t}}|\varphi_{HME}\right)\right) \quad (2)$$

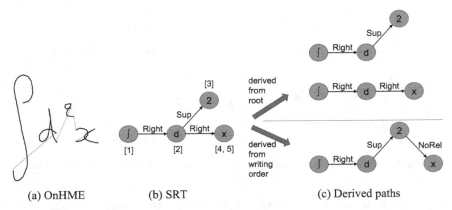

(a) OnHME   (b) SRT     (c) Derived paths

**Fig. 2.** Paths derived from the SRT: derived from the root, or from writing order.

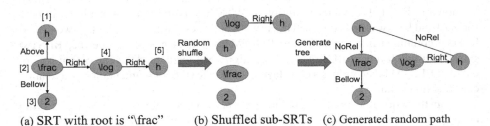

(a) SRT with root is "\frac"  (b) Shuffled sub-SRTs (c) Generated random path

**Fig. 3.** Random path generation.

**Learning of the Model.** Local CTC [3] constrains the output of symbols and relations to the specific strokes and off-strokes. However, the model does not constraint the output of relations to the exact locations, which affects relation classification since the model would be confused on many possible output locations.

We use a single feature point representing an off-stroke. We make the model learn precise relations by the constraint loss, which is the combination of the cross-entropy loss function $loss_{CE}$ and the CTC loss function $loss_{CTC}$, where the former $loss_{CE}$ is computed as shown in Eq. (3), and the loss function to train the model is computed as in Eq. (4):

$$loss_{CE} = -\sum_{i=0}^{n-1} log\left(1 - \sum P_{rel}(s_i|\varphi_{HME})\right) \quad (3)$$

$$loss = loss_{CTC} + loss_{CE} \quad (4)$$

**Training Path Extraction.** As we mentioned above, there are multiple derived paths in the SRT for an OnHME. From the SRT, we extract all of them, with each representing a path of strokes and off-strokes as well as their corresponding labels to prepare data for training the symbol-relation temporal classifier.

We propose the following three path extraction rules (PE-rules):

PE-rule 1: trace all paths from the root to the leaves of an SRT.
PE-rule 2: trace the path by writing order. When there is no relation between two consecutive nodes, NoRel is added.
PE-rule 3: extract random paths. The rule simulates various writing orders by randomly shuffling the order of sub-trees connected to the root node.

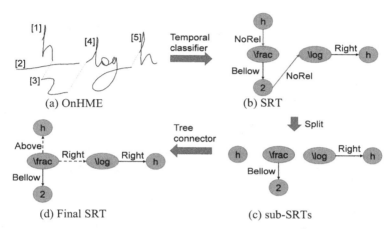

(a) OnHME    (b) SRT

(d) Final SRT    (c) sub-SRTs

**Fig. 4.** Processes of recognizing an HME pattern: $\frac{h}{2}\log h$.

PE-rule 1 extracts all the spatial relations along a path except NoRel. PE-rule 2 and PE-rule 3 assign NoRel when tracing a derived path containing two consecutive symbols without a spatial relation between them. Figure 2 shows an example of applying PE-rule 1 and PE-rule 2 to produce the derived paths from the root and the derived path by writing order. Figure 3 shows an example of applying PE-rule 3 to generate one of the random paths. Note that PE-rule 3 generates more training patterns by shuffling all sub-SRTs, which is hard for other LaTeX based methods.

### 3.2 Tree Reconstruction

For a list of strokes in an OnHME pattern, the temporal classifier generates an SRT in 1D as a sequence of several derived paths. Each derived path represents the symbol segmentation and relation classification results sequentially based on the order of input strokes. In the SRT, two consecutive symbols have a suitable relation between them. Otherwise, no relation is displayed. Therefore, we cut the tree into multiple sub-SRTs at the point that the relation is NoRel and then connect these discrete sub-SRTs to build up a final SRT that represents the whole OnHME.

The temporal classifier recognizes the whole input sequence into the sequence of symbols and spatial relations based on the order of them in the input sequence. First, sub-SRTs are obtained by splitting the temporal classification results of symbols and spatial relations. Then, sub-SRTs are connected into the SRT by additional spatial relations classification by the temporal classifier. Figure 4 illustrates our recognition method for an HME pattern: $\frac{h}{2} \log h$.

---

**Algorithm 1**: Graph cut and connection

**Input:**

　　A sequence of strokes $S = (s_0, \dots, s_{n-1})$ and a trained symbol-relation temporal classifier (SRTC).

**Output:**

　　SRT describing the OnHME.

| | |
|---|---|
| 1 | Let L is the SRT output of the temporal classifier: $L = SRTC(s_0, \dots, s_{n-1})$ |
| 2 | Let $L_2$ is the list of sub-SRTs when cutting L at the point that there is NoRel between two symbols. |
| 3 | Sort $L_2$ based on its component's position. |
| 4 | **repeat** |
| 5 | 　**for** i = 1, ..., length $(L_2) - 1$ **do** |
| 6 | 　　Let $l_i$ is the $i^{th}$ sub-SRT in $L_2$ |
| 7 | 　　Let m is the length of $L_2$ |
| 8 | 　　#local_connect($l_i, l_{i+1}$) |
| 9 | 　　Let $L_3$ is the list of leaf nodes or nodes that do not have Right child in $l_i$ |
| 10 | 　　Let $relation_i = \mathrm{argmax}_{n_j\ in\ L_3}\ P_{rel}\left(n_j, l_{i+1} | SRTC(n_j, l_{i+1})\right)$. |
| 11 | 　　If $relation_i$ is valid, connect $l_i$ with $l_{i+1}$, remove $l_{i+1}$ from $L_2$, break. |
| 12 | 　　#global_connect($l_i, l_{1:i,\ i+1:length(L_2)}$) |
| 13 | 　　Let |
| | 　　$relation_i = \mathrm{argmax}_{n_j\ in\ L_3, k=[1:i,\ i+1:length(L_2)]}\ P_{rel}\left(n_j, l_k | SRTC(n_j, l_k)\right)$. |
| 14 | 　　If $relation_i$ is valid, connect $l_i$ with $l_{i+1}$, remove $l_{i+1}$ from $L_2$, break. |
| 15 | 　　#can not connect |
| 16 | 　　flag($l_i$) = True |
| 17 | 　**end** |
| 18 | **until** length $(L_2) = 1$ or all flag of $L_2$ is True |
| 19 | **return** $L_2$ |

---

Based on the idea, we propose a tree connector that recognizes an OnHME pattern. Algorithm 1 presents the precise details on how to recognize an input OnHME using the temporal classifier. For an input OnHME pattern, we first get a sequence of strokes $S = (s_0, \dots, s_{n-1})$ and then pass it to the symbol-relation temporal classifier to recognize the 1D SRT, a sequence of symbols, and relations between them. Next, we cut the 1D-SRT into sub-SRTs and sort them by the information of their bounding boxes. Finally, we connect the discrete sub-SRTs using local and global connections.

To solve the writing order variation problem, we propose a method to sort the sub-SRTs before connecting them. We sort the sub-SRTs using their bounding box coordinates by the following sorting rules (S-rules):

S-rule 1: If a sub-SRT A is entirely in the left position of another sub-SRT B, A is sorted before B.

S-rule 2: If S-rule 1 is not satisfied and a sub-SRT A is entirely in the above position of another sub-SRT B, A is sorted before B.

S-rule 3: If S-rule 1 and S-rule 2 are not satisfied, the sub-SRTs are sorted along the x-axis.

The sorting step solves the problem of writing order variation at the symbol level. For example, the symbol-relation temporal classifier might make a false symbol recognition or redundant recognition for a symbol with non-consecutive strokes (a part of the symbol written after). There is room to improve the performance by solving the writing order problem at the stroke level.

In order to build the final SRT from the sorted list of sub-SRTs, the tree connector verifies whether two sub-SRTs are appropriate to connect by a local or global connection and then connect them. For each sub-SRT, the local connection denotes that the tree connector finds its adjacent sub-SRTs in the sorted list to connect them. If it does not have any adjacent sub-SRT, the tree connector considers all other sub-SRTs as the global connection. Next, the tree connector looks up all the symbols without Right node (candidate symbols) in the first sub-SRT. Then, the temporal classifier predicts the relation probabilities between the candidate symbols and the second sub-SRT. Consequently, the highest relation probability indicates the best pair of a candidate symbol in the first sub-SRT and the second sub-SRT.

## 4  Evaluation

### 4.1  Dataset

Data samples and evaluation metrics were introduced in CROHME [5, 6]. Revisions of the datasets and metrics from CROHME 2011 to CROHME 2016 were made for more precise evaluation. We use the CROHME 2014 training set to train the proposed model. For model validation and selection, we use the CROHME 2013 testing set. For evaluation, we use the CROHME 2014 and 2016 testing sets.

In our experiments, we use the CROHME tool LgEval to evaluate our proposed model. We mainly use the expression recognition rate (ExpRate) for the metrics, which shows the ratio of successfully recognized OnHMEs over all OnHMEs. We also use the Precision and Recall rates, which are provided by the LgEval tool [6].

### 4.2  Experiments

We evaluate the effects of the data generation method and the mathematical LM. We compare our OnHME recognition system with the other systems on the CROHME 2014 and 2016 testing sets. We show the effectiveness of the proposed system by comparing it with the benchmark proposed in [3].

**Result of HME Recognition.**  In this section, we evaluate the proposed method on the CROHME 2014 and 2016 testing sets. Table 1 and Table 2 show the evaluation results on the CROHME 2014 testing set at the symbol and expression levels, respectively. Then, Table 3 and Table 4 show those on the CROHME 2016 testing set, respectively. Table 1 and Table 3 consist of recall and precision rates for symbol segmentation (Segments), symbol segmentation and recognition (Segment + Class), and spatial relation classification (Tree relations). A spatial relation prediction between two symbols is correct if the relation is correctly classified and the two symbols are correctly segmented and recognized. Table 2 and Table 4 compare the HME recognition rates of the proposed methods with the other methods on the CROHME 2014 and 2016 testing sets, respectively.

**Table 1.** Symbol level evaluation on CROHME 2014 testing set.

| System | Segments (%) | | Segment+Class (%) | | Tree relations (%) | |
|---|---|---|---|---|---|---|
| | Recall | Precision | Recall | Precision | Recall | Precision |
| MyScript [5] | 98.42 | 98.13 | 93.91 | 93.63 | 94.26 | 94.01 |
| Valencia [5] | 93.31 | 90.72 | 86.59 | 84.18 | 84.23 | 81.96 |
| Nantes [5] | 89.43 | 86.13 | 76.53 | 73.71 | 71.77 | 71.65 |
| RIT-CIS [5] | 88.23 | 84.20 | 78.45 | 74.87 | 61.38 | 72.70 |
| RIT-DRPL [5] | 85.52 | 86.09 | 76.64 | 77.15 | 70.78 | 71.51 |
| Tokyo [5] | 83.05 | 85.36 | 69.72 | 71.66 | 66.83 | 74.81 |
| Sao Paulo [5] | 76.63 | 80.28 | 66.97 | 70.16 | 60.31 | 63.74 |
| Tree BLSTM* [3] | 95.52 | 91.31 | 89.55 | 85.60 | 78.08 | 74.64 |
| Our system | 87.69 | 98.11 | 82.62 | 92.44 | 82.28 | 93.02 |

"*" denotes an ensemble of multiple recognition models.

**Table 2.** Expression level evaluation on CROHME 2014 testing set.

| System | Correct (%) | ≤1 error | ≤2 errors | ≤3 errors |
|---|---|---|---|---|
| MyScript [5] | 62.68 | 72.31 | 75.15 | 76.88 |
| Valencia [5] | 37.22 | 44.22 | 47.26 | 50.20 |
| Nantes [5] | 26.06 | 33.87 | 38.54 | 39.96 |
| Tokyo [5] | 25.66 | 33.16 | 35.90 | 37.32 |
| RIT-DRPL [5] | 18.97 | 28.19 | 32.35 | 33.37 |
| RIT-CIS [5] | 18.97 | 26.37 | 30.83 | 32.96 |
| Sao Paulo [5] | 15.01 | 22.31 | 26.57 | 27.69 |
| TAP [4] | 50.41 | – | – | – |
| Tree BLSTM* [3] | 29.91 | 39.94 | 44.96 | 50.15 |
| Our system | 44.12 | 52.94 | 56.29 | 58.62 |

"*" denotes an ensemble of multiple recognition models.

In Table 1 and Table 2, the top-ranked system MyScript is built on the principle that segmentation, recognition, and interpretation have to be handled concurrently at the same level to produce the best candidate. They used a large number of extra training samples of HME patterns. System Valencia parsed expressions using two-dimensional stochastic context-free grammars. System TAP [4] used an end-to-end network to learn directly LaTeX sequences from OnHME patterns with a built-in language model. Tree BLSTM [3] is the benchmark to compare with our system, where it used a tree-BLSTM-based recognition system. Details of works in Table 1 and Table 2 can be found in the CROHME 2014 [5].

**Table 3.** Symbol level evaluation on CROHME 2016 testing set.

| System | Segments (%) | | Segment + Class (%) | | Tree relations (%) | |
|---|---|---|---|---|---|---|
| | Recall | Precision | Recall | Precision | Recall | Precision |
| MyScript | 98.89 | 98.95 | 95.47 | 95.53 | 95.11 | 95.11 |
| Wiris | 96.49 | 97.09 | 90.75 | 91.31 | 90.17 | 90.79 |
| Tokyo | 91.62 | 93.25 | 86.05 | 87.58 | 82.11 | 83.64 |
| Sao Paulo | 92.91 | 95.01 | 86.31 | 88.26 | 81.48 | 84.16 |
| Nantes | 94.45 | 89.29 | 87.19 | 82.42 | 73.20 | 68.72 |
| Tree BLSTM* [3] | 95.64 | 91.44 | 89.84 | 85.90 | 77.23 | 74.08 |
| Our system | 88.78 | 97.85 | 83.53 | 92.06 | 82.85 | 92.26 |

"*" denotes an ensemble of multiple recognition models.

**Table 4.** Expression level evaluation on CROHME 2016 testing set.

| System | Correct (%) | $\leq 1$ error | $\leq 2$ errors | $\leq 3$ errors |
|---|---|---|---|---|
| MyScript | 67.65 | 75.59 | 79.86 | – |
| Wiris | 49.61 | 60.42 | 64.69 | – |
| Tokyo | 43.94 | 50.91 | 53.70 | – |
| Sao Paulo | 33.39 | 43.50 | 49.17 | – |
| Nantes | 13.34 | 21.02 | 28.33 | – |
| TAP* [4] | 55.37 | – | – | – |
| Tree BLSTM* [3] | 27.03 | 35.48 | 42.46 | 27.03 |
| Our system | 41.76 | 49.43 | 52.40 | 54.84 |

"*" denotes an ensemble of multiple recognition models.

For symbol segmentation, recognition, and relation classification, our system archives better precision than the benchmark with nearly equal to the MyScript team. Our system achieves a 4.2 points higher recall rate with 82.28% compared to 78.08% of the benchmark for relation classification. However, the recall of our system is not better than the benchmark for symbol segmentation and recognition, with around 8 points lower. Our system reaches the level between the second-ranked and the third-ranked systems in CROHME 2014. The global expression recognition rate of our system is 44.12%, which is higher than the other systems that use the traditional approach without extra training data. Within the systems that use global context sharing for all subtasks, the expression recognition rate of our system is higher than the benchmark but lower than the TAP system. Note that TAP used a built-in language model.

In Table 3 and Table 4, MyScript used a large number of extra training samples of HME patterns, as mentioned above. The team Wiris won the CROHME 2016 competition, but in their work, they trained a language model using a Wikipedia formula corpus consisting of more than 592,000 formulas. Details of other works in Table 3 and Table 4 can be found in the CROHME [6].

For the symbol level evaluation, our system accounts for a competitive result compared with the other participating systems and the benchmark Merge 9, where the precision stands at the level between the first and the second team. However, the recall is still limited as compared with the other teams and the benchmark. There is room for improvement.

For the expression levels, TAP* [4] achieved the best OnHME recognition rate with 55.37% among the systems without using extra samples. However, they use an ensemble of 4 different models and a gated recurrent unit-based language model. Our system accounts for the ExpRate of 41.76%, a competitive result with the other participant systems in the contest without extra samples.

**Error Analysis.** In this section, we make an in-depth error analysis of our system's recognition results to understand better and explore the directions for improving recognition rate in the future using the CROHME validation tool [6].

**Table 5.** Node label errors of our system on CROHME 2014 testing set.

| Output label | Ground truth label (no. of nodes with this label) | No. of occurrences (percentage) |
| --- | --- | --- |
| X | x (890) | 36 (4.04%) |
| P | p (76) | 22 (28.95%) |
| \times | x (890) | 20 (2.25%) |
| C | c (90) | 16 (17.78%) |
| Y | y (223) | 16 (7.17%) |
| \ldots | . (18) | 13 (72.22%) |
| \div | + (599) | 12 (2.0%) |
| 1 | COMMA (87) | 12 (13.79%) |
| 2 | z (116) | 11 (9.48%) |
| V | v (53) | 11 (20.75%) |
| 9 | q (25) | 10 (40.0%) |
| S | s (25) | 10 (40.0%) |
| \lamda | x (890) | 10 (1.12%) |

**Table 6.** Edge label errors of our system on CROHME 2014 testing set.

| Prediction | G-truth | | | | | | | |
|---|---|---|---|---|---|---|---|---|
| | * (9044) | Above (592) | Below (627) | Inside (377) | Right (13698) | Sub (1115) | Sup (923) | NoRel (261528) |
| * | 486 | 2 | 1 | 2 | 33 | 3 | 1 | 76 |
| Above | 5 | | | | 5 | | | 52 |
| Below | 5 | | | | | 1 | | 17 |
| Inside | | 3 | 3 | | | | | 5 |
| Right | 65 | | | 11 | | 103 | 22 | 593 |
| Sub | 3 | | 1 | 1 | 43 | | 2 | 9 |
| Sup | 3 | 1 | | | 18 | | | 32 |
| NoRel | 1017 | 189 | 193 | 35 | 2021 | 174 | 191 | |

Table 5 lists the types of node label errors by our system where the number of errors is larger than or equals 10 on the CROHME 2014 testing set. The first column gives the output node labels by the classifier; the second column provides the ground truth node labels and the number of nodes with each label; the last column records the number of occurrences and the percentages. As can be seen from the table, the most frequent error $(x \to X, 36)$ belongs to the type of lowercase-uppercase errors. Moreover, $(P \to p, 22)$, $(C \to c, 16)$, and $(Y \to y, 16)$ also belong to the same type of lowercase-uppercase errors. Another type of common errors is the confusion between the symbols having similar shapes, such as $(\times \to x, 20)$, $(\ldots \to ., 13)$, $(\div \to +, 12)$, $(1 \to COMMA, 12)$, and so on. Another improvement would be to integrate a language model explicitly to promote frequent symbols.

Table 6 provides the edge label errors on the CROHME 2014 testing set using our OnHME recognition system. The first column represents the output labels; the first row offers the ground truth labels, the number of edges with each label; the other cells in this table provide the corresponding no. of occurrences. '*' represents segmentation edges within a symbol.

Since the Right edges are the most common edges among six spatial relations, the number of confusions to Right edges is the largest among the spatial relations. However, there is no confusion of Above and Below edges to Right edges. Additionally, there are only 11 over 377 Inside edges being confused to Right edges. The result shows that our temporal classifier could learn spatial relations effectively with the global context.

The current system still encounters the problem of missing relations or determine them as NoRel. Two reasons could produce the problem. First, the temporal classifier may fail to detect symbols or misclassified spatial relations into NoRel. The other reason is that the proposed method might skip some sub-SRTs in the SRT reconstruction step in some cases where the system cannot connect two sub-SRTs with local and global connections. Moreover, this is also why the precision rate is high, but the recall rate is low on the CROHME testing sets. Therefore, there is room to improve the tree reconstruction method.

## 5   Conclusion

In this work, we proposed an LSTM-based temporal classifier that used a shared context to learn from OnHME patterns to solve symbol recognition and relation classification. We used the temporal classifier to build a tree-based OnHME recognition system. Our recognition system has achieved the expression recognition rates of 44.12% and 41.76% on the CROHME 2014 and 2016 testing sets, respectively. They are inferior to the best recognition rates but better than the related approach of 29.91% and 27.03% by the previous tree-based OnHME recognition system [3]. The proposed system learns better relation classification with higher recognition rates, and there is no massive drop in the Recall rate of relation classification. We plan to improve the symbol-relation temporal classifier by sorting the strokes to avoid the stroke order variation problem in our future work.

**Acknowledgement.** This work is being partially supported by the Grant-in-Aid for Scientific Research (A) 19H01117 and that for Early-Career Scientists 21K17761.

## References

1. Álvaro, F., Sánchez, J.A., Benedí, J.M.: Recognition of on-line handwritten mathematical expressions using 2D stochastic context-free grammars and hidden Markov models. Pattern Recogn. Lett. **35**, 58–67 (2014)
2. Hu, L., Zanibbi, R.: MST-based visual parsing of online handwritten mathematical expressions. In: Proceedings of the 15th International Conference on Frontiers in Handwriting Recognition, pp. 337–342 (2016)
3. Zhang, T., Mouchère, H., Viard-Gaudin, C.: A tree-BLSTM-based recognition system for online handwritten mathematical expressions. Neural Comput. Appl. **32**(9), 4689–4708 (2018)
4. Zhang, J., Du, J., Dai, L.: Track, attend, and parse (TAP): an end-to-end framework for online handwritten mathematical expression recognition. IEEE Trans. Multimed. **21**, 221–233 (2019)
5. Mouchere, H., Viard-Gaudin, C., Zanibbi, R., Garain, U.: ICFHR 2014 competition on recognition of on-line handwritten mathematical expressions. In: Proceedings of the 14th International Conference on Frontiers in Handwriting Recognition, pp. 791–796 (2014)
6. Mouchère, H., Viard-Gaudin, C., Zanibbi, R., Garain, U.: ICFHR 2016 competition on recognition of online handwritten mathematical expressions. In: Proceedings of the 15th International Conference on Frontiers in Handwriting Recognition, pp. 607–612 (2016)
7. Zhang, T., Mouchere, H., Viard-Gaudin, C.: Online handwritten mathematical expressions recognition by merging multiple 1D interpretations. In: Proceedings of the 15th International Conference on Frontiers in Handwriting Recognition, pp. 187–192 (2016)
8. Blostein, D., Grbavec, A.: Recognition of mathematical notation. In: Wang, P.S.P., Bunke, H. (eds.) Handbook on Optical Character Recognition in Document Analysis, pp. 557–582 (1996)

9. Anderson, R.H.: Syntax-directed recognition of hand-printed two-dimensional mathematics. In: Interactive Systems for Experimental Applied Mathematics – 1967 Proceedings of the Association for Computing Machinery Inc. Symposium, pp. 436–459. ACM (1967)

10. Chang, S.K.: A method for the structural analysis of two-dimensional mathematical expressions. Inf. Sci. (Ny) **2**, 253–272 (1970)

11. Yamamoto, R., Sako, S., Nishimoto, T., Sagayama, S.: On-line recognition of handwritten mathematical expressions based on stroke-based stochastic context-free grammar. In: Proceedings of the 10th International Workshop on Frontiers in Handwriting Recognition, pp. 249–254 (2006)

12. MacLean, S., Labahn, G.: A new approach for recognizing handwritten mathematics using relational grammars and fuzzy sets. Int. J. Doc. Anal. Recognit. **16**, 139–163 (2013)

13. Zanibbi, R., Blostein, D., Cordy, J.R.: Recognizing mathematical expressions using tree transformation. IEEE Trans. Pattern Anal. Mach. Intell. **24**, 1455–1467 (2002)

14. Průša, D., Hlaváč, V.: Mathematical formulae recognition using 2D grammars. In: Proceedings of the 9th International Conference on Document Analysis and Recognition, pp. 849–853 (2007)

15. Alvaro, F., Sanchez, J.A., Benedi, J.M.: Offline features for classifying handwritten math symbols with recurrent neural networks. In: Proceedings of the 22nd International Conference on Pattern Recognition, pp. 2944–2949 (2014)

16. Dai Nguyen, H., Le, A.D., Nakagawa, M.: Deep neural networks for recognizing online handwritten mathematical symbols. In: Proceedings of the 3rd IAPR Asian Conference on Pattern Recognition, pp. 121–125 (2016)

17. Nguyen, C.T., Truong, T.N., Ung, H.Q., Nakagawa, M.: Online handwritten mathematical symbol segmentation and recognition with bidirectional context. In: Proceedings of the 17th International Conference on Frontiers in Handwriting Recognition, pp. 355–360 (2020)

18. Zhelezniakov, D., Zaytsev, V., Radyvonenko, O.: Acceleration of online recognition of 2D sequences using deep bidirectional LSTM and dynamic programming. In: Rojas, I., Joya, G., Catala, A. (eds.) IWANN 2019. LNCS, vol. 11507, pp. 438–449. Springer, Cham (2019). https://doi.org/10.1007/978-3-030-20518-8_37

# Subject Adaptive EEG-Based Visual Recognition

Pilhyeon Lee[1], Sunhee Hwang[4], Seogkyu Jeon[1], and Hyeran Byun[1,2,3(✉)]

[1] Department of Computer Science, Yonsei University, Seoul, South Korea
{lph1114,jone9312,hrbyun}@yonsei.ac.kr
[2] Graduate School of Artificial Intelligence, Yonsei University, Seoul, South Korea
[3] Graduate Program of Cognitive Science, Yonsei University, Seoul, South Korea
[4] AI Imaging Tech. Team, LG Uplus, Seoul, South Korea
sunheehwang@lguplus.co.kr

**Abstract.** This paper focuses on EEG-based visual recognition, aiming to predict the visual object class observed by a subject based on his/her EEG signals. One of the main challenges is the large variation between signals from different subjects. It limits recognition systems to work only for the subjects involved in model training, which is undesirable for real-world scenarios where new subjects are frequently added. This limitation can be alleviated by collecting a large amount of data for each new user, yet it is costly and sometimes infeasible. To make the task more practical, we introduce a novel problem setting, namely *subject adaptive EEG-based visual recognition*. In this setting, a bunch of pre-recorded data of existing users (source) is available, while only a little training data from a new user (target) are provided. At inference time, the model is evaluated solely on the signals from the target user. This setting is challenging, especially because training samples from source subjects may not be helpful when evaluating the model on the data from the target subject. To tackle the new problem, we design a simple yet effective baseline that minimizes the discrepancy between feature distributions from different subjects, which allows the model to extract subject-independent features. Consequently, our model can learn the common knowledge shared among subjects, thereby significantly improving the recognition performance for the target subject. In the experiments, we demonstrate the effectiveness of our method under various settings. Our code is available at here (https://github.com/DeepBCI/Deep-BCI).

**Keywords:** Brain-computer interface · Electroncephalography · Visual recognition · Subject adaptation · Deep learning

## 1 Introduction

Brain-computer interface (BCI) has been a long-standing research topic for decoding human brain activities, playing an important role in reading the human mind with various applications [21,32,40,44]. For instance, BCI systems enable a

© Springer Nature Switzerland AG 2022
C. Wallraven et al. (Eds.): ACPR 2021, LNCS 13189, pp. 322–334, 2022.
https://doi.org/10.1007/978-3-031-02444-3_24

**Training**                                    **Inference**

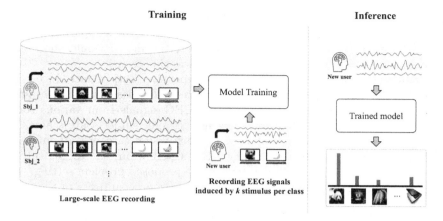

**Fig. 1.** An illustration of *Subject Adaptive EEG-based Visual Recognition*. During the large-scale EEG recording step, abundant sample images are observed by various subjects (source) and we collect their EEG signals. Afterwards, we record EEG signals from a new user (target) induced by only $k$ stimuli per class. We train the model on the EEG signals from the source and the target subject and expect the trained model to correctly predict the visual classes given unseen EEG signals from the target subject.

user to comfortably control machines without requiring any peripheral muscular activities [3,27]. In addition, BCI is especially helpful for people suffering from speech or movement disorders, allowing them to freely communicate and express their feelings by thinking [4,7,12,24]. It also can be utilized to identify abnormal states of brains, such as seizure state, sleep disorder, and dementia [33,34,41,43]. Recently, taking it to the next level, numerous works attempt to decode brain signals for figuring out what audiovisual stimulus is being taken by a person, providing deeper insight for analyzing human perception [1,13,26,37].

There are different ways to collect brain signals, *e.g.*, electroencephalography (EEG), magnetoencephalography (MEG), and functional magnetic resonance imaging (fMRI). Among them, EEG is considered the most favorable one to analyze human brain activities since it is non-invasive and promptly acquirable. With its numerous advantages, EEG-based models have been largely explored by researchers and developed for various research fields such as disorder detection [2, 29], drowsy detection [17,23], emotion recognition [14,15,30], *etc.*.

In this paper, we tackle the task of visual recognition based on EEG signals, whose goal is to classify visual stimuli taken by subjects. Recently, thanks to the effectiveness of deep neural networks (DNNs), existing models have shown impressive recognition performances [15,23,36,37]. However, they suffer from the large inter-subject variability of EEG signals, which greatly restricts their scalability. Suppose that a model faces a new user not included in the training set – note that this is a common scenario in the real world. Since the EEG signals from the user are likely to largely differ from those used for training, the model would fail to recognize the classes. Therefore, in order to retain the performance, it is inevitable to collect EEG signals for training from the new subject, which requires additional costs proportional to the number of the samples. If we have sufficient training samples for the new subject, the model would show great performance, but it is not the case for the real-world scenario.

To handle this limitation and bypass the expensive cost, we introduce a new practical problem setting, namely *subject adaptive EEG-based visual recognition*. In this setting, we have access to abundant EEG signals from various source subjects, whereas the signals from a new user (target subject) are scarce, *i.e.*, only a few samples ($k$-shot) are allowed for each visual category. At inference, the model should correctly classify the EEG signals from the target subject. Figure 1 provides a graphical illustration of the proposed problem setting.

Naturally, involving the copious samples from source subjects in the model training would bring about performance gains compared to the baseline using only signals from the target subject. However, as aforementioned, the signals obtained from the source and the target subjects are different from each other, and thus the performance improvements are limited. To maximize the benefits of pre-acquired data from source subjects, we here provide a simple yet effective baseline method. Our key idea is to allow the model to learn subject-agnostic representations for EEG-based visual recognition. Technically, together with the conventional classification loss, we design a loss to minimize maximum mean discrepancy (MMD) between feature distributions of EEG signals from different subjects. On the experiments under a variety of circumstances, our method shows consistent performance improvements over the vanilla method.

Our contributions can be summarized in three-fold.

- We introduce a new realistic problem setting, namely subject-adaptive EEG-based visual recognition. Its goal is to improve the recognition performance for the target subject whose training samples are limited.
- We design a simple baseline method for the proposed problem setting. It encourages the feature distributions between different subjects to be close so that the model learns subject-independent representations.
- Through the experiments on the public benchmark, we validate the effectiveness of our model. Specifically, in the extreme 1-shot setting, it achieves the performance gain of 6.4% upon the vanilla model.

## 2    Related Work

### 2.1    Brain Activity Underlying Visual Perception

Over recent decades, research on visual perception has actively investigated to reveal the correlation between brain activity and visual stimuli [9,31,35]. Brain responses induced by visual stimuli come from the occipital cortex that is a brain region for receiving and interpreting visual signals. In addition, visual information obtained by the occipital lobe is transmitted to nearby parietal and temporal lobes to perceive higher-level information. Based on this prior knowledge, researchers have tried to analyze brain activities induced by visual stimuli.

Eroğlu *et al.* [8] examine the effect of emotional images with different luminance levels on EEG signals. They also find that the brightness of visual stimuli can be represented by the activity power of the brain cortex. Stewart *et al.* [38] attempt to distinguish the presence of visual stimuli within a single trial in EEG recordings. It is revealed in their analyses that the individual components of EEG signals are spatially located in the visual cortex and are effective in classifying visual states. More recently, Spampinato *et al.* [37] tackle the problem of EEG-based visual recognition by learning a discriminative manifold of brain activities on diverse visual categories. Besides, they build a large-scale EEG dataset for training deep networks and demonstrate that human visual perception abilities can be transferred to deep networks. Kavasidis *et al.* [20] propose to reconstruct the observed images by decoding EEG signals. They find that EEG contains some patterns related to visual contents, which can be used to effectively generate images that are semantically coherent to the visual stimuli.

In line with these works, we build a visual recognition model to decode EEG signals induced by visual stimuli. In addition, we design and tackle a new practical problem setting where a limited amount of data is allowed for new users.

### 2.2 Subject-Independent EEG-Based Classification

Subject-dependent EEG-based classification models have widely been studied, achieving the noticeable performances [5,14,16,19,30]. However, EEG signal patterns greatly vary among individuals, building a subject-independent model remains an important research topic to be solved. Hwang *et al.* [15] train a subject-independent EEG-based emotion recognition model by utilizing an adversarial learning approach to make the model not able to predict the subject labels. Zhang *et al.* [42] propose a convolutional recurrent attention model to classify movement intentions by focusing on the most discriminative temporal periods from EEG signals. In [17], an EEG-based drowsy driving detection model is introduced, which is trained in an adversarial manner with gradient reversal layers in order to encourage feature distribution to be close between subjects.

Besides, to eliminate the expensive calibration process for new users, zero-training BCI techniques are introduced which does not require the re-training. Lee *et al.* [25] try to find the network parameters that generalize well on common features across subjects. Meanwhile, Grizou *et al.* [11] propose a zero-training BCI method that controls virtual and robotic agents in sequential tasks without requiring calibration steps for new users.

Different from the works above, we tackle the problem of EEG-based visual recognition. Moreover, we propose a new problem setting to reduce the cost of acquiring labeled data for new users, as well as introduce a strong baseline.

## 3   Dataset

Before introducing the proposed method, we first present the dataset details for experiments. We use the publicly available large-scale EEG dataset collected

**Table 1.** The list of object classes utilized for collecting EEG signals with ImageNet [6] class indices.

| n02106662 German shepherd | n02951358 Canoe | n03445777 Golf ball | n03888257 Parachute |
|---|---|---|---|
| n02124075 Egyptian cat | n02992529 Cellular telephone | n03452741 Grand piano | n03982430 Pool table |
| n02281787 Lycaenid | n03063599 Coffee mug | n03584829 Iron | n04044716 Radio telescope |
| n02389026 Sorrel | n03100240 Convertible | n03590841 Jack-o'-lantern | n04069434 Reflex camera |
| n02492035 Capuchin | n03180011 Desktop computer | n03709823 Mailbag | n04086273 Revolver |
| n02504458 African elephant | n03197337 Digital watch | n03773504 Missile | n04120489 Running shoe |
| n02510455 Giant panda | n03272010 Electric guitar | n03775071 Mitten | n07753592 Banana |
| n02607072 Anemone fish | n03272562 Electric locomotive | n03792782 Mountain bike | n07873807 Pizza |
| n02690373 Airliner | n03297495 Espresso maker | n03792972 Mountain tent | n11939491 Daisy |
| n02906734 Broom | n03376595 Folding chair | n03877472 Pajama | n13054560 Bolete |

by [37] that consists of 128-channel EEG sequences lasting for 440 ms from six different subjects (five male and one female). The EEG signals are filtered using a notch filter (49–51 Hz) and a band-pass filter (14–72 Hz) to include two frequency bands, *i.e.*, Beta and Gamma. The dataset contains 40 easily distinguishable object categories from ImageNet [6], which are listed in Table 1. The number of image samples looked at by subjects is 50 for each class, constituting a total of 2,000 samples. We use the official splits, keeping the ratio of training, validation, and test sets as 4:1:1. The dataset contains a total of 6 splits and we measure the mean and the standard deviation of performance of 6 runs in the experiments. We refer readers to the original paper [37] for further details about the dataset.

# 4    Method

In this section, we first define the proposed problem setting (Sect. 4.1). Then, we introduce a baseline method with subject-independent learning to tackle the problem. Its network architecture is illustrated in Sect. 4.2, followed by the detailed subject-independent learning scheme (Sect. 4.3). An overview of our method is depicted in Fig. 2.

## 4.1    Subject Adaptive EEG-Based Visual Recognition

We start by providing the formulation of the conventional EEG-based visual recognition task. Let $\mathcal{D}^s = \{(x_i^s, y_i^s)\}_{i=1}^{N^s}$ denote the dataset collected from the $s$-th subject. Here, $x_i^s \in \mathbb{R}^{D \times T}$ denotes the $i$-th EEG sample of subject $s$ with its channel dimension $D$ and the duration $T$, while $y_i^s \in \mathbb{R}^K$ is the corresponding ground-truth visual category observed by the subject and $N^s$ is the number of the samples for subject $s$. In general, the EEG samples are abundant for each subject, *i.e.*, $N^s \gg 0$. To train a deep model, multiple datasets from different subjects are assembled to build a single training set $\mathcal{D} = \{\mathcal{D}^1, \mathcal{D}^2, ..., \mathcal{D}^S\}$, where $S$ is the total number of subjects. At inference, given an EEG sample $x^{s'}$, the model should predict its category. Here, it is assumed that the input signal at test time is obtained by one of the subjects whose samples are used during the training stage, *i.e.*, $s' \in [1, S]$. However, this conventional setting is impractical especially for the case where EEG data from new subjects are scarce.

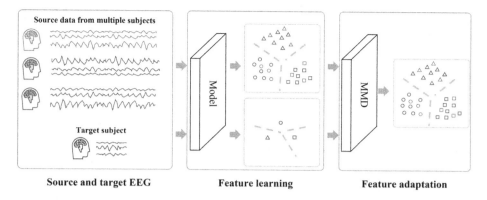

Source and target EEG            Feature learning            Feature adaptation

**Fig. 2.** An overview of the proposed method. Colors and shapes respectively represent subject identities and classes. During feature learning, we train the model to accurately predict the class from the EEG signals. To alleviate the feature discrepancy of source and target signals, we propose a feature adaptation stage which minimizes the maximum mean discrepancy. Consequently, both source and target features are projected on the same manifold, enabling accurate predictions on target signals during inference.

Instead, we propose a more realistic problem setting, named *Subject Adaptive EEG-based Visual Recognition*. In this setting, we aim to utilize the knowledge learned from abundant data of source subjects to classify signals from a target subject whose samples are rarely accessible. For that purpose, we first divide the training set into source and target sets, *i.e.*, $\mathcal{D}_{src}$ and $\mathcal{D}_{trg}$. We choose a subject and set it to be the target while the rest become the sources. For example, letting subject $S$ be the target, $\mathcal{D}_{src} = \{\mathcal{D}^1, \mathcal{D}^2, ..., \mathcal{D}^{S-1}\}$ and $\mathcal{D}_{trg} = \hat{\mathcal{D}}^S \subset \mathcal{D}^S$. Based on the sparsity constraint, the target dataset contains only a few examples, *i.e.*, $\hat{\mathcal{D}}^S = \{(x_j^S, y_j^S)\}_{j=1}^{\hat{N}^S}$, where $\hat{N}^S \ll N^S$. In practice, we make the target set have only $k$ samples with their labels per class ($k$-shot). Note that we here use the $S$-th subject as the target, but any subject can be the target without loss of generality. After trained on $\mathcal{D}_{src}$ and $\mathcal{D}_{trg}$, the model is supposed to predict the class of an unseen input signal $x^S$ which is obtained from the target subject $S$.

## 4.2 Network Architecture

In this section, we describe the architectural details of the proposed simple baseline method. Our network is composed of a sequence encoder $f$, an embedding layer $g$, and a classifier $h$. The sequence encoder $f(\cdot)$ is a single-layer gated recurrent unit (GRU), which takes as input an EEG sample and outputs the extracted feature representation $z = f(x) \in \mathbb{R}^{D_{seq}}$, where $\mathbb{R}^{D_{seq}}$ is the feature dimension. Although the encoder produces the hidden representation for every timestamp, we only use the last feature and discard the others since it encodes the information from all timestamps. Afterwards, the feature $z$ is embedded to the semantic manifold by the embedding layer $g(\cdot)$, *i.e.*, $w = g(z) \in \mathbb{R}^{D_{emb}}$, where $\mathbb{R}^{D_{emb}}$ is the dimension of embedded features. The embedding layer $g(\cdot)$ is composed of a fully-connected (FC) layer with an activation function. As the final step, we feed the embedded feature $w$ to the classifier $h(\cdot)$ consisting of a FC layer with the softmax activation, producing the class probability $p(\mathbf{y}|x;\theta) = h(w) \in \mathbb{R}^K$. Here, $\theta$ is a set of the trainable parameters in the overall network. To train our network for the classification task, we minimize the cross-entropy loss as follows.

$$\mathcal{L}_{\text{cls}} = \frac{-1}{|\mathcal{D}_{src}| + |\mathcal{D}_{trg}|} \sum_{(x_i, y_i) \in \mathcal{D}_{src} \cup \mathcal{D}_{trg}} y_i \log p(y_i|x_i; \theta), \tag{1}$$

where $|\mathcal{D}_{src}|$ and $|\mathcal{D}_{trg}|$ indicate the number of samples in source and target sets.

### 4.3   Subject-Independent Feature Learning

In spite of the learned class-discriminative knowledge, the model might not fully benefit from the data of source subjects due to the feature discrepancy from different subjects. To alleviate this issue and better exploit the source set, we propose a simple yet effective framework, where subject-independent features are learned by minimizing the divergence between feature distributions of source and target subjects. Concretely, for the divergence metric, we estimate the multi-kernel maximum mean discrepancy (MK-MMD) [28] between the feature distributions $Z^{s_i}$ and $Z^{s_j}$ from two subjects $s_i$ and $s_j$ as follows.

$$\text{MMD}(Z^{s_i}, Z^{s_j}) = \left\| \frac{1}{N^{s_i}} \sum_{n=1}^{N^{s_i}} \phi(z_n^{s_i}) - \frac{1}{N^{s_j}} \sum_{m=1}^{N^{s_j}} \phi(z_m^{s_j}) \right\|_F, \tag{2}$$

where $\phi(\cdot) : \mathcal{W} \to \mathcal{F}$ is the mapping function to the reproducing kernel Hilbert space, while $\|\cdot\|_F$ indicates the Frobenius norm. $z_n^{s_i}$ denotes the $n$-th feature from subject $s_i$ encoded by the sequence encoder $f$, whereas $N^{s_i}$ and $N^{s_j}$ are the total numbers of samples from the $s_i$-th and the $s_j$-th subjects in the training set, respectively. In practice, we use the samples in an input batch rather than the whole training set due to the memory constraint. We note that the embedded feature $w_n^i$ could also be utilized to compute the discrepancy, but we empirically find that it generally performs inferior to the case of using $z_n^i$ (Sect. 5.3).

Reducing the feature discrepancy between different subjects allows the model to learn subject-independent features. To make feature distributions from all subjects close, we compute and minimize the MK-MMD of all possible pairs of the subjects. Specifically, we design the discrepancy loss that is formulated as:

$$\mathcal{L}_{\text{disc}} = \frac{2}{S(S-1)} \sum_{s_i=1}^{S} \sum_{\forall s_j \neq s_i} \text{MMD}(Z^{s_i}, Z^{s_j}), \tag{3}$$

where $S$ is the number of the subjects in the training data including the target.

By minimizing the discrepancy loss, our model could learn subject-independent features and better utilize the source data to improve the recognition performance for the target subject. The overall training loss of our model is a weighted sum of the losses, which is computed as follows:

$$\mathcal{L}_{\text{total}} = \mathcal{L}_{\text{cls}} + \lambda \mathcal{L}_{\text{disc}}, \tag{4}$$

where $\lambda$ is the weighting factor, which is empirically set to 1.

**Table 2.** Quantitative comparison of methods by changing the target subject. For evaluation, we select one subject as a target and set the rest as sources, then compute the top-$k$ accuracy for the test set from the target subject. Note that only a single target sample for each class is included in training, *i.e.*, 1-shot setting. We measure the mean and the standard deviation of a total of 5 runs following the official splits.

| Validation set | | | | | | |
|---|---|---|---|---|---|---|
| Subject | Top-1 accuracy (%) | | | Top-3 accuracy (%) | | |
| | $k$-shot | Vanilla | Ours | $k$-shot | Vanilla | Ours |
| #0 | $13.5_{\pm2.1}$ | $29.3_{\pm1.9}$ | $\mathbf{35.7}_{\pm1.9}$ | $22.6_{\pm2.8}$ | $51.6_{\pm3.0}$ | $\mathbf{58.1}_{\pm2.9}$ |
| #1 | $12.6_{\pm2.1}$ | $21.8_{\pm2.3}$ | $\mathbf{29.0}_{\pm3.6}$ | $22.3_{\pm2.5}$ | $41.0_{\pm5.1}$ | $\mathbf{49.5}_{\pm3.5}$ |
| #2 | $17.0_{\pm1.6}$ | $25.3_{\pm0.9}$ | $\mathbf{30.8}_{\pm2.2}$ | $29.8_{\pm2.2}$ | $44.4_{\pm2.1}$ | $\mathbf{53.1}_{\pm2.6}$ |
| #3 | $27.8_{\pm1.7}$ | $28.8_{\pm2.2}$ | $\mathbf{31.9}_{\pm3.9}$ | $41.6_{\pm2.1}$ | $47.8_{\pm4.1}$ | $\mathbf{52.6}_{\pm3.7}$ |
| #4 | $16.3_{\pm2.8}$ | $25.9_{\pm1.9}$ | $\mathbf{36.2}_{\pm3.3}$ | $25.9_{\pm2.3}$ | $44.4_{\pm2.7}$ | $\mathbf{61.0}_{\pm4.7}$ |
| #5 | $9.2_{\pm1.4}$ | $20.7_{\pm2.9}$ | $\mathbf{25.8}_{\pm1.7}$ | $16.9_{\pm2.5}$ | $40.1_{\pm3.9}$ | $\mathbf{47.5}_{\pm3.4}$ |
| Test set | | | | | | |
| Subject | Top-1 accuracy (%) | | | Top-3 accuracy (%) | | |
| | $k$-shot | Vanilla | Ours | $k$-shot | Vanilla | Ours |
| #0 | $12.2_{\pm2.1}$ | $24.3_{\pm0.9}$ | $\mathbf{29.6}_{\pm4.9}$ | $20.4_{\pm2.5}$ | $48.3_{\pm2.3}$ | $\mathbf{56.8}_{\pm4.1}$ |
| #1 | $10.3_{\pm2.2}$ | $18.1_{\pm2.7}$ | $\mathbf{25.4}_{\pm2.4}$ | $20.8_{\pm2.1}$ | $39.0_{\pm1.9}$ | $\mathbf{49.0}_{\pm2.4}$ |
| #2 | $15.5_{\pm2.9}$ | $23.9_{\pm3.0}$ | $\mathbf{29.2}_{\pm3.7}$ | $29.9_{\pm3.4}$ | $44.3_{\pm4.3}$ | $\mathbf{54.5}_{\pm3.1}$ |
| #3 | $26.2_{\pm3.2}$ | $27.4_{\pm3.2}$ | $\mathbf{32.1}_{\pm4.3}$ | $41.7_{\pm3.9}$ | $47.9_{\pm4.2}$ | $\mathbf{53.6}_{\pm4.0}$ |
| #4 | $15.2_{\pm1.9}$ | $22.7_{\pm1.2}$ | $\mathbf{35.3}_{\pm3.6}$ | $24.5_{\pm2.0}$ | $44.8_{\pm3.5}$ | $\mathbf{60.7}_{\pm4.9}$ |
| #5 | $7.0_{\pm1.0}$ | $18.9_{\pm2.9}$ | $\mathbf{21.4}_{\pm2.6}$ | $15.3_{\pm1.8}$ | $38.4_{\pm4.1}$ | $\mathbf{45.0}_{\pm4.1}$ |

## 5    Experiments

### 5.1    Implementation Details

The input signals for our method contain a total of 128 channels ($D = 128$) with a recording unit of 1 $ms$, each of which lasts for 440 $ms$. Following [37], we only use the signals within the interval of 320–480 $ms$, resulting in the temporal dimension $T = 160$. As described in Sect. 4.2, our model consists of a single-layer gated recurrent unit (GRU) followed by two fully-connected layers respectively for embedding and classification. For all layers but the classifier, we set their hidden dimensions to the same one with input signals to preserve the dimensionality, *i.e.*, $D_{seq} = D_{emb} = 128$. For non-linearity, we put the Leaky ReLU activation after the embedding layer $g$ with $\alpha = 0.2$. To estimate multi-kernel maximum mean discrepancy, we use the radial basis function (RBF) kernel [39] as the mapping function. For effective learning, we make sure that all the subjects are included in a single batch. Technically, we randomly pick 200 examples from each source dataset and take all samples in the target dataset to configure a batch. Our model is trained in an end-to-end fashion from scratch without pre-training. For model training, we use the Adam [22] optimizer with a learning rate of $10^{-3}$.

## 5.2  Quantitative Results

To validate the effectiveness of our method, we compare it with two different competitors: $k$-shot baseline and the vanilla model. First, the $k$-shot method is trained exclusively on the target dataset. As the amount of target data is limited, the model is expected to poorly perform and it would serve as the baseline for investigating the benefit of source datasets. Next, the vanilla model is a variant of our method that discards the discrepancy loss. Its training depends solely on the classification loss without considering subjects, and thus it can demonstrate the effect of abundant data from other unrelated subjects.

**Table 3.** Quantitative comparison of methods by changing the number of target samples per class provided during training. The value of $k$ means that only $k$ samples of the target subject are used for training. We measure the mean and the standard deviation of a total of 5 runs for all subjects following the official splits.

| Validation set | | | | | | |
|---|---|---|---|---|---|---|
| $k$ | Top-1 accuracy (%) | | | Top-3 accuracy (%) | | |
| | $k$-shot | Vanilla | Ours | $k$-shot | Vanilla | Ours |
| 1 | $16.0_{\pm0.6}$ | $25.3_{\pm1.0}$ | $\mathbf{31.7}_{\pm1.5}$ | $26.5_{\pm0.9}$ | $44.9_{\pm1.3}$ | $\mathbf{53.6}_{\pm1.9}$ |
| 2 | $33.2_{\pm1.2}$ | $41.7_{\pm1.9}$ | $\mathbf{46.3}_{\pm1.8}$ | $50.1_{\pm1.0}$ | $65.2_{\pm2.0}$ | $\mathbf{70.2}_{\pm1.6}$ |
| 3 | $49.9_{\pm0.4}$ | $54.4_{\pm1.0}$ | $\mathbf{58.9}_{\pm0.7}$ | $68.5_{\pm0.7}$ | $77.6_{\pm0.7}$ | $\mathbf{80.8}_{\pm1.2}$ |
| 4 | $61.9_{\pm2.0}$ | $64.6_{\pm1.5}$ | $\mathbf{67.5}_{\pm1.2}$ | $79.6_{\pm1.7}$ | $85.1_{\pm1.1}$ | $\mathbf{86.8}_{\pm1.2}$ |
| 5 | $70.0_{\pm1.6}$ | $72.0_{\pm1.3}$ | $\mathbf{73.5}_{\pm1.1}$ | $85.6_{\pm1.7}$ | $89.6_{\pm0.9}$ | $\mathbf{90.0}_{\pm1.0}$ |
| Test set | | | | | | |
| $k$ | Top-1 accuracy (%) | | | Top-3 accuracy (%) | | |
| | $k$-shot | Vanilla | Ours | $k$-shot | Vanilla | Ours |
| 1 | $14.4_{\pm1.6}$ | $22.5_{\pm0.8}$ | $\mathbf{28.8}_{\pm1.2}$ | $25.4_{\pm1.8}$ | $43.8_{\pm1.6}$ | $\mathbf{53.3}_{\pm1.9}$ |
| 2 | $31.2_{\pm1.2}$ | $39.9_{\pm2.0}$ | $\mathbf{43.8}_{\pm1.4}$ | $49.3_{\pm2.0}$ | $65.1_{\pm2.1}$ | $\mathbf{69.5}_{\pm1.4}$ |
| 3 | $48.2_{\pm2.6}$ | $52.6_{\pm1.7}$ | $\mathbf{56.4}_{\pm1.7}$ | $67.2_{\pm1.7}$ | $77.0_{\pm1.5}$ | $\mathbf{80.4}_{\pm1.1}$ |
| 4 | $60.4_{\pm0.9}$ | $62.4_{\pm1.7}$ | $\mathbf{64.7}_{\pm1.6}$ | $79.4_{\pm1.1}$ | $84.3_{\pm0.9}$ | $\mathbf{85.9}_{\pm1.1}$ |
| 5 | $68.1_{\pm1.6}$ | $69.5_{\pm1.1}$ | $\mathbf{70.1}_{\pm1.0}$ | $85.6_{\pm1.3}$ | $89.0_{\pm0.5}$ | $\mathbf{89.2}_{\pm0.5}$ |

*Comparison in the 1-Shot Setting.* We first explore the most extreme scenario of our subject adaptive EEG-based visual classification, *i.e.*, the 1-shot setting. In this setting, only a single example for each visual category is provided for the target subject. The experimental results are summarized in Table 2. As expected, the $k$-shot baseline performs the worst due to the scarcity of training data. When including the data from source subjects, the vanilla setting improves the performance to an extent. However, we observe that the performance gain is limited due to the representation gap between subjects. On the other hand, our model manages to learn subject-independent information and brings a large performance boost upon the vanilla method without regard to the choice of the target subject. Specifically, the top-1 accuracy of subject #1 on the validation set is improved by 7.2% from the vanilla method. This clearly validates the effectiveness of our approach.

*Comparison with Varying k.* To investigate the performance in diverse scenarios, we evaluate the models with varying $k$ for the $k$-shot setting. Specifically, we change $k$ from 1 to 5 and the results are provided in Table 3. Obviously, increasing $k$ leads to performance improvements for all the methods. On the other hand, it can be also noticed that regardless of the choice of $k$, our method consistently outperforms the competitors with non-trivial margins, indicating the efficacy and the generality of our method. Meanwhile, the performance gaps between the methods get smaller as $k$ grows, since the benefit of source datasets vanishes as the volume of the target dataset increases. We note, however, that a large value of $k$ is impractical and sometimes even unreachable in the real-world setting.

**Table 4.** Ablation on the location of feature adaptation. We compare two variants that minimize discrepancy after the sequence encoder $f$ and the embedding layer $g$, respectively. We measure the mean and the standard deviation of a total of 5 runs for all subjects.

| $k$ | Top-1 accuracy (%) | | Top-3 accuracy (%) | |
|---|---|---|---|---|
| | After $f$ | After $g$ | After $f$ | After $g$ |
| 1 | $31.7_{\pm1.5}$ | $\mathbf{32.4}_{\pm0.7}$ | $53.6_{\pm1.9}$ | $\mathbf{54.8}_{\pm1.1}$ |
| 2 | $\mathbf{46.3}_{\pm1.8}$ | $46.0_{\pm1.8}$ | $\mathbf{70.2}_{\pm1.6}$ | $69.6_{\pm1.9}$ |
| 3 | $\mathbf{58.9}_{\pm0.7}$ | $58.3_{\pm1.3}$ | $\mathbf{80.8}_{\pm1.2}$ | $80.4_{\pm1.3}$ |
| 4 | $\mathbf{67.5}_{\pm1.2}$ | $65.6_{\pm1.5}$ | $\mathbf{86.8}_{\pm1.2}$ | $86.0_{\pm0.9}$ |
| 5 | $\mathbf{73.5}_{\pm1.1}$ | $72.3_{\pm1.3}$ | $\mathbf{90.0}_{\pm1.0}$ | $89.7_{\pm0.7}$ |

### 5.3   Analysis on the Location of Feature Adaptation

Our feature adaptation with the discrepancy loss (Eq. 3) can be adopted into any layer of the model. To analyze the effect of its location, we compare two variants that minimize the distance of feature distributions after the sequence encoder $f$ and the embedding layer $g$, respectively. The results are shown in Table 4, where the variant "after $f$" generally shows better performance compared to "after $g$" except for the case where $k$ is set to 1. We conjecture that this is because it is incapable for a single GRU encoder (*i.e.*, $f$) to align feature distributions from different subjects well when the amount of the target dataset is too small. However, with a sufficiently large $k$, the variant "after $f$" consistently performs better with obvious margins. Based on these results, we compute the MK-MMD on the features after the sequential encoder $f$ by default.

## 6   Concluding Remarks

In this paper, we introduce a new setting for EEG-based visual recognition, namely *subject adaptive EEG-based visual recognition*, where plentiful data from source subjects and sparse samples from a target subject are provided for training. This setting is cost-effective and practical in that it is often infeasible to acquire sufficient samples for a new user in the real-world scenario. Moreover, to better exploit the abundant source data, we introduce a strong baseline that minimizes the feature discrepancy between different subjects. In the experiments with various settings, we clearly verify the effectiveness of our method compared to the vanilla model. We hope this work would trigger further research under realistic scenarios with data scarcity, such as subject generalization [10,18].

**Acknowledgment.** This work was supported by Institute for Information & Communications Technology Planning & Evaluation (IITP) grant funded by the Korea government (MSIT) (No. 2017-0-00451: Development of BCI based Brain and Cognitive Computing Technology for Recognizing Users Intentions using Deep Learning, No. 2020-0-01361: Artificial Intelligence Graduate School Program (YONSEI UNIVERSITY)).

# References

1. An, W.W., et al.: Decoding music attention from "EEG headphones": a user-friendly auditory brain-computer interface. In: ICASSP 2021–2021 IEEE International Conference on Acoustics, Speech and Signal Processing (ICASSP), pp. 985–989. IEEE (2021)
2. Anuragi, A., Sisodia, D.S.: Alcohol use disorder detection using EEG signal features and flexible analytical wavelet transform. Biomed. Signal Process. Control **52**, 384–393 (2019)
3. Bos, D.O., Reuderink, B.: Brainbasher: a BCI game. In: Extended Abstracts of the International Conference on Fun and Games, pp. 36–39. Eindhoven University of Technology Eindhoven, The Netherlands (2008)
4. Chambayil, B., Singla, R., Jha, R.: Virtual keyboard BCI using eye blinks in EEG. In: 2010 IEEE 6th International Conference on Wireless and Mobile Computing, Networking and Communications, pp. 466–470. IEEE (2010)
5. Dai, M., Zheng, D., Na, R., Wang, S., Zhang, S.: EEG classification of motor imagery using a novel deep learning framework. Sensors **19**(3), 551 (2019)
6. Deng, J., Dong, W., Socher, R., Li, L.J., Li, K., Fei-Fei, L.: ImageNet: a large-scale hierarchical image database. In: 2009 IEEE Conference on Computer Vision and Pattern Recognition, pp. 248–255 (2009). https://doi.org/10.1109/CVPR.2009.5206848
7. Eidel, M., Kübler, A.: Wheelchair control in a virtual environment by healthy participants using a p300-BCI based on tactile stimulation: training effects and usability. Front. Hum. Neurosci. **14** (2020)
8. Eroğlu, K., Kayıkçıoğlu, T., Osman, O.: Effect of brightness of visual stimuli on EEG signals. Behav. Brain Res. **382**, 112486 (2020)
9. Foxe, J.J., Simpson, G.V., Ahlfors, S.P.: Parieto-occipital 10 hz activity reflects anticipatory state of visual attention mechanisms. NeuroReport **9**(17), 3929–3933 (1998)
10. Ghifary, M., Kleijn, W.B., Zhang, M., Balduzzi, D.: Domain generalization for object recognition with multi-task autoencoders. In: Proceedings of the IEEE International Conference on Computer Vision, pp. 2551–2559 (2015)

11. Grizou, J., Iturrate, I., Montesano, L., Oudeyer, P.Y., Lopes, M.: Calibration-free BCI based control. In: Proceedings of the AAAI Conference on Artificial Intelligence, vol. 28 (2014)
12. Huang, H., et al.: An EEG-based brain computer interface for emotion recognition and its application in patients with disorder of consciousness. IEEE Trans. Affect. Comput. **12**(4), 832–842 (2019)
13. Hwang, S., Hong, K., Son, G., Byun, H.: EZSL-GAN: EEG-based zero-shot learning approach using a generative adversarial network. In: 2019 7th International Winter Conference on Brain-Computer Interface, BCI, pp. 1–4 (2019). https://doi.org/10.1109/IWW-BCI.2019.8737322
14. Hwang, S., Hong, K., Son, G., Byun, H.: Learning CNN features from de features for EEG-based emotion recognition. Pattern Anal. Appl. **23**(3), 1323–1335 (2020)
15. Hwang, S., Ki, M., Hong, K., Byun, H.: Subject-independent EEG-based emotion recognition using adversarial learning. In: 2020 8th International Winter Conference on Brain-Computer Interface, BCI, pp. 1–4 (2020). https://doi.org/10.1109/BCI48061.2020.9061624
16. Hwang, S., Lee, P., Park, S., Byun, H.: Learning subject-independent representation for EEG-based drowsy driving detection. In: 2021 9th International Winter Conference on Brain-Computer Interface, BCI, pp. 1–3 (2021). https://doi.org/10.1109/BCI51272.2021.9385364
17. Hwang, S., Park, S., Kim, D., Lee, J., Byun, H.: Mitigating inter-subject brain signal variability for EEG-based driver fatigue state classification. In: ICASSP 2021–2021 IEEE International Conference on Acoustics, Speech and Signal Processing, ICASSP, pp. 990–994 (2021). https://doi.org/10.1109/ICASSP39728.2021.9414613
18. Jeon, S., Hong, K., Lee, P., Lee, J., Byun, H.: Feature stylization and domain-aware contrastive learning for domain generalization. In: Proceedings of the 29th ACM International Conference on Multimedia (2021)
19. Jin, Z., Zhou, G., Gao, D., Zhang, Y.: EEG classification using sparse bayesian extreme learning machine for brain-computer interface. Neural Comput. Appl. **32**(11), 6601–6609 (2020)
20. Kavasidis, I., Palazzo, S., Spampinato, C., Giordano, D., Shah, M.: Brain2Image: converting brain signals into images. In: Proceedings of the 25th ACM International Conference on Multimedia, pp. 1809–1817 (2017)
21. Khurana, V., et al.: A survey on neuromarketing using EEG signals. IEEE Trans. Cogn. Dev. Syst. (2021). https://doi.org/10.1109/TCDS.2021.3065200
22. Kingma, D.P., Ba, J.: Adam: a method for stochastic optimization. In: International Conference on Learning Representations (2015)
23. Ko, W., Oh, K., Jeon, E., Suk, H.I.: VIGNet: a deep convolutional neural network for EEG-based driver vigilance estimation. In: 2020 8th International Winter Conference on Brain-Computer Interface, BCI, pp. 1–3. IEEE (2020)
24. Kumar, P., Saini, R., Roy, P.P., Sahu, P.K., Dogra, D.P.: Envisioned speech recognition using EEG sensors. Pers. Ubiquit. Comput. **22**(1), 185–199 (2018)
25. Lee, J., Won, K., Kwon, M., Jun, S.C., Ahn, M.: CNN with large data achieves true zero-training in online P300 brain-computer interface. IEEE Access **8**, 74385–74400 (2020). https://doi.org/10.1109/ACCESS.2020.2988057
26. Lee, S.H., Lee, M., Lee, S.W.: Neural decoding of imagined speech and visual imagery as intuitive paradigms for BCI communication. IEEE Trans. Neural Syst. Rehabil. Eng. **28**(12), 2647–2659 (2020)
27. Li, M., et al.: The MindGomoku: an online P300 BCI game based on bayesian deep learning. Sensors **21**(5), 1613 (2021)

28. Long, M., Cao, Y., Wang, J., Jordan, M.I.: Learning transferable features with deep adaptation networks. In: Proceedings of the 32nd International Conference on International Conference on Machine Learning, pp. 97–105 (2015)
29. Mahato, S., Paul, S.: Detection of major depressive disorder using linear and non-linear features from EEG signals. Microsyst. Technol. **25**(3), 1065–1076 (2019)
30. Placidi, G., Di Giamberardino, P., Petracca, A., Spezialetti, M., Iacoviello, D.: Classification of emotional signals from the deap dataset. In: International Congress on Neurotechnology, Electronics and Informatics, vol. 2, pp. 15–21. SCITEPRESS (2016)
31. Qin, W., Yu, C.: Neural pathways conveying novisual information to the visual cortex. Neural Plast. **2013**, 864920 (2013)
32. Ramsey, N.F., Van De Heuvel, M.P., Kho, K.H., Leijten, F.S.: Towards human BCI applications based on cognitive brain systems: an investigation of neural signals recorded from the dorsolateral prefrontal cortex. IEEE Trans. Neural Syst. Rehabil. Eng. **14**(2), 214–217 (2006)
33. Runnova, A., Selskii, A., Kiselev, A., Shamionov, R., Parsamyan, R., Zhuravlev, M.: Changes in EEG alpha activity during attention control in patients: association with sleep disorders. J. Personalized Med. **11**(7), 601 (2021)
34. Rutkowski, T.M., Koculak, M., Abe, M.S., Otake-Matsuura, M.: Brain correlates of task-load and dementia elucidation with tensor machine learning using oddball BCI paradigm. In: ICASSP 2019–2019 IEEE International Conference on Acoustics, Speech and Signal Processing, ICASSP, pp. 8578–8582. IEEE (2019)
35. Salenius, S., Kajola, M., Thompson, W., Kosslyn, S., Hari, R.: Reactivity of magnetic parieto-occipital alpha rhythm during visual imagery. Electroencephalogr. Clin. Neurophysiol. **95**(6), 453–462 (1995)
36. Schirrmeister, R.T., et al.: Deep learning with convolutional neural networks for EEG decoding and visualization. Hum. Brain Mapp. **38**(11), 5391–5420 (2017)
37. Spampinato, C., Palazzo, S., Kavasidis, I., Giordano, D., Souly, N., Shah, M.: Deep learning human mind for automated visual classification. In: Proceedings of the IEEE Conference on Computer Vision and Pattern Recognition, pp. 6809–6817 (2017)
38. Stewart, A.X., Nuthmann, A., Sanguinetti, G.: Single-trial classification of EEG in a visual object task using ICA and machine learning. J. Neurosci. Methods **228**, 1–14 (2014)
39. Vert, J.P., Tsuda, K., Schölkopf, B.: A primer on kernel methods. Kernel Methods Comput. Biol. **47**, 35–70 (2004)
40. Wolpaw, J.R., et al.: Brain-computer interface technology: a review of the first international meeting. IEEE Trans. Rehabil. Eng. **8**(2), 164–173 (2000)
41. Yuan, Y., Xun, G., Jia, K., Zhang, A.: A multi-view deep learning framework for EEG seizure detection. IEEE J. Biomed. Health Inform. **23**(1), 83–94 (2018)
42. Zhang, D., Yao, L., Chen, K., Monaghan, J.: A convolutional recurrent attention model for subject-independent EEG signal analysis. IEEE Signal Process. Lett. **26**(5), 715–719 (2019). https://doi.org/10.1109/LSP.2019.2906824
43. Zhou, M., et al.: Epileptic seizure detection based on EEG signals and CNN. Front. Neuroinform. **12**, 95 (2018)
44. Zickler, C., et al.: BCI applications for people with disabilities: defining user needs and user requirements. In: Assistive Technology from Adapted Equipment to Inclusive Environments, AAATE, vol. 25, pp. 185–189 (2009)

# Spectro-Spatio-Temporal EEG Representation Learning for Imagined Speech Recognition

Wonjun Ko[1], Eunjin Jeon[1], and Heung-Il Suk[1,2(✉)]

[1] Department of Brain and Cognitive Engineering, Korea University,
Seoul 02841, Republic of Korea
{wjko,eunjinjeon,hisuk}@korea.ac.kr
[2] Department of Artificial Intelligence, Korea University,
Seoul 02841, Republic of Korea

**Abstract.** In brain–computer interfaces, imagined speech is one of the most promising paradigms due to its intuitiveness and direct communication. However, it is challenging to decode an imagined speech EEG, because of its complicated underlying cognitive processes, resulting in complex spectro-spatio-temporal patterns. In this work, we propose a novel convolutional neural network structure for representing such complex patterns and identifying an intended imagined speech. The proposed network exploits two feature extraction flows for learning richer class-discriminative information. Specifically, our proposed network is composed of a spatial filtering path and a temporal structure learning path running in parallel, then integrates their output features for decision-making. We demonstrated the validity of our proposed method on a publicly available dataset by achieving state-of-the-art performance. Furthermore, we analyzed our network to show that our method learns neurophysiologically plausible patterns.

**Keywords:** Brain–computer interface · Convolutional neural network · Electroencephalogram · Imagined speech

## 1 Introduction

Brain–computer interface (BCI) is in the limelight among recent promising technologies as it provides a communication pathway between a user and an external device without normal peripheral pathways [18]. Among various monitoring methods, electroencephalogram (EEG) has gained widespread acceptances in recent BCIs thanks to its portability and non-invasiveness [18,26]. In regard

This work was supported by Institute for Information & Communications Technology Promotion (IITP) grant funded by the Korea government under Grant 2017-0-00451 (Development of BCI based Brain and Cognitive Computing Technology for Recognizing User's Intentions using Deep Learning) and Grant 2019-0-00079 (Department of Artificial Intelligence, Korea University).

C. Wallraven et al. (Eds.): ACPR 2021, LNCS 13189, pp. 335–346, 2022.
https://doi.org/10.1007/978-3-031-02444-3_25

to inducing brain activities, there have been various strategies including event-related and spontaneous (or self-paced) paradigms [1,27]. In this work, we focus on the imagined speech, getting the popularity recently, which can be defined as an internal pronunciation of a word/sentence without any articulatory movement. Hence, with an imagined speech-based BCI, a user only has to simply think, for example, 'Yes' or 'No,' to express his/her intention.

Since the verbal communication is one of the most generally used and fastest communication ways, imagined speech has a great potential to build intuitive BCIs. Notably, imagined speech involves very complex internal cognitive processes [15], thus it is challenging to engineer class-discriminative feature representation from EEG signals. In this regard, recent approaches have adopted linear [2,15,22] or deep and hierarchical [5,11] machine learning models, thanks to their caliber for EEG representation learning.

In conventional machine learning methods, DaSalla et al. [6] used a *common spatial pattern* (CSP) method for feature extraction, which is one of the most widely used spatial filtering, and applied *support vector machine* (SVM). Matsumoto and Hori [20] extracted features of low-pass filtered imagined speech EEG and classified the features using SVM and *relevance vector machine* (RVM). Brigham and Kumar [3] constructed a univariate *autoregressive* (AR) model to characterize imagined speech EEG. Deng et al. [7] tried to classify imagined syllables by analyzing Hilbert spectrum to extract features. Then, the features were classified by *linear discriminant analysis* (LDA). Bakhshali et al. [2] used the Riemannian distance of *correntropy spectral density* (R-CSD) and a $k$-nearest neighbors ($k$-NN) classifier.

Cooney et al. [5] conducted both five vowels and six words imagined speech classification tasks using many machine learning methods. *Relative wavelet energy* (RWE) features with SVM, RWE with *random forest* (RF), and filter bank CSP (FBCSP) features with LDA showed plausible performance. Additionally, hyperparameters of the machine learning methods used in their work were automatically searched. Furthermore, Cooney et al. also explored calibers of deep neural network methods for imagined speech EEG representation. In addition, the authors applied a hyperparmeter optimization technique in the intra-subject and the subject-specific manner. Specifically, *Shallow ConvNet* [24], *Deep ConvNet* [24], and *EEGNet* [14] were used in their classification experiments.

Among various machine learning and deep learning methods that demonstrated the ability for EEG analysis, convolutional neural networks (CNNs) have been one of the most powerful methods [11,12,14,24] aiming at discovering representations inherent in EEGs. In the viewpoint of EEG analysis, three types of convolutional layers are commonly used [11,14], namely, a spectral convolution, a spatial convolution, and a temporal convolution, which represent an input EEG in regards to frequency, topological relations among electrodes, and temporal dynamics, respectively.

In combination of the three types convolutional operations, many existing CNN architectures can be categorized into two groups according to the order of convolution types: (1) spatial-temporal learning [5,14,24] and (2) temporal/spectral-spatial learning [11,13,23]. Note that those two approaches

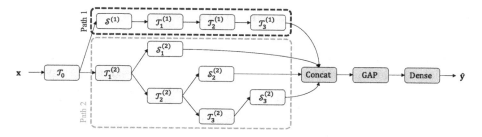

**Fig. 1.** Graphical overview of the proposed network. In the proposed network, an input EEG **x** is fed into a spectral convolution $\mathcal{T}_0$. Then, spatial filtering information is learned through the Path 1 in the red-dotted box and multi-scale temporal structure information is learned through the Path 2 in the green-dotted box. Finally, the feature representations from each path are concatenated (Concat), global average pooled (GAP), and fed into the densely connected layer (Dense) to identify the user's intention $\hat{\mathbf{y}}$. Note that $\mathcal{T}_i^j$ and $\mathcal{S}_i^{(j)}$, $i \in \{1, ..., k\}$ (in this figure, $k = 3$), $j \in \{1, 2\}$ denote, respectively, the $i^{\text{th}}$ temporal and spatial convolution of the path $j$. (Color figure online)

have their own characteristics in learning representations, while limiting their power of discovering representations constrained by the respective network architectures. It is desirable to jointly utilize those network architectures to learn enriched representations by obtaining complementary information, thereby enhancing a model's decoding power. To this end, in this work, we propose a novel CNN architecture to enjoy both aforementioned pathways. Precisely, we combine those two mainstream architectures and effectively use multi-scale intermediate features.

## 2 Methods

In this section, we propose a novel CNN architecture in Fig. 1, which is designed to represent imagined speech EEG by learning spectro-spatio-temporal representation.

### 2.1 Three Convolution Types for EEG Analysis

Let us assume that there is a given EEG trial $\mathbf{x} \in \mathbb{R}^{C \times T}$, where $C$ and $T$ denote the number of electrode channels and timepoints, respectively. A CNN is commonly composed of a spatial convolution $\mathcal{S}(\cdot)$ with $C \times 1$ kernel size and temporal convolutions $\mathcal{T}_i(\cdot)$ with $1 \times t_i$, $\forall t_i \leq T$ kernel, where $i$ denotes an index of the convolution layer. Then, the spatial filtering path [24] can be generalized as $\mathcal{T}_k \circ \cdots \circ \mathcal{T}_1 \circ \mathcal{S}(\cdot)$, whereas the temporal structure learning path [13] is described as $\mathcal{S} \circ \mathcal{T}_k \circ \cdots \circ \mathcal{T}_1(\cdot)$, where $k$ is the number of temporal convolutions. Furthermore, a spectral convolution, $\mathcal{T}_0(\cdot)$ with a $1 \times F_s/2$ kernel, where $F_s$ denotes a sampling rate of the input EEG [11,14], is preceding to both paths. This architecture is directly comparable to the existing work of [11] $(\mathcal{S} \circ \mathcal{T}_k \circ \cdots \circ \mathcal{T}_1 \circ \mathcal{T}_0(\cdot))$ and [14] $(\mathcal{T}_k \circ \cdots \circ \mathcal{T}_1 \circ \mathcal{S} \circ \mathcal{T}_0(\cdot))$.

## 2.2  Spectro-Spatio-Temporal EEG Representation

Many successful CNNs [11,14,24] for EEG representation consist of three types of convolutions, and can be categorized into two groups according to the order of a spatial convolution and temporal convolutions. Our proposed network system-ically exploits both architectures to learn spatial filtering information [24] and temporal structure information [11] from an imagined speech EEG. Besides, the proposed CNN also exploits a shared spectral convolution preceding each path, as depicted in Fig. 1.

In our proposed architecture, the topological dynamics over the whole brain are characterized and represented through the upper stream (Path 1), while the channel-wise temporal dynamics are represented in multiple scales via skip con-nections through the lower stream (Path 2). Then, the output features from dif-ferent streams with more diverse and complementary information are integrated via a series of operations, i.e., concatenation, *global average pooling* (GAP) [16], before being fed into the dense classifier. The detailed explanation on these pro-cesses is given below.

**Spectral Convolution.** Note that a spectral convolution $\mathcal{T}_0$ first convolves the $l^{\text{th}}$ input EEG trial $\mathbf{x}_l \in \mathbb{R}^{C \times T}$. To be specific, the spectral convolution temporally embeds in a channel-wise manner with a kernel of $1 \times (F_s/2)$ in size to expand the number of feature maps, i.e., depths. Thus, the activated feature has the form of $\mathcal{T}_0(\mathbf{x}_l) \in \mathbb{R}^{C \times T' \times D_{\mathcal{T}_0}}$, where $T' = T - (F_s/2) + 1$ and $D_{\mathcal{A}}$ denotes the depth dimension of a convolution layer $\mathcal{A}$. For the kernel size of $1 \times (F_s/2)$, since the kernel can only learn wave properties that have two or more periods within its size, thus the spectral convolution hereby captures spectral information 2 Hz or above [11,14]. Besides, $\mathcal{T}_0(\mathbf{x}_l)$ has the expanded dimension $D_{\mathcal{T}_0}$, hence it is expected that each feature slice of $\mathcal{T}_0(\mathbf{x}_l)$ that has the size of $C \times T'$ learns different kinds of information in frequency.

**Path 1.** After the spectral convolution, our proposed network extracts class-discriminative features in two different streams. First, the Path 1 embeds the input features using a spatial convolution $\mathcal{S}^{(1)}$. Because the spatial convolu-tion uses $C \times 1$ kernel, the extracted feature has the form of $\mathcal{S}^{(1)} \circ \mathcal{T}_0(\mathbf{x}_l) \in \mathbb{R}^{1 \times T' \times D_{\mathcal{S}^{(1)}}}$. Since the kernel size is constrained to be identical with the num-ber of EEG acquisition channels, similar to many successful CNN-based EEG representation methods [11,14,24], this convolution extracts spatial or topolog-ical information from the raw EEG channel distributions. In other words, the spatial convolution learns functional relations among channels over the whole brain in an imagined speech EEG, thus interpretable from a neurophysiological point of view.

After the spatial embedding, a sequence of temporal convolutions $\mathcal{T}_k \circ \cdots \circ \mathcal{T}_1(\cdot)$ are followed. It is worth noting that we exploit a separable convolution [4] for each temporal convolution, same as the previous work [14]. The main benefits of using the separable convolutions are an appreciable reduction of the number of trainable parameters. Moreover, it efficiently and explicitly decouples the relationship between the temporal and the depth dimensions during training, because it learns kernels separately from each feature map. It means that the separable convolution allows the system to learn temporal kernels without any feature map coupling (by a depthwise convolution [4]) and also enables an enhanced complexity of the feature maps (using a pointwise convolution). Further, each temporal convolution in the proposed network uses the zero padding to keep the feature size to be $T'$, thereby being able to exploit features learned from Path 1 and Path 2. The stacked temporal convolutions represent different time-scales information in EEG [11]. Therefore, the temporal convolutions can summarize the EEG trial $\mathbf{x}_l$ of $T$-temporal dimension to a $T'$-temporal dimensional features. The finally learned feature of the $l^{\text{th}}$ EEG trial from the spatial filtering path $\mathbf{f}_l^{(1)}$ can be defined as follows:

$$\mathbf{f}_l^{(1)} = \mathcal{T}_k^{(1)} \circ \cdots \mathcal{T}_1^{(1)} \circ \mathcal{S}^{(1)} \circ \mathcal{T}_0^{(1)}(\mathbf{x}_l) \in \mathbb{R}^{1 \times T' \times D_{\mathcal{T}_k^{(1)}}}. \tag{1}$$

**Path 2.** While Path 1 learns the important information of spatial/topological dynamics over the whole brain for the imagined speech EEG representation, Path 2 is dedicated to learn the temporal dynamics of individual channels in a multi-scale manner and combine such information over the brain topology. Note that both streams share the spectrally convolved feature $\mathcal{T}_0(\mathbf{x}_l)$. Because a separable convolution learns its kernel individually from its depths [4], hierarchical temporal convolutions, which are consisted of separable convolutions after the spectral convolution, represent independent information in time. It means that the initially divided frequency bands after the spectral convolution in $\mathcal{T}_0$ can keep their unmixedness from each other through a series of temporal convolutions $\mathcal{T}_k^{(2)} \circ \cdots \circ \mathcal{T}_1^{(2)}(\cdot)$. Thus, the temporal convolutions in this path also effectively encapsulates temporal information similar to the spatial filtering structure, but independently among the electrodes.

After the temporal structure learning, a spatial convolution is also applied to the learned feature to represent spatial distribution. Hence a feature learned from this path can be formulated as:

$$\mathbf{f}_l^{(2)} = \mathcal{S}^{(2)} \circ \mathcal{T}_k^{(2)} \circ \cdots \circ \mathcal{T}_1^{(2)} \circ \mathcal{T}_0^{(2)}(\mathbf{x}_l) \in \mathbb{R}^{1 \times T' \times D_{\mathcal{T}_k^{(2)}}}. \tag{2}$$

Meanwhile, we focus on designing our network to capture multi-scale information similar to the recent work in [11] because the multi-scale representation is one of the most important characteristics for EEG analysis. In this temporal structure learning path, we add supplemental spatial convolutions to extract intermediate features after each temporal convolution layer. Therefore, another form of features from this pathway can be subdivided as follows:

$$\mathbf{f}_{l,i}^{(2)} = \mathcal{S}_i^{(2)} \circ \mathcal{T}_i^{(2)} \circ \cdots \circ \mathcal{T}_1 \circ \mathcal{T}_0(\mathbf{x}_l) \in \mathbb{R}^{1 \times T' \times D_{\mathcal{S}_i^{(2)}}}, \tag{3}$$

where $\mathbf{f}_{l,i}^{(2)}$, $i = \{1, ..., k\}$, is the $i^{\text{th}}$ intermediate representation of the temporal features. In this pathway, we extract features of different levels of temporal information. It is noteworthy that unlike many stacked CNNs for representing EEG [14,24], our proposed network exploits intermediate activations and creates the power to represent multi-range of temporal information in an imagined speech EEG.

**Classifier.** For the classification, because our proposed network extracts many types of features, i.e., features of topological dynamics over the whole brain and multi-scale temporal dynamics of individual electrodes along with their spatial relations, we integrate such diverse information by concatenating along the depth dimension as follows:

$$\mathbf{f}^{\text{Concat}} = \text{Concat}\left(\mathbf{f}_l^{(1)}, \mathbf{f}_{l,1}^{(2)}, ..., \mathbf{f}_{l,k}^{(2)}\right) \in \mathbb{R}^{1 \times T' \times \left(D_{\mathcal{T}_k^{(1)}} + \sum_i^k D_{\mathcal{S}_i^{(2)}}\right)}, \tag{4}$$

where Concat denotes a concatenation operation.

Assuming $N_o$ possible user's intentions or interest, a single densely connected layer can be constructed with the number of $T' \times \left(D_{\mathcal{T}_k^{(1)}} + \sum_i^k D_{\mathcal{S}_i^{(2)}}\right) \times N_o$ parameters (note that we disregard bias terms for simplicity). However, as, $T'$ is hundreds in size, we introduce GAP [16] to reduce the dimension. Note that it also allows to get the insights of which sources of representations are informative for making a decision at the end. It averages all elements along the predefined axis, thus there is no requirement for setting window size or stride. Our proposed network applies GAP $\mathcal{G}(\cdot)$ to the concatenated feature $\mathbf{f}^{\text{Concat}}$ along the temporal dimension as follows:

$$\mathcal{G}_2\left(\mathbf{f}^{\text{Concat}}\right) \in \mathbb{R}^{1 \times 1 \times \left(D_{\mathcal{T}_k^{(1)}} + \sum_i^k D_{\mathcal{S}_i^{(2)}}\right)}, \tag{5}$$

where $\mathcal{G}_s$ denotes the GAP along the $i^{\text{th}}$ axis. More formally, $\mathcal{G}_s$ of an input $\mathbf{v}$ is defined as:

$$\mathcal{G}_s(\mathbf{v}) = \frac{1}{\text{Dim}_{\mathbf{e}_s}(\mathbf{v})} \sum_{\mathbf{e}_s} \mathbf{v}_{\mathbf{e}_s}, \tag{6}$$

where $\text{Dim}_{\mathbf{e}_s}$ and $\sum_{\mathbf{e}_s}$ respectively denote the dimension of the $s^{\text{th}}$ axis and the summation along the $s^{\text{th}}$ axis.

Finally, a single densely connected layer with a softmax activation function infers the user's intention $\hat{\mathbf{y}}$:

$$\hat{\mathbf{y}} = \text{softmax}\left(\mathbf{W}_o^\top \times \mathcal{G}\left(\mathbf{f}^{\text{Concat}}\right) + \mathbf{b}_o\right) \in \{1, 0\}^{N_o}, \tag{7}$$

where $\mathbf{W}_o \in \mathbb{R}^{\left(D_{\mathcal{T}_k^{(1)}} + \sum_i^k D_{\mathcal{S}_i^{(2)}}\right) \times N_o}$ and $\mathbf{b}_o \in \mathbb{R}^{N_o}$ denote respectively a weight matrix and a bias of the classifier network.

## 3    Experiments

In this section, we describe a dataset, experimental settings, and baseline settings used for our experiments. In addition, we also present the experimental results of the proposed network as well as the competing methods considered in this work.

### 3.1   Dataset and Preprocessing

In this study, we used a publicly available imagined speech EEG dataset of BCI Competition V-3 dataset[1] to demonstrate the validity of the proposed network. The dataset consists of five different imagination of speech: 'Hello,' 'Help me,' 'Stop,' 'Thank you,' and 'Yes,' that are acquired from 15 subjects. All EEG signals were recorded from 64 electrode channels according to the standard 10–20 system and sampled at 256 Hz, i.e., $F_s = 256$. For each subject, 70 trial-label pairs per class are released, thus we used 350 trials for each subject.

For the preprocessing, we first applied a notch filter to remove the 60 Hz line noise contamination and the 120 Hz noise harmonic. We then performed a band-pass filtering at 0.5–125 Hz range, a large Laplacian filtering, a baseline correction, and rejected the first and the last signals of 0.5 s length from each trial. Finally, we applied a Gaussian normalization.

### 3.2   Experimental Settings

In our classification experiments, we conducted a five-fold cross-validation for each subject. Further, for each fold, we used 10% of the training samples as a validation set to tune the hyperparameters. We kept the class balance for every dataset division. Moreover, we compared the proposed method with two conventional machine learning methods and three deep neural networks.

- CSP + SVM: We built a CSP feature extraction combined with an SVM classifier. For the CSP, the number of spatial filters was searched by a Bayesian hyperparameter optimization [25]. For the SVM, we used a linear kernel.
- R-CSD + $k$-NN [2]: We implemented an R-CSD. Then, we built a $k$-NN classifier by setting $k = 5$.
- Deep ConvNet [24]: For Deep ConvNet, except for activation functions and the spatial convolution kernel size, all hyperparameters such as the temporal kernel sizes, depth dimensions, pooling parameters were optimized by a Bayesian hyperparameter optimization.
- EEGNet [14]: Similar to Deep ConvNet, we performed hyperparameter searching for all temporal kernel sizes and all depth dimensions by a Bayesian hyperparameter optimization. Note that EEGNet does not have any pooling layer.
- MSNN [11]: Like all CNNs used in this study, we also found the optimal temporal kernel sizes and depth dimensions via a Bayesian optimization method. Note that there is also no pooling layer in MSNN except for the GAP layer.

For our proposed network, we set a mini-batch size of 28, an exponentially decreasing learning rate, and an Adam optimizer. We regarded the initial learning rate, all temporal convolution kernel sizes $t_i^{(j)}$ where $i = \{1, 2, ..., k\}$ and $j = \{1, 2\}$, and all depth dimensions $D_A$ as hyperparameters to be explored via a Bayesian optimization method. In our proposed network, we selected $k = 3$. In

---

[1] Available at: https://osf.io/pq7vb/.

addition, an exponential linear unit function activated all layer outputs except for the final decision making layer, for which a softmax function was used. All tunable model parameters were regularized by an elastic net regularizer ($\ell_1 = 0.01$ and $\ell_2 = 0.001$) and initialized by a Xavier initializer [8]. Meanwhile, hyperparameters of the network such as temporal kernel sizes are optimized by a Bayesian optimization technique, whereas some predefined parameters, i.e., the number of channels and the sampling frequency, are fixed. For the Bayesian hyperparameter optimization [25], we used a *Gaussian processes* with an RBF kernel as a surrogate model. As for the acquisition function which is used to propose sampling points in the hyperparameter searching space, we used an expected improvement function. The overall procedure is optimized by the limited memory Broyden-Fletcher-Goldfarb-Shanno (BFGS) algorithm [17].

### 3.3   Experimental Results

We summarized the performance of the comparative methods in Table 1. Our proposed network clearly outperformed the other competing methods for the imagined speech EEG classification task. More precisely, our proposed network achieved the higher accuracy than the other deep neural networks specially designed for the spontaneous EEG classification. Furthermore, our method was superior to the conventional machine learning methods combined with the features engineered for the imagined speech EEG classification. With this clear improvement in performance, we expect that the proposed method can be a good candidate for the intuitive BCI.

## 4   Analysis

In this section, we analyzed our proposed network by investigating the characteristics of features represented from two different streams, i.e., Path 1 and Path 2 in Fig. 1. Additionally, we estimated and visualized the activation pattern maps [9] and the relevance scores [21] to demonstrate the effectiveness of our method from a neurophysiological viewpoint.

**Table 1.** Performance comparison among the competing methods and our proposed method.

| Method | Mean $\pm$ SD | Median | Max $-$ Min |
|---|---|---|---|
| CSP + SVM | $36.16 \pm 13.80$ | 38.57 | $64.29 - 18.57$ |
| R-CSD + $k$-NN [2] | $48.91 \pm 11.44$ | 48.57 | $80.00 - 27.14$ |
| Deep ConvNet [24] | $65.11 \pm 8.54$ | 68.57 | $87.14 - 44.29$ |
| EEGNet [14] | $68.53 \pm 10.80$ | 71.43 | $88.57 - 55.71$ |
| MSNN [11] | $67.21 \pm 8.20$ | 70.00 | $82.86 - 61.43$ |
| Proposed | $\mathbf{70.19 \pm 7.29}$ | 71.43 | $88.57 - 64.29$ |

### 4.1  Difference Between Features Extracted from Each Path

The strategy of exploiting two pathways is one of the most important aspects of our proposed network. Here, we calculated cosine similarity values between features, learned from Path 1 and Path 2 in Fig. 1. In the proposed architecture, there are four different information learning pathways, i.e., $\mathbf{f}_l^{(1)}$, $\mathbf{f}_{l,1}^{(2)}$, $\mathbf{f}_{l,2}^{(2)}$, and $\mathbf{f}_{l,3}^{(2)}$. In order to measure the similarity between features of two arbitrary paths $\mathbf{f}$ and $\mathbf{f}'$, we estimated an average similarity $\sigma(\mathbf{f}, \mathbf{f}')$ as follows:

$$\sigma(\mathbf{f}, \mathbf{f}') = \frac{1}{N_{\text{train}}} \sum_{l=1}^{N_{\text{train}}} \left| \text{CosSim}\left( \mathcal{G}_3(\mathbf{f}_l), \mathcal{G}_3(\mathbf{f}_l') \right) \right|, \tag{8}$$

where $N_{\text{train}}$ is the number of training samples and $\text{CosSim}(\mathbf{v}, \mathbf{w})$ is the cosine similarity between $\mathbf{v}$ and $\mathbf{w}$, i.e., $\text{CosSim}(\mathbf{v}, \mathbf{w}) = \frac{\mathbf{v}^\top \mathbf{w}}{\|\mathbf{v}\| \|\mathbf{w}\|}$.

We first estimated all averaged similarities on each subject and each fold. Then, we averaged the acquired similarities and calculated mean and standard deviation values. All results are summarized in Table 2. Based on our observation, each feature representation path learns different information from each other. Especially, the similarity values between Path 1 and Path 2, i.e., $\sigma\left( \mathbf{f}^{(1)}, \mathbf{f}_k^{(2)} \right)$, $k \in \{1, 2, 3\}$, showed much smaller values than the similarities between intermediate features of Path 2 at different scale, i.e., $\sigma\left( \mathbf{f}_k^{(2)}, \mathbf{f}_j^{(2)} \right)$, $k \neq j, k, j \in \{1, 2, 3\}$. From these quantitative results, we concluded that the represented features of different paths, especially from the topological dynamics learning and the electrode-wise temporal dynamics learning paths, extract different sources of information from an input EEG.

### 4.2  Towards Neurophysiological Representation

We also investigated our proposed network using *layer-wise relevance propagation* (LRP) [21] and *activation pattern* [9] mapping. In particular, we used the LRP method to show the relevance scores of the learned feature $\mathcal{G}_2(\mathbf{f}^{\text{concat}})$ for explanation of the output decision. Besides, we visualized topological activation pattern maps of the optimized spatial convolution kernels.

In Fig. 2, we plotted *power spectral densities* (PSDs) of a 'Hello' class sample within six different cortical areas, namely, Broca's and Wernicke's areas, visual cortex, auditory cortex, motor cortex, prefrontal cortex, and sensory cortex,

**Table 2.** Averaged cosine similarity values between each pair of feature representations in our proposed network. The first row denotes two compared features extracted from each path and the second row reports the estimated cosine similarity values.

| $\left(\mathbf{f}^{(1)}, \mathbf{f}_1^{(2)}\right)$ | $\left(\mathbf{f}^{(1)}, \mathbf{f}_2^{(2)}\right)$ | $\left(\mathbf{f}^{(1)}, \mathbf{f}_3^{(2)}\right)$ | $\left(\mathbf{f}_1^{(2)}, \mathbf{f}_2^{(2)}\right)$ | $\left(\mathbf{f}_2^{(2)}, \mathbf{f}_3^{(2)}\right)$ | $\left(\mathbf{f}_1^{(2)}, \mathbf{f}_3^{(2)}\right)$ |
|---|---|---|---|---|---|
| $0.13 \pm 0.21$ | $0.08 \pm 0.18$ | $0.09 \pm 0.17$ | $0.29 \pm 0.31$ | $0.26 \pm 0.29$ | $0.23 \pm 0.27$ |

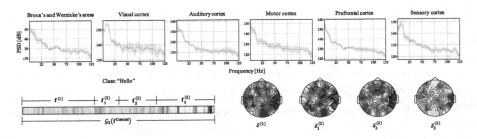

**Fig. 2.** Visualization of the power spectral density curves of six different cortical groups (top), relevance scores (bottom-left), and activation pattern maps of the spatial convolution kernels (bottom-right) estimated from a 'Hello' class imagined speech EEG sample.

based on [15,22]. Then, we estimated their corresponding relevance scores and activation patterns. In this example, we observed high PSD values at the visual and the sensory cortex in lower frequency range and high PSD values at the Broca's/Wernicke's areas, the auditory cortex, and the sensory cortex. In the meantime, the relevance scores are highlighted in the lower frequency, i.e., $\mathbf{f}_3^{(2)}$ range and in the higher frequency, i.e., $\mathbf{f}_1^{(2)}$ range. Generally, in computer vision tasks, a *low-level* convolution has a small *field-of-view* [19]. Similarly, in BCI tasks, a low-level temporal convolution tends to embed a shorter range of the input, thus represents high frequency properties of the input. Therefore, stacked CNNs can rarely learn low spectral features because they exploit only the finally acquired features. In the contrary, our proposed architecture effectively learned a wide frequency range of the input data and exploited all of the learned features to decide a user's intention.

In the activation patterns analysis, the spatial convolution of the topological dynamics modeling path showed an activated pattern near the Broca's and Wernicke's areas, visual cortex, and auditory cortex. In the electrode-wise temporal dynamics learning path, scale paths learned different patterns. The first spatial convolution $\mathcal{S}_1^{(2)}$ showed an activation at the visual cortex and the sensory cortex. The second spatial convolution $\mathcal{S}_2^{(2)}$ was activated at the auditory cortex, the prefrontal cortex, and the visual cortex. Finally, the third spatial convolution $\mathcal{S}_3^{(3)}$ showed a relatively prominent pattern in the auditory cortex, and Broca's and Wernicke's areas. From these promising results, we identified that our proposed network discovers the neurophysiological features induced by an imagined speech reasonably.

## 5    Conclusion

In this work, we proposed a novel deep CNN that can learn spectro-spatio-temporal representations of an imagined speech EEG. Based on the superiority of our proposed method in performance to the competing methods as well as the neurophysiologically informative features, we conclude that the proposed network can be beneficial to the intuitive BCIs. From a practical standpoint, it will be our forthcoming research issue to extend the proposed network for subject-invariant application towards zero-calibration [10].

# References

1. Ang, K.K., Chin, Z.Y., Zhang, H., Guan, C.: Filter bank common spatial pattern (FBCSP) in brain-computer interface. In: 2008 IEEE International Joint Conference on Neural Networks, pp. 2390–2397. IEEE (2008)
2. Bakhshali, M.A., Khademi, M., Ebrahimi-Moghadam, A., Moghimi, S.: EEG signal classification of imagined speech based on Riemannian distance of correntropy spectral density. Biomed. Signal Process. Control **59**, 101899 (2020)
3. Brigham, K., Kumar, B.V.: Imagined speech classification with EEG signals for silent communication: a preliminary investigation into synthetic telepathy. In: 2010 4th International Conference on Bioinformatics and Biomedical Engineering, pp. 1–4. IEEE (2010)
4. Chollet, F.: Xception: deep learning with depthwise separable convolutions. In: Proceedings of the IEEE Conference on Computer Vision and Pattern Recognition, pp. 1251–1258 (2017)
5. Cooney, C., Korik, A., Folli, R., Coyle, D.: Evaluation of hyperparameter optimization in machine and deep learning methods for decoding imagined speech EEG. Sensors **20**(16), 4629 (2020)
6. DaSalla, C.S., Kambara, H., Sato, M., Koike, Y.: Single-trial classification of vowel speech imagery using common spatial patterns. Neural Netw. **22**(9), 1334–1339 (2009)
7. Deng, S., Srinivasan, R., Lappas, T., D'Zmura, M.: EEG classification of imagined syllable rhythm using Hilbert spectrum methods. J. Neural Eng. **7**(4), 046006 (2010)
8. Glorot, X., Bengio, Y.: Understanding the difficulty of training deep feedforward neural networks. In: Proceedings of the Thirteenth International Conference on Artificial Intelligence and Statistics, pp. 249–256. JMLR Workshop and Conference Proceedings (2010)
9. Haufe, S., et al.: On the interpretation of weight vectors of linear models in multivariate neuroimaging. Neuroimage **87**, 96–110 (2014)
10. Ko, W., Jeon, E., Jeong, S., Phyo, J., Suk, H.I.: A survey on deep learning-based short/zero-calibration approaches for EEG-based brain-computer interfaces. Front. Hum. Neurosci. **15**, 643386 (2021)
11. Ko, W., Jeon, E., Jeong, S., Suk, H.I.: Multi-scale neural network for EEG representation learning in BCI. IEEE Comput. Intell. Mag. **16**(2), 31–45 (2021)
12. Ko, W., Oh, K., Jeon, E., Suk, H.I.: VigNet: a deep convolutional neural network for EEG-based driver vigilance estimation. In: 2020 8th International Winter Conference on Brain-Computer Interface, BCI, pp. 1–3. IEEE (2020)
13. Ko, W., Yoon, J., Kang, E., Jun, E., Choi, J.S., Suk, H.I.: Deep recurrent spatio-temporal neural network for motor imagery based BCI. In: 2018 6th International Conference on Brain-Computer Interface, BCI, pp. 1–3. IEEE (2018)
14. Lawhern, V.J., Solon, A.J., Waytowich, N.R., Gordon, S.M., Hung, C.P., Lance, B.J.: EEGNet: a compact convolutional neural network for EEG-based brain-computer interfaces. J. Neural Eng. **15**(5), 056013 (2018)

15. Lee, S.H., Lee, M., Lee, S.W.: Neural decoding of imagined speech and visual imagery as intuitive paradigms for BCI communication. IEEE Trans. Neural Syst. Rehabil. Eng. **28**(12), 2647–2659 (2020)
16. Lin, M., Chen, Q., Yan, S.: Network in network. arXiv preprint http://arxiv.org/abs/1312.4400 (2013)
17. Liu, D.C., Nocedal, J.: On the limited memory BFGS method for large scale optimization. Math. Program. **45**(1), 503–528 (1989)
18. Lotte, F., Roy, R.N.: Brain-Computer Interface Contributions to Neuroergonomics. In: Neuroergonomics, pp. 43–48. Elsevier (2019)
19. Lowe, D.G.: Distinctive image features from scale-invariant keypoints. Int. J. Comput. Vision **60**(2), 91–110 (2004)
20. Matsumoto, M., Hori, J.: Classification of silent speech using support vector machine and relevance vector machine. Appl. Soft Comput. **20**, 95–102 (2014)
21. Montavon, G., Lapuschkin, S., Binder, A., Samek, W., Müller, K.R.: Explaining nonlinear classification decisions with deep Taylor decomposition. Pattern Recogn. **65**, 211–222 (2017)
22. Nguyen, C.H., Karavas, G.K., Artemiadis, P.: Inferring imagined speech using EEG signals: a new approach using Riemannian manifold features. J. Neural Eng. **15**(1), 016002 (2017)
23. Sakhavi, S., Guan, C., Yan, S.: Parallel convolutional-linear neural network for motor imagery classification. In: 2015 23rd European Signal Processing Conference, EUSIPCO, pp. 2736–2740. IEEE (2015)
24. Schirrmeister, R.T., et al.: Deep learning with convolutional neural networks for EEG decoding and visualization. Hum. Brain Mapp. **38**(11), 5391–5420 (2017)
25. Snoek, J., Larochelle, H., Adams, R.P.: Practical Bayesian optimization of machine learning algorithms. In: Advances in Neural Information Processing Systems, vol. 25 (2012)
26. Suk, H.I., Lee, S.W.: A novel Bayesian framework for discriminative feature extraction in brain-computer interfaces. IEEE Trans. Pattern Anal. Mach. Intell. **35**(2), 286–299 (2012)
27. Wang, Y., Jung, T.P., et al.: Visual stimulus design for high-rate SSVEP BCI. Electron. Lett. **46**(15), 1057–1058 (2010)

# Is Notable EEG Feature Extracted Over Time-Dependent Cognitive Load Variation During Intelligence Tests?

Jinyoung Choi, Sehyeon Jang, and Sung Chan Jun[✉]

School of Electrical Engineering and Computer Science, Gwangju Institute of Science
and Technology, Gwangju, South Korea
scjun@gist.ac.kr

**Abstract.** In this study, we collected electroencephalography (EEG) data during
an intelligence test to understand the tendency of neurophysiologic change according to task difficulty or mental fatigue. Four healthy subjects were recruited for
the study. Subjects solved problem sets (Raven's APM Set II problems) without
a time limit in random order for measuring their intellectual quotient level. We
measured EEG activity as participants performed the task. We used spectral power
as a feature and introduced XGBoost as the predictor of cognitive load. When we
trained the network of XGBoost using the feature of EEG labeled in problem
order (ordered by difficulty), the root mean squared error (RMSE) from the test
data was significantly larger ($12.5 \pm 1.3$) than the same measure from a regressor
trained by a feature aligned by time ($9.6 \pm 1.4$, $p < 0.001$ from unpaired student's
t-test). Moreover, we found a stronger correlation from the prediction result of
a time-dependent feature learning network ($0.7 \pm 0.1$) compared to the prediction of a difficulty-dependent feature learning network ($0.39 \pm 0.1$, $p < 0.001$
from unpaired students' t-test). In summary, we found a better predictive performance in networks trained with time-dependent features compared to networks
with difficulty-dependent features. We propose that these results may explain EEG
feature variability biased by mental state changes during intellectual tasks.

**Keywords:** EEG · XGBoost · Cognitive load

## 1 Introduction

Cognitive load is a major concern as it is related to the task performance and problem-
solving capacity of individuals. It affects the mental state of a person who performs
a specific task or experiences a particular situation, accompanying cortical activity to
processing information and preparing job procedures. The intellectual quotient (IQ) is
a standard item for measuring personal problem-solving capacity, and here are various
tests for assessing personal IQ levels, including a wide range of items related to specific
higher-mental activity domains. Friedman et al., [1] reported a successful prediction
of cognitive load using EEG data that was collected during individuals' IQ tests. They
introduced XGBoost [2] for as a predictor and trained it with feature data extracted

© Springer Nature Switzerland AG 2022
C. Wallraven et al. (Eds.): ACPR 2021, LNCS 13189, pp. 347–355, 2022.
https://doi.org/10.1007/978-3-031-02444-3_26

from EEGs with the label of problem difficulty, and reported a significant correlation between prediction results and true labels, but they did not mention the salient feature information of the predictor, except for the top-10 EEG channels which affected the predictor dominantly.

In this study, we attempted to reproduce the predictors of cognitive load and reveal the feature characteristics that can offer clues for understanding neurophysiology as it relates to cognitive load. Although we recruited a small number of participants, we introduced the same model (XGBoost) and same feature (spectral power of EEG) as Friedman et al. We will explain the details of the experiment in the next chapter, followed by the results and discussion to provide a useful perspective for understanding EEG characteristics related to a cognitive task.

## 2   Method

### 2.1   Participants

We recruited six, right-handed healthy graduate students (five males, $29 \pm 1.7$) who were familiar with EEG recording experiments. They reported no cigarette usage, and they had not taken any kind of intelligence test in the previous three months. During the post-analysis, we discarded the EEG data of two subjects; we found that the EEG data of subjects 5 and 6 were contaminated by movement artifacts or abnormal high band power (gamma) caused by EMG. As a result, we used four subjects' data (task performance and EEG data) for the analysis.

### 2.2   Experiment Procedure

Each subject was equipped with an EEG recording system with dry electrodes (DSI-24 system, wearable sensing) before the experiment. We introduced Raven's APM Set II problems [3] for the problem set of intellectual testing. It is known that the difficulty increases along with the problem index of the Raven's test. The problem set included 48 problems, and half the subjects (subjects 1 and 3) solved problems in the regular sequence, and the others (subjects 2 and 4) solved the problems in a random order. We introduced the random problem sequence to examine the effect of elapsed time during the task (e.g., effect of fatigue on EEG as a result of the cognitive task), which may be more significant than the effect of problem difficulty. We recorded 19 channels (placed in 10–20 system locations) of EEG data during the test (sampling frequency: 300 Hz), and this was divided into epochs per problem. Subjects pressed a number on the keyboard to answer each problem, and we used EEG epochs from correct answers given [1].

### 2.3   Predictor

We used XGBoost as a predictor and trained it with EEG feature data. We used delta (1–4 Hz), theta (4–8 Hz), alpha (8–13 Hz), beta (13–30 Hz), and gamma (30–50 Hz) band power from each of the 19-channel EEG data epochs per correct answer. Therefore, there were 95 features for each correct answer. We pre-processed the EEG epochs before measuring the feature: this process included re-referencing with the common average for every channel, band-pass filtering in the 1–50 Hz band, independent component analysis (ICA) for artifact removal, and manual data inspection to eliminate noisy data epochs. We collected 128 epochs of 19-channel EEG data from four subjects after the pre-processing.

We used 80% of the data to train the predictor and used 20% of the data to test the performance of the predictor. We trained predictors in two different ways: (1) with feature data labeled with a problem number (P-order), and (2) with feature data labeled with the number of sequences in time order (T-order).

**Feature Data Labeled with Problem Number (P-order).** The problem number of the Raven's test is related to difficulty, and one can expect that the cognitive load in increases as problem number of the problem set increases. Therefore, we labeled features with problem numbers from the problem set.

**Feature Data Labeled with Solving Sequence (T-order).** In this experiment, two subjects solved the problem set in the regular order, from problem numbers 1 to 48 of the problem set. Meanwhile, the others (subjects 2 and 4) solved the problem set in a random order. In this case, we allocated an index of solving order for the label of the feature data. we expected that such labeling could affect the time-dependent variability of the feature data, even at the cost of losing difficulty-related feature information.

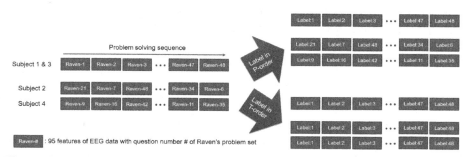

**Fig. 1.** Two different ways for feature data labeling. For the P-order, we labeled the feature data with problem numbers from the Raven's problem set. In this case, labels indicated problem difficulty. For the T-order, labels indicated the solving sequence, which was arranged by time.

## 2.4  Validation

By introducing two different ways of training, we could produce two types of predictors: the P-order predictor and the T-order predictor. For each predictor, we picked the 80% feature data set randomly and trained it to predict the label number of the test feature data set (remaining 20% of data set).

For training, we optimized the hyperparameter by the gird-search algorithm to ensure the best prediction performance. Specific parameter values are shown below (Table 1):

**Table 1.** Hyperparameters for predictors.

| Parameter name | Value | Meaning of parameter |
|---|---|---|
| Number of estimators | 500 | Maximum iteration of training |
| Alpha | 6 | L1 regularization term on weights |
| Gamma | 0.04 | Minimum threshold for making a new node |
| Learning rate | 0.3 | Learning rate for the training data |
| Max depth | 5 | Maximum depth of the tree |
| Colsample_bytree | 0.1 | Feature sampling ratio per tree depth |

We repeated the training-test evaluation for each predictor 100 times, and we used different training-test data sets for each evaluation. For validation, we calculated the root-mean-squared error (RMSE) and Pearson's correlation between the true label and predicted label.

### 2.5 Feature Analysis

We examined the details of feature information after training the predictors. First, we extracted the top 10 features that affected label prediction dominantly. Then, we compared the variation of the top features based on the label order. We expected that such a review of feature characteristics could offer perspectives to understanding cognitive load or the neurophysiology of intellectual activity.

## 3   Results

### 3.1   Feature Importance

We used the absolute power of the spectral band (five bands) for each epoch of 19 channels of EEG data. Among 95 features, we found the top 10 features for the predictors (Fig. 2). The most affected feature was the theta power from the C4 channel. When we arranged features in time order, there was a decreasing trend for the theta power in this feature for subject 4. Meanwhile, there was no clear trend in the same feature for subject 4 when aligning the feature with problem number (order of difficulty).

Three types of features from the F3 channel were ranked in the top 10 features (delta, gamma, and beta), and the gamma power in four channels were selected as important features (F3, Fp1, and F4). The delta power in the F3, P3, and F7 channels were picked for the top features; the theta power from the central channels (C4 and Cz) also could be considered as an important feature.

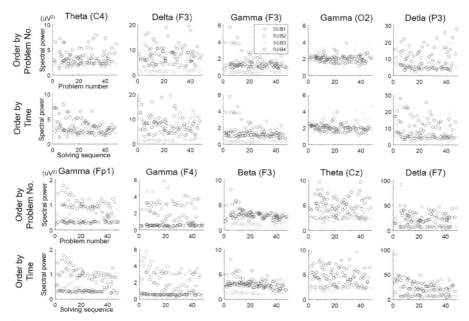

**Fig. 2.** Top 10 features for the predictors. The most important feature is the theta power from the C4 channel, and other ($2^{nd}$ to $10^{th}$) features are arranged by importance ranking. Each circle on the figure was a feature value for a specific EEG data epoch labeled by problem number (P-order) or solving sequence (arranged in time series: T-order).

## 3.2 Feature Variation

Next, we plotted the feature variation per subject for a clear view of the trend in the top 5 features (Fig. 3). Subjects 1 and 3 solved problems in the order of problem number, so their features were indexed with the problem number (P-order) of the Raven's problem set. Subjects 2 and 4 solved problems in random order, so we arranged features in two different ways: (1) P-order and (2) order of time (T-order) as the given label with the sequence of problem-solving during the test.

To highlight the trend of the variation in each feature, we plotted the relative feature value change based on the average feature value from $1^{st}$ to $10^{th}$ labeled data. As a result, we can see the decreasing trend from the blue lines from subjects 1, 2, and 4, which were arranged in time sequence. Subject 3 showed a large variation around the $30^{th}$-$40^{th}$ labeled feature, but there is a decreasing trend between the $1^{st}$ and $27^{th}$ labeled data. The orange line (feature variation rearranged by problem index) showed some fluctuation. For example, one can find a decreasing trend in the gamma power at the F4 channel for subject 2 (Fig. 2) in the T-order. The largest feature is shown in the fourth trial from the T-order, and the same feature may act as a distractor of the trend of the Q-order (the actual problem number is 19).

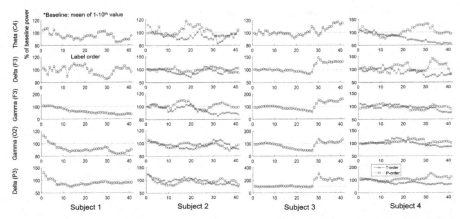

**Fig. 3.** Variation of the top 5 features for each subject. Circle points indicate relative feature value variation in the order of problem number from the Raven's test. Cross points indicate relative feature value variation in the order of time (problem-solving sequence for each subject).

### 3.3    Performance Comparison: P-order vs. T-order

Lastly, we compared the prediction performance between P-order labeled data and T-order labeled data. For each predictor, we performed 100 evaluations of training and tests. We randomly picked 102 samples of feature data for predictor training (80% of total data) and tested them with 26 samples for each evaluation. We measured RMSE and Pearson's correlation using the prediction results from the 26-test data and the true label of the test data.

After all evaluations, we plotted every prediction result for each predictor respectively (upper panels in Fig. 4). The total evaluation samples (2,600 samples for each predictor) were scattered with the true label and prediction results. We gathered 100 samples of average RMSE data and Pearson's correlation value for each predictor. When we compare the RMSE, the predictor with the T-order labeled data showed a lower RMSE value (12.5 ± 1.3) than the predictor with the P-order labeled data (9.6 ± 1.4), and this difference is statistically significant (p < 0.001 in unpaired student's t-test). The correlation between the true label and the prediction results is also stronger in the predictor with the T-order labeled data (0.7 ± 0.1) than it is for the predictor with P-order labeled data (0.39 ± 0.1), showing a significant difference (p < 0.001 in unpaired student's t-test) (Table 2).

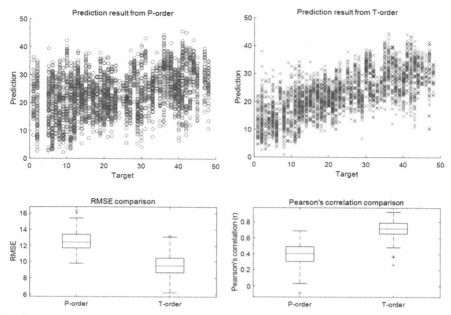

**Fig. 4.** Scatter plot for prediction results from each type of predictor (upper panels) and boxplot for evaluation matric (RMSE and Pearson's correlation) for each predictor (lower panels).

**Table 2.** Performance evaluation results.

| Evaluation matric | Value | p-value for comparison |
|---|---|---|
| P-order RMSE | $12.5 \pm 1.3$ | <0.001 |
| T-order RMSE | $9.6 \pm 1.4$ | |
| P-order Pearson's correlation | $0.39 \pm 0.1$ | <0.001 |
| T-order Pearson's correlation | $0.7 \pm 0.1$ | |

## 4    Discussion

### 4.1    Cognitive Load vs. Time-Dependent Mental State Variation

In this study, we tried to reconstruct the cognitive load predictor reported in [1]. We provided Raven's problems in random order for some subjects so that we could consider the time order and problem difficulty (which is related to the problem index from the Raven's test) for EEG feature analysis.

Interestingly, when we used the problem difficulty for the label of the feature data, the performance of the predictor is quite lower (Pearson's correlation = 0.39) than the reference predictor (from Friedman et al., 2019; Pearson's correlation = 0.8 [1]). Also, the predictor which is trained with the feature data of a time-sequence label showed comparable performance (Pearson's correlation = 0.7) with the reference predictor. We guessed that such a result may imply that the EEG feature of the cognitive task may vary in a time-dependent manner and is not strongly affect by cognitive load (or problem difficulty). Yet, there is a weak trend in the prediction result from the P-order data set, so we cannot exclude the predictor's function of cognitive load measure. However, in our results, the top 5 features showed decreasing trends along with time. Such a phenomenon may affect the training sequence of the regressor (XGBoost), and the test data is also highly correlated with time labels. We suggest dominant EEG features may vary according to the mental state of subjects during the intellectual test, and such a trend affects regressors' ability to predict the variation of mental state from EEG features.

There are limitations in our results due to the small number of subjects in our sample size, which may be not sufficient to provide data for training and testing the neural network. Problem difficulty also cannot be measured in an intuitive way, such as by calculating the correct ratio for each problem. Therefore, these results may suggest the existence of implicit time-dependent characteristics (such as mental fatigue) for the EEG feature data for the cognitive load predictor, which should be verified with additional experiments including a greater number of subjects.

### 4.2   Neurophysiology Phenomenon from the Intellectual Test

Among the top 10 features of predictors, we found the contribution of delta and gamma-band power from the frontal channels (F3, Fp1, F4, and F7) for the prediction. The delta wave is related to cognitive processing [4], and the frontal delta is generally known as being related to event-related potentials (ERPs) during the awake state [5]. An increase in delta power is associated with mental task capacity and concentration [6]. Therefore, the delta decrement along with time flow in our data (Fig. 3) could be understood as a loss of cognitive capacity or a decrement of mental condition.

There is evidence of gamma power increase, especially in the occipital lobe, during the task of working memory [6], which is related to memory load. The author suggested that gamma oscillation in the occipital lobe may occur during working memory tasks associated with primary visual processing activity. Our result data also showed the 4th important feature as gamma power from the O2 channel. The problem of the Raven's test is composed of diagrams for reasoning and inference. Therefore, we suggest that visual processing from the occipital area elicits gamma oscillation, which is the main feature of cognitive load for solving the Raven's test problem set.

## 5   Conclusion

In this study, we generated predictors for cognitive load and mental state. We used the spectral band power of EEG as feature data for training and testing predictors. There was a correlation between the true label and prediction result from the cognitive load predictor, but it showed error and a lower correlation compared to the predictor that was trained with time-dependent feature data. We suggest these results imply the importance of considering time-dependent parameters, such as mental state or fatigue, for predicting cognitive load.

**Acknowledgment.** This research was supported by the Institute of Information & Communications Technology Planning & Evaluation (IITP) grant, funded by the Korean government (No. 2017–0-00451; Development of BCI based Brain and Cognitive Computing Technology for recognizing User's Intentions using Deep Learning).

# References

1. Friedman, N., Fekte, T., Gal, K., Shriki, O.: EEG-Based prediction of cognitive load in intelligence tests. Front. Hum. Neurosci. **13**, 191 (2019)
2. Chen, T., Guestrin, C.: XGBoost: a scalable tree boosting system. In: Proceedings of the 22nd ACM SIGKDD International Conference on Knowledge Discovery and Data Mining, pp. 785–794. Association for Computing Machinery, New York (2016)
3. Raven, J., Raven, C., Court, H.: Raven's Standard Progressive Matrices (SPM). England, Oxford (1998)
4. Eggermont, J., Brain Oscillations, Synchrony and Plasticity, 1st edn. Elsevier (2021)
5. Malik, A., Amin U., Designing EEG Experiments for Studying the Brain, 1st edn. Elsevier (2017)
6. Harmony, T.: The functional significance of delta oscillations in cognitive processing. Front. Integr. Neurosci. **7**, 83 (2013)
7. Meltzer, J., et al.: Effects of working memory load on oscillatory power in human intracranial EEG. Cereb. Cortex **18**(8), 1843–1855 (2008)

# A Self-attention Based Model for Offline Handwritten Text Recognition

Nam Tuan Ly[✉] [ID], Trung Tan Ngo [ID], and Masaki Nakagawa [ID]

Tokyo University of Agriculture and Technology, Tokyo, Japan
namlytuan@gmail.com, trungngotan94@gmail.com,
nakagawa@cc.tuat.ac.jp

**Abstract.** Offline handwritten text recognition is an important part of document analysis and it has been receiving a lot of attention from numerous researchers for decades. In this paper, we present a self-attention-based model for offline handwritten textline recognition. The proposed model consists of three main components: a feature extractor by CNN; an encoder by a BLSTM network and a self-attention module; and a decoder by CTC. The self-attention module is complementary to RNN in the encoder and helps the encoder to capture long-range and multi-level dependencies across an input sequence. According to the extensive experiments on the two datasets of IAM Handwriting and Kuzushiji, the proposed model achieves better accuracy than the state-of-the-art models. The self-attention map visualization shows that the self-attention mechanism helps the encoder capture long-range and multi-level dependencies across an input sequence.

**Keywords:** Self-attention · Multi-head · Handwritten text recognition · CNN · BLSTM · CTC

## 1 Introduction

Offline handwritten text recognition is an important part of document analysis and it has been receiving a lot of attention from numerous researchers for decades. Starting with the recognition of isolated handwritten characters and digits, the focus has shifted to the recognition of words and sentences. Recognizing them is significantly more difficult than characters because of a large vacabulary in each language, and multiple touches between characters. Other challengings of offline handwritten recognition are various backgrounds, noises, and diversity of writing styles. Most of early works in handwritten Japanese/Chinese text recognition often took the segmentation-based approach that segmented or over-segmented text into characters and fragments and then merged the fragments in the recognition state [1, 2]. This segmentation-based approach is costly and error-prone because the segmentation of characters directly affects the whole system's performance. On the other hand, segmentation-free methods can avoid segmentation errors and have been employed for western handwritten documents based on the Hidden Markov Model (HMM) [3, 4] so far. However, a weakness of HMMs is the local modeling, which cannot capture long-term dependencies in an input sequence.

© Springer Nature Switzerland AG 2022
C. Wallraven et al. (Eds.): ACPR 2021, LNCS 13189, pp. 356–369, 2022.
https://doi.org/10.1007/978-3-031-02444-3_27

In recent years, many segmentation-free methods have been proposed and proven to be powerful for both western and oriental text recognition [5–13] based on Recurrent Neural Network (RNN) and Connectionist Temporal Classification (CTC). The core recognition engine has been shifted from Hidden Markov Models (HMMs) to RNNs with CTC. The RNNs, such as Gated recurrent unit (GRU) or Long-short term memory (LSTM), are good at sequence modeling and solve the weakness of the local modeling of HMMs. However, the number of hidden nodes in RNNs is usually fixed, which implies all historical information is compressed into a fixed-length vector, so that RNNs are difficult to capture long-range context. Recently, A. Vaswani et al. [14] proposed a self-attention mechanism in the Transformer model, which achieved the state-of-the-art performance in some machine translation tasks. The self-attention mechanism can capture the dependencies between different positions of arbitrary distance in an input sequence and replaces the LSTM in both the encoder and the decoder of the sequence-to-sequence models.

In this paper, we present a self-attention-based model for offline handwritten textline recognition. The proposed model consists of three main components: a feature extractor by CNN; an encoder by a BLSTM network and a self-attention module; and a decoder by CTC. The self-attention module complements RNN in the encoder and helps the encoder capture long-range and multi-level dependencies across an input sequence. According to our extensive experiments on the two datasets of IAM Handwriting and Kuzushiji, the proposed model achieves better accuracy than the state-of-the-art models. Furthermore, the self-attention map visualization shows that the self-attention mechanism helps the encoder capture the dependencies between different positions of arbitrary distance in an input sequence.

The rest of this paper is organized as follows: Sect. 2 describes the related work. Section 3 presents an overview of the proposed model. Section 4 reports our experiments, results and analysis. Finally, Sect. 5 draws conclusions.

## 2 Related Work

In recent years, based on Deep Neural Networks, many segmentation-free methods have been proposed and shown to be effective, especially for recognizing noisy, complex, and handwritten text [5–10]. They can be categorized into two main approaches: CTC and attention-based sequence-to-sequence methods.

Early works of the CTC-based approach were introduced by A. Graves et al. [5, 6]. They proposed BLSTM followed by CTC for recognizing both online and offline handwritten English text and achieved better accuracy than HMM-based methods [5]. They also presented Multi-Dimensional LSTM (MDLSTM) with CTC for offline handwritten Arabic text recognition [6]. Following the works in [6], V. Pham et al. presented an end-to-end MDLSTM with dropout followed by CTC for handwritten text recognition [7]. B. Shi et al. proposed the combination of CNN and BLSTM, followed by CTC, which is called Convolutional Recurrent Neural Network (CRNN) for image-based sequence recognition [8]. Based on the CRNN model, T. Bluche et al. proposed the Gated Convolutional Recurrent Neural Networks (GCRNN) for Multilingual Handwriting Recognition [9]. At the same time, N. T. Ly et al. presented the pre-trained CNN with sliding window followed by BLSTM with CTC to recognize offline handwritten Japanese text and achieve better accuracy than the traditional segmentation-based method [10]. J. Puigcerver et al. applied MDLSTM or CNN + LSTM, both followed by CTC for offline handwritten English and French text recognition [13].

The sequence-to-sequence (seq2seq) model with the attention mechanism has been proven to be a powerful model for many tasks, such as machine translation [15] and speech recognition [16]. Based on the attention-based seq2seq model, many segmentation-free models have been studied for image-based sequence recognition tasks [17–22]. J. Sueiras et al. presented an attention-based seq2seq model using a horizontal sliding window for handwritten English and French text recognition [17]. T. Bluche et al. proposed an attention-based end-to-end model with an MDLSTM network in the encoder for handwritten paragraph recognition [18, 19]. N. T. Ly et al. also proposed an attention-based seq2seq model with residual LSTM for recognizing multiple textlines in Japanese historical documents [20, 21]. Zhang et al. presented an attention-based seq2seq model with a CNN-encoder and a GRU decoder for robust text image recognition [22]. Following the success of the self-attention mechanism in the Transformer model [14], L. Kang et al. presented the CNN-Transformer model for handwritten text line recognition [23]. Meanwhile, N. T. Ly et al. presented an Attention Augmented Convolutional Recurrent Network with a self-attention mechanism for Handwritten Japanese Text Recognition [24].

Recently, Trung et al. proposed the pretrained ResNet32 followed by RNN-Transducer for Japanese and Chinese offline handwritten text line recognition and achieved state-of-the-art accuracies on the SCUT-EPT and Kuzushiji datasets [25].

## 3   The Proposed Method

### 3.1   Self-attention Mechanism

The self-attention mechanism is one of the main ideas of the Transformer model [14]. It uses all position-pairs in an input sequence to extract more expressive representations of the input. Therefore, the self-attention mechanism helps the model capture long-range and multi-level dependencies across the input sequence. To obtain these representations, the input sequence is linearly projected to get the *queries Q, keys K,* and *values V*. Then, the self-attention mechanism performs Scaled Dot-Product Attention to the *queries, keys,* and *values* to compute the output as shown in Eq. (1).

$$\text{Attention}(Q, K, V) = \text{softmax}\left(\frac{QK^T}{\sqrt{d_k}}\right)V \tag{1}$$

where $Q \in R^{T_q \times d_k}$, $K \in R^{T_k \times d_k}$, and $V \in R^{T_k \times d_v}$; $T$ and $d$ are the number of features and the dimension of the feature in $Q$, $K$, $V$, respectively.

The self-attention mechanism can be further extended to the multi-head self-attention mechanism, which jointly attends to information from different representation subspaces at different positions. The multi-head self-attention mechanism firstly obtains $h$ different representations of ($Q$, $K$, $V$) by linear projections and then independently performs the self-attention mechanism to each representation to get $h$ heads. Finally, $h$ heads are concatenated and then projected to produce the output encodings, as following:

$$\text{head}_i = \text{Attention}\left(QW_i^Q, KW_i^K, VW_i^V\right) \tag{2}$$

$$\text{MultiHead}(Q, K, V) = [\text{head}_1, \ldots, \text{head}_h]W^o \tag{3}$$

where $h$ is the number of heads, $W_i^Q \in R^{d_{\text{model}} \times d_k}$, $W_i^K \in R^{d_{\text{model}} \times d_k}$, $W_i^V \in R^{d_{\text{model}} \times d_v}$, and $W^o \in R^{d_{\text{model}} \times d_{\text{model}}}$ are parameter matrices of the linear projections, $d_{\text{model}}$ is the dimension of the input sequence, $d_K = d_V = d_{\text{model}}/h$.

The self-attention layer in Transformer [14] consists of two main components: a multi-head self-attention component and a position-wise fully connected feed-forward layer, as shown in Fig. 1. A residual connection followed by layer normalization is applied after each of the two sub-components.

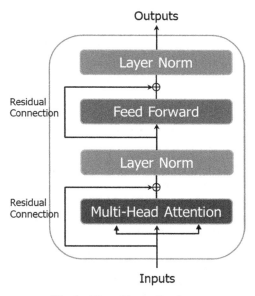

**Fig. 1.** The self-attention layer.

## 3.2 Self-attention Based Convolutional Recurrent Neural Network

In this work, we propose a model of Self-Attention based Convolutional Recurrent Neural Network for recognizing each handwritten textline. The proposed model is composed of three main components: a feature extractor, an encoder, and a CTC-decoder, as shown in Fig. 2. They are described in the following sections.

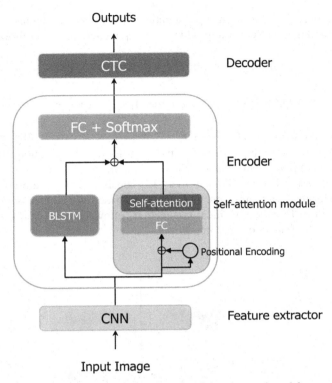

**Fig. 2.** The network architecture of the proposed model.

**Feature Extractor:** At the bottom of the model, the feature extractor extracts a feature sequence from an input textline image. In this work, we use a standard CNN network without softmax and fully connected layers to build the feature extractor. Given an input image of size $w \times h \times c$ (where $w$, $h$, and $c$ are the width, height and color channels of the image, respectively), the CNN network extracts a feature gird $F$ of size $w' \times h' \times k$, where $k$ is the number of feature maps in the last convolutional layer, and $w'$ and $h'$ depend on the $w$ and $h$ of input images and the number of pooling layers in the CNN network. Then, the feature grid $F$ is unfolded into a feature sequence. Finally, the feature sequence will be fed into the encoder component.

**Encoder:** At the top of the feature extractor, the encoder converts the feature sequence extracted from the previous component into a sequence of label-probabilities. Mathematically, the encoder predicts label-probabilities from each feature in the feature sequence. In this model, the encoder consists of two main parts: a self-attention module and a BLSTM network. The self-attention module helps the encoder to capture long-range and multi-level dependencies across an input sequence. Meanwhile, the BLSTM network helps the encoder focus on the dependencies of nearby positions. The self-attention module consists of three sub-layers: a positional encoding layer which helps the model to exploit the order of the feature sequence; a fully connected layer which reduces the dimensions of the features; and several self-attention layers, as shown in Fig. 2.

Firstly, the feature sequence from the previous component is fed to the self-attention module and the BLSTM network. Then, the output of the self-attention module and the BLSTM network are concatenated and fed to the fully connected layer, which converts the output dimension to the size of the character set. Finally, one softmax layer is placed in the end to predict the label-probabilities at each time step. Let $F = (f_1, f_2 \cdots f_n)$, and $E = (e_1, e_2 \cdots e_n)$ denote the feature sequence, and the sequence of label probabilities, respectively, where $n$ is the number of feature vectors. Then, we have:

$$E = \text{Softmax}(\text{Concat}(\text{BLSTM}(F), \text{SelfAttn}(F))) \tag{4}$$

**Decoder:** At the top of the encoder, the decoder decodes the sequence of label probabilities made by the encoder into a final target sequence. Mathematically, the decoding process finds the final label sequence with the highest probability conditioned on the sequence of label probabilities. In this work, we use the CTC [26] algorithm to build the decoder to obtain conditional probability.

The whole model is trained end-to-end using stochastic gradient descent algorithms to minimize the CTC loss. For the decoding process in the testing phase, we apply the CTC beam search with the *beamwidth* of 2 to obtain the final label sequence with the highest probability conditioned.

## 4  Experiments

To evaluate the performance of the proposed model, we conducted experiments on the two datasets: IAM handwriting and Kuzushiji datasets. The information of the datasets is given in Sect. 4.1; the implementation details are described in Sect. 4.2; the results of the experiments are presented in Sect. 4.3; and the analysis is shown in Sect. 4.4.

### 4.1  Datasets

In this paper, we use two datasets for experiments. IAM Handwriting is offline hand-written English text dataset compiled by the FKI-IAM Research Group. The dataset is composed of 13,353 textlines extracted from 1,539 pages of scanned handwritten English text which were written by 657 different writers. We employ the shared Aachen data splits by T. Bluche from RWTH Aachen University to split the dataset into three subsets: 6,482 lines for training, 2,915 lines for testing, and 976 lines for validation. There are 79 different characters in the dataset, including the space character. The summary of the IAM handwriting is given in Table 1.

Kuzushiji is a dataset of the pre-modern Japanese documents prepared by the National Institute of Japanese Literature (NIJL). The first version of the Kuzushiji (Kuzushiji_v1) dataset consists of 15 pre-modern Japanese books composing of 2,222 pages and was released in 2016 [27]. For every character in each page, its bounding box, location and Shift_JIS code are annotated. The Kuzushiji_v1 textline dataset, consisting of 25,875 textline images, was compiled from the Kuzushiji_v1 dataset. We use all

**Table 1.** IAM Handwriting dataset.

|  | IAM Handwriting | | |
|  | Train set | Valid set | Test set |
|---|---|---|---|
| Text lines | 6,482 | 976 | 2,915 |
| Pages | 747 | 116 | 336 |

textline images collected from the 15th book as the testing set. The remaining images are divided randomly from the training and validation sets with a ratio of 9:1. Table 2 shows the profile of the Kuzushiji_v1 textline dataset.

**Table 2.** Kuzushiji_v1 textline dataset.

|  | Kuzushiji_v1 textline | | |
|  | Train set | Valid set | Test set |
|---|---|---|---|
| Samples | 19,797 | 2,200 | 3,878 |
| Books | 1st –14th | | 15th |

## 4.2 Implementation Details

In the experiments, the architecture of the CNN network in the feature extractor is deployed as shown in Table 3. It consists of five (six for the Kuzushiji_v1 textline dataset) convolutional (Conv) blocks. Each Conv block consists of one Conv layer with a kernel size of $3 \times 3$ pixels and a stride of $1 \times 1$ pixel followed by the Batch normalization [28] and the ReLU activation. To reduce overfitting, we apply dropout at the input of the last three Conv blocks (with dropout probability equal to 0.2).

At the encoder, we use a Deep BLSTM network with 256 hidden nodes of three layers (two layers for the Kuzushiji_v1 textline dataset). To prevent overfitting when training the model, the dropout (dropout rate = 0.5) is also applied in each layer of the Deep BLSTM network. The self-attention module consists of six self-attention layers

**Table 3.** Network configurations of the CNN in the feature extractor.

| Config | Values | |
|  | IAM | Kuzushiji_v1 textline |
|---|---|---|
| Input | $128 \times w$ | $128 \times w$ |
| Conv Block | 16 - 32 - 48 - 64 - 80 | 16 - 32 - 48 - 64 - 80 - 128 |
| Max-Pooling | (2,2) - (2,2) - (1,2) - (2,1) - No | (2,2) - (2,2) - (2,2) - (1,2) - (2,1) - No |
| Dropout | 0 - 0 - 0.2 - 0.2 - 0.2 | 0 - 0 - 0 - 0.2 - 0.2 - 0.2 |

where each self-attention layer is composed of eight heads and 2,048 nodes of a single full connected layer. the BLSTM network and the self-attention module are followed by a fully connected layer and a softmax layer with the node size equal to the character set size (n = 80 for IAM and 4,818 for Kuzushiji).

## 4.3   Experiment Results

In order to evaluate the performance of the proposed model, we use the terms of Character Error Rate (CER), Word Error Rate (WER), and Sequence Error Rate (SER) that are defined as follows:

$$CER(h,S') = \frac{1}{Z} \sum_{(x,z) \in S'} ED(h(x),z) \tag{5}$$

$$WER(h,S') = \frac{1}{Z_{word}} \sum_{(x,z) \in S'} ED_{word}(h(x),z) \tag{6}$$

$$SER(h,S') = \frac{100}{|S'|} \sum_{(x,z) \in S'} \begin{cases} 0 \text{ if } h(x) = z \\ 1 \text{ otherwise} \end{cases} \tag{7}$$

where Z is the total number of target labels in S' and $ED(p, q)$ is the edit distance between two sequences $p$ and $q$, while $Z_{word}$ is the total number of words in S', and $ED_{word}(p, q)$ is the word-level edit distance between two sequences $p$ and $q$.

### 4.3.1   Effects of the Self-attention Mechanism

In the first experiment, we evaluate the effectiveness of the self-attention module and the fully connected layer in the self-attention module. We prepared two variations. The first one is the same as the proposed model (called SA-CRNN) except using the self-attention module, which is named SA-CRNN_w/o_SelfAttn. The second one is the same as the proposed model except the fully connected layer in the self-attention module, which is named SA-CRNN_w/o_FC. Table 4 compares their recognition error rates with the proposed model on the test set of the IAM Handwriting dataset. The proposed model slightly outperforms SA-CRNB_w/o_SelfAttn. The results imply that the self-attention module in the encoder improves the performance of the CRNN model for handwritten text recognition. This seems to be due to the self-attention module that

**Table 4.** Recognition error rates (%) with different encoders.

| Model | IAM | |
|---|---|---|
| | CER | WER |
| SA-CRNN_w/o_SelfAttn | 7.54 | 24.06 |
| SA-CRNN_w/o_FC | 7.59 | 23.85 |
| SA-CRNN | **7.22** | **22.87** |

helps the encoder capture long-range dependencies in an input sequence. The proposed model again slightly outperforms SA-CRNN_w/o_FC. The results show that the fully connected layer in the self-attention module improves the performance of the proposed model.

The second experiment explores the effect of head number in the self-attention mechanism. We performed experiments with a different head numbers of 1, 2, 4, and 8 on the IAM dataset. The results are shown in Table 5. As can be seen, the proposed model obtained its best CER when the head number was 8, while the best WER was obtained with the head number of 4.

**Table 5.** Recognition error rates (%) with a different head numbers.

| Head Number | IAM | |
|---|---|---|
| | CER | WER |
| 1 | 7.51 | 23.97 |
| 2 | 7.45 | 23.43 |
| 4 | 7.28 | **22.80** |
| 8 | **7.22** | 22.87 |

### 4.3.2 Comparison with the State-of-the-Art

The third experiment evaluates the performance of the proposed model and compares it with the previous works on the IAM Handwriting dataset in terms of CER and WER. To fairly compare with the previous models [7, 9, 13, 17, 19, 22, 23, 29], we do not use any data augmentation techniques as well as linguistic context information. The results are shown in Table 6. The proposed model achieved CER of 7.22% and WER of 22.87%. These results show that the proposed model achieves state-of-the-art accuracy and outperforms the best model in [23] by about 6% of CER and 9% of WER on the IAM Handwriting dataset without data augmentation techniques as well as linguistic context information.

**Table 6.** Recognition error rates (%) on the IAM dataset.

| Model | IAM | |
|---|---|---|
| | CER | WER |
| CNN-1DLSTM (Moysset et al. [29]) | 11.52 | 35.64 |
| MDLSTM (Pham et al. [7]) | 10.80 | 35.10 |
| GNN-1DLSTM (Bluche et al. [9])* | 10.17 | 32.88 |

(*continued*)

**Table 6.** (*continued*)

| Model | IAM | |
|---|---|---|
| | CER | WER |
| 2DLSTM (Moysset et al. [29]) | 8.88 | 29.15 |
| 2DLSTM-X2 (Moysset et al. [29]) | 8.86 | 29.31 |
| CNN-Seq2Seq (Sueiras et al. [17]) | 8.80 | 23.80 |
| CNN-Seq2Seq (Zhang et al. [22]) | 8.50 | 22.20 |
| CNN-1DLSTM (Puigcerver et al. [13]) | 8.20 | 25.40 |
| 2DLSTM (Bluche et al. [19]) | 7.90 | 24.60 |
| CNN-1DLSTM (Puigcerver et al. [13])* | 7.73 | 25.22 |
| CNN-Transformers (Kang et al. [23]) | 7.62 | 24.54 |
| The Proposed Model (Ours) | **7.22** | **22.87** |

* Experiments run by Moysset et al. [29]

In the second experiment, we evaluate the performance of the proposed model and compare it with the previous works [11, 20, 24, 25] on the Kuzushiji_v1 textline dataset in terms of CER and SER. We also do not use any data augmentation techniques as well as linguistic context information. As shown in Table 7, the proposed model achieved CER of 20.25% and SER of 94.53% on the test set of the Kuzushiji_v1 textline dataset, which is best among the previous methods without data augmentation and linguistic context. Furthermore, the proposed model also has lower CER than the RNN-Transducer model

**Table 7.** Recognition error rates (%) on the Kuzushiji_v1 textline dataset.

| Model | Kuzushiji_v1 textline | |
|---|---|---|
| | CER | SER |
| End-to-End DCRN [11] | 28.34 | 97.27 |
| Attention-based seq2seq model [20] | 31.38 | 98.07 |
| AACRN [24] | 21.48 | 94.97 |
| The proposed model (Ours) | **20.25** | **94.53** |
| RNN-Transducer [25] * | 20.33 | – |

* Data augmentations + Pretrained ResNet32 on ImageNet.

in the works of [25] which applied data augmentation techniques during the training process.

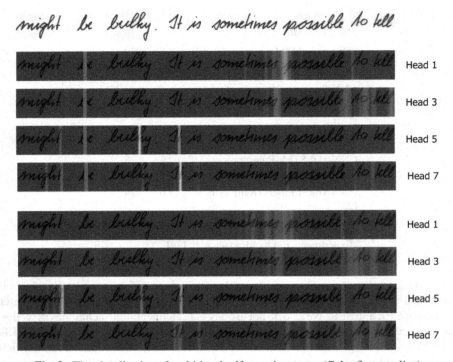

**Fig. 3.** The visualization of multi-head self-attention maps. (Color figure online)

### 4.4 Analysis

Figure 3 shows the visualization of the multi-head self-attention maps for one image. The top image is the original input image, while each of the two groups of four images shows one query column with the color-coded location (blue and red) and four self-attention maps of four attention heads (eight attention heads in total) for that query column. These visualizations show that the self-attention mechanism helps the encoder capture long-range and multi-level dependencies across the input sequence.

Figure 4 shows some correctly recognized and misrecognized samples in the Kuzushiji_v1 textline dataset by the proposed model. For each misrecognized sample, the image on the left is an input image, the text bounded by the blue rectangular shows the ground-truth, and the text bounded by the red rectangular shows the recognition resulted.

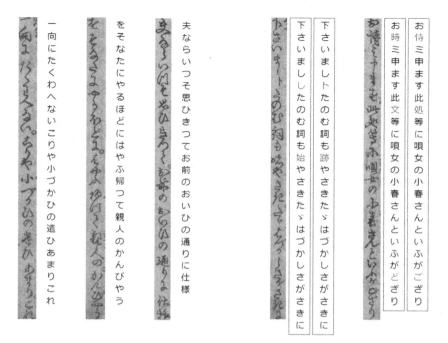

a). Correctly recognized samples.      b). Misrecognized samples.

**Fig. 4.** Correctly recognized and misrecognized samples by the proposed model. (Color figure online)

## 5 Conclusion

In this paper, we proposed an self-attention-based model for recognizing offline handwritten textlines. We introduced the self-attention mechanism into the encoder component to help the encoder to capture long-range and multi-level dependencies across an input sequence. The proposed model achieves better accuracy than the state-of-the-art models on the two datasets of IAM Handwriting and Kuzushiji_v1 textline. We also visualized the self-attention map and observed that the self-attention mechanism helps the encoder capture long-range and multi-level dependencies across an input sequence.

In future works, we will conduct experiments of the proposed model with other text recognition tasks such as scene text recognition and historical text recognition. We also plan to apply data augmentations and incorporate language models into the proposed model to improve its performance.

**Acknowledgments.** This research is being partially supported by the grant-in-aid for scientific research (S) 18H05221 and (A) 18H03597.

# References

1. Nguyen, K.C., Nguyen, C.T., Nakagawa, M.: A segmentation method of single- and multiple-touching characters in offline handwritten Japanese text recognition. IEICE Trans. Inf. Syst. **E100.D**, 2962–2972 (2017)
2. Wang, Q.-F., Yin, F., Liu, C.-L.: Handwritten Chinese text recognition by integrating multiple contexts. IEEE Trans. Pattern Anal. Mach. Intell. **34**, 1469–1481 (2012)
3. El-Yacoubi, A., Gilloux, M., Sabourin, R., Suen, C.Y.: An HMM-based approach for off-line unconstrained handwritten word modeling and recognition. IEEE Trans. Pattern Anal. Mach. Intell. **21**, 752–760 (1999)
4. España-Boquera, S., Castro-Bleda, M.J., Gorbe-Moya, J., Zamora-Martinez, F.: Improving offline handwritten text recognition with hybrid HMM/ANN models. IEEE Trans. Pattern Anal. Mach. Intell. **33**, 767–779 (2011)
5. Graves, A., Liwicki, M., Fernandez, S., Bertolami, R., Bunke, H., Schmidhuber, J.: A novel connectionist system for unconstrained handwriting recognition. IEEE Trans. Pattern Anal. Mach. Intell. **31**, 855–868 (2009)
6. Graves, A., Schmidhuber, J.: Offline handwriting recognition with multidimensional recurrent neural networks. In: Advances Neural Information Processing System 21, NIPS 2021, pp. 545–552 (2008)
7. Pham, V., Bluche, T., Kermorvant, C., Louradour, J.: Dropout improves recurrent neural networks for handwriting recognition. In: Proceedings of International Conference on Frontiers in Handwriting Recognition, ICFHR, pp. 285–290 (2014)
8. Shi, B., Bai, X., Yao, C.: An end-to-end trainable neural network for image-based sequence recognition and its application to scene text recognition. IEEE Trans. Pattern Anal. Mach. Intell. **39**, 2298–2304 (2017)
9. Bluche, T., Messina, R.: Gated convolutional recurrent neural networks for multilingual handwriting recognition. In: Proceedings of the International Conference on Document Analysis and Recognition, ICDAR, pp. 646–651 (2017)
10. Ly, N.-T., Nguyen, C.-T., Nguyen, K.-C., Nakagawa, M.: Deep convolutional recurrent network for segmentation-free offline handwritten Japanese text recognition. In: Proceedings of the International Conference on Document Analysis and Recognition (ICDAR), pp. 5–9 (2017)
11. Ly, N.T., Nguyen, C.T., Nakagawa, M.: Training an end-to-end model for offline handwritten japanese text recognition by generated synthetic patterns. In: Proceedings of the International Conference on Frontiers in Handwriting Recognition (ICFHR), pp. 74–79 (2018)
12. Ly, N.T., Nguyen, K.C., Nguyen, C.T., Nakagawa, M.: Recognition of anomalously deformed kana sequences in Japanese historical documents. IEICE Trans. Inf. Syst. **E102D** (2019)
13. Puigcerver, J.: Are Multidimensional recurrent layers really necessary for handwritten text recognition? In: Proceedings of the International Conference on Document Analysis and Recognition, ICDAR, pp. 67–72 (2017)
14. Vaswani, A., et al.: Attention is all you need. In: Advances in Neural Information Processing Systems, pp. 5999–6009 (2017)
15. Luong, T., Pham, H., Manning, C.D.: Effective approaches to attention-based neural machine translation. In: Proceedings of the Conference on Empirical Methods in Natural Language Processing, pp. 1412–1421 (2015)
16. Bahdanau, D., Chorowski, J., Serdyuk, D., Brakel, P., Bengio, Y.: End-to-end attention-based large vocabulary speech recognition. In: Proceedings of the International Conference on Acoustics, Speech and Signal Processing (ICASSP), pp. 4945–4949 (2016)
17. Sueiras, J., Ruiz, V., Sanchez, A., Velez, J.F.: Offline continuous handwriting recognition using sequence to sequence neural networks. Neurocomputing **289**, 119–128 (2018)

18. Bluche, T., Louradour, J., Messina, R.: Scan, Attend and Read: End-to-End Handwritten Paragraph Recognition with MDLSTM Attention. In: Proceedings of the International Conference on Document Analysis and Recognition (ICDAR), pp. 1050–1055 (2017)
19. Bluche, T.: Joint line segmentation and transcription for end-to-end handwritten paragraph recognition. Neural Inf. Process. Syst. (2016)
20. Ly, N.T., Nguyen, C.T., Nakagawa, M.: An attention-based end-to-end model for multiple text lines recognition in japanese historical documents. In: Proceedings of the International Conference on Document Analysis and Recognition, ICDAR, pp. 629–634 (2019)
21. Ly, N.T., Nguyen, C.T., Nakagawa, M.: An attention-based row-column encoder-decoder model for text recognition in Japanese historical documents. Pattern Recognit. Lett. **136**, 134–141 (2020)
22. Zhang, Y., Nie, S., Liu, W., Xu, X., Zhang, D., Shen, H.T.: Sequence-to-sequence domain adaptation network for robust text image recognition. In: Proceedings of the IEEE Computer Society Conference on Computer Vision and Pattern Recognition, pp. 2735–2744 (2019)
23. Kang, L., Riba, P., Rusiñol, M., Fornés, A., Villegas, M.: Pay attention to what you read: non-recurrent handwritten text-line recognition. arXiv (2020)
24. Ly, N.T., Nguyen, C.T., Nakagawa, M.: Attention augmented convolutional recurrent network for handwritten Japanese text recognition. In: Proceedings of International Conference on Frontiers in Handwriting Recognition, ICFHR, pp. 163–168 (2020)
25. Ngo, T.T., Nguyen, H.T., Ly, N.T., Nakagawa, M.: Recurrent neural network transducer for Japanese and Chinese offline handwritten text recognition. arXiv (2021)
26. Graves, A., Fernández, S., Gomez, F., Schmidhuber, J.: Connectionist temporal classification: labelling unsegmented sequence data with recurrent neural networks. In: Proceedings of the ACM International Conference Proceeding Series, pp. 369–376 (2006)
27. Kuzushiji dataset. http://codh.rois.ac.jp/char-shape/book/. Accessed 07 Mar 2020
28. Ioffe, S., Szegedy, C.: Batch normalization: accelerating deep network training by reducing internal covariate shift. In: Proceedings of the International Conference on Machine Learning, ICML 2015, pp. 448–456 (2015)
29. Moysset, B., Messina, R.: Are 2D-LSTM really dead for offline text recognition? In: International Journal on Document Analysis and Recognition, pp. 193–208 (2019)

# Coarse-to-Fine Learning Framework for Semi-supervised Multimodal MRI Synthesis

Kun Yan[1,2], Zhizhe Liu[1,2], Shuai Zheng[1,2], Zhenyu Guo[1,2], Zhenfeng Zhu[1,2(✉)], and Yao Zhao[1,2]

[1] Institute of Information Science, Beijing Jiaotong University, 100091 Beijing, China
[2] Beijing Key Laboratory of Advanced Information Science and Network Technology, Beijing, China
{kunyan,zhzliu,zs1997,zhyguo,zhfzhu,yzhao}@bjtu.edu.cn

**Abstract.** Since multi-modal data contains more information than the single-modal, it is widely leveraged in medical domain. For example, different tissues have distinct visual effects in multimodal MRI, which allows doctors to use multimodal MRI to assist in the diagnosis of a variety of diseases. However, due to scan time, acquisition cost, noise pollution and other reasons in practice, the multimodal MRI of a patient is often not completely acquired. Given a set of available MRI multimodal data, our goal is to develop a semi-supervised (In this paper, semi-supervised learning refers to training using a large amount of unpaired data and a small amount of paired data, unsupervised learning refers to using only unpaired data and supervised learning refers to using only paired data, where paired data refers to MR images of two modalities from the same patient and unpaired data refers to MR images of two modalities from different patients.) deep learning model to synthesize their missing modal data in a coarse-to-fine manner, thereby avoiding the burden of traditional supervised approaches requiring collecting enough paired data for training of synthesis model. Specifically, to unveil the difference and content consistency among modalities of different distributions, large amounts of easily collected unpaired multimodal data were utilized to establish the cross-modal distribution mapping through adversarial learning, thus coarsely generating the reference image for missing MRI modality. Considering the detail differences between different modal images within the same subject, an enhancement network, trained with only a very small amount of available paired multimodal data, is used to further refine the generated reference image. Extensive experiments on BRATS2015 [13] dataset demonstrate that the proposed model outperforms both the unsupervised and the supervised methods quantitatively and qualitatively, and the latter requires a large amount of complete multimodal training data.

**Keywords:** Multi modal data · Semi-supervised learning · Cross-modal synthesis · Missing modal completion · Magnetic resonance imaging

© Springer Nature Switzerland AG 2022
C. Wallraven et al. (Eds.): ACPR 2021, LNCS 13189, pp. 370–384, 2022.
https://doi.org/10.1007/978-3-031-02444-3_28

# 1  Introduction

Based on the principle of "the more modalities, the more information", multiple modalities are often used in medical applications. For instance, magnetic resonance imaging(MRI) is widely utilized in current clinical practice since the powerful ability to capture various contrasts (*i.e.* modalities) of distinct soft tissues and the advantage of none radiation. In the actual situation, however, MR images collected by some patients may have certain modalities missing or completely unusable due to allergies to some contrasts agents, incorrect machine settings, excessive noise and scan costs, which will adversely affect clinical diagnosis and treatment. Under this condition, many downstream analysis models that require complete multimodal data often fails to achieve desired results. A simple solution is to directly discard the data with missing modalities and barely employ the remaining complete multi-modal data, but this will lead to disregard a lot of useful information. Therefore, it has potential value to study how to synthesize missing or damaged modalities from other successfully acquired modalities.

To address the above issue, cross-modal medical image synthesis has attached great research interest. The relevant synthesis methods can be divided into two main categories: traditional methods and deep learning-based methods. Traditional methods for medical image synthesis often learn nonlinear patch mapping and generate corresponding target modality patch [9,11,18,19], a setup that requires learning pixel intensity nonlinear mappings from patch of the source modal image or volume to the corresponding patch of the target modal using various techniques. Another approach is atlas-based [3,14], which use co-registered images from source and target modality to generate an atlas and then synthesize images of the desired target modality by combining the atlas and computing the geometric transformation of different subjects image within the same modality. Apart from these, sparse dictionary representation is proposed for cross-modal medical image synthesis [8,17]. Currently, deep learning has been widely applied to cross modal medical image synthesis with great success. Among them, important applications involve CT to PET synthesis [1,2], MR to CT synthesis [16,20], CT to MR synthesis [4], and retinal vascular map to color retinal image synthesis [6]. There are also many effective methods in the field of multi-contrast MRI synthesis, for example supervised learning models such as Multimodal [5], pGAN [7], EaGANs [21], Hi-Net [22], and unsupervised learning models such as cGAN [7].

However, among these methods, supervised learning models [5,7,21,22] require a large amount of complete paired multimodal data for training which is often scarce due to actual conditions, thus the performance of the model is difficult to guarantee. While unsupervised learning models, such as the cGAN proposed in [7], can solve this dilemma to some extent, the quality of the synthesized images is difficult to ensure due to the lack of sample level information. Considering this problem, we propose a coarse-to-fine learning framework for semi-supervised multimodal MRI synthesis[1], which can combine the use of

---

[1] Note that our data in this paper are all image data, while [12] focuses on generating image data from non-image data.

paired and unpaired data. Our framework is divided into two training phases. In the first phase, we learn the modality distribution information and cross-modal mapping relationships by generate network using unpaired data composed of all subjects while coarsely generate the reference image for missing MRI modality. Then in the second stage, we refine the coarse synthesis result to make it more clinically meaningful visually by using the multimodal supervised sample level information embedded in the paired data through our enhancement network.

In summary, contributions of this paper are as follows:

- In the field of multimodal MRI synthesis, we have conducted a new kind of exploration: how to apply deep learning technique to better synthesize MR images under the premise of a large amount of unpaired data and a small subset of complete data pairs in the dataset.
- In order to solve the above problem, we propose a semi-supervised multimodal MRI synthesis framework, which adopts the coarse-to-fine learning strategy. It can combine the use of the distribution level information in both the unpaired and paired data and the sample level information only in the paired data to synthesize MR imaging. After the model is trained, it can synthesize the image of the corresponding target modality given any modality.

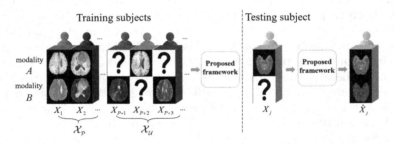

**Fig. 1.** Semi-supervised cross-modal MR image synthesis illustration. The dataset contains a small number of subjects with complete two modality images, and the remaining plenty of subjects have randomly missing images of one modality. Our goal is to build such a deep learning model that can learn how to better perform cross-modality MR image synthesis from such dataset.

## 2   Methodology

### 2.1   Problem Definition

As shown in Fig. 1, we denote the whole training data of modality $A$ and modality $B$ by $\mathcal{X}^A$ and $\mathcal{X}^B$, respectively. To be more specific, for a patient $i$, the modality $A$ data is denoted by $X_i^A$ and the modality $B$ data is denoted by $X_i^B$. In addition to this, suppose that there are a total of $N$ patients in the training set, of which $P$ patients have complete multimodal data, $i.e.$,

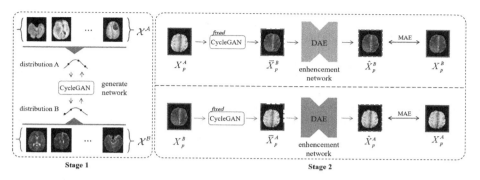

**Fig. 2.** Schematic diagram of our coarse-to-fine learning framework. The parameters of CycleGAN are updated only in the stage one of training, and are fixed in the stage two.

$\mathcal{X}_{\mathcal{P}} = \left\{ \left(X_1^A, X_1^B\right), \left(X_2^A, X_2^B\right), \dots, \left(X_P^A, X_P^B\right) \right\}$, and $N-P$ patients have missing data for a certain modality denoted as $\mathcal{X}_{\mathcal{U}}$. Our task is to mine the multimodal sample level image detail difference using $\mathcal{X}_{\mathcal{P}}$ and the cross-modal distribution mapping relationships of all modalities data, $i.e.$, $\mathcal{X}_{\mathcal{P}} \cup \mathcal{X}_{\mathcal{U}}$, to better synthesize MR reference images. Concretely speaking, for testing subject $j$, $X_j$, if the $A$ modality data $X_j^A$ is missing, we can coarsely synthesize $A$ modality data $\hat{X}_j^A$ from available $B$ modality data $X_j^B$ then $\bar{X}_j^A$ is enhanced by DAE to get $\hat{X}_j^A$ as the final output, and vice versa.

## 2.2 Coarse-to-Fine Learning Framework

**Overview of Framework.** For multimodal data, there are cross-modal distribution mapping relationships between different contrasts while exists the image detail differences between multiple modalities of the same subject. Therefore, our framework, as shown in Fig. 2, includes two networks - a generate network and an enhancement network (CycleGAN [23] is used as the generate network and DAE as the enhancement network in this paper) - and is trained in two phases. In the first stage, we leverage the unsupervised learning advantage of Cycle-GAN to learn cross-modal distribution mapping relationships from $\mathcal{X}_{\mathcal{P}} \cup \mathcal{X}_{\mathcal{U}}$ and coarsely synthesize image. In the second stage, in order to let the enhancement network mine the detail difference between diverse modalities within the same patient and to fully utilize the good generalization ability of DAE, we use the set of paired data $\mathcal{X}_{\mathcal{P}}$ and the generate network CycleGAN which has been trained in the previous stage to adjust the enhancement network parameters. In particular, for the paired data $\left(X_p^A, X_p^B\right)$ in the set $\mathcal{X}_{\mathcal{P}}$, if we take modality $A$ as the source modality and $B$ as the target modality, we first input $X_p^A$ into the trained CycleGAN by cross-modal mapping to get the coarse synthesis result $\bar{X}_p^B$, and then input $\bar{X}_p^B$ into DAE to get the output $\hat{X}_p^B$. To introduce multimodal sample level detail information in training DAE to achieve the enhancement effect, we do MAE constraint on $\hat{X}_p^B$ and $X_p^B$. The process is similar when the B modality is used as the source modality and the A modality is used as the target modality.

**Distribution Level.** In terms of multimodal data, if we view each modality as a domain, then each domain has a corresponding distribution of data. Therefore, to achieve cross-modal synthesis, we have to find the mapping relationship between each domain distribution, and map the data in the source domain to the target domain through the mapping relationship. Adversarial learning, allowing networks to learn distribution mappings of data domains, was introduced by generative adversarial networks. The generative adversarial network consists of generator and discriminator, where the generator is responsible for trying to generate data from the source domain that is similar to the data in the target domain, while the discriminator aims to distinguish the generated target domain data from the real data. Through adversarial learning, we can make model acquire domain mapping without the need for multimodal paired data, which can greatly avoid many supervised learning models from underperforming due to the limited amount of multimodal training data. In this paper, Cycle-GAN, which is used to learn the mapping relationship between bi-directional domain distributions from multimodal data, utilizes both adversarial loss and cycle consistency loss in its training in order to improve the accuracy of the mapping. After training, the mapping relationships learned by CycleGAN can be used to map a given source modality image to the target modality to achieve coarse synthesis of the reference image.

**Sample Level.** Since different tissues have different visual effects in images of different modalities, it is difficult to synthesize clinically meaningful target modal images directly from source modal images by the domain mapping learned by CycleGAN alone. Therefore the image synthesized by CycleGAN can be regarded as real images with some kind of noise added. In order to eliminate the noise, improve the image quality and make the synthetic image more valuable for clinical application, we introduce the enhancement network(DAE). The corrupted input and uncorrupted output force the denoising autoencoder to learn the important features of the image and ignore the unimportant ones, and the use of bottleneck middle layer gives it a strong generalization capability. Considering this feature, to ensure the spatial correlation between the synthesized target modality image and the real image, we use a small amount of paired data in the dataset to train a denoising autoencoder in a supervised learning manner to enhance the coarsely synthesized images of CycleGAN.

## 2.3   Optimization

The loss function can determine the effect of the model to a large extent. For the purpose of exploring the mapping relationships between different modalities, in the first stage of training we construct plenty of unpaired MR images and apply the loss introduced in [23], so that generate network can achieve preliminary cross-modal synthesis. Since the images of different contrasts of the same subject have the image detail difference, our enhancement network is trained with paired data, and the images obtained from the generate network are used as input to do the mean absolute error(MAE) constraint with the real target modality images.

$$MAE = E_{h,w}[||\hat{X}_p^C - X_p^C||_1] \tag{1}$$

In the above equation, $h$ and $w$ denote the height and width of the image respectively, $\hat{X}_i^A$ denotes enhanced synthetic result for contrast $C \in \{A, B\}$ of subject $p$, $X_p^C$ denotes the corresponding groundtruth.

## 3    Experiments and Results

### 3.1    Dataset

To evaluate our method, we use the multimodal brain tumor segmentation challenge 2015 (BRATS2015) dataset [13]. This dataset has co-registered T1, T2, T1c and Flair skull-stripped MR volumes for every subjects, each modal volume is $155 \times 240 \times 240$ which can be considered as an image sequence. In this study, we use a total of 54 volumes of T1, T2 modality of low grade glioma, of which 42 volumes are used for training, 6 for validation and 6 for testing, where the pixel intensity values of each volume were linearly normalized to [-1, 1]. Since our model utilizes 2D axial slices, we cropped the size of each slice to $192 \times 160$ in order to reduce the effect of the background during training and to fit our twice down-sampling and up-sampling network structure.

### 3.2    Benchmark Methods

To validate the effectiveness of the proposed semi-supervised synthesis framework, paired data for a certain proportion of patients and unpaired data consisting of all patients were used and several sets of experiments were done with different proportions. Due to the nature of supervised models themselves, we can only use paired data when train these models. While training unsupervised models, we use unpaired data consisting of all patients. The proposed model is compared with five models, including three supervised models and two unsupervised models, details of which are given below:

**Supervised Models.** Pix2pix [10] is a conditional GAN [15] model, which synthesizes images by focusing on confining the pixel-wise intensity difference, here we use it to synthesize MR images. Multimodal is a CNN-based model with an encoder-decoder structure to synthesize MR images slice-by-slice. pGAN utilizes both adversarial loss and pixel-level loss while also considering contextual information contained in multiple consecutive cross-sections for training, and can generate target contrast MR images from given source contrast MR images after training is completed.

**Unsupervised Models.** CycleGAN achieves cross-modal image synthesis by exploiting cycle consistent loss and adversarial loss without the need for paired data. Compared to CycleGAN, cGAN additionally takes into account the contextual information contained in multiple consecutive cross-sections during training, and it has the same network structure as pGAN.

### 3.3 Implementation Details

For the proposed framework, we follow the generator network structure of pGAN to build our denoising autoencoder network. But since our DAE performs an enhancement task which difficulty is less than the cross-modal synthesis task and to reduce the number of model parameters and boost computational speed, we retain only the four residual blocks of the generator network of pGAN in comparison experiments with other methods. Meanwhile, we further explore the effect of different number of residual blocks on the generated images in Subsect. 3.6. In terms of constructing training data, we considered the registered volumes of five different proportions of the patients in the training set to form paired data: 100%, 50%, 20%, 10% and just one patient which is the most extreme case. At the same time, for remaining subjects, we disrupt the modal alignment within subject and combine the volumes of one modality for each subject with the volumes of another modality for another subject to form a large number of unpaired data. For instance, for two patients A and B, the T1 volume of patient A is combined with the T2 volume of patient B to construct unpaired data.

### 3.4 Results Comparison

In order to avoid the impact on the model performance due to the biased distribution of the selected samples, we performed five experimental setup for paired data ratio: 100%, 50%, 20%, 10% and only one subject, where in 50%, 20%, 10% and only one subject cases we performed a quintuple sampling to construct paired data. At the same time, aiming to illustrate the effectiveness of our coarse-to-fine learning framework, the experimental results of CycleGAN here are the results we obtained from testing with CycleGAN after the first phase of pre-training. In all our experiments, the number of consecutive cross-sections of the input pGAN and cGAN was 3 (k=3).

Here we present the results of a series of experiments examining our proposed model in the case of 50% and 20% paired data respectively in two tasks, *i.e.*, using T1 modality image to synthesize T2 modality image and vice versa. Table 1 and Table 2 shows the quantitative evaluation results for two experimental scenarios respectively, and the final results of the proposed method and supervised methods of three metrics (MSE, SSIM and PSNR) are presented as mean ± standard deviation due to quintuple sampling. Since both unsupervised models are trained with unpaired data from all subjects, the results of the unsupervised methods have only the mean of each metric without standard deviation.

**Table 1.** Quantitative evaluation of T1→T2 and T2→T1 synthesis results (mean±standard deviation) in the case of 50% paired data.

| | | MSE(↓) | SSIM(↑) | PSNR(↑) |
|---|---|---|---|---|
| T1→T2 | pix2pix | 0.0076±0.0002 | 0.8893±0.0009 | 22.43±0.15 |
| | MM | 0.0075±0.0011 | 0.9120±0.0036 | 23.40±0.34 |
| | pGAN | 0.0052±0.0004 | 0.8788±0.0032 | 23.23±0.26 |
| | cGAN | 0.0070 | 0.885 | 22.58 |
| | CycleGAN | 0.0052 | 0.893 | 23.51 |
| | **Proposed** | **0.0050±0.0001** | **0.9110±0.0007** | **24.38±0.037** |
| T2→T1 | pix2pix | 0.0227±0.0050 | 0.8651±0.0122 | 17.13±1.03 |
| | MM | 0.0313±0.0015 | 0.8671±0.0027 | 16.07±0.26 |
| | pGAN | 0.0060±0.0008 | 0.8850±0.0042 | 22.63±0.68 |
| | cGAN | 0.0122 | 0.8860 | 19.67 |
| | CycleGAN | 0.0062 | 0.9040 | 23.36 |
| | **Proposed** | **0.0037±0.0001** | **0.9272±0.0009** | **24.48±0.12** |

**Table 2.** Quantitative evaluation of T1→T2 and T2→T1 synthesis results (mean±standard deviation) in the case of 20% paired data.

| | | MSE(↓) | SSIM(↑) | PSNR(↑) |
|---|---|---|---|---|
| T1→T2 | pix2pix | 0.0088±0.0007 | 0.8808±0.0032 | 21.47±0.31 |
| | MM | 0.0078±0.0009 | 0.9025±0.0066 | 22.74±0.80 |
| | pGAN | 0.0081±0.0008 | 0.8704±0.0016 | 21.75±0.31 |
| | cGAN | 0.0070 | 0.885 | 22.58 |
| | CycleGAN | 0.0052 | 0.893 | 23.51 |
| | **Proposed** | **0.0054±0.0002** | **0.9047±0.0011** | **23.85±0.108** |
| T2→T1 | pix2pix | 0.0224±0.0025 | 0.8690±0.0046 | 17.18±0.61 |
| | MM | 0.0307±0.0022 | 0.8680±0.0052 | 16.06±0.48 |
| | pGAN | 0.0059±0.0008 | 0.8903±0.0020 | 22.86±0.71 |
| | cGAN | 0.0122 | 0.8860 | 19.67 |
| | CycleGAN | 0.0062 | 0.9040 | 23.36 |
| | **Proposed** | **0.0049±0.0002** | **0.9207±0.0017** | **23.79±0.17** |

From Table 1 and Table 2, as it can be seen that our method significantly outperforms all comparison methods in all three metrics when 50% and 20% of the subjects have available multimodal paired data. This suggests that in our experimental setup, using both modal distribution information hidden in unpaired data and sample level detail information in paired data can be effective in enhancing image synthesis. Interestingly, for supervised models, we find that the performance of these models does not improve observably with the increasing amount

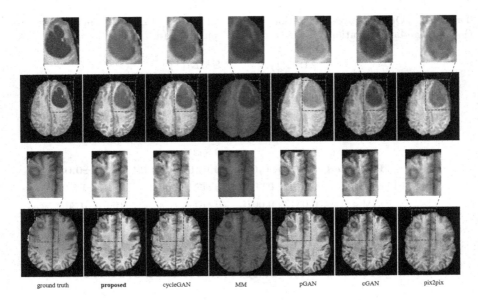

**Fig. 3.** Qualitative comparison between the proposed synthesis method and other synthesis methods for the T2→T1 task.

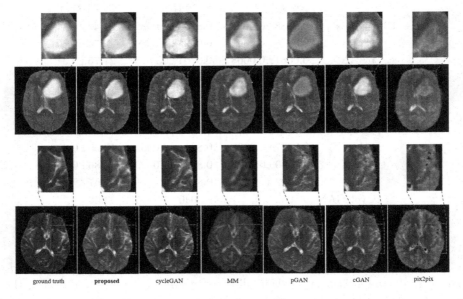

**Fig. 4.** Qualitative comparison between the proposed synthesis method and other synthesis methods for the T1→T2 task.

of available training data in the task of synthesizing T1 modalities from T2 modalities. This may be due to the fact that obtaining supervised information from paired data alone and lacking information on the data distribution of each modality is not sufficient to gain enough knowledge, which is particularly evident in this task. At the same time, for unsupervised models, we found that cGAN was not as effective as CycleGAN under this experimental condition, which may be due to the fact that cGAN can only be trained in two synthesis directions separately and cannot be synthesized in both directions at the same time as CycleGAN can leverage modal collaboration to promote each other's synthesis effect. These unsupervised models do not perform as well as our approach because the lack of supervised image detail information does not guarantee the synthesis quality.

We show the visual effects of the resulting synthetic images in an experimental setup with 20% paired training data. Figure 3 and Fig. 4 show a qualitative comparison between our method and other comparative methods of synthesis images in both cases with and without lesions in the T1 and T2 synthesis task.

As shown in the second row and first row of Fig. 3 and Fig. 4 respectively, our method can achieve relatively satisfactory visual effects in both lesion-free detailed structures and lesion areas which may be more critical in assisting physicians in the clinical diagnosis of disease. In contrast, the supervised model is difficult to guarantee the model performance due to the lack of training data, and the quality of the generated images is not satisfactory. Compared with unsupervised methods, our method outperforms them visually because it takes into account the pixel-wise detail between multimodal images. Note that the overall darkness of the Multimodal synthesized image is due to the mean normalization applied to the MR volumes [5].

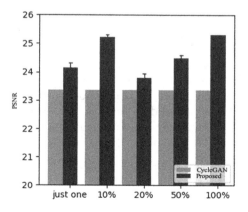

**Fig. 5.** Variation of CycleGAN and the proposed method PSNR metrics for different paired data ratio settings in the task of T2→T1.

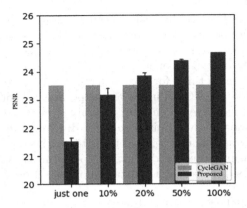

**Fig. 6.** Variation of CycleGAN and the proposed method PSNR metrics for different paired data ratio settings in the task of T1→T2.

To further illustrate the effectiveness of our coarse-to-fine framework for semi-supervised learning, we show the variation of our method and CycleGAN in PSNR metrics for the five paired data ratio settings mentioned in the previous section. Since CycleGAN is trained using unpaired data consisting of all patients, its results have only mean values and no standard deviation. It should be noted that the results of our method do not have standard deviations when the proportion of paired data reaches 100% because only one sampling can be performed. As we can see from Fig. 5, our method outperforms CycleGAN in all experimental settings even when paired data of just one subject is available for the task of synthesizing T1 modalities, and achieves optimal results especially when all pairs of data are available.

In another synthesis task (synthesis of T2 modality from T1 modality), as shown in Fig. 6, our model is less effective than CycleGAN in the case of minimal paired data, probably because denoising autoencoder does not have strong enough learning ability to learn sufficiently general features from such limited data. However, as the available paired data increases the performance of our method becomes better and better, and our model outperforms CycleGAN when the percentage of available paired data reaches 10%. These experiments demonstrate the effectiveness of our coarse-fo-fine semi-supervised learning model.

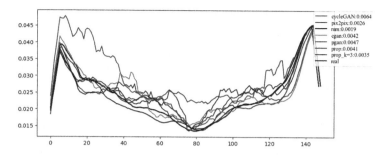

**Fig. 7.** Stability of MRI sequences synthesized by different models in T1→T2 task

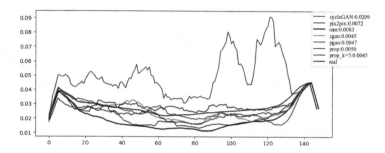

**Fig. 8.** Stability of MRI sequences synthesized by different models in T2→T1 task

### 3.5   Synthesis Stability

Our method inputs data on a slice by slice basis, but MRI is a 3D volume with contextual correlation between neighboring slices. Therefore stability when synthesizing MRI slices is crucial. Inspired by [7], we try to introduce contextual information in the input of enhancement network to improve the synthesis stability, which is done by changing the input of the denosing autoencoder from a single slice to three consecutive neighboring slices(k=3).

To measure the synthesis sequence stability of different methods, we calculate the KL divergence of slice and neighboring slice of real volume and each model synthesized volume in all testing subject and plot the line chart. As can be seen from Fig. 7 and Fig. 8[2], in terms of the closeness to the stability curve of real volume, our method has a significant improvement compared to CycleGAN. At the same time, the images synthesized after considering contextual information in the input of our proposed model are more stable than when they are not considered. And compared with other methods, our model that adds contextual information to the input has the best stability in synthesizing T1 modality task and competitive stability in synthesizing T2 modality task.

---

[2] The value in the upper right legend indicates the average absolute error of the KL divergence sequence of neighboring slices between the volume synthesized by each method and the real volume.

**Table 3.** Quantitative evaluation of the synthesis results affected by different number of residual blocks.

| | T1→T2 | | | T2→T1 | | |
|---|---|---|---|---|---|---|
| | MSE($\downarrow$) | SSIM($\uparrow$) | PSNR($\uparrow$) | MSE($\downarrow$) | SSIM($\uparrow$) | PSNR($\uparrow$) |
| $n=0$ | 0.0052 | 0.9077 | 24.08 | 0.0042 | 0.9247 | 24.56 |
| $n=1$ | 0.0051 | 0.9056 | 24.07 | 0.0043 | 0.9217 | 24.26 |
| $n=2$ | 0.0054 | 0.9032 | 23.78 | 0.0047 | 0.9224 | 24.07 |
| $n=4$ | **0.0052** | **0.9080** | **24.08** | **0.0041** | **0.9250** | **24.56** |
| $n=6$ | 0.0054 | 0.9056 | 23.84 | 0.0049 | 0.9240 | 23.78 |

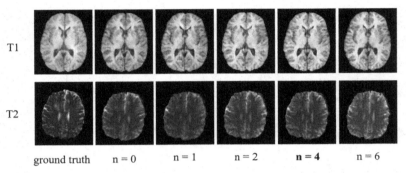

**Fig. 9.** The difference in the visual effect of the synthesis results affected by different number of residual blocks.

## 3.6  Ablation Study

Taking into account the effectiveness of the model with respect to computation time and cost, we investigated the effect of different number of residual blocks (n=0, 1, 2, 4 or the 6 blocks in the original pGAN [7]) on the synthesis effect, and the experimental quantitative results are shown in Table 3 and the qualitative results are shown in Fig. 9.

In general, these results show that the quantitative index of the synthesized image is high but the visual effect is blurred when the number of residual blocks is small or even absent. On the contrary, the quantitative index of the synthesized image is relatively low when the number of residual blocks is high, but the visual effect is good and the details of structure and organization are clear. Therefore, in order to pursue the balance of all aspects, four residual blocks are used in our scheme to construct the denoising autoencoder network.

## 4  Conclusion

In this paper, we propose a coarse-to-fine semi-supervised cross-modal MRI synthesis deep learning architecture and validate the effectiveness of the scheme through extensive experiments. In the future, our work has two potential research directions: exploring cross-modal synthesis of three or more modal data and cross-modal synthesis of non-image modal (*e.g.*, structured data) data.

**Acknowledgements.** This work was supported in part by Science and Technology Innovation 2030 - "New Generation Artificially Intelligence" Major Project under Grant 2018AAA-0102101, in part by the National Natural Science Foundation of China under Grant 61976018 and Grant 61532005.

# References

1. Ben-Cohen, A., Klang, E., Raskin, S.P., Amitai, M.M., Greenspan, H.: Virtual pet images from CT data using deep convolutional networks: initial results. In: Tsaftaris, S.A., Gooya, A., Frangi, A.F., Prince, J.L. (eds.) Simulation and Synthesis in Medical Imaging, pp. 49–57. Springer, Cham (2017)
2. Bi, L., Kim, J., Kumar, A., Feng, D., Fulham, M.: Synthesis of positron emission tomography (pet) images via multi-channel generative adversarial networks (GANs). In: Cardoso, M.J., et al. (eds.) Molecular Imaging, Reconstruction and Analysis of Moving Body Organs, and Stroke Imaging and Treatment, pp. 43–51. Springer, Cham (2017)
3. Burgos, N., et al.: Attenuation correction synthesis for hybrid pet-MR scanners: application to brain studies. IEEE Trans. Med. Imaging **33**(12), 2332–2341 (2014)
4. Chartsias, A., Joyce, T., Dharmakumar, R., Tsaftaris, S.A.: Adversarial image synthesis for unpaired multi-modal cardiac data. In: Tsaftaris, S.A., Gooya, A., Frangi, A.F., Prince, J.L. (eds.) SASHIMI 2017. LNCS, vol. 10557, pp. 3–13. Springer, Cham (2017). https://doi.org/10.1007/978-3-319-68127-6_1
5. Chartsias, A., Joyce, T., Giuffrida, M.V., Tsaftaris, S.A.: Multimodal MR synthesis via modality-invariant latent representation. IEEE Trans. Med. Imaging **37**(3), 803–814 (2017)
6. Costa, P., et al.: End-to-end adversarial retinal image synthesis. IEEE Trans. Med. Imaging **37**(3), 781–791 (2017)
7. Dar, S.U., Yurt, M., Karacan, L., Erdem, A., Erdem, E., Çukur, T.: Image synthesis in multi-contrast MRI with conditional generative adversarial networks. IEEE Trans. Med. Imaging **38**(10), 2375–2388 (2019)
8. Huang, Y., Shao, L., Frangi, A.F.: Cross-modality image synthesis via weakly coupled and geometry co-regularized joint dictionary learning. IEEE Trans. Med. Imaging **37**(3), 815–827 (2017)
9. Huynh, T., et al.: Estimating CT image from MRI data using structured random forest and auto-context model. IEEE Trans. Med. Imaging **35**(1), 174–183 (2015)
10. Isola, P., Zhu, J.Y., Zhou, T., Efros, A.A.: Image-to-image translation with conditional adversarial networks. In: Proceedings of the IEEE Conference on Computer Vision and Pattern Recognition, pp. 1125–1134 (2017)
11. Jog, A., Roy, S., Carass, A., Prince, J.L.: Magnetic resonance image synthesis through patch regression. In: 2013 IEEE 10th International Symposium on Biomedical Imaging, pp. 350–353. IEEE (2013)
12. Li, D., Du, C., He, H.: Semi-supervised cross-modal image generation with generative adversarial networks. Pattern Recogn. **100**, 107085 (2020)

13. Menze, B.H., Jakab, A., Bauer, S., Kalpathy-Cramer, J., Farahani, K., Kirby, J., Burren, Y., Porz, N., Slotboom, J., Wiest, R., et al.: The multimodal brain tumor image segmentation benchmark (brats). IEEE Trans. Med. Imaging **34**(10), 1993–2024 (2014)

14. Miller, M.I., Christensen, G.E., Amit, Y., Grenander, U.: Mathematical textbook of deformable neuroanatomies. Proc. Natl. Acad. Sci. **90**(24), 11944–11948 (1993)

15. Mirza, M., Osindero, S.: Conditional generative adversarial nets. arXiv preprint arXiv:1411.1784 (2014)

16. Nie, D., Trullo, R., Lian, J., Wang, L., Petitjean, C., Ruan, S., Wang, Q., Shen, D.: Medical image synthesis with deep convolutional adversarial networks. IEEE Trans. Biomed. Eng. **65**(12), 2720–2730 (2018)

17. Roy, S., Carass, A., Prince, J.L.: Magnetic resonance image example-based contrast synthesis. IEEE Trans. Med. Imaging **32**(12), 2348–2363 (2013)

18. Roy, S., Chou, Y.Y., Jog, A., Butman, J.A., Pham, D.L.: Patch based synthesis of whole head MR images: application to epi distortion correction. In: Tsaftaris, S.A., Gooya, A., Frangi, A.F., Prince, J.L. (eds.) Simulation and Synthesis in Medical Imaging, pp. 146–156. Springer International Publishing, Cham (2016)

19. Vemulapalli, R., Van Nguyen, H., Zhou, S.K.: Unsupervised cross-modal synthesis of subject-specific scans. In: Proceedings of the IEEE International Conference on Computer Vision, pp. 630–638 (2015)

20. Wolterink, J.M., Dinkla, A.M., Savenije, M., Seevinck, P.R., van den Berg, C., Išgum, I.: MR-to-CT synthesis using cycle-consistent generative adversarial networks. In: Proceedings Neural Information Processing Systems (NIPS) (2017)

21. Yu, B., Zhou, L., Wang, L., Shi, Y., Fripp, J., Bourgeat, P.: EA-GANs: edge-aware generative adversarial networks for cross-modality MR image synthesis. IEEE Trans. Med. Imaging **38**(7), 1750–1762 (2019)

22. Zhou, T., Fu, H., Chen, G., Shen, J., Shao, L.: Hi-net: hybrid-fusion network for multi-modal MR image synthesis. IEEE Trans. Med. Imaging **39**(9), 2772–2781 (2020)

23. Zhu, J.Y., Park, T., Isola, P., Efros, A.A.: Unpaired image-to-image translation using cycle-consistent adversarial networks. In: Proceedings of the IEEE International Conference on Computer Vision, pp. 2223–2232 (2017)

# Computer Vision and Robot Vision

Computer Vision and Control Systems

# Intelligent Recognition of Point Source Target Image Control Points with Simulation Datasets

Kai Li[1(✉)], Weiming Yang[1], Lei Zhang[2], and Zhenchao Zhang[2]

[1] Academy of Military Sciences, Academy of System Engineering, Beijing, China
likai_rs@163.com
[2] School of Geospatial Information, Strategic Support Force Information Engineering
University, Zhengzhou, China

**Abstract.** The point source target (PST) can provide high object and image positioning accuracy and is expected to play an important role in the precise geometric processing of optical remote sensing sensors in the future. This paper proposes a method for intelligently recognizing PST image control points (ICPs) from satellite imagery, which can improve the intelligent level of geometric processing of optical remote sensing sensors. Two deep convolutional neural networks (DCNNs), Faster R-CNN and CenterNet are selected to complete the recognition task. Due to the lack of training data, a large number of simulated samples are generated considering the PST image characteristics. The simulated and real PST ICPs are then used to test the trained DCNNs. The two DCNNs complete the recognition task on the simulated dataset successfully. The Recall and Precision values of the two DCNNs are close to 100%. The performance of the two DCNNs on real PST ICPs is worse than that on the simulated data, but the recognition task is also well completed when the quality of PST ICPs is good. The Recall values of both models are above 95%, and the Precision values are close to 100%. Experiment results also show that the performance of CenterNet is better than Faster R-CNN and the image quality has a great impact on the recognition performance.

**Keywords:** Point source target (PST) · Image control point (ICP) · Deep convolutional neural networks (DCNNs) · Faster R-CNN · CenterNet

## 1 Introduction

Satellites equipped with remote sensing sensors are the main equipment for carrying out target reconnaissance, positioning and mapping. During the on-orbit operation of the remote sensing sensors, the geometric positioning accuracy is in the process of dynamic change due to orbit perturbation, environment change, and device aging [1–3]. The laboratory calibration results before satellite launch and the limited auxiliary equipment test on the satellite is an open-loop detection method, which cannot ensure a high calibration accuracy of the parameters of sensors. The accuracy and reliability of satellite positioning results will be greatly affected if the geometric parameters are not corrected for on-orbit sensors [4–7].

© Springer Nature Switzerland AG 2022
C. Wallraven et al. (Eds.): ACPR 2021, LNCS 13189, pp. 387–401, 2022.
https://doi.org/10.1007/978-3-031-02444-3_29

The trend for high-precision and reliable positioning of remote sensing sensors is to establish a large-scale ground calibration field. When the satellite transits the area, on-orbit geometric calibration based on the large-scale calibration field is carried out. The key geometric parameters of the sensors are continuously and dynamically solved, and the updated parameters are used to compensate for the variation, so as to ensure the authenticity, reliability and accuracy of the satellite positioning results [8–14].

The ground geometry calibration field is actually a control network composed of many high-precision Ground Control Points (GCPs). The images of the GCPs on the satellite imagery are generally called the Image Control Points (ICPs). Natural features with good geometric properties, such as road intersections, playground corners, etc., are usually chosen as GCPs even in nowadays [15–17]. Some artificial targets with good measurement performance are also used to meet the demand for quantity of GCPs [18]. These control points have very high precision 3D coordinates provided by Real-time kinematic (RTK) positioning technique. However, these traditional GCPs have some drawbacks. First, the ICPs of the GCPs are recognized mainly rely on visual interpretation of the surveyor [15–17, 19], thus bringing a lot of manual work. Although methods such as deep learning can be used to recognize images such as road intersections, it is not easy to find the specific road intersection corresponding to the GCP because such features are widespread in nature. Second, it is difficult to lay out artificial target GCP due to the large area. For example, the artificial target used by the Chinese Ziyuan-3 satellite is a square cloth with a side length of 40 m. Third, due to the relatively low resolution and poor quality of satellite imagery, the image extraction accuracy of ICP of the traditional GCP is not high and the error of manual interpretation can reach 0.5–1 pixels [16, 19, 20].

For geometry applications of remote sensing images, point source target (PST) is a new type of target, but it has been used for many years in radiation applications for some sensors, such as Landsat-5 TM [21] and Quickbird II [22]. PST can be used for MTF (Modulation Transfer Function) measurement and radiation calibration due to its imaging characteristics. For on-orbit satellite sensors, PST can be seen as an ideal point source and its image pixel values in the satellite imagery are the discrete values of the PSF (Point Spread Function). In other words, the PST image can be accurately described with specific function. High precision geometry and radiation parameters then can be restored from the function. Radiation information of the PST image have been fully utilized these years [21–23], however, the geometry information is left out though it has been proved to provide high-precision image position information.

PSTs are clearly an ideal alternative to traditional GCPs. PSTs are easy to lie, and the image extraction accuracy of PST images is much higher. Thus, the second and third drawbacks of traditional GCPs are overcome by PSTs. In this paper, we focus on the first drawback of traditional GCPs and propose a method to recognize the PST ICPs intelligently without manual intervention.

The deep convolutional neural network (DCNN) has excellent performance for the recognition and detection of specific targets in the image. Therefore, the PST can be regarded as a special kind of ground object. Through the train with a large number of PST image samples, a stable neural network model can be obtained to realize the fast and intelligent recognition of PST ICPs. Unlike natural features such as road intersections, PST images have some particularities that may bring difficult for recognition tasks. First, there are no PSTs in nature and the number of PSTs manually deployed is also limited. Therefore, it is now impossible to obtain enough PST image samples for neural network training. Second, the PST image features are not rich enough, while the DCNN is usually designed for the recognition and classification of objects with rich features, such as face, vehicle, animals and plants, buildings, etc. Finally, the PST image has a very small size with a scale of only 3–7 pixels, which is rarely seen in the application of the DCNN.

DCNN cannot work without a sufficient number of samples. To recognize the PST ICPs, we first constructed a PST image simulation dataset based on the image characteristics of PST image. Then two popular DCNNs Faster R-CNN [24] and CenterNet [25] are trained with the simulation dataset to obtain the test model. Simulated and real PST ICPs are then used to test the performance of the trained models.

## 2   PST Image Characteristics

When any image system collects information of real-world scenes, it will cause the image to degrade to varying degrees. The factors that cause the degradation include design defects in sensor photosensitive elements, channel noise during image transmission, the interference of the atmosphere, etc. We can use mathematical formulas to describe the degradation process of an image. Assuming that the input original real world scene is $f(x, y)$, after the action of the system $H$, it is added to the Gaussian noise $n(x, y)$ to obtain a degraded image $g(x, y)$. This process can be expressed as.

$$g(x, y) = H(f(x, y)) + n(x, y) \tag{1}$$

In the formula, the operation $H$ of the imaging system contains the effects of all degradation factors except for noise. $H$ can be expressed as the convolution of the original image $f$ with the degeneration function $h(x, y)$.

$$H(f(x, y)) = f(x, y) * h(x, y) \tag{2}$$

The degeneration function $h(x, y)$ is also called the spatial response function of the imaging system. Equation (1) and (2) can be further expressed in the form of integrals as follows

$$g(x, y) = \int_{-\infty}^{+\infty} \int_{-\infty}^{+\infty} f(\mu, v) \cdot h(x - \mu, y - v) d\mu dv + n(x, y) \tag{3}$$

Consider the case where the scene contains only one ideal point source. In this case, the point source can be regarded as a unit impulse function $\delta(x, y)$. The radiant energy at the origin is infinite, and the area outside the origin is zero. The integral of the function is 1, so we have

$$\delta(x, y) * h(x, y) = \int_{-\infty}^{+\infty} \int_{-\infty}^{+\infty} \delta(\mu, v) \cdot h(x - \mu, y - v) d\mu dv = h(x, y) \tag{4}$$

It can be seen from Eq. (4) that $h(x, y)$ is the degraded image generated by an ideal light spot after the degradation of imaging system, so it is also called the point spread function. For optical remote sensing satellites capable of clear imaging, the defocusing effect of the optical system during imaging can be neglected, and the two-dimensional Gaussian function is usually used to simulate the PSF [26–28], which is also the most commonly used degradation function of optical camera systems.

$$h(x, y) = \frac{1}{2\pi\sigma\xi} \exp\left(-\frac{(x - x_0)^2}{2\sigma^2} - \frac{(y - y_0)^2}{2\xi^2}\right) \tag{5}$$

Equation (1) to (5) describe degradation of a scene of continuous energy, however the digital image is discretized. The spatial distribution of the pixel values of the PST image is obtained by sampling and quantizing Eq. (5) at pixel intervals and adding Gaussian noise

$$g_p(i, j) = K \cdot \exp\left(-\frac{(i - x_0)^2}{2\sigma^2} - \frac{(j - y_0)^2}{2\xi^2}\right) + N_w(i, j) \tag{6}$$

where $i$ and $j$ are the row and column coordinates of the PST image, respectively. $K$ represents the pixel value of the center of the PST image. $N_w(i, j)$ is the discretized Gaussian white noise. $x_0$ and $y_0$ are the peak positions of the PSF, respectively. $\sigma$ and $\xi$ are the standard deviations of the PSF. For PST image, $x_0$ and $y_0$ provider the exact position of the point source image. The energy distribution of the background is not considered in Eq. (6). When the background energy distribution is uniform, the background pixel value is a constant $b$. The final PST image then can be generated by adding Eq. (6) with the background pixel value $b$.

## 3    Methodology

This paper intends to use the DCNN to realize the intelligent recognition of PST image ICPs, but there is not enough number of PST image sample data. Therefore, the key problem to be solved in this paper is to construct a simulation dataset of PST image ICPs. The data set should simulate PST imaging results under various imaging conditions as much as possible. Then, we use two classical DCNNs to train the data set, get the network model, and use it to detect the real PST image.

### 3.1    Generation of Simulation Dataset

Section 2 introduces the characteristics of PST images and also provides a theoretical basis for generating PST simulated images. A PST simulated image can be generated with Eq. (6) if all the parameters in the equation and the background pixel value b are known. The values of these parameters are affected by the internal structure of the imaging sensor and external environmental factors. These factors and their relationship with the parameters in Eq. (6) are listed as follows.

### 3.1.1 Position of PST Image Center

The position $(x_0, y_0)$ is the center of PST image. The fractional part of $x_0$ and $y_0$ is called the phase of the PST image in this paper. Figure 1 shows the spatial distribution of the pixel values of the PST image when the phase of the point source image is (0, 0) and (0.6, 0.8) (in pixels) in the ideal case without noise. From Fig. 1 we can see that when $(x_0, y_0)$ is changed, the PST imaging result also changes. Therefore, when generating PST simulated image, the phase of the image should be randomly selected from 0 to 1.

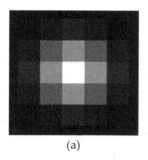          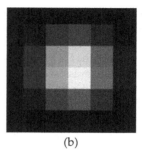

(a)                                                          (b)

**Fig. 1.** PST simulated image. (a) Phase of image is (0, 0); (b) Phase of image is (0.6, 0.8).

### 3.1.2 Standard Deviations of PSF

PSF is the degradation function of the image and this function spreads the PST imaging result to an image patch with a length of 3–7 pixels. The parameters $\sigma$ and $\xi$ in the PSF function determine the size of the imaging result, and also affect the value of each pixel in the PST image. When generating a simulated image, the value of $\sigma$ and $\xi$ should be considered. Some experiments use Gaussian functions to fit the PSFs of sensors such as Landsat 4/5, Quickbird II, GF-2, and GF-4, and the results show that the standard deviation of the PSFs of these sensors is generally between 0.5 and 1 pixel.

### 3.1.3 Noise in the Imaging System

Noise is inevitable in real images. Design defects in the sensor's photosensitive elements, channel noise during image information transmission, and other factors can cause noise in the imaging result. In this paper, Gaussian noise with different signal-to-noise ratio (SNR) is added to generate PST images to simulate the influence of noise.

### 3.1.4 Brightness of PST Image Center

The PST acquires a large luminous flux by reflecting sunlight, thereby forming a bright spot on the satellite imagery. When the light path between the sun, the target mirror, and the satellite entrance is strictly aligned, the sensor obtains the largest luminous flux. However, in practical applications, due to the deviation of the orbit prediction, there is generally an error in the optical path, which causes the imaging brightness of the PST image to change. In addition, the illumination conditions also directly affect the imaging brightness. The influence of these factors should be fully considered when generating the PST simulated image.

### 3.1.5 Contrast of PST Image Center

The contrast here refers to the contrast between the center of the target image and the background, which is mainly determined by the ratio of the reflectance of the PST mirror to the background. In practice, a black bottom net is usually laid under the target, which can increase the imaging contrast on the one hand, and avoid the influence of pixel mixing effect caused by complex background on the other hand. However, this practice also has drawbacks, especially for low-resolution sensors, which require a large area of black bottom net, and the difficulty of experimental preparation is greatly increased. In fact, the reflectance of the PST mirror is about 80%, while the bare ground surface reflectance is 10%–25%, the grassland surface reflectance is 15%–25%. Therefore, there is a large contrast between the PST mirror surface and bare land or grassland. Imaging results with higher contrast can also be obtained if the PST is placed in an open bare ground or grassland. In this paper, different imaging contrasts are considered when generating simulated images, so that the trained neural network model can be used for PST image recognition under various contrast conditions.

By using Eq. (6) and setting different imaging parameters, the PST simulated images under different conditions can be obtained. The PST simulated image is an image patch with size of $w \times w$ pixels. The PST simulated image obtained now is not sample data for training. Since the 3D coordinate of the PST is known, the corresponding ICP position can be predicted according to the strict imaging model, so it is not necessary to recognize the PST ICP in the whole imagery. We randomly selected an image patch with the size of $W \times W$ (the value of $W$ is set according to the positioning error of the sensor) pixels from a satellite imagery, then place the PST simulated image into anywhere in the image patch to replace the corresponding pixel values. Thus, a sample of data for training is generated.

### 3.2 Faster R-CNN and CenterNet

The purpose of generating a simulated dataset is to train it with a DCNN and obtain a detection model of PST ICPs. Target detection based on deep learning can be generally divided into two categories: one is the one-stage algorithm, and the other is two-stage algorithm. The two-stage algorithm first generate a series of generate region proposals for the target, and then classify each region proposals by a neural network, while one-stage algorithm does not generate region proposals, and the detection result is directly obtained. In general, the one-stage algorithm is faster than the two-stage algorithm.

This paper selects a representative DCNN algorithm from each of the two categories of algorithms to train the simulated dataset. The first DCNN algorithm is Faster R-CNN, a two-stage algorithm. Before the emergence of Faster R-CNN, there were already R-CNN [29] and Fast R-CNN [30]. Faster R-CNN improves some of the shortcomings of R-CNN and Fast R-CNN, such as the inability to implement end-to-end training and the time-consuming of the selective search process. Faster R-CNN integrates convolutional layer, region proposal network, ROI pooling, and classification into a network, and the target detection speed has been greatly improved. The second DCNN algorithm is Centernet, a one-stage algorithm. CenterNet is an improved algorithm for another one-stage algorithm, CornerNet [31]. CenterNet determines a target by detecting three key points for each target instead of two used by CornerNet, thus improving the accuracy and recall of the model.

## 4  Experiments and Results

### 4.1  Experimental Data

#### 4.1.1  Simulated Datasets

According to Sect. 3, the range of values for each parameter when generating the PST simulated image is shown in Table 1. Table 1 takes the various possible scenarios that affect imaging into account, including very poor imaging conditions. Thus, the model trained by the simulated dataset can have stronger recognition ability and greater applicability. When generating a PST simulated image, the parameter values are randomly selected from the range of values of each parameter in Table 1. In this paper, a total of 14000 PST simulated images are generated, and the size of PST simulated image is $7 \times 7$ pixels. In Fig. 2, a plurality of PST simulated images is randomly selected for display, and the image is enlarged in order to be clearly observed.

**Table 1.** Parameter ranges for generating PST image.

| Parameters | Parameter ranges |
|---|---|
| phase | x axis:0–1 pixels, y axis:0–1 pixels |
| standard deviation of PSF | $\sigma$:0.5–1 pixels, $\xi$:0.5–1 pixels |
| SNR | 20dB-40dB |
| pixel value of the center of PST image ($K$) | $(0.5–1) \times N_{max}$* |
| reflectance ratio between PST and background | 2–20 |

* $N_{max}$ is the maximum pixel value of satellite imagery.

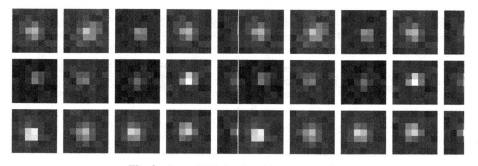

**Fig. 2.** Some PST simulated images samples.

The PST simulated images are then placed into an image patch with a size of $W \times W$ pixels randomly selected from the satellite imagery (Fig. 4(a), introduced in Sect. 4.1.2).

Here we set $W$ to 60 because the positioning error of state-of-the-art mapping satellite usually does not exceed this value. Thus, 14000 samples are generated. Figure 3 shows two samples of the simulated dataset.

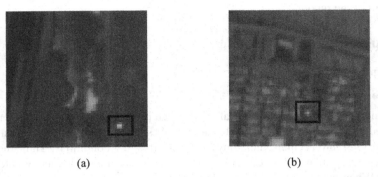

(a)                                    (b)

**Fig. 3.** Two samples of the generated dataset, in which the PST images are marked with a red frame.

### 4.1.2   Satellite Imagery and PST Image Data

The satellite imagery was provided by the Chinese TH-1 satellite, as show in Fig. 4(a). The TH-1 satellite is an optical remote sensing satellite with an orbital altitude of 500 km and an orbital inclination of 97.3°. The size of the imagery is 12000 × 12000 pixels and the spatial resolution of the imagery is 5 m. 16 PSTs were placed in a 4 × 4 array form on the ground with a distance about 40 m between any two targets before imaging. Figure 4(b) shows the scene of a part of the PSTs in the experiment. The imaging result of the 16 PSTs on the satellite imagery is shown in Fig. 4(c). A large black bottom net is placed under the target as shown in Fig. 4(b), so the background of the PST images is black.

The PSTs are deployed for radiation calibration in a very small area and are not suitable for geometric calibration, which requires the ICPs to be distributed throughout the entire imagery evenly. In order to test the DCNN models, we extracted each PST image in Fig. 4(c) and placed it into an image patch with a size of 60 × 60 pixels as done in Sect. 4.1.1. The 16 PST ICPs are reused to generate a test dataset with a total of 1000 samples. This paper refers to the dataset as Dataset I. Figure 4(d) shows one sample of the dataset, in which the PST image is marked with a red frame.

Although 16 PST images were scattered in 1000 image slices, this only fully examined the recognition effect of PSTs in a sufficiently complex background. We also want to test the model's ability to recognize more PST images. It can be seen from Fig. 4(d) that the quality of the PST images is good, which reduces the difficulty of recognition. Therefore, we change the brightness of the PST images in Fig. 4(d) using Eq. (7), and derive several test datasets of different brightness from the real data.

$$f'_k = k \cdot \left(f - N_{bg}\right) + N_{bg} \tag{7}$$

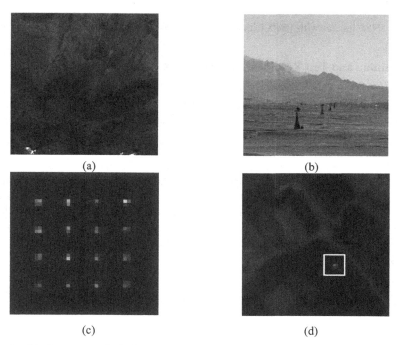

**Fig. 4.** Satellite imagery and PST image data. (a) The satellite imagery; (b) the PST; (c) the scene of the PSTs; (d) the imaging result of the 16 PSTs.

In Eq. (7), $f$ is the image in Fig. 4(c); $N_{bg}$ is the average pixel value of the background area pixels in image $f$; $k$ is the coefficient to change the brightness of the PST image; $f_a'$ is the new image. $k$ is set to 0.8, 0.5, and 0.2, respectively, and the corresponding new images with 16 PST images are shown in Fig. 5. Three datasets with 1000 test samples each then can be generated using the same method as Dataset I. The three datasets are hereinafter referred to as data sets II, III, and IV, respectively.

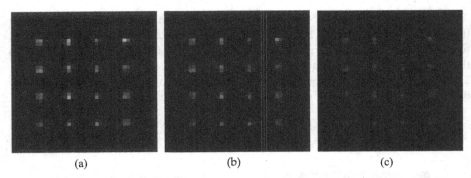

(a)             (b)             (c)

**Fig. 5.** New images with 16 PST images generated using Eq. (7) with different value of $k$.

### 4.2 Training and Test Results of Simulated Dataset

Faster R-CNN and CenterNet were implemented using TenserFlow and Pytorch respectively. Both the two DCNNs use the stochastic gradient descent (SGD) as the optimization method. When training data using Faster R-CNN and CenterNet, the training set contains 10000 samples, and both the test set and the verification set contain 2000 samples. Both neural networks are trained 10000 times to obtain the test model.

The test set samples are input into the test models to obtain the recognition results of Faster R-CNN and CenterNet. The test results of the two models are shown in Table 2. It can be seen from Table 2 that the test results of the two models on the simulated data set are very successful. The Recall and Precision values of the two models are close to 100%. Although the test data is simulated data, the experimental results show that these two DCNNs have great application potential in recognizing small scenes with single features like the PST ICPs.

**Table 2.** Recognition results of the test models using the simulated samples. *

| Model | TN | TP | FP | FN | Recall | Precision |
|---|---|---|---|---|---|---|
| Faster R-CNN | 2000 | 1999 | 7 | 1 | 99.95% | 99.65% |
| CenterNet | 2000 | 1992 | 2 | 8 | 99.60% | 99.90% |

* TN = Total Number; TP = True Positive; FP = False Positive; FN = False Negative.

Comparing the confidence scores of each recognition target in the test results, it is found that the target recognized by Faster R-CNN generally has a high confidence score, and most of them are above 0.99. The target confidence scores of CenterNet are relatively low and the values are more dispersed. Therefore, when using the same confidence threshold of 0.5 for test, there is almost no targets are missed in the Faster R-CNN model. The scores of fake targets in the CenterNet model are low, so there are fewer False Positives, while some real targets are also missed due to low scores. Figure 6 shows the different recognition results of the two models in the same picture. In Fig. 6(a), the simulated PST image is successfully recognized by Faster R-CNN with a score of

0.997, while the CenterNet model failed to detect the target in Fig. 6(b) for that the confidence score of the target is less than 0.5. In Fig. 6(c), a false alarm occurred and the building was recognized as a target by Faster R-CNN with a score of 0.957. The real target was also detected with a score of 0.997. The CenterNet model accurately judged the false alarm and only the real target was detected with a score of 0.778. The results also indicate that the building is easily recognized as a target, and the PST should be placed as far as possible from such objects.

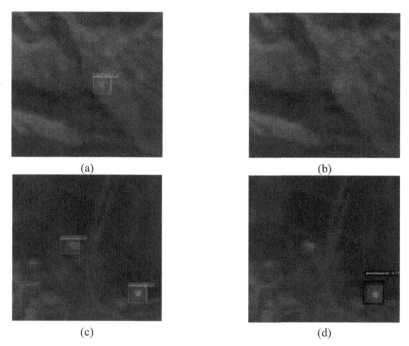

(a)                                        (b)

(c)                                        (d)

**Fig. 6.** Examples of recognition results of two models. (a) and (b), (c) and (d) are the different recognition results of the same sample. (a) and (c) shows the recognition results of Faster R-CNN model. (b) and (d) shows the recognition results of CenterNet model.

## 4.3   Recognition Result of PST ICPs

The data sets I, II, III, and IV generated by real PST images are input into the Faster R-CNN and CenterNet models respectively, and the test results of each dataset are shown in Table 3. There is no processing inside the PST images in Dataset I. Therefore, the test results of Dataset I can best reflect the recognition performance of the models on PST images. It can be seen from Table 3 that the test performance of the two models in Dataset I is worse than the simulated data test results, but the recognition tasks of Dataset I are also well completed. The Recall values of both models are above 95%, and the Precision values are close to 100%. The Recall value of CenterNet is 2.60% higher than Faster R-CNN, and the Precision value is 1.15% higher than Faster R-CNN. The comprehensive recognition performance of CenterNet is better than the Faster R-CNN model. The experimental results show that the DCNN model trained by the simulated data can be used for the recognition of real PST ICPs, and can achieve good results when the image quality of the PST image is good.

From Dataset I to IV, the brightness of the PST images, the contrast between the PST image and the background are gradually reduced. For the traditional recognition algorithm or visual interpretation, the recognition difficulty is gradually increased. Table 3 shows that the test results of the Faster R-CNN and CenterNet network models also follow this rule, that is, from datasets I to IV, the Recall and Precision values of the recognition results are gradually decreasing. For example, for Dataset IV, the Recall value of the Faster R-CNN and CenterNet models are reduced to 37.20% and 50.60% respectively, and the two models are no longer able to effectively work. For the same Dataset, the CenterNet still yields better results than Faster R-CNN. As the image quality of PSTs decreases, the advantages of the CenterNet become more obvious. Figure 7 shows the different test results for a PST image sample and three sample data derived from it. The four samples from left to right in Fig. 7(a) and Fig. 7(b) belong to Dataset I to IV respectively. Faster R-CNN can only recognize targets in the first two samples in Fig. 7(a), while CenterNet can recognize targets in all samples in Fig. 7(b). This shows that CenterNet can better adapt to the recognition of PST images for poor imaging conditions.

**Table 3.** Recognition results of the test models using the simulated samples

| Dataset | Model | TN | TP | FP | FN | Recall | Precision |
|---------|-------|----|----|----|----|--------|-----------|
| I | Faster R-CNN | 1000 | 951 | 12 | 49 | 95.10 | 98.75 |
|   | CenterNet | 1000 | 977 | 1 | 23 | 97.70 | 99.90 |
| II | Faster R-CNN | 1000 | 892 | 11 | 108 | 89.20 | 98.78 |
|    | CenterNet | 1000 | 965 | 3 | 35 | 96.50 | 99.69 |
| III | Faster R-CNN | 1000 | 726 | 11 | 274 | 72.60 | 98.51 |
|     | CenterNet | 1000 | 885 | 11 | 115 | 88.50 | 98.77 |
| IV | Faster R-CNN | 1000 | 372 | 11 | 628 | 37.20 | 97.13 |
|    | CenterNet | 1000 | 506 | 53 | 494 | 50.60 | 90.52 |

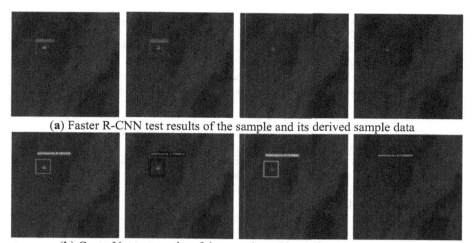

(a) Faster R-CNN test results of the sample and its derived sample data

(b) CenterNet test results of the sample and its derived sample data

**Fig. 7.** Different test results of a source target image sample and three sample data derived therefrom.

## 5   Conclusions

This paper proposes a method for intelligently recognizing PST ICPs from satellite imagery. DCNN is a good way to achieve target recognition, so we chose two DCNNs to complete the recognition of PST ICPs. A large number of simulated samples are generated based on the characteristics of PST image as the training samples for the DCNNs. The experiment results show that the DCNN models trained with simulated dataset can recognize the simulated and real PST ICPs with high accuracy. However, when the imaging quality of the PST image is degraded, the detection result of the model also deteriorates. In practical applications, experiments should be carried out under good illumination to obtain high-quality PST images.

## References

1. Zhang, Y., Zheng, M., Xiong, J., Lu, Y., Xiong, X.: On-orbit geometric calibration of ZY-3 three-line array imagery with multistrip data sets. IEEE T. Geosci. Remote. **52**, 224–234 (2014)
2. Takaku, J., Tadono, T.: PRISM on-orbit geometric calibration and DSM performance. IEEE T. Geosci. Remote. **47**(12), 4060–4073 (2009)
3. Jiang, Y., Wang, J., Zhang, L., Zhang, G., Li, X., Wu, J.: Geometric processing and accuracy verification of Zhuhai-1 Hyperspectral satellites. Remote Sens. **11**(9), 996 (2019)
4. Zhang, G., Wang, J., Jiang, Y., Zhou, P., Zhao, Y., Xu, Y.: On-orbit geometric calibration and validation of Luojia 1–01 night-light satellite. Remote Sens. **11**(3), 264 (2019)
5. Jeong, J., Han, H., Park, Y.J.: A geometric accuracy analysis of the geostationary ocean color imager (GOCI) level 1B product. Opt. Express **28**(5), 7634–7653 (2019)
6. Westin, T.: Inflight calibration of SPOT CCD detector geometry. Photogramm. Eng. Rem. S. **58**(9), 1313–1319 (1992)

7.  Srivastava, P.K., Medha, S.A.: Inflight calibration of IRS-1C imaging geometry for data products. ISPRS J. Photogram. **52**(5), 215–221 (1997)
8.  Seo, D., Oh, J., Lee, C., et al.: Geometric calibration and validation of Kompsat-3A AEISS-A camera. Sensors. **16**(10), 1776 (2016)
9.  Poli, D., Remondino, F., Angiuli, E., et al.: Radiometric and geometric evaluation of GeoEye-1, WorldView-2 and Pléiades-1A stereo images for 3D information extraction. ISPRS J. Photogram. **100**, 35–47 (2015)
10. Wang M., Cheng Y., Tian Y., et al.: A new on-orbit geometric self-calibration approach for the high-resolution geostationary optical satellite GaoFen4. IEEE J. Sel. Top. Appl. Earth Observ. Remote Sens. **11**(5), 1670–1683 (2018)
11. Qinghong, S., Qi, W., Hui, X., et al.: Research on geometric calibration of spaceborne linear array whiskbroom camera. Sensors. **18**(1), 247 (2018)
12. Dowman, I., Reuter, H.I.: Global geospatial data from Earth observation: status and issues. Int J. Digit. Earth. **10**, 328–341 (2017)
13. Wang, J., Wang, R., Hu, X., Su, Z.: The on-orbit calibration of geometric parameters of the Tian-Hui 1 (TH-1) satellite. ISPRS J. Photogram. **124**, 144–151 (2017)
14. Gascon, F., et al.: Copernicus Sentinel-2A calibration and products validation status. Remote Sens. **9**, 584 (2017)
15. Tang X.M., Zhou P., Zhang G., Wang X., Jiang Y., Guo L., Liu, S.: Verification of ZY-3 satellite imagery geometric accuracy without ground control points. IEEE Geosci. Remote Sens. Lett. **12**(10), 2100–2104 (2015)
16. Zhang, G., Jiang, Y., Li, D., et al.: In-orbit geometric calibration and validation of ZY-3 linear array sensors. Photogramm. Rec. **29**(145), 68–88 (2014)
17. Gaparovi, M., Dobrini, D., Medak, D.: Geometric accuracy improvement of WorldView-2 imagery using freely available DEM data. Photogramm. Rec. **34**, 266–281 (2019)
18. Jiang, Y.H., Zhang, G., Tang, X.M., et al.: Geometric calibration and accuracy assessment of ZiYuan-3 multispectral images. IEEE T. Geosci. Remote. **52**(7), 4161–4172 (2014)
19. Cao, J., Yuan, X., Gong, J.: In-orbit geometric calibration and validation of ZY-3 three-line cameras based on CCD-detector look angles. Photogramm. Rec. **30**(150), 211–226 (2015)
20. Li, K., Zhang, Y., Zhang, Z., Yu, Y.: An Automatic recognition and positioning method for point source targets on satellite images. ISPRS Int. J. Geo-Inf. **7**(11), 434 (2018)
21. Rauchmiller, R.F., Robert, A.S.: measurement of the landsat thematic mapper modulation transfer function using an array of point sources. Opt. Eng. **27**(4), 334–343 (1988)
22. Rangaswamy, M.K., Quickbird, II.: Two-dimensional on-orbit modulation transfer function analysis using convex mirror array. M.S. thesis, Dept. Electr. Eng., South Dakota State Univ., SD, USA (2003)
23. Schiller, S.J., Silny, J.: The SPecular Array Radiometric Calibration (SPARC) method: a new approach for absolute vicarious calibration in the solar reflective spectrum. In: Proc, p. 78130E. SPIE, San Diego, California, USA (2010)
24. Ren, S., He, K., Girshick, R., Sun, J.: Faster R-CNN: towards real-time object detection with region proposal networks. IEEE Trans. Pattern Anal. Mach. Intell. **39**(6), 1137–1149 (2017)
25. Duan, K., Bai, S., Xie, L., Qi, H., Huang, Q., Tian, Q.: CenterNet: object detection with keypoint triplets. In: 2019 IEEE/CVF International Conference on Computer Vision (ICCV) (2019)
26. Chander, G., et al.: Landsat-5 TM reflective-band absolute radiometric calibration. IEEE T. Geosci. Remote. **42**(12), 2747–2760 (2004)
27. Czapla-Myers, J., et al.: The ground-based absolute radiometric calibration of Landsat 8 OLI. Remote Sens. **7**(1), 600–626 (2015)
28. Chao, X., Zhaoli, L., Guanglei, H.: Simulation of the Impact of a Sensor's PSF on mixed pixel decomposition: 1 Nonuniformity Effect. Remote Sens. **8**(5), 437 (2016)

29. Girshick, R., Girshick, J., Darrell, T., Malik, J.: Rich feature hierarchies for accurate object detection and semantic, segmentation. In: Proceedings of the IEEE International Conference on Computer Vision and Pattern Recognition, Columbus, Ohio, pp. 580–587, 24–27 June 2014

30. Girshick, R.: Fast R-CNN. In: Proceedings of the IEEE International Conference on Computer Vision, Santiago, Chile, pp. 1440–1448. 13–16 December 2015

31. Law, H., Deng, J.: Cornernet: detecting objects as paired keypoints. In: European Conference on Computer Vision, Santiago, Chile, 8–14 September 2018

# Image Registration Between Real Image and Virtual Image Based on Self-supervised Keypoint Learning

Sangwon Kim[1] , In-Su Jang[2], and Byoung Chul Ko[1]([✉]) 

[1] Keimyung University, Daegu, South Korea
niceko@kmu.ac.kr
[2] Electronics and Telecommunications Research Institute, Daegu, South Korea
jef1015@etri.re.kr

**Abstract.** A digital twin is a next-generation technology that connects virtual and physical environments into a single world. Although the virtual environment of a digital twin models the real world, the technology used to match the real world with the virtual environment has yet to be studied. The existing deep-learning-based image registration methods aim to extract feature points and descriptors and show a good registration performance in real images. However, these methods are difficult to apply in an actual digital twin environment because 3D and real 2D images have a significant difference in terms of the external and physical characteristics of the image itself. In this paper, we propose a deep learning model that self-learns the difference between virtual and real environments using a generative-adversarial network and self-supervised learning. Image registration between virtual environments with real-world images is a new method that has not been previously achieved, and we have demonstrated experimentally that the proposed method is applicable to various virtual environments and real-world image matching.

**Keywords:** Digital twin · Keypoint detection · Self-supervised learning · GAN · 3D-2D registration

## 1 Introduction

A digital twin is a technology implementing a real-world environment into a virtual environment and analyzing and simulating various real-world scenarios within the virtual environment for effective operation within the real world. In recent years, digital twins have advanced beyond manufacturing, becoming increasingly sophisticated in various fields such as transportation, energy, geographic information, urbanization, retail, and disaster prediction. Beyond a simple virtual prototyping, Hicks [1] defined a digital twin as a proper synchronization of a virtual space with a physical object. In other words, it is viewed as a type of information flow where the physical and virtual states converge at a single intersection. The virtual environment of a digital twin is produced based on the real world, and the predicted results in the virtual environment must be

© Springer Nature Switzerland AG 2022
C. Wallraven et al. (Eds.): ACPR 2021, LNCS 13189, pp. 402–410, 2022.
https://doi.org/10.1007/978-3-031-02444-3_30

reflected in the real world. By contrast, it should also be possible to quickly determine which part of the real world the physical information corresponds to within the virtual environment. However, research on real-time registration (3D-2D image registration) between real- and virtual-world images remains at a relatively basic level compared to digital twin studies on mirroring the real world. In the medical field, there has been limited research on matching 3D models of organ parts to actual 2D images [2], and studies on the matching of large-scale virtual environments and real-world images have yet to be conducted. This paper focuses on the development of a technology that allows a virtual space and the real world to quickly synchronize through the real-time matching of a model implemented in a virtual 3D space and a 2D image captured in the real world.

The existing traditional image matching method follows the matching of similar key points between two images through a detection of the key points and feature descriptors. Recent convolutional neural network (CNN)-based image matching algorithms show an excellent image matching performance. The CNN-based keypoint detection method can be divided into supervised, self-supervised, and unsupervised learning according to the learning approach. Self-supervised, which can learn with only a small dataset, has been mainly studied rather than supervised learning. SuperPoints [9], a representative method of self-supervised learning, shares the Siamese network structure to extract feature points and descriptors using unlabeled images, and image feature points and descriptors are simultaneously extracted from each image pair and used for matching. method was proposed. R2D2 [10] also proposed a fully convolutional network that can simultaneously learn the repeatability and reliability of keypoints based on self-supervised learning. KeyReg [11] proposed a method for training keypoint regressors by combining a multi-layer random forest and a single-layer random forest module in a coarse-to-fine manner. This method was able to improve the matching performance by alleviating the existing problems of self-supervised and unsupervised learning approaches based on CNNs.

Although CNN-based image registration has shown reasonable and accurate results, there is a limitation in that they target only 2D images with similar physical characteristics.

Therefore, in this paper, we propose a new method for quickly matching the real-world 2D images captured by a CCD camera and a digital twin environment that implements a real terrain into a virtual 3D space. The technology used to match a virtual digital twin environment with physical real-world images in real time is a new approach that has not previously been achieved.

## 2 Methods

In general, an image matching method using deep learning is applied using an image pair and homography, which share completely identical spatial information. However, it is difficult to acquire homography between a virtual space and real-world images in a digital twin, and it is a costly task to find a corresponding pair between 3D and 2D images for producing learning data. In this paper, 3D → 2D and 2D → 3D image pairs are therefore generated using a cycle generative adversarial network (CycleGAN) [3]; in addition, self-supervised learning, which enables effective keypoint and feature descriptor learning without the use of learning labels is proposed.

## 2.1  2D ↔ 3D Image Pair Generation Using CycleGAN

To apply keypoint matching using a virtual 3D space and a real-world image, an image pair maintaining the same spatial information is required. Although data are collected while maintaining the same coordinate system as that of the location where the real-world images were acquired, a large error occurs depending on the viewpoint of the camera, the shooting angle, and the distortion rate. Therefore, in this study, instead of finding each training image for constructing a corresponding 2D ↔ 3D image pair, we secure various image pairs by alternately generating 3D and 2D images using CycleGAN. Using CycleGAN, it is possible to convert an image obtained from 3D into a 2D image, or inversely, transform a 2D image into a 3D image for different images that are not formed in pairs. because it is extremely difficult to produce a pair of images that share the exact same spatial information in the real world, this characteristic of CycleGAN is extremely useful for generating data for self-supervised learning.

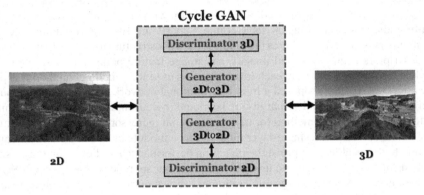

**Fig. 1.** CycleGAN model used to create 2D ↔ 3D image pair

Figure 1 shows the corresponding 2D ↔ 3D image pair generation process using CycleGAN. CycleGAN learns to simulate the target image for the input image. As the most important characteristic of CycleGAN, it learns to reproduce the shape of the input through the process of inversely transforming the simulated target image during the learning process. Therefore, by using the trained CycleGAN model, a virtual image and a real-world image can be generated in both directions and can thus be used for various learning data.

## 2.2  Self-supervised Learning Model Design

For network learning used to detect and match the keypoints from an image, a pre-defined keypoint and a descriptor for an image are required. However, it is difficult to clearly define the keypoints representing important characteristics of an image, which is a task requiring a large cost, and thus there is a limit to designating a learning label in advance. Therefore, in this paper, we propose a self-supervised learning technique in which a deep learning model finds important keypoints on its own and learns the descriptors. Self-supervised keypoint learning teaches how to generate a heat map from a given image pair such that frequently overlapping parts are learned to be regarded as more important parts, and identical parts of an image pair are learned to generate the same feature descriptor.

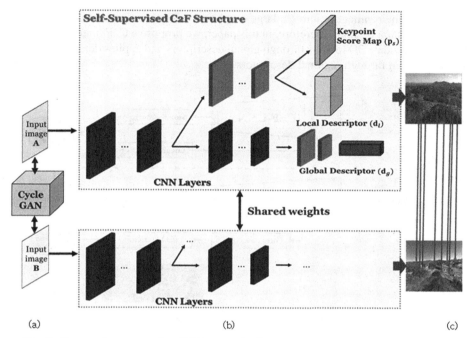

**Fig. 2.** Proposed coarse-to-fine (C2F) type of self-supervised keypoint learning structure

Figure 2 shows the learning process of the proposed coarse-to-fine (C2F) self-supervised keypoint learning model. After creating a 2D ↔ 3D image pair with the same spatial information from CycleGAN (Fig. 2(a)), the pair is input into the same CNN model that shares the weight (Fig. 2(b)). The backbone network of the proposed CNN model consists of eight convolutional layers, and the two sub-networks are each comprised of two convolutional layers.

In the first branch network, the local information of the image is learned to emphasize the keypoint score map $\mathbf{p}_s$, which is a weight tensor of keypoints, and to generate the local descriptor $\mathbf{d}_l$ tensor containing each local descriptor. The second branch network enables C2F inference by learning to emphasize the global information of the image and generate the global descriptor $\mathbf{d}_g$ tensor. Tensors generated by the other CNN model that shares the weights are redefined as $\hat{\mathbf{p}}_s$, $\hat{\mathbf{d}}_s$, and $\hat{\mathbf{d}}_g$. The loss function ($L$) is calculated by measuring the distances of the three descriptors to apply self-supervised learning (Fig. 2(c)).

$$L = \|\mathbf{d}_g - \hat{\mathbf{d}}_g\|_2^2 + \|\mathbf{d}_l - \hat{\mathbf{d}}_l\|_2^2 - \sum \hat{\mathbf{p}}_s \log(\mathbf{p}_s) \qquad (1)$$

Network training is conducted 40,000 times in the direction of minimizing the loss function ($L$) using the stochastic gradient descent optimizer.

### 2.3 Coarse-to-Fine Image Registration

The process of matching a 2D image given by a CCD camera in a vast 3D virtual digital twin environment requires a large number of computations, and thus real-time registration is impossible. Therefore, in this paper, we propose a C2F matching method that finds candidate 3D regions through global descriptors and applies detailed keypoint matching again through regional descriptors.

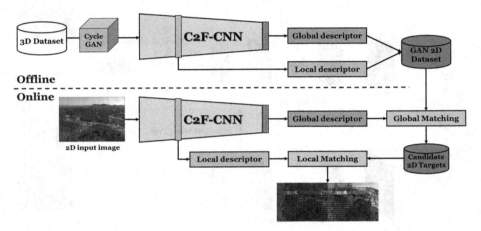

**Fig. 3.** 2D ↔ 3D image matching through coarse-to-fine matching

Figure 3 shows the C2F inference operation used to find the same virtual environment location for the input 2D image. First, global descriptors and local descriptors are extracted from the 3D dataset transformed using CycleGAN during the offline phase. When a global descriptor is extracted from a given input image, 3D images with the most similar descriptors are searched from the database. Keypoint extraction and local descriptor matching are conducted for the input 2D image and the searched 3D images. Finally, local matching is applied to the 2D image and corresponding 3D image.

## 3    Experiments

In this paper, we propose a self-supervised learning technique and a new C2F matching algorithm for digital twin matching between virtual and real-world images. The data for training consist of 275 pairs (550 pieces), and are applied for C2F network learning through 2D → 3D and 3D → 2D conversion using CycleGAN. The test was conducted using 82 pairs (164) of 2D and 3D image data.

To evaluate the performance of the proposed model, five traditional keypoint extractors (SIFT [4], SURF [5], FAST [6], ORB [7], and AKAZE [8]) and the most recently released deep learning base (SuperPoint [9] and R2D2 [10]) are applied.

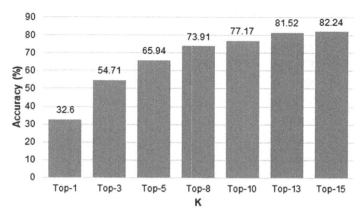

**Fig. 4.** Performance comparison of global descriptor matching

First, Fig. 4 shows the global image matching performance of the proposed algorithm. The consistency of the global image was evaluated for the top-K results, showing a high similarity when comparing only the global descriptors between the input 2D image and the target virtual 3D image. The global matching algorithm showed a higher accuracy as the ranking of the top-K result increased and achieved an accuracy of 82.24% for the top-15, indicating its suitability as a coarse step for quickly searching for candidate 3D images.

Apart from the matching performance for global descriptors, the purpose of matching local descriptor images is to measure the similarity between keypoints, and thus instead of applying the top-K accuracy, keypoint repeatability and the mean matching accuracy (MMA), which are standard methods for comparing the keypoint matching performance, were used. The repeatability is a method for detecting the keypoints for a given pair of images and evaluating the precision regarding the detection of a keypoint for the same object in each image. The MMA is a method for evaluating whether the keypoints of the same object are actually matched through a process of matching those points with a high similarity using a local descriptor. During each experiment, five traditional keypoint detection algorithms (i.e., [4–8]) were compared with two modern deep learning-based keypoint detection algorithms (i.e., [9] and [10]).

In Table 1, the traditional algorithms showed a low result of less than 50% in the case of the repeatability. Traditional methods must rely on the shape of the image, and thus they cannot correctly reflect the physical difference between a virtual image and a real-world image. Although deep-learning-based algorithms show better results than traditional algorithms, because the keypoint detection performance is not uniform, there are no significant differences in performance between the conventional methods and SuperPoint [9]. In addition, R2D2 [10] achieves a performance approximately 26% worse than that of the proposed method.

Table 1. Local descriptor image matching performance comparison

| Methods | Repeatability (%) | MMA (%) |
|---|---|---|
| FAST [4] | 34.96 | 42.03 |
| SIFT [5] | 35.54 | 86.41 |
| SURF [6] | 35.12 | 86.52 |
| ORB [7] | 44.64 | 33.71 |
| AKAZE [8] | 37.02 | 69.59 |
| SuperPoint [9] | 35.70 | 83.57 |
| R2D2 [10] | 72.05 | 99.27 |
| **Ours** | **99.92** | **99.97** |

By contrast, the self-supervised C2F-CNN is trained to extract the most similar global and local descriptors and overcome any differences. As a result, it demonstrated an extremely high performance of 99.92%.

In the MMA comparison experiment, the traditional algorithms were unable to fully reflect the morphological and physical differences between the virtual image and the real-world image, and thus the performance and repeatability were significantly degraded. In particular, a phenomenon occurred in which the keypoints of the 2D image were frequently matched with unrelated keypoints of the 3D image (clouds and forests). Unlike traditional algorithms that depend on the shape, deep-learning-based algorithms showed better results because they process feature maps in several stages. In the case of R2D2 [10], the matching performance of the keypoints extracted from 2D and 3D images was high because the network was trained to extract keypoints and feature descriptors reflecting the repeatability and reliability. The proposed algorithm showed a 99.97% performance in terms of the MMA, which is 0.7% higher than that of R2D2, because it was trained to fully grasp the differences between the virtual and real-world images.

Figure 5 shows the result of C2F inference using the proposed algorithm. As shown in the figure, although 2D and 3D images have completely different physical characteristics, it can be seen that a precise image registration is possible through image matching of global and local engineers.

The development environment of the C2F CNN-based 2D ↔ 3D matching algorithm proposed in this paper is as follows. Training and testing were conducted on a Windows PC with 16 GB of RAM, an i7-7700 CPU, and a GTX 1080Ti GPU, and the 3D virtual environment was developed using Unity.

**2D**              **3D**

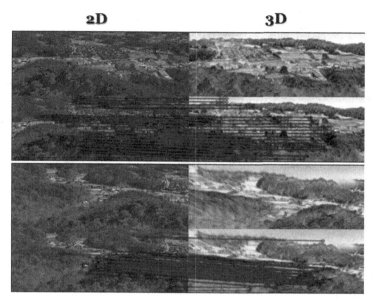

**Fig. 5.** Matching results of 2D image input from CCD camera and 3D image in a virtual space

## 4  Conclusion

Digital twins are attracting attention as a new research field connecting both virtual and real-worlds. In this paper, a new algorithm for keypoint matching, i.e., applying a 3D map implemented in a virtual environment and a CCD image captured in the real-world, is proposed. The proposed deep learning algorithm uses a self-supervised learning technique to learn important keypoints of an image and shows an excellent matching performance for a vast image dataset through coarse-to-fine inference. In particular, because it is possible to generate image pairs that share the same spatial information using CycleGAN for self-supervised keypoint learning, there is an advantage in that it can be used for the matching of various digital twins.

**Acknowledgement.** This research was supported by Basic Science Research Program through the National Research Foundation of Korea (NRF) funded by the Ministry of Education (2021R1A6A3A13039438) and partially supported by Electronics and Telecommunications Research Institute (ETRI) grant funded by the Korean government. [21ZD1120, Development of ICT Convergence Technology for Daegu-Gyeongbuk Regional Industry].

## References

1. Hicks, B.: Industry 4.0 and Digital Twins: Key Lessons From NASA. https://www.thefuture factory.com/blog/24. Accessed 09 June 2021

2. Lange, A., Heldmann, S.: Multilevel 2D-3D intensity-based image registration. In: Špiclin, Ž, McClelland, J., Kybic, J., Goksel, O. (eds.) WBIR 2020. LNCS, vol. 12120, pp. 57–66. Springer, Cham (2020). https://doi.org/10.1007/978-3-030-50120-4_6oop

3. Zhu, J.Y., Park, T., Isola, P., Efros, A.A.: Unpaired image-to-image translation using cycle-consistent adversarial networks. In: ICCV, pp. 2223–2232. IEEE, Venice (2017)

4. Rosten, E., Drummond, T.: Machine learning for high-speed corner detection. In: Leonardis, A., Bischof, H., Pinz, A. (eds.) ECCV 2006. LNCS, vol. 3951, pp. 430–443. Springer, Heidelberg (2006). https://doi.org/10.1007/11744023_34

5. Lowe, D.G.: Object recognition from local scale-invariant features. In: ICCV, pp. 1150–1157. IEEE, Kerkyra (1999)

6. Bay, H., Tuytelaars, T., Van Gool, L.: SURF: speeded up robust features. In: Leonardis, A., Bischof, H., Pinz, A. (eds.) ECCV 2006. LNCS, vol. 3951, pp. 404–417. Springer, Heidelberg (2006). https://doi.org/10.1007/11744023_32

7. Rublee, E., Rabaud, V., Konolige, K., Bradski, G.: ORB: an efficient alternative to SIFT or SURF. In: ICCV, pp. 2564–2571. IEEE, Barcelona (2011)

8. Alcantrilla, P.F., Solutions, T.: Fast explicit diffusion for accelerated features in nonlinear scale spaces. IEEE TPAMI **34**(7), 1281–1298 (2011)

9. DeTone, D., Malisiewicz, T., Rabinovich, A.: Superpoint: self-supervised interest point detection and description. In: CVPR Workshops, pp. 224–236. IEEE, Long Beach (2018)

10. Revaud, J., et al.: R2D2: repeatable and reliable detector and descriptor. arXiv preprint arXiv: 1906.06195 (2019)

11. Kim, S., Jeong, M., Ko, B.C.: Self-supervised keypoint detection based on multi-layer random forest regressor. IEEE ACCESS **9**, 40850–40859 (2021)

# Fast Deep Asymmetric Hashing for Image Retrieval

Chuangquan Lin[1], Zhihui Lai[1,2(✉)], Jianglin Lu[1], and Jie Zhou[1]

[1] Computer Vision Institute, College of Computer Science and Software Engineering,
Shenzhen University, Shenzhen 518060, China
lai_zhi_hui@163.com
[2] Shenzhen Institute of Artificial Intelligence and Robotics for Society,
Shenzhen, China

**Abstract.** Recently, by exploiting asymmetric learning mechanism, asymmetric hashing methods achieve superior performance in image retrieval. However, due to the discrete binary constraint, these methods typically rely on a special optimization strategy of discrete cyclic coordinate descent (DCC), which is time-consuming since it must learn the binary codes bit by bit. To address this problem, we propose a novel deep supervised hashing method called Fast Deep Asymmetric Hashing (FDAH), which learns the binary codes of training and query sets in an asymmetric way. FDAH designs a novel asymmetric hash learning framework using the inner product of the output of deep network and semantic label regression to approximate the similarity and minimize the discriminant reconstruction error between the deep representation and the binary codes. Instead of using the DCC optimization strategy, FDAH avoids using the quadratic term of binary variables and the binary code of all bits can be optimized simultaneously in one step. Moreover, by incorporating the semantic information in binary code learning and the quantization process, FDAH can obtain more discriminative and efficient binary codes. Extensive experiments on three well-known datasets show that the proposed FDAH can achieve state-of-the-art performance with less training time.

**Keywords:** Image retrieval · Asymmetric hashing · Deep learning

## 1 Introduction

As one of the most popular approximate nearest neighbor (ANN) [1] search techniques, hashing has attracted considerable attention in different scenarios, including sketch retrieval [21], large-scale clustering [26] and objective recognition [25]. By encoding data through a set of binary codes, hashing methods can reduce the memory storage and speed up retrieval with efficient pairwise comparison of Hamming distance.

With the rapid development of machine learning, learning-based hashing has become a hot topic, because it can greatly improve the retrieval performance by

C. Wallraven et al. (Eds.): ACPR 2021, LNCS 13189, pp. 411–420, 2022.
https://doi.org/10.1007/978-3-031-02444-3_31

learning the hashing function from a large number of data. Generally, learning-based hashing methods can be categorized into unsupervised and supervised methods. Unsupervised hashing methods, including Spectral Hashing (SH) [23], Binary Reconstructive Embedding (BRE) [11], Iterative Quantization (ITQ) [6], Jointly Sparse Hashing (JSH) [13], aim at constructing hash functions by exploiting inherent structures of data. On the other hand, supervised hashing methods fully exploit labeled information to obtain more discriminative binary codes, such as Supervised Discrete Hashing (SDH) [20], Fast Supervised Discrete Hashing (FSDH) [7] and Column Sampling Based Discrete Supervised Hashing (COSDISH) [10]. However, the above-mentioned hashing methods learn hash functions based on hand-crafted features, which cannot perform feature learning to generate more effective binary codes. To address this problem, some hashing methods based on deep neural network have been proposed [3,4,12,22,24]. Some representative deep hashing methods including Deep Pairwise Supervised Hashing (DPSH) [15], Deep Supervised Discrete Hashing (DSDH) [14] and Deep Discrete Supervised Hashing (DDSH) [8] integrate deep feature learning and hash code learning into a end-to-end framework and then obtain a great retrieval performance.

Due to the high computation cost, most deep hashing methods will select a subset from the dataset for training, which cannot fully utilize the supervised information. Therefore, some deep asymmetric hashing methods have been proposed [9,19,27]. One of the representative methods is Asymmetric Deep Supervised Hashing (ADSH) [9]. By treating query set and training set in an asymmetric way, ADSH can fully exploit the supervised information during the iterative learning procedure. However, because of using discrete cyclic coordinate descent (DCC) algorithm [20], ADSH still needs high computation cost to solve discrete optimization with the increasing length of binary codes. Meanwhile, ADSH does not fully exploit the semantic information of data in binary codes learning and the quantization process, resulting in inevitable information loss. To address these problems, this paper proposes a novel deep hashing method called Fast Deep Asymmetric Hashing (FDAH) for image retrieval, which learns the binary codes of training and query sets in an asymmetric way. Specifically, we use the commonly-used objective function of asymmetric hashing and assume that the binary codes of training set can be obtained by regressing their semantic labels. As such, we can avoid using the quadratic term of binary variables and solve the discrete optimization with a closed-form solution instead of DCC algorithm. Moreover, we consider the accumulated quantization error and incorporate the semantic information in quantization process, which can reduce the inevitable information loss and obtain more discriminative and efficient binary codes. Extensive experiments on three well-known datasets show that the proposed FDAH can achieve state-of-the-art performance with less training time.

## 2   The Proposed Method

In this paper, boldface uppercase letters are used to denote matrices, e.g., $\mathbf{X}$, and boldface lowercase letters are used to denote vectors, e.g., $\mathbf{x}$. $\mathbf{X}_{ij}$ denote The i-th

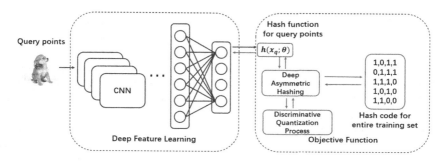

**Fig. 1.** The overview of FDAH

row and j-th column element of matrix X. The Frobenius norm and transpose of matrix X are defined as $\|\mathbf{X}\|_F$ and $\mathbf{X}^T$, respectively. Furthermore, the binary function is presented by $sgn(\cdot)$, which outputs $+1$ for positive numbers and $-1$ for negative number. The Hadamard product is presented by $\odot$. $\mathbf{I}$ and $\mathbf{1}$ indicate an identity matrix and a matrix with all elements equaling to 1.

Suppose that the training set $\mathbf{X} = \{\mathbf{x}_i\}_{i=1}^n$ includes n training samples, and the corresponding labels matrix are denoted by $\mathbf{Y} = \{\mathbf{y}_i\}_{i=1}^n \in \{0,1\}^{c \times n}$, where $c$ is the number of classes and $\mathbf{Y}_{ji} = 1$ if $\mathbf{x}_i$ belongs to the j-th class. Meanwhile, the query set is denoted as $\mathbf{Q} = \{\mathbf{q}_j\}_{j=1}^m$ including m query samples, which are randomly sampled from the training set. The purpose of our designed model FDAH is to learn the binary codes $\mathbf{B} = \{\mathbf{b}_i\}_{i=1}^n \in \{-1,+1\}^{l \times n}$ for the whole training set and $\mathbf{U} = \{\mathbf{u}_j\}_{j=1}^m \in \{-1,+1\}^{l \times m}$ for the query set, respectively, where $l$ is the length of binary codes.

### 2.1  The Idea and Model Formulation

Our method FDAH integrates deep feature learning and binary code learning into an end-to-end framework. The overview of FDAH framework is shown in Fig. 1. The deep feature learning adopts a CNN model from [2], i.e., CNN-F model. Furthermore, the objective function of FDAH mainly contains two significant parts: deep asymmetric hashing part and discriminative quantization process part.

**Deep Asymmetric Hashing.** We attempt to learn the binary codes $\mathbf{B}$ of the whole training set $\mathbf{X}$ and the binary codes $\mathbf{U}$ of the query set $\mathbf{Q}$. Therefore, we consider the commonly-used objective function [16] of asymmetric hashing, that is:

$$\min_{\mathbf{B},\Theta} J_1 = \sum_{i=1}^n \sum_{j=1}^m \|\mathbf{b}_i^T \mathbf{u}_j - c\mathbf{S}_{ij}\|^2$$

$$s.t. \quad \mathbf{B} \in \{-1,+1\}^{c \times n}, \mathbf{U} \in \{-1,+1\}^{c \times m} \tag{1}$$

where $S$ is the asymmetric semantic similarity matrix. Specifically, $\mathbf{S}_{ij} = +1$ if $\mathbf{x_i}$ and $\mathbf{q_j}$ belong to the same class, $\mathbf{S}_{ij} = -1$, otherwise.

To make full use of asymmetry, we attempt to directly learn the binary codes $\mathbf{B}$ of training set while the binary codes $\mathbf{U}$ of query set can be generated by training a deep hashing function. Thus, we set $\mathbf{U} = sgn(F(\mathbf{Q}; \Theta))$, where $F(\mathbf{Q}; \Theta)$ is the output of the feature learning part, and $\Theta$ is the parameters of the neural network. Due to the non-differentiability of $sgn(\cdot)$ function, we decide to use $tanh(\cdot)$ function to replace the $sgn(\cdot)$ function for ease of optimization.

Moreover, because of the quadratic term of binary variables, the natural idea to solve the discrete optimization of the binary codes $\mathbf{B}$ is to use the discrete cyclic coordinate descent (DCC) algorithm, which is time-consuming. To tackle this problem, inspired by [7], we assume that the binary codes $\mathbf{B}$ of training set can be learned by regressing their semantic labels, i.e., $\mathbf{B} = sgn(\mathbf{W}^T\mathbf{Y})$, where $\mathbf{W} \in \mathbb{R}^{c \times l}$ is regression matrix. It is worth noting that integrating semantic information into the representation learning can generate more discriminative and efficient binary codes. Then we relax the $sgn(\cdot)$ function with its signed magnitude in our objective function. We can rewrite (1) as follows:

$$\min_{\mathbf{B},\Theta} J_1 = \gamma_1 \sum_{i=1}^{n} \sum_{j=1}^{m} ||(\mathbf{W}^T\mathbf{y}_i)^T tanh[F(\mathbf{q}_j; \Theta)] - c\mathbf{S}_{ij}||^2 \qquad (2)$$

where $\gamma_1$ is a hyper-parameter.

**Discriminative Quantization Process.** Due to the relaxed strategy, we need to consider the accumulated quantization error in the binary code learning procedure. Thus, For the binary codes $\mathbf{B}$ of training set, we impose a discriminant term to keep $\mathbf{B}$ and $\mathbf{W}^T\mathbf{Y}$ as close as possible. Besides, we adopt an asymmetric graph regularization term [17] to minimize the distance between network outputs $tanh[F(\mathbf{q}_j; \Theta)]$ and the binary codes:

$$\min_{\mathbf{B},\Theta} J_2 = \gamma_2 \sum_{i=1}^{n} \sum_{j=1}^{m} \frac{1}{\tau_j} ||\mathbf{b}_i - tanh(F(\mathbf{q}_j; \Theta))||^2 \mathbf{A}_{ij}$$

$$+ \gamma_3 \sum_{i=1}^{n} ||\mathbf{b}_i - \mathbf{W}^T\mathbf{y}_i||^2 \qquad (3)$$

$$s.t. \quad \mathbf{B} \in \{-1, +1\}^{c \times n}$$

where $\gamma_2$, $\gamma_3$ are hyper-parameters, and $\tau_j$ is the total number of data points that have the same class with $\mathbf{q}_j$, which is designed to avoid class-imbalance effect. $\mathbf{A} \in \mathbb{R}^{n \times m}$ is an asymmetric affinity matrix, and if $\mathbf{x}_i$ and $\mathbf{q}_j$ belong to the same class, $\mathbf{A}_{ij} = 1$. Otherwise, $\mathbf{A}_{ij} = 0$. As can be seen from (3), we take full advantage of semantic information in the quantization process, which can improve the discriminative capabilities of the network model and reduce the inevitable information loss.

**Overall Framework.** Finally, by integrating $J_1$ and $J_2$ into a jointly framework, we obtain the final objective function of FDAH as follow:

$$\min_{\mathbf{B},\Theta} J = J_1 + J_2 \quad s.t. \quad \mathbf{B} \in \{-1, +1\}^{c \times n} \qquad (4)$$

## 2.2   Optimization Algorithm

In this part, we will solve the minimization problem (4) by using an iterative algorithm.

**Given B and W, Update $\Theta$.** For simplicity, we define $\mathbf{z}_j = F(\mathbf{q}_j; \Theta)$ and $\tilde{\mathbf{u}}_i = tanh(F(\mathbf{q}_j; \Theta))$. From (4), we rewrite the problem as:

$$\min_{\Theta} J = \gamma_1 tr(\tilde{\mathbf{U}}^T(\mathbf{W}^T\mathbf{Y})(\mathbf{W}^T\mathbf{Y})^T\tilde{\mathbf{U}} - 2\tilde{\mathbf{U}}^T\mathbf{W}^T\mathbf{Y}\tilde{\mathbf{S}})$$
$$+ \gamma_2 tr(\tilde{\mathbf{U}}\tilde{\mathbf{U}}^T - 2\mathbf{B}\tilde{\mathbf{A}}\tilde{\mathbf{U}}^T) \tag{5}$$

where $\tilde{\mathbf{S}} = c\mathbf{S}$ and $\tilde{\mathbf{A}}_{ij} = \frac{1}{\tau_j}\mathbf{A}_{ij}$. We can update $\Theta$ by using back-propagation (BP) algorithm [18]. Thus, we can compute the gradient of $\mathbf{Z}$:

$$\frac{\partial J}{\partial \mathbf{Z}} = [2\gamma_1((\mathbf{W}^T\mathbf{Y})(\mathbf{W}^T\mathbf{Y})^T\tilde{\mathbf{U}} - 2\mathbf{W}^T\mathbf{Y}\tilde{\mathbf{S}})$$
$$+ 2\gamma_2(\tilde{\mathbf{U}} - \mathbf{B}\tilde{\mathbf{A}})] \odot (1 - \tilde{\mathbf{U}} \odot \tilde{\mathbf{U}}) \tag{6}$$

**Given $\Theta$ and B, Update W.** From (4), By taking the partial derivative with respect to $\mathbf{W}$ to be zero, we obtain:

$$\mathbf{W} = (\mathbf{Y}\mathbf{Y}^T)^{-1}(\gamma_1\mathbf{Y}\mathbf{S}\tilde{\mathbf{U}}^T + \gamma_3\mathbf{Y}\mathbf{B}^T)(\gamma_1\tilde{\mathbf{U}}\tilde{\mathbf{U}}^T + \gamma_3\mathbf{I})^{-1} \tag{7}$$

**Given $\Theta$ and W, Update B.** By expanding the objective function (4) and discarding the constant terms, we derive the following maximization problem:

$$\max_{\mathbf{B}} tr(\gamma_2\mathbf{B}^T\tilde{\mathbf{U}}\tilde{\mathbf{A}}^T + \gamma_3\mathbf{B}^T\mathbf{W}^T\mathbf{Y})$$
$$s.t. \quad \mathbf{B} \in \{-1, +1\}^{c \times n} \tag{8}$$

Thus, **B** can be solved with a closed-form solution as follows:

$$\mathbf{B} = sgn(\gamma_2\tilde{\mathbf{U}}\tilde{\mathbf{A}}^T + \gamma_3\mathbf{W}^T\mathbf{Y}) \tag{9}$$

The same training strategy in ADSH [9] is adopted in our method. Specifically, we repeat the learning procedure for several times and each time we randomly sample a query set. After training, the learned neural network can be used to generate the binary codes of testing samples, i.e., $\mathbf{b}_{test} = sgn(F(\mathbf{x}_{test}; \Theta))$, where $\mathbf{x}_{test}$ is a testing sample and $\mathbf{b}_{test}$ is its corresponding binary codes.

## 3   Experiments

In this part, we evaluate the proposed FDAH and baselines on three datasets: Fashion-MNIST, CIFAR-10 and NUS-WIDE.

**Table 1.** The MAP (%) results with varying bits on three datasets. The best results are shown in bold face.

| Method | Fashion-MNIST | | | | CIFAR-10 | | | | NUS-WIDE | | | |
|---|---|---|---|---|---|---|---|---|---|---|---|---|
| | 12 | 24 | 32 | 48 | 12 | 24 | 32 | 48 | 12 | 24 | 32 | 48 |
| LSH | 22.46 | 24.56 | 27.35 | 33.08 | 15.21 | 15.68 | 14.40 | 16.27 | 39.44 | 41.87 | 41.07 | 45.68 |
| SH | 35.56 | 31.57 | 31.84 | 29.46 | 20.27 | 18.27 | 17.94 | 17.53 | 41.91 | 41.00 | 40.63 | 43.21 |
| BRE | 33.85 | 42.90 | 42.41 | 44.33 | 18.26 | 21.26 | 23.13 | 23.80 | 46.03 | 47.49 | 46.68 | 51.72 |
| ITQ | 36.94 | 39.68 | 40.23 | 40.31 | 21.76 | 19.03 | 19.85 | 20.53 | 53.53 | 53.70 | 53.17 | 53.88 |
| SDH | 62.91 | 79.10 | 80.43 | 80.14 | 54.02 | 66.94 | 67.40 | 68.33 | 64.86 | 65.45 | 65.10 | 67.10 |
| FSDH | 77.70 | 79.86 | 80.69 | 81.10 | 60.95 | 65.73 | 66.38 | 68.41 | 57.64 | 58.21 | 67.19 | 58.33 |
| DPSH | 77.81 | 79.97 | 80.72 | 82.16 | 69.01 | 72.70 | 71.38 | 73.35 | 68.43 | 71.39 | 72.32 | 72.88 |
| DSDH | 79.67 | 81.58 | 82.40 | 82.59 | 72.02 | 77.41 | 79.86 | 80.72 | 67.18 | 69.34 | 70.13 | 70.12 |
| DDSH | 77.32 | 84.82 | 85.82 | 85.91 | 71.37 | 81.08 | 81.73 | 81.94 | 65.95 | 68.81 | 68.86 | 69.42 |
| ADSH | 91.36 | 93.35 | 93.93 | 94.22 | 87.06 | 91.20 | 92.93 | 93.46 | 76.70 | 80.28 | **81.23** | **83.16** |
| FDAH | **94.18** | **94.19** | **94.39** | **94.48** | **93.66** | **93.32** | **93.59** | **94.31** | **78.77** | **80.34** | 80.65 | 81.66 |

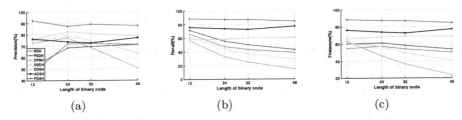

(a)          (b)          (c)

**Fig. 2.** Experimental results in (a) Precision, (b) Recall, and (c) F-measure of different methods on CIFAR-10 dataset.

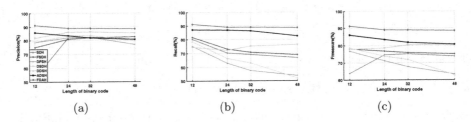

(a)          (b)          (c)

**Fig. 3.** Experimental results in (a) Precision, (b) Recall, and (c) F-measure of different methods on Fashion-MNIST dataset.

## 3.1 Datasets and Experimental Settings

The Fashion-MNIST includes 70,000 images which belong to 10 classes. From each class, we randomly select 6,000 images for training and the rest 1,000 images for testing. The CIFAR-10 contains 60,000 images from 10 classes. From each class, we randomly select 5,900 images for training and the rest 100 images for testing. The NUS-WIDE is a multi-labeled dataset which includes 21 classes, and we select more than 190,000 images for training and 2,100 for testing.

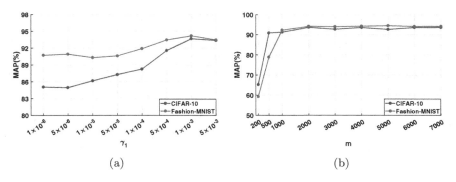

**Fig. 4.** The MAP results versus different hyper-parameters (a) $\gamma_1$ and (b) the size of query set $m$ on CIFAR-10 and Fashion-MNIST datasets

We compare our proposed method with some traditional hashing methods including LSH [5], SH [23], BRE [11], ITQ [6], SDH [20], FSDH [7] and some representative deep methods including DPSH [15], DSDH [14], DDSH [8], ADSH [9]. For traditional hashing methods, we use the whole training set to learn the hashing function, and we first obtain deep features extracted by CNN-F model pre-trained on the ImageNet. For deep hashing methods, DPSH, DSDH and DDSH select 5,000 images from training set on Fashion-MNIST and CIFAR-10 datasets, and 10,500 images from training set on NUS-WIDE dataset for training. ADSH and our proposed FDAH select 2,000 images on CIFAR-10 and Fashion-MNIST, and 5,000 images on NUS-WIDE as query set. For fair comparison, all the deep hashing methods iterate 150 times for convergence and apply the same network model [2], i.e., CNN-F model. The learning rate is tuned from $\{10^{-2}, ..., 10^{-6}\}$ and the batch size is 128. For FDAH, we set $\gamma_1 = 10^{-3}$, $\gamma_2 = 10$, and $\gamma_3 = 1$. Mean average precision (MAP), Precision rate, Recall rate and F-measure rate are adopted to evaluate the retrieval performance.

**Table 2.** The MAP (%) results and training time (in minute) of different methods with varying bits on CIFAR-10 dataset

| Method | 12 bits | 24 bits | 32 bits | 48 bits |
|---|---|---|---|---|
| DPSH-A | 92.01 | 92.95 | 93.16 | 92.95 |
|  | 334.2 m | 337.5 m | 348.1 m | 368.3 m |
| DSDH-A | 92.94 | 93.83 | 93.65 | 94.25 |
|  | 327.4 m | 350.6 m | 362.2 m | 391.6 m |
| DDSH-A | 75.89 | 86.79 | 90.85 | 93.36 |
|  | 276.2 m | 282.1 m | 292.7 m | 310.8 m |
| ADSH | 87.06 | 91.20 | 92.93 | 93.46 |
|  | 24.7 m | 30.9 m | 35.8 m | 47.6 m |
| FDAH | 93.66 | 93.32 | 93.59 | 94.31 |
|  | 10.5 m | 11.5 m | 11.7 m | 12.1 m |

## 3.2   Discussion

The MAP results of different methods are presented in Table 1. Obviously, by integrating feature learning and binary codes learning into a end-to-end framework, deep hashing methods can achieve better retrieval performance than traditional methods. We can find that the deep asymmetric hashing methods ADSH and our proposed FDAH can greatly outperform other deep symmetric hashing methods such as DPSH, DSDH and DDSH. The reason is that deep asymmetric methods can fully utilize the supervised information of the whole training set with the asymmetric learning mechanism. Compared with ADSH, FDAH can obtain a better performance in most cases since FDAH incorporates the semantic information in binary codes learning and the quantization process. ADSH can obtain higher accuracy with the increasing length of binary codes on NUS-WIDE dataset. The results on precision, recall and F-measure of different methods on CIFAR-10 and Fashion-MNIST datasets are shown in Fig. 2 and Fig. 3. As the figure shows, FDAH can always outperform the other methods on precision, recall and F-measure, which can be always around 90%.

Deep asymmetric hashing methods ADSH and FDAH adopt the whole training set for training to obtain high retrieval performance with the asymmetric mechanism. Therefore, we further test other deep hashing methods which utilize the whole training set. Table 2 shows the MAP results and training time of different methods on CIFAR-10. DPSH-A, DSDH-A and DDSH-A denote the corresponding deep hashing methods which utilize the whole training set. As Table 2 shows, DPSH-A, DSDH-A and DDSH-A obtain similarly high retrieval performance with much more training time. Because of using DCC algorithm, ADSH also need much training time as the length of binary codes increases. By using a closed-form solution instead of DCC algorithm, our proposed FDAH can achieve highest accuracy with less and steady training time.

Figure 4 shows the sensitivity to hyper-parameters of the proposed FDAH on CIFAR-10 and Fashion-MNIST datasets. We shows the MAP results by tuning one of the parameters and fixing others. From Fig. 4(a), we can see that FDAH obtains the best performance when $\gamma_1 = 10^{-3}$. Figure 4(b) presents the MAP results versus the size of query set $m$. FDAH can achieve stable performance when $m >= 2000$, because FDAH can utilize the whole training set when $m$ is greater than 2000. Besides, FDAH is not sensitive to $\gamma_2$ and $\gamma_3$ in a range from $10^{-4}$ to $10^2$ in practice.

## 4   Conclusion

In this paper, we propose a novel deep hashing method called Fast Deep Asymmetric Hashing (FDAH). The proposed FDAH assumes that the binary codes of training set can be obtained by regressing their semantic labels and avoids using the quadratic term of binary variables in the final hashing loss. As a result, FDAH can learn the binary codes of all bits with a closed-form solution to speed up the training procedure. Moreover, FDAH can obtain more discriminative and efficient binary codes by incorporating the semantic information in binary codes learning and the quantization process. Extensive experiments on three well-known datasets show that the proposed FDAH can achieve state-of-the-art performance with less training time.

**Acknowledgement.** This work was supported in part by the Natural Science Foundation of China under Grant 61976145, Grant 62076164 and Grant 61802267, in part by the Guangdong Basic and Applied Basic Research Foundation (No. 2021A1515011861), and in part by the Shenzhen Municipal Science and Technology Innovation Council under Grants JCYJ20180305124834854 and JCYJ20190813100801664.

# References

1. Andoni, A., Razenshteyn, I.P.: Optimal data-dependent hashing for approximate near neighbors. In: STOC, pp. 793–801 (2015)
2. Chatfield, K., Simonyan, K., Vedaldi, A., Zisserman, A.: Return of the devil in the details: delving deep into convolutional nets. In: BMVC (2014)
3. Chen, Y., Lai, Z., Ding, Y., Lin, K., Wong, W.K.: Deep supervised hashing with anchor graph. In: ICCV, pp. 9795–9803 (2019)
4. Cui, H., Zhu, L., Li, J., Yang, Y., Nie, L.: Scalable deep hashing for large-scale social image retrieval **29**, 1271–1284 (2020)
5. Datar, M., Indyk, P., Immorlica, N., Mirrokni, V.: Locality-sensitive hashing scheme based on p-stable distributions. In: ASCG, pp. 253–262 (2004)
6. Gong, Y., Lazebnik, S., Gordo, A., Perronnin, F.: Iterative quantization: a procrustean approach to learning binary codes for large-scale image retrieval. IEEE Trans. Pattern Anal. Mach. Intell. **35**(12), 2916–2929 (2013)
7. Gui, J., Liu, T., Sun, Z., Tao, D., Tan, T.: Fast supervised discrete hashing. IEEE Trans. Pattern Anal. Mach. Intell. **40**, 490–496 (2018)
8. Jiang, Q., Cui, X., Li, W.: Deep discrete supervised hashing. IEEE Trans. Image Process. **27**, 5996–6009 (2018)
9. Jiang, Q., Li, W.: Asymmetric deep supervised hashing. In: AAAI, pp. 3342–3349 (2018)
10. Kang, W., Li, W., Zhou, Z.: Column sampling based discrete supervised hashing. In: AAAI, pp. 1230–1236 (2016)
11. Kulis, B., Darrell, T.: Learning to hash with binary reconstructive embeddings. In: NIPS, pp. 1042–1050 (2009)
12. Lai, H., Pan, Y., Liu, Y., Yan, S.: Simultaneous feature learning and hash coding with deep neural networks. In: CVPR, pp. 3270–3278 (2015)
13. Lai, Z., Chen, Y., Wu, J., Wong, W.K., Shen, F.: Jointly sparse hashing for image retrieval. IEEE Trans. Image Process. **27**(12), 6147–6158 (2018)
14. Li, Q., Sun, Z., He, R., Tan, T.: Deep supervised discrete hashing. In: NIPS, pp. 2482–2491 (2017)
15. Li, W., Wang, S., Kang, W.: Feature learning based deep supervised hashing with pairwise labels. In: IJCAI, pp. 1711–1717 (2016)
16. Liu, W., Wang, J., Ji, R., Jiang, Y., Chang, S.: Supervised hashing with kernels. In: CVPR, pp. 2074–2081 (2012)
17. Liu, W., Wang, J., Kumar, S., Chang, S.: Hashing with graphs. In: ICML, pp. 1–8 (2011)
18. Rumelhart, D.E., Hinton, G.E., Williams, R.J.: Learning representations by back propagating errors. Nature **323**, 533–536 (1986)

19. Shen, F., Gao, X., Liu, L., Yang, Y., Shen, H.T.: Deep asymmetric pairwise hashing. In: ACM MM, pp. 1522–1530 (2017)
20. Shen, F., Shen, C., Liu, W., Shen, H.T.: Supervised discrete hashing. In: CVPR, pp. 37–45 (2015)
21. Shen, Y., Liu, L., Shen, F., Shao, L.: Zero-shot sketch-image hashing. In: CVPR, pp. 3598–3607 (2018)
22. Wang, X., Shi, Y., Kitani, K.M.: Deep supervised hashing with triplet labels. In: Lai, S.-H., Lepetit, V., Nishino, K., Sato, Y. (eds.) ACCV 2016. LNCS, vol. 10111, pp. 70–84. Springer, Cham (2017). https://doi.org/10.1007/978-3-319-54181-5_5
23. Weiss, Y., Torralba, A., Fergus, R.: Spectral hashing. In: NIPS, pp. 1753–1760 (2008)
24. Xia, R., Pan, Y., Lai, H., Liu, C., Yan, S.: Supervised hashing for image retrieval via image representation learning. In: AAAI, pp. 2156–2162 (2014)
25. Xie, G., et al.: Attentive region embedding network for zero-shot learning. In: CVPR, pp. 9384–9393 (2019)
26. Zhang, Z., Liu, L., Shen, F., Shen, H.T., Shao, L.: Binary multi-view clustering. IEEE Trans. Pattern Anal. Mach. Intell. 41, 1774–1782 (2019)
27. Zhao, S., Wu, D., Zhang, W., Zhou, Y., Li, B., Wang, W.: Asymmetric deep hashing for efficient hash code compression. In: ACM MM, pp. 763–771 (2020)

# Siamese Tracking with Bilinear Features

Zhixiong Pi$^{(\boxtimes)}$, Changxin Gao, and Nong Sang

Key Laboratory of Image Processing and Intelligent Control, School of Artificial
Intelligence and Automation, HuaZhong University of Science and Technology,
Wuhan, China
{pzxiong,cgao,nsang}@hust.edu.cn

**Abstract.** Bilinear features arise in fine-grained visual recognition.
They are advantageous to encode detailed representations and attributes
to differentiate visually similar objects. The apparent similarity is challenging in visual tracking where background distractors interfere siamese
trackers to localize the target object. Especially when distractors and the
target belong to the same object category. To increase the discrimination between similar appearance objects, we propose an efficient bilinear
encoding method for siamese tracking. The proposed method consists of a
self-bilinear encoder and an cross-bilinear encoder. The bilinear features
generated via the self-bilinear encoder and the cross-bilinear encoder
represent target variations itself and target distractor difference, respectively. To this end, the proposed bilinear encoders advance siamese trackers to capture target appearance variations while differentiating the target and background distractors. Experiments on the benchmark datasets
show the effectiveness of bilinear features. Our tracker performs favorably
against state-of-the-art approaches.

**Keywords:** Siamese network · Bilinear feature · Visual tracking

## 1 Introduction

There has been a continuous need to localize the target object in video sequences.
The performance of existing trackers are significantly improved via using deep
neural networks. Among these CNN based approaches, siamese trackers receive
huge attention [1,45] because of its efficient online prediction. A siamese network
consists of a template branch and a search branch. The target appearance in the
initial frame is preserved in the template branch and is matched to the content
in the current frame (i.e., search branch). The detection based trackers [24,58]
and correlation filter based trackers [11,57] can also be formulated within the
siamese network to improve the computational efficiency.

Visual trackers suffer from target awareness that the target object is only
identified via a single annotation bounding box in the first frame. A challenging scenario appears that when the background contains similar objects (i.e.,

**Supplementary Information** The online version contains supplementary material
available at https://doi.org/10.1007/978-3-031-02444-3_32.

C. Wallraven et al. (Eds.): ACPR 2021, LNCS 13189, pp. 421–435, 2022.
https://doi.org/10.1007/978-3-031-02444-3_32

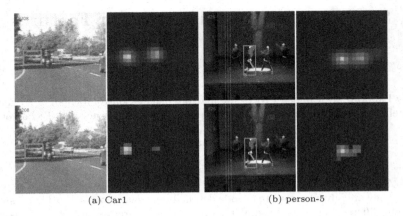

(a) Carl                                    (b) person-5

**Fig. 1.** Response maps of PrDiMP50 (the first line) and our BiDiMP (the second line).

distractors), the appearance models maintained in each tracker need to discriminate the target from the distractors. Meanwhile, the appearance of target varies during the whole sequence. It is difficult to capture both target appearance variations while differentiating background distractors. For example, part-based trackers [30,56] focus on the global movement of object parts while underestimating the interference from similar distractor parts. The detection based trackers [38,41] use a discriminative classifier to exclude background distractors as well as heavily varied target. For siamese trackers, CNN feature representations are very important as the matching process purely relies on them. As various challenges like background distraction and target variation occur during the tracking process, it is necessary to encode more reliable features in siamese trackers.

In this paper, we propose two bilinear encoders within the siamese network to capture target appearance variations while differentiating background distractors. Our motivation is from the bilinear features [29,33] that has been widely adopted in fine-grained visual recognition. We integrate the proposed bilinear encoders into the siameseFC framework, SiamDW [57] and PrDiMP [9] for joint training. We use a local and a global branch to separately map CNN features from both search patch and template patch into the local and global representations. The self-bilinear feature is obtained by the fusion of local and global representations from the same branch via an outer product operation. The cross-bilinear feature is obtained by the fusion of local and global representations from different branches. As a result, the proposed tracker is able to account for target appearance variations via self-bilinear features while differentiating background distractors via cross-bilinear features. Experiments on the benchmark datasets demonstrate the effectiveness of these two bilinear features upon siameseFC improvement. By integrating the proposed bilinear features in PrDiMP [9], the tracker performs favorably against state-of-the-art approaches.

## 2    Related Work

There are extensive surveys on visual tracking in the literature [40,52]. In this section, we discuss the representative visual trackers and the bilinear modules for the fine-grained recognition.

### 2.1    Visual Tracking

The state-of-the-art visual tracking methods can typically be categorized as one-stage regression framework and two-stage classification framework. The one-stage framework regresses CNN features or hand-craft features into a Gaussian response via discriminative correlation filters (DCF) [6,7,10,35,48,55] to localize the target object. The two-stage framework, namely tracking-by-detection framework [17,38,39], first generates multiple bounding box proposals and then classifies each as either the target object or the background. Recently, the siamese network has been widely used for visual tracking because of its high efficiency and precision. Starting from the SiamFC [1] which verifies the template patch and search patch via a siamese network, many extensions are proposed. Some methods use bounding box regression in siamese framework to track the target more precisely [24,25]. SiamMask [45] and D3S [34] further utilize a segmentation branch tracking and segmenting targets at the same time. SiamFCTri [11] designs a triplet loss to train the network better. ATOM [8] and DiMP [2] propose the efficient online updating methods to adapt to the appearance changes. There are also other extensions from the perspectives of residual attention [44], flow calibration [59] and recurrently memory [50]. In this paper, we propose a method to encode the bilinear features in the siamese network. Different from existing siamese based trackers, our method is more powerful in mining the useful details and the localized attributes. We conduct the experiments based on two siamese trackers, SiamDW [57] and PrDiMP [9].

### 2.2    Bilinear Model in Fine-Grained Recognition

In the fine-grained recognition field, the bilinear deep model is firstly used by Lin et al. [33] to extract the highly localized attributes and details which can replace the part-based representations. They demonstrate several widely-used texture encoders such as BOVW and VLAD can be represented by an outer product of two hand-designed features and generalizing the part-based representations as an outer product of two CNN features. Then a series of bilinear models are proposed either to speed up the feature extracting process [15,29,46,54] or to encode the bilinear feature more elaborately [5,27,32,53]. Drawing the lessons from these bilinear models, we design a bilinear feature encoding module in the siamese tracking network to obtain the bilinear relationships between the feature channels. However, different from the recognition task, the target need to be located in the visual tracking. Considering the locating requirement and the efficiency, we design a new bilinear feature encoding module to extract the bilinear feature with the unchanged spatial resolution.

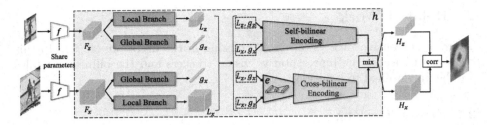

**Fig. 2.** Pipeline of the siamese bilinear tracking.

## 3 Proposed Approach

In Fig. 2, we shows the pipeline overview of our approach where self- and cross-bilinear encoders reorganize CNN features before the correlation for response map generation. We first revisit bilinear features and then illustrate the details of bilinear encoders.

### 3.1 Revisiting Bilinear Features

The bilinear feature is introduced in CNN [33] for fine-grained image classification. We define two features $\mathbf{x} \in \mathbb{R}^{m_1 \times 1}$ and $\mathbf{y} \in \mathbb{R}^{m_2 \times 1}$, the bilinear feature can be written as:

$$\mathbf{b}_{xy} = \begin{bmatrix} b_{xy}^1 \\ b_{xy}^2 \\ \vdots \\ b_{xy}^N \end{bmatrix} = \begin{bmatrix} x^1 w^1 y^1 \\ x^1 w^2 y^2 \\ \vdots \\ x^{m_1} w^N y^{m_2} \end{bmatrix} \tag{1}$$

where $N = m_1 \cdot m_2$ and $\mathbf{b}_{xy}$ is the bilinear feature that represents the channel correlation between $\mathbf{x}$ and $\mathbf{y}$. In a CNN, the feature maps with a size of h × w × n can be reorganized as $\mathbf{X}$ with a size of hw × n. After reorganization, there is a vector $\mathbf{x}^i$ representing each spatial location in the CNN feature maps. The size of vector $\mathbf{x}^i$ is n × 1 and $i \in [1, 2, ..., h \times w]$.

Figure 3(a) shows how bilinear feature suites fine-grained image classification. For an input CNN feature $\mathbf{X}$, there are two streams A and B to separately map $\mathbf{X}$ to $\mathbf{F}_A$ and $\mathbf{F}_B$. An outer product operation is used to individually fuse each channel of $\mathbf{F}_A$ and $\mathbf{F}_B$ to generate the bilinear features. Then, a global average pooling is performed by vectorizing the outer product result for globalization. As a result, the output bilinear feature models the relationships between feature channels of $\mathbf{F}_A$ and $\mathbf{F}_B$. We show how we improve this original bilinear model to for siamese tracking adaption in the following.

### 3.2 Self-bilinear Encoder

The structure of self-bilinear encoder is shown in Fig. 3(b). Given an input CNN feature $\mathbf{X}$, we use a local branch and a global branch to map $\mathbf{X}$ to $\mathbf{L}$ and $\mathbf{g}$,

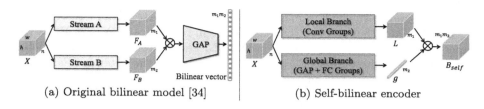

(a) Original bilinear model [34]          (b) Self-bilinear encoder

**Fig. 3.** Overview of the original bilinear model [33] and our self-bilinear encoder.

respectively. The local branch consists of fully convolutional groups to retain part-based spatial sensitivity. The global branch consists of a global average pooling and fully connected layers to formulate a vectorized global representation. We denote each spatial location in $\mathbf{L}$ as $\mathbf{l}^i$ that is a vector of size $m_1 \times 1$. The size of $\mathbf{g}$ is $m_2 \times 1$. The outer product of $\mathbf{L}$ and $\mathbf{g}$ generates a self-bilinear feature. Each spatial location of this feature can be represented as:

$$\mathbf{b}_{\text{self}}^i = vec(\mathbf{l}^i \cdot \mathbf{g}^\top) \tag{2}$$

where $\mathbf{b}_{\text{self}}^i \in \mathbb{R}^{m_1 m_2 \times 1}$ is a vector representing the fusion of global and local branch outputs. The self-bilinear feature maintains both spatial sensitivity and global consistency of the input feature $\mathbf{X}$.

Equation 2 can be illustrated via a toy example. We assume there is only one convolutional layer in the local branch, and a fully connected layer following GAP in the global branch. We denote the parameters of the convolutional layer as $\mathbf{W}_1 \in \mathbb{R}^{m_1 \times n}$, the parameters of the fully connected layer as $\mathbf{W}_2 \in \mathbb{R}^{m_2 \times n}$, the input feature as $\mathbf{X} \in \mathbb{R}^{n \times hw}$ whose row is $\mathbf{x}^i \in \mathbb{R}^{n \times 1}$, and the GAP output as $\overline{\mathbf{x}} \in \mathbb{R}^{n \times 1}$. Equation 2 can be written as:

$$\mathbf{b}_{\text{self}}^i = vec(\mathbf{W}_1 \mathbf{x}^i \cdot \overline{\mathbf{x}}^\top \mathbf{W}_2^\top) = vec(\begin{bmatrix} \mathbf{W}_1^1 \mathbf{x}^i \\ \mathbf{W}_1^2 \mathbf{x}^i \\ \vdots \\ \mathbf{W}_1^{m_1} \mathbf{x}^i \end{bmatrix} \begin{bmatrix} \mathbf{W}_2^1 \overline{\mathbf{x}} \\ \mathbf{W}_2^2 \overline{\mathbf{x}} \\ \vdots \\ \mathbf{W}_2^{m_2} \overline{\mathbf{x}} \end{bmatrix}^\top) \tag{3}$$

where $vec(.)$ operator can be unfolded as follows:

$$\mathbf{b}_{\text{self}}^i = \begin{bmatrix} \mathbf{x}^{i\top} \cdot \mathbf{W}_1^{1\top} \mathbf{W}_2^1 \cdot \overline{\mathbf{x}} \\ \mathbf{x}^{i\top} \cdot \mathbf{W}_1^{1\top} \mathbf{W}_2^2 \cdot \overline{\mathbf{x}} \\ \vdots \\ \mathbf{x}^{i\top} \cdot \mathbf{W}_1^{p\top} \mathbf{W}_2^q \cdot \overline{\mathbf{x}} \\ \vdots \\ \mathbf{x}^{i\top} \cdot \mathbf{W}_1^{m_1\top} \mathbf{W}_2^{m_2} \cdot \overline{\mathbf{x}} \end{bmatrix}, \tag{4}$$

where $p \in [1, 2, ..., m_1]$ and $q \in [1, 2, ..., m_2]$. The term $\mathbf{W}_1^{p\top} \mathbf{W}_2^q \in \mathbb{R}^{n \times n}$ is a relationship matrix that describes the co-occurrence tendency of these feature pairs.

In the siamese tracking framework (i.e., Fig. 2), we first obtain CNN features $\mathbf{F}_z$ and $\mathbf{F}_x$ from the template and search patch, respectively. We use $\mathbf{F}_z$ as the input to the self-bilinear encoder and obtain $\mathbf{L}_z$ and $\mathbf{g}_z$ from the local and global branches. Similarly, we map $\mathbf{F}_x$ to $\mathbf{L}_x$ and $\mathbf{g}_x$. We take the outer product of $\mathbf{L}_z$ and $\mathbf{g}_z$ to generate a self-bilinear feature $\mathbf{B}_z^{\text{self}}$, and take the outer product of $\mathbf{L}_x$ and $\mathbf{g}_x$ to generate a self-bilinear feature $\mathbf{B}_x^{\text{self}}$. Specifically, we can write the outer product operation as follows:

$$\mathbf{B}_z^{\text{self}} = \mathbf{L}_z \times \mathbf{g}_z,$$
$$\mathbf{B}_x^{\text{self}} = \mathbf{L}_x \times \mathbf{g}_x. \tag{5}$$

where the outer product is executed following Eq. 2 in practice. These two self-bilinear features will be fused with cross-bilinear features to form a joint representation of the search and template patches.

### 3.3 Cross-Bilinear Encoder

In cross-bilinear encoder, we also use a local branch and a global branch following Sect. 3.2. These two branches contain the same parameters as those in the self-bilinear encoder. So we can obtain $\mathbf{L}_z$, $\mathbf{g}_z$, $\mathbf{L}_x$ and $\mathbf{g}_x$, which are the same as those in self-bilinear encoder. The motivation of encoding cross-bilinear features is to extract pairwise relationships between the template and search patch CNN features. An extra convolution group, taking $\mathbf{g}_z$ and $\mathbf{g}_x$ as the inputs, extracts the interaction feature $\mathbf{e}_z$ and $\mathbf{e}_x$:

$$\mathbf{e}_z = e(\mathbf{g}_z), \mathbf{e}_x = e(\mathbf{g}_x), \tag{6}$$

where $e(.)$ denotes the extra convolution group. Then, the encoder calculates the outer product to generate the cross-bilinear features:

$$\mathbf{B}_z^{\text{cross}} = \mathbf{L}_z \times \mathbf{e}_x,$$
$$\mathbf{B}_x^{\text{cross}} = \mathbf{L}_x \times \mathbf{e}_z. \tag{7}$$

After obtaining the self-bilinear features and the cross-bilinear features, we fuse these features following [29] to via a mixture operation. The final features of the template and the search region can be written as:

$$\mathbf{H}_z = \mathbf{B}_z^{\text{self}} + \mathbf{B}_z^{\text{cross}} + \mathbf{F}_z,$$
$$\mathbf{H}_x = \mathbf{B}_x^{\text{self}} + \mathbf{B}_x^{\text{cross}} + \mathbf{F}_x, \tag{8}$$

where the $\mathbf{H}^{\text{self}}$ and $\mathbf{H}^{\text{cross}}$ represent the self-bilinear features and the cross-bilinear features, respectively. The mixed features $\mathbf{H}_z$ and $\mathbf{H}_x$ are sent into the correlation operation for target response map generation.

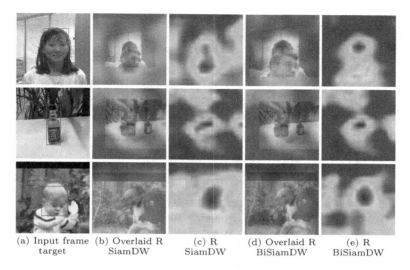

|  (a) Input frame | (b) Overlaid R | (c) R | (d) Overlaid R | (e) R |
|  target | SiamDW | SiamDW | BiSiamDW | BiSiamDW |

**Fig. 4.** Visualizations of the response maps (i.e., R). The input frames are shown in (a). The response maps generated by the original siamese network are shown in (c). They are overlaid to the input frames in (b). The response maps generated by the proposed siamese network are shown in (e) and overlaid to the input frames in (d). (Color figure online)

## 3.4    Discussions and Visualizations

The proposed bilinear features improve the representation to capture target variations while differentiating the background distractions. We show the bilinear features contribute to the tracking performance in practice.

Figure 4 shows the response maps of our BiSiamDW and its baseline SiamDW [57]. The input frames are shown in (a) and the response maps from the baseline siamese tracker (i.e., siamDW [57] with ResNet22 as feature backbone) and the proposed tracker are shown in (c) and (e). We also overlay these response maps on the input frames to show the values around the target object in (b) and (d). The higher values in the response maps are marked in red while lower values are marked in blue.

Figure 5 shows the response map comparison of DiMP50 [2], PrDiMP50 [9], and our BiDiMP. We select three challenging sequences, including 'elephant-12' and 'giraffe-10' in the LaSOT [12] dataset, and 'Human4-2' in the OTB-2015 [47] dataset to compare the results. in the 'elephant-12' sequence, DiMP50 [2] and PrDiMP50 [9] are distracted by the similar objects easily, while our BiDiMP can distinguish the real target from the distractors, with the help of the bilinear features in the 'giraffe-10' sequence, when the occlusion happens, DiMP50 [2] and PrDiMP50 [9] wrongly track the man or the arm, but BiDiMP can tell the wrong target and generate a low response in the 'Human4-2' sequence, there are two similar men. DiMP50 [2] is influenced by the similar distractor, and generates a double-peak response. PrDiMP50 [9] shifts to the middle of the two men. However, our BiDiMP still can find the real target with certainty.

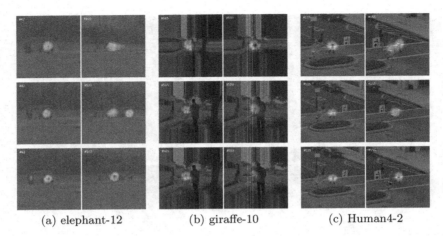

(a) elephant-12          (b) giraffe-10          (c) Human4-2

**Fig. 5.** Response map comparison of some state-of-the-art trackers. We compare the response maps from DiMP50, PrDiMP50, and our BiDiMP. The response maps from DiMP50, PrDiMP50, and BiDiMP are in the first, second, and third line, respectively. The subfigure (a) shows the results from the sequence 'elephant-12'. The subfigure (b) shows the results from the sequence 'giraffe-10'. The subfigure (c) shows the results from the sequence 'Human4-2'.

## 4    Experiments

In this section, we illustrate our implementation details and evaluate the performance of integrating the proposed module in SiamDW [57] and PrDiMP [9] trackers. The evaluation process consists of ablation studies and state-of-the-art comparisons. The benchmark datasets include OTB-2015 [47], VOT-2017 [22], VOT-2019 [23], LaSOT [12] and GOT-10K [21] where there are 100, 60, 60, 280 and 180 test video sequences, respectively. We follow standard evaluation protocols for comparison. On the OTB-2015 [47] and LaSOT [12] dataset, we use distance precision (Prec.) rates at a threshold of 20 pixels and overlap success (AUC) rates. On the VOT [22,23] datasets, we use expected average overlap (EAO), accuracy values (Av) and robustness values (Rv). On the GOT-10K [21], we evaluate the performance via average overlap (AO), and success rates (SR) at overlap threshold of 0.5 and 0.75.

### 4.1    Implementation Details

*Network Architecture.* We integrate our bilinear feature encoder in the siamese based trackers SiamDW [57] and PrDiMP [9] to get our new trackers named BiSiamDW and BiDiMP, respectively. The backbones of BiSiamDW and BiDiMP are resnet22 [18] and resnet50 [18], respectively. The bilinear feature encoder consists of a local branch, a global branch, and an extra convolutional group.

**Table 1.** Ablation studies on OTB-2015 and LaSOT datasets.

| Method | OTB2015 | | LaSOT | | |
|---|---|---|---|---|---|
| | AUC↑ | Prec.↑ | AUC↑ | Prec.↑ | N.Prec.↑ |
| SiamDW | 0.644 | 0.869 | 0.381 | 0.381 | 0.474 |
| +CrossBilinear | 0.659 | 0.875 | 0.394 | 0.398 | 0.485 |
| +SelfBilinear | 0.656 | 0.875 | 0.392 | 0.394 | 0.484 |
| +SelfCrossBilinear | 0.663 | 0.882 | 0.401 | 0.407 | 0.492 |
| PrDiMP50 | 0.693 | 0.893 | 0.603 | 0.612 | 0.693 |
| +CrossBilinear | 0.695 | 0.902 | 0.627 | 0.645 | 0.719 |
| +SelfBilinear | 0.697 | 0.911 | 0.631 | 0.652 | 0.724 |
| +SelfCrossBilinear | 0.703 | 0.919 | 0.648 | 0.677 | 0.742 |

*Training Strategy.* The parameters of the proposed bilinear feature encoder are set randomly in the initialization process. Then we train the whole model end-to-end. For the tracker BiSiamDW, we train the model by 50 epochs with a SGD solver, like SiamDW [57] does, using GOT-10K [21] as the training dataset. An epoch includes 234400 iterations. The training batch size is set to 32. For the tracker BiDiMP, we train the model by 50 epochs with an ADAM solver, like DiMP [2] does, using GOT-10K [21], TrackingNet [37], COCO [31], and LaSOT [12] as the training datasets. An epoch includes 2000 iterations. The training batch size is set to 32.

*Online Tracking.* BiSiamDW tracks the targets without any online update or initial fine-tuning. We always extract the feature of the target patch in the initial frame as the template of the current video sequence. The average speed of BiSiamDW is 50 FPS with a nvidia TITAN X GPU. BiDiMP uses the online updating strategy and does the initial fine-tuning to get the template like DiMP [2]. The average speed of BiDiMP is 22 FPS with a nvidia TITAN X GPU.

## 4.2 Ablation Studies

We evaluate the effectiveness of the proposed module to the siamese tracking framework. First, we construct a baseline tracking framework which does not encode any bilinear features. Then we add the self-bilinear feature and the cross-bilinear feature in the model separately. The performance of the final model with both the two kinds of bilinear features is illustrated also. We generate the tracking results produced by each configuration on the OTB and LaSOT datasets as shown in Table 1. Based on SiamDW [57], the cross-bilinear feature improves the AUC scores by 1.5% and 1.3% on the OTB-2015 and the LaSOT, respectively. The self-bilinear feature improves the AUC score by 1.2% and 1.1% on the OTB-2015 and the LaSOT, respectively. The best performance can be reached when combining the two kinds of bilinear features. Based on PrDiMP [9], the results on OTB dataset can be improved from 69.3% to 70.3% AUC score, by

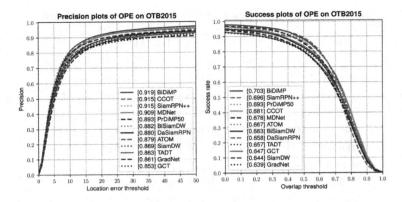

**Fig. 6.** Precision success plots and overlap success plots on OTB-2015 dataset.

encoding the bilinear feature. On the LaSOT dataset, the tracker obtains 2.4% and 2.8% gains in terms of the AUC score, by integrating the cross-bilinear module and the self-bilinear module alone, respectively. When integrating both the two bilinear modules, we can obtain 64.8% AUC score, which is higher than the baseline PrDiMP50 [9] by 4.5%.

### 4.3    Results on OTB Dataset

We compare the proposed tracker with existing trackers on OTB-2015 dataset. We evaluate all the results with the standard toolkit of the OTB dataset. BiSiamDW and BiDiMP are our proposed trackers. SiamDW [57] and PrDiMP50 [9] are our baselines. Expected the baseline, we further compare our tracker with more state-of-the-art trackers, including GradNet [26], GCT [14], TADT [28], DaSiamRPN [58], ATOM [8], MDNet [38], PrDiMP50 [9], and SiamRPN++ [24]. Figure 6 shows the evaluation results, where BiDiMP performs favorably against the state-of-the-arts.

On the OTB-2015 dataset, the proposed BiDiMP tracker achieves state-of-the-arts, and obtain higher scores than these siamese trackers SiamRPN++ [24], PrDiMP50 [9], ATOM [8], DaSiamRPN [58], and SiamDW [57] both in AUC and precision. Compared with the state-of-the-art trackers PrDiMP50 [9] and SiamRPN++ [24], which also use the resnet50 [18] to extract backbone features, our tracker BiDiMP outperforms them by 0.7% and 1.0% in terms of the AUC score. Our BiSiamDW also outperforms its baseline SiamDW [57].

### 4.4    Results on VOT Dataset

In this section, we evaluate the proposed tracker on the VOT-2017 [22] and VOT-2019 [23] datasets. On the VOT-2017 [22] dataset, we compare the results with the state-of-the-art trackers, including CFWCR [19], CCOT [10],

MCPF [55], CRT [3], ECOhc [7], SiamDW [57], and SiamFC [1]. On the VOT-2019 [23] dataset, we show and compare the performances of the state-of-the-art trackers, including DiMP50 [2], SiamBAN [4], ATOM [8], SiamMask [45], SiamRPN++ [24], ROAM++ [51], SPM [43], TADT [28], and our tracker BiDiMP. The standard evaluation toolkit is utilized.

**Table 2.** EAO scores, Av, and Rv of the state-of-the-art trackers on VOT-2017 dataset. The color red and **blue** notate the best and the second best results.

|     | SiamFC | SiamDW | ECOhc | CRT | MCPF | CCOT | CFWCR | BiSiamDW | BiDiMP |
|-----|--------|--------|-------|-----|------|------|-------|----------|--------|
| EAO | 0.188 | 0.229 | 0.239 | 0.245 | 0.248 | 0.267 | 0.301 | 0.252 | 0.370 |
| Av  | 0.454 | 0.541 | 0.495 | 0.467 | 0.510 | 0.494 | 0.484 | 0.543 | 0.611 |
| Rv  | 0.585 | 0.493 | 0.435 | 0.337 | 0.427 | 0.318 | 0.267 | 0.357 | 0.262 |

**Table 3.** EAO scores, Av, and Rv of the state-of-the-art trackers on VOT-2019 dataset. The color red and **blue** notate the best and the second best results.

|     | TADT | SPM | ROAM++ | SiamRPN++ | SiamMask | ATOM | SiamBAN | DiMP50 | BiDiMP |
|-----|------|-----|--------|-----------|----------|------|---------|--------|--------|
| EAO | 0.207 | 0.275 | 0.281 | 0.285 | 0.287 | 0.292 | 0.327 | 0.379 | 0.392 |
| Av  | 0.516 | 0.577 | 0.561 | 0.599 | 0.594 | 0.603 | 0.602 | 0.594 | 0.617 |
| Rv  | 0.677 | 0.507 | 0.431 | 0.482 | 0.461 | 0.411 | 0.396 | 0.278 | 0.279 |

Our proposed tracker BiDiMP obtaining 0.37 EAO score performs better than all the compared trackers. According to Table 2, BiDiMP also gets the highest tracking accuracy and robustness with 0.611 Av and 0.262 Rv. BiSiamDW achieves 0.252 EAO score on the VOT-2017 dataset, which is also outperforms its baseline SiamDW [57] by 0.023. On Table 3, we compare the performances of our tracker BiDiMP with other 8 state-of-the-art trackers on VOT-2019 dataset. In terms of the EAO and Av score, BiDiMP performs the best among all these state-of-the-art trackers.

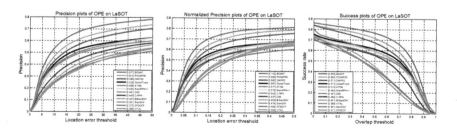

**Fig. 7.** Precision success plots, normalized precision success plots and overlap success plots on the LaSOT dataset.

### 4.5    Results on LaSOT Dataset

We evaluate our BiSiamDW and BiDiMP on the large-scale visual tracking dataset LaSOT and compare them with other state-of-the-art trackers, including GFSDCF [48], SiamDW [57], VITAL [41], C-RPN [13], D3S [34], SiamRPN++ [24], ATOM [8], GlobalTrack [20], DiMP50 [2], and PrDiMP50 [9]. We illustrate the precision plots, normalized precision plots and success plots of these trackers on the LaSOT testing set, as shown in Fig. 7. The proposed BiDiMP method obtains the highest scores in terms of the AUC, precision, and normalized precision scores. BiDiMP tracker achieves 64.8% AUC score and 74.2% normalized precision score. Compared with the trackers with the resnet50 [18] backbone, such as PrDiMP50 [9], DiMP50 [2], SiamRPN++ [24], and D3S [34], our BiDiMP tracker outperforms them significantly.

### 4.6    Results on GOT-10K Dataset

GOT-10K [21] dataset has more than 10,000 video sequences. 180 of these sequences are used for testing. We show the state-of-the-art comparison on Table 4 in terms of the standard metrics which are evaluated on the official server. The comparison trackers are RPT [36], SiamRCNN [42], PrDiMP50 [9], DiMP50 [2], SiamCAR [16], ATOM [8], SiamFC++ [49], SPM [43], and our BiDiMP.

Our tracker BiDiMP achieves the best AO value and $SR_{0.75}$ value. The AO value of BiDiMP is 68.4%, which is higher than the baseline PrDiMP50 by 4.8%. Compared with the RPT [36] tracker, the $SR_{0.50}$ value of our BiDiMP tracker is slightly lower, while our BiDiMP obtains the better AO and $SR_{0.75}$ value.

**Table 4.** Average overlap (AO), and success rates (SR) at overlap threshold of 0.5 and 0.75 of the state-of-the-art trackers on GOT-10K dataset. The color red and **blue** notate the best and the second best results.

|            | SPM   | SiamFC++ | ATOM  | CRT   | SiamCAR | DiMP50 | PrDiMP50 | SiamRCNN | RPT   | BiDiMP |
|------------|-------|----------|-------|-------|---------|--------|----------|----------|-------|--------|
| AO         | 0.513 | 0.526    | 0.556 | 0.245 | 0.581   | 0.611  | 0.636    | 0.649    | 0.682 | 0.684  |
| $SR_{0.50}$ | 0.593 | 0.625    | 0.634 | 0.467 | 0.683   | 0.717  | 0.739    | 0.728    | 0.803 | 0.795  |
| $SR_{0.75}$ | 0.359 | 0.347    | 0.402 | 0.337 | 0.441   | 0.492  | 0.529    | 0.597    | 0.583 | 0.601  |

## 5    Conclusion

Bilinear features have been shown to be effective for the challenge of distinguishing two objects that are only different in the subtle details at fine-grained recognition. In this paper, we encode the bilinear features in the siamese tracking network with very low computational burden. The proposed bilinear encoders extract the self- and cross-bilinear features at the same time, to enrich the capabilities of distinguishing the target from similar distractors and adapting to target deformations. The tracking results on several widely-used tracking datasets show that the bilinear features are useful for the visual tracking task.

# References

1. Bertinetto, L., Valmadre, J., Henriques, J.F., Vedaldi, A., Torr, P.H.S.: Fully-convolutional Siamese networks for object tracking. In: Hua, G., Jégou, H. (eds.) Computer Vision – ECCV 2016 Workshops: Amsterdam, The Netherlands, October 8-10 and 15-16, 2016, Proceedings, Part II, pp. 850–865. Springer, Cham (2016). https://doi.org/10.1007/978-3-319-48881-3_56
2. Bhat, G., Danelljan, M., Gool, L.V., Timofte, R.: Learning discriminative model prediction for tracking. In: ICCV, pp. 6182–6191 (October 2019)
3. Chen, K., Tao, W.: Convolutional regression for visual tracking. TIP **27**(7), 3611–3620 (2018)
4. Chen, Z., Zhong, B., Li, G., Zhang, S., Ji, R.: Siamese box adaptive network for visual tracking. In: CVPR, pp. 6668–6677 (2020)
5. Cui, Y., Zhou, F., Wang, J., Liu, X., Lin, Y., Belongie, S.: Kernel pooling for convolutional neural networks. In: CVPR (July 2017)
6. Dai, K., Wang, D., Lu, H., Sun, H., Li, J.: Visual tracking via adaptive spatially-regularized correlation filters. In: CVPR, June 2019 (2019)
7. Danelljan, M., Bhat, G., Khan, F.S., Felsberg, M.: ECO: efficient convolution operators for tracking. In: CVPR (2017)
8. Danelljan, M., Bhat, G., Khan, F.S., Felsberg, M.: ATOM: accurate tracking by overlap maximization. In: CVPR, June 2019 (2019)
9. Danelljan, M., Gool, L.V., Timofte, R.: Probabilistic regression for visual tracking. In: CVPR, pp. 7183–7192 (2020)
10. Danelljan, M., Robinson, A., Shahbaz Khan, F., Felsberg, M.: Beyond correlation filters: learning continuous convolution operators for visual tracking. In: Leibe, B., Matas, J., Sebe, N., Welling, M. (eds.) ECCV 2016. LNCS, vol. 9909, pp. 472–488. Springer, Cham (2016). https://doi.org/10.1007/978-3-319-46454-1_29
11. Dong, X., Shen, J.: Triplet loss in Siamese network for object tracking. In: Ferrari, V., Hebert, M., Sminchisescu, C., Weiss, Y. (eds.) ECCV 2018. LNCS, vol. 11217, pp. 472–488. Springer, Cham (2018). https://doi.org/10.1007/978-3-030-01261-8_28
12. Fan, H., et al.: LaSOT: a high-quality benchmark for large-scale single object tracking. In: CVPR, pp. 5374–5383 (2019)
13. Fan, H., Ling, H.: Siamese cascaded region proposal networks for real-time visual tracking. In: CVPR, June 2019 (2019)
14. Gao, J., Zhang, T., Xu, C.: Graph convolutional tracking. In: CVPR, June 2019 (2019)
15. Gao, Y., Beijbom, O., Zhang, N., Darrell, T.: Compact bilinear pooling. In: CVPR, June 2016 (2016)
16. Guo, D., Wang, J., Cui, Y., Wang, Z., Chen, S.: SiamCAR: Siamese fully convolutional classification and regression for visual tracking. In: CVPR, June 2020, pp. 6269–6277 (2020)
17. Han, B., Sim, J., Adam, H.: BranchOut: regularization for online ensemble tracking with convolutional neural networks. In: CVPR (2017)
18. He, K., Zhang, X., Ren, S., Jian, S.: Deep residual learning for image recognition. In: CVPR, pp. 770–778 (2016)
19. He, Z., Fan, Y., Zhuang, J., Dong, Y., Bai, H.: Correlation filters with weighted convolution responses. In ICCV, October 2017 (2017)
20. Huang, L., Zhao, X., Huang, K.: GlobalTrack: a simple and strong baseline for long-term tracking. In: AAAI, vol. 34, pp. 11037–11044 (2020)

21. Huang, L., Zhao, X., Huang, K.: GOT-10k: a large high-diversity benchmark for generic object tracking in the wild. TPAMI **43**(5), 1562–1577 (2021)
22. Kristan, M., et al.: The visual object tracking vot2017 challenge results. In: ICCV (2017)
23. Kristan, M., et al.: The seventh visual object tracking VOT2019 challenge results. In ICCV, October 2019 (2019)
24. Li, B., Wu, W., Wang, Q., Zhang, F., Xing, J., Yan, J.: SiamRPN++: evolution of Siamese visual tracking with very deep networks. In: CVPR, June 2019 (2019)
25. Li, B., Yan, J., Wu, W., Zhu, Z., Hu, X.: High performance visual tracking with Siamese region proposal network. In: CVPR, June 2018 (2018)
26. Li, P., Chen, B., Ouyang, W., Wang, D., Yang, X., Lu, H.: GradNET: gradient-guided network for visual object tracking. In: ICCV, pp. 6162–6171 (2019)
27. Li, P., Xie, J., Wang, Q., Gao, Z.: Towards faster training of global covariance pooling networks by iterative matrix square root normalization. In: CVPR, June 2018 (2018)
28. Li, X., Ma, C., Wu, B., He, Z., Yang, M.-H.: Target-aware deep tracking. In: CVPR, pp. 1369–1378 (2019)
29. Li, Y., Wang, N., Liu, J., Hou, X.: Factorized bilinear models for image recognition. In: ICCV, pp. 2079–2087 (2017)
30. Li, Y., Zhu, J., Hoi, S.C.: Reliable patch trackers: robust visual tracking by exploiting reliable patches. In: CVPR, June 2015 (2015)
31. Lin, T.-Y.: Microsoft COCO: common objects in context. In: Fleet, D., Pajdla, T., Schiele, B., Tuytelaars, T. (eds.) ECCV 2014. LNCS, vol. 8693, pp. 740–755. Springer, Cham (2014). https://doi.org/10.1007/978-3-319-10602-1_48
32. Lin, T.-Y., Maji, S., Koniusz, P.: Second-order democratic aggregation. In: Ferrari, V., Hebert, M., Sminchisescu, C., Weiss, Y. (eds.) ECCV 2018. LNCS, vol. 11207, pp. 639–656. Springer, Cham (2018). https://doi.org/10.1007/978-3-030-01219-9_38
33. Lin, T.-Y., RoyChowdhury, A., Maji, S.: Bilinear CNN models for fine-grained visual recognition. In: ICCV, December 2015 (2015)
34. Lukezic, A., Matas, J., Kristan, M.: D3S - a discriminative single shot segmentation tracker. In: CVPR, pp. 7133–7142 (2020)
35. Ma, C., Huang, J.-B., Yang, X., Yang, M.-H.: Hierarchical convolutional features for visual tracking. In: ICCV (2015)
36. Ma, Z., Wang, L., Zhang, H., Lu, W., Yin, J.: RPT: learning point set representation for Siamese visual tracking. In: Bartoli, A., Fusiello, A. (eds.) ECCV 2020. LNCS, vol. 12539, pp. 653–665. Springer, Cham (2020). https://doi.org/10.1007/978-3-030-68238-5_43
37. Müller, M., Bibi, A., Giancola, S., Alsubaihi, S., Ghanem, B.: TrackingNet: a large-scale dataset and benchmark for object tracking in the wild. In: Ferrari, V., Hebert, M., Sminchisescu, C., Weiss, Y. (eds.) ECCV 2018. LNCS, vol. 11205, pp. 310–327. Springer, Cham (2018). https://doi.org/10.1007/978-3-030-01246-5_19
38. Nam, H., Han, B.: Learning multi-domain convolutional neural networks for visual tracking. In: CVPR (2016)
39. Pu, S., Song, Y., Ma, C., Zhang, H., Yang, M.-H.: Deep attentive tracking via reciprocative learning. In: NeurIPS (2018)
40. Smeulders, A.W., Chu, D.M., Cucchiara, R., Calderara, S., Dehghan, A., Shah, M.: Visual tracking: an experimental survey. TPAMI **36**, 1442–1468 (2014)
41. Song, Y., et al.: VITAL: visual tracking via adversarial learning. In: CVPR, pp. 8990–8999 (2018)

42. Voigtlaender, P., Luiten, J., Torr, P.H., Leibe, B.: Siam R-CNN: visual tracking by re-detection. In: CVPR, pp. 6578–6588 (2020)
43. Wang, G., Luo, G., Xiong, Z., Zeng, W.: SPM-tracker: series-parallel matching for real-time visual object tracking. In: CVPR, pp. 3643–3652, June 2019 (2019)
44. Wang, Q., Teng, Z., Xing, J., Gao, J., Hu, W., Maybank, S.: Learning attentions: residual attentional Siamese network for high performance online visual tracking. In: CVPR (2018)
45. Wang, Q., Zhang, L., Bertinetto, L., Hu, W., Torr, P.H.: Fast online object tracking and segmentation: a unifying approach. In: CVPR, June 2019 (2019)
46. Wei, X., Zhang, Y., Gong, Y., Zhang, J., Zheng, N.: Grassmann pooling as compact homogeneous bilinear pooling for fine-grained visual classification. In: Ferrari, V., Hebert, M., Sminchisescu, C., Weiss, Y. (eds.) ECCV 2018. LNCS, vol. 11207, pp. 365–380. Springer, Cham (2018). https://doi.org/10.1007/978-3-030-01219-9_22
47. Wu, Y., Lim, J., Yang, M.-H.: Object tracking benchmark. TPAMI **37**, 1834–1848 (2015)
48. Xu, T., Feng, Z.-H., Wu, X.-J., Kittler, J.: Joint group feature selection and discriminative filter learning for robust visual object tracking. In: ICCV, October 2019 (2019)
49. Xu, Y., Wang, Z., Li, Z., Yuan, Y., Yu, G.: SiamFC++: towards robust and accurate visual tracking with target estimation guidelines. In: AAAI, vol. 34, pp. 12549–12556 (2020)
50. Yang, T., Chan, A.B.: Learning dynamic memory networks for object tracking. In: Ferrari, V., Hebert, M., Sminchisescu, C., Weiss, Y. (eds.) ECCV 2018. LNCS, vol. 11213, pp. 153–169. Springer, Cham (2018). https://doi.org/10.1007/978-3-030-01240-3_10
51. Yang, T., Xu, P., Hu, R., Chai, H., Chan, A.B.: ROAM: recurrently optimizing tracking model. In: CVPR, pp. 6718–6727, June 2020 (2020)
52. Yazdi, M., Bouwmans, T.: New trends on moving object detection in video images captured by a moving camera: a survey. Comput. Sci. Rev. **28**, 157–177 (2018)
53. Yu, C., Zhao, X., Zheng, Q., Zhang, P., You, X.: Hierarchical bilinear pooling for fine-grained visual recognition. In: Ferrari, V., Hebert, M., Sminchisescu, C., Weiss, Y. (eds.) ECCV 2018. LNCS, vol. 11220, pp. 595–610. Springer, Cham (2018). https://doi.org/10.1007/978-3-030-01270-0_35
54. Yue, K., Sun, M., Yuan, Y., Zhou, F., Ding, E., Xu, F.: Compact generalized non-local network. In: NeurIPS, November 2018 (2018)
55. Zhang, T., Xu, C., Yang, M.-H.: Multi-task correlation particle filter for robust object tracking. In: CVPR (2017)
56. Zhang, Y., Wang, L., Qi, J., Wang, D., Feng, M., Lu, H.: Structured Siamese network for real-time visual tracking. In: Ferrari, V., Hebert, M., Sminchisescu, C., Weiss, Y. (eds.) ECCV 2018. LNCS, vol. 11213, pp. 355–370. Springer, Cham (2018). https://doi.org/10.1007/978-3-030-01240-3_22
57. Zhang, Z., Peng, H.:L Deeper and wider Siamese networks for real-time visual tracking. In: CVPR, June 2019 (2019)
58. Zhu, Z., Wang, Q., Li, B., Wu, W., Yan, J., Hu, W.: Distractor-aware Siamese networks for visual object tracking. In: Ferrari, V., Hebert, M., Sminchisescu, C., Weiss, Y. (eds.) ECCV 2018. LNCS, vol. 11213, pp. 103–119. Springer, Cham (2018). https://doi.org/10.1007/978-3-030-01240-3_7
59. Zhu, Z., Wu, W., Zou, W., Yan, J.: End-to-end flow correlation tracking with spatial-temporal attention. In: CVPR (2018)

# Deep Siamese Network with Co-channel and Cr-Spatial Attention for Object Tracking

Fan Gao[✉], Ying Hu, and Yan Yan

Nanjing University of Science and Technology, Nanjing 210094, China
gaofan@njust.edu.cn

**Abstract.** Siamese trackers with offline training strategies have recently drawn great attention because of their balanced accuracy and speed. However, some limitations still remain to overcome, i.e., trackers cannot robustly discriminate target from similar background so far. In this paper, we propose a novel real-time co-channel and spatial attention based deeper Siamese network (DCANet). Our approach aims at dealing with some challenging situations like appearance variations, similar distractors, etc. Different from replacing the backbone network Alexnet with VGG16 directly, we modified the structure of VGG16 which has no fully connective layer and padding operation. In addition, co-channel and spatial attention mechanisms were applied to our method to enhance feature representation capability. Channel attention and spatial attention were proposed towards computer vision problems before. However, considered the special structure of siamese network, we designed Co-channel attention module which helps to emphasize the important areas in the two branches simultaneously. When we directly add spatial attention to our tracker, the tracking effect falls. However with a crop operation placed after spatial attention our tracker can tracking better. We perform extensive experiments on several benchmark datasets, including OTB-2013, OTB-2015, VOT-2017, LaSOT and GOT-10k, which demonstrate that our DCANet gains a competitive tracking performance, with a running speed of more than 60 frames per second.

**Keywords:** Siamese network · Single object tracking · Attention mechanism

## 1 Introduction

Visual object tracking is a critical issue in many areas of computer vision such as visual surveillance [1], pose estimation [18], etc. Trackers demand to efficiently locate the target object defined in the initial frame with a bounding box. In order to achieve robust tracking results, challenging cases should be taken into consideration, including occlusion, appearance variation, background distractors, etc.

Siamese network-based trackers have recently drawn great attention. The pioneering work SiamFC [2] treats tracking as learning similarity. By adopting

© Springer Nature Switzerland AG 2022
C. Wallraven et al. (Eds.): ACPR 2021, LNCS 13189, pp. 436–446, 2022.
https://doi.org/10.1007/978-3-031-02444-3_33

offline tracking strategies, SiamFC achieves real-time speed. Because of its simple architecture and high speed, SiamFC has become the cornerstone of most Siamese network based trackers. However, the tracker cannot adapt to challenging cases. Further research is needed to improve the adaptability and discriminability of tracking network. Many trackers have extended the SiamFC architecture [5,6,8,15,16]. EAST [8] formulates tracking as a decision-making process to speed up the tracker. CFNet [15] embeds a correlation filter layer into the Siamese network so that it can benefit from historical information and meanwhile keep high speed. SA-Siam [6] introduces a semantic branch which comes from classification task to learn semantic features. DSiam [5] proposes a dynamic Siamese network, which can effectively learn the appearance variation. SiamRPN [11] introduces Region proposal network (RPN) and place it after a siamese network. The RPN structure transforms tracking into a binary classification task and a bounding box regression task. SiamRPN and its succeeding works [10,11,19] usually can achieve a more accurate output but with too many parameters introduced which need a long-time training process. Although trackers above have been improved a lot, there remains one problem to be addressed that is how to enhance the discriminative ability of the neural network and keep in a high running speed.

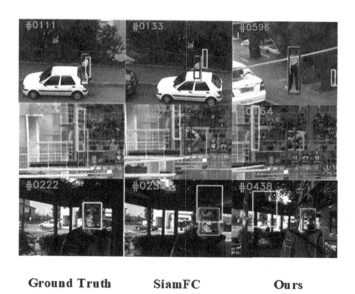

**Ground Truth**          **SiamFC**              **Ours**

**Fig. 1.** Comparison of tracking performance results between SiamFC and DCANet. Benefiting from deeper backbone and Co-channel and Cr-spatial attention mechanisms, our tracker can locate the target successfully when SiamFC fails, especially towards some challenging tracking scenarios like scale change, occlusion, etc.

In this paper, we propose a novel Co-channel and Cr-spatial attention mechanism for visual object tracking. We squeeze the template feature as the channel weight and use the learned weight to excite both of the two branches. This modification is designed to make the instance branch keep pace with the template branch and enhance the discriminative capacity of the tracker. A spatial attention module modified from CBAM [17] is also adopted to take advantage of spatial information.

Our contributions are summarized as follows. (i) We propose a Co-channel attention module to associate two branches and emphasis channels related to the target category, which will enhance the discriminative capacity of the tracker. (ii) We place a Cr-spatial attention module into the instance branch to take advantage of spatial information. An additional crop operation is placed after the attention module to mitigate the effect of padding. (iii) Fig. 1 shows the comparison of tracking results between SiamFC and DCANet, it seems that our tracker gains better performance towards some challenging tracking scenarios like scale change, occlusion, etc. To show the effectiveness of the proposed idea more qualitatively, we evaluate our DCANet on OTB-2015, VOT-2017 and LaSOT [3] datasets, which demonstrate that our proposed DCANet tracker can gain competitive performance on these tracking benchmarks.

## 2   Related Work

### 2.1   Trackers Based on Siamese Network

Siamese trackers [2,5,6,8,15,16] convert the tracking problem into a similarity learning problem to overcome the low-frame-rate challenge in traditional tracking methods. Siamese network based trackers use Siamese network as feature extraction module. Most trackers use shallow AlexNet as backbone network until SiamDW [19] and SiamRPN++ [10] come out. SiamDW investigates the destruction of translation invariance caused by padding operation and introduces cropping-inside residual (CIR) units into the model. SiamRPN++ propose an offset sampling strategy to mitigate the effect of padding. VGGNets [14] shows that deeper network could significantly improve the representative ability of features. Inspired by CIR units, we adopt a modified VGG16 model with cropping operations as the backbone to get a better feature extraction result.

### 2.2   Attention Mechanisms

In order to enhance the discriminability of network, we take attention mechanisms into consideration. Attention mechanisms originated from neuroscience field and have been widely used in computer vision. DAVT [4] adopts discriminative spatial attention. CSR-DCF [12] introduces color histograms to restrict correlation filter learning, which finally constructs a target spatial reliability map. Squeeze-and-Excitation (SE) block [7] models the interdependencies between channels to adaptively recalibrate channel-wise feature responses. RASNet [16] exploits SEblock to emphasize useful channel information. SASiam [6] also adopts the SEblock as a channel attention module in the semantic branch. CBAM [17] takes both SEblock and spatial attention mechanism into consideration.

# 3   The Proposed Algorithm

We propose a real-time tracker with Co-channel and Cr-spatial attention mechanism based on SiamFC. Figure 2 shows the architecture of our proposed tracker. The fundamental idea behind this design is that better feature representation, better output.

## 3.1   Siamese Tracker with Modified Backbone

Object tracking can be addressed as a learning similarity problem. Trackers are required to calculate the value function $f(x, z)$, which makes a comparison between template image $z$ and instance image $x$.

Towards fully-convolutional Siamese architecture like SiamFC, the function $\varphi$ represents the feature extraction part. $*$ denotes a cross-correlation operation which generates the output score map $f$. Thus, the final score map can be calculated by:

$$f(z, x) = \varphi(z) * \varphi(x) \tag{1}$$

the maximum score refers to the position of the tracking target by frames.

In our proposed approach, we change the backbone from AlexNet to modified VGG16, which helps us get more discriminative features by a deeper but not too complex feature extraction network. Some recent studies apply more deeper backbone like ResNet, which means it will need expand the training set and take a much longer time to train the network. With a single RTX 2080Ti GPU, it will need about a month to train the network with ResNet backbone. However, the modified VGG16 which selects the layers without padding operations from VGG16 can gain a better tracking result while not extending the training time much. The training process of our tracker can be completed in less than a day with a single RTX 2080Ti GPU.

## 3.2   Co-channel Attention Module

It is mentioned that objects belong to the same type will have a high response on particular channels. Meanwhile, the responses of other channels are suppressed. To enhance the learning of convolutional features by explicitly modeling channel interdependencies, SEblock [7] was proposed. This representative module takes advantage of the channel information and has been widely used in single-branch networks. Siamese network is a two-branch network so that we propose a Co-attention module to multiply the channel weight not only on the template branch but also on the instance branch. The two branches deal with the same object, which obviously belongs to the same categories. Thus we can process the channel

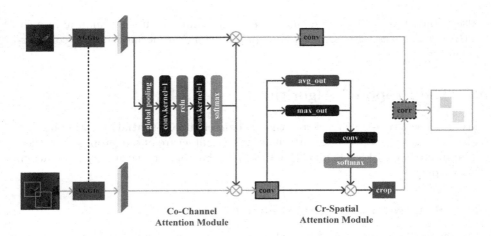

**Fig. 2.** The overall architecture of our DCANet tracker, which can be divided into four parts. First, a deeper backbone was applied to get better-extracted features. Second, we propose a Co-channel attention module to correlate the exemplar and search images and enhance channel information related to the target in parallel. Third, we adopt the spatial-attention module with a crop operation to take advantage of spatial information and mitigate the effect of padding. The last part is a cross-correlation operation, which plays a role in combination and finally calculates the output score map.

information on two branches in parallel. Synchronous weight operation makes the tracker pay attention to the discriminative information in the tracking process. The proposed approach can be described as follows.

Given the template feature $Z \in \mathbb{R}^{H \times W \times C}$, first, we squeeze $Z$ by embedding global information to obtain channel weight $V = [v_1, v_2, ..., v_c]$, where $v_c$ refers to the information learned from the $c-$th filter parameters. Then use a convolution operator to recalibrate the channel weight of input $X$ and input $Z$ in parallel. Final output of proposed Co-channel attention mechanism are two feature maps $U \in \mathbb{R}^{H \times W \times C} = [u_1, u_2, ..., u_c]$ and $N \in \mathbb{R}^{H \times W \times C} = [n_1, n_2, ..., n_c]$. The transformation can be presented as follows.

$$u_c = v_c * X = \sum_{s=1}^{C} v_c^s * x^s \tag{2}$$

$$n_c = v_c * Z = \sum_{s=1}^{C} v_c^s * z^s \tag{3}$$

## 3.3   Cr-Spatial Attention Module

In this part, we propose a module to take advantage of the spatial informa-
tion. With a given input $X \in \mathbb{R}^{H \times W \times C}$, Cr-spatial attention module needs
to generate a weight map $Q_s(X) \in \mathbb{R}^{H \times W}$ which records spatial information
and indicates whether the place should be emphasized or suppressed. However,
spatial attention module includes a padding operation which harms the translation invariance property of network. In our proposed model, we employ a crop
operation placed after spatial attention module to overcome this problem. The
proposed Cr-spatial attention can be computed as:

$$
\begin{aligned}
X' &= Cr(X * Q_s(X)) \\
&= Cr(X * \sigma(f^{3 \times 3}([X_{avg}^s; X_{max}^s])))
\end{aligned}
\tag{4}
$$

where $X_{avg}^s$ and $X_{max}^s$ respectively refer to average-pooled features and max-
pooled features. $f^{3 \times 3}$ represents a $3 \times 3$ filter size convolution operation with
padding equals to 1. $\sigma$ refers to a sigmoid function. $Cr$ means crop 1 element
around the tensor of input.

# 4   Experiments

## 4.1   Implementation Details

We apply a pretrained VGG16 as the backbone network. The training dataset
is GOT-10k [9] which is a large database for generic object tracking in the wild.
In order to obtain robust results, we adopt data enhancement method. In detail,
we generate images in advance by adding transformations to sequences. During
training, we randomly select two pictures from the same sequence for each time.
One as the template image resized to $127 \times 127$ pixels, another as the instance
image resized to $255 \times 255$ pixels.

After offline end-to-end training, we perform our tracker and evaluate online
tracking with the help of got-10k toolkit [9].

## 4.2   Evaluation Results of Visual Object Tracking

We evaluate the proposed DCANet on three different benchmarks including
OTB-2013, OTB-2015, LaSOT, VOT-2017 and GOT-10k. The evaluation results
are shown in Fig. 3 and Fig. 4. All of illustrations are obtained by OTB, VOT
and LaSOT toolkit.

**OTB2013 and OTB-2015 Dataset.** OTB-2013 dataset has 50 image
sequences and OTB-2015 dataset has 100 image sequences in the benchmark. We
make a comparison between the DCANet tracker and others, including SiamFC,
Muster, MEEM, STRUCK, SCM, CXT, ASLA, TLD and CSK. As illustrated
in Fig. 3, our method gains a better performance than SiamFC.

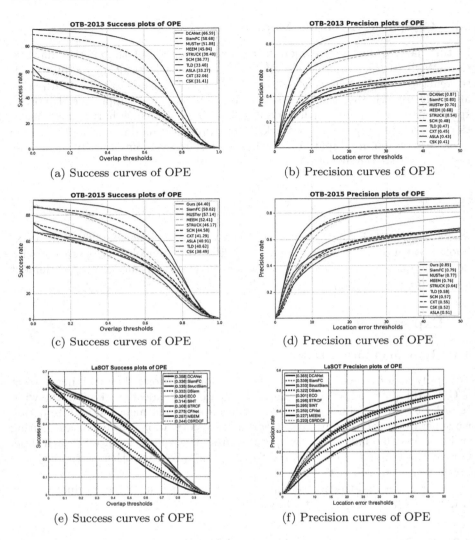

**Fig. 3.** Experiment results on the OTB2013, OTB-2015 and LaSOT dataset. (a) and (b) are the results of the evaluation on OTB-2013 with other trackers, (c) and (d) are the results of the evaluation on OTB-2015 with other trackers, (e) and (f) are the results of the evaluation on LaSOT with other trackers.

**LaSOT Dataset.** We compare the proposed tracker with several representative approaches, including SiamFC, StructSiam, DSiam, ECO, SINT, STRCF, CFNet, MEEM and CSRDCF. The results showed in Fig. 3 demonstrate that our DCANet outperforms other trackers.

**VOT-2017 Dataset.** VOT2017 dataset consists of 60 sequences and the performance on this dataset is measured by accuracy, robustness and a comprehensive measurement named EAO. We make a comparison between our tracker and others on VOT-2017. The EAO results are shown in Fig. 4, which demonstrates that the DCANet tracker gains a competitive performance and runs in real-time.

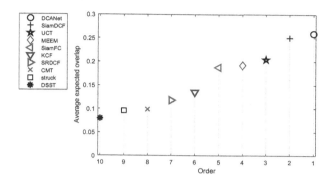

**Fig. 4.** EAO rank results on the VOT-2017 dataset. We only choose 10 trackers [13] to show for clarity. The measurement EAO involved in this dataset can show us the balance between tracking speed and precision. The higher the better.

**GOT-10k Dataset.** GOT-10k is a large, high-diversity, one-shot database for generic object tracking in the wild. Different from other datasets above, we use this dataset as our training data. The test set embodies 84 object classes and 32 motion classes with only 180 video segments, allowing for efficient evaluation. As shown in Table1, DCANet achieves the best performance among these trackers.

**Table 1.** Comparative results on GOT10k dataset.

| Tracker | AO | SR $_{0.5}$ | SR $_{0.75}$ |
|---|---|---|---|
| KCF | 0.203 | 0.177 | 0.065 |
| CSK | 0.205 | 0.174 | 0.056 |
| DSST | 0.247 | 0.223 | 0.081 |
| CFNet | 0.293 | 0.235 | 0.068 |
| MDNet | 0.299 | 0.303 | 0.099 |
| ECO | 0.316 | 0.309 | 0.111 |
| GOTURN | 0.347 | 0.375 | 0.124 |
| SiamFC | 0.348 | 0.353 | 0.098 |
| **DCANet** | **0.403** | **0.466** | **0.150** |

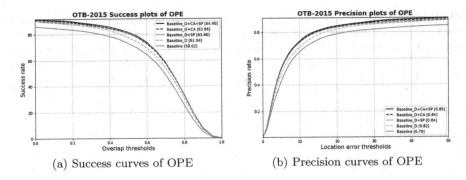

(a) Success curves of OPE          (b) Precision curves of OPE

**Fig. 5.** (a) and (b) are the results of ablation studies on OTB-2015. As shown above, our tracker DCANet gain the best performance with all components.

### 4.3   Ablation Studies

We ablate our method on several components to verify the effectiveness of each part. Take the SiamFC tracker as a baseline. First, we change the backbone of the network from Alexnet to a pretrained VGG16 (Baseline_D). Second, we employ the Co-channel attention module in both of the two branches(Baseline_D+CA). Third, we adopt a Cr-spatial attention module in the instance branch (Baseline_D+SP). In the end, we combine both of the two parts and get the final output (Baseline_D+CA+SP). As shown in Fig. 5, the results on OTB-2015 demonstrate the effectiveness of each component in DCANet. Obviously, our DCANet achieves the best performance and gains a great improvement than the baseline SiamFC tracker by more than 6%.

## 5   Conclusion

In this paper, we propose an effective DCANet tracker. First, we propose a Co-channel attention mechanism to emphasize the channels related to target in both of template branch and instance branch. Second, we employ a Cr-spatial attention mechanism to take full advantage of spatial information. Benefits from modifications above, our DCANet achieves competitive tracking performance and runs in real-time. The results of experiments on OTB2013, OTB-2015, VOT-2017, and LaSOT datasets show the superiority of our proposed DCANet tracker.

## References

1. Ali, A., et al.: Visual object tracking-classical and contemporary approaches. Front. Comp. Sci. **10**, 167–188 (2016)

2. Bertinetto, L., Valmadre, J., Henriques, J.F., Vedaldi, A., Torr, P.H.S.: Fully-convolutional Siamese networks for object tracking. In: Hua, G., Jégou, H. (eds.) ECCV 2016. LNCS, vol. 9914, pp. 850–865. Springer, Cham (2016). https://doi.org/10.1007/978-3-319-48881-3_56
3. Fan, H., et al.: LaSOT: a high-quality benchmark for large-scale single object tracking. In: Proceedings of the IEEE Conference on Computer Vision and Pattern Recognition (CVPR), June 2019
4. Fan, J., Wu, Y., Dai, S.: Discriminative spatial attention for robust tracking. In: Daniilidis, K., Maragos, P., Paragios, N. (eds.) ECCV 2010. LNCS, vol. 6311, pp. 480–493. Springer, Heidelberg (2010). https://doi.org/10.1007/978-3-642-15549-9_35
5. Guo, Q., Feng, W., Zhou, C., Huang, R., Wan, L., Wang, S.: Learning dynamic Siamese network for visual object tracking. In: Proceedings of the IEEE International Conference on Computer Vision (ICCV), October 2017
6. He, A., Luo, C., Tian, X., Zeng, W.: A twofold Siamese network for real-time object tracking. In: Proceedings of the IEEE Conference on Computer Vision and Pattern Recognition (CVPR), June 2018
7. Hu, J., Shen, L., Sun, G.: Squeeze-and-excitation networks. In: Proceedings of the IEEE Conference on Computer Vision and Pattern Recognition (CVPR), June 2018
8. Huang, C., Lucey, S., Ramanan, D.: Learning policies for adaptive tracking with deep feature cascades. In: Proceedings of the IEEE International Conference on Computer Vision (ICCV), October 2017
9. Huang, L., Zhao, X., Huang, K.: GOT-10k: a large high-diversity benchmark for generic object tracking in the wild. IEEE Trans. Pattern Anal. Mach. Intell. **43**, 1562–1577 (2019)
10. Li, B., Wu, W., Wang, Q., Zhang, F., Xing, J., Yan, J.: SiamRPN++: evolution of Siamese visual tracking with very deep networks. In: Proceedings of the IEEE Conference on Computer Vision and Pattern Recognition (CVPR), June 2019
11. Li, B., Yan, J., Wu, W., Zhu, Z., Hu, X.: High performance visual tracking with Siamese region proposal network. In: Proceedings of the IEEE Conference on Computer Vision and Pattern Recognition (CVPR), June 2018
12. Lukezic, A., Vojir, T., Cehovin Zajc, L., Matas, J., Kristan, M.: Discriminative correlation filter with channel and spatial reliability. In: Proceedings of the IEEE Conference on Computer Vision and Pattern Recognition (CVPR), July 2017
13. Mishra, D., Matas, J.: The visual object tracking VOT2017 challenge results. In: 2017 IEEE International Conference on Computer Vision Workshops (ICCVW), pp. 1949–1972, October 2017. https://doi.org/10.1109/ICCVW.2017.230
14. Simonyan, K., Zisserman, A.: Very deep convolutional networks for large-scale image recognition. arXiv preprint arXiv:1409.1556 (2014)
15. Valmadre, J., Bertinetto, L., Henriques, J., Vedaldi, A., Torr, P.H.S.: End-to-end representation learning for correlation filter based tracking. In: Proceedings of the IEEE Conference on Computer Vision and Pattern Recognition (CVPR), July 2017
16. Wang, Q., Teng, Z., Xing, J., Gao, J., Hu, W., Maybank, S.: Learning attentions: residual attentional Siamese network for high performance online visual tracking. In: Proceedings of the IEEE Conference on Computer Vision and Pattern Recognition (CVPR), June 2018
17. Woo, S., Park, J., Lee, J.-Y., Kweon, I.S.: CBAM: convolutional block attention module. In: Ferrari, V., Hebert, M., Sminchisescu, C., Weiss, Y. (eds.) ECCV 2018. LNCS, vol. 11211, pp. 3–19. Springer, Cham (2018). https://doi.org/10.1007/978-3-030-01234-2_1

18. Xiao, B., Wu, H., Wei, Y.: Simple baselines for human pose estimation and tracking. In: Ferrari, V., Hebert, M., Sminchisescu, C., Weiss, Y. (eds.) ECCV 2018. LNCS, vol. 11210, pp. 472–487. Springer, Cham (2018). https://doi.org/10.1007/978-3-030-01231-1_29

19. Zhang, Z., Peng, H.: Deeper and wider Siamese networks for real-time visual tracking. In: Proceedings of the IEEE Conference on Computer Vision and Pattern Recognition (CVPR), June 2019

# Hierarchical Multi-scale Architecture Search for Self-supervised Monocular Depth Estimation

Jian Ren, Jin Xie$^{(\boxtimes)}$, and Zhong Jin

PCA Lab, Key Lab of Intelligent Perception and Systems for High-Dimensional Information of Ministry of Education, Nanjing University of Science and Technology, Nanjing, China
{renjian,csjxie,zhongjin}@njust.edu.cn

**Abstract.** Self-supervised learning has shown great promising in monocular depth estimation task, using images as the only source of supervision. Most existing methods design the network architecture in a handcrafted manner, which is usually time-consuming and not specific to depth estimation task. To reduce the human efforts in network design, we propose a hierarchical multi-scale Neural Architecture Search framework for self-supervised monocular depth estimation, named Auto-Depth. Specially, our method consists of a two-level search space: cell level and network level. In the cell level, we explore the possible hierarchical connections within one single cell to enhance the ability of multi-scale information representation. In the network level, we search the depth and width of network to balance the accuracy and computational complexity. Furthermore, the two-level path binarization is adopted to reduce the computational cost in searching stage, which only activate one operation path among several candidate operations. Extensive experiments on the KITTI and Make3D datasets show that our searched network yields better performance than previous state-of-the-art monocular depth estimation methods.

**Keywords:** Neural Architecture Search · Monocular depth estimation · Deep learning

## 1 Introduction

Depth estimation is important for many applications such as autonomous driving [44], augmented reality [25], scene reconstruction [43] and robotics [16]. Many traditional methods [27,30] estimate the depth of image based on the assumption of multiple observations. To break the limitation of this assumption, several methods [7,19,23] predict the depth map from single image by supervised learning approach, which requires a large amount of ground truth depth. Despite

This work was supported by the National Science Fund of China (Grant Nos. 61872188, U1713208), Shanghai Automotive Industry Science and Technology Development Foundation (No. 1917).

these methods have obtained great success, collecting these data by depth sensors is expensive and time-consuming. As an alternative, self-supervised methods [9,12,46] have shown comparable results without using ground truth depth.

Recent studies have demonstrated that training monocular depth estimation model is feasible with stereo pairs [4,12,31] or monocular videos [3,13,26]. With these approaches, we can replace ground truth depths with image samples which are easily collected. However, most existing methods directly use networks designed for image classification as backbones (e.g., Monodepth2 [13] uses ResNet [14] as backbone). The network architecture might be sub-optimal because image classification focuses on what kind of an image is, and monocular depth estimation aims at finding the depth of each pixel in an image. Therefore, it is meaningful to design a specific network architecture for depth estimation.

The number of possible network architectures for depth estimation task is so larger that it is difficult to design effective network in a hand-craft manner. Recently, Neural Architecture Search (NAS) has demonstrated promising ability to discover excellent network architecture in a huge design space. Many methods achieve similar or even better results than the hand-crafted networks in various high-level tasks such as image classification [2,15,38], object detection [11,32,39], and semantic segmentation [5,21]. It can reduce the efforts of human in designing task-specific network architecture. Inspired by [2], we apply NAS to monocular depth estimation task to search network architecture with better performance.

In this paper, we present a novel NAS framework named Auto-Depth for monocular depth estimation task to search a more suitable and effective architecture. We design a hierarchical multi-scale search space for the entire network architecture, including cell level and network level. In the cell level search space, we explore more granular multi-scale cell architecture by constructing hierarchical connections within one single cell. The designed cell can extract information of multiple receptive field sizes. In the network level search space, we can choose operations of different expansion ratio for each layer to control the overall architecture of network. Furthermore, in order to alleviate the problem of memory consumption, we binarize the architecture parameters and activate only one operation in multiple candidate operations, while the others are released from memory. Extensive experiments demonstrate that our method obtains better performance compared to existing state-of-the-art methods.

In summary, our main contributions are as follows:

1. To the best of our knowledge, we make the first effort to search the whole network architecture for self-supervised monocular depth estimation.
2. We design a hierarchical multi-scale search space including cell level and network level, and propose a two-level path binarization to reduce the memory consumption during searching.
3. Experiments on the KITTI and Make3D datasets demonstrate that our method can achieve better performance compared with state-of-the-art monocular depth estimation methods.

## 2    Related Work

### 2.1    Monocular Depth Estimation

There are numerous literatures on monocular depth estimation from images. Saxena *et al.* [36] proposed Make3D that first crops the image into patches and then uses Markov Random Field (MRF) to estimate 3D location and orientation. Liu *et al.* [20] used segmentation information to construct the two-layer MRF model to obtain the depth result. With the development of deep learning, various of works applied it in monocular depth estimation task. Eigen *et al.* [7] proposed coarse-scale and fine-scale networks to predict the depth of image. Laina *et al.* [19] employed smaller convolution kernel and efficient upsampling module to improve the result of network.

However, these methods need a large amount of labeled data to train the model, which are difficult to collect in realistic scene. Recently, self-supervised methods remove the need for a large quantity of ground truth depth in the form of stereo pairs [9,12,31] or monocular video [3,13,46]. Garg *et al.* [9] predicted continuous disparity to reconstruct the original images as supervisory signal. Godard *et al.* [12] proposed to estimate the binocular disparities and added a left-right depth consistency loss to ensure the epipolar geometric constraints. On the other hand, Zhou *et al.* [46] trained the network based on monocular videos by reconstruction loss between the adjacent frames. Godard *et al.* [13] proposed minimum reprojection loss and auto-masking to improve the performance of depth estimation.

### 2.2    Neural Architecture Search

NAS aims to automatically discover a model from the predefined search space using different methods, such as random search, evolutionary algorithms, reinforcement learning (RL), gradient-based methods. Evolutionary algorithms [33, 34] were widely used in the early period which evolves network architecture by crossovers and mutations. RL methods [32,38,47] use controller to explore the search space and use the performance of current network as the reword to update the controller. Although promising, these methods are often computationally expensive since the searched model has to be trained from scratch. To reduce the burden, weight-sharing methods [1,29] are proposed in which searched models share operations weights from super network, and the optimization process is only performed once. These weight-sharing methods are faster and product comparable performance with the previous methods. A mainstream way of weight-sharing methods is based on gradient [2,21,22]. The core idea of them is continuous relaxation of architecture parameters, thus allowing the differentiable update strategies.

## 3    Method

We use gradient-based strategy in our Auto-Depth to search for the whole network architecture. We build a two-level multi-scale search space including cell

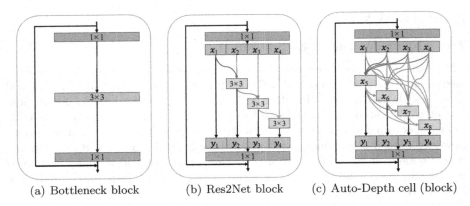

(a) Bottleneck block     (b) Res2Net block     (c) Auto-Depth cell (block)

**Fig. 1.** Comparison between Bottleneck block [14], Res2Net block [8] and our Auto-Depth cell (block) architecture.

level and network level. Furthermore, we adopt path binarization to reduce memory cost during searching. In this section, we introduce the novel cell level architecture search using continuous relaxation strategy. Then we propose network level search space to optimize the width and depth of final network. Finally, we present our design of search algorithm and loss function.

### 3.1  Cell Level Architecture Search

As shown in Fig. 1, Res2Net [8] replaces the $3 \times 3$ filter in ResNet block [14] with several smaller filters and connects them in a hierarchical manner. Instead of building the connections by hand, we use NAS to search the connections and operations between features, as shown in Fig. 1 (c). Specifically, we define the cell as a directed acyclic graph which contains a sequence of $N$ nodes. Each node $x_i$ is a feature map and each directed edge $(i, j)$ is candidate operations $O_{i,j}$ between node $x_i$ and node $x_j$. We first split the input feature into $s$ groups, denoted by $x_i$, where $i \in \{1, 2, ..., s\}$. Each feature map $x_i$ has the same resolution size (H $\times$ W) and channel size $(1/s)$ compared to the input feature. These feature maps are the input nodes of the cell. There are $s$ intermediate nodes connected to input nodes and previous intermediate nodes, denoted by $x_i$, where $i \in \{s + 1, s + 2, ..., 2 \times s\}$. The output of the cell is the concatenation of all intermediate nodes. Each intermediate node is calculated by the following equation:

$$x_j = \sum_{i<j} o_{i,j}(x_i) \tag{1}$$

and $o_{i,j}$ is:

$$o_{i,j}(x) = \sum_{r=1}^{K} p_{i,j}^r o_{i,j}^r(x) = \sum_{r=1}^{K} \frac{\exp(\alpha_{i,j}^r)}{\sum_{s=1}^{K} \exp(\alpha_{i,j}^s)} o_{i,j}^r(x) \tag{2}$$

where $o_{i,j}^r$ is the $r$-th operation between node $x_i$ and node $x_j$, $p_{i,j}^r$ is the weight of $o_{i,j}^r$ which is implemented through softmax, and $\alpha_{i,j}$ is weight vector of all possible operations of dimension $|K|$. After the completion of search phase, we can obtain a normal architecture by choosing the most likely operation of each edge, i.e., $o_{i,j} = o_{i,j}^{r^*}, r^* = \arg\max_r \alpha_{i,j}^r$. Following [22], we only retain the top-$m$ strongest operations for each intermediate node.

Like ResNet [14], we add two $1 \times 1$ convolution to change the channel size of the cell and add a residual connection between input and output features. We use $e$ to represent this ratio of change for the number of channels. Specially, the input channel size is $C_{in}$, and after the first $1 \times 1$ convolution, it becomes $C_{in}/e$. It keeps the same until the last $1 \times 1$ convolution and becomes $C_{out}$. Instead of sharing the architecture parameters $\alpha$ to obtain several types of cells and stacking them into the final network, we search the cell architecture for each layer independently, so that each layer can flexibly choose cell architecture according to its need.

**Candidate Operation.** In our designed cell architecture, the receptive field of the feature will become larger than previous via multiple convolution operations, as shown in Fig. 1 (c). Thus we do not need some operations (e.g., dilated convolutions, pooling operations) in DARTS [22] to enlarge the receptive field. Besides, the computational complexity increases linearly w.r.t. the number of choices, so we remove some unnecessary operations and remain two main operations {$3 \times 3$ convolution, skip connection}. $3 \times 3$ convolution is the basic operation while the skip connection can form residual structure and promote the fusion of information.

## 3.2 Network Level Architecture Search

The whole network is built by many candidate cells with different expansion rates, as shown in Fig. 2. The first stage (fixed cell in Fig. 2) of network is designed by hand while the others are searched by NAS. Each stage has several layers, in which contains candidate cells with different expansion ratios. For the entire network architecture, we define the resolutions and input/output channels of each layer. At the beginning of the network, we first downsample the input image to $1/2$ original resolution size in first stage with a $7 \times 7$ convolution. Then we design four-stage searchable architecture changing the resolution of feature map to $1/32$ compared with original input image. In the decoder part, we first upsample the feature map and concatenate it with the results of skip connection. Then the feature map passes through several cells and reaches the next stage. We obtain the disparity predictions in the last four stages of the network, which have different resolution sizes at different scales.

Generally, convolution network doubles the width of feature map if the spatial resolution is halved. However, it may be sub-optimal in dense regression task. Based on this, we propose to search the width of each layer and depth of each stage.

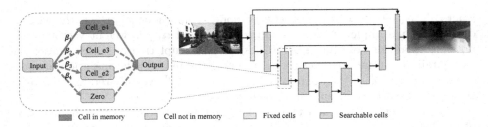

**Fig. 2.** Network level search space. We illustrate our candidate operations for each layer (left) and the whole network (right). The architecture of yellow layer is fixed, and the architectures of blue layers are searched by our algorithm. (Color figure online)

**Width Search.** Instead of directly controlling the width of each cell, we use the expansion ratio $e$ to adjust the number of filters in each cell, which expresses how much we expand the channel size after the first $1 \times 1$ convolution compared with the input channel size. For each layer in network, the set of candidate expansion ratio is $\{2, 3, 4\}$. We design three searchable blocks with different expansion ratio and assign a weight to each block. The output result is the weighted sum of all candidate cells with different expansion ratio. We use $\beta$ to represent this weight vector and optimize it by gradient like $\alpha$.

**Depth Search.** For the depth of the network, existing methods determine the number of layers in a handcraft manner. To make the network architecture more flexible, we search the number of layers of each stage independently by adding zero operation to candidate operations. The zero operation represents that the output of cell is equal to the input, which makes the feature map can skip current cell. Thus, the network can adjust the number of layers by choosing zero operation.

### 3.3 Auto-Depth Search Algorithm

**Loss Functions.** In process of optimization, our Auto-Depth uses the gradient descent strategy to optimize the model. The architecture parameters $\alpha$, $\beta$ and weight parameters $w$ are optimized alternately in searching process using the same loss. Following the Monodepth [12], we calculate loss for the last four stages in decoder, and the total loss are formed as the sum $\mathcal{L}_{total} = \sum_{s=1}^{4} \mathcal{L}_s$. $\mathcal{L}_s$ includes three main terms and is formulated as:

$$\mathcal{L}_s = \alpha_{re}(\mathcal{L}_{re}^l + \mathcal{L}_{re}^r) + \alpha_{ds}(\mathcal{L}_{ds}^l + \mathcal{L}_{ds}^r) + \alpha_{lr}(\mathcal{L}_{lr}^l + \mathcal{L}_{lr}^r) \tag{3}$$

Each term is calculated with the left image, the right image and the network predictions. We only introduce our loss about left image since the right image versions are the same designs. The first term $\alpha_{re}$ represents the photometric reconstruction error, which is used to measure the difference between the input image and the reconstructed image. It is the weighted sum of $L1$ and Structural

Similarity (SSIM) [42] loss between the input image $I_{i,j}^l$ and reconstructed image $\widetilde{I}_{i,j}^l$,

$$\mathcal{L}_{re}^l = \frac{1}{N} \sum_{i,j} \alpha \frac{1 - \text{SSIM}(I_{i,j}^l, \widetilde{I}_{i,j}^l)}{2} + (1 - \alpha)\|I_{i,j}^l - \widetilde{I}_{i,j}^l\| \tag{4}$$

The disparity smoothness term $\mathcal{L}_{ds}^l$ encourages the predictions to be smooth and continuous. We weight the L1 penalty with the image gradient $\partial I$,

$$\mathcal{L}_{ds}^l = \frac{1}{N} \sum_{i,j} |\partial_x d_{i,j}^l| e^{-\|\partial_x I_{i,j}^l\|} + |\partial_y d_{i,j}^l| e^{-\|\partial_y I_{i,j}^l\|} \tag{5}$$

The last term is the left-right disparity consistency error $\mathcal{L}_{lr}^l$. The predictions of network include both left and right disparities, which have epipolar geometric constraints. To ensure the consistency of disparity, the left disparity map $d_{i,j}^l$ needs to correspond to the projected right disparity map,

$$\mathcal{L}_{lr}^l = \frac{1}{N} \sum_{i,j} |d_{i,j}^l - d_{i,j+d_{i,j}^l}^r| \tag{6}$$

The other three terms are same as these, except the input is right image. At test phase, network predicts the disparity at the last scale which has the same resolution as the input image. Using the focal length $f$ and baseline $b$ of camera from the training set, we convert the disparity $D_{disparity}$ to final depth map with $D_{depth} = f * b / D_{disparity}$.

**Path Binarization.** Because of the continuous relaxation strategy, the output result of mixed operation is weighted sum of $K$ candidate operations results, which need $K$ times GPU memory compared to normal operation. To reduce the memory consumption, we use the path binarization strategy in [2] and transform the path weights $p_{i,j}^r$ in Eq. (2) to binary gates in searching phase,

$$g_{i,j}^r = \begin{cases} [1, 0, ..., 0], \text{ with probability } p_{i,j}^1 \\ ... \\ [0, 0, ..., 1], \text{ with probability } p_{i,j}^K \end{cases} \tag{7}$$

Based on this, the output of the mixed operation is updated to:

$$o_{i,j}^{binary}(x) = \sum_{r=1}^{K} g_{i,j}^r o_{i,j}^r(x) = \begin{cases} o_{i,j}^1(x), \text{ with probability } p_1 \\ ... \\ o_{i,j}^K(x), \text{ with probability } p_K \end{cases} \tag{8}$$

With this method, we only active one path in memory at training phase, while the other paths are released from memory. The memory consumption of our method is reduced to the same level of training a normal network. Since our search space is two-level, we activate only one cell from the candidate cells and activate one operation from the candidate operations between different nodes in this cell.

**Optimization and Decoding.** Following [22], we split the training set into two disjoint parts $D_{train}$ and $D_{val}$. With continuous relaxation and path binarization, the weight parameters $w$ and architecture parameters $\alpha, \beta$ are optimized alternately on $D_{train}$ and $D_{val}$: update weight parameters $w$ by $\nabla_w \mathcal{L}_{train}(w, \alpha, \beta)$; update architecture parameters $\alpha, \beta$ by $\nabla_{\alpha, \beta} \mathcal{L}_{val}(w, \alpha, \beta)$.

When the optimization is finished, we decode the final network architecture by remaining the two strongest operations for each intermediate node in cells. In the network level, we simply choose the strongest cell to replace the mixed cells. Then we retrain the final network to obtain the final monocular depth estimation performance.

## 4 Experiments

In this section, we first present our results on the KITTI [10] and Make3D [37] datasets compared with existing methods. Then we illustrate our network architecture searched by Auto-Depth. Last, the ablation study of Auto-Depth on KITTI dataset [10] is presented to evaluate the effectiveness of our method.

### 4.1 Implementation Details

Our framework is implemented with PyTorch [28]. In all experiments, we resize the input images to $256 \times 512$ and use the data augmentation described in [12]. During optimization, we set the weights $\alpha_{re} = 1$ and $\alpha_{lr} = 1$ in Eq. (3). The weight of $\alpha_{ds} = 0.1/r$, where $r$ is the downscaling factor of current feature map (*e.g.*, 1, 2, 4, 8), where $\alpha = 0.85$ in Eq. (4).

During the architecture search time, we use Adam [18] to optimize the weight parameters and architecture parameters of network, respectively. We random sample 5000 images from the training data to optimize the architecture parameters. We warm up our model for 20 epochs before search and train the network for 50 epochs with a batch size of 16. We use an initial learning rate of $10^{-4}$ to optimize weight parameters which is reduced by half every 10 epochs after 30 epochs. For optimizing architecture parameters, the learning rate is $10^{-3}$. Search stage takes about 6 GPU days on TITAN RTX GPU.

After obtaining the final network architecture, we retrain the network with a batch size of 8 and initial learning rate of $10^{-3}$ to present better performance. Other parameters are same as search stage. We use the post-processing proposed in [12] to improve the quantitative performance of model. This stage costs about 21 GPU hours on TITAN RTX GPU.

### 4.2 Results

**KITTI Quantitative Result.** We train and evaluate our method on the KITTI dataset [10], using the Eigen data split [7]. We use 697 images as test data covering 29 scenes, while 22,600 image pairs are used for training and remaining images are used for validation. We use the crop operation from [9] to reduce the

**Table 1.** Results on KITTI [10] using the Eigen split. Best results in each category are in **bold**. M: motion. S: stereo. †: the new results. Original: raw depth maps in [7]. Improved: annotated depth maps in [40]. Red metrics : lower is better. Green metrics : higher is better. R50: ResNet50 [14].

| | Method | Train | Abs Rel | Sq Rel | RMSE | RMSE log | $\delta < 1.25$ | $\delta < 1.25^2$ | $\delta < 1.25^3$ |
|---|---|---|---|---|---|---|---|---|---|
| Original [6] | SfMLeaner [46] | M | 0.183 | 1.595 | 6.709 | 0.270 | 0.734 | 0.902 | 0.959 |
| | Struct2depth [3] | M | 0.141 | 1.026 | 5.291 | 0.215 | 0.816 | 0.945 | **0.979** |
| | Sadek et al. [35] | M | 0.162 | 1.126 | 5.284 | 0.221 | 0.823 | 0.935 | 0.971 |
| | Monodepth2 [13] | M | 0.132 | 1.044 | 5.142 | 0.210 | 0.845 | 0.948 | 0.977 |
| | HR-Depth [26] | M | 0.128 | 0.967 | 5.028 | **0.205** | 0.852 | **0.950** | 0.978 |
| | Garg et al. [9] † | S | 0.152 | 1.226 | 5.849 | 0.246 | 0.784 | 0.921 | 0.967 |
| | Monodepth [12] † | S | 0.129 | 1.020 | 5.351 | 0.225 | 0.830 | 0.937 | 0.972 |
| | 3Net (R50) [31] | S | 0.126 | 0.961 | 5.205 | 0.220 | 0.835 | 0.941 | 0.974 |
| | Monodepth2 [13] | S | 0.130 | 1.144 | 5.485 | 0.232 | 0.831 | 0.932 | 0.968 |
| | SceneNet [4] | S | 0.118 | 0.905 | 5.096 | 0.211 | 0.839 | 0.945 | 0.977 |
| | Auto-Depth (**ours**) | S | **0.116** | **0.880** | **4.927** | 0.207 | **0.857** | 0.949 | 0.977 |
| Improved [40] | SfMLeaner [46] | M | 0.176 | 1.532 | 6.129 | 0.244 | 0.758 | 0.921 | 0.971 |
| | GeoNet [45] | M | 0.132 | 0.994 | 5.240 | 0.193 | 0.833 | 0.953 | 0.985 |
| | DDVO [41] | M | 0.126 | 0.866 | 4.932 | 0.185 | 0.851 | 0.958 | 0.986 |
| | EPC++ [24] | M | 0.120 | 0.789 | 4.755 | 0.177 | 0.856 | 0.961 | 0.987 |
| | Monodepth2 [13] | M | 0.112 | 0.715 | 4.502 | 0.167 | 0.876 | 0.967 | 0.990 |
| | HR-Depth [26] | M | **0.099** | 0.608 | 4.134 | 0.150 | 0.896 | 0.975 | 0.992 |
| | Monodepth [12] | S | 0.109 | 0.811 | 4.568 | 0.166 | 0.877 | 0.967 | 0.988 |
| | 3Net (R50) [31] | S | 0.102 | 0.675 | 4.293 | 0.159 | 0.881 | 0.969 | 0.991 |
| | Monodepth2 [13] | S | 0.110 | 0.849 | 4.580 | 0.173 | 0.875 | 0.962 | 0.986 |
| | Auto-Depth (**ours**) | S | 0.107 | **0.503** | **3.672** | **0.146** | **0.899** | **0.980** | **0.995** |

errors caused by object occlusion and motion. The maximum evaluation distance in all methods is 80m. Since our purpose is to search for a network architecture for depth estimation task, we evaluate our method without pretraining on other datasets.

Table 1 shows the comparison performance of our method with other methods using either original depth maps from [7] or annotated depth maps from [40]. It can be seen that we achieve better performance compared with existing monocular video based methods and stereo based methods. Notably, SceneNet [4] use additional segmentation information to train the depth network, while our model is only trained with image pairs. Since our method can build multi-scale cell architecture and adjust the expansion ratio for each layer, our model achieves higher accuracy, especially in the $\delta < 1.25$.

**KITTI Qualitative Result.** In Fig. 3, we illustrate the performance of Auto-Depth and other methods. It is apparent that our Auto-Depth has better representation ability and more sharp depth contour even for tiny or thin objects (*e.g.*, traffic sign poles, trees). Our method maintains the continuous depth of objects by extracting multi-scale information, such as the vehicle and traffic sign.

| Input | Monodepth | Monodepth2 | **Auto-Depth** |

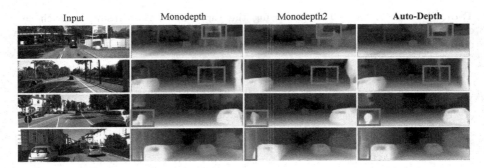

**Fig. 3.** Comparison results of monocular depth estimation on KITTI Eigen split. Our method has a better representation of details.

**Table 2.** Make3D results. D: depth supervision. M: motion supervision. S: stereo supervision.

| Method | Train | Abs Rel | Sq Rel | RMSE | $\log_{10}$ |
|---|---|---|---|---|---|
| Karsch *et al.* [17] | D | 4.894 | 0.417 | 8.172 | 0.144 |
| Liu *et al.* [23] | D | 0.475 | 6.562 | 10.05 | 0.165 |
| Laina *et al.* [19] | D | **0.204** | **1.840** | **5.683** | **0.084** |
| SfMLearner [46] | M | 0.383 | 5.321 | 10.470 | 0.478 |
| DDVO [41] | M | 0.387 | 4.720 | 8.090 | 0.204 |
| Monodepth [12] | S | 0.544 | 10.94 | 11.760 | 0.193 |
| Auto-Depth (**ours**) | S | 0.464 | 4.833 | 9.706 | 0.279 |
| Auto-Depth (**ours**, median) | S | **0.345** | **4.194** | **7.875** | **0.171** |

Benefiting from the ability of extracting multi-scale information, the searched model has better performance for details.

**Make3D Quantitative Result.** To evaluate the generalization of our searched model, we present our performance on Make3D dataset [37] using our model trained on KITTI dataset, as shown in Table 2. We use the same data processing as in [13] to solve the misalignment of ground truth and input image. Since monocular video methods are ambiguous in scale, they need to scale the median of prediction value to the median of ground truth. Our model can achieve better results than them if we also use the median scaling. Despite our network is searched in KITTI [10], it also yields better performance than other methods on the Make3D dataset, which demonstrates the strong generalization of our searched model.

### 4.3   Visualization of Search Results

As shown in Fig. 4, we visualize the three cells searched by our method. Since there are many different cells in our network, we just only show three kinds of

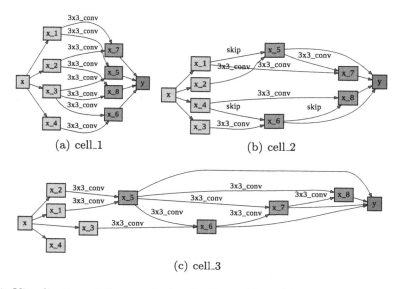

**Fig. 4.** Visualization of the searched cells. From (a) to (c), the intermediate nodes connect more previous intermediate nodes instead of input nodes, so that the cell can obtain larger receptive field.

them. We find that cell_1 is often shown in front and back of the network, and cell_3 is often in middle of the network, while cell_2 is between them. At the shallow level of network, the cells focus on details and their receptive fields are small. With the network going deeper, nodes in the current cell use more intermediate nodes as input, thereby the receptive fields of them become larger and the ability of extracting contextual information become better. In the subsequent manual network design process, we can refer this principle to design a well-performing network architecture. Besides, it also demonstrates the necessity to search cell architecture for each layer independently.

### 4.4 Ablation Study

**Comparison with Baseline.** In order to demonstrate the effectiveness of our algorithm, we perform an ablation study in Table 3. Monodepth [12] is the baseline of our method, and the cell architecture of our Auto-Depth is inspired by Res2Net [8]. Our Auto-Depth outperforms them with an improved margin of 10.08% and 5.7% for Abs Rel, while the computational cost is 37.3 GFLOPs, which is similar to Res2Net and less than Monodepth. This shows that NAS algorithm can discover the model with better performance for monocular depth estimation task.

**Effectiveness of Search Space and Algorithm.** To evaluate the effectiveness of our search algorithm, we compare our results with random search using the same search space. In random search, we randomly sample 8 networks from our designed search space for training to ensure the search time is similar to our Auto-Depth and present the best result among them. We observe that there are many zero operations in this network, so it has the lowest GFLOPs. This result is significantly better than the baseline models, and the computational complexity is lower, which proves our search space is well designed. Compared with the result of random search, our model yields better performance although it produces more GFLOPs, *e.g.*, 4.1% for Abs Rel. Our algorithm can search better model in the same search space than random search, which demonstrates the effectiveness of our search algorithm.

**Benefits of Independent Search.** We also explore the impact of searching each layer independently by replacing all cells in searched model with one type of cell. The three cell architectures are mentioned in Fig. 3. Compared with them, our model has similar computational cost and better performance. Although these cell architectures are searched by our method, the combination of different cell architectures is also important to the final performance, so it is necessary to search each cell architecture for network independently.

**Table 3.** Comparison results with other methods, random search and replacing all cells in network with one cell.

| Method | GFLOPs | Abs Rel | Sq Rel | RMSE | RMSE log | $\delta < 1.25$ | $\delta < 1.25^2$ | $\delta < 1.25^3$ |
|---|---|---|---|---|---|---|---|---|
| Monodepth [12] | 45.2 | 0.129 | 1.020 | 5.351 | 0.225 | 0.830 | 0.937 | 0.972 |
| Res2Net50 [8] | 35.6 | 0.123 | 0.928 | 5.189 | 0.217 | 0.836 | 0.943 | 0.975 |
| Random Search | 20.8 | 0.121 | 0.928 | 5.122 | 0.214 | 0.844 | 0.944 | 0.976 |
| Auto-Depth, Cell_1 | 39.0 | 0.122 | 0.956 | 5.216 | 0.218 | 0.840 | 0.943 | 0.975 |
| Auto-Depth, Cell_2 | 30.6 | 0.128 | 1.013 | 5.224 | 0.222 | 0.835 | 0.940 | 0.974 |
| Auto-Depth, Cell_3 | 38.9 | 0.130 | 1.320 | 5.353 | 0.224 | 0.839 | 0.941 | 0.973 |
| Auto-Depth (**ours**) | 37.3 | **0.116** | **0.880** | **4.927** | **0.207** | **0.857** | **0.949** | **0.977** |

## 5    Conclusion

In this paper, we proposed a novel NAS method which makes the first effort to search the whole network architecture for monocular depth estimation task. We explored more granular multi-scale cell architecture to enhance the ability of extracting information from different receptive fields and control the depth and width of the network. Besides, we used two-level path binarization for the hierarchical search space to reduce the memory-consuming. On KITTI and Make3D datasets, our method can yield better results than existing state-of-the-art monocular depth estimation methods.

# References

1. Brock, A., Lim, T., Ritchie, J.M., Weston, N.: SMASH: one-shot model architecture search through hypernetworks. arXiv preprint arXiv:1708.05344 (2017)
2. Cai, H., Zhu, L., Han, S.: ProxylessNAS: direct neural architecture search on target task and hardware. In: ICLR (2019)
3. Casser, V., Pirk, S., Mahjourian, R., Angelova, A.: Depth prediction without the sensors: leveraging structure for unsupervised learning from monocular videos. In: AAAI (2019)
4. Chen, P.Y., Liu, A.H., Liu, Y.C., Wang, Y.C.F.: Towards scene understanding: unsupervised monocular depth estimation with semantic-aware representation. In: CVPR (2019)
5. Chen, W., Gong, X., Liu, X., Zhang, Q., Li, Y., Wang, Z.: FasterSeg: searching for faster real-time semantic segmentation. arXiv preprint arXiv:1912.10917 (2019)
6. Eigen, D., Fergus, R.: Predicting depth, surface normals and semantic labels with a common multi-scale convolutional architecture. In: ICCV (2015)
7. Eigen, D., Puhrsch, C., Fergus, R.: Depth map prediction from a single image using a multi-scale deep network. In: Advances in Neural Information Processing Systems (2014)
8. Gao, S., Cheng, M.M., Zhao, K., Zhang, X.Y., Yang, M.H., Torr, P.H.: Res2Net: a new multi-scale backbone architecture. IEEE Trans. Pattern Anal. Mach. Intell. **43**, 652–662 (2019)
9. Garg, R., Bg, V.K., Carneiro, G., Reid, I.: Unsupervised CNN for single view depth estimation: geometry to the rescue. In: Leibe, B., Matas, J., Sebe, N., Welling, M. (eds.) ECCV 2016. LNCS, vol. 9912, pp. 740–756. Springer, Cham (2016). https://doi.org/10.1007/978-3-319-46484-8_45
10. Geiger, A., Lenz, P., Urtasun, R.: Are we ready for autonomous driving? The KITTI vision benchmark suite. In: CVPR (2012)
11. Ghiasi, G., Lin, T.Y., Le, Q.V.: NAS-FPN: learning scalable feature pyramid architecture for object detection. In: CVPR (2019)
12. Godard, C., Mac Aodha, O., Brostow, G.J.: Unsupervised monocular depth estimation with left-right consistency. In: CVPR (2017)
13. Godard, C., Mac Aodha, O., Firman, M., Brostow, G.J.: Digging into self-supervised monocular depth estimation. In: ICCV (2019)
14. He, K., Zhang, X., Ren, S., Sun, J.: Deep residual learning for image recognition. In: CVPR (2016)
15. Huang, S.Y., Chu, W.T.: Searching by generating: flexible and efficient one-shot NAS with architecture generator. In: CVPR (2021)
16. Kalia, M., Navab, N., Salcudean, T.: A real-time interactive augmented reality depth estimation technique for surgical robotics. In: ICRA (2019)
17. Karsch, K., Liu, C., Kang, S.B.: Depth transfer: depth extraction from video using non-parametric sampling. IEEE Trans. Pattern Anal. Mach. Intell. **36**, 2144–2158 (2014)
18. Kingma, D.P., Ba, J.: Adam: a method for stochastic optimization. arXiv preprint arXiv:1412.6980 (2014)
19. Laina, I., Rupprecht, C., Belagiannis, V., Tombari, F., Navab, N.: Deeper depth prediction with fully convolutional residual networks. In: 3DV (2016)
20. Liu, B., Gould, S., Koller, D.: Single image depth estimation from predicted semantic labels. In: CVPR (2010)

21. Liu, C., et al.: Auto-DeepLab: hierarchical neural architecture search for semantic image segmentation. In: CVPR (2019)
22. Liu, H., Simonyan, K., Yang, Y.: DARTS: differentiable architecture search. In: ICLR (2019)
23. Liu, M., Salzmann, M., He, X.: Discrete-continuous depth estimation from a single image. In: CVPR (2014)
24. Luo, C., et al.: Every pixel counts++: joint learning of geometry and motion with 3D holistic understanding. IEEE Trans. Pattern Anal. Mach. Intell. **42**, 2624–2641 (2019)
25. Luo, X., Huang, J.B., Szeliski, R., Matzen, K., Kopf, J.: Consistent video depth estimation. In: ACM SIGGRAPH (2020)
26. Lyu, X., et al.: HR-depth: high resolution self-supervised monocular depth estimation. In: AAAI (2021)
27. Mur-Artal, R., Montiel, J.M.M., Tardós, J.D.: ORB-SLAM: a versatile and accurate monocular SLAM system. IEEE Trans. Robot. **31**, 1147–1163 (2015)
28. Paszke, A., et al.: Automatic differentiation in PyTorch (2017)
29. Pham, H., Guan, M., Zoph, B., Le, Q., Dean, J.: Efficient neural architecture search via parameters sharing. In: International Conference on Machine Learning (2018)
30. Pire, T., Fischer, T., Castro, G., De Cristóforis, P., Civera, J., Berlles, J.J.: S-PTAM: stereo parallel tracking and mapping. Robot. Auton. Syst. **93**, 27–42 (2017)
31. Poggi, M., Tosi, F., Mattoccia, S.: Learning monocular depth estimation with unsupervised trinocular assumptions. In: 3DV (2018)
32. Rashwan, A., Du, X., Yin, X., Li, J.: Dilated SpineNet for semantic segmentation. In: CVPR (2021)
33. Real, E., Aggarwal, A., Huang, Y., Le, Q.V.: Regularized evolution for image classifier architecture search. In: AAAI (2019)
34. Real, E., et al.: Large-scale evolution of image classifiers. In: ICML (2017)
35. Sadek, A., Chidlovskii, B.: Self-supervised attention learning for depth and ego-motion estimation. arXiv preprint arXiv:2004.13077 (2020)
36. Saxena, A., Chung, S.H., Ng, A.Y.: 3-D depth reconstruction from a single still image. Int. J. Comput. Vis. **76**, 53–69 (2008). https://doi.org/10.1007/s11263-007-0071-y
37. Saxena, A., Sun, M., Ng, A.Y.: Make3D: learning 3D scene structure from a single still image. IEEE Trans. Pattern Anal. Mach. Intell. **31**, 824–840 (2008)
38. Tan, M., Le, Q.: EfficientNet: rethinking model scaling for convolutional neural networks. In: ICML (2019)
39. Tan, M., Pang, R., Le, Q.V.: EfficientDet: scalable and efficient object detection. In: CVPR (2020)
40. Uhrig, J., Schneider, N., Schneider, L., Franke, U., Brox, T., Geiger, A.: Sparsity invariant CNNs. In: 3DV (2017)
41. Wang, C., Buenaposada, J.M., Zhu, R., Lucey, S.: Learning depth from monocular videos using direct methods. In: CVPR (2018)
42. Wang, Z., Bovik, A.C., Sheikh, H.R., Simoncelli, E.P.: Image quality assessment: from error visibility to structural similarity. IEEE Trans. Image Process. **13**, 600–612 (2004)
43. Wimbauer, F., Yang, N., von Stumberg, L., Zeller, N., Cremers, D.: MonoRec: semi-supervised dense reconstruction in dynamic environments from a single moving camera. In: CVPR (2021)
44. Xue, F., Zhuo, G., Huang, Z., Fu, W., Wu, Z., Ang, M.H.: Toward hierarchical self-supervised monocular absolute depth estimation for autonomous driving applications. In: IROS (2020)

45. Yin, Z., Shi, J.: GeoNet: unsupervised learning of dense depth, optical flow and camera pose. In: CVPR (2018)
46. Zhou, T., Brown, M., Snavely, N., Lowe, D.G.: Unsupervised learning of depth and ego-motion from video. In: CVPR (2017)
47. Zoph, B., Le, Q.V.: Neural architecture search with reinforcement learning. In: ICLR (2017)

# Visualizing the Embedding Space to Explain the Effect of Knowledge Distillation

Hyun Seung Lee[1] and Christian Wallraven[1,2(✉)]

[1] Department of Artificial Intelligence, Korea University, Seoul, Korea
hslrock@korea.ac.kr, wallraven@korea.ac.kr
[2] Department of Brain and Cognitive Engineering, Korea University, Seoul, Korea

**Abstract.** Recent research has found that knowledge distillation can be effective in reducing the size of a network and in increasing generalization. A pre-trained, large teacher network, for example, was shown to be able to bootstrap a student model that eventually outperforms the teacher in a limited label environment. Despite these advances, it still is relatively unclear *why* this method works, that is, what the resulting student model does 'better'. To address this issue, here, we utilize two non-linear, low-dimensional embedding methods (t-SNE and IVIS) to visualize representation spaces of different layers in a network. We perform a set of extensive experiments with different architecture parameters and distillation methods. The resulting visualizations and metrics clearly show that distillation guides the network to find a more compact representation space for higher accuracy already in earlier layers compared to its non-distilled version.

**Keywords:** Knowledge distillation · Transfer learning · Computer vision · Limited data learning · Visualization

## 1 Introduction

The field of image recognition has rapidly developed with convolutional neural networks that allow for efficient computation of filters learned from large amounts of data. Researchers were able to stack multiple convolutional layers and form a "deep" network [13,28] to increase performance. Empirically, it was found that *deeper* networks have higher accuracy in many benchmark datasets. At the same time, however, *deeper* networks require more computational resources. To address this issue, researchers have developed different methods to compress the network without significant loss of performance, including pruning and quantization [12].

Here, we focus on knowledge distillation [14], another method designed to *compress* the network by *transferring* the knowledge through soft targets from a trained network. Based on this approach, additional distillation schemes have been developed (such as attention-based, quantized, and multi-teacher) that

© Springer Nature Switzerland AG 2022
C. Wallraven et al. (Eds.): ACPR 2021, LNCS 13189, pp. 462–475, 2022.
https://doi.org/10.1007/978-3-031-02444-3_35

further improve efficiency [11,16,19,23]. Recently, SimCLR2 [9] was proposed - an architecture, which is effective in limited data training through interactions between a well-trained, large teacher network and another, smaller student network. Surprisingly, the distillation method showed that the student model could even *outperform* the teacher in certain cases. Therefore, knowledge distillation has become one of the commonly-used techniques in transfer learning and other, similar application areas. Attempts to *explain* the mechanism behind the knowledge distillation, however, are non-trivial since distillation relies on one black-box model's output to train another, new black-box model. To our knowledge, it is still largely unclear *how* distilled and undistilled networks differ in their representation of the classification problem.

This paper aims to investigate the effect of distillation in terms of accuracy, correlations, and - most importantly - representation space. To obtain the latter, we compare two different non-linear, low-dimensional embedding methods (t-SNE [20], and the neural-network-based Ivis [30]). We use different metrics from these embeddings to measure the effect of distillation and also visualize the representation spaces for qualitative exploration of the networks' generalization ability.

This paper has three main key contributions: First, we examine the effect of the knowledge distillation methods in different few-shot learning scenarios. Second, we show that distillation better captures the mutual information among class labels. Third, we use the embedding methods to visualize the representation spaces to explore the effect of distillation.

## 2   Related Work

### 2.1   Dimensionality Reduction

In a deep network, the latent space is of *"high dimensionality"*. However, this high-dimensionality is often a problem in explaining the network since its decision pattern is not easy to visualize. Therefore, researchers have developed different methods to reduce the number of dimensions while trying to preserve as much of the original information as possible.

Principal component analysis (PCA) is one such reduction method based on the correlation within dimensions. However, it is a linear mapping making it not suitable for data containing non-linearities. t-SNE [20] was developed to specifically produce a non-linear, low-dimensional visualization using stochastic neighbor embedding. Specifically, this method computes the probability distribution of multiple embeddings assigning higher probability to more similar embeddings and vice versa. After this, it uses the calculated probability distributions to determine the most similar distribution in the target dimensionality. One common issue with t-SNE is that it has numerous different parameters that influence the result and has high computational cost in for a large number of input dimensions [34]. Also, t-SNE by design often creates clustered data points even with unclustered random data input (see below). Despite this, t-SNE has been a popular methods to visualize the representation space of neural networks (see [4] for an early recommendation of using t-SNE and [27] for an early review). In practice, however, research has mostly employed t-SNE either on the raw, small-scale input or on comparatively low-dimensional parts of the network, such as vectorized words [1,37] given its computational cost for higher-dimensional inputs (but see [35]).

Recently, Benjamin et al. [30] developed an alternative reduction model called Ivis. This is a neural network-based approach that learns a parametric mapping from a higher, input dimensionality to a lower, target dimensionality by minimizing the *triplet loss* of a Siamese network. The networks use anchor, positive, and negative comparison pairs from the input data sampled using a nearest neighbor algorithm. Through the shared Siamese parallel network, the framework reduces the input to the target dimensionality. Later, the network computes the triplet loss between samples and fits its parameters towards the best embedding generator - see Sect. 3. Overall, Ivis showed *higher* effectiveness in capturing the global data structures compared to other methods [30].

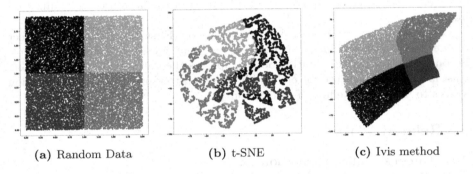

(a) Random Data          (b) t-SNE          (c) Ivis method

**Fig. 1.** 2D uniform noise (a) projected to 15 dimensions and re-embedded with b) t-SNE and c) Ivis.

Figure 1 illustrates a dimensionality reduction result for uniform random noise (color-labelled into four 2D quadrants), comparing t-SNE and Ivis for illustration. We projected this 2D random noise input into a higher dimension ($\Re^2 \longrightarrow \Re^{15}$) by performing both linear and non-linear mappings ($x + y, x - y, x^2, y^2, sin(x + y), e^x, x^3, y^3$ ...) and then applied the two methods. As the figure shows, Ivis is better able to preserve the global information compared to the cluster-biased t-SNE method.

One of the advantages of using the structure-preserving Ivis method while explaining the network's behavior is that humans can directly observe and understand the network's representation spaces. Figure 2 compares two-dimensional embeddings from the Ivis method and the t-SNE method from an embedding of the popular CIFAR-100 dataset [17] (see below for more details). As it is not possible to determine ground truth, we rely on a preliminary, qualitative analyses first. In line with Fig. 1a, we observe that Ivis produces a smoother distribution of the test dataset of CIFAR-100, compared to t-SNE, which often creates outlier points. At the same time, Ivis has a significantly lower computational budget: 600 s to fit 10000 samples with 16384 dimensions, compared to t-SNE's computation time with 3700 s at a perplexity of 150 (but see [8] for GPU-enabled computation of t-SNE, which may decrease its execution time).

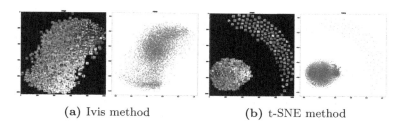

(a) Ivis method             (b) t-SNE method

**Fig. 2.** Two-dimensional embedding of the CIFAR-100 dataset, comparing Ivis and t-SNE.

The goal of this paper is to compare these two methods to visualize the high-dimensional representation spaces of distilled and undistilled networks.

## 2.2 Transfer Learning

*Transfer learning* refers to the use of a model (pre-)trained for a certain task in another, second task [38]. Most current applications use such pre-trained network for weight initialization and subsequent fine-tuning. Canziani et al. [7] showed that this approach can achieve higher accuracy compared to random weight initialization. Fine-tuning the network was shown to be especially effective when the network needs to work in a domain with a small sample size. Additional approaches to address such limited sample situations make use of data augmentation, label mixing, and consistency regularization [2,6,24,29,31].

Compared to standard transfer learning, which directly uses the pre-trained weights, *knowledge distillation* is another method that is analogous to an interaction between a teacher and their student. Hinton et al. [14] pioneered this method by using the (soft) outputs from a large teacher network for training a smaller student network (this method bears similarity to label smoothing [21]). In their experiments, the student's performance showed similar performance compared to the teacher - importantly, follow-up studies showed that distillation actually resulted in *better performing* student networks in a limited label setting in [9,18,32].

Recently, the so-called FixMatch [29] approach was proposed that uses self-interaction inside the training model to improve consistency and confidence without out a separate teacher model. It does this by using weak and strong augmentations, where weak augmentation flips and shifts input images, whereas strong augmentations consists of randomly-selected unrestricted transformations. For all augmentations, the goal of the final model was to match its outputs on both augmented images. This method has achieved state-of-the-art performance on CIFAR-10,100 and SVHN in limited label settings. One issue with this approach, however, is that the optimal augmentation strategy that does not affect the essential features of input images needs to be hand-crafted for each dataset - knowledge distillation in contrast is a more automated process.

### 2.3 Explaining Knowledge Distillation

Although knowledge distillation created a new field in transfer learning, it remained a black box. According to a recent study by Wang et al. [33], knowledge distillation maximizes the mutual information between the teacher and the student as shown through Bayes' rule: by fitting to the general teacher's information, an effective student can be trained. Phuong et al. [22] showed that distillation is equivalent to learning with a favored data distribution, unbiased information, and strong monotonicity. Finally, Cheng et al. [10] presented a mathematical model trying to quantify the discarded information throughout the layers in the models with and without distillation - they showed that the student seems to discard task-irrelevant information, learns faster, and optimizes with fewer detours.

To our knowledge, however, further *visualizations* of the representation space of the different layers of distilled and undistilled networks in the contexts of limited-label setting and transfer learning have not been explored so far, which is the focus of the present work. Note, that we use the term "limited-label setting" for investigating approaches on how to use knowledge from a large amount of unlabeled data to improve classification when given only a small amount of labeled data - other relevant contexts for our work are the semi-supervised learning or few-shot learning fields.

## 3     Methods

### 3.1     Distillation Training

This paper uses a *Wide-Resnet* as a student model and a standard *Resnet* as a teacher network [13,36]. These two network architectures have become "standard" backbone networks used often in smaller-scale classification tasks such as CIFAR-100 [17]. Irwan et al. [3] showed that a large Resnet remains at the top rank for CIFAR-100 with modification of the training methods, achieving 89.3% accuracy without any extra data used. For our distillation experiments, we used a Wide-Resnet with a width multiplier of one and a depth scale of 28, denoting this network as *WideRes-28-1*. For the "larger" Resnet, we used a Resnet-18 that was *pre-trained* on ImageNet. The ratio of parameters in WideRes-28-1 to Resnet-18 is 3% with 0.37 million parameters for the former. We added an extra upsampling layer at the top of Resnet-18 for fine-tuned with CIFAR-100 for size-matching.

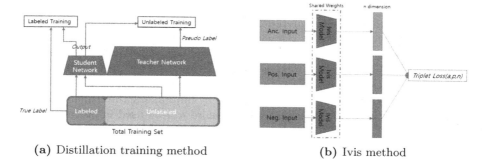

**(a)** Distillation training method    **(b)** Ivis method

**Fig. 3.** Training methods used in the experiment

In experiments on limited sample settings, we extract subsets of CIFAR-100 using balanced sampling. We refer to the labeled and unlabeled data as $x^l \in R^n$ and $x^{ul} \in R^n$. We initially train without any interaction between the student network and teacher network, where we label the untrained student as $f(x)$ and the teacher as $F(x)$. After the teacher network finishes its fine-tuning on the supplied training set, we use $F(x^{ul})$ to train a distilled student network, $g(x)$. As Fig. 3 shows, we undergo cyclical update of $g(x)$ by first training with $x^l$, then we compute $F(x^{ul})$ for unlabeled data and update $g(x)$'s weights using the loss function, Eq. (1).

$$\sum_{x^{ul} \in X^{ul}} KL(softmax(\frac{g(x^{ul})}{T}), softmax(\frac{F(x^{ul})}{T})) \tag{1}$$

This loss decreases the distributional difference between the two networks, with temperature $T$ as a smoothing factor.

## 3.2   Ivis Analysis

After training, we analyzed the difference between the two models, $f(x)$ and $g(x)$. For our initial analysis, we employed the Ivis method of dimensionality reduction with the test dataset of CIFAR-100 (see below for a comparison with t-SNE).

As expressed in Fig. 3, Ivis selects the anchor, positive, and negative samples from the input data. Then, it decreases each input embedding dimension with size $n$ through three networks with shared parameters. The network then modifies its parameters based on the *triplet loss* between the embeddings:

$$\sum_{i}^{N}[||I(x_i^a) - I(x_i^p)||_2^2 - ||I(x_i^a) - I(x_i^n)||_2^2 + \alpha] \tag{2}$$

As shown in Eq. (2), the triplet loss is computed using the comparison of an anchor input distance with positive and negative inputs [26]. The positive and negative samples are selected through nearest-neighbor sampling in an *unsupervised* method, known as *Annoy* index [5] - the closest sample being the positive sample and the furthest being the negative one. The network maximizes the distance between negative and anchor samples and minimizes it between positive and anchor samples. The loss includes $\alpha$ as the threshold for the margin between positive and negative pairs. Thus, we can obtain an embedding with a reduced dimension that keeps its original information by minimizing the triplet loss. This reduced embedding and the converged loss score will be used in our analysis.

## 4    Experiments

### 4.1    Datasets

We analyzed the effect on the standard classification dataset of CIFAR-100 [17], which consists of 100 classes with 600 images per class. Originally, the data is split into 500 training and 100 test images per class, but given our limited sample setting, we only used a subset of these for training and testing. Additionally, CIFAR-100 has extra-label information called a 'superclass', which group the 100 labels more coarsely. The Resnet-18 teacher network was first trained using the ImageNet database [25], which is a large dataset containing more than 14 million images in 1000 classes.

### 4.2    Implementation Details

Both teacher and student networks used *cross-entropy loss*, and for the distillation, $T = 4$ was used (lower values did not result in significant effects, whereas too high values led to divergence). We used the SGD optimizer for updating the weights. The initial learning rate was 0.1 with step-size decay per 60 epochs with multiplicity of 0.2. We set the batch size to 64. For augmentations, only random horizontal flips were applied during training.

For the CIFAR-100 dataset, we tested the distillation with 400, 2500, 5000, 10000, 20000 total labeled data budgets (balanced in each class). For comparison in this limited sample setting, below, we also report results shown in the recent FixMatch work [29] and other related work. FixMatch used a much larger WideResnet-28-8 for their training, so that we also used their framework with a comparably-sized WideResnet-28-1. For all analyses of distillation effects, we report average accuracy and standard deviation across five random folds.

Figure 4 shows some of the test accuracies of WideResnet-28-1 and Resnet-18 with different number of labels in CIFAR-100. As visible, a pre-trained Resnet-18 has better performance in the presence of limited labeled data, compared to the untrained WideResnet-28-1. When using 20,000 labels (equivalent to 40% of the full training set), however, the Wide-Resnet approaches similar to higher performance

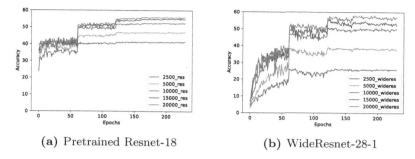

(a) Pretrained Resnet-18                    (b) WideResnet-28-1

**Fig. 4.** Accuracy comparison for a pre-trained Resnet vs a "vanilla" Wide-Resnet in various, limited sample settings.

# 5    Results and Discussion

## 5.1    Classification Accuracy

Table 1 presents detailed results for distillation. With more than 20,000 samples, there is no clear effect of distillation with similar performance between distilled and undistilled student networks and the teacher network. This result may represent the capacity limit of the student network. In this context, it is important to note that the pattern of degradation in the performance of the state-of-the-art FixMatch approach is similar to the distilled model with the same (reduced) model size. Overall, the distilled model also showed similar, high robustness to reductions in label budget comparable with the teacher's network. Similar to other distillation research, the student network can perform better compared to the teacher network in highly-constrained budgets (bold values in Table 1).

## 5.2    Correlation of Final Outputs

We next explored correlations for the final outputs as represented by the real-valued vote towards each label in CIFAR-100. Figure 5 shows this correlation, which was computed as the mean correlation value between all labels contained *in the same superclass* for distilled ($D_*$) and undistilled networks ($UD_*$). As can be seen, the distilled model often can represent the inter-class correlation better compared to the undistilled model. This is especially the case when coarse labels inside a superclass have high visual similarity: for example, the people class has a large effect on correlation strength as it contains man, woman, baby, girl, and boy as visually similar categories. For this superclass, distillation on 2500 labels yields a difference in correlation of 0.11 ($UD_{2500}$ vs $D_{2500}$); training with more data labels can obtain a similar value (0.420 vs 0.421, $D_{2500}$ vs $UD_{10000}$). This value, however, increases to an even higher value (0.69; $D_{10000}$) with distillation.

**Table 1.** Accuracy for CIFAR-100 for different limited label methods. FixMatch [29] performed best overall, but with reduction of the model's backbone to a Wide-Resnet-28-1, performance became similar in most conditions in our experiments (below horizontal line; UD = undistilled, D = distilled).

| Method | CIFAR-100 | | | | |
|---|---|---|---|---|---|
| | 400 | 2500 | 5000 | 10000 | 20000 |
| II-Model [24] | – | $42.75_{\pm 0.48}$ | – | $62.12_{\pm 0.11}$ | – |
| Pseudo-Labeling [31] | – | $42.62_{\pm 0.46}$ | – | $63.79_{\pm 0.19}$ | – |
| Mean Teacher [29] | – | $46.09_{\pm 0.57}$ | – | $64.17_{\pm 0.24}$ | – |
| MixMatch [6] | $32.39_{\pm 1.32}$ | $60.06_{\pm 0.37}$ | – | $71.69_{\pm 0.33}$ | – |
| FixMatch [29] | $51.15_{\pm 1.75}$ | $71.71_{\pm 0.11}$ | – | $77.40_{\pm 0.12}$ | – |
| FixMatch (Reduced) | 25.90 | 45.63 | – | 60.35 | |
| WResnet-28-1(UD) | $5.60_{\pm 0.82}$ | $24.24_{\pm 1.30}$ | $35.77_{\pm 1.67}$ | $48.33_{\pm 0.98}$ | $\mathbf{57.18_{\pm 1.94}}$ |
| WResnet-28-1(D) | $23.75_{\pm 0.85}$ | $\mathbf{46.22_{\pm 0.61}}$ | $50.15_{\pm 0.80}$ | $\mathbf{54.24_{\pm 1.69}}$ | $56.51_{\pm 1.43}$ |
| Resnet-18 | $26.18_{\pm 0.51}$ | $41.48_{\pm 0.77}$ | $47.11_{\pm 0.06}$ | $52.11_{\pm 0.12}$ | $\mathbf{55.97_{\pm 0.41}}$ |

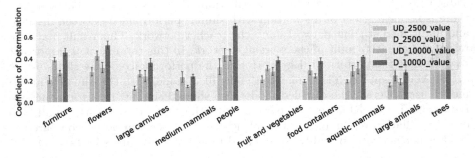

**Fig. 5.** Correlation comparison ($r^2$) between coarse labels in a single super class

### 5.3   Ivis Result

Next, we used the Ivis embeddings to analyze the effects of distillation on each model's layer-wise outputs. Figure 6 shows the five different positions at which we calculated such embeddings. Table 2 shows the loss at convergence from the Ivis framework.

We did not observe any *significant* pattern of distillation at early positions A and B. However, the total variability in loss decreased as the embedding moved closer to the final layers from $\pm 0.121$ to $\pm 0.016$, showing that the embeddings created in early layers had notable fluctuation with different folds. Indeed, we observed that with very few labels (400), the loss for distilled network embeddings was always considerably higher - this should be taken with caution, however, given that the undistilled network may not produce reliable embeddings with only four images per class to begin with.

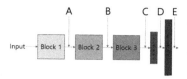

**Fig. 6.** Extraction point of the embeddings

**Table 2.** Ivis convergence loss at the different output stages (Fig. 6). The error across five folds is given as max-min range and was similar across undistilled (UD) and distilled (D) networks.

| Labels | A (±0.121) | | B (±0.071) | | C (±0.024) | | D (±0.015) | | E (±0.016) | |
|--------|------|------|------|------|------|------|------|------|------|------|
| | UD | D | UD | D | UD | D | UD | D | UD | D |
| 400 | 0.255 | 0.606 | 0.360 | 0.513 | 0.229 | 0.309 | 0.181 | 0.240 | 0.146 | 0.174 |
| 2500 | 0.274 | 0.533 | 0.375 | 0.530 | 0.380 | 0.312 | 0.317 | 0.246 | 0.240 | 0.180 |
| 5000 | 0.442 | 0.571 | 0.473 | 0.507 | 0.392 | 0.323 | 0.297 | 0.243 | 0.220 | 0.168 |
| 10000 | 0.462 | 0.498 | 0.474 | 0.515 | 0.391 | 0.305 | 0.289 | 0.227 | 0.204 | 0.156 |
| 20000 | 0.436 | 0.472 | 0.535 | 0.520 | 0.260 | 0.299 | 0.249 | 0.215 | 0.176 | 0.154 |

Interestingly, we also observed few significant differences in distilled networks as a function of label budget. This is most likely due to using the additional number of unlabeled data for extra training. In contrast, more labels made the loss of the undistilled network slowly follow its respective distilled network. Most importantly, we also found that the distilled network had reduced loss at the later C, D, and E layers with more than 2500 labels compared to its undistilled cousin.

Overall, we were able to detect several effects of distillation on the converging loss. Since the embeddings were independent of the test output of each classifier model, the only cause for such different losses would be due to differences in the raw representation space of the test dataset. Based on the overall loss criteria of the Ivis model, we suggest that the distilled network's lower layers has increased potential to separate negative and move closer positive pairs, resulting in "simpler" embeddings especially in low label-budget conditions.

## 5.4 Quantitative Analysis of Representation Space

As an additional, quantitative test we computed the boundary of a single class (plate) in CIFAR-100 over the whole test representation space using Gaussian density estimation (see Fig. 7). Here, we can see that the distilled network has earlier, tight clustering of this class in its representation space, confirming our earlier analyses of correlations above.

Figure 8 shows the computation of the mean class area to the whole area for different label budgets across extraction points (layers). There was no change in this ratio across layers for the undistilled network in the 400 label case, as

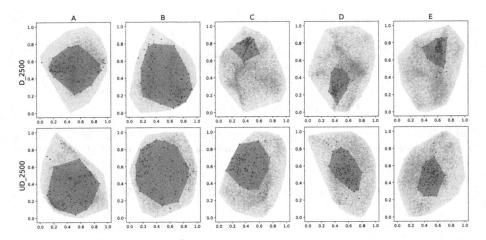

**Fig. 7.** Single class ("plate") distribution of whole data

the network was not able to distribute the classes into different chunks. However, even here the distilled network already showed crucial differences between the early and the late layers of the network. This difference was visible for all label budgets, separating the early layers A and B from the later layers C-E. In addition, with increasing label budget, the gap between the two networks was slowly reduced across layers, matching our earlier loss analysis. Again, this analysis confirms that the distilled network finds a more tight (potentially effective) representation faster (i.e., in earlier layers) in the network for low label budgets.

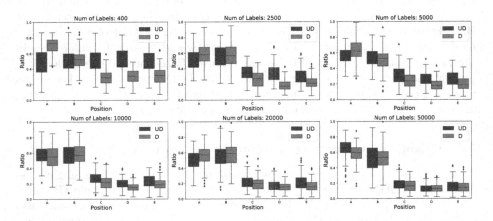

**Fig. 8.** Box plot of area ratio for all classes

# 6    Conclusion and Future Work

All our results clearly showed how distillation provides the network with increased robustness at low label budgets. Crucially, we verified this not only in terms of accuracy, but also with our detailed loss analysis and class measurements using the Ivis method. This increased robustness comes in part due to the additional provision of unlabeled data, which represents one advantage of the distillation framework given the abundance of unlabeled data in the wild.

We also showed that Ivis is able to visualize representation spaces even in relatively high-dimensional layers. With this visualization, we observed more compact class representations in distilled networks in general, happening at earlier layers. We presume that the teacher network's pseudo-outputs provide large amounts of feature information feedback to the student, leading the distilled network to make every layer work more independently and effectively. In our case, the first block in the Wide-Resnet has 16 filters per inner convolution layers, followed by 32 and 64 filters later. The best possible outcome would occur when every filter detects different features - an argument made in [15], which showed that the performance of deeper networks is better due to the kernels capturing more independent information. We argue that distillation also works in a similar fashion, resulting in better performance. In addition, our preliminary comparisons with t-SNE indicated that Ivis may be better suited for such high-dimensional visualizations, but further studies also on a larger variety of datasets will be necessary to validate this observation.

In our results, we also observed a large degree of similarity between the recent FixMatch approach and distillation training with a similar model architecture on CIFAR-100 training - future work will need to analyze different model architectures with better, overall performance in more detail. FixMatch's main idea was to match the distribution of output with soft augmented and hard augmented images without damaging the essential features of the input source - distillation is actually similar to this approach as the large network's output preserves the important feature information. One limitation of FixMatch compared to distillation is that the augmentation methods of the former need to be handcrafted, which varies from dataset to dataset (faces vs objects, for example). We cautiously suggest therefore that distillation overall has the better potential to generalize to other dataset domains, but this remains to be shown in future work as well.

**Acknowledgments.** This work was supported by Institute of Information Communications Technology Planning Evaluation (IITP) grant funded by the Korean government (MSIT) (No. 2019-0-00079), Department of Artificial Intelligence, Korea University

# References

1. Aljalbout, E., Golkov, V., Siddiqui, Y., Cremers, D.: Clustering with deep learning: taxonomy and new methods. arXiv preprint arXiv:1801.07648 (2018)

2. Arazo, E., Ortego, D., Albert, P., O'Connor, N.E., McGuinness, K.: Pseudo-labeling and confirmation bias in deep semi-supervised learning. In: 2020 International Joint Conference on Neural Networks (IJCNN), pp. 1–8. IEEE (2020)
3. Bello, I., et al.: Revisiting ResNets: improved training and scaling strategies. arXiv preprint arXiv:2103.07579 (2021)
4. Bengio, Y.: Practical recommendations for gradient-based training of deep architectures. In: Montavon, G., Orr, G.B., Müller, K.-R. (eds.) Neural Networks: Tricks of the Trade. LNCS, vol. 7700, pp. 437–478. Springer, Heidelberg (2012). https://doi.org/10.1007/978-3-642-35289-8_26
5. Bernhardsson, E.: Approximate Nearest Neighbors in C++/Python optimized for memory usage and loading/saving to disk (2018). https://github.com/spotify/annoy
6. Berthelot, D., Carlini, N., Goodfellow, I., Papernot, N., Oliver, A., Raffel, C.: MixMatch: a holistic approach to semi-supervised learning. arXiv preprint arXiv:1905.02249 (2019)
7. Canziani, A., Paszke, A., Culurciello, E.: An analysis of deep neural network models for practical applications. arXiv preprint arXiv:1605.07678 (2016)
8. Chan, D.M., Rao, R., Huang, F., Canny, J.F.: T-SNE-CUDA: GPU-accelerated t-SNE and its applications to modern data. In: 2018 30th International Symposium on Computer Architecture and High Performance Computing (SBAC-PAD), pp. 330–338. IEEE (2018)
9. Chen, T., Kornblith, S., Swersky, K., Norouzi, M., Hinton, G.: Big self-supervised models are strong semi-supervised learners. arXiv preprint arXiv:2006.10029 (2020)
10. Cheng, X., Rao, Z., Chen, Y., Zhang, Q.: Explaining knowledge distillation by quantifying the knowledge. In: Proceedings of the IEEE/CVF Conference on Computer Vision and Pattern Recognition, pp. 12925–12935 (2020)
11. Gou, J., Yu, B., Maybank, S.J., Tao, D.: Knowledge distillation: a survey. Int. J. Comput. Vis. **129**(6), 1789–1819 (2021)
12. Han, S., Mao, H., Dally, W.J.: Deep compression: compressing deep neural networks with pruning, trained quantization and Huffman coding. arXiv preprint arXiv:1510.00149 (2015)
13. He, K., Zhang, X., Ren, S., Sun, J.: Deep residual learning for image recognition. In: Proceedings of the IEEE Conference on Computer Vision and Pattern Recognition, pp. 770–778 (2016)
14. Hinton, G., Vinyals, O., Dean, J.: Distilling the knowledge in a neural network (2015)
15. Huh, M., Mobahi, H., Zhang, R., Cheung, B., Agrawal, P., Isola, P.: The low-rank simplicity bias in deep networks. arXiv preprint arXiv:2103.10427 (2021)
16. Komodakis, N., Zagoruyko, S.: Paying more attention to attention: improving the performance of convolutional neural networks via attention transfer. In: ICLR (2017)
17. Krizhevsky, A., Hinton, G., et al.: Learning multiple layers of features from tiny images. University of Toronto (2009)
18. Lin, Z.Q., Wong, A.: Progressive label distillation: learning input-efficient deep neural networks. arXiv preprint arXiv:1901.09135 (2019)
19. Liu, Y., Zhang, W., Wang, J.: Adaptive multi-teacher multi-level knowledge distillation. Neurocomputing **415**, 106–113 (2020)
20. Van der Maaten, L., Hinton, G.: Visualizing data using t-SNE. J. Mach. Learn. Res. **9**(11), 2579–2605 (2008)
21. Müller, R., Kornblith, S., Hinton, G.: When does label smoothing help? arXiv preprint arXiv:1906.02629 (2019)

22. Phuong, M., Lampert, C.: Towards understanding knowledge distillation. In: International Conference on Machine Learning, pp. 5142–5151. PMLR (2019)

23. Polino, A., Pascanu, R., Alistarh, D.: Model compression via distillation and quantization. arXiv preprint arXiv:1802.05668 (2018)

24. Rasmus, A., Valpola, H., Honkala, M., Berglund, M., Raiko, T.: Semi-supervised learning with ladder networks. arXiv preprint arXiv:1507.02672 (2015)

25. Russakovsky, O.: ImageNet large scale visual recognition challenge. Int. J. Comput. Vis. **115**(3), 211–252 (2015)

26. Schroff, F., Kalenichenko, D., Philbin, J.: FaceNet: a unified embedding for face recognition and clustering. In: Proceedings of the IEEE Conference on Computer Vision and Pattern Recognition, pp. 815–823 (2015)

27. Seifert, C.: Visualizations of deep neural networks in computer vision: a survey. In: Cerquitelli, T., Quercia, D., Pasquale, F. (eds.) Transparent Data Mining for Big and Small Data. SBD, vol. 11, pp. 123–144. Springer, Cham (2017). https://doi.org/10.1007/978-3-319-54024-5_6

28. Simonyan, K., Zisserman, A.: Very deep convolutional networks for large-scale image recognition. arXiv preprint arXiv:1409.1556 (2014)

29. Sohn, K., et al.: FixMatch: simplifying semi-supervised learning with consistency and confidence. arXiv preprint arXiv:2001.07685 (2020)

30. Szubert, B., Cole, J.E., Monaco, C., Drozdov, I.: Structure-preserving visualisation of high dimensional single-cell datasets. Sci. Rep. **9**(1), 1–10 (2019)

31. Tarvainen, A., Valpola, H.: Mean teachers are better role models: weight-averaged consistency targets improve semi-supervised deep learning results. arXiv preprint arXiv:1703.01780 (2017)

32. Thiagarajan, J.J., Kashyap, S., Karargyris, A.: Distill-to-label: weakly supervised instance labeling using knowledge distillation. In: 2019 18th IEEE International Conference on Machine Learning And Applications (ICMLA), pp. 902–907. IEEE (2019)

33. Wang, L., Yoon, K.J.: Knowledge distillation and student-teacher learning for visual intelligence: a review and new outlooks. IEEE Trans. Pattern Anal. Mach. Intell. (2021)

34. Wattenberg, M., Viégas, F., Johnson, I.: How to use t-SNE effectively. Distill **1**(10), e2 (2016)

35. Yu, W., Yang, K., Bai, Y., Yao, H., Rui, Y.: Visualizing and comparing convolutional neural networks. arXiv preprint arXiv:1412.6631 (2014)

36. Zagoruyko, S., Komodakis, N.: Wide residual networks. arXiv preprint arXiv:1605.07146 (2016)

37. Zhu, L., Xu, Z., Yang, Y., Hauptmann, A.G.: Uncovering the temporal context for video question answering. Int. J. Comput. Vis. **124**(3), 409–421 (2017)

38. Zhuang, F.: A comprehensive survey on transfer learning. Proc. IEEE **109**(1), 43–76 (2020)

# Adversarial Training Inspired Self-attention Flow for Universal Image Style Transfer

Kaiheng Dang[1], Jianhuang Lai[1,2,3(✉)], Junhao Dong[1], and Xiaohua Xie[1,2,3]

[1] School of Computer Science and Engineering,
Sun Yat-sen University, Guangzhou, China
{dangkh,dongjh8}@mail2.sysu.edu.cn, {stsljh,xiexiaoh6}@mail.sysu.edu.cn
[2] Guangdong Key Laboratory of Information Security Technology, Guangzhou,
China
[3] Key Laboratory of Machine Intelligence and Advanced Computing,
Ministry of Education, Guangzhou, China

**Abstract.** Flow-based model receives more and more attention and has been recently applied to image style transfer. While these methods can achieve splendid performance, there remains a problem that the stacked convolutions are inefficient and cannot focus on valuable features. Starting with training an adversarial robust model, we find that no matter in the perceptual loss network or the transfer model, robust features are beneficial for performing better universal style transfer (UST) results. Based on this initial conclusion, we improve the current Glow model by applying self-attention mechanism with three different blocks using ViT, non-local and involution, respectively. Designed feature extraction blocks can capture more valuable deep features with fewer parameters, making Glow more effective and efficient in UST. Our improved Glow can generate artistic images that look nicer and more stable. Both visual results and quantitative metrics are compared to prove that our improvement makes Glow more suitable for UST.

**Keywords:** Image style transfer · Flow-based model · Adversarial robust feature

## 1 Introduction

Image style transfer task aims to synthesize two images, a content image and a style image, into a single one with the former's global content and the latter's artistic effects. Recent years have witnessed the substantial development of neural style transfer. Several excellent methods have been published after the initial successful attempt of Gatys [1]. Similar approaches appeared a lot that used feed-forward networks and iterative optimization [2–4]. Universal style transfer

This work was supported in part by the NSFC under Grant 62076258 and in part by the Key-Area Research and Development Program of Guangzhou under Grant 202007030004.

(UST) can handle the generalization ability and perform good results for arbitrary style and content. The most representative methods include AdaIN [5], WCT [6], Avatar-Net [7] and Linear Transformation [8]. These methods explore the second-order statistical transformation from style image features onto content image features via different transformations.

A recent work named ArtFlow [9] proposed an unbiased style transfer framework based on Glow [10]. With perfect mathematical support, flow-based models can generate confidential image results in many image generation tasks. ArtFlow contains a chain of revertible operators proposed by Glow, including activation normalization layers, invertible $1 \times 1$ convolutions, and affine coupling layers. A simple reverse operation can be performed to reconstruct the image since the flow-based model is reversible.

Despite DNNs superior performance, there exists tailored examples to disturb DNNs called adversarial examples [12,16,30]. These examples are inputs to machine learning models that deliberately add some subtle interference by attackers imperceptible in human vision. The discussion of adversarial examples [31] has shown us non-robust features dominates in the style transfer mission. Specifically, VGG-based networks perform poorly in adversarial training tasks yet outperform other networks like ResNet and Inception regarding style transfer.

Although there is no doubt that we can obtain beautiful transfer results with the powerful flow-based model, there is still some weakness of the framework. Researchers do not attend flow-based models for many years due to their weak feature representation ability. To improve the feature extraction ability, we start by exploring the relationship between robust features and the style transfer model based on Glow. Experiments show adversarial robust features are not only useful in iterative optimization methods but also can work well in UST. Based on the finding, we try to improve the expression of the flow-based model to make it capture more valuable features in transfer image style. We have an attempt with vision transformer first because [22] finds that ViTs has a better performance than convolution layers in the adversarial training mission. Then we further design two blocks with non-local [24] and involution [25], respectively. Both visual results and quantitative comparisons show our improved Glow can generate more excellent images. There are two main contributions of this work:

1. We confirm the effectiveness of adversarial robust features in UST by performing experiments. Robust features are helpful both as loss calculating and transfer features. The conclusion will broaden the road of future study of relative areas.
2. We improve the performance of flow-based model by replacing the current convolution layers. The original feature extraction block contains a simple stack of convolutions, which needs extra parameters and will not necessarily capture useful information. We design feature extraction blocks with self-attention, which use fewer parameters and focus on significant features. Experiments are conducted to prove our redesigned Glow is capable of capturing more valuable features for image style transfer.

## 2  Related Works

**Image Style Transfer.** Traditional methods can paint high-quality images yet may take much time, which means they have to trade-off between quality and costs. This problem has been a hindrance until Gatys [1] first introduce the neural network to extract deep features and represent image styles by Gram matrix. The iterative optimization process has a high computational cost. Numerous neural style transfer methods emerge then, which can be roughly divided into three categories. One style per model method [2,13,14] trains feed-forward neural networks to minimize the same feature reconstruction loss and style loss. Multiple-style per model methods [3,15,32] represent several styles with a single model, which can perform multiple image style transfer. Universal style transfer methods [3,5,6,8,17,18] aim to improve the generalization ability of neural style transfer by matching statistical variables like mean and variance, generating excellent results for arbitrary style and content images.

**Flow-Based Model.** The flow-based model was first proposed by the work of NICE [11], which extracts high dimension features with a stack of affine coupling layers. It has not been pay much attention to because of its weak feature expression capability, which is the consequence of ensuring reversibility. Subsequent work of Glow [10] improves flow with flexible reversible $1 \times 1$ convolution, increasing the performance of the flow-based model in an extensive range. Recent proposed flow-based models [19] are capable of synthesizing high-quality images and realistic speech data. ArtFlow has just been made public using the architecture of Glow, which can handle content leak problems and is capable of performing unbiased image style transfer.

**Adversarial Examples.** Existing models achieve good results except for a particular case which is named adversarial examples. These examples may cause the model to give an erroneous output with high confidence. Andrew et al. [20] does some experiments and proposes that adversarial examples are due to non-robust features that are highly predictive but imperceptible to humans. This conclusion arises many works in various fields. Wang et al. [21] rethink the difference of architectural between VGG and ResNet and their performance in the style transfer task, further proposing a simple solution to improve the robustness of ResNet.

## 3  Method

### 3.1  Robust Features and Style Transfer

We first state the initial conclusion about the relationship between robust features and image style transfer. The discussion [31] about robust features [20] gives us hints that VGG is more suitable in image style transfer tasks, but other networks like the most popular ResNet cannot work very well without tricks.

**(a) Content**          **(b) Style**     **(c) Non-robust ResNet**     **(c) Robust ResNet**

**Fig. 1.** Glow-based Style transfer results with non-robust and robust ResNet-50. Robust one generate more reasonable results.

VGG is far behind compared to other models like ResNet, Inception-v3 and DenseNet when it comes to the adversarial training tasks. This phenomenon can easily conclude that it is just because VGG is unable to capture non-robust features as efficient as other architectures that make it capable of performing confidential style transfer outputs. [31] does some quick experiments and shows the first four layers of VGG are almost as robust as the layers of robust ResNet.

[21] conducts more experiments and finds the residual connection is unsuitable in style transfer and adds a simple trick on loss function to create a more uniform distribution of activations, which is beneficial to produce good style transfer with ResNet. Although this is useful, we find the trick can only be used for iterative optimization methods, which can only transfer one pair of style and content once, similar to Gatys [1], and cannot work well when it comes to universal style transfer. We attempt to apply the solution to ArtFlow and only get noisy results, with the loss and gradient values being strange.

To expand the current conclusion to a universal case, we first train Art-Flow with a robust perceptual loss network [2] to verify that robust feature is still working for UST. Figure 1 shows the results of ArtFlow using standard and robust ResNet-50 as the perceptual loss network. The transferring is not really working well with standard ResNet-50. Nevertheless, the outputs become far better with robust cases, which indicates that a robust network can indeed capture features that are useful to style transfer.

We further consider that since robust features are more critical in evaluating the distance of features from loss networks, it is more reasonable to perform the transfer with robust features than non-robust ones. Table 1 shows quantitative metrics of robust and non-robust ArtFlow.

**Algorithm 1.** Affine coupling with reverse.

**Input:** input feature tensor $x_{in}$    **Output:** output feature tensor $y_{out}$

1: $x_a, x_b = split(x_{in})$
2: $(logs, t) = NN(x_b)$
3: $s = exp(logs)$
4: $y_a = s \odot x_a + t$
5: $y_b = x_b$
6: $y_{out} = concat(y_b, y_a)$
7: **return** $y_{out}$

### 3.2   Glow Architecture

ArtFlow [9] introduces the flow-based model to solve the content leak problem of style transfer mission, whose overall architecture is the same with Glow [10], including a chain of three reversible transformations, i.e., affine coupling, invertible $1 \times 1$ convolution, and Actnorm [10]. Different from the widely used auto-encoder methods, the flow-based model can perform as both encoder and decoder. The following are detailed descriptions of the main reversible transformations of the network.

**Actnorm.** Early used batch normalization (BN) is subject to the batch size, which may add noise and cause performance to degrade. Actnorm is then proposed for activation normalization, which performs an affine transformation of the activations using a scale and bias per channel. Parameters are initialized to make the activations have zero mean and unit variance, which will output the initial minibatch of data. Actnorm performs per channel as:

$$y_{i,j} = \omega \odot x_{i,j} + b \tag{1}$$

where $i, j$ denote the position on the feature tensor. $\omega$ and b are the scale and bias and are learnable in training, which is similar to BN.

**Invertible   $1 \times 1$ Convolution.** Since affine coupling layers only process half of the features, it is necessary to permute the channels of the feature maps. Instead of fixed permutation in flow-based models before, Glow uses a learnable invertible $1 \times 1$ convolution. This convolution part is the main reason for the performance increase of the flow-based model. The operation can be represented by:

$$y_{i,j} = W x_{i,j} \tag{2}$$

where $W \in \mathcal{R}^{c \times c}$ is the weight matrix with c being the channel dimension of the feature tensor.

**Affine Coupling Layers.** The essential part of the flow-based model is the expressive reversible transformation named affine coupling proposed by Dinh

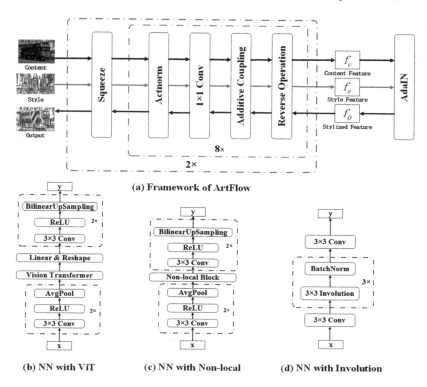

**Fig. 2.** (a) The overall framework of ArtFlow used to perform Style Transfer, adding the reverse operation. (b) NN with ViT uses average pooling to downsample the feature to reduce the calculation. Linear and Reshape layers transform the tokens back into features tensors. (c) NN with Non-local is similar to the previous one and doesn't need Linear since the shape will not change through the non-local block. (d) NN with Involution performs better with a convolution layer to increase the number of channels first and remains the same count of channels inside. A BatchNorm layer helps handle outliers.

et al. [11]. Roughly speaking, an affine coupling layer splits the input tensor into two parts along the channel dimension. The first part unchanged to be the first half of the output tensor, and the second part does affine transformation using the transformed result of the first part.

**Reverse Operation.** Inspired by the conclusion of [21] that residual connections may interfere style transfer task, we make a slight change of the affine coupling layer. Although the sophisticated $1 \times 1$ convolution is indeed able to learn an appropriate permutation of the input, it is well known that a good initialization can speed up the model convergence and get better results. To reduce the tendency of delivering the same half of the tensor multiple times directly, we add a simple reverse operation to exchange the two parts of the output of the

**Algorithm 2.** Pseudo PyTorch code of involution.

**Input:** $x \in \mathcal{R}^{B \times C \times H \times W}$    **Output:** $y \in \mathcal{R}^{B \times C \times H \times W}$

```
# K: kernal size, s: stride, r: reduction ratio
# initialization
1: o = AvgPool2d(s, s) if s > 1 else Identity()
2: reduce = Conv2d(C, C//r, 1)
3: span = Conv2d(C//r, K*K, 1)
4: unfold = Unfold(K, padding=K//2, s)
5: weight1 = Parameter((1,1,H,W))
6: weight2 = Parameter((1,1,H,W))
# forward
1: weighted_sum = ReLU(BN(mul(weight1, x))).sum(dim=(2,3)) # B, C
2: weighted_sum = weighted_sum.unsqueeze().unsqueeze()# B, C, 1, 1
3: weighted_sum = mul(weighted_sum, weight2) # B, C, H, W
4: x_unfolded = unfold(x).view(B, C, K*K, H, W)
5: kernel = reduce(o(x+weighted_sum)) # B, C//r, H, W
6: kernel = span(ReLU(BN(kernel))).view(B, 1, K*K, H, W)
7: y = mul(kernel, x_unfolded).sum(dim=2) # B, C, 1, H, W
8: return y.squeeze()
```

affine coupling layer. The affine coupling with reverse is summarized in Algorithm 1. An additive coupling layer is a simplified case with $s = 1$, which is the one exactly used in ArtFlow.

### 3.3 Improve Feature Extraction

There is no doubt that robust features are beneficial to performing more wonderful image style transfer results, but adversarial training is very time-consuming. To increase the performance while holding the efficiency, it is a better idea to improve the architecture of the network. As we can see from the modules, affine coupling layer consists of the only feature extraction Neural Network (NN) in Glow since the $1 \times 1$ convolution is for feature shuffling. Aiming to capture robust features, we need to use a more suitable structure. Shao et al. [22] has recently published a work about the adversarial robustness of ViTs [23]. It can be inferred from their experiments that ViTs possess better adversarial robustness compared with convolutional neural networks, which raises an assumption that self-attention is playing an essential role in this question.

As shown in Fig. 2, we design three different neural network blocks for the affine coupling block to increase the feature extraction ability, using vision transformer, non-local [24] and involution [25], respectively. To be clear, non-local is a widely used attention mechanism in the computer vision area, which is a lighter weight module than ViT. Involution is a neural network operator whose kernel parameters are shared along the channel dimension, which is different from convolution, whose kernel remains the same along pixels. The kernels are transform results of the vectors along the channel dimension with a kernel generation function. The involution operator can be a general form of self-attention by replacing the generation function. To let each channel receive the global information, which is important in style expression, we add a global weighted sum along the channel dimension to the channels. Furthermore, we use one more weight matrix to learn the importance of the global information to the current channel. The global information we add only need $2 \times H \times W$ more parameters and can obtain much promotion. We accept the group number, reduction ratio and dilation to be all 1. Algorithm 2 is the pseudo-PyTorch code of involution we apply. Experiments show that involution is actually capable of capturing helpful features.

## 3.4   Loss Function

Gatys [1] propose the Gram matrix to represent the style of an image and soon becomes the general criterion of style transfer. The perceptual loss [2] further extends the usage with a loss network, which brings up the development of Universal Style Transfer. Loss networks, usually VGG-19, maps an image into a set of feature maps $\{F^l(x_0)\}_{l=1}^L$ where $F^l$ is the mapping from the image to the activations of the $l^{th}$ layer. Suppose the activation to be $\mathcal{R}^{C_l \times W_l \times H_l}$ and can also be reshaped into a matrix $F^l(x_0) \in \mathcal{R}^{C_l \times M_l}$, where $M_l = W_l \times H_l$. The Gram matrix $G^l \in \mathcal{R}^{C_l \times C_l}$ is computed by the inner product between the feature maps in layer l:

$$G_{ij}^l = \sum_k F_{ik}^l F_{jk}^l \tag{3}$$

then with $x_s$ representing the style image and $x$ the output image, the style loss can be measured by $\mathcal{L}_{style}$, as:

$$\mathcal{L}_{style}(x_s, x) = \sum_{l=1}^L \frac{\omega_l}{4 C_l^2 M_l^2} ||G^l(F^l(x)) - G^l(F^l(x_s))||_2^2 \tag{4}$$

where $\omega_l \in \{0, 1\}$ are factors using to choose which layers will contribute to the style loss. Content loss $\mathcal{L}_content$ is a simple mean square error as:

$$\mathcal{L}_{content}(x_c, x) = \frac{1}{2} ||F^l(x) - F^l(x_c)||_2^2 \tag{5}$$

where $x_c$ is the content image and $x$ the output. $l$ here represents the feature used to measure the content distance, usually the deepest layer. The total loss function $\mathcal{L}_{total}$ is a weighted sum of style loss and content loss as:

$$\mathcal{L}_{total}(x, x_c, x_s) = \lambda_{content} \mathcal{L}_{content}(x, x_c) + \lambda_{style} \mathcal{L}_{style}(x, x_s) \tag{6}$$

It is necessary to clarify that VGG-19 is used as the perceptual loss network. There is no fixed statement about which layers to use. According to experiments of [8], we adopt the combination of four outputs of the first ReLU layer of the first four VGG blocks as *relu1_1, relu2_1, relu3_1, relu4_1*, respectively. As for

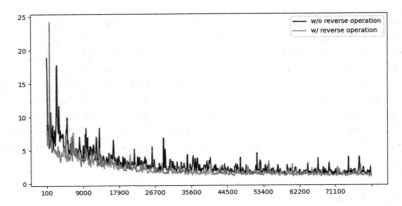

**Fig. 3.** Training Loss of Glow with and without the reverse operation. Applying reverse can accelerate the training procedure and makes it more stable.

ResNet used in the comparison experiment of Sect. 4.2, we refer to the approach of [31] and choose layers of *relu2_3*, *relu3_4*, *relu4_6*, *relu5_3* considering the fair comparison with VGG.

## 4  Experiments

In this section, we explain the experiment details of three main terms. We first prove the adversarial training has a positive influence on universal style transfer. Then we conduct a fast experiment of the effect of the Reverse Operation. Moreover, extensive experiments are performed to show the enhancement of the improved Glow.

### 4.1  Experiment Settings

**Datasets.** Following the existing image style transfer methods, we use the MS-COCO dataset [26] as our content images and the WikiArt dataset [27] as style images. The input images are resized to $512 \times 512$ and then randomly cropped to $256 \times 256$. In the experiment of adversarial training, we follow the current study to train the Glow on cifar-10 [28], then use the pretrained model to transfer the style of our test set.

**Network Structure.** We adopt the structure of ArtFlow [9] using two Glow blocks, with each block containing eight combinations of the three reversible transformations. The author has discussed that additive coupling is sufficient for style transfer and is more stable, which is the same with our attempts, no matter which NN we use.

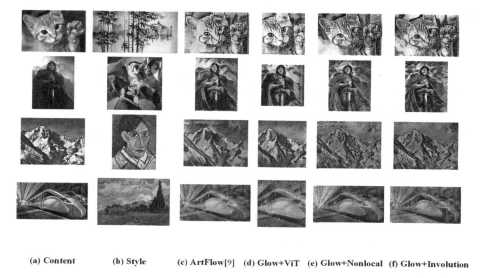

(a) Content     (b) Style     (c) ArtFlow[9]   (d) Glow+ViT   (e) Glow+Nonlocal   (f) Glow+Involution

**Fig. 4.** Visual results compared to original ArtFlow. Our ViT block requires the content feature to be in certain sizes, so we randomly crop the input content image. Our improved ArtFLow generates more beautiful and stable images, especially the details and textures. Please zoom in to confirm.

**Training.** We implement all experiments on the PyTorch framework. Standard training on cifar-10 takes about 15 h for 250 epochs on an RTX 2080Ti GPU. Adversarial training needs 4 h for one epoch, and the loss is usually becoming stable after 40 epochs. We adopt the widely used TRADES [29] to perform adversarial training with step size, epsilon, number of perturbation iterations to be 0.003, 0.031, 7, respectively. For the training of Glow, the loss weights are set to 0.1 for $\lambda_{content}$ and 1 for $\lambda_{style}$ based on previous work experience. Adain is used as the style transfer module because of its simplicity and effectiveness. We perform 100000 iterations using Adam with the initial learning rate of 1e−4 and decay of 5e−5. The original architecture takes about 22 h with a batch size of 4 on an RTX 2080Ti GPU or 21 h with a batch size of 2 on a GTX 1080Ti GPU.

**Metrics.** Visual results are first compared to show the superiority of our methods. We choose different kinds of style and content images as the test set. A good style transfer result should remain more overall content and generate vivid hues and detailed textures. In addition, we also make quantitative comparisons. The perceptual loss value of the test set is a common metric among image synthesis tasks. We use the content loss to measure the content preservation and the Gram matrix loss to measure the style transfer ability. The efficiency is important as well, so we compare the transfer speed and the model size.

**Table 1.** Quantitative evaluation comparisons. The first two rows are the result of Sect. 4.2 training on cifar-10. The rest are the results of Sect. 4.3. Transfer time is evaluated on 256 × 256 images using an TITAN RTX GPU.

| Models | Style loss | Content loss | NLL loss | Time (s) | Model size (MB) |
|---|---|---|---|---|---|
| Standard Glow | 11.1 | 1.924 | 3.39 | 0.144 | 74.38 |
| Robust Glow | 8.5 | 1.997 | 3.49 | 0.144 | 74.38 |
| ArtFlow [9] | 3.905 | 3.199 | 3.39 | **0.144** | 74.38 |
| Glow+ViT (ours) | 4.631 | **2.902** | 3.42 | 0.221 | 239.36 |
| Glow+nonlocal (ours) | 3.55 | 3.003 | 3.44 | 0.185 | 51.62 |
| Glow+Involution (ours) | **3.110** | 2.939 | 3.52 | 0.157 | **34.46** |

## 4.2   Comparing Adversarial and Standard Networks

We first show that robust features are still working when it comes to universal style transfer. Since adversarial training is very time-consuming, we directly use the pretrained robust ResNet. The Glow used in this part remains the same with ArtFlow. As shown in Fig. 1, the first row are the results of standard ResNet-50, and the second row is from robust ResNet-50. Obviously, standard ResNet-50 is not really performing style transfer, yet the robust one makes better performance.

Then we compare the robust Glow and the standard Glow. With the training setting stated before, we use the pretrained Glow models to transfer the style of images. The pretrained model is not able to perform reasonable image results. However, from the loss comparison, we can see the robust model extracts more useful features for style transfer, leading to a lower Gram matrix loss.

## 4.3   Improved Glow

**Ablation Experiment.** Firstly, we prove that training will be accelerated with the simple reverse operation. We use the original Glow to perform this part of experiments. Figure 3 shows training procedures of the two cases, one of which uses the reverse operation. It is clear that with the reverse operation, training loss descends faster, which confirms our assumption that the parameters of the $1 \times 1$ convolution in the network are trained to have similar behaviour.

Secondly, we demonstrate that with a more suitable design for NN, Glow can obtain more excellent style transfer results. Visual comparisons are shown in Fig. 4. The attention mechanism can enrich details of the image results, and the textures are described better. The designed block with involution achieves relatively better performance than others, with generated images being rich in details and seems stable in the meantime. Quantitative comparisons are made with the testing loss aforementioned. We also compare the negative-log-likelihood loss when training Glow models with cifar-10. NLL is the most common loss function to train flow-based models and can show their classification ability. As we can see in Table 1, our blocks make the classification a little bit worth but

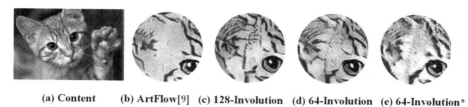

(a) Content     (b) ArtFlow[9]  (c) 128-Involution   (d) 64-Involution  (e) 64-Involution*

**Fig. 5.** Detail comparisons. (c) Our involution block with 128 dimensions of hidden layers and is the one used in the previous section. (d) The same structure of (c) with 64-dimension hidden layers. (e) Pure involution without the convolutions in Fig. 2. Model sizes (MB) are 34.46, 10.86, 4.20, respectively.

facilitate style transfer, which also confirms our point of view that style-transfer-useful features may have some degrees of difference with those in recognition tasks. ViT gets a similar score with original convolutions. Our blocks with non-local and involution obtain lower style and content loss, indicating the model transfers more artistic effects while preserving the global content. The model size is smaller since our blocks can capture more valuable features. Using the involution block reduces the scale more than twice. The time cost rises a little, owing to the time-consuming calculations of self-attention.

**Detail Comparison.** We compare the details of our involution block of different sizes. As shown in Fig. 5, our involution block can generate more textures of the corresponding artistic effect, which benefits both content and style loss. After further comparisons, we can find that as the parameters decrease (from c to e), the performance of colour begins to degrade first, and then the textures (notice the purple part of the ear). This phenomenon indicates that our involution block has a more powerful ability to capture the global stroke of the style image, which is more complex than capturing colours. The promotion is due to the self-attention mechanism and the weighted sum we add, both of which are able to increase the overall awareness.

## 5   Conclusions

In this paper, we first explore the relationship between adversarial robust features and universal image style transfer. Although standard ResNet-50 is not suitable to be the perceptual loss network in UST, using an adversarial robust ResNet-50 makes things different and generates confidential results. Experiments prove robust features are helpful not only during loss calculating but also in the transfer procedure. Based on the conclusion, we improve the existing Glow model by enhancing the original feature extraction block with self-attention mechanism, making it perform more pleasing and more stable style transfer results. Three different blocks are used with ViT, non-local and involution, respectively. Our block with involution gets the best results while significantly reducing the model size.

# References

1. Gatys, L.A., Ecker, A.S., Bethge, M.: Image style transfer using convolutional neural networks. In: Proceedings of the IEEE Conference on Computer Vision and Pattern Recognition, pp. 2414–2423 (2016)
2. Johnson, J., Alahi, A., Fei-Fei, L.: Perceptual losses for real-time style transfer and super-resolution. In: Leibe, B., Matas, J., Sebe, N., Welling, M. (eds.) ECCV 2016. LNCS, vol. 9906, pp. 694–711. Springer, Cham (2016). https://doi.org/10.1007/978-3-319-46475-6_43
3. Zhang, H., Dana, K.: Multi-style generative network for real-time transfer. In: Leal-Taixé, L., Roth, S. (eds.) ECCV 2018. LNCS, vol. 11132, pp. 349–365. Springer, Cham (2019). https://doi.org/10.1007/978-3-030-11018-5_32
4. Chen, D., Yuan, L., Liao, J., Yu, N., Hua, G.: StyleBank: an explicit representation for neural image style transfer. In: Proceedings of the IEEE Conference on Computer Vision and Pattern Recognition, pp. 1897–1906 (2017)
5. Huang, X., Belongie, S.: Arbitrary style transfer in real-time with adaptive instance normalization. In: Proceedings of the IEEE International Conference on Computer Vision, pp. 1501–1510 (2017)
6. Li, Y., Fang, C., Yang, J., Wang, Z., Lu, X., Yang, M.H.: Universal style transfer via feature transforms. arXiv preprint arXiv:1705.08086 (2017)
7. Sheng, L., Lin, Z., Shao, J., Wang, X.: Avatar-Net: multi-scale zero-shot style transfer by feature decoration. In: Proceedings of the IEEE Conference on Computer Vision and Pattern Recognition, pp. 8242–8250 (2018)
8. Li, X., Liu, S., Kautz, J., Yang, M.H.: Learning linear transformations for fast image and video style transfer. In: Proceedings of the IEEE/CVF Conference on Computer Vision and Pattern Recognition, pp. 3809–3817 (2019)
9. An, J., Huang, S., Song, Y., Dou, D., Liu, W., Luo, J.: ArtFlow: unbiased image style transfer via reversible neural flows. In: Proceedings of the IEEE/CVF Conference on Computer Vision and Pattern Recognition, pp. 862–871 (2021)
10. Kingma, D.P., Dhariwal, P.: Glow: generative flow with invertible $1 \times 1$ convolutions. arXiv preprint arXiv:1807.03039 (2018)
11. Dinh, L., Krueger, D., Bengio, Y.: NICE: non-linear independent components estimation. arXiv preprint arXiv:1410.8516 (2014)
12. Moosavi-Dezfooli, S.M., Fawzi, A., Frossard, P.: DeepFool: a simple and accurate method to fool deep neural networks. In: Proceedings of the IEEE Conference on Computer Vision and Pattern Recognition, pp. 2574–2582 (2016)
13. Ulyanov, D., Lebedev, V., Vedaldi, A., Lempitsky, V.S.: Texture networks: feed-forward synthesis of textures and stylized images. In: ICML, June 2016, vol. 1, no. 2, p. 4 (2016)
14. Ulyanov, D., Vedaldi, A., Lempitsky, V.: Improved texture networks: maximizing quality and diversity in feed-forward stylization and texture synthesis. In: Proceedings of the IEEE Conference on Computer Vision and Pattern Recognition, pp. 6924–6932 (2017)
15. Dumoulin, V., Shlens, J., Kudlur, M.: A learned representation for artistic style. arXiv preprint arXiv:1610.07629 (2016)
16. Szegedy, C., et al.: Intriguing properties of neural networks. arXiv preprint arXiv:1312.6199 (2013)
17. Gu, S., Chen, C., Liao, J., Yuan, L.: Arbitrary style transfer with deep feature reshuffle. In: Proceedings of the IEEE Conference on Computer Vision and Pattern Recognition, pp. 8222–8231 (2018)

18. Shen, F., Yan, S., Zeng, G.: Neural style transfer via meta networks. In: Proceedings of the IEEE Conference on Computer Vision and Pattern Recognition, pp. 8061–8069 ((2018))

19. Ho, J., Chen, X., Srinivas, A., Duan, Y., Abbeel, P.: Flow++: improving flow-based generative models with variational dequantization and architecture design. In: International Conference on Machine Learning, pp. 2722–2730. PMLR (May 2019)

20. Ilyas, A., Santurkar, S., Tsipras, D., Engstrom, L., Tran, B., Madry, A.: Adversarial examples are not bugs, they are features. arXiv preprint arXiv:1905.02175 (2019)

21. Wang, P., Li, Y., Vasconcelos, N.: Rethinking and improving the robustness of image style transfer. In: Proceedings of the IEEE/CVF Conference on Computer Vision and Pattern Recognition, pp. 124–133 (2021)

22. Shao, R., Shi, Z., Yi, J., Chen, P.Y., Hsieh, C.J.: On the adversarial robustness of visual transformers. arXiv preprint arXiv:2103.15670 (2021)

23. Dosovitskiy, A., et al.: An image is worth $16 \times 16$ words: transformers for image recognition at scale. arXiv preprint arXiv:2010.11929 (2020)

24. Wang, X., Girshick, R., Gupta, A., He, K.: Non-local neural networks. In: Proceedings of the IEEE Conference on Computer Vision and Pattern Recognition, pp. 7794–7803 (2018)

25. Li, D., et al.: Involution: inverting the inherence of convolution for visual recognition. In: Proceedings of the IEEE/CVF Conference on Computer Vision and Pattern Recognition, pp. 12321–12330 (2021)

26. Lin, T.-Y., et al.: Microsoft COCO: common objects in context. In: Fleet, D., Pajdla, T., Schiele, B., Tuytelaars, T. (eds.) ECCV 2014. LNCS, vol. 8693, pp. 740–755. Springer, Cham (2014). https://doi.org/10.1007/978-3-319-10602-1_48

27. Nichol, K.: Painter by numbers, wikiart (2016). https://www.kaggle.com/c/painter-by-numbers

28. Krizhevsky, A., Hinton, G.: Learning multiple layers of features from tiny images (2009)

29. Zhang, H., Yu, Y., Jiao, J., Xing, E., El Ghaoui, L., Jordan, M.: Theoretically principled trade-off between robustness and accuracy. In: International Conference on Machine Learning, May 2019, pp. 7472–7482. PMLR (2019)

30. Dong, J., Xie, X.: Visually maintained image disturbance against deepfake face swapping. In 2021 IEEE International Conference on Multimedia and Expo (ICME), pp. 1–6. IEEE (July 2021)

31. Nakano: A discussion of 'Adversarial Examples Are Not Bugs, They Are Features': adversarially robust neural style transfer. Distill (2019). https://distill.pub/2019/advex-bugs-discussion/

32. Ma, J., Yu, W., Liang, P., Li, C., Jiang, J.: FusionGAN: a generative adversarial network for infrared and visible image fusion. Inf. Fus. **48**, 11–26 (2019)

# Symbolizing Visual Features
# for Pre-training with Unlabeled Images

Yuichi Kamata[1(✉)], Moyuru Yamada[1], Keizo Kato[1], Akira Nakagawa[1],
and Takayuki Okatani[2]

[1] Fujitsu Ltd., Kawasaki, Kanagawa 211-8588, Japan
{kamata.yuichi,yamada.moyuru,kato.keizo,anaka}@fujitsu.com
[2] Graduate School of Information Sciences, Tohoku University, Sendai, Japan
okatani@vision.is.tohoku.ac.jp

**Abstract.** Multi-layer Transformers, which have shown good performance in natural language processing (NLP), have recently started to be used in multi-modal learning tasks that involve both texts and images. In the NLP part of the multi-modal learning, the approach of pre-training the parameters of Transformers from large unlabeled text data has been shown to contribute to an increase in accuracy. On the other hand, for the image part of the Transformer, there are no reports to show the validity of pre-training, even though, intuitively, the prospect of leveraging knowledge obtained from large amounts of unlabeled image data is appealing. This paper aims to construct a single modal pre-training model based on a Transformer in the image domain for multi-modal learning of texts and images. We have found that, unlike the case of discrete values representing word embeddings, current Transformers have trouble handling continuous values like image features. In order to overcome this limitation, we propose a Transformer with the list of features named SymboList which convert the continuous image features of detected objects into discrete ones by referring to a discrete key list. We demonstrate that our proposed method leads to effective image pre-training and is beneficial to the multi-modal down-stream task.

**Keywords:** Multi-modal transformer · Image pre-training · Visual Question Answering

## 1 Introduction

Visual understanding is one of the key challenges for developing artificial intelligence. To advance this area of research, it is important to address not only the capturing of visual features but also the associated semantic information found in linguistic knowledge. As such, multi-modal learning for vision and language is currently a very hot area of research [3,11,22].

In the field of natural language processing (NLP), Transformer-based [19] architectures and their pre-training on large text corpora, such as in the case of BERT [5], have been shown to boost performance. The fundamental intuition

© Springer Nature Switzerland AG 2022
C. Wallraven et al. (Eds.): ACPR 2021, LNCS 13189, pp. 490–503, 2022.
https://doi.org/10.1007/978-3-031-02444-3_37

behind BERT, which is widely used in NLP, is that the meaning of a word can be determined by its context, especially by considering the co-occurrence of words. This intuition can be extended to multi-modal learning, by considering the co-occurrence between image instances and language. This lead to extensions of the Transformer architecture to vision and language [3,11,22].

In the above, even in the context of multi-modal learning, it has been shown that it is effective to use the co-occurrence of the words or contextualize the word embeddings [11,22]. Note that contextualized word embeddings in the linguistic domain are pre-trained in an unsupervised way.

On the other hand, the effects of pre-training the Transformer in the image-domain have not yet been studied in the context of multi-modal learning. Intuitively, information learned by analyzing co-occurrences between objects in the images should provide us with valuable insight. For example, given an image of a pasture, one is likely to imagine the presence of some domestic animals. However, to the best of our knowledge, the use of pre-trained image models for contextualizing visual features is an area of research not yet explored.

The aim of this study is to reveal what hinders the acquisition of useful knowledge from co-occurrence in the image domain and propose a method to overcome the obstacles. The contributions of this paper are as follows:

- We first examine whether the current Transformer-based architecture can sufficiently capture the co-occurrence in the image domain by executing masked object prediction experiments, which leads to an important insight. In terms of learning co-occurrences, the current Transformer architecture works well for discrete features such as word embedding, but it may not be appropriate for continuous features such as those associated with images.
- Based on the above insight, we propose a novel architecture to obtain discrete object features where the query generated from the object feature references symbolized key lists. We experimentally validated that the proposed method helps to learn co-occurrences in the image domain.
- Finally, the pre-training in the image-domain using our method achieves the boost in the performance of multi-modal down-stream task.

## 2   Related Work

Most existing pre-trained computer vision (CV) models are based on multi-layer CNN, such as VGG [16], ResNet [6] and DenseNet [7]. These models are trained using large-scale annotated image datasets such as ImageNet [4] in a supervised-manner. Faster-RCNN [14] is one of the object detection models which are designed on top of the above pre-trained backbone models. Such object detection models are widely used to detect the objects in an image and extract object features. The extracted object features might contain their shapes and attributes, since object detection models are trained to predict their class label, but do not pay attention to visual and positional relations, i.e., co-occurrence of objects in an image. By contrast, our pre-trained model focuses on learning those relations by predicting masked objects in the image.

Recent studies show significant improvements in NLP tasks with pre-trained language models. These models are based on multi-layer Transformer, such as GPT [13], BERT [5], XLNet [21], and RoBERTa [10]. These models are trained using large-scale text corpora. They learn the co-occurrence of words in a sentence by predicting masked word tokens based on their contexts, and output their contextualized word representations. The language models split a sentence into words using tokenizers such as WordPiece [20] and convert the word tokens to embedding vectors. While word embeddings can be treated in a discrete space, visual object features are in a continuous, high-dimensional space. This fundamental difference between text and visual features is the reason why we need to introduce a novel pre-training model for learning the co-occurrence of objects in an image.

Recently, inspired by pre-trained language models, multi-layer Transformers have been utilized in multi-modal models for vision and language tasks. MCAN [22] proposed a Transformer based architecture for Visual Question Answering (VQA) and achieved state-of-the-art performance. They used the attention mechanism to fuse question-image pairs. UNITER [3] and VL-BERT [17] proposed a single-stream architecture like BERT, which fuses two modalities (vision and language) as a sequence of tokens. Unicoder-VL [9] also adopted a single-stream 12 layer Transformer, with weights initialized from BERT-base, which is pre-trained on text data only. The model of ViLBERT [11] consists of two single-modal streams, and has a language Transfomer followed by a cross-modal Transformer. ViLBERT also borrowed the initial weights from BERT-base for the language part. Different from ViLBERT, LXMERT [18] proposed two multi-layer Transformers for each modality before the cross-modal attentions, i.e., the language Transformer and the vision Transformer. Each of them focuses only on a single modality. They trained both Transformers only on multi-modal pre-training tasks and did not evaluate the effect of the pre-training for the vision transformer using only image corpus as we proposed in this paper.

## 3    Analysis of Transformer-Based Visual Understanding

Our purpose is to construct a pre-trained image model analogous to BERT in order to improve the performance of the multi-modal down-stream tasks. This section explains an analysis of our proposed Vision BERT, a simple BERT-like model for image pre-training. By analyzing the experimental results, we find that Vision BERT pre-trained with discrete object classes gives better performance than the model pre-trained with continuous object features.

### 3.1    Vision BERT Model

Vision BERT consists of multi-layer bidirectional Transformers which take a visual object sequence as input and uses mask prediction for pre-training.

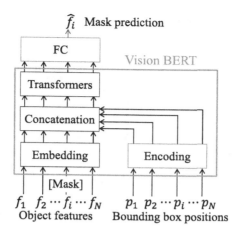

**Fig. 1.** Our Vision BERT model for pre-training. The inputs of Vision BERT are sequences of object features and their bounding box positions extracted by Faster R-CNN. In pre-training, Vision BERT predicts object features that are randomly selected and are masked out. The masked object features are reconstructed by applying the FC layer to outputs of Vision BERT.

**Embeddings of Visual Objects.** As shown in Fig. 1, we use Faster R-CNN to extract $N$ object features $\{f_1, \cdots, f_N\}$ and bounding box positions $\{p_1, \cdots, p_N\}$ in the image, where $N$ and $i$ denote a number of objects in an image and object index respectively. Each object feature is converted to feature embedding by using a fully-connected (FC) layer. Each bounding box position $p_i$ for the $i$-th object is given by the eight dimensional position encoding:

$$
\begin{aligned}
( &\sin \frac{x_{c(i)}}{2}\pi, \sin \frac{y_{c(i)}}{2}\pi, \cos \frac{x_{c(i)}}{2}\pi, \cos \frac{y_{c(i)}}{2}\pi, \\
&\sin \frac{x_{s(i)}}{2}\pi, \sin \frac{y_{s(i)}}{2}\pi, \cos \frac{x_{s(i)}}{2}\pi, \cos \frac{y_{s(i)}}{2}\pi)
\end{aligned}
\tag{1}
$$

where $(x_{c(i)}, y_{c(i)})$ and $(x_{s(i)}, y_{s(i)})$ denote the center position and the region size (i.e., width and height) of the bounding box respectively, where the values are normalized by dividing by the longitude size of the image. The feature embeddings and the position encodings are concatenated and fed to Transformer blocks.

**Loss Function in Pre-training.** In pre-training, mask prediction is used. Outputs of Vision BERT are converted to object feature predictions $\widehat{f}_i$ by applying the FC layer. Following, 15% of object indices, denoted by $M$, are randomly selected and their features are masked. The cosine similarity for masked objects, between the predicted features and input features, is maximized by the loss function shown below.

$$
E_{\mathbf{f},\ i \in M}\left(1 - CosineSimilarity\left(\widehat{f}_i, f_i\right)\right)
\tag{2}
$$

## 3.2  Pre-training of Vision BERT

Vision BERT is pre-trained with the collection of three datasets: Conceptual Captions [15], SBU Captions [12] and COCO 2017 unlabeled images. The Conceptual Captions dataset contains 3.3M pairs of images and captions harvested from the web, and is widely used in pre-training for down-stream tasks that use image and text for input or output, such as VQA and text-image retrieval. Due to inaccessible URLs, only 2.8M data items were used for our pre-training. The SBU Captions dataset contains 1M pairs of images and captions collected from Flickr, which is also used in multi-modal pre-training along with Conceptual Captions. Due to inaccessible URLs, the number of pairs used for our pre-training is about 870k. The COCO 2017 unlabeled images dataset consists of 120k images. Annotations such as object bounding boxes or image captions are not provided, however the objects follow the same class distribution as in the labeled images of the COCO datasets.

To prepare the visual features and regional positions of objects as input to Visual BERT, we use Faster R-CNN with ResNet-101 backbone [6] pre-trained on the Visual Genome dataset [8]. More specifically, we use the Bottom-Up and Top-Down attention [1] method. The number of ROIs (i.e., objects) is limited to 36 and the dimension of the visual features is set to 2048. The positional encoding has eight dimensions, as described in Sect. 3.1. The number of Transformer blocks is set to four and each Transformer block has 1032 hidden units and 12 attention heads.

We train models on four Tesla V100 GPUs with a total batch size of 256 for 10 epochs. The Adam optimizer is used with learning rates of 2e−4. The weight decay is set to zero.

## 3.3  Evaluation of Performance on Multi-modal Task

First, Vision BERT is applied to VQA, a task which requires to answer a question posed in natural language about paired images. We extend the MCAN model by feeding the output of the pre-trained Vision BERT to MCAN. Then, the model is trained and evaluated on the VQA 2.0 dataset [2]. The model parameters of MCAN and training conditions are the same as described in [22] except that the batch size is 128. As shown in Table 1, our obtained model accuracy is 0.11% lower than the original MCAN on VQA 2.0 test-dev, which is contrary to our expectations.

**Table 1.** VQA accuracy by applying Vision BERT to MCAN.

| Model | Overall (test-dev) |
|---|---|
| MCAN [22] | 70.70 |
| MCAN + Vision BERT (ours) | 70.59 |

## 3.4   Analysis of Co-occurrence in Pre-trained Model

To understand whether the co-occurrence can be obtained by pre-training on image data, we introduce two types of Vision BERT pre-training, and evaluate the prediction accuracy. To avoid the influence of the Faster R-CNN object detection accuracy, we use the Visual Genome dataset with the ground truth of objects.

**Pre-training Configuration and Derivation of Prediction Accuracy.** In our evaluation, we compare two types of pre-training: masked object prediction and masked class prediction. Figure 2 shows an overview of the masked object prediction task for analyzing the co-occurrence in the pre-trained model. We extract a small dataset for analysis from the Visual Genome dataset. We select 78 COCO class labels except for two classes (i.e., "hair drier" and "sport ball") because they have only a few samples. For each selected class, we sample 40 pairs of an object matching that class and the image containing that object.

For Vision BERT with masked object prediction, we execute the following steps. First, we reconstruct the masked object feature as a prediction. Next, we retrieve the most similar top 20 objects from all sampled objects by cosine similarity. Finally, we calculate the accuracy to predict whether the retrieved objects belong to the same class as the masked object. In pre-training, Vision BERT learns to reconstruct masked object features. In prediction, a particular object feature of the target class (i.e., one of 78 classes) in a single image is masked and reconstructed.

For Vision BERT with masked class prediction, object classes are defined by regarding object names in the annotations as classes (82.8k classes, total). The output of Vision BERT is connected to the FC layer like in Fig. 2, then the softmax activation function is used to select one of the 78 classes. We pre-train the Vision BERT using all 82.8k class outputs of the FC layer. In prediction, the Vision BERT applies the argmax function to the 78 outputs of the FC layer that are ignored the other classes. Then we obtain object classification in the same model and evaluate the classification accuracy.

**Comparison Between Masked Object Prediction and Masked Class Prediction.** Table 2 shows the comparison of the prediction accuracy of Vision BERT using object feature prediction and object class prediction. The top 10 accurate classes by using object features are listed. When using masked object feature prediction, classes such as "giraffe", "zebra", and "elephant" can be predicted with high accuracy. This proved that, to some extent, the co-occurrence of these classes has been successfully learned. However, the overall accuracy of the 78 classes is much lower than for the case when using masked class prediction. This result implies that co-occurrence is improved by using the discrete class (or token), which is analogous to the language case.

**Comparison with Exclusion of Position.** To analyze whether the object positions are significant for learning co-occurrence, we pre-train Vision BERT

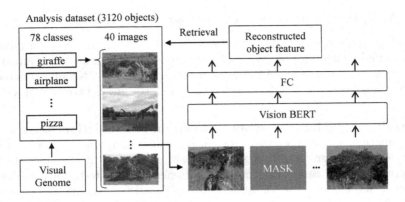

**Fig. 2.** Overview of masked object prediction task. The analysis dataset is extracted from the Visual Genome dataset and consists of pairs of an object matching the 78 class labels (40 objects, for each class; 3120 objects, total) and the image containing that object. The masked object prediction task takes the following steps: First, Vision BERT reconstructs the masked object feature. Then, we retrieve the most similar top 20 objects from all objects in the analysis dataset.

using only object class information (i.e., excluding bounding box positions). The manners of pre-training and the derivation of accuracy are the same as in Sect. 3.4.

Table 3 and 4 show the comparison of prediction accuracy with/without the bounding box position encoding. In these tables, the classes with the top 10 and bottom 10 accuracy differences are listed. As shown in these tables, the accuracy values without bounding box information are lower except for "toaster". Therefore, we find that the position information is essential to learn the co-occurrence of objects.

## 4 Proposed Model

Pre-training Vision BERT using object classes instead of object features achieves higher performance in mask prediction, as shown in Sect. 3. We assume one of the reasons for degraded accuracy is that object features are continuous, unlike symbolized word embeddings (i.e., used in language model BERT). Even if the object is the same, its object feature changes by posture, lighting, and so on. In order to overcome the problem, we propose SymVoL BERT, which combines Vision BERT and a list of object features. We name this list SymboList. SymboList converts continuous object features into discrete symbols by referencing a list with fixed number of elements. Then, via an attention mechanism, SymboList learns the representing state by attention from queries and keys and the co-occurrence by values. As shown in Fig. 3, the SymboList projects feature $\mathbf{y}_n^{l-1}$ from the $(l-1)$-th Transformer block to a query with a matrix $\mathbf{Q} = [\mathbf{Q}^1 \ldots \mathbf{Q}^H]^T$. To compute the similarity, the dot product of a query with all keys is taken.

**Table 2.** Prediction accuracy for object feature prediction and object class prediction. Classes with the top 10 prediction accuracy for object feature prediction are listed. "Overall" indicates the overall accuracy of all 78 classes.

| Class name | Object feature | Object class | Difference |
|---|---|---|---|
| Giraffe | 0.722 | 0.846 | −0.124 |
| Zebra | 0.722 | 0.760 | −0.038 |
| Elephant | 0.709 | 0.843 | −0.134 |
| Airplane | 0.502 | 0.853 | −0.351 |
| Horse | 0.472 | 0.724 | −0.252 |
| Pizza | 0.472 | 0.672 | −0.200 |
| Train | 0.464 | 0.698 | −0.234 |
| Motorcycle | 0.447 | 0.635 | −0.188 |
| Broccoli | 0.441 | 0.531 | −0.090 |
| Sheep | 0.426 | 0.705 | −0.279 |
| Overall | 0.212 | 0.534 | −0.323 |

The similarity is converted to attention via the softmax function. The attention weighted value for the $h$-th attention head is computed:

$$\mathbf{s}_n^{l,\,h} = \sum_{m=1}^{M} softmax\left(\frac{(\mathbf{Q}^h \mathbf{y}_n^{l-1}) \cdot \mathbf{k}_m^h}{\sqrt{d_k}}\right) \mathbf{v}_m^h \tag{3}$$

The feature $\mathbf{x}_n^l$ to $l$-th of the Transformer block are normalized after adding attention weighted value $\mathbf{s}_n^l = [\mathbf{s}_n^{l,\,1} \dots \mathbf{s}_n^{l,\,H}]$ to the feature $\mathbf{y}_n^{l-1}$:

$$\mathbf{x}_n^l = LayerNorm\left(\mathbf{y}_n^{l-1} + \mathbf{s}_n^l\right) \tag{4}$$

$M$ and $H$ indicate the number of SymboList elements and attention heads, $\mathbf{x}_n^l$ and $\mathbf{y}_n^{l-1}$ indicate the $l$-th layer input and the $(l-1)$-th layer output for the $n$-th object, and $\mathbf{k}_m = [\mathbf{k}_m^1 \dots \mathbf{k}_m^H]$ and $\mathbf{v}_m = [\mathbf{v}_m^1 \dots \mathbf{v}_m^H]$ denote element $m$ of keys and values, respectively. The projection matrix $\mathbf{Q}$, the keys $\{\mathbf{k}_1, \cdots, \mathbf{k}_M\}$ and the values $\{\mathbf{v}_1, \cdots, \mathbf{v}_M\}$ are learnable parameters in the SymboList.

## 5    Experiment on SymVoL BERT

SymVoL BERT replaces object features with symbols representing similar concepts, which enables it to learn co-occurrence relations. In this section, we present evaluation results for SymVoL BERT in a masked object prediction task and a VQA task (described in Sect. 3). We use same Vision BERT and pre-train SymVoL BERT on the mask prediction task with Conceptual Captions, SBU Captions and COCO 2017 unlabeled images (described in Sect. 3.2). SymboList has 100 elements of keys and values and 24 attention heads. By combining Vision BERT with SymboList, learnable parameters increase by 2.4 percents (from 55.1M to 56.4M).

**Table 3.** Prediction accuracy with/without bounding box position encoding. Classes with the top 10 difference of prediction accuracy are listed. "Overall" indicates the overall accuracy of all 78 classes.

| Class name | W/ bounding box | W/o bounding box | Difference |
|---|---|---|---|
| Microwave | 0.652 | 0.137 | 0.515 |
| Laptop | 0.530 | 0.137 | 0.393 |
| Traffic light | 0.542 | 0.153 | 0.390 |
| Couch | 0.579 | 0.200 | 0.379 |
| Mouse | 0.699 | 0.320 | 0.378 |
| Bench | 0.543 | 0.183 | 0.360 |
| Umbrella | 0.537 | 0.177 | 0.360 |
| Oven | 0.613 | 0.258 | 0.356 |
| Stop sign | 0.469 | 0.122 | 0.346 |
| Dining table | 0.399 | 0.067 | 0.333 |
| Overall | 0.534 | 0.322 | 0.213 |

## 5.1  Masked Object Prediction

We first examine the performance of SymVoL BERT on the masked object prediction task by comparing it with results obtains for Vision BERT. As reported in Table 5, SymVoL BERT improves the overall accuracy by 11.7% points (from 0.212 to 0.329). This result supports our hypothesis that SymboList facilitates learning of co-occurrences among objects in the image.

## 5.2  Experimental Results on VQA

We show experimental results on the VQA task for SymVoL BERT applied to MCAN and UNITER. In the case of MCAN, we use the same setting as detailed in Sect. 3.3. In the case of UNITER, following the approach described in [3], we first pre-trained on in-domain data (COCO + Visual Genome) for 200k steps with a batch size of 5120. We use AdamW optimizer with an initial learning rate of 1e−4 and a weight decay of 0.1. Then, VQA tasks was trained for 6k steps with a batch size of 5120 using AdamW optimizer with an initial learning rate of 8e−5 and a weight decay of 0.1. Table 6 shows the experimental results for applying SymboList and pre-training for the collection of three datasets. In the case of MCAN, even if there was no pre-training, SymVoL BERT performs better than Vision BERT (70.03 vs 69.82). The performance gain is further widened with pre-training (70.59 vs 71.02). In the case of UNITER, SymVoL BERT has little advantage as compared to Vision BERT when there is no image pre-training (72.64 vs 72.59). With image pre-training, SymVoL BERT performs better than Vision BERT (72.62 vs 72.70), but this improvement is less than that case of MCAN. We suppose pre-training with pairs of images and text can give more informative co-occurrence information, while pre-training with images only

**Table 4.** Prediction accuracy with/without bounding box position encoding. Classes with the bottom 10 difference of prediction accuracy are listed.

| Class name | W/ bounding box | W/o bounding box | Difference |
|---|---|---|---|
| Toaster | 0.113 | 0.117 | −0.004 |
| Dog | 0.440 | 0.396 | 0.044 |
| Toilet | 0.658 | 0.607 | 0.051 |
| Train | 0.698 | 0.645 | 0.052 |
| Zebra | 0.760 | 0.676 | 0.085 |
| Spoon | 0.248 | 0.155 | 0.093 |
| Snowboard | 0.451 | 0.358 | 0.093 |
| Bear | 0.397 | 0.302 | 0.094 |
| Handbag | 0.125 | 0.024 | 0.101 |
| Cow | 0.662 | 0.553 | 0.109 |

**Table 5.** Accuracy for masked object prediction.

| Model | Overall |
|---|---|
| Vision BERT | 0.212 |
| SymVoL BERT | 0.329 |

is weaker in comparison. Finally, our method outperforms the original model in both cases of MCAN and UNITER. Merely attaching self-attention like in Vision BERT does not achieve such performance. We argue that thanks to SymVol BERT, useful knowledge is learned from the co-occurrence of objects, which helps multi-modal learning as well.

**Table 6.** VQA accuracy of MCAN and UNITER, + Vision VERT, and + SymVol BERT.

| Model | Pre-trained | VQA 2.0 Overall (test-dev) | |
|---|---|---|---|
| | | MCAN [22] | UNITER [3] |
| Original | | 70.70 | 72.47 |
| + Vision BERT | | 69.82 | 72.59 |
| + Vision BERT | ✓ | 70.59 | 72.62 |
| + SymVoL BERT | | 70.03 | 72.64 |
| + SymVoL BERT | ✓ | **71.02** | **72.70** |

## 5.3   Ablation Study 1: Key Size of SymboList

Table 7 shows VQA accuracy of SymVoL BERT for different size of SymboList keys. When we fix the number of attention heads to 24 as in the previous sections,

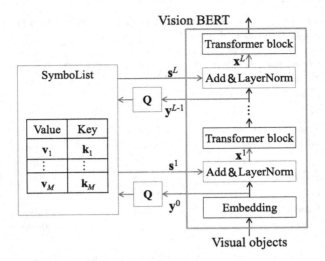

**Fig. 3.** Proposed SymVoL BERT model applying SymboList. SymboList is a list with fixed pairs of a key and a value representing co-occurrences of object features. SymVoL BERT references discrete object features in SymboList by using an attention mechanism.

VQA accuracy is the same as when the keys in SymboList are over 100. We leave for future work a detailed investigation of the relation between the concepts, attention heads and SymboList.

**Table 7.** VQA accuracy (test-dev) of SymVoL BERT with different SymboList size.

| SymboList keys | MCAN + SymVol BERT | UNITER + SymVol BERT |
|---|---|---|
| 25 | 70.93 | 72.49 |
| 100 | 71.02 | 72.70 |
| 400 | **71.05** | 72.69 |
| 800 | 71.00 | **72.73** |

## 5.4   Ablation Study 2: Effect of Dataset Size on Pre-training

As described in Sect. 3.2, about 3.8M sets of objects are used for pre-training on visual modality. To study how the amount of image data used for pre-training affects the accuracy on the VQA task, we test with reduced amounts of pre-training data. While decreasing the amount of pre-training data we increase the number of training epochs so that the total number of training iterations remains the same. As Table 8 shows, a greater amount of pre-training data results in higher VQA accuracy. Since the pre-training of SymVoL BERT is unsupervised,

(a) Attention head: 3, key element: 62          (b) Attention head: 23, key element: 19

**Fig. 4.** Examples of objects with high attention to SymboList. They show visual concepts in SymboList keys on the top Transformer block of Vision BERT.

larger amount of data are available without the need of time-consuming labeling. Therefore, it is possible to obtain further performance gains by increasing the amount of data used for pre-training.

**Table 8.** VQA accuracy (test-dev) for different amount of pre-training data.

| Data quantity | Pre-training epochs | MCAN + SymVol BERT | UNITER + SymVol BERT |
|---|---|---|---|
| 10% | 100 | 70.86 | 72.58 |
| 25% | 40 | 70.89 | 72.62 |
| 50% | 20 | 70.96 | 72.67 |
| 100% | 10 | **71.02** | **72.70** |

## 5.5   Analysis of SymboList

We analyze discretized features of objects in the pre-trained SymboList. Figure 4 shows the objects that cause high attention to a particular attention head of SymboList keys on the top Transformer block of Vision BERT. Objects in the left figure seem to show the concept 'head' of persons. Objects in the right figure seem to show the concept 'forehead or neck' of persons or animals, while they are entangled with the background involving the sky. For further symbolization, we will extend SymboList architecture to capture disentangled features.

## 6   Conclusion

We have proposed the pre-training of the image model inside a Transformer for vision and language, which boosts the performance in the multi-modal downstream task. From our preliminary experiments, we have obtained the intuition that while the current Transformer can learn co-occurrence relations well for discrete features, such as word embeddings, this is not the case for continuous features such as images. To capture the co-occurrences in the image domain, we designed a novel architecture where the query generated from the object feature references symbols in a list. We have experimentally validated that our model boosted the performance of VQA. In future work, we will apply our pre-trained image model to other down-stream tasks such as image retrieval and visual grounding.

# References

1. Anderson, P., et al.: Bottom-up and top-down attention for image captioning and visual question answering. In: Proceedings of the IEEE Conference on Computer Vision and Pattern Recognition (CVPR), pp. 6077–6086 (2018). https://doi.org/10.1109/CVPR.2018.00636
2. Antol, S., et al.: VQA: visual question answering. In: Proceedings of the International Conference on Computer Vision (ICCV), pp. 2425–2433 (2015). https://doi.org/10.1109/ICCV.2015.279
3. Chen, Y.-C., et al.: UNITER: UNiversal Image-TExt Representation learning. In: Vedaldi, A., Bischof, H., Brox, T., Frahm, J.-M. (eds.) ECCV 2020. LNCS, vol. 12375, pp. 104–120. Springer, Cham (2020). https://doi.org/10.1007/978-3-030-58577-8_7
4. Deng, J., Dong, W., Socher, R., Li, L.J., Li, K., Fei-Fei, L.: ImageNet: a large-scale hierarchical image database. In: Proceedings of the IEEE Conference on Computer Vision and Pattern Recognition (CVPR), pp. 248–255 (2009). https://doi.org/10.1109/CVPR.2009.5206848
5. Devlin, J., Chang, M.W., Lee, K., Toutanova, K.: BERT: pre-training of deep bidirectional transformers for language understanding. In: Proceedings of the Conference of the North American Chapter of the Association for Computational Linguistics: Human Language Technologies, pp. 4171–4186 (2019)
6. He, K., Zhang, X., Ren, S., Sun, J.: Deep residual learning for image recognition. In: Proceedings of the IEEE Conference on Computer Vision and Pattern Recognition (CVPR), pp. 770–778 (2016). https://doi.org/10.1109/CVPR.2016.90
7. Huang, G., Liu, Z., Van Der Maaten, L., Weinberger, K.Q.: Densely connected convolutional networks. In: Proceedings of the IEEE Conference on Computer Vision and Pattern Recognition (CVPR), pp. 2261–2269 (2017). https://doi.org/10.1109/CVPR.2017.243
8. Krishna, R.: Visual genome: connecting language and vision using crowdsourced dense image annotations. Int. J. Comput. Vis. **123**(1), 32–73 (2017). https://doi.org/10.1007/s11263-016-0981-7
9. Li, G., Duan, N., Fang, Y., Gong, M., Jiang, D., Zhou, M.: Unicoder-VL: a universal encoder for vision and language by cross-modal pre-training. In: Proceedings of the AAAI Conference on Artificial Intelligence (AAAI), pp. 11336–11344 (2020). https://doi.org/10.1609/aaai.v34i07.6795
10. Liu, Y., et al.: RoBERTa: a robustly optimized BERT pretraining approach. arXiv preprint arXiv:1907.11692 (2019)
11. Lu, J., Batra, D., Parikh, D., Lee, S.: ViLBERT: pretraining task-agnostic visiolinguistic representations for vision-and-language tasks. In: Advances in Neural Information Processing Systems, vol. 32, pp. 13–23 (2019)

12. Ordonez, V., Kulkarni, G., Berg, T.L.: Im2Text: describing images using 1 million captioned photographs. In: Advances in Neural Information Processing Systems, vol. 24, pp. 1143–1151 (2011)
13. Radford, A., Narasimhan, K., Salimans, T., Sutskever, I.: Improving language understanding by generative pre-training (2018)
14. Ren, S., He, K., Girshick, R., Sun, J.: Faster R-CNN: towards real-time object detection with region proposal networks. In: Advances in Neural Information Processing Systems, vol. 28, pp. 91–99 (2015)
15. Sharma, P., Ding, N., Goodman, S., Soricut, R.: Conceptual captions: a cleaned, hypernymed, image alt-text dataset for automatic image captioning. In: Proceedings of the 56th Annual Meeting of the Association for Computational Linguistics (ACL), pp. 2556–2565 (2018)
16. Simonyan, K., Zisserman, A.: Very deep convolutional networks for large-scale image recognition. In: Proceedings of the International Conference on Learning Representations (ICLR) (2015)
17. Su, W., et al.: VL-BERT: pre-training of generic visual-linguistic representations. In: Proceedings of the International Conference on Learning Representations (ICLR) (2020)
18. Tan, H., Bansal, M.: LXMERT: learning cross-modality encoder representations from transformers. In: Proceedings of the 2019 Conference on Empirical Methods in Natural Language Processing and the 9th International Joint Conference on Natural Language Processing (EMNLP-IJCNLP), pp. 5100–5111 (2019)
19. Vaswani, A., et al.: Attention is all you need. In: Advances in Neural Information Processing Systems, vol. 30, pp. 5998–6008 (2017)
20. Wu, Y., et al.: Google's neural machine translation system: bridging the gap between human and machine translation. arXiv preprint arXiv:1609.08144 (2016)
21. Yang, Z., Dai, Z., Yang, Y., Carbonell, J., Salakhutdinov, R.R., Le, Q.V.: XLNet: generalized autoregressive pretraining for language understanding. In: Advances in Neural Information Processing Systems, vol. 32, pp. 5753–5763 (2019)
22. Yu, Z., Yu, J., Cui, Y., Tao, D., Tian, Q.: Deep modular co-attention networks for visual question answering. In: Proceedings of the IEEE Conference on Computer Vision and Pattern Recognition (CVPR), pp. 6274–6283 (2019). https://doi.org/10.1109/CVPR.2019.00644

# Interactive Learning for Assisting Whole Slide Image Annotation

Ashish Menon[✉], Piyush Singh, P. K. Vinod, and C. V. Jawahar

International Institute of Information Technology, Hyderabad, India
{ashish.menon,piyush.singh}@research.iiit.ac.in,
{vinod.pk,jawahar}@iiit.ac.in

**Abstract.** Owing to the large dimensions of the histopathology whole slide images (WSI), visually searching for clinically significant regions (patches) is a tedious task for a medical expert. Sequential analysis of several such images further increases the workload resulting in poor diagnosis. A major impediment towards automating this task using deep learning models is that it requires a huge chunk of laboriously annotated data in the form of WSI patches. Our work suggests a novel CNN-based, expert feedback-driven interactive learning technique to mitigate this issue. The proposed method seeks to acquire labels of the most informative patches in small increments with multiple feedback rounds to maximize the throughput. It requires the expert to query a patch of interest from one slide and provide feedback to a set of unlabelled patches chosen using the proposed sampling strategy from a ranked list. The experiments on a large patient cohort of colorectal cancer histological patches (100K images with nine classes of tissues) show a significant reduction ($\approx$ 95%) in the amount of labelled data required to achieve state-of the-art results when compared to other existing interactive learning methods (35%–50%). We also demonstrate the utility of the proposed technique to assist a WSI tumor segmentation annotation task using the ICIAR breast cancer challenge dataset ($\approx$ 12.5K patches per slide). The proposed technique reduces the scanning and searching area to about 2% of the total area of WSI (by seeking labels of $\approx$ 250 informative patches only) and achieves segmentation outputs with 85% IOU. Thus our work helps avoid the routine procedure of exhaustive scanning and searching during annotation and diagnosis in general.

**Keywords:** Deep learning · Interactive learning · Whole slide image annotation · Histopathology · Sampling strategies · Expert-in-the-Loop

## 1 Introduction

Histopathology is considered the gold standard for cancer diagnosis [6,21]. A histopathologic Whole Slide Image (WSI) represents a digitized image of a tissue sample characterized by a large size of up to $10^9$ pixels at maximum resolution. A significant bottleneck in WSI diagnosis is locating certain classes of tissues

© Springer Nature Switzerland AG 2022
C. Wallraven et al. (Eds.): ACPR 2021, LNCS 13189, pp. 504–517, 2022.
https://doi.org/10.1007/978-3-031-02444-3_38

[1] or regions of prognostic importance within the WSI. Hence it becomes essential to automate the detection of such regions using deep learning models. The requirement of large amounts of annotated data for deep learning models and their robustness to adapt to different datasets is an issue of concern. Thus, a model that interactively learns with minimal expert involvement without having labelled data upfront would be an appropriate solution.

## 1.1  Why Patch Level Analysis of WSI?

Interactive learning methods proposed in the past had experts providing feedback as pen strokes on specialized devices or drawing regions of interest by carefully delineating tissue regions [14], marking nuclei and cellular level details [16] on the WSI. These methods needed continuous involvement of the pathologist in correcting the model's prediction to obtain nuclei and cellular level features used as input for an ML model. With the advancements in deep learning and its capability to obtain powerful representations, recent focus has shifted to analysing WSI tiles(patches). Recent approaches have shown the effectiveness of patch level analysis of a WSI to detect regions of prognostic values such as survival prediction [8,24], mutation prediction [5,13], tumor grading and staging [12,22]. Several medical imaging challenges have provided patch-level annotated datasets highlighting regions of biological relevance [2,3,18] to facilitate patch analysis using deep learning methods.

## 1.2  Related Work

Interactive learning methods for patch labelling include active learning-based techniques to acquire the most informative samples for training, thereby reducing the need for large amounts of annotated data. One such technique selects the most informative samples from a relatively smaller cohort of patients with 5000 patches [10] using a variational drop-out-based uncertainty sampling [20]. At each step 160 most informative images were selected to be reviewed by the expert. This method achieved a scale reduction of 45% in the training set. A novel method of identifying the most informative patches was proposed [23] using conditional random fields in a spatially adaptive manner. This method showed a scale reduction in the training set by 38.0%. These approaches often required large batches of patches to be reviewed, which can be an overhead to the expert and the overall workflow. A deep active learning work for biomedical image segmentation [25] proposed a framework combining fully convolutional networks and active learning to determine the most representative and uncertain areas for annotation. They obtained state-of-the-art segmentation performance using only 50% of training data for gland segmentation in Colon histology images, with gland segmented image patches of a WSI as ground truth. An attention gated FCN (ag-FCN) and distribution-discrepancy based active learning algorithm [11] was demonstrated for gland segmentation. This work achieved state-of-the-art results using 50% training data and beat the state-of-the-art using full training data. DeepScribble [4] proposed an interactive segmentation method that corrects the segmented boundaries from deep neural networks with user interactions. This method used two networks, one trained with annotated WSI patches generated an initial segmentation output. While the other refines the segmentation iteratively based on user inputs.

### 1.3    Our Contribution

Most of the previously mentioned interactive learning have used uncertainty based criteria to select the most informative samples. These methods have reported using patches or have used carefully delineated tumorous subregions of a WSI (gland segmentation). We select the most informative samples using distance metric learning combined with a classifier approach in our proposed technique. We also demonstrate the utility of our method in helping annotation (tumor segmentation) of an unannotated WSI. The key contributions of the proposed technique include

(i) Put forward a novel method of sampling from a ranked list of patches to pick the most informative samples to be labelled, resulting in a significant scale reduction in the training set (95%–97%) to achieve state-of-the-art results.

(ii) Demonstrate the utility of an ImageNet pre-trained model (last few layers trainable) without any architectural modification for this task, thereby resulting in quick and memory-efficient training

(iii) Assisting annotation of large WSI for a segmentation task by obtaining segmentation mask predictions with minimal expert efforts

(iv) Our method can also give segmentation predictions on multiple WSI using a single slide understudy without going through all the slides.

## 2    Proposed Interactive Learning Technique

Our method is developed by assuming that there is a database of patches of undiagnosed or unseen slides. An expert is ready to search for clinically important patches of one such slide and provide feedback to a set of patches chosen by a deep learning model. The proposed strategy of sampling from a ranked list is used to select these patches. Based on the expert requirement, the patches chosen for feedback could be the patches from the same slide or patches from multiple slides. The feedback input can either be relevant/irrelevant or explicit class labels of the patches and thus avoids complex expert interactions at the cellular and nuclei level details as seen in the previous interactive learning strategies [16].

Inspired by the idea of [19], our work demonstrates the utility of pre-trained CNNs for this task. When finetuned with the proposed sampling strategy, the last few layers of an ImageNet pre-trained model representation generalize well on unseen data within a minimal number of expert feedback rounds (less labelled data). The major steps of the proposed work is explained in the following subsections, before which we will introduce the following frequently used terms.

**Retrieval**: nearest neighbour retrieval using the deep learning representations with images ranked in the increasing order of their distance from the query image in the higher dimensional space. **Session**: for every query, there is a session that consists of $r$ rounds of review. **Review**: the step where we obtain relevance feedback (0/1) or explicit class labels by presenting to the expert a set of $K$ samples. **Sampling from ranked list**: to obtain the most informative samples to be reviewed at each review step. **Finetuning**: the trainable layers of the ImageNet pre-trained ResNet-18 model (layer4.1) is finetuned with the samples reviewed. Two models are trained, one for retrieval and the other for classification using a triplet loss with hard negative mining and cross-entropy loss respectively (Fig. 1).

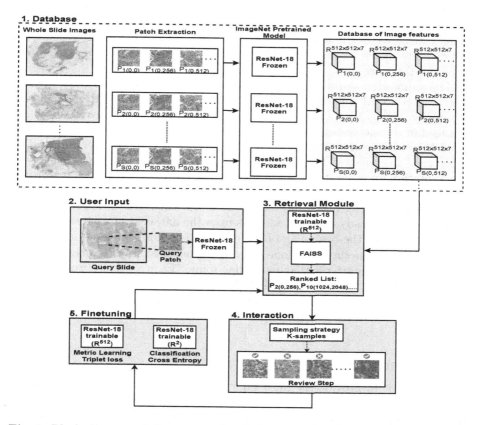

**Fig. 1.** Block diagram of the proposed technique. **1. Database:** The unannotated WSI are stored in the form of features ($R^{(512 \times 512 \times 7)}$) extracted from an ImageNet pretrained ResNet-18. **2. User Input:** Highlights a rectangular patch of interest on the WSI as the input. **3. Retrieval Module:** Nearest neighbour retrieval powered by FAISS [7]. **4. Interaction:** The expert provides feedback either as relevant/irrelevant or as explicit class label. Sampling from the ranked list ensures that the feedback is provided for the most informative samples. **5. Finetuning:** ResNet18 used as a feature extractor and as classifier are trained using the samples reviewed.

## 2.1  Assisting WSI Annotation

In this paper, we perform the task of annotating tumorous regions of multiple WSIs as a use case of the proposed interactive learning technique. The underlying assumption is that the group of patches deemed relevant to the query patch or provided with a specific class label by the expert are closely clustered in a higher-dimensional space. We pose the annotation task to be equivalent to a WSI patch classification using a deep learning model. The goal is to achieve a satisfactory annotation with as few feedback sessions as possible. Towards this, we propose a novel sampling strategy by sampling from a ranked list of patches from the search database, ranked based on the Euclidean distance to the query in a higher dimensional space learnt by another deep learning model using a distance metric learning approach. Both models used for classification and distance metric learning are trained using the same set of reviewed samples across feedback sessions.

The annotation starts by querying a patch of interest from the WSI. Nearest neighbour retrieval is performed using an ImageNet pre-trained ResNet-18 representation ($R^{512}$) to obtain a ranked list of patches from the search database arranged in the increasing order of their distance to the query patch. This is followed by sampling $K$ patches from the ranked list, review and finetuning. The same steps are repeated for the subsequent rounds using the finetuned model representation and a refined query for retrieval. Query refinement is performed by assuming that the original query lies far from the cluster of relevant images in the feature space [19]. It is important to note that the retrieval is performed by leaving out the already reviewed samples from the database at each step. A new query would mark the beginning of the next session, and the same procedure is carried forward. Finetuning is done at every round/session using the data accumulated from the start till that particular round. Each session is restricted to '$r$' rounds of review; the model presents $K$ samples to be reviewed by the expert for every round. Thus the expert ends up having to review $r \times K$ images per query. At the end of $N$ sessions, we would have $N \times r \times K$ reviewed images with true labels.

## 2.2  Sampling Strategy

It is important to provide the most informative samples (samples that are not obvious for the model) for review during the interactive feedback. A strategy of sampling from a ranked list is proposed to pick such samples at every review step. We experiment on the following sampling strategies: **random, top-K** and **front-mid-end** sampling to pick K samples from the front middle and the end of the ranked list. The **Closest Negative Farthest Positive (CNFP)** sampling uses predictions of a classifier trained on the samples reviewed till $(k-1)^{th}$ step, to pick the $K/2$ closest negatives and $K/2$ farthest positives from the ranked list. Finally, we also investigate a **hybrid** scheme, which uses the combination of CNFP and front-mid-end. **Entropy-based** sampling, which is a standard uncertainty measure for sampling by using the entropy of classifier prediction and choosing the samples with the highest entropy for review.

**Algorithm 1:** Pseudocode for retrieval and annotation using the proposed interactive learning technique. **S**:Images of Search database, **Q**:Images of Query database, **M**:Number of images in the search database, **N**:Number of images in the query database, $\mathbf{f_{ret}}$:Pre-trained deep learning model used for retrieval, $\mathbf{f_{cl}}$:Pre-trained deep learning model used for classification **r**:Number of feedback rounds/steps, **K**:Number of images to be reviewed per step, $\hat{\mathbf{f}}$:model that has learnt the new feature space

---

**Input**: Query image $\mathbf{Q_{sample}}$ , deep learning models $\mathbf{f_{ret}}, \mathbf{f_{cl}}$, number of feedback rounds $\mathbf{r}$, number of images to be reviewed per step $\mathbf{K}$

**Output**: $Y = \{y_i\}_{i=1}^{M}$ ; // labels for image in the database

for $Q_{sample}$ in $Q$ do

   $q = f_{ret}(Q_{sample}), s = f_{ret}(S)$ ; // embedding computation ($R^{512}$)

   $\hat{S} = retrieval(q, s)$ ; // ranked list of images from search database

   for $i \leftarrow 1$ to $r$ do

      $\hat{S}_K = SAMPLE(\hat{S}, K)$

      $S_{0i}$ , $S_{1i} = feedback(\hat{S}_K)$

      $S_0.append(S_{0i})$ , $S_1.append(S_{1i})$

      $\hat{f}_{ret} \leftarrow train(f_{ret}, S_0, S_1, Q)$

      $\hat{f}_{cl} \leftarrow train(f_{cl}, S_0, S_1, Q)$

      $S \leftarrow \{S\} - \{\hat{S}_K\}; q \leftarrow \hat{f}_{ret}(Q); q \leftarrow mean(q, \hat{f}_{ret}(S_{1i}))$

      $\hat{S} = retrieval(q, \hat{f}_{ret}(S))$

   end

end

if $annotation$ then

   $\hat{Y} = \hat{f}_{cl}(S)$ ; // Prediction step using classifier

---

**Algorithm 2:** Sampling strategy. $S$ represents unannotated set of Images, $s$ represents the sampling strategy, $K$ represents number of images to sample, $M$ indicates number of images in the list

---

**Input**: Set of Images $S$ , Sampling strategy $s$, number of samples $K$, number of images in the list $M$

**Output**: $S_K$ ; // K number of samples

if $s == top - k$ then

   $S_K \leftarrow \{S_i\}_{i=1}^{K}$

if $s == front - mid - end$ then

   $N_{front} = \lceil M/3 \rceil; N_{end} = \lfloor M/3 \rfloor; N_{mid} = M - N_{front} - N_{end}$

   $S_K \leftarrow \{S_i\}_{i=1}^{N_{front}} \cup \{S_i\}_{i=M/2-N_{mid}/2}^{M/2+N_{mid}/2} \cup \{S_i\}_{i=M-N_{end}}^{M}$

if $s == CNFP$ then

   $S' \leftarrow S[:: -1]$ ; // Reversed ranked list

   $S_1 \leftarrow \{S_i' \ni f_{cl}(S_i') == 1\}_{i=1}^{M}, S_0 \leftarrow \{S_i \ni f_{cl}(S_i) == 0\}_{i=1}^{M}$

   $S_k \leftarrow \{S_{1i}\}_{i=1}^{i=K/2} \cup \{S_{0i}\}_{i=1}^{i=K/2}$

## 3    Implementation

### 3.1    Dataset and Database Formation

To validate and demonstrate our work, we use two publicly available datasets.

**CRC Dataset** [9]: Consists of 100,000 non overlapping image patches from H&E stained slides of human colorectal cancer (CRC). All images are 224 × 224 pixels. It consists of the following tissue classes cancer-associated stroma **STR**, colorectal adenocarcinoma epithelium **TUM**, adipose **ADI**, mucus **MUC**, smooth muscle **MUS**, debris **DEB**, lymphocytes **LYM**, background **BACK**, normal colon mucosa **NORM**. These were extracted from 86 cancer tissue slides. The prognostic importance of some of these tissues was demonstrated in predicting the overall survival prediction of colorectal cancer patients [8]. Due to the availability of ground truth patch labels, a pseudo feedback [19] technique was used to automate the manual feedback. We created a query database of 10 random patches from each class to simulate querying a patch of interest. The remaining patches formed the search database (Table 1).

**Table 1.** The dataset distribution of the CRC dataset.

| Class labels | MUC | MUS | NORM | STR | TUM | ADI | BACK | DEB | LYM |
|---|---|---|---|---|---|---|---|---|---|
| Search DB | 8886 | 13526 | 8753 | 10436 | 14307 | 10397 | 10556 | 11502 | 11547 |
| Held out test set | 1035 | 592 | 741 | 421 | 1233 | 1338 | 847 | 339 | 634 |
| Query DB | 10 | 10 | 10 | 10 | 10 | 10 | 10 | 10 | 10 |

**ICIAR BACH Challenge Dataset** [18]: is used to demonstrate the application of the proposed technique towards slide annotation. ICIAR dataset is composed of H&E stained Breast cancer histology microscopy and WSI. It provides annotations of pixel coordinates belonging to 4 different classes **normal, benign, invasive, insitu** for 10 WSIs. We group the insitu, invasive and benign classes as tumor class. Patches of 256 × 256 were extracted from these WSI using a sliding window approach with no overlap at the maximum magnification resolution. A patch was labelled as tumor if at least 50% of it consisted of the annotated pixels. Noisy and background patches are filtered out [24] during the patch extraction process. Patches with the fractal structure were rejected by considering only those patches with at least ten connected components present in their binarized format. During annotation of a given slide, 10 random tumor patches from it formed the query database, and the remaining patches of the slide formed the search database. The search database can contain patches of one slide or could be expanded to contain patches of multiple slides based on the use case. This step expands the annotation or finds tumorous patches across multiple slides using a single slide under study.

## 3.2   Classification and Metric Learning

An ImageNet pre-trained ResNet-18 was used as the base model. We first save the image features obtained from the frozen layers (upto layer4.0, $R^{512 \times 7 \times 7}$), which are fed as input to the respective trainable modules during training. So the database consists of images features instead of images. Benefits of this setup include quick and memory efficient training, avoid overfitting, and non-linearity introduced during training by layer 4.1. The images were normalized using the mean and standard deviation calculated across all the RGB channels on the entire dataset before obtaining the features.

The trainable module for the metric learning consisted of layer4.1 and the global average pooling (GAP) layer of ResNet-18. Thus the metric learning output would be an $R^{512}$ embedding. The trainable module for the classification step consisted of layer4.1, Global Average pooling layer (GAP), followed by the fully connected layer with $N$ neurons as output. Depending on the type of feedback, $N$ could vary from 2 to the number of classes under analysis. Thus the classifier output would be an $R^N$ embedding.

Every session consists of 5 rounds of review, with 5 images reviewed per round for the ICIAR dataset annotation and 10 images reviewed per round for the CRC dataset. If the type of feedback is relevant/irrelevant, two sets of images are maintained, a relevant set and an irrelevant set. Relevant set consists of those reviewed patches that share the same label as the queried patch, and the irrelevant set consists of patches otherwise. We used 50 training epochs and an Adam optimizer with a learning rate of 0.0001 for the metric learning and the classification steps. The metric learning was performed using triplet loss with hard triplet mining following the implementation suggested in [15] with the margin for triplet loss set to 0.2. The classifier was trained using the cross-entropy loss function. FAISS [7] was used for the nearest neighbour retrieval using Euclidean distance.

# 4   Results and Discussion

## 4.1   Evaluation on CRC Dataset

We validate the efficacy of the proposed approach on a held-out test set of 7180 patches from slides belonging to 50 patients that had no overlap with patients of the training set. Figure 2 indicates that the proposed interactive learning technique can achieve results for classification and retrieval in par with [17] with fewer labelled data. This was obtained using a standard ImageNet pre-trained ResNet-18 (with weights frozen up to layer4.1) for finetuning without additional architectural modification. Among all the proposed sampling strategies, the CNFP sampling strategy (Ref. 2.2) gives the best result. The state-of-the-art performance was obtained within 80 sessions which evaluates to an average of requiring 10 query images from each class and providing feedback to 4000 patches ($\approx 4.34\%$ of the labelled samples per class). The proposed CNFP sampling technique also performs better than the standard entropy-based sampling

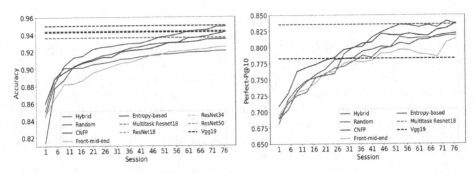

**Fig. 2. Held out test set**: performance of proposed interactive learning technique across feedback sessions on the heldout test set of the CRC dataset [9] in comparison to baseline methods [17] that were trained using all the annotated data. The image on the left is the accuracy, the image on the right is the macro averaged perfect P@10 score.

technique, a commonly used sampling strategy in the active learning literature. This demonstrates the efficiency and relevance of the proposed interactive learning over learning from a fully annotated dataset available upfront.

### 4.2 Evaluation on ICIAR Dataset

The segmentation masks are obtained from the patch label predictions of the classifier by assigning the colour code (green represents tumor and black represents normal patch). Patch locations lost during the patch extraction process are assigned black by default. Figure 3 indicates the performance of the proposed technique in the segmentation annotation task.

We notice that the annotation performance using CNFP sampling strategy (Ref. 2.2) increases with prolonged interaction, whereas the performance

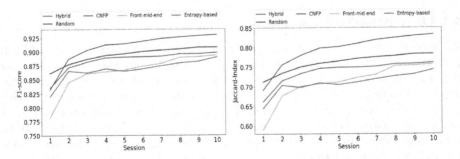

**Fig. 3. Annotation performance**: across feedback sessions using different sampling strategies on the ICIAR dataset. The image on the left is the slide wise macro averaged patch classification F1 score and the image on the right is the slide wise macro averaged Jaccard index score. (Color figure online)

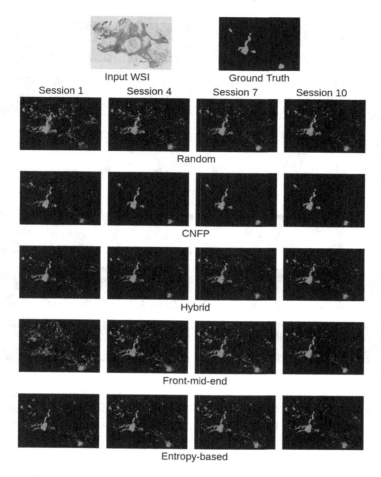

Fig. 4. **Annotation** output of a sample slide across feedback sessions using different sampling strategies on the ICIAR challenge dataset. The CNFP sampling strategy performs the best with segmentation output being less noisy and closest to the groundtruth

using other sampling strategies saturates. The CNFP sampling strategy (Ref. 2.2) achieves an average F1 score of 0.94 and an average Jaccard index score (represents the amount of overlap with the ground truth segmentation mask) of 0.85 within 10 sessions per slide. This includes providing 10 random tumor query patches and reviewing 250 patches ($\approx$ 2% of total patches per slide). It is important to note that though the entropy-based sampling strategy shows a similar trend, its performance is poor during the initial sessions. Figure 4 shows the segmentation output of a sample slide using the proposed interactive

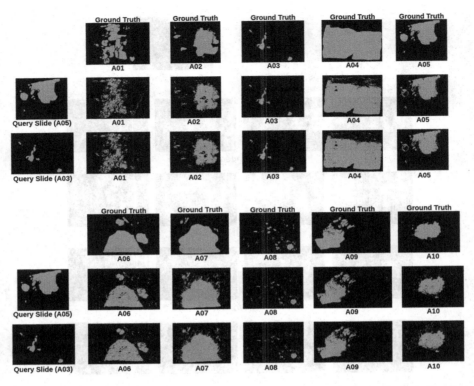

**Fig. 5. Inter slide annotation**: annotation results across slides with a single slide under review using the CNFP sampling strategy. The segmentation output results show that the proposed method is robust to the queried slide and is able to find anomalous patterns existing across multiple slides

learning technique. The improvement of segmented output using different sampling strategies over feedback sessions is shown. We can observe that the CNFP sampling strategy (Ref. 2.2) performs better than the other sampling strategies by obtaining a segmentation output with a Jaccard index of ($\approx 0.98$) at the end of 10 sessions.

Figure 5 shows the inter slide annotation results. Here the patches sampled for feedback belong to a slide different from the one understudy. The technique can be useful to help annotate multiple slides concurrently using patches queried from one slide. The segmentation results shown here are the results across 10 feedback sessions. From a diagnostic viewpoint, this could be helpful to search across multiple slides for anomalous patterns present in a slide that was already diagnosed.

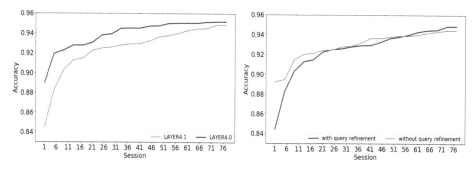

**Fig. 6. Ablation studies**: showing the effect of layers used for finetuning the model and query refinement on the final results using the CRC dataset [9]

## 4.3   Ablation Studies

We analysed two aspects for the ablation purpose on the final results. The layers used for finetuning and the effect of query refinement. Figure 6 shows the results of the ablation study performed on the CRC dataset [9].

For the finetuning experiment, we compared the performance obtained by finetuning layer4.0 of ResNet-18 and finetuning layer4.1 of ResNet-18. The model finetuned from layer4.0 reached the desired accuracy faster (20 sessions earlier) than the one finetuned from layer4.1. However, the number of trainable parameters resulting in finetuning from layer4.0 is about 78% more than layer4.1. This would increase both the time duration between every feedback session and memory for training. Hence we chose layer4.1 by prioritising the efficiency and time over the number of feedback sessions taken to achieve the desired accuracy.

We also analysed the effect of query refinement on the final results. It was observed that experiments without query refinement initially had good accuracy, but it saturates within 50 feedback sessions. The experiments performed using query refinement had a low initial accuracy but continued to increase over feedback sessions.

## 5   Conclusion

We propose expert feedback-driven interactive learning, which effectively reduces the requirement of large amounts of patch-level annotated images for a deep-learning-based WSI analysis. Our technique also assists WSI tumor(anomalous) region annotations and WSI diagnosis with minimal expert involvement. The proposed technique requires multiple rounds of expert feedback on informative patches selected using a novel method of sampling from a ranked list of patches. Experimentation results show that the proposed technique required only 5% of the total annotated patches to achieve state-of-the-art results. Experimentation on WSI annotation shows that the proposed technique reduces the expert efforts by requiring feedback of only 250 patches which is about 2% of total patches per slide, to obtain segmentation outputs with 85% IOU. Inter slide annotation results also show that the proposed technique can annotate anomalous regions across multiple slides using a single slide under review. These annotated data can further be refined and used to build AI models aimed at being used as potential prognostic and diagnostic tools.

**Acknowledgements.** We thank IHub-Data, International Institute of Information and Technology, Hyderabad for financial support.

# References

1. Aeffner, F., et al.: Commentary: roles for pathologists in a high-throughput image analysis team. Toxicologic Pathol. **44**(6), 825–34 (2016)
2. Bándi, P., et al.: From detection of individual metastases to classification of Lymph node status at the patient level: The CAMELYON17 challenge. IEEE Trans. Med. Imaging **38**, 550–560 (2019)
3. Bejnordi, B.E., et al.: Diagnostic assessment of deep learning algorithms for detection of Lymph node metastases in women with Breast Cancer. JAMA **318**, 2199–2210 (2017)
4. Cho, S., et al.: DeepScribble: interactive pathology image segmentation using deep neural networks with scribbles. In: 2021 IEEE 18th International Symposium on Biomedical Imaging (ISBI), pp. 761–765 (2021)
5. Coudray, N., et al.: Classification and mutation prediction from non-small cell lung cancer histopathology images using deep learning. Nat. Med. **24**(10), 1559–1567 (2018)
6. Jeelani, S., et al.: Histopathological examination of nail clippings using PAS staining (HPE-PAS): gold standard in diagnosis of Onychomycosis. Mycoses **58**, 27–32 (2015)
7. Johnson, J., Douze, M., Jégou, H.: Billion-scale similarity search with GPUs. arXiv preprint arXiv:1702.08734 (2017)
8. Kather, J.N., et al.: Predicting survival from colorectal cancer histology slides using deep learning: a retrospective multicenter study. PLoS Med. **16**(1), e1002730 (2019)
9. Kather, J.N., Halama, N., Marx, A.: 100,000 histological images of human colorectal cancer and healthy tissue. Version v0.1, April 2018. https://doi.org/10.5281/zenodo.1214456
10. Kather, D.J.N., et al.: Collection of textures in colorectal cancer histology, May 2016. https://doi.org/10.5281/zenodo.53169
11. Li, H., Yin, Z.: Attention, suggestion and annotation: a deep active learning framework for biomedical image segmentation. In: Martel, A.L., et al. (eds.) MICCAI 2020. LNCS, vol. 12261, pp. 3–13. Springer, Cham (2020). https://doi.org/10.1007/978-3-030-59710-8_1
12. Li, W., et al.: Path R-CNN for prostate cancer diagnosis and Gleason grading of histological images. IEEE Trans. Med. Imaging **38**, 945–954 (2019)
13. Liao, H., et al.: Deep learning-based classification and mutation prediction from histopathological images of hepatocellular carcinoma. Clin. Transl. Med. **10**, e102 (2020)
14. Lindvall, M., et al.: TissueWand, a rapid histopathology annotation tool. J. Pathol. Inform. **11**, 27 (2020)

15. Musgrave, K., Belongie, S., Lim, S.-N.: PyTorch metric learning. arXiv: 2008.09164 [cs.CV] (2020)
16. Nalisnik, M., et al.: Interactive phenotyping of large-scale histology imaging data with HistomicsML. Sci. Rep. **7**, 14588 (2017)
17. Peng, T., Boxberg, M., Weichert, W., Navab, N., Marr, C.: Multi-task learning of a deep K-nearest neighbour network for histopathological image classification and retrieval. In: Shen, D., et al. (eds.) MICCAI 2019. LNCS, vol. 11764, pp. 676–684. Springer, Cham (2019). https://doi.org/10.1007/978-3-030-32239-7_75
18. Polónia, A., Eloy, C., Aguiar, P.: BACH dataset: grand challenge on breast cancer histology images. Med. Image Anal. **56**, 122–139 (2019). https://doi.org/10.5281/zenodo.3632035
19. Putzu, L., Piras, L., Giacinto, G.: Convolutional neural networks for relevance feedback in content based image retrieval. Multimedia Tools Appl. **79**, 26995–27021 (2020)
20. Raczkowski, Ł, et al.: ARA: accurate, reliable and active histopathological image classification framework with Bayesian deep learning. Sci. Rep. **9**, 14347 (2019)
21. Sardanelli, F., et al.: Sensitivity of MRI versus mammography for detecting foci of multifocal, multicentric breast cancer in Fatty and dense breasts using the whole-breast pathologic examination as a gold standard. AJR Am J. Roentgenol. **183**(4), 1149–57 (2004)
22. Shaban, M., et al.: Context-aware convolutional neural network for grading of colorectal cancer histology images. IEEE Trans. Med. Imaging **39**, 2395–2405 (2020)
23. Shen, Y., Ke, J.: Representative region based active learning for histological classification of colorectal cancer. In: 2021 IEEE 18th International Symposium on Biomedical Imaging (ISBI), pp. 1730–1733 (2021)
24. Tabibu, S., Vinod, P.K., Jawahar, C.: Pan-Renal Cell Carcinoma classification and survival prediction from histopathology images using deep learning. Sci. Rep. **9**, 10509 (2019)
25. Yang, L., Zhang, Y., Chen, J., Zhang, S., Chen, D.Z.: Suggestive annotation: a deep active learning framework for biomedical image segmentation. In: Descoteaux, M., Maier-Hein, L., Franz, A., Jannin, P., Collins, D.L., Duchesne, S. (eds.) MICCAI 2017. LNCS, vol. 10435, pp. 399–407. Springer, Cham (2017). https://doi.org/10.1007/978-3-319-66179-7_46

# Label Quality in AffectNet: Results of Crowd-Based Re-annotation

Doo Yon Kim[1] and Christian Wallraven[2(✉)]

[1] Department of Artificial Intelligence, Korea University, Seoul, Korea
kdoodoo@korea.ac.kr
[2] Department of Artificial Intelligence and Department of Brain and Cognitive
Engineering, Korea University, Seoul, Korea
wallraven@korea.ac.kr

**Abstract.** AffectNet is one of the most popular resources for facial expression recognition (FER) on relatively unconstrained in-the-wild images. Given that images were annotated by only one annotator with limited consistency checks on the data, however, label quality and consistency may be limited. Here, we take a similar approach to a study that re-labeled another, smaller dataset (FER2013) with crowd-based annotations, and report results from a re-labeling and re-annotation of a subset of difficult AffectNet faces with 13 people on both expression label, and valence and arousal ratings. Our results show that human labels overall have medium to good consistency, whereas human ratings especially for valence are in excellent agreement. Importantly, however, crowd-based labels are significantly shifting towards neutral and happy categories and crowd-based affective ratings form a consistent pattern different from the original ratings. ResNets fully trained on the original AffectNet dataset do not predict human voting patterns, but when weakly-trained do so much better, particularly for valence. Our results have important ramifications for label quality in affective computing.

**Keywords:** Facial expression recognition · Crowd annotation · AffectNet · Affective computing

## 1 Introduction

Despite recent advances in facial expression recognition (FER) from images, FER on so-called in-the-wild images taken in less constrained contexts still has much lower performance when compared with FER on controlled datasets. Recent performance on one of the most popular in-the-wild datasets - AffectNet [15] - is "only" around 61% [11]. This performance falls far short of performance levels on controlled datasets, such as the CK+ dataset [1] with 99.69% [2] and other in-the-wild datasets, such as the (smaller) FER+ dataset [4] with 89.75% [5]. For a more in-depth review of the current state-of-the-art in deep-learning-based FER, see [3,9,12,13,16].

© Springer Nature Switzerland AG 2022
C. Wallraven et al. (Eds.): ACPR 2021, LNCS 13189, pp. 518–531, 2022.
https://doi.org/10.1007/978-3-031-02444-3_39

Interestingly, for FER+, an earlier version that was annotated by the original dataset creators [10] called FER2013, had a much lower recognition baseline of 70.22%. Whereas the FER2013 dataset was annotated by only one individual, a follow-up study [4] re-labeled the data based on crowd annotation and showed that the resulting maximum vote label also provided a better computational recognition performance.

Since label quality directly determines performance outcomes, providing good and consistent labels has been a recent focus in the machine learning field [6]. Performance increases can not only come from more advanced architectures, but much more "trivially", from annotating the data with clean, correct labels. Issues of label quality have, for example, been highlighted in the recent work by [19]—the authors showed that there is an average of 3.4% errors in several of the surveyed datasets, and that by omitting 6% of correctly labeled images, a smaller ResNet18 can perform better than a larger ResNet50.

Given the relatively lower levels of performance on AffectNet, here we wanted to revisit this dataset with a similar approach to that taken to create FER+. As an example of the potential issues with AffectNet, see Fig. 1, which shows four examples of images from AffectNet that seem to have problematic labels. Given the large size of AffectNet, we here first report results of a pilot test that uses a subset of (difficult-to-recognize) images of the different expression categories of AffectNet. We re-labeled these both in terms of expression label and also in terms of affective rating of valence and arousal by 13 naive annotators. We compare the consistency of annotators and also how well the images fit to the predictions made by a deep-learning model naively trained on the original AffectNet before and after crowd-relabeling.

**Fig. 1.** Four images of AffectNet (originally labeled as anger, surprise, happy, and sad (from left)) illustrating the challenges in uniquely labeling expressions.

## 2   Experiment

Originally, AffectNet is composed of 11 different categories that also include labels such as "No face", for example. Here, we solely focused on the seven emotional expressions plus the neutral category, resulting in: Neutral, Happy, Sad, Disgust, Surprise, Contempt, Fear, and Anger as labels. From each expression, 100 potentially-confusing images were selected by pre-screening the original images, resulting in a total of 800 images for re-annotation.

## 2.1  ResNet50

As our deep neural network (DNN) backbone, we used a standard, ImageNet pre-trained ResNet-50, which is one of the most widely used standard architectures in image classification tasks [20]. The architecture is based on 50 blocks of convolutional filters of size 3 × 3 with residual connections that allow the optimizer to skip a whole convolutional layer, thereby increasing the effectiveness of the total network.

Implementation details for training the ResNet50 architecture on AffectNet were as follows: for augmentation, we added intensity normalization of the color data into 0 to 1, as well as clockwise and anti-clockwise rotations of up to 10 degrees, affine shearing up to 0.1, as well as horizontal flips. Class weights (given the imbalance in label categories) were used for a weighted cross-entropy loss that was optimized with Adam at an initial learning rate of 0.0001.

This model was trained with 256 × 256px color images of the AffectNet training set of 287,561 images for 50 epochs and a batch size of 64, after which it reached a validation accuracy of 53.15% (ResNet50 50 epoch) - its best validation accuracy throughout the run, however, was 59.25% (ResNet50 Best), which is only less than two percent worse than the state-of-the-art in AffectNet on eight classes with a much more involved architecture [11]. To look at the early performance of this model, we also saved its snapshot after the first epoch (ResNet50 1 epoch).

Finally, we set up another training scheme that would perhaps be more akin to human learning, in which one epoch used only 512 randomly-chosen images, but we trained for much longer (1000 epochs). Interestingly, this very weakly-trained model achieved also a reasonable accuracy of around 53.5%. All models are compared in Table 1.

For valence and arousal, we followed the same model structure and created two regression models for each rating based on mean squared error (MSE) loss. These models were trained for 10 epochs (again, relatively weakly-trained), and resulted in comparable validation losses of 0.0177 (valence) and 0.0167 (arousal).

**Table 1.** Parameters and validation performance for our ResNet50 architectures.

| Model | Epoch | Pre-trained | Steps per epoch | Val accuracy/Loss |
|---|---|---|---|---|
| ResNet50 50Epoch | 50 | ImageNet | 287,651/batch size | 0.5315 |
| ResNet50 Best | 50 | ImageNet | 287,651/batch size | 0.5925 |
| ResNet50 1Epoch | 1 | ImageNet | 287,651/batch size | 0.4972 |
| ResNet50 8Step | 1000 | ImageNet | 8 | 0.5353 |
| ResNet50 Valence | 10 | ImageNet | 287,651/batch size | 0.0177 |
| ResNet50 Arousal | 10 | ImageNet | 287,651/batch size | 0.0167 |

## 2.2   Selecting 800 Images for Re-annotation

In total, there are 420,299 images in AffectNet. For our pilot exploration of label quality, we first pre-screened 100 images from each class to have a more manageable dataset size. To pick these images, we designed a HTML-based GUI that allowed us to quickly loop through all images for a class and select those exemplars that the trained annotator deemed "confusing".

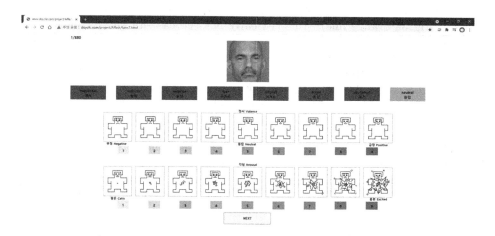

**Fig. 2.** Screenshot of the annotation GUI for the main experiment showing the image, the category selector and the SAM manikins for affective ratings.

## 2.3   Annotation Experiment

For the experiment, we designed a software application based on HTML shown in Fig. 2. For each image, participants were asked to make three annotations: in the first row, they were to click on one of the eight categories that best described the expression content of the image; the second and third row showed self-assessment manikins (SAM, [21]) for rating of valence and arousal at 9 different rating levels.

The experiment was conducted in a quiet room and supervised in real-time by the experimenter. Participants were first instructed about the experimental procedure and were familiarized with expression labels and valence and arousal ratings. The experimenter also demoed the experiment with one dummy picture to instruct participants about how to pick the expression, to rate valence and arousal, and to move on to the next picture. Unlike AffectNet, we did *not* constrain valence and arousal values to pre-defined ranges (see [15]), so as not to affect participants' intuitive evaluations of the affective content.

We recruited a total of N = 13 people. (7 female, 6 male, mean age (STD) = 33.23 (12.39) years) from the population of Korea University. Participants were naive as to the purpose of the experiment, and reported no neurological or psychological issues that would interfere with emotion processing.

# 3    Re-annotation Results

## 3.1    Expression Categories

The total number of votes added up to 10,400—as a first, omnibus result, we observed that of these votes, 8,658 (83.25%) did *not* agree with the original AffectNet labels, indicating that these labels may have issues.

Figure 3a shows the overall results for participants' votes[1] in more detail (as box plots). The original AffectNet data was uniformly distributed across the eight classes (Fig. 3a orange line)—this is clearly not the case for the median votes, however: On average, participants chose a much higher proportion of neutral and happy labels and much lower proportions of contempt, fear, sad, and disgust. We also observed variability across expression categories in the voting patterns, especially for the neutral, and to lesser degrees for the happy and sad categories, indicating that there was less agreement among participants for these category labels.

The overall consistency of participants on voting was evaluated by taking each participant's individual voting pattern per expression and correlating this with all other participants' voting patterns. The average value of the upper triangular part of the resulting correlation matrix is a measure of *relative* consistency and was determined to be $r_{expr} = 0.551$, indicating medium to good consistency levels.

Figure 3a also shows the original number of images in each category in Affect-Net (blue line, normalized). We can see that this distribution—as an extremely weak measure of a "real-life" distribution of these facial expression categories—fits somewhat better to the median voting pattern (the correlation value for the human voting data to this data is $r = 0.71$, see also Fig. 8b below). This may be an indication that participants implicitly fitted their overall voting strategy to some sort of "hidden distribution"; for example, one would expect that most of the time, faces display no strong facial emotion and hence will be neutral. The next most common expression may be happy followed by the other categories with contempt and disgust being perhaps the least commonly-encountered expressions.

Figure 3b displays a type of confusion matrix, which shows how the original AffectNet labels and the maximum vote labels are connected. As can be seen, the matrix does not exhibit any diagonal structure owing to the large number of differing votes we received. Many contempt images, for example, got relabelled as happy or neutral. At the same time, and in line with the results in Fig. 3a, many images originally annotated with an emotional label received votes for the neutral expression.

---

[1] In determining the final vote to be counted, we also experimented with different kinds of maximum (modal) voting, such as maximum vote across all votes, maximum votes for each image with different ways of breaking ties (counting the first tie, the second, or the third). We found that the average voting pattern was not affected by these methods, and hence used this pattern in the remainder of this paper.

Human Vote on AffectNet Label

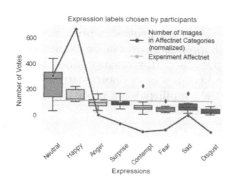

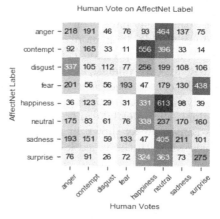

(a) Box-whisker plot showing the results of the human re-annotation in comparison to the constant AffectNet label distribution (orange line) and the distribution of all images in AffectNet (blue line).

(b) Confusion-type matrix showing which label participants chose depending on the original AffectNet label.

**Fig. 3.** Voting results and confusion matrix (Color figure online)

Overall, our results so far on the 800, pre-screened images suggest that the original expression labels in AffectNet for these difficult images are far from ideal.

### 3.2   Valence and Arousal

To better compare our data with those from AffectNet, we mapped the 1–9 scale into an −1.0 to 1.0 range. Figure 4a) shows the full data of our experiment with our arousal and valence ratings colored by the maximum vote labels. First of all, we see a clear "rotated U"-shape that is reminiscent of the data from affective ratings obtained for the International Affective Picture System (IAPS, [22])—in other words, as valence increases positively and negatively arousal increases into the positive direction in both cases. This pattern is a well-established result for affective ratings of pictures and videos [17,22].

In this context, it is important to mention that the AffectNet annotations for valence and arousal were collected in a different way compared to ours: their annotation scheme used a software application in which the annotator clicked into a pre-defined region within a two-dimensional coordinate system (see [15]). In our case, the two annotations were obtained in a more "traditional" fashion using the SAM method and without restricting participants to certain value ranges, depending on the label, which may explain some of the differences in rating pattern.

One of the reasons for the different annotation scheme for the original Affect-Net ratings may have been to ensure a better consistency for valence and arousal evaluations. To look more closely into this matter, Fig. 4 also shows coloring based on the expression categories obtained from the maximum votes, which clearly fit this valence/arousal space well: the green neutral expression stays near the center, whereas red anger and grey happiness clearly move to the upper positive and bottom negative quadrants of the space. If we change labels to the original AffectNet labels, however, the space becomes much more scattered and less consistent as shown in Fig. 4b. Hence, the overall pattern of ratings seems consistent with the voted labels in our experiment.

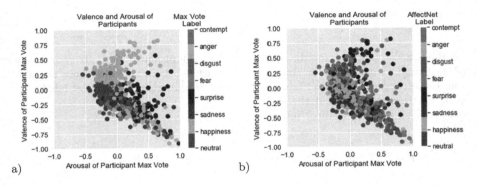

**Fig. 4.** a) Arousal-Valence space colored with our max vote labels. b) Same space colored with original AffectNet labels (Color figure online)

To reinforce this point, in Fig. 5 we show the overall distribution of valence and arousal votes when labeled with the chosen, maximum vote. Here, the distributions also have peaks at expected values (neutral being at 0, happy peaking at positive valence values, and anger peaking at positive arousal values).

We next analyzed the standard deviation of valence and arousal ratings within each category selected by participants—these results are shown in Fig. 6a,b. As can be seen, overall standard deviations were in the range from 0.2 to 1.0 and were lowest for neutral and contempt for both valence and arousal. Valence seemed to have similar variability for each expression compared to arousal ratings. Overall, *absolute* agreement on the rating values was relatively high at these low levels of variability.

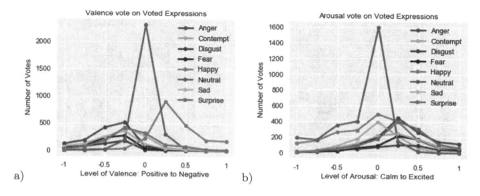

**Fig. 5.** Human votes on a) valence and b) arousal for voted expressions. In Fig. 5, it shows how people annotated valence and arousal related to their votes to the expressions. For example, we can clearly see when people voted for 'neutral' they also voted mostly on middle point of both valence and arousal.

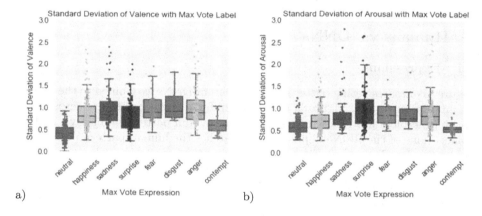

**Fig. 6.** Standard deviations of a) valence and b) arousal ratings across participants based on the chosen maximum vote label.

We again analyzed the overall correlations among participants in the same manner as done for the expressions. These matrices are shown in Fig. 7. The average correlations measuring consistency in *relative* voting pattern among human participants was $r_{val} = 0.865$ for valence and $r_{aro} = 0.476$ for arousal. Relative agreement was very high for valence, but only at medium levels for arousal due to some participants choosing a different rating profile (see Fig. 7b, Participant 10, for example). By flipping the arousal ratings of participant 3 and 10, our final result becomes $r_{aro} = 0.669$ Our results show that participants can agree much better on valence and arousal ratings of the expressions than on the label.

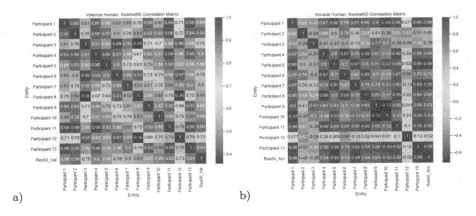

**Fig. 7.** Correlation matrix between participants for a) valence and b) arousal ratings (see text for discussion of participants 3 and 10). The matrix also includes an extra row for the ResNet model (see analysis below).

## 4   Humans vs. DNNs

### 4.1   Expressions

Figure 8 compares voting patterns of the different DNNs we trained to the human re-annotation results. Figure 8a shows the different voting patterns across categories (line-plots were chosen to highlight the overall pattern similarity). At first glance, none of the ResNets' predictions matches the human pattern perfectly—however, when looking at Fig. 8b, which plots the correlation values among all voting patterns, we can see that the most similar voting pattern to human performance is obtained for the ResNet trained very weakly with only 8 images for 1000 epochs. This is at similar levels to the correlation for human votes to the AffectNet label distribution (blue line).

Overall, we find that ResNets trained on the AffectNet original label distribution cannot capture the human voting pattern well, except for a model that was only weakly-trained (yet still achieved a relatively high performance on the AffectNet validation set).

### 4.2   Valence and Arousal

We found that agreement with human valence ratings was very high for the simple ResNet we trained for only 10 epochs as shown in the scatter plot in Fig. 9a. The coloring in this figure was done according to the human maximum voting label and shows the expected distribution of expression categories along the valence range (from angry in red to happy in grey). Conversely, if we color the same data according to the original AffectNet labels, the plot looks much less well-structured (Fig. 9b).

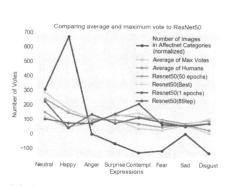

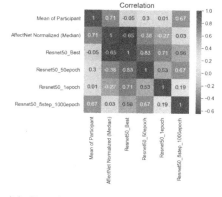

(a) Average voting for the four different ResNet models compared to the average human vote (green) and the number of images in AffectNet categories (blue).

(b) Correlation matrix showing similarities in voting pattern for all curves in Figure 8a

**Fig. 8.** Comparison of human and machine voting patterns. (Color figure online)

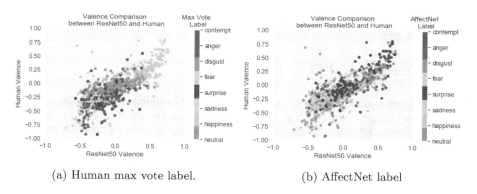

(a) Human max vote label.

(b) AffectNet label

**Fig. 9.** Valence comparison between ResNet50 and humans.

Results for arousal also show good agreement of the ResNet model with human data (Fig. 10a). Again, the human maximum vote coloring produces the desired relationship of arousal to expression category label (cf. neutral at the bottom part to anger and surprised expressions towards the top). Compared to the valence data, however, arousal seems to have more spread—this may be due in part to the fact that arousal values did not span the whole scale, which could have resulted in worse generalization performance for the network. Again, Fig. 10b, which uses the original AffectNet labels does not produce consistent relationships between ratings and expression categories.

The last rows in Fig. 7 show the correlations of the trained ResNet models with the human ratings. The overall, average correlation of the DNN with valence

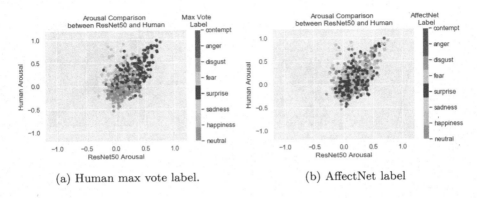

(a) Human max vote label.          (b) AffectNet label

**Fig. 10.** Arousal comparison between ResNet50 and humans.

is $r_{val,DNN} = 0.862$ and for arousal $r_{aro,DNN} = 0.744$ ($r_{aro,DNN} = 0.619$ before correcting participant 3 and 10). These results confirm the previous analysis and show that, indeed, the ResNet with minimal training of 10 epochs is capable of capturing the valence ratings on our newly-annotated images well. The relative agreement with the arousal ratings is at medium levels—similar to human-human consistency values obtained above.

## 5 Discussion and Conclusion

Given the recent discussion in the field about label quality in datasets [19] and the "success" that crowd-based re-annotation had for the FER+ dataset, here we presented results of re-annotation experiments on the popular AffectNet dataset.

Thirteen participants re-annotated our pre-screened dataset of 800, difficult-to-parse images with expression category and affective ratings. Overall, we found that expression category votes agreed only very weakly with the original Affect-Net labels: only 13% of votes kept the same label. Indeed, participants instead seemed to follow an implicit bias to real-life frequencies in their voting with large numbers of votes falling into the neutral category, for example. Adding the neutral category is relatively rare in human annotation experiments as participants usually are forced to choose one out of seven emotional categories from among expressive faces - this may bias the results, however, as shown, for example, in [7,8] as participants cannot select a "non-signal". It will be interesting, nonetheless, to repeat the annotation with different amounts of categories or with a ranking strategy (similar to the TopN-accuracy results reported for large-scale classification tasks). Overall, our results so far clearly confirm the difficulty to assign unique labels to facial expressions out-of-context (that is, without temporal or auditory contextual information)—an issue that was also visible in the large variability in some of the expression categories. Importantly, this issue was also highlighted in a recent review paper in affective psychology [18], which cast doubt on context-free, unambiguous labeling of facial expressions.

The issue of labels is circumvented to some degree by the affective ratings we obtained in the annotation. Here, participants had less variability overall, but also showed clear, systematic, and consistent deviations from the original Affect-Net ratings. In line with a large number of other results [17,22], we obtained a valence-arousal space that showcased dependencies between the two dimensions. This may in part be due to the difference in methods, where the AffectNet annotations placed implicit and explicit restrictions on participants' rating pattern—a topic that will be interesting to follow up in future studies. The observed rating patterns, however, did match well with the average expression categories and were consistent among participants with little variability.

Finally, we compared the human crowd annotations with predictions of DNNs. In terms of expression categories, we found no good match, except for a weakly-trained, somewhat "unconventional" DNN that showed good correlations. Given that the human data did not match well with the AffectNet labels, the failure of the AffectNet-trained DNNs to capture human voting patterns is perhaps not surprising. Only a much more extensive re-annotation of AffectNet will be able to shed final light on potential performance gains (and better fitting quality), as here we were only able to test a first set of 800 images. This work is currently underway.

In terms of valence and arousal, however, we found much better agreement between the ResNets and human performance, especially for valence but also to high degree for arousal. Since the number of networks we tested for these ratings, was limited, however, we can only cautiously suggest that this could be due to the fact that affective ratings for our (difficult) images suffered less from ambiguity compared to the labels (see human results). Future work will need to test the degree to which the weakly-trained networks used in our work are better at capturing the label- and/or rating space of human annotations.

Overall, our results clearly highlight issues with expression labeling and point to the need for the field to use also other, continuous annotation schemes (like valence and arousal, but more evaluative dimensions are possible [14]) and/or focus on analysis of affective data in more contextually rich environments.

**Acknowledgments.** This work was supported by Institute of Information Communications Technology Planning Evaluation (IITP; No. 2019-0-00079, Department of Artificial Intelligence, Korea University) and National Research Foundation of Korea (NRF; NRF-2017M3C7A1041824) grant funded by the Korean government (MSIT).

# References

1. Lucey, P., Cohn, J.F., Kanade, T., Saragih, J., Ambadar, Z., Matthews, I.: The extended Cohn-Kanade dataset (CK+): a complete dataset for action unit and emotion-specified expression. In: 2010 IEEE Computer Society Conference on Computer Vision and Pattern Recognition - Workshops, CVPRW 2010, July, pp. 94–101 (2010). https://doi.org/10.1109/CVPRW.2010.5543262

2. Meng, D., Peng, X., Wang, K., Qiao, Y.: Frame attention networks for facial expression recognition in videos. In: Proceedings - International Conference on Image Processing, ICIP, 2019-September, pp. 3866–3870 (2019). https://doi.org/10.1109/ICIP.2019.8803603

3. Savchenko, A.V.: Facial expression and attributes recognition based on multi-task learning of lightweight neural networks (2021). http://arxiv.org/abs/2103.17107

4. Barsoum, E., Zhang, C., Ferrer, C.C., Zhang, Z.: Training deep networks for facial expression recognition with crowd-sourced label distribution. In: ICMI 2016 - Proceedings of the 18th ACM International Conference on Multimodal Interaction, pp. 279–283 (2016). https://doi.org/10.1145/2993148.2993165

5. Vo, T.H., Lee, G.S., Yang, H.J., Kim, S.H.: Pyramid with super resolution for in-the-wild facial expression recognition. IEEE Access **8**, 131988–132001 (2020). https://doi.org/10.1109/ACCESS.2020.3010018

6. Guan, M.Y., Gulshan, V., Dai, A.M., Hinton, G.E.: Who said what: modeling individual labelers improves classification. In: 32nd AAAI Conference on Artificial Intelligence, AAAI 2018, pp. 3109–3118 (2018)

7. Nusseck, M., Cunningham, D.W., Wallraven, C., Bülthoff, H.H.: The contribution of different facial regions to the recognition of conversational expressions. J. Vis. **8**(8), 1–23 (2008). https://doi.org/10.1167/8.8.1

8. Russell, J.: Is there universal recognition of emotion from facial expression? A review of the cross-cultural studies. Psychol. Bull. **115**(1), 102–141 (1994)

9. Zhou, H., et al.: Exploring emotion features and fusion strategies for audio-video emotion recognition. In: ICMI 2019 - Proceedings of the 2019 International Conference on Multimodal Interaction, pp. 562–566 (2019). https://doi.org/10.1145/3340555.3355713

10. Goodfellow, I.J., et al.: Challenges in representation learning: a report on three machine learning contests. Neural Netw. **64**, 59–63 (2015). https://doi.org/10.1016/j.neunet.2014.09.005

11. Li, S., Deng, W.: Deep facial expression recognition: a survey. IEEE Trans. Affect. Comput. 1–25 (2020). https://doi.org/10.1109/TAFFC.2020.2981446

12. Wang, K., Peng, X., Yang, J., Meng, D., Qiao, Y.: Region attention networks for pose and occlusion robust facial expression recognition. IEEE Trans. Image Process. **29**(February), 4057–4069 (2020). https://doi.org/10.1109/TIP.2019.2956143

13. Mostafa, A., El-Sayed, H., Belal, M.: Facial expressions recognition via CNNCraftnet for static RGB images. Int. J. Intell. Eng. Syst. **14**(4), 410–421 (2021). https://doi.org/10.22266/ijies2021.0831.36

14. Derya, D., Kang, J., Kwon, D.Y., Wallraven, C.: Facial expression processing is not affected by Parkinson's disease, but by age-related factors. Front. Psychol. **10**, 1–14 (2019). https://doi.org/10.3389/fpsyg.2019.02458

15. Mollahosseini, A., Hasani, B., Mahoor, M.H.: AffectNet: a database for facial expression, valence, and arousal computing in the wild. IEEE Trans. Affect. Comput. **10**(1), 18–31 (2019). https://doi.org/10.1109/TAFFC.2017.2740923

16. Albanie, S., Nagrani, A., Vedaldi, A., Zisserman, A.: Emotion recognition in speech using cross-modal transfer in the wild. In: MM 2018 - Proceedings of the 2018 ACM Multimedia Conference, pp. 292–301 (2018). https://doi.org/10.1145/3240508.3240578

17. Castillo, S., Wallraven, C., Cunningham, D.W.: The semantic space for facial communication. Comp. Anim. Virtual Worlds **25**, 223–231 (2014). https://doi.org/10.1002/cav.1593

18. Barrett, L.F., Adolphs, R., Marsella, S., Martinez, A.M., Pollak, S.D.: Emotional expressions reconsidered: challenges to inferring emotion from human facial movements. Psychol. Sci. Public Interest **20**(1), 1–68 (2019). https://doi.org/10.1177/1529100619832930

19. Northcutt, C.G., Athalye, A., Mueller, J.: Pervasive label errors in test sets destabilize machine learning benchmarks (2021). http://arxiv.org/abs/2103.14749

20. He, K., Zhang, X., Ren, S., Sun, J.: Deep residual learning for image recognition. In: Proceedings of the IEEE Computer Society Conference on Computer Vision and Pattern Recognition, December 2016, pp. 770–778 (2016). https://doi.org/10.1109/CVPR.2016.90

21. Bradley, M.M., Lang, P.J.: Measuring emotion: the self-assessment manikin and the semantic differential. J. Behav. Ther. Exp. Psychiatry **25**(1), 49–59 (1994). PMID: 7962581. https://doi.org/10.1016/0005-7916(94)90063-9

22. Lang, P.J.: The emotion probe: studies of motivation and attention. Am. Psychol. **50**(5), 372–385 (1995). https://doi.org/10.1037/0003-066X.50.5.372

# Hybrid Contrastive Learning with Cluster Ensemble for Unsupervised Person Re-identification

He Sun, Mingkun Li, and Chun-Guang Li[✉]

School of Artificial Intelligence, Beijing Univsersity of Posts and Telecommunications,
Beijing 100876, People's Republic of China
{sunhe123,mingkun.li,lichunguang}@bupt.edu.cn

**Abstract.** Unsupervised person re-identification (ReID) aims to match a query image of a pedestrian to the images in gallery set without supervision labels. The most popular approaches to tackle unsupervised person ReID are usually performing a clustering algorithm to yield pseudo labels at first and then exploit the pseudo labels to train a deep neural network. However, the pseudo labels are noisy and sensitive to the hyper-parameter(s) in clustering algorithm. In this paper, we propose a Hybrid Contrastive Learning (HCL) approach for unsupervised person ReID, which is based on a hybrid between instance-level and cluster-level contrastive loss functions. Moreover, we present a Multi-Granularity Clustering Ensemble based Hybrid Contrastive Learning (MGCE-HCL) approach, which adopts a multi-granularity clustering ensemble strategy to mine priority information among the pseudo positive sample pairs and defines a priority-weighted hybrid contrastive loss for better tolerating the noises in the pseudo positive samples. We conduct extensive experiments on two benchmark datasets Market-1501 and DukeMTMC-reID. Experimental results validate the effectiveness of our proposals.

**Keywords:** Unsupervised person ReID · Contrastive learning · Cluster ensemble · Multi-granularity

## 1 Introduction

Person Re-identification (ReID) is a popular and important task in pattern recognition and computer vision, aiming to find the images of the same pedestrian in gallery to match the given probe image. The common approaches are to sort the gallery images according to the similarity between the probe image and the images in the gallery. Early works are usually based on supervised learning, which trains a deep model with a large amount of labeled data. However, the performance of the supervised ReID model will often seriously degenerate when facing the open-world data because the models are usually trained with limited data with supervision information. Thus it is crucial to exploit the hidden guidance information from the images without supervision.

In recent years, unsupervised methods for person ReID have attracted a lot of attention. In unsupervised setting, the most popular methods [5–7,27] are based on training a deep neural network with pseudo labels, which are generated by clustering algorithm

© Springer Nature Switzerland AG 2022
C. Wallraven et al. (Eds.): ACPR 2021, LNCS 13189, pp. 532–546, 2022.
https://doi.org/10.1007/978-3-031-02444-3_40

(e.g., $k$-means, DBSCAN [3]). For instance, $k$-means is used in [5] to generate the pseudo labels for different part of the images and DBSCAN is used in [6,7,27].

The basic assumption behind the pseudo labels-based unsupervised methods is that the samples in the same cluster are more likely with the same class label. Unlike the ground-truth labels, however, the pseudo labels obtained via a clustering algorithm are unavoidably noisy. Thus it is critic to tackle the noises in pseudo labels. For example, in [6], a mutual learning strategy via a temporal mean net is leveraged; in [5], a multi-branch network from [19] is adopted to perform clustering with different part of images. Besides, some works [15,24] attempt to exploit the neighborhood relationship instead of using traditional clustering methods.

More recently, in [7], contrastive learning is introduced to unsupervised person ReID, in which a hybrid memory bank is used to store all the features and a unified contrastive loss based on the similarity of inputs and all features is adopted to train a deep neural network. While remarkable improvements in performance are reported, all these methods depend upon performing clustering method with a delicate hyper-parameter (e.g., the neighborhood ratio parameter $d$ in DBSCAN). Unfortunately, the performance might dramatically degenerate if an improper hyper-parameter is used.

In this paper, we present a simple yet effective contrastive learning-based framework for unsupervised person ReID, in which the noisy pseudo labels are used to define a hybrid contrastive loss—which aims to "attract" the pseudo positive samples in the current cluster and at the meantime "dispel" all the remaining samples (i.e., the pseudo negative samples) with respect to the current cluster. Moreover, we introduce a cluster ensemble strategy to generate multi-granularity clustering information—which is encoded into priority weights, and adopt the priority weights to define a weighted hybrid contrastive loss. The cluster ensemble strategy aims to alleviate the sensitivity of using a single hyper-parameter in clustering algorithm by using a range of the hyper-parameter to perform clustering ensemble instead; whereas the priority-weighting mechanism in the contrastive loss aims to better tolerate the noises in pseudo labels.

**Paper Contributions.** The contributions of the paper can be summarized as follows.

- We propose a novel hybrid contrastive paradigm for unsupervised person ReID, which is able to better exploit the noisy pseudo labels.
- We adopt a multi-granularity clustering ensemble strategy to depict the confidence of positive samples and hence present a priority-weighted hybrid contrastive loss for better tolerating the noises in pseudo positive samples.
- We conduct extensive experiments on two benchmark datasets and the experimental results validate the effectiveness of our proposals.

## 2   Related Works

This section provides a brief review on the relevant work in unsupervised person ReID and contrastive learning.

**Unsupervised Person ReID.** The prior work in unsupervised person ReID can be grouped into two categories: a) Unsupervised Domain Adaptation (UDA) based methods and b) pure Unsupervised Learning (USL) based methods. UDA is a transfer learning paradigm where both labeled data in source domain and unlabeled data in target domain are required. However, UDA needs labeled source data and it works only when the distributions of the data in target domain and the data in source domain are closer. On the contrary, the USL methods only need the unlabeled data. Most recent works in USL for unsupervised reID, e.g., [6,7,14,25] use pseudo labels to train a deep network, in which the pseudo labels are generated by a clustering algorithm, such as $k$-means, DBSCAN [3] and so on. Unfortunately, the pseudo labels are unavoidably noisy, and the clustering results are very sensitive to the hyper-parameter used in the clustering algorithm.

**Contrastive Learning.** Contrastive learning is a hot topic in recent years. Many contrastive learning methods [1,8,10,16] are developed to learn the hidden information from image samples themselves by minimizing the similarity between different augmented samples of the inputs. In [16], InfoNCE loss is proposed and proved that minimizing the InfoNCE loss is equivalent to maximizing the mutual information loss. In [1] and [10], a siamese network based framework and a momentum updating paradigm are developed, respectively. More recently, contrastive learning strategy has also been introduced to person ReID task, e.g., [7,16]. Inspired by the InfoNCE loss [22], a unified contrastive loss for UDA based person ReID is presented in [7]. Different from the previous work, in this paper, we develop a hybrid contrastive learning based unsupervised person ReID baseline at first, and then we present a novel priority-weighted contrastive loss, which effectively encodes a multi-granularity clustering results.

## 3    Contrastive Learning Based Unsupervised Person ReID

This section provides some basics on contrastive learning and then present a simple but effective framework for contrastive learning based unsupervised person ReID.

### 3.1    Instance-Level and Cluster-Level Contrastive Learning: A Revisit

According to the way to exploit the (pseudo) supervision information, contrastive learning can be divided into two paradigms: (a) instance-level contrastive learning, and (b) cluster-level contrastive learning. Instance-level contrastive learning depends on sample augmentation. Given an input sample, a set of class-preserving samples are generated and fed into a siamese network. In such a paradigm, the sample augmentation is assumed to be class-preserving and thus the augmented samples are treated as *positive samples* and all the remaining samples in a batch are considered as *negative samples*. Therefore, instance-level contrastive learning mainly leverages self-supervision information from each sample itself individually, without taking into account of the structure or correlation in samples.

In cluster-level contrastive learning, cluster information (i.e., pseudo labels), is generated by a clustering algorithm, and the similarity of the feature of the input image and the cluster centers (i.e., the mean vector of each cluster) is used to build an InfoNCE-like loss as follows:

$$\mathcal{L}_{con} = -\frac{1}{|\mathcal{B}|} \sum_{i=1}^{|\mathcal{B}|} \log \frac{\exp(\langle \boldsymbol{f}_{x_i}, \boldsymbol{\mu}_+ \rangle / \tau)}{\sum_{j=1}^{C} \exp(\langle \boldsymbol{f}_{x_i}, \boldsymbol{\mu}_j \rangle / \tau))}, \tag{1}$$

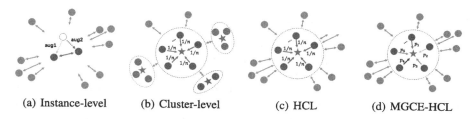

|(a) Instance-level|(b) Cluster-level|(c) HCL|(d) MGCE-HCL|

**Fig. 1. Illustration for different contrastive learning paradigms.** Red arrows in a), b) and c): pulling together; Green arrows: pushing away. (a) For instance-level paradigm, two augmented samples (red points) of original input (red circle) are pulled together and push all others away. (b) For cluster-level paradigm, positive samples (red points) are pushed to the cluster center (red star), and different clusters are mutually exclusive. (c) In our HCL, different from (a) and (b), we consider all negative samples (grey points) individually as individual class. (d) In MGCE-HCL, we further use the priority to weight the similarity between positive samples. (Color figure online)

where $\tau > 0$ is a temperature constant[1], $\mathcal{B}$ denotes a mini-batch of samples, $|\mathcal{B}|$ denotes the number of the samples in $\mathcal{B}$, $C$ denotes the number of clusters, $\boldsymbol{f}_{x_i}$ is the feature representation of an input $x_i$, and $\boldsymbol{f}_{M_i}$ denotes the feature from memory bank with index $i$, in which $\boldsymbol{f}_{x_i}$ and $\boldsymbol{f}_{M_i}$ are defined as

$$\boldsymbol{f}_{M_i} \leftarrow \gamma \boldsymbol{f}_{x_i} + (1 - \gamma)\boldsymbol{f}_{M_i}, \tag{2}$$

$$\boldsymbol{f}_{M_i} \leftarrow \frac{\boldsymbol{f}_{M_i}}{\|\boldsymbol{f}_{M_i}\|_2}, \tag{3}$$

and $\boldsymbol{\mu}_+$ denotes the mean vector of the samples (i.e., positive sample) of the cluster to which $x_i$ belongs, and $\boldsymbol{\mu}_j$ denotes the mean vector of the samples in the $j$-th cluster. The reason to use the memory bank $\mathcal{M}$ is that the features from memory bank is relative static and thus are not only more suitable to perform clustering algorithm for generating pseudo labels but also used as a reference for contrastive learning. Nevertheless, the dynamic features $\boldsymbol{f}_{x_i}$ extracted from the backbone are more appropriate for dynamic inputs due to containing more information from the random sample augmentation.

For clarity, we illustrate the mechanisms in instance-level contrastive learning and cluster-level contrastive learning in Fig. 1(a) and (b). Note that both instance-level contrastive learning and cluster-level contrastive learning have shortcomings. Instance-level contrastive learning digs self-supervision information individually for each sample, ignoring the structure or correlation information among samples (e.g., cluster information), which is of vital importance especially for positive samples. For cluster-level contrastive learning, while it has been applied to the task such as person ReID, it introduces too much structural information for negative samples, which is usually useless in practice.

---

[1] By default, we set $\tau = 0.05$.

## 3.2  Hybrid Contrastive Learning (HCL) Based Unsupervised Person ReID

To tackle the deficiencies mentioned above, we present a modified contrastive learning paradigm, which is a hybrid between the instance-level paradigm and the cluster-level paradigm, and thus is termed Hybrid Contrastive Learning (HCL).

The HCL framework consists of three components: a) an encoder module for learning convolution feature, b) a memory bank to store the updated features of the whole dataset, and c) a clustering module for generating pseudo labels. We adopt ResNet-50 [11] without the full-connection (FC) layer as the encoder module and denote the memory bank as $\mathcal{M} = \{f_{M_i}\}_{i=1}^{N}$ which is used to store all the features during the training, where $N$ denotes the total number of samples in the dataset. The memory bank is initialized by the normalized features extracted from ResNet-50, which is pre-trained with ImageNet.

In training phase, we feed a batch of images, denoted as $\mathcal{B}$, into the backbone and then update the memory bank $\mathcal{M}$ with the new features via Eq. (2), where $f_{M_i}$ denotes the feature representation of the sample $x_i$ in the memory $\mathcal{M}$ and $f_{x_i}$ is the convolution feature of the input $x_i$ extracted by the backbone. We adopt the DBSCAN algorithm [3] with a fixed parameter $d$ to generate the pseudo labels. While the pseudo labels are noisy, there are still rich supervision information for contrastive learning.

In this paper, to remedy the deficiencies in instance-level and cluster-level contrastive learning, we propose a hybrid contrastive loss as follows:

$$\mathcal{L}_{HCL} = -\frac{1}{|\mathcal{B}|}\sum_{i=1}^{|\mathcal{B}|} \log \frac{\exp(\langle f_{x_i}, \mu_+\rangle/\tau)}{\exp(\langle f_{x_i}, \mu_+\rangle/\tau) + \sum_{j \notin \omega_+}\exp(\langle f_{x_i}, f_{M_j}\rangle/\tau)}, \quad (4)$$

where $\mu_+$ denotes the mean of the positive samples of $f_{x_i}$, $|\mathcal{B}|$ denotes the batch size, and $j \notin \omega_+$ denotes to the index set of samples that do not belong to the current cluster $\omega_+$ which corresponds to $\mu_+$. For clarity, we illustrate the hybrid contrastive paradigm in Fig. 1(c).

**Remark 1.** In the modified contrastive loss Eq. (4), we reserve the cluster information for positive samples (i.e., which corresponds to positive cluster) which is able to pull the similar samples together, and at the same time, we treat all the remaining samples—other than the positive samples—as negative samples, rather than using the mean vectors of other (negative) clusters. The reasons are two-folds: a) since that the primal goal of the contrastive learning is to pull positive samples together and push all negative samples away, it is not needed to care the cluster information of the negative samples; and b) more negative samples are used, more contrasting information can be provided and thus help to avoid obtaining a trivial solution [9, 16].

## 4  Hybrid Contrastive Learning with Multi-Granularity Cluster Ensemble (MGCE-HCL)

This section presents a Hybrid Contrastive Learning framework with Multi-Granularity Clustering Ensemble (MGCE-HCL) for unsupervised person ReID.

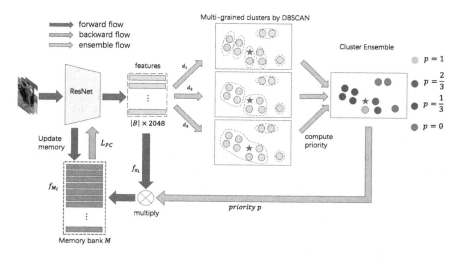

**Fig. 2. Architecture of MGCE-HCL.** The figure shows the case that three clustering results are assembled. Each batch of images are fed into ResNet50 to obtain the features, and then DBSCAN with parameter $d$ is used to perform clustering with the features in the memory bank. After that, we compute priority matrix with multiple granularity cluster results. In Cluster Ensemble (CE) module, different colors of points denote different value of priority and the red star denotes the convolution features of the current sample. To compute $\mathcal{L}_{PC}$, we compute the cosine similarity between the input features and the features in memory bank with priority-weighting mechanism. (Color figure online)

Compared to HCL, the key differences of MGCE-HCL are two-folds: a) rather than performing DBSCAN with a single neighborhood parameter $d$ to yield a clustering result, we perform DBSCAN multiple times with parameter $d$ sampled in a range to generate a multi-granularity clustering results and encode the obtained clustering results into priority weights; and b) we introduce the priority weights into the hybrid contrastive loss, which automatically exploits the confidence of the positive sample pairs.

**Multi-Granularity Clustering Ensemble (MGCE).** To remedy the sensitivity to the hyper-parameter in DBSCAN, we perform DBSCAN $T$ times, each time using a different neighborhood parameter $d^{(\ell)}$, in which $\{d^{(\ell)}\}_{\ell=1}^{T}$ are sampled from a range with an interval $\delta$. Let $c^{(\ell)}$ be the obtained cluster index of the $\ell$-th clustering with parameter $d^{(\ell)}$, where $\ell = 1, \cdots, T$. Accordingly we define an affinity matrix $A^{(\ell)}$, which is calculated as follows:

$$A_{i,j}^{(\ell)} = \begin{cases} 1, & c_i^{(\ell)} = c_j^{(\ell)} \\ 0, & c_i^{(\ell)} \neq c_j^{(\ell)}. \end{cases} \tag{5}$$

Note that $A_{i,j}^{(\ell)}$ is obtained with the neighborhood parameter taking the value $d^{(\ell)}$ and thus we view $A_{i,j}^{(\ell)}$ as the affinity under a specific granularity indexed with $d^{(\ell)}$. By taking an average over the $T$ results, we have a **priority** weight as follows:

$$p_{i,j} = \frac{1}{T} \sum_{\ell=1}^{T} A_{i,j}^{(\ell)}, \tag{6}$$

where $0 \leq p_{i,j} \leq 1$ approximately quantifies the confidence of two samples being grouped into the same cluster.

**Remark 2.** From a geometrical perspective, the priority is to describe the neighboring relationship between any two samples. This is because that if two samples lie close enough—they are more likely to be grouped into the same small cluster and thus are certainly to be grouped into larger cluster, resulting a higher priority value according to Eq. (6). From the probabilistic perspective, the priority also measures the confidence that the two samples are in the same cluster. Briefly, the higher the priority is, the two samples are more likely to be closer and the sample pairs are more credible to be positive samples. On contrary, when the priority of two samples is 0, it is reasonable to consider them as negative samples.

**Priority-Weighted Hybrid Contrastive Loss.** Given the priority weights, we propose a priority-weighted hybrid contrastive loss as follows:

$$\mathcal{L}_{PC} = -\frac{1}{|\mathcal{B}|} \sum_{i=1}^{|\mathcal{B}|} \log \frac{s_i^+}{s_i^+ + s_i^-}, \tag{7}$$

in which $s_i^+$ and $s_i^-$ are defined as the exponential similarity between the input and the positive samples and between the input and the negative samples, respectively, i.e.,

$$s_i^+ = \exp(\frac{\sum_{j=1}^{N} p_{i,j} \langle \boldsymbol{f}_{x_i}, \boldsymbol{f}_{M_j} \rangle / \tau}{\sum_{j=1}^{N} p_{i,j}}), \tag{8}$$

$$s_i^- = \sum_{j=1}^{N} \mathbb{I}(p_{i,j} = 0) \exp(\langle \boldsymbol{f}_{x_i}, \boldsymbol{f}_{M_j} \rangle / \tau), \tag{9}$$

where $\mathbb{I}(\cdot)$ is an indicator function, $\mathbb{I}(p_{i,j} = 0)$ outputs 1 if $p_{i,j} = 0$, and $\langle \cdot, \cdot \rangle$ denotes the inner product. Note that $s_i^+$ is computed by the inner product between the feature of the input image and the features from the memory bank $\mathcal{M}$ and are weighted by the nonzero priority; whereas $s_i^-$ is computed by the samples whose priority being 0 which are considered as negative samples and each negative sample pair is treated individually ignoring their cluster information.

For clarity, we provide the flowchart of the MGCE-HCL framework in Fig. 2. The input image is shown as the red star in the cluster ensemble module. After obtaining the confidence of all sample pairs, we weight each sample pair with the accumulated priority to train the whole model.

**Remark 3.** Note that priority-weighted similarity defined in Eq. (8) can bring more information for positive samples pairs because, the priority is able to describe the density of samples. For the computation of positive scores, we use priority to weight the positive samples of different distance but the cluster-level contrastive loss and HCL only compute the similarity between the input and the mean vector of all positive samples, which is equivalent to give each positive sample the same weight. For the negative samples, both MGCE-HCL and HCL consider each negative sample individually without using cluster information. For clarity, the difference between HCL and MGCE-HCL is illustrated in Fig. 1(d).

# 5   Experiments

## 5.1   Datasets and Evaluation Metrics

**Datasets.** We evaluate our method with two benchmark datasets: Market-1501 [28] and DukeMTMC-reID [17]. Market1501 has total 12,936 images of 751 identities in the training set, and in total 19,732 images of 750 identities; whereas DukeMTMC-reID has total 16,522 images of 702 identities in the training set, and in total 19,989 images of 702 identities.

**Evaluation Metrics.** We use two popular metrics for person ReID, including Cumulative Match Characteristic (CMC) and mean Average precision (mAP). For CMC, we only use top-1 to evaluate the performance.

## 5.2   Implementation Details

Our MGCE-HCL adopts ImageNet to pretrain ResNet50 as the backbone. Each input is resized to $256 \times 128$, and is transformed by horizontal flip and random erasing [29], whose probabilities are all set to 0.5. The range of the parameter $d$ in MGCE are set as $[0.4, 0.6]$ with interval $\delta = 0.05$. The parameter $\tau$ in the loss $\mathcal{L}_{PC}$ in Eq. (7) is set to 0.05 and the momentum parameter $\gamma$ in Eq. (2) is set to 0.2. During the training, following the protocol in the prior work, we select 16 *pseudo* identities[2] and 4 samples per identity as each mini-batch, and train totally 50 epochs. In experiments, we utilize the Adam optimizer [12] to optimize the network with a weight decay rate $5 \times 10^{-4}$.

## 5.3   Ablation Study

To validate the effectiveness of each component in our proposals, we conduct a set of ablation experiments.

**HCL vs. Cluster-level and Instance-level based Methods.** In HCL, we use the negative samples without any clustering structural information. To validate the effectiveness of our approach, we compare our HCL approach with the cluster-level contrastive learning method, which is marked as "clusterNCE", and the instance-level contrastive learning method which is represented by MoCo [10]. We conduct a set of experiments with the commonly used best-performing parameter $d$ in DBSCAN as in prior works [6,7,20,27]. Experimental results are reported in Table 1. We can read from the table that our HCL outperforms the instance-level and cluster-level contrastive learning methods in all cases. This is because that our hybrid contrastive learning paradigm can well

---

[2] We should note that the pseudo identities are obtained from clustering result rather than using the ground-truth labels.

grasp the useful information and effectively eliminate the impact of negative samples compared to MoCo and clusterNCE.

**MGCE-HCL vs. HCL.** In HCL, we perform DBSCAN with a fixed neighborhood radius parameter $d$ to obtain a specific clustering result and thus the pseudo labels; whereas in MGCE, we perform DBSCAN for multiple times, each time with a different parameter $d$, to obtain multiple clustering results. In previous DBSCAN based methods, it has been reported that the best-performing results are obtained usually when $d$ is taking the value from 0.4 to 0.6. This means that performing clustering with $d$ in such an interval will gain the most useful clustering information. To demonstrate the effectiveness of our clustering ensemble strategy, we compare our MGCE-HCL with HCL, in which both of them use $d$ taking from 0.4 to 0.6 in an interval of 0.05. The experimental results are shown in Table 2. We can observe that HCL performs best when $d$ is set to 0.5 for Market-1501 and 0.55 or 0.6 for DukeMTMC; whereas MGCE-HCL outperforms all the cases of HCL on both Market-1501 and DukeMTMC-reID.

**Table 1.** HCL vs. clusterNCE and MoCo. The results of MoCo are cited from [7].

| Method | Market-1501 | | DukeMTMC-reID | |
|---|---|---|---|---|
| | mAP | top-1 | mAP | top-1 |
| MoCo [10] | 6.1 | 12.8 | 5.6 | 10.7 |
| clusterNCE ($d = 0.4$) | 69.2 | 86.8 | 59.0 | 76.2 |
| **HCL** ($d = 0.4$) | 74.6 | 89.4 | 61.1 | 77.2 |
| clusterNCE ($d = 0.5$) | 73.9 | 87.9 | 63.6 | 79.2 |
| **HCL** ($d = 0.5$) | **79.4** | **91.7** | 66.2 | <u>81.3</u> |
| clusterNCE ($d = 0.6$) | 68.9 | 85.5 | 62.5 | 78.6 |
| **HCL** ($d = 0.6$) | <u>77.2</u> | <u>90.1</u> | **67.4** | **81.8** |

**Table 2.** Comparison of MGCE-HCL and HCL with different $d$

| Method | Market-1501 | | DukeMTMC-reID | |
|---|---|---|---|---|
| | mAP | top-1 | mAP | top-1 |
| HCL ($d = 0.40$) | 74.6 | 89.4 | 61.1 | 77.2 |
| HCL ($d = 0.45$) | 77.4 | 90.9 | 63.3 | 78.2 |
| HCL ($d = 0.50$) | <u>79.4</u> | <u>91.7</u> | 66.2 | 81.3 |
| HCL ($d = 0.55$) | 79.0 | 91.2 | 67.0 | **82.5** |
| HCL ($d = 0.60$) | 77.2 | 90.1 | <u>67.4</u> | <u>81.8</u> |
| MGCE-HCL ($d \in [0.4, 0.6]$) | **79.6** | **92.1** | **67.5** | **82.5** |

**Evaluation on Parameter Range for MGCE-HCL.** To explore the proper range to sample the parameter $d$, we conduct experiments with $d$ sampled in different ranges and show the results in Table 3. Since that the parameter $d$ is used to determine the

**Table 3.** Evaluation on MGCE-HCL with different parameter ranges.

| Ensemble Range | Market-1501 | | DukeMTMC-reID | |
|---|---|---|---|---|
| | mAP | top-1 | mAP | top-1 |
| 0.1–0.3 | 39.3 | 63.3 | 48.8 | 67.6 |
| 0.2–0.3 | 49.5 | 74.0 | 51.8 | 71.1 |
| 0.1–0.4 | 65.6 | 84.7 | 58.9 | 75.9 |
| 0.2–0.4 | 68.2 | 86.8 | 58.4 | 75.5 |
| 0.3–0.4 | 73.3 | 89.1 | 60.1 | 77.0 |
| 0.1–0.5 | 75.8 | 90.3 | 63.4 | 79.7 |
| 0.2–0.5 | 77.5 | 91.3 | 63.5 | 79.2 |
| 0.3–0.5 | 78.2 | 91.1 | 64.6 | 80.1 |
| 0.4–0.5 | 79.3 | 91.4 | 64.9 | 80.7 |
| 0.1–0.6 | 79.0 | 91.5 | 67.0 | 81.7 |
| 0.2–0.6 | 79.1 | 91.0 | 67.2 | 81.9 |
| 0.3–0.6 | 79.4 | 91.8 | 66.8 | 81.3 |
| 0.4–0.6 | **79.6** | **92.1** | **67.5** | **82.5** |
| 0.5–0.6 | 78.1 | 91.3 | 67.3 | 81.5 |
| 0.3–0.7 | 17.7 | 35.4 | 7.8 | 15.1 |
| 0.4–0.7 | 50.0 | 74.0 | 46.8 | 64.7 |

**Table 4.** Evaluation on MGCE-HCL with different interval $\delta$.

| Interval $\delta$ | Market-1501 | | DukeMTMC-reID | |
|---|---|---|---|---|
| | mAP | top-1 | mAP | top-1 |
| 0.05 | **79.6** | **92.1** | **67.5** | **82.5** |
| 0.02 | 78.8 | 91.2 | 67.0 | 81.8 |
| 0.01 | 79.5 | 91.7 | 67.2 | 81.5 |

**Table 5.** Evaluation on MGCE-HCL with different $\gamma$.

| $\gamma$ | Market-1501 | | DukeMTMC-reID | |
|---|---|---|---|---|
| | mAP | top-1 | mAP | top-1 |
| 0.1 | 78.8 | 91.1 | 67.1 | 81.6 |
| 0.2 | **79.6** | **92.1** | **67.5** | **82.5** |
| 0.3 | **79.6** | 92.0 | 67.0 | 81.4 |
| 0.4 | 79.3 | 91.7 | 66.0 | 80.5 |
| 0.5 | 79.0 | 91.4 | 64.3 | 79.9 |

**Table 6.** Comparison to SOTA methods on Market-1501 and DukeMTMC.

| Type | Method | Reference | Market-1501 | | DukeMTMC-reID | |
|------|--------|-----------|------|-------|------|-------|
| | | | mAP | top-1 | mAP | top-1 |
| UDA | PTGAN [21] | CVPR'18 | 15.7 | 38.6 | 13.5 | 27.4 |
| | SPGAN [2] | CVPR'18 | 26.7 | 58.1 | 26.4 | 46.9 |
| | HHL [30] | ECCV'18 | 31.4 | 62.2 | 27.2 | 46.9 |
| | ECN [31] | CVPR'19 | 43.0 | 75.1 | 40.4 | 63.3 |
| | SSG [5] | ICCV'19 | 58.3 | 80.0 | 53.4 | 73.0 |
| | MMCL [18] | CVPR'20 | 60.4 | 84.4 | 51.4 | 72.4 |
| | ECN++ [32] | TPAMI'20 | 63.8 | 84.1 | 54.4 | 74.0 |
| | AD-cluster [26] | CVPR'20 | 68.3 | 86.7 | 54.1 | 72.6 |
| | MMT [6] | ICLR'20 | 73.8 | 89.5 | 62.3 | 76.3 |
| | SpCL [7] | NeuIPS'20 | 76.7 | 90.3 | 68.8 | 82.9 |
| USL | LOMO [13] | CVPR'15 | 8.0 | 27.2 | 4.8 | 12.3 |
| | BoW [28] | ICCV'15 | 14.8 | 35.8 | 8.5 | 17.1 |
| | PUL [4] | TOMM'18 | 22.8 | 51.5 | 22.3 | 41.1 |
| | CAMEL [23] | ICCV'17 | 26.3 | 54.4 | 19.8 | 40.2 |
| | BUC [14] | AAAI'19 | 30.6 | 61.0 | 21.9 | 40.2 |
| | SSL [15] | CVPR'20 | 37.8 | 71.7 | 28.6 | 52.5 |
| | HCT [25] | CVPR'20 | 56.4 | 80.0 | 50.1 | 69.6 |
| | SpCL [7] | NeurIPS'20 | 72.6 | 87.7 | 65.3 | 81.2 |
| | CAP [20] | AAAI'21 | <u>79.2</u> | <u>91.4</u> | 67.3 | 81.1 |
| | **HCL** | This paper | 77.2 | 90.1 | <u>67.4</u> | <u>81.8</u> |
| | **MGCE-HCL** | This paper | **79.6** | **92.1** | **67.5** | **82.5** |

neighborhood, it is not reasonable to set it too large and the same for the upper bound of the parameter range in MGCE. According to the experience, when $d$ is set in the range of $[0.4, 0.6]$, the cluster results might combine positive samples and moderate noises which contain rich and reliable clustering information. To make full use of such clustering information in the range of $[0.4, 0.6]$, we set the upper bound of the parameter range as $0.5, 0.6, 0.7$, respectively, and increase the lower bound of the range from 0.1 and using an interval $\delta = 0.05$ for fair comparison. We also add the experiments with the upper bound of 0.4 to validate the robustness of our MGCE-HCL. Experiments are shown in Table 3. We can read that when the upper bound is 0.6, MGCE-HCL yields better performance. Especially when the lower bound is set as 0.4, MGCE-HCL achieves the best performance. This result suggests that the range of $[0.4, 0.6]$ for the parameter $d$ to perform DBSCAN contains the richest clustering information and it is consistent with the common practice for setting the parameter $d$ in prior works [6,7,20,27]. Moreover, we find that decreasing the lower bound may cause slight drop on the performance. The reason is that when the upper bound is fixed, decreasing the lower bound will decrease the priority of samples from clusters of larger size, which may contain more useful information. It is worth to note that MGCE-HCL is insensitive to the lower bound of ensemble range and not that sensitive to the upper bound of the range when the upper bound is not over-large. This hints that we can obtain reasonably good performance with a relatively larger range for clustering ensemble and an appropriate upper bound even if we do not know the exact best parameter $d$. However, as shown in Table 3, the results might sharply drop when we set the upper bound up to 0.7. It is because that the clustering results will be too noisy when using an over-large parameter $d$.

**Evaluation on $\delta$ in Cluster Ensemble.** To evaluate the effect of the interval in the ensemble range, we fix the parameter range to pick $d$ as $[0.4, 0.6]$ and change the sampling interval $\delta$ to $\{0.05, 0.02, 0.01\}$, individually. Experimental results are shown in Table 4. Using a smaller $\delta$ leads to a larger $T$, i.e., the times of running DBSCAN. The results show that MGCE-HCL is also insensitive to the interval $\delta$.

**Evaluation on Momentum Factor $\gamma$.** As shown in Eq. 2, parameter $\gamma$ is the momentum factor to update memory bank. In our method, memory bank is used to store relatively static features (i.e.smoothed features), rather than using the features directly extracted from the output of the backbone. Therefore, the momentum factor $\gamma$ should not be too large. To evaluate the effect of using different parameter $\gamma$, we conduct a set of experiments to compare the performance with different $\gamma$ in Table 5. The results show that $\gamma = 0.2$ achieves the best performance and the performance gradually drops when $\gamma$ is larger than 0.2.

## 5.4   Comparison to State-of-the-art Methods

Finally, we compare the performance of our proposed MGCE-HCL method to the state-of-the-art methods on Market-1501 and DukeMTMC-reID. The experimental results are shown in Table 6.

**Compared to USL-based methods.** We compare the most unsupervised works recent years, including BoW [28], LOMO [13], PUL [4], CAMEL [23], BUC [14], SSL [15], HCT [25], SpCL [7] and CAP [20]. In the USL-based methods, only the unlabeled data is used. In most recent works, e.g., BUC, HCT, SpCL and CAP, they are based on a clustering method (e.g., $k$-means, DBSCAN, or hierarchical clustering) to yield the pseudo labels. Among them, SpCL and CAP also use cluster-based contrastive learning method. SpCL learns with a self-paced strategy and CAP introduces the camera information to boost training. Compared to CAP, our HCL obtains the comparable results on Market-1501 and obtains 0.7% top-1 and 0.1% mAP performance gain on DukeMTMC-reID, and our MGCE-HCL obtains 0.7% top-1 and 0.4% mAP performance gain on Market-1501, and obtains 1.4% top-1 gain and 0.2% mAP gain on DukeMTMC-reID, respectively.

**Compared to UDA-based methods.** We also list the results for UDA based methods at the upper part in Table 6. The UDA-based methods exploit the information from source domain to improve the performance of unlabeled target domain. In the UDA part, the column of Market-1501 shows the results where model is transferred from DukeMTMC-reID to Market-1501, and vice versa for the column of DukeMTMC-reID. Note that our methods without any label annotation can outperform SpCL on Market-1501 and are on par with SpCL on DukeMTMC-reID.

## 6    Conclusions

We have proposed a hybrid contrastive learning (HCL) paradigm for unsupervised person ReID, in which the cluster structure of positive samples are reserved but the clusters of the negative samples are ignored. Moreover, we have presented a multi-granularity cluster ensemble (MGCE) approach to weight the positive samples in different granularity with a priority, and developed a priority-weighted hybrid contrastive loss for training, by which the noises especially from larger granularity clusters can be reduced to some extent. We conducted extensive experiments on two benchmark datasets and the results shown that our HCL paradigm notably outperforms the instance-level contrastive learning paradigm and cluster-level contrastive learning paradigm, and our MGCE-HCL approach achieves the better performance compared to state-of-the-art methods.

**Acknowledgment.** This work is supported by the National Natural Science Foundation of China under Grant 61876022.

## References

1. Chen, T., Kornblith, S., Norouzi, M., Hinton, G.: A simple framework for contrastive learning of visual representations. In: International Conference on Machine Learning, pp. 1597–1607. PMLR (2020)
2. Deng, W., Zheng, L., Ye, Q., Kang, G., Yang, Y., Jiao, J.: Image-image domain adaptation with preserved self-similarity and domain-dissimilarity for person re-identification. In: IEEE Conference on Computer Vision and Pattern Recognition, pp. 994–1003 (2018)
3. Ester, M., Kriegel, H.P., Sander, J., Xu, X.: A density-based algorithm for discovering clusters in large spatial databases with noise. In: Proceedings of the Second International Conference on Knowledge Discovery and Data Mining, pp. 226–231 (1996)
4. Fan, H., Zheng, L., Yan, C., Yang, Y.: Unsupervised person re-identification: clustering and fine-tuning. ACM Trans. Multimed. Comput. Commun. Appl. **14**(4), 83 (2018)
5. Fu, Y., Wei, Y., Wang, G., Zhou, Y., Shi, H., Huang, T.S.: Self-similarity grouping: A simple unsupervised cross domain adaptation approach for person re-identification. In: Proceedings of the IEEE/CVF International Conference on Computer Vision, pp. 6112–6121 (2019)
6. Ge, Y., Chen, D., Li, H.: Mutual mean-teaching: pseudo label refinery for unsupervised domain adaptation on person re-identification. In: International Conference on Learning Representations (2020)
7. Ge, Y., Zhu, F., Chen, D., Zhao, R., Li, H.: Self-paced contrastive learning with hybrid memory for domain adaptive object RE-ID. In: Advances in Neural Information Processing Systems (2020)
8. Grill, J.B., et al.: Bootstrap your own latent: A new approach to self-supervised learning. arXiv preprint arXiv:2006.07733 (2020)
9. Gutmann, M., Hyvärinen, A.: Noise-contrastive estimation: a new estimation principle for unnormalized statistical models. J. Mach. Learn. Res. **9**, 297–304 (2010)
10. He, K., Fan, H., Wu, Y., Xie, S., Girshick, R.: Momentum contrast for unsupervised visual representation learning. In: Proceedings of the IEEE/CVF Conference on Computer Vision and Pattern Recognition, pp. 9729–9738 (2020)
11. He, K., Zhang, X., Ren, S., Sun, J.: Deep residual learning for image recognition. In: Proceedings of the IEEE Conference on Computer Vision and Pattern Recognition, pp. 770–778 (2016)

12. Kingma, D.P., Ba, J.: Adam: a method for stochastic optimization. arXiv preprint arXiv:1412.6980 (2014)
13. Liao, S., Hu, Y., Zhu, X., Li, S.Z.: Person re-identification by local maximal occurrence representation and metric learning. In: IEEE Conference on Computer Vision and Pattern Recognition, pp. 2197–2206 (2015)
14. Lin, Y., Dong, X., Zheng, L., Yan, Y., Yang, Y.: A bottom-up clustering approach to unsupervised person re-identification. In: The Association for the Advancement of Artificial Intelligence, vol. 33, pp. 8738–8745 (2019)
15. Lin, Y., Xie, L., Wu, Y., Yan, C., Tian, Q.: Unsupervised person re-identification via softened similarity learning. In: IEEE Conference on Computer Vision and Pattern Recognition (2020)
16. Oord, A.v.d., Li, Y., Vinyals, O.: Representation learning with contrastive predictive coding. arXiv preprint arXiv:1807.03748 (2018)
17. Ristani, E., Tomasi, C.: Features for multi-target multi-camera tracking and re-identification. In: Proceedings of the IEEE Conference on Computer Vision and Pattern Recognition, pp. 6036–6046 (2018)
18. Wang, D., Zhang, S.: Unsupervised person re-identification via multi-label classification. In: Proceedings of the IEEE/CVF Conference on Computer Vision and Pattern Recognition, pp. 10981–10990 (2020)
19. Wang, G., Yuan, Y., Chen, X., Li, J., Zhou, X.: Learning discriminative features with multiple granularities for person re-identification. In: Proceedings of the 26th ACM international conference on Multimedia, pp. 274–282 (2018)
20. Wang, M., Lai, B., Huang, J., Gong, X., Hua, X.S.: Camera-aware proxies for unsupervised person re-identification. In: Proceedings of the AAAI Conference on Artificial Intelligence (AAAI) (2021)
21. Wei, L., Zhang, S., Gao, W., Tian, Q.: Person transfer GAN to bridge domain gap for person re-identification. In: IEEE Conference on Computer Vision and Pattern Recognition, pp. 79–88 (2018)
22. Wu, Z., Xiong, Y., Yu, S.X., Lin, D.: Unsupervised feature learning via non-parametric instance discrimination. In: Proceedings of the IEEE Conference on Computer Vision and Pattern Recognition, pp. 3733–3742 (2018)
23. Yu, H.X., Wu, A., Zheng, W.S.: Cross-view asymmetric metric learning for unsupervised person re-identification. In: IEEE International Conference on Computer Vision, pp. 994–1002 (2017)
24. Yu, H.X., Zheng, W.S., Wu, A., Guo, X., Gong, S., Lai, J.H.: Unsupervised person re-identification by soft multilabel learning. In: Proceedings of the IEEE/CVF Conference on Computer Vision and Pattern Recognition, pp. 2148–2157 (2019)
25. Zeng, K., Ning, M., Wang, Y., Guo, Y.: Hierarchical clustering with hard-batch triplet loss for person re-identification. In: IEEE Conference on Computer Vision and Pattern Recognition, pp. 13657–13665 (2020)
26. Zhai, Y., et al.: Ad-cluster: augmented discriminative clustering for domain adaptive person re-identification. In: Proceedings of the IEEE/CVF Conference on Computer Vision and Pattern Recognition, pp. 9021–9030 (2020)
27. Zhai, Y., Ye, Q., Lu, S., Jia, M., Ji, R., Tian, Y.: Multiple expert brainstorming for domain adaptive person re-identification. In: Vedaldi, A., Bischof, H., Brox, T., Frahm, J.-M. (eds.) ECCV 2020. LNCS, vol. 12352, pp. 594–611. Springer, Cham (2020). https://doi.org/10.1007/978-3-030-58571-6_35
28. Zheng, L., Shen, L., Tian, L., Wang, S., Wang, J., Tian, Q.: Scalable person re-identification: a benchmark. In: IEEE International Conference on Computer Vision, pp. 1116–1124 (2015)
29. Zhong, Z., Zheng, L., Kang, G., Li, S., Yang, Y.: Random erasing data augmentation. In: Proceedings of the AAAI Conference on Artificial Intelligence, vol. 34, pp. 13001–13008 (2020)

30. Zhong, Z., Zheng, L., Li, S., Yang, Y.: Generalizing a person retrieval model hetero- and homogeneously. In: Ferrari, V., Hebert, M., Sminchisescu, C., Weiss, Y. (eds.) ECCV 2018. LNCS, vol. 11217, pp. 176–192. Springer, Cham (2018). https://doi.org/10.1007/978-3-030-01261-8_11

31. Zhong, Z., Zheng, L., Luo, Z., Li, S., Yang, Y.: Invariance matters: exemplar memory for domain adaptive person re-identification. In: Proceedings of the IEEE/CVF Conference on Computer Vision and Pattern Recognition, pp. 598–607 (2019)

32. Zhong, Z., Zheng, L., Luo, Z., Li, S., Yang, Y.: Invariance matters: exemplar memory for domain adaptive person re-identification, pp. 598–607 (2019)

# Robust Multi-view Registration of Point Sets with Laplacian Mixture Model

Jin Zhang[1], Mingyang Zhao[2,3], Xin Jiang[1,4(✉)], and Dong-Ming Yan[3]

[1] Key Laboratory of Mathematics, Informatics and Behavioral Semantics, School of Mathematical Science, Beihang University, Beijing, China
{theigrams,jiangxin}@buaa.edu.cn
[2] Beijing Academy of Artificial Intelligence, Beijing, China
[3] National Key Laboratory of Pattern Recognition, Institute of Automation, Chinese Academy of Sciences (CAS), Beijing, China
zhaomingyang16@mails.ucas.ac.cn
[4] Peng Cheng Laboratory, Shenzhen, Guangdong, China

**Abstract.** Point set registration is an essential step in many computer vision applications, such as 3D reconstruction and SLAM. Although there exist many registration algorithms for different purposes, however, this topic is still challenging due to the increasing complexity of various real-world scenarios, such as heavy noise and outlier contamination. In this paper, we propose a novel probabilistic generative method to simultaneously align multiple point sets based on the heavy-tailed Laplacian distribution. The proposed method assumes each data point is generated by a *Laplacian Mixture Model* (LMM), where its centers are determined by the corresponding points in other point sets. Different from the previous *Gaussian Mixture Model* (GMM) based method, which minimizes the quadratic distance between points and centers of Gaussian probability density, LMM minimizes the sparsity-induced $L_1$ distance, thereby it is more robust against noise and outliers. We adopt *Expectation-Maximization* (EM) framework to solve LMM parameters and rigid transformations. We approximate the $L_1$ optimization as a linear programming problem by exponential mapping in Lie algebra, which can be effectively solved through the *interior point method*. To improve efficiency, we also solve the $L_1$ optimization by *Alternating Direction Multiplier Method* (ADMM). We demonstrate the advantages of our method by comparing it with representative state-of-the-art approaches on benchmark challenging data sets, in terms of robustness and accuracy.

**Keywords:** Point set registration · $L_1$ optimization · GMM · LMM

## 1 Introduction

Point set registration is a fundamental problem that has wide applications in computer vision [26], robotics [25], computer graphics [12], medical image analysis [19] and so on. With the advent of sensors such as LiDAR (Light Detection

© Springer Nature Switzerland AG 2022
C. Wallraven et al. (Eds.): ACPR 2021, LNCS 13189, pp. 547–561, 2022.
https://doi.org/10.1007/978-3-031-02444-3_41

and Ranging) and depth cameras, it becomes relatively easy to capture real-world 3D scene data. However, one usually attains partial point clouds at once due to the 3D nature of the objects. To accurately reconstruct the 3D model, it is necessary to align multiple point clouds acquired from multi views of the object into a unified coordinate system.

Point set registration has been extensively studied in literature, and many efforts are devoted to the pair-wise (two sets) registration problem. Among these methods, the most classical one is the *Iterative Closest Point* (ICP) algorithm [18], in which the registration is decomposed as the alternative implementation of point correspondence and transformation estimation. Given a set of data points, the rigid transformation of ICP is solved by minimizing the summation of the squared distance of the closest point pairs. However, ICP tends to get trapped in a local optimum because of the hard assignment scheme, improper initialization, occlusions, and the interference of noise and outliers.

In contrast to the hard assignment scheme of ICP, previous works also explore the use of statistical models for registration, such as GMM [13], which replaces the previous binary assignment with probability. These methods formulate point set registration as a probability density estimation, where the mean of each component is initialized as the point location. In principle, probability registration can provide better estimation for convergence and geometric matching, thereby they are further extended for multi-view registration [8]. Most existing probability methods rely on GMM for registration, nevertheless, Gaussian distribution minimizes the quadratic distance between the data points and their means, which makes GMM susceptible to noise with heavy tail and sensitive to outliers [10].

In this paper, to address the aforementioned problems, we propose a novel and robust multi-view registration method based on the LMM composed by the Laplacian distribution. Due to the heavy-tail property and the sparsity-induced $L_1$ norm, LMM is more robust against outliers. We formulate point set registration as a likelihood estimation problem, which can be solved by EM framework. To handle the $L_1$ optimization, we customize the rotation estimation to a linear programming problem by exponential mapping and name it as *linear programming approximation* (LPA). Moreover, inspired by [4], we also use ADMM to solve $L_1$ optimization, which has higher efficiency without significant accuracy decreasing. We test and compare the proposed methods (including LPA and ADMM) with representative state-of-the-art approaches in terms of accuracy and robustness, and the results indicate that our methods outperform previous ones with higher accuracy and are more robust against noise and outliers.

In a nutshell, the main contributions of this paper are twofold as follows:

- We propose a novel multi-view registration method for point clouds based on the sparsity-induced Laplacian mixture model. Due to the $L_1$ norm of Laplacian distribution, the proposed method is more robust against noise and outliers;
- To handle $L_1$ optimization, we customize it as a linear programming problem via exponential mapping, which can be effectively solved by the interior

point method. For efficiency, we further deduce it into the ADMM framework, thereby it can also be solved by the ADMM algorithm.

## 2   Related Work

We briefly review the related work of point set registration from the perspective of pair-wise registration and multi-view registration.

### 2.1   Pair-Wise Registration

The objective of pair-wise registration is to align two point sets by solving a transformation matrix. The most popular algorithm of pair-wise registration is ICP [18], which composes two iterative steps: 1) correspondence step in which the point correspondence between two point sets is established, and 2) transformation step in which the transformation matrix based on the current correspondence is updated. ICP takes the least-squares estimator as the objective function, thereby the closed-form solution in each step can be attained through *singular value decomposition* (SVD). However, as the Gauss-Markov theorem [21] pointed, the least-squares estimator is sensitive to outliers. Moreover, ICP requires good initialization and fails to handle non-overlapping point sets. To improve performance, many variants of ICP have been proposed. Fitzgibbon [9] adopts M-estimator for registration error minimization and solves the problem by non-linear Levenberg-Marquardt optimization, thereby proper initialization is required. Chetverikov *et al.* [6] propose a trim scheme named TrICP to automatically remove non-overlapping regions for accurate registration. For efficiency, Rusu *et al.* [22] introduce Fast Point Feature Histograms (FPFH) to describe the local geometry around a point to reduce the computational complexity. Lei *et al.* [15] compute eigenvalues and normals from multiple scales and take them as local descriptors to speed up matching. However, descriptor-based methods [11,15] are susceptible to point sets with noise and low overlapping. Recently, deep learning-based methods such as [1] are also proposed to estimate the transformation matrix. Nevertheless, the lack of comprehensive registration datasets results in a hard time for the learning methods to grasp all shape variations.

Alternatively, probability registration methods adopt GMM to represent data points, such as Robust Point Matching [7], Coherent Point Drift [17], and GMM-Reg [13]. These methods either simultaneously model the source and the target point sets by GMM, and the transformation matrix is solved by minimizing the discrepancy between the two GMMs, or singly model the source point set as GMM, and then evoke maximum likelihood estimation to fit the target point set. However, GMM fails to attain accurate registration results under the contamination of noise with a heavy tail. Moreover, since GMM minimizes the quadratic distance between the points and its means, it suffers from severe outliers. In contrast, we introduce Laplacian mixture models to model data distribution, which adopt the $L_1$ norm for error evaluation, thereby it is more robust against outliers for registration.

## 2.2   Multi-view Registration

Multi-view registration aims to simultaneously register multiple point sets from different views, which is often solved through sequential pair-wise registration. Transformation parameters are sequentially updated by ICP or probability methods if a new point set is added. Except for the drawbacks from pair-wise registration, these methods also suffer from error accumulation and propagation. Bergevin et al. [3] propose a star-network and sequentially put one point set in the center of it, then pair-wise registration by ICP is implemented to align the central point set with the other ones. In contrast, Williams et al. [24] simultaneously compute the correspondence between all point sets, which is time-consuming. Mateo et al. [16] introduce the Bayesian perspective to assign different weights for different correspondences, with the detection of false correspondences. Although the registration accuracy is improved, it needs to compute many variables.

Additionally, information theoretic measures are also customized for multi-view registration task. Wang et al. [23] first represent point sets by cumulative distribution function (CDF), and then minimize the Jensen-Shannon divergence between CDFs for multi-view registration. Later, Chen et al. [5] use the Havrda-Charvat divergence to evaluate the differences between CDFs, compared with previous Jensen-Shannon divergence, this method is more efficient. Nevertheless, information theory based approaches are still with low efficiency.

Recently, GMM is generalized for multi-view registration by [8] named JRMPC, which assumes data points are generated by a central GMM, and then casts the registration task as a clustering process. By this, global information of point sets is combined to avoid the error accumulation. Zhu et al. [27] propose a method named EMPMR, which assumes that each data point is generated from a GMM whose Gaussian centroids are composed of corresponding points from other point sets. Nevertheless, GMM suffers from heavy-tail noise, and is sensitive to severe outliers due to the $L_2$ norm. Based on JMRPC, TMM [20] achieves better robustness by replacing the Gaussian distribution with a $t$-distribution, however, its time consumption is relatively considerable. To address these drawbacks, we propose a novel and robust multi-view registration method based on the sparsity-induced $L_1$ norm, which is effectively solved by LPA or ADMM.

## 3   Methodology

### 3.1   Multivariate Laplacian Distribution

Suppose $\dot{\mathbf{x}} \in \mathbb{R}^d$ is a random variable following the multivariate Laplacian distribution, with the probability density function as

$$\mathcal{L}\left(\boldsymbol{x};\boldsymbol{\mu},b\right) = \frac{1}{(2b)^d} \exp\left(-\frac{\|\boldsymbol{x}-\boldsymbol{\mu}\|_1}{b}\right), \tag{1}$$

where $\boldsymbol{\mu}$ and $b$ represent the mean and the scale parameter of the $d$-dimensional Laplacian distribution, respectively, and $\|\cdot\|_1$ denotes the sparsity-induced $L_1$

norm, summarizing the absolute values of all elements of a vector. Previous work has shown that the Gaussian distribution is sensitive to heavy outliers because of its short tails [2,10], while the Laplacian distribution has heavier tails.

## 3.2  Laplacian Mixture Model

Let $\mathcal{X} = \{X_i\}_{i=1}^{M}$ be the union of $M$ point sets, and $X_i = [x_{i1}, x_{i2}, \ldots, x_{iN_i}] \in \mathbb{R}^{3 \times N_i}$ be the $i$-th point set, where $x_{il}$ is the $l$-th point of $X_i$ and $N_i$ is the cardinality of $X_i$. The task of multi-view registration is to align the multiple point sets in $\mathcal{X}$ to the same center frame. To this end, we solve the rotation matrix $R_i$ and the translation vector $t_i$ for each $X_i$, and represent the transformed coordinates as $\hat{x}_{il} = R_i x_{il} + t_i$. Due to the influence of noise, it is hard to hope that corresponding points in different frames will have the same coordinate after alignment. In contrast, we assume the multi-view point sets will constitute multiple clusters.

Suppose each data point $\hat{x}_{il}$ is generated from a unique LMM, where the Laplacian centers are composed of the corresponding points in other frames after alignment. However, it is difficult to directly get the accurate correspondence relationship between different point sets. Here we adopt the *nearest neighbor search* based on the *kd-tree* to approximate the corresponding points. In specific, for point $\hat{x}$ of the center frame, we denote $c_j(\hat{x})$ as the nearest neighbor of $\hat{x}$ from the $j$-th point set, which can be defined as:

$$c_j(\hat{x}) = \arg\min_{\{\hat{x}_{jh}\}_{h=1}^{N_j}} \|\hat{x} - \hat{x}_{jh}\|_1. \tag{2}$$

For simplicity, we use isotropic covariance $b$ and equal membership probability for all LMM components. Thereby, the LMM of $x \in X_i$ is defined as

$$P(x) = \sum_{\substack{j=1 \\ j \neq i}}^{M} \frac{1}{M-1} \mathcal{L}(R_i x + t_i; c_j(\hat{x}), b). \tag{3}$$

Note that different from previous GMM based methods, in which a uniform distribution has to be added to account for noise and outliers, there is no need for our LMM based method, since Laplacian distribution has a heavy tail and is sparse enough to accommodate outliers.

We adopt the *maximum likelihood estimation* (MLE) to solve unknown parameters. The log-likelihood function of observed data points is

$$L(\Theta; \mathcal{X}) = \log P(\mathcal{X} \mid \Theta) = \sum_{i=1}^{M} \sum_{l=1}^{N_i} \log \left( \sum_{\substack{j=1 \\ j \neq i}}^{M} \frac{1}{M-1} \mathcal{L}(\hat{x}_{il}; c_j(\hat{x}_{il}), b) \right), \tag{4}$$

where $\Theta = \left\{ \{R_i, t_i\}_{i=1}^{M}, b \right\}$ represents all parameters. It is intractable to directly solve the maximum likelihood solution for such a complex model. Instead, we adopt the effective EM framework by introducing latent variables for solving, as presented in the following.

## 4  Registration by EM Algorithm

To estimate the parameters by EM algorithm, we first define a set of latent variables $\mathcal{Z} = \{Z_{il} \mid 1 \leq i \leq M,\ 1 \leq l \leq N_i\}$, where $Z_{il} = j$ means that $\hat{\boldsymbol{x}}_{il}$ is generated from the $j$-th component of the LMM. Given all observed data $\mathcal{X}$, model parameters can be estimated by maximizing the expectation of the log-likelihood function:

$$
\mathcal{E}\left(\Theta; \mathcal{X}, \mathcal{Z}\right) = \mathbb{E}_{\mathcal{Z}}\left[\log P\left(\mathcal{X}, \mathcal{Z}; \Theta\right)\right] = \sum_{\mathcal{Z}} P\left(\mathcal{Z} \mid \mathcal{X}; \Theta\right) \log P\left(\mathcal{X}, \mathcal{Z}; \Theta\right)
$$

$$
= \sum_{\mathcal{Z}} P\left(\mathcal{Z} \mid \mathcal{X}; \Theta\right)\left(\log P\left(\mathcal{X} \mid \mathcal{Z}; \Theta\right) + \log P\left(\mathcal{Z}; \Theta\right)\right). \tag{5}
$$

Since we regard each Laplacian component equal, the prior probability $P(\mathcal{Z}; \Theta)$ is a constant term. In addition, $P(\mathcal{X} \mid \mathcal{Z}; \Theta)$ can be derived from Eq. (3), namely, $P\left(\boldsymbol{x}_{il} \mid Z_{il} = j; \Theta\right) = \mathcal{L}\left(\hat{\boldsymbol{x}}_{il}; c_j\left(\hat{\boldsymbol{x}}_{il}\right), b\right).$

After ignoring constant terms, the objective function of Eq. (5) is reformulated as

$$
f\left(\Theta\right) = \sum_{i=1}^{M}\sum_{l=1}^{N_i}\sum_{j\neq i}^{M} \alpha_{ilj} \log \mathcal{L}\left(\hat{\boldsymbol{x}}_{il}; c_j(\hat{\boldsymbol{x}}_{il}), b\right)
$$

$$
= -\sum_{i,l,j} \alpha_{ilj}\left(\frac{1}{b}\|\hat{\boldsymbol{x}}_{il} - c_j(\hat{\boldsymbol{x}}_{il})\|_1 + d\log 2b\right), \tag{6}
$$

where $\alpha_{ilj} = P(Z_{il} = j \mid \boldsymbol{x}_{il}; \Theta)$ denotes the posterior and $d$ denotes the data dimension ($d = 3$ in our case). Therefore, the multi-view registration problem is cast into a constrained optimization problem as follows:

$$
\hat{\Theta} = \arg\max_{\Theta} f(\Theta), \quad \text{s.t. } \boldsymbol{R}_i \in \mathrm{SO}(3), \quad \forall i \in [1, ..., M]. \tag{7}
$$

In order to maximize $f(\Theta)$ by EM algorithm, we alternatively perform E-step and M-step as follows, after which the transformation parameters of multi-view registration are attained.

### 4.1  E-Step

Given data point set $\mathcal{X}$ and currently estimated parameters $\Theta^{(k)}$, E-step calculates the distribution of latent variable $\mathcal{Z}$, which can be divided into two steps. The first step is to establish point correspondence. For point $\boldsymbol{x}_{il}$ in $i$-th point set, it is initially transformed into the center frame with new coordinate $\hat{\boldsymbol{x}}_{il}^{(k)} = \boldsymbol{R}_i^{(k)}\boldsymbol{x}_{il} + \boldsymbol{t}_i^{(k)}$. Then the corresponding point in $j$-th frame can be approximated by the nearest neighbour of $\hat{\boldsymbol{x}}_{il}^{(k)}$:

$$
c_j\left(\hat{\boldsymbol{x}}_{il}^{(k)}\right) = \arg\min_{\{\hat{\boldsymbol{x}}_{jh}\}_{h=1}^{N_j}} \left\|\hat{\boldsymbol{x}}_{il}^{(k)} - \hat{\boldsymbol{x}}_{jh}^{(k)}\right\|_1. \tag{8}
$$

The second step updates $\alpha_{ilj}^{(k+1)} = P(Z_{il} = j \mid \boldsymbol{x}_{il}; \Theta^{(k)})$, which represents the posterior probability of point $\boldsymbol{x}_{il}$ generated from $j$-th component of LMM. According to Bayesian formula, we have

$$\alpha_{ilj}^{(k+1)} = \frac{\mathcal{L}\left(\hat{\boldsymbol{x}}_{il}^{(k)}; c_j(\hat{\boldsymbol{x}}_{il}^{(k)}), b^{(k)}\right)}{\sum_{j \neq i}^{M} \mathcal{L}\left(\hat{\boldsymbol{x}}_{il}^{(k)}; c_j(\hat{\boldsymbol{x}}_{il}^{(k)}), b^{(k)}\right)} = \frac{\beta_{ilj}^{(k+1)}}{\sum_{j \neq i}^{M} \beta_{ilj}^{(k+1)}}, \tag{9}$$

where $\beta_{ilj}$ denotes the probability density of Laplacian distribution:

$$\beta_{ilj}^{(k+1)} = \frac{1}{\left(2b^{(k)}\right)^d} \exp\left(-\frac{\left\|\hat{\boldsymbol{x}}_{il}^{(k)} - c_j(\hat{\boldsymbol{x}}_{il}^{(k)})\right\|_1}{b^{(k)}}\right). \tag{10}$$

## 4.2   M-Step

M-step estimates the parameters $\Theta^{(k+1)}$ by maximizing the expectation $f(\Theta)$ with current values $\alpha_{ilj}^{(k+1)}$ and $c_j(\hat{\boldsymbol{x}}_{il}^{(k)})$. Since it is difficult to directly estimate all parameters in $\Theta = \{\{\boldsymbol{R}_i, \boldsymbol{t}_i\}_{i=1}^{M}, b\}$, we first solve transformation parameters $\{\boldsymbol{R}_i, \boldsymbol{t}_i\}$ and then solve the variance scale $b$. Transformation parameters are estimated by

$$\begin{cases} \underset{\boldsymbol{R}_i, \boldsymbol{t}_i}{\arg\min} & \sum_{l=1}^{N_i} \sum_{j \neq i}^{M} \alpha_{ilj}^{(k+1)} \left\|\boldsymbol{R}_i \boldsymbol{x}_{il} + \boldsymbol{t}_i - c_j(\hat{\boldsymbol{x}}_{il}^{(k)})\right\|_1 \\ \text{s.t.} & \boldsymbol{R}_i^T \boldsymbol{R}_i = \boldsymbol{I} \text{ and } |\boldsymbol{R}_i| = 1. \end{cases} \tag{11}$$

The above equation is a *weighted least absolute value* (WLAV) problem with SO(3) constraint. Although there is lack of a closed-form solution, we propose two methods to iteratively solve it in Sect. 4.3. After updating transformation parameters, we take the partial derivative of $f(\Theta)$ with respect to $b$ and equate it to zero, then the update of $b^{(k+1)}$ is

$$b^{(k+1)} = \frac{\sum_{i,j,l} \alpha_{ilj}^{(k+1)} \left\|\hat{\boldsymbol{x}}_{il}^{(k+1)} - c_j(\hat{\boldsymbol{x}}_{il}^{(k+1)})\right\|_1}{d \sum_i N_i}, \tag{12}$$

where $N_i$ denotes the cardinality of the $i$-th point set. As can be seen, $b$ presents the weighted average of the deviations.

## 4.3   WLAV Subproblem

Previous GMM based approaches usually need to solve a weighted least square problem, and the closed-form solution can be attained through SVD. However, due to the $L_1$ norm optimization, WLSV problem requires iterative solving. In this work, we propose two methods to solve this kind of problem, namely, LPA based and ADMM based methods, as presented in the following.

**LPA Method.** We first transform the sub-problem (11) into a canonical form:

$$\min_{R,t} \quad \sum_{i=1}^{n} w_i \|Rp_i + t - q_i\|_1 \quad \text{s.t. } R \in SO(3), \tag{13}$$

where $P = [p_1, \ldots, p_n] \in \mathbb{R}^{3 \times n}$ and $Q = [q_1, \ldots, q_n] \in \mathbb{R}^{3 \times n}$ represent the source point set and the target point set respectively, while $w_i$ represents the weight. By exponential mapping, the rotation matrix $R$ can be written as:

$$R = \exp\left([r]_\times\right) = I + [r]_\times + \frac{1}{2!}[r]_\times^2 + \frac{1}{3!}[r]_\times^3 + \cdots, \tag{14}$$

where $[r]_\times$ represents the skew-symmetric matrix of $r \in \mathbb{R}^3$, expressed as

$$[r]_\times = \begin{bmatrix} 0 & -r_3 & r_2 \\ r_3 & 0 & -r_1 \\ -r_2 & r_1 & 0 \end{bmatrix}. \tag{15}$$

To eliminate the SO(3) constraint, we linearly approximate the rotation matrix $R$ by neglecting the higher-order terms of (14). Then the deviation can be approximated as

$$Rp - q + t \approx \begin{bmatrix} -[p]_\times & I_{3\times3} \end{bmatrix} \begin{bmatrix} r \\ t \end{bmatrix} + p - q, \tag{16}$$

since $[r]_\times p = -[p]_\times r$.

Then the objective function can be reformulated as:

$$\sum_{i=1}^{N} w_i \|Rp_i - q_i + t\|_1 \approx \left\| \begin{bmatrix} -w_1[p_1]_\times & I_3 \\ \vdots & \vdots \\ -w_N[p_N]_\times & I_3 \end{bmatrix} \begin{bmatrix} r \\ t \end{bmatrix} - \begin{bmatrix} -w_1(p-q) \\ \vdots \\ -w_N(p-q) \end{bmatrix} \right\|_1 = \|Ax - b\|_1, \tag{17}$$

where $x$ denotes $[r, t]^T$. Let $u = |Ax - b|$, the original WLAS problem is transformed into a linear programming problem:

$$\min_{u,x} \quad \sum_{i=1}^{N} u_i, \quad \text{s.t. } -u + Ax - b \le 0 \text{ and } -u - Ax + b \le 0, \tag{18}$$

which can be efficiently solved by interior point methods [14]. Moreover, we deduce another method to solve $L_1$ optimization based on the ADMM in the following. We name the two optimizations as Ours-LPA and Ours-ADMM, respectively, and compare them with previous approaches in Sect. 5.

**ADMM Method.** Considering the constraint $z_i = w_i(Rp_i + t - q_i)$, Eq. (13) can be reformulated as:

$$\begin{aligned} \min_{R,t} \quad & \sum_{i=1}^{n} \|z_i\|_1 \\ \text{s.t.} \quad & R \in SO(3), \\ & z_i = w_i(Rp_i + t - q_i), \quad i = 1, \ldots, n. \end{aligned} \tag{19}$$

Then the augmented Lagrangian function of ADMM is

$$L_\rho \left( \boldsymbol{R}, \boldsymbol{t}, \boldsymbol{z}, \lambda \right) = \sum_{i=1}^{n} \left( \|\boldsymbol{z}_i\|_1 + \frac{\rho}{2} \left\| \boldsymbol{z}_i - \boldsymbol{s}_i + \frac{1}{\rho} \boldsymbol{\lambda}_i \right\|_2^2 - \frac{1}{2\rho} \|\boldsymbol{\lambda}_i\|_2^2 \right), \qquad (20)$$

where we replace $\boldsymbol{w}_i \left( \boldsymbol{R} \boldsymbol{p}_i + \boldsymbol{t} - \boldsymbol{q}_i \right)$ by $\boldsymbol{s}_i$ to simplify the formula. Due to the space limit, we directly present the iterative steps as

$$\boldsymbol{z}^{(k+1)} := \arg\min_{\boldsymbol{z}} L_\rho \left( \boldsymbol{R}^{(k)}, \boldsymbol{t}^{(k)}, \boldsymbol{z}, \boldsymbol{\lambda}^{(k)} \right), \qquad (21)$$

$$\boldsymbol{R}^{(k+1)}, \boldsymbol{t}^{(k+1)} := \arg\min_{\boldsymbol{R}, \boldsymbol{t}} L_\rho \left( \boldsymbol{R}, \boldsymbol{t}, \boldsymbol{z}^{(k+1)}, \boldsymbol{\lambda}^{(k)} \right), \qquad (22)$$

$$\boldsymbol{\lambda}_i^{(k+1)} := \boldsymbol{\lambda}_i^{(k)} + \rho \left( \boldsymbol{z}_i^{(k)} - \boldsymbol{s}_i^{(k)} \right), \quad i = 1, \ldots, n, \qquad (23)$$

where sub-problem (21) can be solved efficiently by the following shrinkage operator:

$$\boldsymbol{z}_i^{(k+1)} = \mathcal{S}_{1/\rho} \left( \boldsymbol{s}_i^{(k)} - \frac{1}{\rho} \boldsymbol{\lambda}^{(k)} \right), \qquad \mathcal{S}_\lambda \left( x \right) = \begin{cases} x - \lambda & \text{if } x > \lambda; \\ x + \lambda & \text{if } x < \lambda; \\ 0 & \text{otherwise}. \end{cases}, \qquad (24)$$

while sub-problem (22) can be solved by SVD.

## 5    Experiments

In this section, we compare the performance of the proposed method with three representative state-of-the-art approaches for multi-view registration, namely, JRMPC [8], TMM [20], and EMPMR [27]. The implementation of all compared methods is publicly available. All experiments in the following are performed on a laptop with a 6-core 2.2 GHz Intel CPU and 16 GB RAM.

### 5.1    Data Sets and Evaluation Measure

We use six 3D data sets from the Stanford 3D Scanning Repository[1] (Bunny, Buddha, Dragon, and Armadillo) and the AIM@SHAPE Repository[2] (Bimba and Olivier hand) for test. To quantitatively evaluate the registration performance of different methods, we compute the error by

$$e_{\boldsymbol{R}} = \frac{1}{M} \sum_{i=1}^{M} \arccos \left( \frac{\text{tr} \left( \boldsymbol{R}_i \left( \boldsymbol{R}_i^G \right)^T \right) - 1}{2} \right), \quad e_t = \frac{1}{M} \sum_{i=1}^{M} \left\| \boldsymbol{t}_i - \boldsymbol{t}_i^G \right\|_2, \quad (25)$$

where $\left\{ \boldsymbol{R}_i^G, \boldsymbol{t}_i^G \right\}_{i=1}^{M}$ and $\{\boldsymbol{R}_i, \boldsymbol{t}_i\}_{i=1}^{M}$ denote the ground truth and the estimated rigid transformation, respectively.

[1] http://graphics.stanford.edu/data/3Dscanrep.
[2] http://visionair.ge.imati.cnr.it/ontologies/shapes.

**Table 1.** Statistics of registration errors of all compared methods, where the *italic* and **bold** fonts indicate the best and the second-best performance for each metric. The proposed method Ours-LPA attains the overall best performance.

| Methods | | Armadillo | Bimba | Buddha | Bunny | Dragon | Hand |
|---|---|---|---|---|---|---|---|
| Initial | $e_R$ | 0.037378 | 0.04016 | 0.034194 | 0.036776 | 0.033269 | 0.038187 |
| | $e_t$ | 0.000000 | 0.000000 | 0.000000 | 0.000000 | 0.000000 | 0.000000 |
| TMM [20] | $e_R$ | 0.165546 | 0.182914 | 0.150696 | 0.204346 | 0.152766 | 0.085944 |
| | $e_t$ | 0.001657 | 0.003268 | 0.009475 | 0.008532 | 0.011171 | 0.002163 |
| JRMPC [8] | $e_R$ | **0.004748** | 0.067163 | 0.024169 | **0.007340** | **0.002504** | 0.312689 |
| | $e_t$ | 0.000087 | 0.001867 | 0.000615 | 0.000246 | 0.000259 | 0.001234 |
| EMPMR [27] | $e_R$ | 0.042555 | 0.008452 | 0.021825 | 0.029602 | 0.032349 | 0.010282 |
| | $e_t$ | *0.000008* | *0.000005* | *0.000019* | *0.000021* | *0.000028* | *0.000003* |
| Ours-ADMM | $e_R$ | 0.008538 | **0.001002** | **0.004597** | 0.008356 | 0.004588 | **0.002335** |
| | $e_t$ | 0.000120 | 0.000075 | 0.000301 | 0.000713 | 0.000326 | 0.000080 |
| Ours-LPA | $e_R$ | *0.002954* | *0.000353* | *0.001519* | *0.001953* | *0.001181* | *0.000896* |
| | $e_t$ | **0.000051** | **0.000019** | **0.000114** | **0.000159** | **0.000101** | **0.000023** |

## 5.2 Comparison Results

We first downsample each data set to 4,000 points, and crop them along the $xy$-plane to generate the missing overlapping, then we rotate them around the $x$, $y$ and $z$-axes with the rotation angle uniformly distributed between $[-20°, 20°]$. Moreover, we add Gaussian noise to each data point with the signal-to-noise ratio (SNR) equal to 70 dB and 30% outliers following the uniform distribution.

The comparison results are reported in Table 1. We color the best in *italic* and the second-best in **bold** for each metric. As observed, compared with initial errors, TMM has larger rotation deviations for all data sets, JRMPC and EMPMR also suffer from rotation estimation, such as the Bunny and the Armadillo data sets. In contrast, our proposed methods including Ours-ADMM and Ours-LPA achieve fewer rotation errors than initial cases for all data sets. Moreover, the proposed Ours-LPA attains the highest accuracy for rotation estimation than all competitors. EMPMR has the overall lowest translation error, but its rotation errors are relatively large. Our proposed method Ours-LPA attains the second highest accuracy for translation estimation, and the deviations are small enough. Thereby, the proposed method Ours-LPA achieves the overall best performance. We present several test examples in Fig. 1.

We further report the time consumption of different methods in Table 2. As observed, due to the closed-form solution of EMPMR based on the $L_2$ norm, it consumes relatively less time. Our proposed method Ours-ADMM has the second fastest speed, and its time consumption is quite close to EMPMR. Moreover, from Table 1, we find that Ours-ADMM has fewer rotation errors than EMPMR, meanwhile with acceptable translation deviations. Ours-LPA consumes relatively more time than Ours-ADMM, however, it is still faster than TMM and JRMPC. Therefore, to register point sets with high efficiency and comparable accuracy, we suggest Ours-ADMM for use.

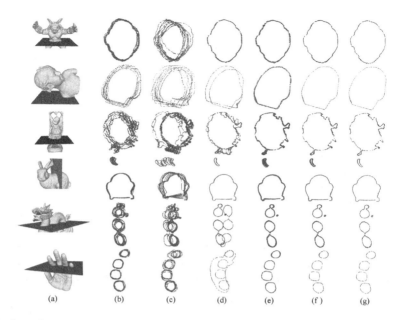

**Fig. 1.** Sample registration results presented in the form of cross section. (a) 3D models. (b) Initial poses. (c) TMM. (d) JRMPC. (e) EMRPC . (f) Ours-ADMM. (g) Ours-LPA.

**Table 2.** Time consumption of all compared methods.

| Methods | Armadillo | Bimba | Buddha | Bunny | Dragon | Hand |
|---------|-----------|-------|--------|-------|--------|------|
| TMM [20] | 416.048315 | 306.375451 | 428.698706 | 215.150639 | 456.21449 | 328.926923 |
| JRMPC [8] | 260.635473 | 234.189799 | 315.937198 | 69.655174 | 73.304373 | 163.161366 |
| EMPMR [27] | 14.298502 | 7.159238 | 10.059491 | 5.108593 | 6.233101 | 4.700202 |
| Ours-ADMM | 21.439405 | 8.915458 | 51.801415 | 8.883673 | 26.442176 | 8.690539 |
| Ours-LPA | 108.499447 | 36.490062 | 161.175015 | 20.262704 | 96.782577 | 36.421847 |

## 5.3   Robustness Against Outliers

Subsequently, we evaluate the robustness of the proposed method against outliers. We adopt the bunny data set for this purpose. We add 1%–80% outliers to the point cloud. Besides, we contaminate the point cloud with 70 dB Gaussian noise. Several examples are illustrated in Fig. 2. The test results are reported in Table 3. As can be seen, with outlier increasing, the proposed method Ours-LPA exhibits higher robustness than compared ones. EMPMR has fewer deviations at low outlier contamination, but it suffers from severe outliers (more than 30%). JRMPC also shows certain robustness against outliers, whereas its performance is unstable. In contrast, Ours-ADMM attains the quite stable performance for all outlier tests, and it has the a very similar registration accuracy to the first

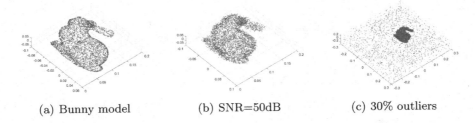

(a) Bunny model          (b) SNR=50dB          (c) 30% outliers

**Fig. 2.** Examples of the Bunny model contaminated by noise and outliers.

**Table 3.** Statistics of registration errors under the contamination of different outliers (%). The proposed method Ours-LPA has the overall best performance.

|            | 1%           | 10%          | 20%          | 30%          | 50%          | 80%          |
|------------|--------------|--------------|--------------|--------------|--------------|--------------|
| Initial    | 0.032794     | 0.034169     | 0.035956     | 0.036776     | 0.028585     | 0.027937     |
| TMM [20]   | 0.010005     | 0.157573     | 0.162055     | 0.204346     | 0.269017     | 0.293706     |
| JRMPC [8]  | **0.004102** | 0.299748     | 0.009423     | **0.007340** | **0.005685** | 0.077505     |
| EMPMR [27] | *0.000342*   | **0.000378** | *0.000500*   | 0.029602     | 0.052858     | 0.094169     |
| Ours-ADMM  | 0.000439     | 0.000572     | 0.008176     | 0.008356     | 0.007888     | **0.034256** |
| Ours-LPA   | 0.000505     | *0.000369*   | **0.000676** | *0.001953*   | *0.002762*   | *0.021861*   |

two winners. TMM has the largest deviations than the others, indicating its weakness in handling outliers.

## 5.4  Robustness Against Noise

We also test the performance of the proposed methods in term of noise. To this end, we first contaminate the point cloud with 30% outliers, and then increase the noise intensity by decreasing the signal-to-noise ratio. The test results are reported in Table 4. As observed, the proposed method Ours-LPA achieves the overall best performance, and its registration errors are even 1,000 times fewer than TMM. JRMPC and Ours-ADMM attain similar results, thereby they have the second-best performance. EMPMR shows shortcomings for noise, especially for low SNR noise.

**Table 4.** Statistics of registration errors of different methods under the contamination of different noise (dB).

|            | 90        | 80        | 70        | 60        | 50        |
|------------|-----------|-----------|-----------|-----------|-----------|
| Initial    | 0.035592  | 0.028818  | 0.036776  | 0.029031  | 0.035445  |
| TMM [20]   | 0.159936  | 0.163456  | 0.204346  | 0.179884  | 0.162614  |
| JRMPC [8]  | 0.093772  | *0.000439* | **0.007340** | 0.065524  | **0.020319** |
| EMPMR [27] | 0.039599  | 0.056480  | 0.029602  | 0.033342  | 0.056580  |
| Ours-ADMM  | **0.008533** | 0.008808  | 0.008356  | **0.009525** | *0.019820* |
| Ours-LPA   | *0.000245* | **0.001216** | *0.001953* | *0.007375* | 0.032890  |

## 6 Conclusion

We have presented a novel and robust multi-view registration method for point clouds based on the Laplacian mixture models (LMM). We adopt Laplacian distribution to represent each data point, and then cast the multi-view registration task as a density estimation problem, which can be efficiently solved through the expectation-maximization framework. Due to the heavy tail and the sparsity-induced $L_1$ norm, LMM is more robust against GMM. To solve the $L_1$ problem, we deduce our objective function into two optimization paradigms, namely, linear programming and ADMM. We test the proposed methods on challenging data sets with contamination of noise and outliers, and compare it with three representative state-of-the-art approaches, and results demonstrate the salient advantages of the proposed method: more robust against noise and outliers, as well as higher accuracy.

**Acknowledgements.** This work was supported by the National Key Research & Development Program of China (2020YFA0713701), the National Natural Science Foundation of China (12171023 and 62172415), and the Open Research Fund Program of State Key Laboratory of Hydroscience and Engineering, Tsinghua University (sklhse-2020-D-07).

## References

1. Aoki, Y., Goforth, H., Srivatsan, R.A., Lucey, S.: PointNetLK: robust & efficient point cloud registration using PointNet. In: Proceedings of the IEEE/CVF Conference on Computer Vision and Pattern Recognition, pp. 7163–7172 (2019)
2. Azam, M., Bouguila, N.: Multivariate bounded support Laplace mixture model. Soft. Comput. **24**, 13239–13268 (2020)
3. Bergevin, R., Soucy, M., Gagnon, H., Laurendeau, D.: Towards a general multi-view registration technique. IEEE Trans. Pattern Anal. Mach. Intell. **18**(5), 540–547 (1996)
4. Bouaziz, S., Tagliasacchi, A., Pauly, M.: Sparse iterative closest point. In: Computer Graphics Forum, vol. 32, pp. 113–123. Wiley Online Library (2013)

5. Chen, T., Vemuri, B.C., Rangarajan, A., Eisenschenk, S.J.: Group-wise point-set registration using a novel CDF-based Havrda-Charvát Divergence. Int. J. Comput. Vis. **86**(1), 111 (2010)

6. Chetverikov, D., Svirko, D., Stepanov, D., Krsek, P.: The trimmed iterative closest point algorithm. In: International Conference on Pattern Recognition, vol. 3, pp. 30545–30545. IEEE Computer Society (2002)

7. Chui, H., Rangarajan, A.: A new point matching algorithm for non-rigid registration. Comput. Vis. Image Underst. **89**(2–3), 114–141 (2003)

8. Evangelidis, G.D., Horaud, R.: Joint alignment of multiple point sets with batch and incremental expectation-maximization. IEEE Trans. Pattern Anal. Mach. Intell. **40**(6), 1397–1410 (2017)

9. Fitzgibbon, A.W.: Robust registration of 2D and 3D point sets. Image Vis. Comput. **21**(13–14), 1145–1153 (2003)

10. Gao, J.: Robust L1 principal component analysis and its Bayesian variational inference. Neural Comput. **20**(2), 555–572 (2008)

11. Guo, J., Wang, H., Cheng, Z., Zhang, X., Yan, D.-M.: Learning local shape descriptors for computing non-rigid dense correspondence. Comput. Vis. Media **6**(1), 95–112 (2020). https://doi.org/10.1007/s41095-020-0163-y

12. Huang, X., Liang, Z., Huang, Q.: Uncertainty quantification for multi-scan registration. ACM Trans. Graph. (TOG) **39**(4), 130:1–130:24 (2020)

13. Jian, B., Vemuri, B.C.: Robust point set registration using gaussian mixture models. IEEE Trans. Pattern Anal. Mach. Intell. **33**(8), 1633–1645 (2010)

14. Kim, S.J., Koh, K., Lustig, M., Boyd, S., Gorinevsky, D.: An interior-point method for large-scale $l_1$-regularized least squares. IEEE J. Sel. Top. Sig. Process. **1**(4), 606–617 (2007)

15. Lei, H., Jiang, G., Quan, L.: Fast descriptors and correspondence propagation for robust global point cloud registration. IEEE Trans. Image Process. **26**(8), 3614–3623 (2017)

16. Mateo, X., Orriols, X., Binefa, X.: Bayesian perspective for the registration of multiple 3D views. Comput. Vis. Image Underst. **118**, 84–96 (2014)

17. Myronenko, A., Song, X.: Point set registration: coherent point drift. IEEE Trans. Pattern Anal. Mach. Intell. **32**(12), 2262–2275 (2010)

18. PaulJ, B., NeilD, M.: A method for registration of 3-D shapes. IEEE Trans. Pattern Anal. Mach. Intell. **14**(2), 239–256 (1992)

19. Rasoulian, A., Rohling, R., Abolmaesumi, P.: Group-wise registration of point sets for statistical shape models. IEEE Trans. Med. Imaging **31**(11), 2025–2034 (2012)

20. Ravikumar, N., Gooya, A., Çimen, S., Frangi, A.F., Taylor, Z.A.: Group-wise similarity registration of point sets using student's t-mixture model for statistical shape models. Med. Image Anal. **44**, 156–176 (2018)

21. Rousseeuw, P.J., Leroy, A.M.: Robust Regression and Outlier Detection, vol. 589. Wiley (2005)

22. Rusu, R.B., Blodow, N., Beetz, M.: Fast point feature histograms (FPFH) for 3D registration. In: 2009 IEEE International Conference on Robotics and Automation, pp. 3212–3217. IEEE (2009)

23. Wang, F., Vemuri, B.C., Rangarajan, A.: Groupwise point pattern registration using a novel CDF-based Jensen-Shannon Divergence. In: 2006 IEEE Computer Society Conference on Computer Vision and Pattern Recognition, CVPR 2006, vol. 1, pp. 1283–1288. IEEE (2006)

24. Williams, J., Bennamoun, M.: Simultaneous registration of multiple corresponding point sets. Comput. Vis. Image Underst. **81**(1), 117–142 (2001)

25. Yang, H., Shi, J., Carlone, L.: TEASER: fast and certifiable point cloud registration. IEEE Trans. Robot. **37**, 314–333 (2020)
26. Yang, J., Li, H., Campbell, D., Jia, Y.: Go-ICP: a globally optimal solution to 3D ICP point-set registration. IEEE Trans. Pattern Anal. Mach. Intell. **38**(11), 2241–2254 (2015)
27. Zhu, J., Guo, R., Li, Z., Zhang, J., Pang, S.: Registration of multi-view point sets under the perspective of expectation-maximization. IEEE Trans. Image Process. **29**, 9176–9189 (2020)

# A Fast and Accurate Point Pattern Matching Algorithm Based on Multi-Hilbert Scans

Jegoon Ryu[1(✉)] and Sei-ichiro Kamata[2]

[1] Information, Production and Systems Research Center,
Waseda University, Kitakyushu, Japan
jkryu@ruri.waseda.jp
[2] Graduate School of Information, Production and Systems,
Waseda University, Kitakyushu, Japan
kam@waseda.jp

**Abstract.** This paper proposes a novel distance measurement using multi-Hilbert scans for matching point patterns on images. A modified Hausdorff distance has been widely used for point pattern matching, recognition tasks, and evaluation of medical image segmentation. However, the computation cost increases sharply with the number of feature points or the increase of data sets. Multi-Hilbert Scanning Distance (MHSD) based on sets of one-dimensional points using Hilbert scans is introduced to overcome this problem. MHSD consists of a combination of four directional Hilbert scans and diagonally shifted Hilbert scans. The proposed method was tested on vehicle images and compared with Hausdorff distance, partial Hausdorff distance, and modified Hausdorff distance. Experimental results show that the proposed method outperforms the compared methods.

**Keywords:** Hausdorff distance (HD) · Modified Hausdorff distance (MHD) · Hilbert scan · Multi-Hilbert Scanning Distance (MHSD) · Point Pattern Matching (PPM)

## 1 Introduction

Point Pattern Matching (PPM) is a fundamental approach for the task of finding correspondences within two arbitrary sets of points [1–4]. The Hausdorff Distance (HD) has often been used for PPM or the similarity between two sets of points in various fields of application, such as object matching, recognition tasks, trajectory matching, and evaluation of medical image segmentation. Furthermore enhanced methods, such as Partial Hausdorff Distance (PHD) and Modified Hausdorff Distance (MHD) have also exhibited good performances [5–12]. Efficient computational algorithms for an accurate and fast HD have been proposed [13–15]. However, MHD still has the weakness that the computation cost increases dramatically as the number of feature points or the increase of data sets.

© Springer Nature Switzerland AG 2022
C. Wallraven et al. (Eds.): ACPR 2021, LNCS 13189, pp. 562–574, 2022.
https://doi.org/10.1007/978-3-031-02444-3_42

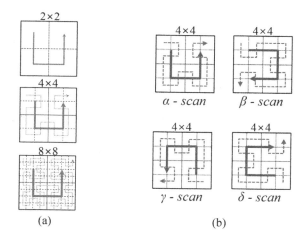

**Fig. 1.** Hilbert scans with Hilbert orders and scanning directions. (a) Hilbert scans according to the change of a Hilbert order. (b) Hilbert scans according to the scanning directions($\alpha$-scan, $\beta$-scan, $\gamma$-scan, and $\delta$-scan).

In this paper, we propose the Multi-Hilbert Scanning Distance (MHSD), which is a novel distance measure based on Hilbert scans. The novel approach of distance measurement for a pattern point matching is introduced by using features of Hilbert scans. The Hilbert scan has some important features that can be utilized for point pattern matching [16, 17]; for example, the Hilbert scan is capable of preserving the coherence between pixels and a one-to-one mapping function between 2-Dimensional (2-D) space and 1-Dimensional (1-D) space. This enables the algorithm to be simplified, speeding up the computation. MHSD is made up of a combination of four directional Hilbert scans and diagonally shifted scans. It computes the minimum value among distances for the nearest point which are obtained by each Hilbert scan. To retain the fast computation time, MHSD utilizes two types of look-up tables which are generated in advance: coordinate loop-up tables and address loop-up tables. As a result, MHSD can have a much lower computation cost than that of the modified Hausdorff distance and shows good performance for matching tasks. In the study, we do not discuss alignment strategies between point sets. Thus, the proposed method is focused on a distance measurement for the point pattern matching between coarsely aligned point sets.

## 2   Multi-Hilbert Scanning Distance

### 2.1   Hilbert Scan

The order $r$ of a Hilbert scan is an important parameter for determining the scanning resolution or the size of the Hilbert curve. When the Hilbert order is $r$, the scanning resolution is $2^r \times 2^r$ in 2-D space $R^2$. Figure 1(a) shows Hilbert scans according to a change in the Hilbert order $r$: $1^{st}$, $2^{nd}$, and $3^{rd}$. It also

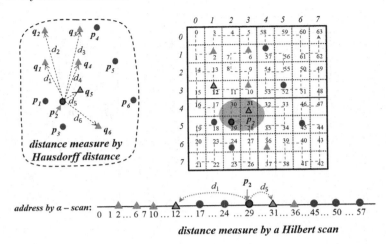

**Fig. 2.** Distance measurements by Hausdorff distance and Hilbert scan on an image with two point sets $P(\bullet)$ and $Q(\blacktriangle)$.

shows the change in the image resolution: $2 \times 2$, $4 \times 4$, and $8 \times 8$. There are four types of Hilbert scans according to the scanning directions. Figure 1(b) shows the four directional Hilbert scans when the Hilbert order is 2. In this study, $\alpha$-scan, $\beta$-scan, $\gamma$-scan, and $\delta$-scan are named according to the scanning directions.

Figure 2 shows distance measurements by the modified Hausdorff distance and a single Hilbert scan on an image including point sets $P(\bullet)$ and $Q(\blacktriangle)$. The modified Hausdorff distance measures distances between all $q$ and $p_2$ for searching the nearest point of $p_2$. However, the single Hilbert scan only needs to measure distances of front and back two neighborhood points for searching the nearest point of $p_2$ in the 1-D sequence. But, the single Hilbert scan can not always guarantee a good performance of a PPM task, because it often misses the nearest point in 2-D space. In the next Section, details on how to measure distance using Hilbert scans will be stated.

## 2.2  Definition of Multi-Hilbert Scanning Distance

A basic concept of distance measurements by $\alpha$-scan and diagonally 1-shifted $\beta$-scan is presented in Fig. 3. In $\alpha$-scan, if the nearest point $q \in Q$ of point $p_4$ is measured, it selects point $q_6$ that is closest to $p_4$ on the 1-D sequence obtained by $\alpha$-scan. The distance between $p_4$ and $q_6$ is 21 on the 1-D sequence. However, the nearest point $q$ of $p_4$ in 2-D space is actually point $q_3$. In the diagonally 1-shifted $\beta$-scan, if the nearest point search of point $p_4$ is performed, the nearest point will be $q_3$, which is the closest point to $p_4$ on the 1-D sequence obtained by the diagonally 1-shifted $\beta$-scan. The distance between $p_4$ and $q_3$ by the diagonally 1-shifted $\beta$-scan is 1 on the 1-D sequence.

Here, we introduce Multi-Hilbert Scans (MHS) to overcome the drawbacks of a single Hilbert scan, which consists of a combination of four directional Hilbert scans and diagonally shifted Hilbert scans. MHS is defined as follows:

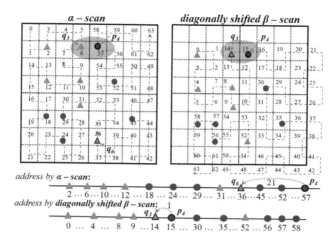

**Fig. 3.** Distance measurements by single Hilbert scan ($k = 0$) and diagonally 1-sifted Hilbert scan ($k = 1$).

$$MHS_K = \{hs^{\alpha,0}, hs^{\beta,1}, hs^{\gamma,2}, hs^{\delta,3}, \cdots, hs^{s,k}, \cdots, hs^{s,K-1}\}, \tag{1}$$

$$s = \begin{cases} \alpha, & \text{if } (k \bmod 4) = 0 \\ \beta, & \text{if } (k \bmod 4) = 1 \\ \gamma, & \text{if } (k \bmod 4) = 2 \\ \delta, & \text{if } (k \bmod 4) = 3 \end{cases}$$

where $K$ is the number of Hilbert scans, $k$ denotes the shift length of the Hilbert scan, and $0 \leq k \leq K - 1$. For example, $hs^{\alpha,0}$, $hs^{\beta,1}$, $hs^{\gamma,2}$, and $hs^{\delta,3}$ denote $\alpha$-scan, diagonally 1-shifted $\beta$-scan, diagonally 2-shifted $\gamma$-scan, diagonally 3-shifted $\delta$-scan, respectively. To measure distances by using Hilbert scan, two point sets $P$ and $Q$ are converted into the new point sets $U$ ($U = \{u_0, u_1, \cdots, u_{M-1}\}$, $\forall u \in \mathbb{Z}$) and $V$ ($V = \{v_0, v_1, \cdots, v_{N-1}\}$, $\forall v \in \mathbb{Z}$), where $u$ and $v$ denote the addresses of points on Hilbert curve. Thus, the new point sets $U^{s,k}$ and $V^{s,k}$ generated from $hs^{s,k}$ are defined as follows:

$$U^{s,k} = \{u_0^{s,k}, u_1^{s,k}, \cdots, u_{M-1}^{s,k}\}, \tag{2}$$

$$V^{s,k} = \{v_0^{s,k}, v_1^{s,k}, \cdots, v_{N-1}^{s,k}\}, \tag{3}$$

where $u^{s,k}$ and $v^{s,k}$ denote the addresses of points on $hs^{s,k}$. According to our statistical analysis, this paper recommends that $K$ has 4: $MHS_4 = \{hs^{\alpha,0}, hs^{\beta,1}, hs^{\gamma,2}, hs^{\delta,3}\}$. The analysis for the combinations of Hilbert scans will be discussed in Sect. 4.1.

To measure distance by using $MHS_4$, we will introduce Multi-Hilbert Scanning Distance. Two point sets $P$ and $Q$ are converted into two new sets $U = \{U^{\alpha,0}, U^{\beta,1}, U^{\gamma,2}, U^{\delta,3}\}$ and $V = \{V^{\alpha,0}, V^{\beta,1}, V^{\gamma,2}, V^{\delta,3}\}$ by the $MHS_4$,

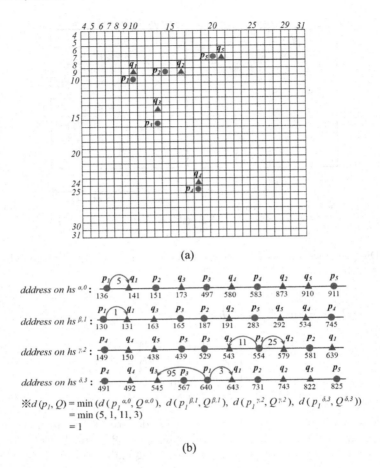

(b)

**Fig. 4.** Distance measurement using $MHS_4$ on an image with two point sets $P$ and $Q$.

respectively. The distance measurement for all $u$ between $U^{s,k}$ and $V^{s,k}$ is defined as follows:

$$d(U^{s,k}, V^{s,k}) = \min(\| u_i^{s,k} - v_t^{s,k} \|, \| u_i^{s,k} - v_{t+1}^{s,k} \|), \qquad (4)$$

where $\| \cdot \|$ is the Euclidean norm distance in 1-D space and $0 \leq i \leq M - 1$. $v_t$ and $v_{t+1}$ are front and back neighbor points of $u_i$ on $hs^{s,k}$. The directed MHSD from $P$ to $Q$ is defined as following:

$$mhsd(P, Q) = \frac{1}{M} \sum_{u \in U} \min_{v \in V}(d(U^{s,k}, V^{s,k})), \qquad (5)$$

where $M$ is the size of the point set $P$ and $0 \leq k \leq 3$ for $MHS_4$. The directed MHSD from $Q$ to $P$ can be computed similarly. MHSD is defined as following:

$$MHSD(P, Q) = \max(mhsd(P, Q), mhsd(Q, P)). \qquad (6)$$

Figure 4 illustrates distance measurement for $p_1$ using $MHS_4$ on an $32\times32$ image. First, two point sets $P$ and $Q$ are converted into the 1-D sequences by $MHS_4$. Then, $d(p_1^{s,k}, Q^{s,k})$ on the each 1-D sequence is calculated by Eq. 4. Lastly, the distance between $p_1$ and $Q$ is determined by minimum value of distances calculated by $d(p_1^{s,k}, Q^{s,k})$. The distances of the other points can be obtained using the same computation.

# 3    Efficient Computation of MHSD

In this study, two kinds of look-up tables are prepared and are called a coordinate look-up table and an address look-up table. The coordinate look-up tables are generated in advance according to the types of Hilbert scans in MHS and are defined as follows:

$$crd\_LUT^{s,k}[i] = (x, y), \qquad (7)$$

where $(s, k)$ denotes types of Hilbert scans in MHS, $i$ is an address on 1-D point sequence of $h^{s,k}$, and $(x, y)$ is a Cartesian coordinate on an image. If the coordinate look-up table of $hs^{\alpha,0}$ is generated by constructing Hilbert curve [16], the coordinate look-up tables of the other $hs^{s,k}$ can be easily obtained by using

---

**Algorithm 1:** $d(U^{\alpha,0}, V^{\alpha,0})$.

**Input:** $U^{\alpha,0}[m]$ and $V^{\alpha,0}[n]$ ($0 \le m \le M - 1$ and $0 \le n \le N - 1$).
1  $k = 0, D^{\alpha,0}[] = 0$ ($D^{\alpha,0}$ is minimum distances of $U^{\alpha,0}$);
2  **for** $(i = 0; i < M; i + +)$ **do**
3      $addr = U^{\alpha,0}[i]$;
4      **while** $k < N$ **do**
5          **if** $(U^{\alpha,0}[i] < V^{\alpha,0}[k])$ **then**
6              **if** $(k == 0)$ **then**
7                  $D^{\alpha,0}[addr] = V^{\alpha,0}[k] - U^{\alpha,0}[i]$;
8                  break;
9              **else**
10                 $temp1 = U^{\alpha,0}[i] - V^{\alpha,0}[k - 1]$;
11                 $temp2 = V^{\alpha,0}[k] - U^{\alpha,0}[i]$;
12                 $D^{\alpha,0}[addr] = \min(temp1, temp2)$;
13                 break;
14         **else if** $(U^{\alpha,0}[i] == V^{\alpha,0}[k])$ **then**
15             k++;
16             break;
17         **else**
18             **if** $(i == M - 1)$ && $(k == N - 1)$ **then**
19                 $D^{\alpha,0}[addr] = U^{\alpha,0}[i] - V^{\alpha,0}[k]$;
20                 break;
21             **else**
22                 k++;
23                 break;
24      **if** $(k == N)$ **then**
25          $D^{\alpha,0}[addr] = U^{\alpha,0}[i] - V^{\alpha,0}[N - 1]$;
26  **return** $D^{\alpha,0}$;

transformation rules. If the coordinate look-up table of $hs^{\alpha,0}$ is $crd\_LUT^{\alpha,0}[i]$ ($crd\_LUT^{\alpha,0}[i] = (x_i^\alpha, y_i^\alpha)$), the other coordinate look-up tables are formulated as follows:

$$crd\_LUT^{\alpha,k}[i] = (x_i^\alpha + k, y_i^\alpha + k), \tag{8}$$

$$crd\_LUT^{\beta,k}[i] = (y_i^\alpha + k, x_i^\alpha + k), \tag{9}$$

$$crd\_LUT^{\gamma,k}[i] = (N - x_i^\alpha + k, N - y_i^\alpha + k) \tag{10}$$

$$crd\_LUT^{\delta,k}[i] = (N - y_i^\alpha + k, N - x_i^\alpha + k) \tag{11}$$

where $N = 2^r$ and $r$ is the Hilbert order for scanning an image. The address look-up tables are generated in advance by using the coordinate look-up tables and are defined as follows:

$$addr\_LUT^{s,k}[x, y] = i. \tag{12}$$

Thus, for $MHS_4$, $addr\_LUT^{\alpha,0}$, $addr\_LUT^{\beta,1}$, $addr\_LUT^{\gamma,2}$, and $addr\_LUT^{\delta,3}$ are generated in advance by using $crd\_LUT^{\alpha,0}$, $crd\_LUT^{\beta,1}$, $crd\_LUT^{\gamma,2}$, and $crd\_LUT^{\delta,3}$, respectively.

---

**Algorithm 2:** $min(d(U^{s,k}, V^{s,k}))$ by $MHS_4$.

---

**Input:** $U^{\alpha,0}$, $D^{\alpha,0}$, $D^{\beta,1}$, $D^{\gamma,2}$, and $D^{\delta,3}$.
1  $MD[] = 0$ ($MD$ is the minimum among minimum distances);
2  **for** $(i = 0; i < M; i + +)$ **do**
3      $addr0 = U^{\alpha,0}[i]$ ;
4      $(x, y) \leftarrow crd\_LUT^{\alpha,0}[addr0]$ ;
5      $d0 = D^{\alpha,0}[addr0]$ ;
6      $addr1 = addr\_LUT^{\beta,1}[x, y]$ ;
7      $d1 = D^{\beta,1}[addr1]$ ;
8      $addr2 = addr\_LUT^{\gamma,2}[x, y]$ ;
9      $d2 = D^{\gamma,2}[addr2]$ ;
10     $addr3 = addr\_LUT^{\delta,3}[x, y]$ ;
11     $d3 = D^{\delta,3}[addr3]$ ;
12     $MD[i] = min(d0, d1, d2, d3)$ ;
13  **return** $MD$ ;

---

The computation of $mhsd(P, Q)$ using $MHS_4$ is summarized as the following steps:

**Step 1.** Convert the point set $P$ to 1-D sequences $U(U = \{U^{\alpha,0}, U^{\beta,1}, U^{\gamma,2}, U^{\delta,3}\})$ by using Eq. 12, and do the same process for 1-D sequences $V(V = \{V^{\alpha,0}, V^{\beta,1}, V^{\gamma,2}, V^{\delta,3}\})$ with the point set $Q$.

**Step 2.** Compute minimum distances of all $p(p \in P)$ on $hs^{\alpha,0}$ with $U^{\alpha,0}$ and $V^{\alpha,0}$ by Eq. 4. The pseudo code for this step is presented in Algorithm 1.

**Step 3.** Repeat Step 2 with ($U^{\beta,1}$ and $V^{\beta,1}$), ($U^{\gamma,2}$ and $V^{\gamma,2}$), and ($U^{\delta,3}$ and $V^{\delta,3}$).

**Step 4.** Compute the minimum among minimum distances obtained from $MHS_4$ for a point $p(p \in P)$. The minimum distance is computed by using address loop-tables and coordinate loop-tables.

**Step 5.** Repeat Step 4 until all $p$ have been processed. The pseudo code for Step 4 and 5 is presented in Algorithm 2.

**Step 6.** Obtain $mhsd(P, Q)$ by calculating the mean value of minimum distances of all $p$.

The process of computing $mhsd(Q, P)$ is the same as the above steps. Finally, MHSD is obtained by choosing the larger one of $mhsd(P, Q)$ and $mhsd(Q, P)$.

## 4    Experimental Results

### 4.1    Statistical Analysis for MHSD

In this Section, we present a statistical analysis of the proposed method and some combined Hilbert scans by using a statistical method [18]. The statistical method analyzes the proportional property of a square Euclidean distance $d = (b_x - a_x)^2 + (b_y - a_y)^2$ and a scanning length $l(l \in [0, R_x \times R_y])$ between the two points $a(a_x, a_y)$ and $b(b_x, b_y)$, where $R_x \times R_y$ is the size of an image. Other scanning methods are combined for the statistical analysis, which are a single Hilbert scan, two Hilbert scans, four Hilbert scans, a single Hilbert scan and four diagonally shifted Hilbert scans, and four Hilbert scans and four diagonally shifted Hilbert scans. Figure 5 shows the relation between the average scanning length and the

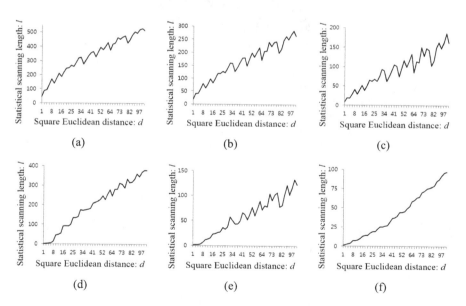

**Fig. 5.** Statistical analysis of scanning length for some combined Hilbert scans and the proposed MHSD. (a) $A - scan$ ($hs^{\alpha,0}$), (b) $B - scann$ ($hs^{\alpha,0}$ and $hs^{\beta,0}$), (c) $C - scan$ ($hs^{\alpha,0}$, $hs^{\beta,0}$, $hs^{\gamma,0}$, and $hs^{\delta,0}$), (d) $D - scan$ ($hs^{\alpha,0}$, $hs^{\alpha,1}$, $hs^{\beta,1}$, $hs^{\gamma,1}$, and $hs^{\delta,1}$), (e) $E - scan$ ($hs^{\alpha,0}$, $hs^{\beta,0}$, $hs^{\gamma,0}$, $hs^{\delta,0}$, $hs^{\alpha,1}$, $hs^{\beta,1}$, $hs^{\gamma,1}$, and $hs^{\delta,1}$), and (f) the proposed Hilbert scans.

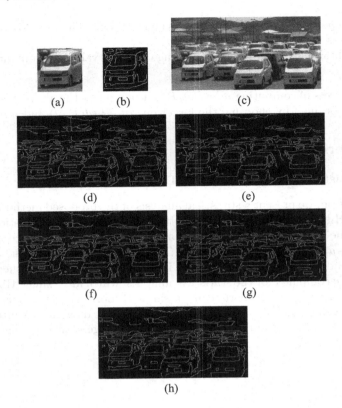

**Fig. 6.** Vehicles image and edge images with different noise levels. All noisy images were made by *imnoise* function in Matlab. (a) Real model of a single vehicle. (b) Edge image of (a). (c) Real image of some similar vehicles. (d) Edge image of (c). (e) Edge image of (c) with Gaussian noise ($\sigma = 0.02$, $\sigma$ means the variance). (f) Edge image of (c) with Poisson noise. (g) Edge image of (c) with salt&pepper noise ($d$=0.2, $d$ is the noise density). (h) Edge image of (c) with Multiplicative noise ($v$=0.2, $v$ means the variance).

square Euclidean distance corresponding to two points. In Fig. 5(a), (b), and (c), the scanning length $l$ fluctuates over a wide range when $d > 25$. Figure 5(a) and (b) have the scanning length greater than 1 when $d = 1$. However, Fig. 5(f) has a small fluctuation and the square Euclidean distance is proportional to $l$.

## 4.2   Evaluation of MHSD on Vehicle Images

The proposed approach was tested with vehicle model images. Firstly, we tested the ability of MHSD to find a vehicle model in an image including many vehicles. Generally, a vehicle model image is smaller than an image including many vehicles. Thus, the directed distance measure from a model to an image is performed

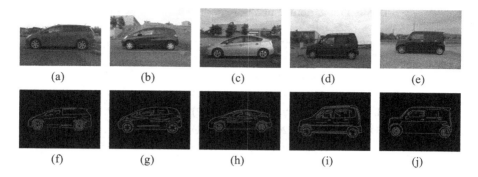

**Fig. 7.** Samples of vehicle model images in a data-set and edge images of the vehicle models.

by translating the model on the fixed image. The minimum value of any distance measure under translation can be computed as follows [19].

$$M_\Psi(A, B) = \min_\psi h(A, B \oplus \psi) \tag{13}$$

where $h$ is any distance measure such as HD, PHD, MHD, single Hilbert scan (SHS) or MHSD, and $\oplus$ is the standard Minkowski sum notation(i.e., $B \oplus \psi = b + \psi | b \in B$). The test sets in Fig. 6 are a vehicle model ($128 \times 128$ size) and an image ($512 \times 256$ size) including some similar vehicles. The proposed method was compared with HD, PHD ($80\%^{th}$ ranked value), Single Hilbert Scan (SHS), and MHD on edge images. Figures 6(a)-(d) show the original images and the binary edge images obtained by Meer [21], and (e)-(h) are the edge images of noisy images adding Gaussian, Poisson, salt&pepper, and Multiplicative noise [20] to Fig. 6(c), respectively. The best matching position of the vehicle model is (20, 111) here. In practice, the best matching position was obtained using graphics tool. Table 1 shows the matching results. The matching position can be evaluated using the Euclidean distance between the best matching positions. The smaller this distance is, the better the distance measure is. From Table 1, the Euclidean distances between the best matching and the HD results are 0, 312, 11, 185, and 200 for (d)-(h), respectively. This shows that HD matching suffers with noisy images. MHD showed good matching results. However, MHSD presented the best matching results for all images.

Secondly, the proposed method was tested by using the real vehicle model images (in Fig. 7). In this study, 40 real vehicles were involved and 200 images were acquired for the experiment. In Fig. 7(f)-(j), the edge images were obtained by applying the edge detection algorithm of Meer [21] and the image size is $512 \times 512$ pixels. The proposed method was compared with HD, PHD ($80\%^{th}$ ranked value), SHS, and MHD on edge images of vehicle models. To evaluate the performance of the proposed method, top-rank order and Bulls-eye statistics were used. Bulls-eye test counts how many of the 5 possible correct matches are presented in the top 10 nearest objects.

**Table 1.** Position results of experiment shown in Fig. 6

| Methods | Matched position $(x, y)$ | | | | |
|---|---|---|---|---|---|
| | (d) | (e) | (f) | (g) | (h) |
| HD | (20,111) | (326,46) | (31,109) | (205,121) | (217,72) |
| PHD | (19,111) | (22,111) | (19,111) | (18,111) | (20,111) |
| SHS | (20,111) | (23,112) | (20,112) | (22,112) | (20,111) |
| MHD | (20,111) | (205,120) | (20,111) | (23,110) | (20,111) |
| MHSD | (20,111) | (21,111) | (20,111) | (20,111) | (20,111) |

**Table 2.** Comparison of recognition rate (%)

| Methods | Matching rate (%) | |
|---|---|---|
| | Top-Ranking | Bulls-eye |
| Hausdorff distance | 92.0 | 90.2 |
| Partial Hausdorff distance | 94.1 | 92.5 |
| Single Hilbert scan | 93.7 | 92.1 |
| Modified Hausdorff distance | 96.5 | 94.4 |
| Multi-Hilbert scanning distance | 97.8 | 95.3 |

**Table 3.** Comparison of running time (sec)

| Methods | Pairs | | |
|---|---|---|---|
| | (f,g) | (f,h) | (f,i) |
| Modified Hausdorff distance (NAVIE) | 0.150 | 0.141 | 0.163 |
| Modified Hausdorff distance (KD-Tree) | 0.033 | 0.031 | 0.037 |
| Multi-Hilbert scanning distance | 0.025 | 0.024 | 0.028 |

Table 2 shows the recognition results by the proposed method and the compared methods. MHD exhibit better performances than HD, PHD, and single Hilbert scan. Nevertheless, the proposed method outperforms the compared methods. For evaluating the computation cost, the proposed method was compared with the NAIVE MHD and the MHD using KD-Tree with samples of vehicle edge images. Table 3 shows that the running time of the proposed method is less than that of the MHD using KD-Tree. The running time of the MHSD algorithm in Table 3 includes the times of converting into 1-D sequences $U$ and $V$. If the 1-D sequences $U$ and $V$ of point sets are registered in advance and distance measurement is performed with those, MHSD can have a much lower computational cost. These experiments demonstrate that the proposed algorithm outperforms the compared algorithms.

# 5    Conclusion

In this study, we propose a multi-Hilbert scanning distance which is a distance measurement for fast and accurate point pattern matching and object recognition. MHSD measures distance using five 1-D point sequences from multi-Hilbert scanning and has two types of look-up tables to lower the computation cost. Evaluation of MHSD was performed using vehicle images. MHSD was compared with other distance measures, such as HD, PHD, SHS, MHD. MHSD showed good performance in terms of matching accuracy and computation cost. Experimental results demonstrate the possibility of the distance measurement for fast and accurate point pattern matching. The future works will aim at applying efficient alignment strategies and extending the application fields.

# References

1. Hu, X.P., Ahuja, N.: Matching point features with ordered geometric, rigidity, and disparity constraints. IEEE Trans. Pattern Anal. Mach. Intell. **16**(10), 1041–1049 (1994)
2. Wen, Y., Zhou, M., Zhang, P., Geng, G.: Matching method of cultural relic fragments constrained by thickness and contour feature. IEEE Access **8**, 25892–25904 (2020)
3. Meng, X., et al.: Multi-feature fusion: a driver-car matching model based on curve comparison. IEEE Access **7**, 83526–83535 (2019)
4. Czovny, R.K., Bellon, O.R.P., Silva, L., Costa, H.S.G.: Minutia matching using 3D pore clouds. In: Proceedings of the International Conference on Pattern Recognition, pp. 3138–3143. IAPR (2018)
5. Dubuisson, M.P., Jain, A.K.: A modified Hausdorff distance for object matching. In: Proceedings of the International Conference on Pattern Recognition, pp. 566–568. IAPR (1994)
6. Yu, C.B., Qin, H.F., Cui, Y.Z., Hu, X.Q.: Finger-vein image recognition combining modified Hausdorff distance with minutiae feature matching. J. Biomed. Sci. Eng. **2**(4), 261–272 (2009)
7. Shao, F., Cai, S., GU, J.: A modified Hausdorff distance based algorithm for 2-dimensional spatial trajectory matching. In: Proceedings of the International Conference on Computer Science and Education, pp. 166–172. IEEE (2010)
8. Schhutze, O., Esquivel, X., Lara, A., Coello, C.A.C.: Using the averaged Hausdorff distance as a performance measure in evolutionary multiobjective optimization. IEEE Trans. Evol. Comp. **16**(4), 504–522 (2012)
9. Kim, J., Kim, M., Kim, T.: Recognition of face orientation angle using modified hausdorff distance. In: Proceedings of International Symposium on Consumer Electronics. IEEE (2014)
10. Sarangi, P.P., Panda, M., Mishra, B.S.P., Dehuri, S.: An automated ear localization technique based on modified hausdorff distance. In: Proceedings of the International Conference on Computer Vision and Image Processing, pp. 229–240. IAPR (2016)
11. Shamai, G., Kimmel, R.: Geodesic distance descriptors. In: Proceedings of the International Conference on Computer Vision and Pattern Recognition, pp. 6410–6418. IEEE (2017)

12. Taha, A.A., Hanbury, A.: Metrics for evaluating 3D medical image segmentation: analysis, selection, and tool. BMC Med. Imaging **15**(29), 1–28 (2015)
13. Taha, A.A., Hanbury, A.: An efficient algorithm for calculating the exact Hausdorff distance. IEEE Trans. Pattern Anal. Mach. Intell. **37**(11), 2153–2163 (2015)
14. Jhang, D., Jou, L., Chen, Y., He, F.: Efficient and accurate Hausdorff distance computation based on diffusion search. IEEE Access **6**, 1350–1361 (2018)
15. Ryu, J., Kamata, S.: An efficient computational algorithm for Hausdorff distance based on points-ruling-out and systematic random sampling. Pattern Recogn. **114**(107857), 1–12 (2021)
16. Kamata, S., Eason, R.O., Bandou, Y.: A new algorithm for n-dimensional Hilbert scanning. IEEE Trans. Image Pro. **8**(7), 964–973 (1999)
17. Hao, P., Kamata, S.: Hilbert scan based bag-of-features for image retrieval. IEICE Trans. Inf. Syst. E94-D(6), 1260–1268 (2011)
18. Zhang, J, Kamata, S., Ueshige, Y.: A pseudo-Hilbert scan for arbitrarily-sized arrays. IEICE Trans. Inf. Syst. E90-A(3), 682–690 (2007)
19. Huttenlocher, D.P., Klanderman, G.A., Rucklidge, W.J.: Comparing images using the Hausdorff distance. IEEE Trans. Pattern Anal. Mach. Intell. **15**, 850–863 (1993)
20. Gonzlez, R.C., Woods, R.E.: Digital Image Processing. Second edn., Prectice Hall, Upper Saddle River (2002)
21. Comaniciu, D., Meer, P.: Edge detection with embedded confidence. IEEE Trans. Pattern Anal. Mach. Intell. **23**(12), 1351–1365 (2001)

# A Multi-feature Embedding Method for Robust Image Matching

Jinhong Yu and Kun Sun[✉]

Hubei Key Laboratory of Intelligent Geo-Information Processing, School of Computer Sciences, China University of Geosciences, Wuhan 430074, China
sunkun@cug.edu.cn

**Abstract.** In this paper, a feature point matching method that integrates both spatial structure and multiple descriptors is proposed. To be specific, given a set of detected keypoints on both images, multiple feature descriptors are extracted at each keypoint. Then, a subspace that simultaneously encodes both spatial structure and multi-feature similarity is computed. In this subspace, two points from different images will be close if their similarity measured by multiple features are high, and two points from the same image will be close if their distance in the original spatial domain is small. The above task is formulated as a Laplacian Embedding problem, which can be solved by eigen decomposition. Finally, vectors in the subspace are treated as new descriptors of the keypoints, and correspondences are established by searching mutual nearest neighbors. Extensive experiments show remarkable improvement in matching accuracy and downstream tasks such as homography and relative pose estimation by combining both structure information and multiple descriptors.

**Keywords:** Image matching · Multi-feature fusion · Spatial structure preserving · Subspace embedding

## 1 Introduction

Establishing sparse feature correspondences between images is a fundamental problem in many computer vision tasks, such as 3D information inferring [1, 13, 14, 24], Structure-from-Motion [22, 36, 40], robot sensing [25] and image retrieval [3, 15]. Given two groups of keypoints, the main steps of image matching are: **i)** computing a high dimensional feature descriptor for each keypoint and **ii)** establishing correspondences between them by for example, finding the nearest neighbor in the feature space. In the above pipeline, feature descriptor is a key factor to improve the final matching result.

In the past two decades, researchers in the community have proposed many excellent handcrafted descriptors [2, 5, 7, 26], as well as modern learned descriptors [10, 16, 29, 32, 43, 44]. Despite their great success, these methods have their own limitations. Firstly, they still suffer from mismatches in challenging situations such as wide baseline and small scene overlap. Secondly, as observed by

C. Wallraven et al. (Eds.): ACPR 2021, LNCS 13189, pp. 575–589, 2022.
https://doi.org/10.1007/978-3-031-02444-3_43

previous studies [18,19], the performance of different descriptors may vary a lot for the same image. A keypoint might be correctly matched by one descriptor but mismatched by another. This difference implies that using a single descriptor hardly applies to all the scenarios, but different descriptors are complementary and they can cooperate. At last, while feature similarity is given much attention, the useful spatial structure information [20,42,45] is overlooked in these methods. This makes the matching result sensitive to local ambiguity. How to integrate multiple features as well as spatial structure constraint still remains an open problem.

In this paper, an image matching method based on multi-feature embedding is proposed. Different form existing methods that use a single feature, it first extracts multiple feature descriptors at each keypoint. Then, a new representation that encodes both multi-feature similarity and keypoint structure is computed via subspace embedding, which is a widely used methodology [23]. There are two properties of this subspace. On the one hand, if the inter-image similarity between two points measured by multiple descriptors is high, they will be close to each other in the embedded subspace. On the other hand, if two points on the same image are spatially close to each other, the distance between them in the new subspace will also be small. As a result, the structure of each point set is preserved and similar points from different point sets are pulled closer. This task is formulated as a Laplacian Embedding problem, which can be solved via eigen decomposition. Vectors in the computed subspace are treated as the new descriptors for the keypoints. In this way, both multi-feature and spatial structure information are utilized by the proposed method.

To summarize, the proposed method distinguishes itself from existing methods in the following aspects. (1) It generates a novel descriptor for each keypoint by computing a subspace, which is equivalent to the Laplacian Embedding problem. (2) The method is a general framework which fuses multiple off-the-shelf descriptors instead of using only one of them. In this way, the embedded descriptor can adapt to more challenging scenarios. (3) The subspace also preserves the spatial structure of the kepoints, which makes the algorithm robust to local appearance ambiguity.

## 2  Related Work

### 2.1  Feature Description Methods

As the most fundamental part of image matching, the performance of feature descriptor is very important. The most famous manual descriptor is SIFT [26], which is obtained by statistical histogram of local image gradient direction of keypoints, and it has been widely used until today. After that, many different kinds of manual feature descriptors have been designed to adapt to different situations, such as faster speed [5,33], smaller memory [7,34], and more robustness [2].

In recent years, feature descriptors based on neural network have developed rapidly, and generally get better matching results than handcrafted descriptors.

Some methods [27,37,43,52] take image patches as input, and can directly calculate the feature vector representations of these patches. HardNet [29] is based on L2-Net [43] network structure, it proposed a triple-network, by introducing a margin and encouraging negative pair feature distance to be greater than the sum of positive pair distance and margin, forcing the network focuses on those negative samples which are most difficult to distinguish. SOSNet [44] achieves better results by using the first-order similarity loss(similar to triplet-loss) and introducing a second-order regularization term between positive matching pairs. Interestingly, one method [53] proposes a *soft margin* relative to *hard margin* in HardNet, it discusses that the traditional *hard margin* is not flexible enough, so this paper proposes a *dynamic soft margin* to overcome this problem.

Another kind of end-to-end methods use image as input to obtain more reliable matching results by calculating dense features. Aiming at a large number of multi-views geometry problems in computer vision, SuperPoint [10] proposes a self supervised training framework of keypoint detection and description, which outputs highly abstract features of the input image. Subsequent end-to-end methods will also compute dense feature representation. D2-Net [11] proposes a "detect-and-describe" method, which uses a single CNN for joint feature detection and description, so an image can only get a 3D tensor. The goal of R2D2 [32] is to learn repeatable and reliable keypoints and powerful descriptors, and its outputs are dense descriptors, reliability map and repeatability map.

The existing deep learning methods all need ground truth correspondences to train, and the acquisition of correspondences is costly in some cases. Therefore, CAPS [47] proposes a method that directly uses the relative camera pose between image pairs as the supervision, thus greatly reducing the training costs. However, dense features tend to occupy more memory and computation is time-consuming.

## 2.2   Feature Matching Methods

Some researchers try to improve the results of image matching from another perspective. The most basic feature matching relationship is usually obtained by finding the mutual nearest neighbor features in feature space. SIFT [26] proposes ratio test based on mutual nearest neighbor searching and greatly improves the matching accuracy. Some methods [12,28,38,39,41,42] use Gaussian mixture model for image matching, where each keypoint in the first image is treated as a Gaussian component, and the probability of each keypoint in the second image being assigned to each Gaussian component is modeled. Other methods [48] to treat the matching problem as a classification problem, in this case, the keypoints in one image can be regarded as cluster centers, while the keypoints in another image are the keypoints to be assigned. Some multi-image matching methods [17,56] can promote the matching accuracy of image pairs to some extent by establishing the cycle-consistency constraint between multiple images.

The feature matching correspondence can also be restored from the feature similarity matrix, which is very common in graph matching [50,55] and multi-graph matching [8,31,46,49]. A spectral method [21] proposes to find the correspondences from the feature similarity matrix, this spectral method is also used in many subsequent graph matching methods. Besides feature similarity, some methods [20,35,42,45] also considers the spatial structure of keypoints in the same image, and the better matching results are obtained by combining feature and spacial information, but this approach only takes into account a single feature. Recently, a novel method, SuperGlue [35], uses neural network to find correspondences, which fully considers the relationship of cross-image keypoints and self-image keypoints, this is also reflected in this paper.

The above image matching methods can not solve the inherent problem of features, that is, a good correspondence basically depends on a good feature descriptor. As we can not guarantee that a certain feature can be widely used in all scenes, from another perspective, the method of fusing multiple different existing features in this paper is a good choice.

### 2.3   Feature Fusion Methods

There are also some matching methods from the perspective of multiple features fusion. Hu et al. proposed in [19] that the best feature can be selected for each keypoint in the homography space for matching, but each keypoint essentially uses a single descriptor information. Yu et al. proposed a multi-feature fusion matching method [51], but their fusion features are geometric, gray, color and texture features. LISRD [30] proposes a method to separate invariants from local descriptors. In its framework, it includes the structure of learning multiple local descriptors, which makes people think it is a multi-feature fusion method. In fact, LISRD does not fuse features.

The goal of this paper is to design a multi-feature fusion method, in which each feature has its own contribution. And for different keypoints, different features have different contributions. In this way, different features complement effectively, and image matching accuracy can also be improved.

## 3   The Proposed Method

Given two images $I_1$ and $I_2$, we detect two groups of keypoints $X_1 \in R^{m \times 2}$ and $Y_2 \in R^{n \times 2}$ on each image. For each keypoint, $K$ kinds of descriptors are extracted, which are denoted as $P_1^k \in R^{m \times d_k}$ and $Q_2^k \in R^{n \times d_k}$. $k = 1,..,K$ is the $k$-th feature and $d_k$ is the dimension of it.

Different from existing methods which use a single descriptor, we want to fuse multiple features and impose structural constraint at the same time. To this end, we compute a new representation $E_1 = \left\{ e_1^1, e_2^1, ..., e_m^1 \right\}^T \in R^{m \times c}$ and $E_2 = \left\{ e_1^2, e_2^2, ..., e_n^2 \right\}^T \in R^{n \times c}$ of the original keypoints by projecting all these keypoints information into a subspace. The superscript 1 or 2 indicates the first or the second image, and $c$ is the dimension of the subspace feature. $E_1$ and $E_2$ can be computed by minimizing the following objective function [45]:

$$\min \sum_{l=1,2} \sum_{i,j} \left\| e_i^l - e_j^l \right\|^2 S_{l,ij} + \sum_{i,j} \left\| e_i^1 - e_j^2 \right\|^2 U_{ij}. \tag{1}$$

The first term in Eq. (1) encodes intra-image spatial information, where $S_{l,ij}$ represents the spatial similarity between keypoints $i$ and $j$ in image $l$. $S_{1,ij}$ and $S_{2,ij}$ can be computed by the following kernel function $K_s\left(\cdot,\cdot\right)$:

$$S_{1,ij} = K_s\left(x_i, x_j\right) = e^{-\frac{\left(x_i - x_j\right)^2}{2\sigma^2}}, \; x_i, x_j \in X_1, \tag{2a}$$

$$S_{2,ij} = K_s\left(y_i, y_j\right) = e^{-\frac{\left(y_i - y_j\right)^2}{2\sigma^2}}, \; y_i, y_j \in Y_2. \tag{2b}$$

According to Eq. (2), if two points on the same image are spatially close to each other, the corresponding similarity in $S_{1,ij}$ would be large. To minimize Eq. (1), their distance in the subspace should be small.

The second term in Eq. (1) encodes inter-image feature information, in which $U_{ij}$ is the feature similarity defined by multiple descriptors between $x_i$ and $y_j$. $U_{ij}$ can be computed from the following equation:

$$U_{ij} = \frac{1}{K}\sum_{k=1}^{K} U_{ij}^k, \tag{3}$$

where

$$U_{ij}^k = K_u\left(p_i^k, q_j^k\right) = e^{-\frac{\left(p_i^k - q_j^k\right)^2}{2\beta^2}}, \; p_i^k \in P_1^k \text{ and } q_j^k \in Q_2^k \tag{4}$$

is a kernel function representing the feature similarity between $x_i$ and $y_j$ with the $k$-th descriptor. As we can see from Eq. (3) and Eq. (4), the feature information in Eq. (1) is jointly defined by multiple descriptors. If two points from different images are similar to each other, the correponding similarity in $U_{ij}$ would be large. To minimize Eq. (1), their distance in the subspace should be small as well. As a result, the subspace defined by Eq. (1) has the following properties: similar points from different images measured by multiple descriptors are pulled closer and the relative structure of points from the same image is preserved.

The feature information and spatial information can be expressed in a compact matrix form, which is shown in Eq. (5).

$$A = \begin{bmatrix} S_1 & U \\ U^T & S_2 \end{bmatrix}. \tag{5}$$

Here $A$ is a $2\times 2$ block matrix. Its diagonal blocks $S_1 \in R^{m\times m}$ and $S_2 \in R^{n\times n}$ are the spatial information matrices computed from Eq. (2). Its off-diagonal block $U \in R^{m\times n}$ is the feature information matrix computed from Eq. (3). Denoting $E = \left[E_1^T, E_2^T\right]$ and applying some simple derivation, Eq. (1) can be rewritten in the following form:

$$\min tr(E^T A E), \tag{6}$$

which can be seen as the Laplacian Embedding problem [6]. The optimal embedding features $E$ in Eq. (6) can be obtained by solving the following problem,

$$\min_{E^T D E = I} tr(E^T L E), \tag{7}$$

where $L = D - A$ is the Laplacian matrix of $A$, and $D$ is a diagonal matrix whose non-zero elements are computed from $D_{ii} = \sum_j A_{ij}$. Equation (7) is a generalized eigenvector problem, whose solution is the eigenvectors corresponding to the $c$ smallest non-zero eigenvalues.

After computing $E$ from Eq. (7), we have a new $c$-dimensional representation for each keypoint in $X_1$ and $Y_2$. This new descriptor not only fuses multi-feature information, but also encodes spatial structure constraint. We then match the keypoints by searching for mutual nearest neighbors in the subspace.

## 4   Experiments

### 4.1   Evaluation Metrics

The experiments are performed on a machine equipped with Xeon E5-2620 2.1GHz, 64GB RAM and one GTX 1080Ti. Following SuperPoint [10], D2-Net [11], UCN [9] and CAPS [47], the proposed method is evaluated in terms of Mean Matching Accuracy (MMA) and several downstream tasks such as homography estimation accuracy and relative pose estimation accuracy.

**Mean Matching Accuracy (MMA).** For a certain keypoint, if the distance between its estimated matching position and the ground truth matching position is smaller than a threshold, this match would be deemed as correct. The Mean Matching Accuracy (MMA) is the ratio of correct correspondences in the whole dataset. Higher MMA is preferable.

**Homography Estimation Accuracy:** Homography is a $3 \times 3$ matrix which plays an important role in a variety of areas such as panorama generation and planar surface detection. It can be estimated from correspondences between two views. To be specific, we use the OpenCV function to estimate the homography matrix and compare it with the ground truth. Following SuperPoint [10], the *four-corner accuracy* is used to check whether the estimated homography is correct. That is, the four corners of an image are warped by the estimated homography and the ground truth homography, respectively. If the average distance error between them is less than a threshold $\varepsilon$, then the estimated homography is admitted to be correct.

**Relative Pose Estimation Accuracy:** Another application of image feature point matching is 3D reconstruction, which requires to estimate the relative pose between two cameras. The pose parameters, *i.e.* the rotation matrix $R \in R^{3\times3}$ and the translation vector $t \in R^{3\times1}$ can also be computed from correspondences. For rotation, we compute the angle error between the estimation and the ground truth. As for translation, we simply compute the directional error with the ground truth because its magnitude is determined up to an unknown scale factor. The estimation is deemed as correct if the error is below a threshold.

### 4.2   Datasets

Similar to CAPS [47], the experiments are carried out on two datasets: HPatches [4] and COLMAP [54].

**Table 1.** The MMA on the HPatches dataset. The pixel threshold is from 1 to 10. Best results are in bold.

| Method | 1 | 2 | 3 | 4 | 5 | 6 | 7 | 8 | 9 | 10 |
|---|---|---|---|---|---|---|---|---|---|---|
| 2-Hand | .177 | .353 | .410 | .441 | .464 | .484 | .501 | .517 | .531 | .542 |
| 2-Depth | **.212** | .413 | .478 | .511 | .535 | .554 | .569 | .581 | .592 | .600 |
| 4-Descs | .197 | .388 | .452 | .486 | .511 | .535 | .554 | .573 | .589 | .602 |
| 4-Depth | **.212** | **.416** | **.483** | **.518** | **.541** | **.561** | **.576** | **.588** | **.598** | **.607** |
| F-Only | .167 | .329 | .384 | .411 | .428 | .440 | .449 | .456 | .460 | .465 |

**Table 2.** Average homography estimation accuracy on HPatches under different thresholds $\varepsilon$. Best results are in bold.

| Method | $\varepsilon = 1$ | $\varepsilon = 3$ | $\varepsilon = 5$ |
|---|---|---|---|
| 2-Hand | 0.303 | 0.497 | 0.595 |
| 2-Depth | 0.322 | 0.541 | 0.654 |
| 4-Descs | 0.311 | 0.534 | 0.663 |
| 4-Depth | **0.325** | **0.560** | **0.690** |
| F-Only | 0.324 | 0.525 | 0.642 |

**HPatches** is used to evaluate MMA and homography estimation accuracy. It consists of 116 scenes, among which 57 scenes are for illumination change and the other 59 scenes are for viewpoint change. Each scene contains 6 images and 5 pairs by matching the first image to the others, leading to a total of 580 image pairs. For every image pair, a homography is provided as the ground truth. SuperPoint [10] is applied to detect at most 1000 keypoints on each image except for the $i\_dc$ scene, because SuperPoint is not able to handle its resolution.

**COLMAP** is used for the evaluation of relative pose estimation accuracy. It contains four scenes: *gerrard*, *graham*, *person* and *south*, with 100, 560, 330 and 128 images respectively. These images, which are captured by different users and collected from the Internet, present great challenges such as viewpoint changes, scaling and occlusion. The camera parameters estimated in a standard SfM pipeline are provided as ground truth. Similar to [47], we divide all the image pairs in this dataset into three groups according to the viewing angle difference: *easy* $[0, 15°]$, *moderate* $[15°, 30°]$ and *hard* $[30°, 60°]$. In each group, we randomly select 200 image pairs, resulting a total of 600 image pairs for testing. SuperPoint [10] is also applied to detect at most 1000 keypoints on each image.

The proposed method is compared with several state-of-the-art descriptors including SIFT [26], RootSIFT [2], HardNet [29], SOSNet [44], SoftMargin [53] and SuperPoint [10]. The first two are famous handcrafted descriptors while the last three are outstanding deep learned descriptors. Our method is also compared with the OS [45] matching algorithm, which is closely related to our method, but it considers only a single descriptor. To evaluate the performance of each descriptor itself, we do not apply ratio test and all the matches are established by simply finding mutual nearest neighbors.

**Table 3.** Average relative pose (*rotation/translation*) estimation accuracy on the COLMAP dataset. The angle threshold is strictly set to 5°. Best results are in bold.

| Method | Easy | Moderate | Hard |
|--------|------|----------|------|
| 2-Hand | 0.550/0.455 | 0.270/0.170 | 0.085/0.050 |
| 2-Depth | **0.695**/0.600 | 0.410/0.325 | 0.225/**0.155** |
| 4-Descs | 0.605/0.520 | 0.390/0.245 | 0.195/0.105 |
| 4-Depth | 0.690/**0.610** | **0.445/0.335** | **0.245**/0.135 |
| F-Only | 0.530/0.445 | 0.360/0.235 | 0.160/0.120 |

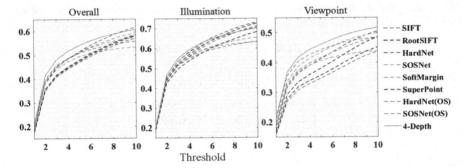

**Fig. 1.** The mean matching accuracy (MMA) for different thresholds on HPatches. From left to right are: results on the whole dataset, the illumination subset and the viewpoint subset.

## 4.3   Ablation Studies

Existing descriptors are either handcrafted or deep learned. Here we test 4 different combinations of them and analyze the results. 2-Hand uses two handcrafted descriptors SIFT and RootSIFT. 2-Depth uses two of the outstanding deep descriptors, HardNet and SOSNet. 4-Descs uses a mixture of both handcrafted and deep learned descriptors. Two of them are from 2-Hand and the others from 2-Depth. 4-Depth uses four deep learned descriptors, including HardNet, SOSNet, SoftMargin and SuperPoint.

The results on MMA, homography estimation accuracy and relative pose estimation accuracy are shown in Table 1, Table 2 and Table 3, respectively. As we can see from the data, when using the same number of descriptors (for example 2-Hand and 2-Depth), deep learned descriptors outperforms traditional handcrafted ones. It also reveals that using more descriptors will improve the results (see 2-Depth and 4-Depth). However, we also find that 4-Descs is lower than 4-Depth and 2-Depth. This indicates that not all the descriptors will contribute to the results. Some descriptors that are not good enough might even make the results worse. Based on the above observations, we recommend to use 4-Depth in the following experiments.

(a) HardNet          (b) SOSNet          (c) 4-Depth

**Fig. 2.** Visualization results of the correspondences on three typical image pairs. *Green* and *red* lines indicate correct and incorrect matches, respectively. (Color figure online)

We also test the role of spatial structure information. According to [45], we replace the diagonal blocks of $A$ in Eq. (5) with identity matrices for the method 4-Depth. In this case, spatial structure information is removed and only feature information is considered. The results, denoted as F-Only, is also shown in Table 1, Table 2 and Table 3. As we can see, F-Only is significantly lower than 4-Depth, showing that integrating spatial structure information is beneficial.

### 4.4  Mean Matching Accuracy Evaluation

Figure 1 shows the result of MMA under different thresholds (from 1 to 10). We plot the statistics on the whole dataset (Overall), as well as two subsets (Illumination and Viewpoint). HardNet (OS) and SOSNet (OS) represent the matching results of [45] when using HardNet and SOSNet, respectively.

The proposed method achieves the best performance on the whole dataset and the viewpoint subset. It also returns the best results on the illumination subset when the threshold is less than 6. HardNet and SOSNet are the top two compared methods. The two handcrafted descriptors, SIFT and RootSIFT, fall behind other learned descriptors on the viewpoint subset but receive good results on the illumination subset. Figure 2 gives some visualization results of the correspondences on some example image pairs. It shows that our method returns more correct and fewer incorrect matches.

### 4.5  Results on Downstream Tasks

Table 4 shows the average homography estimation accuracy on HPatches for different methods. Three thresholds are used. The proposed 4-Depth method achieves the best result for $\varepsilon = 3$ and $\varepsilon = 5$, and ranks second for $\varepsilon = 1$. HardNet(OS) and SOSNet(OS) outperform HardNet and SOSNet, respectively by involving spatial constraint. There is a remarkable improvement between our method and [45], showing that using multiple descriptors is beneficial.

**Table 4.** Average homography estimation accuracy on HPatches under different thresholds $\varepsilon$. A.M.P is the number of Average Matching Points and F.L.R is the Forecast Loss Rate. The best and second best results are in bold and blue.

| Method | $\varepsilon = 1$ | $\varepsilon = 3$ | $\varepsilon = 5$ | F.L.R | A.M.P |
|---|---|---|---|---|---|
| SIFT [26] | 0.296 | 0.499 | 0.588 | 0 | 475.2 |
| RootSIFT [2] | 0.296 | 0.489 | 0.584 | 0 | 467.9 |
| HardNet [29] | 0.315 | 0.513 | 0.638 | 0 | 534.3 |
| SOSNet [44] | 0.322 | 0.529 | 0.650 | 0 | 525.7 |
| SoftMargin [53] | 0.308 | 0.508 | 0.637 | 0 | 526.7 |
| SuperPoint [10] | 0.290 | 0.470 | 0.595 | 0 | 504.5 |
| HardNet(OS) [45] | 0.322 | 0.523 | 0.626 | 0 | 609.5 |
| SOSNet(OS) [45] | **0.329** | 0.525 | 0.671 | 0 | 614.5 |
| 4-Depth | 0.325 | **0.560** | **0.690** | 0 | 625.1 |
| **Un.** | 0.315 | 0.490 | 0.635 | 0 | 858.6 |
| **Vo.** | 0.325 | 0.567 | 0.664 | 0.016 | 287.7 |
| **In.** | 0.283 | 0.464 | 0.565 | 0.049 | 173.4 |

Table 5 shows the average relative pose estimation accuracy on the COLMAP dataset for different methods. The angle thresholds error is strictly set to $5°$. For all these methods, the score drops from *easy* to *hard*. Our 4-Depth method achieves the best results except for translation on the *hard* subset. HardNet (OS) and SOSNet (OS) defeat HardNet and SOSNet, and rank the top two among the remaining compared methods.

To test some other simple feature fusing strategies, we use intersection, union and voting of four deep features in Table 4 and Table 5. They are denoted as **In.**, **Un.** and **Vo.**, respectively. For **Vo.**, a correspondence is required to be found by at least three out of four descriptors. As we can see, **Un.** contains too many false matches so its results are generally not as good as ours. **Vo.** shows much higher score in Table 5, but it's worth noting that the increase of accuracy is at the cost of sacrificing many correct matches. To prove this, we give the number of *Average Matching Points*(A.M.P) and the *Forecast Loss Rate* (F.L.R) in both tables. It shows that **Vo.** sacrifices nearly 50% and 82% matches in Table 4 and Table 5, while the statistics for **In.** is 71% and 93%. Losing too many correspondences may lead to failure when estimating the geometry models due to insufficient data. The Forecast Loss Rate of **Vo.** and **In.** can range from 1% up to 33%. As a result, although **Vo.** and **In.** can achieve higher accuracy in easy situations, they are infeasible in harder situations due to high failure rate.

## 4.6 Parameters and Efficiency

In our method, the dimension $c$ of the subspace is an important parameter. To investigate its influence, an experiment is carried out on the **v_grace** scene of HPatches, in which $c$ increase from 5 to 400 with a step size of 5. The average

**Table 5.** Average relative pose (*rotation/translation*) estimation accuracy. The angle error threshold is strictly set to 5°. A.M.P is the number of Average Matching Points. F.e, F.m and F.h are the Forecast Loss Rate for each subset. The best and second best results are in bold and blue.

| Method | Easy | Moderate | Hard | F.e | F.m | F.h | A.M.P |
|---|---|---|---|---|---|---|---|
| SIFT [26] | .540/.395 | .250/.135 | .105/.050 | 0 | 0 | 0 | 349.4 |
| RootSIFT [2] | .555/.410 | .260/.155 | .105/.050 | 0 | 0 | 0 | 338.3 |
| HardNet [29] | .580/.500 | .340/.215 | .150/.115 | 0 | 0 | 0 | 445.1 |
| SOSNet [44] | .565/.456 | .350/.215 | .160/.080 | 0 | 0 | 0 | 435.9 |
| SoftMargin [53] | .580/.450 | .350/.240 | .150/.090 | 0 | 0 | 0 | 451.4 |
| SuperPoint [10] | .565/.445 | .245/.150 | .125/.065 | 0 | 0 | 0 | 384.2 |
| HardNet(OS) [45] | .615/.515 | .385/.265 | .190/**.140** | 0 | 0 | 0 | 536.3 |
| SOSNet(OS) [45] | .625/.535 | .345/.255 | .170/.130 | 0 | 0 | 0 | 538.6 |
| 4-Depth | **.690/.610** | **.445/.335** | **.245**/.135 | 0 | 0 | 0 | 534.2 |
| **Un.** | .110/.020 | .075/.000 | .040/.010 | 0 | 0 | 0 | 950.2 |
| **Vo.** | .750/.650 | .520/.425 | .285/.220 | .015 | .082 | .097 | 87.9 |
| **In.** | .700/.590 | .330/.260 | .185/.115 | .100 | .333 | .335 | 36.2 |

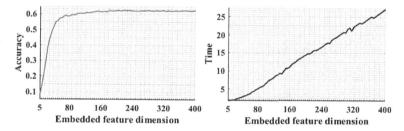

**Fig. 3.** The average matching accuracy and running time for different embedded feature dimension $c$. As a trade-off, we set the embedding feature dimension to $c = 55$ in all the experiments.

matching accuracy and running time are shown in Fig. 3. The results show that the matching accuracy of our method will increase when the embedded dimension becomes higher, but it will cost more time as well. In particular, the running time keeps growing but the average matching accuracy remains stable when the feature dimension $c$ exceeds 60. As a trade-off, we set the embedding feature dimension to $c = 55$ in all the experiments.

## 5   Conclusions

This paper proposes a novel image matching method based on multi-feature fusion and subspace embedding. The basic idea is to compute a subspace, in which intra-image structures of the keypoints are preserved and inter-image multi-feature similarities are encoded. This goal is achieved by solving a Laplacian Embedding problem. The proposed method is tested on a variety of scenes. Both the mean matching accuracy and performance on downstream tasks such as homography estimation and relative pose estimation are evaluated. Results show that the proposed method achieves the best performance when combining four deep descriptors: HardNet, SOSNet, SoftMargin and SuperPoint.

**Acknowledgment.** This work is supported by National Natural Science Foundation of China (62176242, 61802356), also in part by NSFC (41925007, 62076228) and Open Research Project of The Hubei Key Laboratory of Intelligent Geo-Information Processing (KLIGIP-2019B03).

# References

1. Albarelli, A., Rodolà, E., Torsello, A.: Imposing semi-local geometric constraints for accurate correspondences selection in structure from motion: a game-theoretic perspective. Int. J. Comput. Vis. **97**(1), 36–53 (2012)
2. Arandjelovic, R., Zisserman, A.: Three things everyone should know to improve object retrieval. In: CVPR, pp. 2911–2918. IEEE (2012)
3. Babenko, A., Slesarev, A., Chigorin, A., Lempitsky, V.: Neural codes for image retrieval. In: Fleet, D., Pajdla, T., Schiele, B., Tuytelaars, T. (eds.) ECCV 2014. LNCS, vol. 8689, pp. 584–599. Springer, Cham (2014). https://doi.org/10.1007/978-3-319-10590-1_38
4. Balntas, V., Lenc, K., Vedaldi, A., Mikolajczyk, K.: HPatches: a benchmark and evaluation of handcrafted and learned local descriptors. In: CVPR, pp. 3852–3861. IEEE (2017)
5. Bay, H., Tuytelaars, T., Van Gool, L.: SURF: speeded up robust features. In: Leonardis, A., Bischof, H., Pinz, A. (eds.) ECCV 2006. LNCS, vol. 3951, pp. 404–417. Springer, Heidelberg (2006). https://doi.org/10.1007/11744023_32
6. Belkin, M., Niyogi, P.: Laplacian eigenmaps for dimensionality reduction and data representation. Neural Comput. **15**(6), 1373–1396 (2003)
7. Calonder, M., Lepetit, V., Strecha, C., Fua, P.: BRIEF: binary robust independent elementary features. In: Daniilidis, K., Maragos, P., Paragios, N. (eds.) ECCV 2010. LNCS, vol. 6314, pp. 778–792. Springer, Heidelberg (2010). https://doi.org/10.1007/978-3-642-15561-1_56
8. Chen, Z., Xie, Z., Yan, J., Zheng, Y., Yang, X.: Layered neighborhood expansion for incremental multiple graph matching. In: Vedaldi, A., Bischof, H., Brox, T., Frahm, J.-M. (eds.) ECCV 2020. LNCS, vol. 12355, pp. 251–267. Springer, Cham (2020). https://doi.org/10.1007/978-3-030-58607-2_15
9. Choy, C.B., Gwak, J., Savarese, S., Chandraker, M.K.: Universal correspondence network. In: NIPS, pp. 2406–2414. Curran Associates, Inc. (2016)
10. DeTone, D., Malisiewicz, T., Rabinovich, A.: SuperPoint: self-supervised interest point detection and description. In: CVPR, pp. 224–236. IEEE (2018)
11. Dusmanu, M., et al.: D2-Net: a trainable CNN for joint description and detection of local features. In: CVPR, pp. 8092–8101. IEEE (2019)
12. Fang, L., Sun, Z., Lam, K.: An effective membership probability representation for point set registration. IEEE Access **8**, 9347–9357 (2020)

13. Forster, C., Pizzoli, M., Scaramuzza, D.: Appearance-based active, monocular, dense reconstruction for micro aerial vehicles. In: Robotics: Science and Systems X (2014)
14. Gao, X., Luo, J., Li, K., Xie, Z.: Hierarchical RANSAC-based rotation averaging. IEEE Signal Process. Lett. **27**, 1874–1878 (2020)
15. Gordo, A., Almazán, J., Revaud, J., Larlus, D.: Deep image retrieval: learning global representations for image search. In: Leibe, B., Matas, J., Sebe, N., Welling, M. (eds.) ECCV 2016. LNCS, vol. 9910, pp. 241–257. Springer, Cham (2016). https://doi.org/10.1007/978-3-319-46466-4_15
16. Han, X., Leung, T., Jia, Y., Sukthankar, R., Berg, A.C.: MatchNet: unifying feature and metric learning for patch-based matching. In: CVPR, pp. 3279–3286. IEEE (2015)
17. Havlena, M., Schindler, K.: VocMatch: efficient multiview correspondence for structure from motion. In: Fleet, D., Pajdla, T., Schiele, B., Tuytelaars, T. (eds.) ECCV 2014. LNCS, vol. 8691, pp. 46–60. Springer, Cham (2014). https://doi.org/10.1007/978-3-319-10578-9_4
18. Hu, Y., Lin, Y.: Progressive feature matching with alternate descriptor selection and correspondence enrichment. In: CVPR, pp. 346–354. IEEE (2016)
19. Hu, Y., Lin, Y., Chen, H., Hsu, K., Chen, B.: Matching images with multiple descriptors: an unsupervised approach for locally adaptive descriptor selection. IEEE Trans. Image Process. **24**(12), 5995–6010 (2015)
20. Jiang, X., Ma, J., Jiang, J., Guo, X.: Robust feature matching using spatial clustering with heavy outliers. IEEE Trans. Image Process. **29**, 736–746 (2020)
21. Leordeanu, M., Hebert, M.: A spectral technique for correspondence problems using pairwise constraints. In: International Conference on Computer Vision, pp. 1482–1489. IEEE (2005)
22. Li, Z., Snavely, N.: MegaDepth: learning single-view depth prediction from internet photos. In: CVPR, pp. 2041–2050. IEEE (2018)
23. Li, Z., Liu, H., Zhang, Z., Liu, T., Xiong, N.N.: Learning knowledge graph embedding with heterogeneous relation attention networks. IEEE Trans. Neural Netw. Learn. Syst., 1–13 (2021). https://doi.org/10.1109/TNNLS.2021.3055147
24. Liu, H., Fang, S., Zhang, Z., Li, D., Lin, K., Wang, J.: MFDNet: collaborative poses perception and matrix fisher distribution for head pose estimation. IEEE Trans. Multimedia (2021). https://doi.org/10.1109/TMM.2021.3081873
25. Liu, T., Liu, H., Li, Y., Chen, Z., Zhang, Z., Liu, S.: Flexible FTIR spectral imaging enhancement for industrial robot infrared vision sensing. IEEE Trans. Industr. Inform. **16**(1), 544–554 (2020)
26. Lowe, D.G.: Distinctive image features from scale-invariant keypoints. Int. J. Comput. Vis. **60**(2), 91–110 (2004). https://doi.org/10.1023/B:VISI.0000029664.99615.94
27. Luo, Z., et al.: GeoDesc: learning local descriptors by integrating geometry constraints. In: Ferrari, V., Hebert, M., Sminchisescu, C., Weiss, Y. (eds.) ECCV 2018. LNCS, vol. 11213, pp. 170–185. Springer, Cham (2018). https://doi.org/10.1007/978-3-030-01240-3_11
28. Ma, J., Jiang, X., Jiang, J., Gao, Y.: Feature-guided gaussian mixture model for image matching. Pattern Recognit. **92**, 231–245 (2019)
29. Mishchuk, A., Mishkin, D., Radenovic, F., Matas, J.: Working hard to know your neighbor's margins: local descriptor learning loss. In: NIPS, pp. 4826–4837. Curran Associates, Inc. (2017)

30. Pautrat, R., Larsson, V., Oswald, M.R., Pollefeys, M.: Online invariance selection for local feature descriptors. In: Vedaldi, A., Bischof, H., Brox, T., Frahm, J.-M. (eds.) ECCV 2020. LNCS, vol. 12347, pp. 707–724. Springer, Cham (2020). https://doi.org/10.1007/978-3-030-58536-5_42

31. Phillips, S., Daniilidis, K.: All graphs lead to Rome: learning geometric and cycle-consistent representations with graph convolutional networks. CoRR arXiv:1901.02078 (2019)

32. Revaud, J., de Souza, C.R., Humenberger, M., Weinzaepfel, P.: R2D2: reliable and repeatable detector and descriptor. In: NIPS, pp. 12405–12415. Curran Associates, Inc. (2019)

33. Rosten, E., Drummond, T.: Machine learning for high-speed corner detection. In: Leonardis, A., Bischof, H., Pinz, A. (eds.) ECCV 2006. LNCS, vol. 3951, pp. 430–443. Springer, Heidelberg (2006). https://doi.org/10.1007/11744023_34

34. Rublee, E., Rabaud, V., Konolige, K., Bradski, G.R.: ORB: an efficient alternative to SIFT or SURF. In: ICCV, pp. 2564–2571. IEEE (2011)

35. Sarlin, P., DeTone, D., Malisiewicz, T., Rabinovich, A.: SuperGlue: learning feature matching with graph neural networks. In: CVPR, pp. 4937–4946. IEEE (2020)

36. Schönberger, J.L., Frahm, J.: Structure-from-motion revisited. In: CVPR, pp. 4104–4113. IEEE (2016)

37. Simo-Serra, E., Trulls, E., Ferraz, L., Kokkinos, I., Fua, P., Moreno-Noguer, F.: Discriminative learning of deep convolutional feature point descriptors. In: International Conference on Computer Vision, pp. 118–126. IEEE (2015)

38. Sun, J., Sun, Z., Lam, K., Zeng, Z.: A robust point set registration approach with multiple effective constraints. IEEE Trans. Ind. Electron. **67**(12), 10931–10941 (2020)

39. Sun, K., Tao, W., Qian, Y.: Guide to match: multi-layer feature matching with a hybrid Gaussian mixture model. IEEE Trans. Multim. **22**(9), 2246–2261 (2020)

40. Taira, H., et al.: InLoc: indoor visual localization with dense matching and view synthesis. In: CVPR, pp. 7199–7209. IEEE (2018)

41. Tao, W., Sun, K.: Asymmetrical gauss mixture models for point sets matching. In: CVPR, pp. 1598–1605. IEEE (2014)

42. Tao, W., Sun, K.: Robust point sets matching by fusing feature and spatial information using nonuniform gaussian mixture models. IEEE Trans. Image Process. **24**(11), 3754–3767 (2015)

43. Tian, Y., Fan, B., Wu, F.: L2-Net: deep learning of discriminative patch descriptor in Euclidean space. In: CVPR, pp. 6128–6136. IEEE (2017)

44. Tian, Y., Yu, X., Fan, B., Wu, F., Heijnen, H., Balntas, V.: SOSNet: second order similarity regularization for local descriptor learning. In: CVPR, pp. 11016–11025. IEEE (2019)

45. Torki, M., Elgammal, A.M.: One-shot multi-set non-rigid feature-spatial matching. In: CVPR, pp. 3058–3065. IEEE (2010)

46. Wang, Q., Zhou, X., Daniilidis, K.: Multi-image semantic matching by mining consistent features. In: CVPR, pp. 685–694. IEEE (2018)

47. Wang, Q., Zhou, X., Hariharan, B., Snavely, N.: Learning feature descriptors using camera pose supervision. In: Vedaldi, A., Bischof, H., Brox, T., Frahm, J.-M. (eds.) ECCV 2020. LNCS, vol. 12346, pp. 757–774. Springer, Cham (2020). https://doi.org/10.1007/978-3-030-58452-8_44

48. Wang, Y., Mei, X., Ma, Y., Huang, J., Fan, F., Ma, J.: Learning to find reliable correspondences with local neighborhood consensus. Neurocomputing **406**, 150–158 (2020)

49. Yu, T., Yan, J., Liu, W., Li, B.: Incremental multi-graph matching via diversity and randomness based graph clustering. In: Ferrari, V., Hebert, M., Sminchisescu, C., Weiss, Y. (eds.) ECCV 2018. LNCS, vol. 11217, pp. 142–158. Springer, Cham (2018). https://doi.org/10.1007/978-3-030-01261-8_9

50. Yu, T., Yan, J., Wang, Y., Liu, W., Li, B.: Generalizing graph matching beyond quadratic assignment model. In: NIPS, pp. 861–871. Curran Associates, Inc. (2018)

51. Yu, X., Guo, Y., Li, J., Cai, F.: An image patch matching method based on multi-feature fusion. In: 10th International Congress on Image and Signal Processing, BioMedical Engineering and Informatics, 2017, pp. 1–6. IEEE (2017)

52. Zagoruyko, S., Komodakis, N.: Learning to compare image patches via convolutional neural networks. In: CVPR, pp. 4353–4361. IEEE (2015)

53. Zhang, L., Rusinkiewicz, S.: Learning local descriptors with a CDF-based dynamic soft margin. In: International Conference on Computer Vision, pp. 2969–2978. IEEE (2019)

54. Zhao, C., Cao, Z., Li, C., Li, X., Yang, J.: NM-Net: mining reliable neighbors for robust feature correspondences. In: CVPR, pp. 215–224. IEEE (2019)

55. Zhou, F., la Torre, F.D.: Factorized graph matching. IEEE Trans. Pattern Anal. Mach. Intell. **38**(9), 1774–1789 (2016)

56. Zhou, X., Zhu, M., Daniilidis, K.: Multi-image matching via fast alternating minimization. In: International Conference on Computer Vision, pp. 4032–4040. IEEE (2015)

# Author Index